PENGUIN  CLASSICS

ANTI-OEDIPUS:
CAPITALISM AND SCHIZOPHRENIA

GILLES DELEUZE (1925–1995) was a professor of philosophy at the University of Paris (Vincennes) and wrote numerous works, including studies of such philosophers as Kant, Spinoza, and Nietzsche, and such topics as sadomasochism and the logic of meaning.

FELIX GUATTARI (1930–1992) was a militant analyst long active in the anti-psychiatric movement in Europe. He was an active participant in the European Network for Alternatives to Psychiatry, which brought together ex-mental patient groups, radical mental-health workers, and such prominent anti-psychiatrists as R. D. Laing, David Cooper, and Franco Basaglia.

MICHEL FOUCAULT (1926–1984) was an influential thinker of the twentieth century with wide interests in philosophy and psychology.

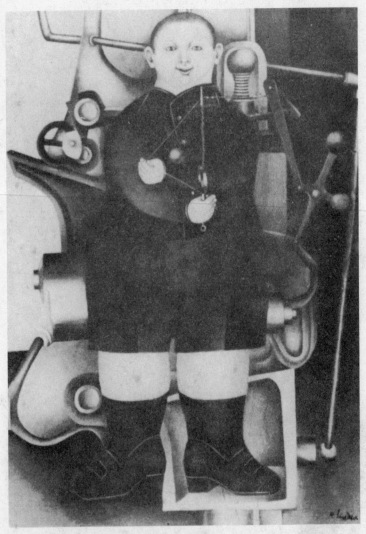

Boy with Machine, Richard Lindner (1954, oil on canvas, 40″ × 30″, Drs. Rosier and Lefer, M.D., P.A. Pension Trust)

GILLES DELEUZE
AND
FÉLIX GUATTARI

Anti-Oedipus

CAPITALISM AND SCHIZOPHRENIA

Preface by MICHEL FOUCAULT
Introduction by MARK SEEM
Translated by ROBERT HURLEY, MARK SEEM, *and* HELEN R. LANE

PENGUIN BOOKS

PENGUIN BOOKS

Published by the Penguin Group
Penguin Group (USA) Inc., 375 Hudson Street, New York, New York 10014, U.S.A.
Penguin Group (Canada), 90 Eglinton Avenue East, Suite 700, Toronto,
Ontario, Canada M4P 2Y3 (a division of Pearson Penguin Canada Inc.)
Penguin Books Ltd, 80 Strand, London WC2R 0RL, England
Penguin Ireland, 25 St Stephen's Green, Dublin 2, Ireland (a division of Penguin Books Ltd)
Penguin Group (Australia), 250 Camberwell Road, Camberwell,
Victoria 3124, Australia (a division of Pearson Australia Group Pty Ltd)
Penguin Books India Pvt Ltd, 11 Community Centre, Panchsheel Park, New Delhi – 110 017, India
Penguin Group (NZ), 67 Apollo Drive, Rosedale, North Shore 0632,
New Zealand (a division of Pearson New Zealand Ltd)
Penguin Books (South Africa) (Pty) Ltd, 24 Sturdee Avenue,
Rosebank, Johannesburg 2196, South Africa

Penguin Books Ltd, Registered Offices:
80 Strand, London WC2R 0RL, England

First published in the United States of America by The Viking Press 1977
Published in Penguin Books 2009

3 5 7 9 10 8 6 4

Copyright © Les Editions de Minuit, 1972
English translation copyright © Penguin Group (USA) Inc., 1977
All rights reserved

Originally published in French as *L'Anti-Oedipe* by Les Editions de Minuit, Paris.

ACKNOWLEDGMENTS
Calder and Boyars Ltd.: From *Collected Works*, Antonin Artaud.
City Lights: From "Kaddish" from *Kaddish & Other Poems* by Allen Ginsberg.
Copyright © 1961 by Allen Ginsberg. From Artaud Anthology by Antonin Artaud.
Copyright © 1956, 1961, 1965 by Editions Gallimard and City Lights Books.
Reprinted by permission of City Lights Books.
Humanities Press Inc. and Athlone Press: From *Rethinking Anthropology* by E. R. Leach.
Mercure de France: From *Nietzsche ou le Cercle Vicieux* by Pierre Klossowski.
Pantheon Books, a Division of Random House, Inc.: From *Madness and Civilization* by Michel Foucault,
translated by Richard Howard. Copyright © 1965 by Random House, Inc.
Presses Universitaires de France: From *L'Affect* by André Green.

THE LIBRARY OF CONGRESS HAS CATALOGED THE HARDCOVER EDITION AS FOLLOWS:
Deleuze, Gilles.
Anti-Oedipus.
Translation of L'anti-OEdipe, v. 1 of Capitalisme et schizophrénie.
"A Richard Seaver book."
Includes bibliographical references and index.
ISBN 0-670-12941-0 (hc.)
ISBN 978-0-14-310582-4 (pbk.)
1. Social psychiatry.   2. Schizophrenia.   3. Capitalism.   I. Guattari, Félix, joint author.   II. Title.
RC455.D42213   150'.19'52   76-47046

Printed in the United States of America
Set in Videocomp Times Roman

CONTENTS

tiations and the nondifferentiated • The second paralogism of psycho-analysis: the Oedipal double-bind • Oedipus wins at every turn • Does the borderline pass between the Symbolic and the Imaginary?

3   SAVAGES, BARBARIANS, CIVILIZED MEN

alliance debt ● Functional disequilibrium: surplus value of code ● It only works by breaking down ● The segmentary machine ● The great fear of decoded flows ● Death which rises from within, but comes from without ●

tal • The transformation of surplus value of code into a surplus value of flux • The two forms of money, the two inscriptions • The falling tendency • Capitalism and deterritorialization • Human surplus value and machinic surplus value • Anti-production • The various aspects of the capitalist immanence • The flows •

4 INTRODUCTION TO SCHIZOANALYSIS

PREFACE

by Michel Foucault

During the years 1945–1965 (I am referring to Europe), there was a certain way of thinking correctly, a certain style of political discourse, a certain ethics of the intellectual. One had to be on familiar terms with Marx, not let one's dreams stray too far from Freud. And one had to treat sign-systems—the signifier—with the greatest respect. These were the three requirements that made the strange occupation of writing and speaking a measure of truth about oneself and one's time acceptable.

Then came the five brief, impassioned, jubilant, enigmatic years. At the gates of our world, there was Vietnam, of course, and the first major blow to the powers that be. But here, inside our walls, what exactly was taking place? An amalgam of revolutionary and antirepressive politics? A war fought on two fronts: against social exploitation and psychic repression? A surge of libido modulated by the class struggle? Perhaps. At any rate, it is this familiar, dualistic interpretation that has laid claim to the events of those years. The dream that cast its spell, between the First World War and fascism, over the dreamiest parts of Europe—the Germany of Wilhelm Reich, and the France of the surrealists—had returned and set fire to reality itself: Marx and Freud in the same incandescent light.

But is that really what happened? Had the utopian project of the thirties been resumed, this time on the scale of historical practice? Or was there, on the contrary, a movement toward political struggles that no longer conformed to the model that Marxist tradition had prescribed? Toward an experience and a technology of desire that were no longer Freudian. It is true that the old banners were raised, but the combat shifted and spread into new zones.

Anti-Oedipus shows first of all how much ground has been covered. But it does much more than that. It wastes no time in discrediting the old idols, even though it does have a great deal of fun with Freud. Most important, it motivates us to go further.

It would be a mistake to read *Anti-Oedipus* as *the* new theoretical reference (you know, that much-heralded theory that finally encompasses everything, that finally totalizes and reassures, the one we are told we "need so badly" in our age of dispersion and specialization where "hope" is lacking). One must not look for a "philosophy" amid the extraordinary profusion of new notions and surprise concepts: *Anti-Oedipus* is not a flashy Hegel. I think that *Anti-Oedipus* can best be read as an "art," in the sense that is conveyed by the term "erotic art," for example. Informed by the seemingly abstract notions of multiplicities, flows, arrangements, and connections, the analysis of the relationship of desire to reality and to the capitalist "machine" yields answers to concrete questions. Questions that are less concerned with *why* this or that than with *how* to proceed. How does one introduce desire into thought, into discourse, into action? How can and must desire deploy its forces within the political domain and grow more intense in the process of overturning the established order? *Ars erotica, ars theoretica, ars politica.*

Whence the three adversaries confronted by *Anti-Oedipus*. Three adversaries who do not have the same strength, who represent varying degrees of danger, and whom the book combats in different ways:

1. The political ascetics, the sad militants, the terrorists of theory, those who would preserve the pure order of politics and political discourse. Bureaucrats of the revolution and civil servants of Truth.

2. The poor technicians of desire—psychoanalysts and semiolo-

gists of every sign and symptom—who would subjugate the multiplicity of desire to the twofold law of structure and lack.

3. Last but not least, the major enemy, the strategic adversary is fascism (whereas *Anti-Oedipus'* opposition to the others is more of a tactical engagement). And not only historical fascism, the fascism of Hitler and Mussolini—which was able to mobilize and use the desire of the masses so effectively—but also the fascism in us all, in our heads and in our everyday behavior, the fascism that causes us to love power, to desire the very thing that dominates and exploits us.

I would say that *Anti-Oedipus* (may its authors forgive me) is a book of ethics, the first book of ethics to be written in France in quite a long time (perhaps that explains why its success was not limited to a particular "readership": being anti-oedipal has become a life style, a way of thinking and living). How does one keep from being fascist, even (especially) when one believes oneself to be a revolutionary militant? How do we rid our speech and our acts, our hearts and our pleasures, of fascism? How do we ferret out the fascism that is ingrained in our behavior? The Christian moralists sought out the traces of the flesh lodged deep within the soul. Deleuze and Guattari, for their part, pursue the slightest traces of fascism in the body.

Paying a modest tribute to Saint Francis de Sales,* one might say that *Anti-Oedipus* is an *Introduction to the Non-Fascist Life.*

This art of living counter to all forms of fascism, whether already present or impending, carries with it a certain number of essential principles which I would summarize as follows if I were to make this great book into a manual or guide to everyday life:

● Free political action from all unitary and totalizing paranoia.

● Develop action, thought, and desires by proliferation, juxtaposition, and disjunction, and not by subdivision and pyramidal hierarchization.

● Withdraw allegiance from the old categories of the Negative (law, limit, castration, lack, lacuna), which Western thought has so long held sacred as a form of power and an access to reality. Prefer what is positive and multiple, difference over uniformity, flows over unities, mobile arrangements over systems. Believe that what is productive is not sedentary but nomadic.

● Do not think that one has to be sad in order to be militant, even though the thing one is fighting is abominable. It is the connection of

---

*A seventeenth-century priest and Bishop of Geneva, known for his *Introduction to the Devout Life.*

desire to reality (and not its retreat into the forms of representation) that possesses revolutionary force.

●Do not use thought to ground a political practice in Truth; nor political action to discredit, as mere speculation, a line of thought. Use political practice as an intensifier of thought, and analysis as a multiplier of the forms and domains for the intervention of political action.

●Do not demand of politics that it restore the "rights" of the individual, as philosophy has defined them. The individual is the product of power. What is needed is to "de-individualize" by means of multiplication and displacement, diverse combinations. The group must not be the organic bond uniting hierarchized individuals, but a constant generator of de-individualization.

●Do not become enamored of power.

It could even be said that Deleuze and Guattari care so little for power that they have tried to neutralize the effects of power linked to their own discourse. Hence the games and snares scattered throughout the book, rendering its translation a feat of real prowess. But these are not the familiar traps of rhetoric; the latter work to sway the reader without his being aware of the manipulation, and ultimately win him over against his will. The traps of *Anti-Oedipus* are those of humor: so many invitations to let oneself be put out, to take one's leave of the text and slam the door shut. The book often leads one to believe it is all fun and games, when something essential is taking place, something of extreme seriousness: the tracking down of all varieties of fascism, from the enormous ones that surround and crush us to the petty ones that constitute the tyrannical bitterness of our everyday lives.

INTRODUCTION

by Mark Seem

"We must die as egos and be
born again in the swarm, not
separate and self-hypnotized, but
individual and related."
        —Henry Miller, *Sexus*

The Anti-Ego

"Lie down, then, on the soft couch which the analyst provides, and try to think up something different. The analyst has endless time and patience; every minute you detain him means money in his pocket. . . . Whether you whine, howl, beg, weep, cajole, pray or curse—he listens. He is just a big ear minus a sympathetic nervous system. He is impervious to everything but truth. If you think it pays to fool him then fool him. Who will be the loser? If you think he can help you, and not yourself, then stick to him until you rot."[1]* So concludes Henry Miller in *Sexus,* and Gilles Deleuze and Felix Guattari are quick to agree in their attack on psychoanalysis' own Oedipus complex (the holy family: daddy-mommy-me), an attack that is at times brutal and without pity, at other times sympathetic and full of a profound love of

*Reference notes begin on page 383.

life, and often enormously amusing. An attack on the ego, on what is all-too-human in mankind, on oedipalized and oedipalizing analyses and neurotic modes of living.

In confronting and finally overturning the Oedipal rock on which Man has chosen to take his stand, *Anti-Oedipus* comes as a kind of sequel to another similar venture, the attack on Christ, Christianity, and the herd in Nietzsche's *The AntiChrist*. For who would deny, *Anti-Oedipus* begins, that psychoanalysis was from the start, still is, and perhaps always will be a well-constituted church and a form of treatment based on a set of beliefs that only the very faithful could adhere to, ie., those who believe in a security that amounts to being lost in the herd and defined in terms of common and external goals? But where do such beliefs originate? What are they based on? For it is absolutely hopeless to think in terms of security, as Miller states in *Sexus;* "there is none. The man who looks for security, even in the mind, is like a man who would chop off his limbs in order to have artificial ones which will give him no pain or trouble" (page 428). No pain, no trouble—this is the neurotic's dream of a tranquilized and conflict-free existence.

Such a set of beliefs, Deleuze and Guattari demonstrate, such a herd instinct, is based on the desire to be led, the desire to have someone else legislate life. The very desire that was brought so glaringly into focus in Europe with Hitler, Mussolini, and fascism; the desire that is still at work, making us all sick, today. *Anti-Oedipus* starts by reviving Reich's completely serious question with respect to the rise of fascism: 'How could the masses be made to desire their own repression?' This is a question which the English and Americans are reluctant to deal with directly, tending too often to respond: "Fascism is a phenomenon that took place elsewhere, something that could only happen to others, but not to us; it's *their* problem." Is it though? Is fascism really a problem for others to deal with? Even revolutionary groups deal gingerly with the fascisizing elements we all carry deep within us, and yet they often possess a rarely analyzed but overriding group 'superego' that leads them to state, much like Nietzsche's man of *ressentiment,* that the *other* is evil (the Fascist! the Capitalist! the Communist!), *and hence that they themselves are good.* This conclusion is reached as an afterthought and a justification, a supremely *self*-righteous rationalization for a politics that can only "squint" at life, through the thick clouds of foul-smelling air that permeates secret meeting places and "security" councils. The man of *ressentiment,* as Nietzsche explains, "loves hiding places, secret paths and back doors, everything covert entices him as *his* world, *his* security, *his* refreshment; he understands how to keep silent, how not to forget, how to wait, how to be provisionally self-deprecating and humble."[2] Such a man, Nietzsche concludes, needs very much to believe in some neutral, independent "subject"—the ego—for he is prompted by an instinct of *self*-affirmation and *self*-preservation that cares little about preserving or affirming life, an instinct "in which every lie is sanctified."[3] This is the realm of the silent majority. And it is into these back rooms, behind the closed doors of the analyst's office, in the wings of the Oedipal theater, that Deleuze and Guattari weave their way, exclaiming as does Nietzsche that it smells bad there, and that what is needed is "a breath of fresh air, a relationship with the outside world."

In examining the problem of the subject, the behind-the-scenes reactive and reactionary man, *Anti-Oedipus* develops an approach that is decidedly *diagnostic* ("What constitutes our sickness today?") and profoundly *healing* as well. What it attempts to cure us of is the cure itself. Deleuze and Guattari term their approach "schizoanalysis," which they oppose on every count to psychoanalysis. Where the latter measures everything against neurosis and castration, schizoanalysis begins with the schizo, his breakdowns and his breakthroughs. For, they affirm, "a schizophrenic out for a walk is a better model than a neurotic lying on the analyst's couch. . . ." Against the Oedipal and oedipalized territorialities (Family, Church, School, Nation, Party), and especially the territoriality of the individual, *Anti-Oedipus* seeks to discover the "deterritorialized" flows of desire, the flows that have not been reduced to the Oedipal codes and the neuroticized territorialities, the *desiring-machines* that escape such codes as *lines of escape* leading elsewhere.

Much like R. D. Laing, Deleuze and Guattari aim to develop a materialistically and experientially based analysis of the "breakdowns" and the "breakthroughs" that characterize *some* of those labeled schizophrenic by psychiatry. Rather than view the creations and productions of desire—all of desiring-production—from the point of view of the norm and the normal, they force their analysis into the sphere of extremes. From paranoia to schizophrenia, from fascism to revolution, from breakdowns to breakthroughs, what is investigated is the process of life flows as they oscillate from one extreme to the other, on a scale of intensity that goes from 0 ("I never asked to be born . . . leave me in peace"), *the body without organs,* to the nth power ("I am all that exists, all the names in history"), *the schizophrenic process of desire.*

The Experience of Delirium

In order to carry out this ambitious undertaking, *Anti-Oedipus* makes joyously unorthodox use of many writers and thinkers, whose concepts flow together with all the other elements in the book in what might well be described as a carefully constructed and executed experiment in delirium.

While Deleuze and Guattari quote frequently from Marx and Freud, it would be an error to view *Anti-Oedipus* as yet another attempt at a Freud/Marx synthesis. For such an attempt always treats political economy (the flows of capital and interest) and the economy of the libido (the flows of desire) as two separate economies, even in the work of Reich, who went as far as possible in this direction. Deleuze and Guattari, on the other hand, postulate one and the same economy, the economy of flows. The flows and productions of desire will simply be viewed as the unconscious of the social productions. Behind every investment of time and interest and capital, an investment of desire, and vice versa.

In order to reach this conclusion a new confrontation was required. Not the standard confrontation between a bourgeois Freud and a revolutionary Marx, where Freud ends up the loser, but a more radical confrontation, between Marx the revolutionary and Nietzsche the madman. The result of this confrontation, as the authors demonstrate convincingly, is that Freud and psychoanalysis (and perhaps even Lacan, although they remain ambiguous on this point) become "impossible."

"Why Marx and Nietzsche? Now that's really mixing things up!" one might protest at this point. But there is really no cause for alarm. Readers of Marx will be happy to learn that Marx fares quite well in this confrontation. One might even say he is trimmed down to bare essentials and improved upon from the point of view of use. Given Deleuze and Guattari's perspective, this confrontation was inevitable. If one wants to do an analysis of the flows of money and capital that circulate in society, nothing is more useful than Marx and the Marxist theory of money. But if one wishes also to analyze the flows of desire, the fears and the anxieties, the loves and the despairs that traverse the social field as intensive notes from the underground (i.e., *libidinal economy*), one must look elsewhere. Since psychoanalysis is of no help, reducing as it does every social manifestation of desire to the familial complex, where is one to turn? To Nietzsche, and the Nietzschean theory of affects and intensity, *Anti-Oedipus* suggests. For here, and especially in *On the Genealogy of Morals,* is a theory of desire and will, of the conscious and the unconscious forces, that relates desire directly to the social field and to a monetary system based on profit. What Nietzsche teaches, as a complement to Marx's theory of alienation, is how the history of mankind is the history of a *becoming-reactive.* And it is Nietzsche,

Deleuze and Guattari stress, whose thought already pointed a *way out* for humanity, whereas Marx and Freud were too ingrained in the culture that they were working against.

One could not really view *Anti-Oedipus* as a purely Nietzschean undertaking, however, for the book would be nothing without the tension between Nietzsche and Marx, between philosophy and politics between thought and revolution; the tension, in short, between Deleuze the philosopher and Guattari the militant. This tension is quite novel, and leads to a combination of the artistic "machine," the revolutionary "machine," and the analytical "machine"; a combination of three modes of knowledge—the *intuitive,* the *practical,* and the *reflective,* which all become joined as bits and pieces of one and the same strategical machine whose target is the ego and the fascist in each of us. Extending thought to the point of madness and action to the point of revolution, theirs is indeed a politics of experience. The experience, however, is no longer that of man, but of what is nonhuman in man, his desires and his forces: a politics of desire directed against all that is egoic—and heroic—in man.

In addition to Nietzsche they also found it necessary to listen to others: to Miller and Lawrence and Kafka and Beckett, to Proust and Reich and Foucault, to Burroughs and Ginsberg, each of whom had different insights concerning madness and dissension, politics and desire. They needed everything they could get their hands on and they took whatever they could find, in an eclectic fashion closer to Henry Miller than it is to Marx or Freud. More poetic, undoubtedly, but also more fun.

While Deleuze and Guattari use many authors and concepts, this is never done in an academic fashion aimed at persuading the reader. Rather, they use these names and ideas as effects that traverse their analyses, generating ever new effects, as points of reference indeed, but also as points of intensity and signs pointing a way out: *points-signs* that offer a multiplicity of solutions and a variety of directions for a new style of politics. Such an approach carries much along with it, in the course of its flow, but it also leaves much behind. Chunks of Marx and Freud that cannot keep up with the fast current will be left behind, buried or forgotten, while everything in Marx and Freud that has to do with how things and people and desires actually flow will be kept, and added to the infernal machine evoked above. This political analysis of desire, this *schizoanalysis,* becomes a mighty tool where schizophrenia as a process—the schiz—serves as a point of departure as well as a point of destination. Like Laing, they encourage mankind to take a journey, the journey through *ego-loss.* They go much further than Laing on this point, however. They urge mankind to strip itself of *all* anthropomorphic and anthropological armoring, all myth and tragedy, and all existentialism, in order to perceive what is nonhuman in man, his will and his forces, his transformations and mutations. The human and social sciences have accustomed us to see the figure of Man behind every social event, just as Christianity taught us to see the Eye of the Lord looking down upon us. Such forms of knowledge project an image of reality, at the expense of reality itself. They talk figures and icons and signs, but fail to perceive forces and flows. They blind us to other realities, and especially the reality of power as it subjugates us. Their function is to tame, and the result is the fabrication of docile and obedient subjects.

Schizoanalysis and Collectivity

To be anti-oedipal is to be anti-ego as well as anti-homo, willfully attacking all reductive psychoanalytic and political analyses that remain caught within the sphere of totality and unity, in order to free the multiplicity of desire from the deadly neurotic and Oedipal yoke. For Oedipus is not a mere psychoanalytic construct, Deleuze and Guattari explain. Oedipus is the figurehead of imperialism, "colonization pursued by other means, it is the interior colony, and we shall see that even here at home . . . it is our intimate colonial education." This internalization of man by man, this "oedipalization," creates a new meaning for suffering, *internal suffering,* and a new tone for life: the depressive tone. Now depression does not just come about one fine day, *Anti-Oedipus* goes on, nor does Oedipus appear one day in the Family and feel secure in remaining there. Depression and Oedipus are agencies of the State, agencies of paranoia, agencies of power, long before being delegated to the family. Oedipus is the figure of power as such, just as neurosis is the result of power on individuals. Oedipus is everywhere.

For anti-oedipalists the ego, like Oedipus, is "part of those things we must dismantle through the united assault of analytical and political forces."[4] Oedipus is belief injected into the unconscious, it is what gives us faith as it robs us of power, *it* is what teaches us to desire our own repression. Everybody has been oedipalized and neuroticized at home, at school, at work. Everybody wants to be a fascist. Deleuze and Guattari want to know how these beliefs succeed in taking hold of a body, thereby silencing the productive machines of the libido. They also want to know how the opposite situation is brought about, where a body successfully wards off the effects of power. Reversing the Freudian distinction between neurosis and psychosis that measures everything against the former, *Anti-Oedipus* concludes: the neurotic is the one on whom the Oedipal imprints take, whereas the psychotic is the one incapable of being oedipalized, even and especially by psychoanalysis. The first task of the revolutionary, they add, is to learn from the psychotic how to shake off the Oedipal yoke and the effects of power, in order to initiate a radical politics of desire freed from all beliefs. Such a politics dissolves the mystifications of power through the kindling, on all levels, of anti-oedipal forces—the schizzes-flows—forces that escape coding, scramble the codes, and flee in all directions: *orphans* (no daddy-mommy-me), *atheists* (no beliefs), and *nomads* (no habits, no territories).

A schizoanalysis schizophrenizes in order to break the holds of power and institute research into a new collective subjectivity and a revolutionary healing of mankind. For we are sick, so sick, of our *selves!*

It is actually not accurate to say that Deleuze and Guattari develop the schizoanalytic approach, for, as they show, it has always been at work in writers like Miller or Nietzsche or Artaud. Stoned thinking based on intensely lived experiences: Pop Philosophy.

To put it simply, as does Miller, "everybody becomes a healer the moment he forgets about himself." And Miller continues: "Reality is here and now, everywhere, gleaming through every reflection that meets the eye. . . . Everybody is a neurotic, down to the last man and woman. The healer, or the analyst, if you like, is only a super-neurotic. . . . To be cured we must rise from our graves and throw off the cerements of the dead. Nobody can do it for another—it is a private affair which is best done collectively."[5] Once we forget about our egos a non-neurotic form of politics becomes possible, where singularity and collectivity are no longer at odds with each other, and where collective expressions of desire are possible. Such a politics does not seek to regiment individuals according to a totalitarian system of norms, but to de-normalize and de-individualize through a multiplicity of new, collective arrangements against power. Its goal is the transformation of human relationships in a struggle against power. And it urges militant groups, as well as lone individuals, to analyze and fight against the effects of power that subjugate them: "For a revolutionary group at the preconscious level remains a *subjugated group,* even in seizing power, as long as this power itself refers to a form of force that continues to enslave and crush desiring-production. . . . A *subject-group,* on the contrary, is a group whose libidinal investments are themselves revolutionary, it causes desire to penetrate into the social field, and subordinates the socius or the forms of power to desiring-production; productive of desire and a desire that produces, the subject-group always invents mortal formations that exorcize the effusion in it of a death instinct; it opposes real coefficients of transversality to the symbolic determinations of subjugation, coefficients without a hierarchy or a group superego." There can be no revolutionary actions, *Anti-Oedipus* concludes, where the the relations between people and groups are relations of exclusion and segregation. Groups must multiply and connect in ever new ways, freeing up territorialities for the construction of new social arrangements. Theory must therefore be conceived as a toolbox, producing tools that work; or as Ivan Illich says, we must learn to construct *tools for conviviality* through the use of counterfoil research.[6] When Illich speaks of "convivial reconstruction," he is very close to Deleuze and Guattari's notion of a "desiring-revolution." Like Deleuze and Guattari, Illich also calls for a radical reversal of the relationships between individuals and tools or machines: "This reversal would permit the evolution of a life-style and of a political system which give priority to the protection, the maximum use, and the enjoyment of the one resource that is almost equally distributed among all people: personal energy under personal control."[7] All three authors agree that such a reversal must be governed by a collective political process, and not by professionals and experts. The ultimate answer to neurotic dependencies on professionals is *mutual self-care*.[8]

Freed from a psychoanalytic framework, the political group or collective cannot, however, push aside the problem of desire. Nor can it leave desire in the hands of new experts. It must analyze the function of desire, in itself and in the groups with which it is involved. What is the function of desire, *Anti-Oedipus* asks, if not one of making connections? For to be bogged down in arrangements from which escape is possible is to be neurotic, seeing an irresolvable crisis where alternatives in fact exist. And as Deleuze and Guattari comment, "perhaps it will be discovered that the only incurable is the neurotic."

We defend so cautiously against our egoically limited experiences, states Laing in *The Politics of Experience,* that it is not surprising to see people grow defensive and panic at the idea of experiencing ego-loss through the use of drugs or collective experiences. But there is nothing pathological about ego-loss, Laing adds; quite the contrary. Ego-loss is the experience of all mankind, "of the primal man, of Adam and perhaps even [a journey] further into the beings of animals, vegetables and minerals."[9] No age, Laing concludes, has so lost touch with this healing process as has ours. Deleuze and Guattari's schizoanalytic approach serves to begin such a healing process. Its major task is to destroy the oedipalized and neuroticized individual dependencies through the forging of a collective subjectivity, a nonfascist subject—anti-Oedipus. Anti-Oedipus is an individual or a group that no longer functions in terms of beliefs and that comes to redeem mankind, as Nietzsche foresaw, not only from the ideals that weighed it down, "but also from that which was bound to grow out of it, the great nausea, the will to nothingness, nihilism; this bell-stroke of noon and of the great decision that liberates the will again and restores its goal to the earth and his hope to man; this AntiChrist and antinihilist. . . *He must come one day.*—"[10]

Unlike Nietzsche's antinihilist, however, Deleuze and Guattari's anti-Oedipus is not alone. Anti-Oedipus is not the superman. It is not transcendent. Where Nietzsche grew progressively more isolated to the point of madness, Deleuze and Guattari call for actions and passions of a collective nature, *here and now.* Madness is a radical break from power in the form of a disconnection. Militancy, in Deleuze and Guattari's framework, would learn from madness but then move beyond it, beyond disconnections and deterritorializations, to ever new connections. A politics of desire would see loneliness and depression as the first things to go. Such is the anti-oedipal strategy: if man is connected to the machines of the universe, if he is in tune with his desires, if he is "anchored," "he ceases to worry about the fitness of things, about the behavior of his fellow-men, about right or wrong and justice and injustice. If his roots are in the current of life he will float on the surface like a lotus and he will blossom and give forth fruit. . . . The life that's in him will manifest itself in growth, and growth is an endless, eternal process. The process is everything."[11] It is this process—of desiring-production—that *Anti-Oedipus* sets out to analyze.

For if desire is repressed in a society, Deleuze and Guattari state, this is hardly because "it is a desire for the mother or for the death of the father; on the contrary, desire becomes that only because it is repressed, it takes that mask on under the reign of the repression that models the mask for it and plasters it on its face. . . . The real danger is elsewhere. If desire is repressed, it is because every position of desire, no matter how small, is capable of calling into question the established order of a society: not that desire is asocial; on the contrary. But it is explosive; there is no desiring-machine capable of being assembled without demolishing entire social sectors."

Deleuze and Guattari conclude that desire, any desiring-machine, is always a combination of various elements and forces of all types. Hence the need to listen not only to revolutionaries but to all those who know how to be truly objective: "Revolutionaries, artists, and seers are content to be objective, merely objective: they know that desire clasps life in its powerfully productive embrace, and reproduces it in a way all the more intense because it has few needs. And never mind those who believe that this is very easy to say, or that it is the sort of idea to be found in books."

ANTI-OEDIPUS

THE DESIRING-MACHINES

Translated by Helen R. Lane, Robert Hurley, and Mark Seem

1 | Desiring-Production

It is at work everywhere, functioning smoothly at times, at other times in fits and starts. It breathes, it heats, it eats. It shits and fucks. What a mistake to have ever said *the* id. Everywhere *it* is machines—real ones, not figurative ones: machines driving other machines, machines being driven by other machines, with all the necessary couplings and connections. An organ-machine is plugged into an energy-source-machine: the one produces a flow that the other interrupts. The breast is a machine that produces milk, and the mouth a machine coupled to it. The mouth of the anorexic wavers between several functions: its possessor is uncertain as to whether it is an eating-machine, an anal machine, a talking-machine, or a breathing-machine (asthma attacks). Hence we are all handymen: each with his little machines. For every organ-machine, an energy-machine: all the time, flows and interruptions. Judge Schreber* has sunbeams in his ass. *A solar anus.* And rest assured that it works: Judge Schreber feels something, produces something, and is capable of explaining the process theoretically. Something is produced: the effects of a machine, not mere metaphors.

A schizophrenic out for a walk is a better model than a neurotic lying on the analyst's couch. A breath of fresh air, a relationship with the outside world. Lenz's stroll, for example, as reconstructed by Büchner. This walk outdoors is different from the moments when Lenz finds himself closeted with his pastor, who forces him to situate himself socially, in relationship to the God of established religion, in relationship to his father, to his mother. While taking a stroll outdoors, on the other hand, he is in the mountains, amid falling snowflakes, with other gods or without any gods at all, without a family, without a father or a mother, with nature. "What does my father want? Can he offer me more than that? Impossible. Leave me in peace."[1] Everything is a machine. Celestial machines, the stars or rainbows in the sky, alpine machines— all of them connected to those of his body. The continual whirr of machines. "He thought that it must be a feeling of endless bliss to be in contact with the profound life of every form, to have a soul for rocks, metals, water, and plants, to take into himself, as in a dream, every element of nature, like flowers that breathe with the waxing and waning of the moon."[1a] To be a chlorophyll- or a photosynthesis-machine, or at least slip his body into such machines as one part among the others. Lenz has projected himself back to a time before the man-nature dichotomy, before all the co-ordinates based on this fundamental dichotomy have been laid down. He does not live nature as nature, but as a process of production. There is no such thing as either man or nature now, only a process that produces the one within the other and couples the machines together. Producing-machines, desiring-machines everywhere, schizophrenic machines, all of species life: the self and the non-self, outside and inside, no longer have any meaning whatsoever.

Now that we have had a look at this stroll of a schizo, let us compare what happens when Samuel Beckett's characters decide to venture outdoors. Their various gaits and methods of self-locomotion constitute, in and of themselves, a finely tuned machine. And then there is the function of the bicycle in Beckett's works: what relationship does the bicycle-horn machine have with the mother-anus machine? "What a

---

*Daniel Paul Schreber was a German judge who began psychiatric treatment in 1884 at the age of forty-two, and spent the remaining twenty-seven years of his life in and out of mental institutions. In 1903, at the age of sixty-one, he published his *Denkwürdigkeiten eines Nervenkranken (Memoirs of a Nervous Illness)*, which Freud used as the basis of his influential 1911 study on paranoia, "Psycho-Analytic Notes" (reference note 7, page 384 of this volume). pp. 390–472. *(Translators' note.)*

rest to speak of bicycles and horns. Unfortunately it is not of them I have to speak, but of her who brought me into the world, through the hole in her arse if my memory is correct."[2] It is often thought that Oedipus* is an easy subject to deal with, something perfectly obvious, a "given" that is there from the very beginning. But that is not so at all: Oedipus presupposes a fantastic repression of desiring-machines. And why are they repressed? To what end? Is it really necessary or desirable to submit to such repression? And what means are to be used to accomplish this? What ought to go inside the Oedipal triangle, what sort of thing is required to construct it? Are a bicycle horn and my mother's arse sufficient to do the job? Aren't there more important questions than these, however? Given a certain effect, what machine is capable of producing it? And given a certain machine, what can it be used for? Can we possibly guess, for instance, what a knife rest is used for if all we are given is a geometrical description of it? Or yet another example: on being confronted with a complete machine made up of six stones in the right-hand pocket of my coat (the pocket that serves as the source of the stones), five stones in the right-hand pocket of my trousers, and five in the left-hand pocket (transmission pockets), with the remaining pocket of my coat receiving the stones that have already been handled, as each of the stones moves forward one pocket, how can we determine the effect of this circuit of distribution in which the mouth, too, plays a role as a stone-sucking machine? Where in this entire circuit do we find the production of sexual pleasure? At the end of *Malone Dies,* Lady Pedal takes the schizophrenics out for a ride in a van and a rowboat, and on a picnic in the midst of nature: an infernal machine is being assembled. "Under the skin the body is an over-heated factory,/ and outside,/ the invalid shines,/ glows,/ from every burst pore."[3]

This does not mean that we are attempting to make nature one of the poles of schizophrenia. What the schizophrenic experiences, both as an individual and as a member of the human species, is not at all any one specific aspect of nature, but nature as a process of production. What do we mean here by process? It is probable that at a certain level nature and industry are two separate and distinct things: from one point of view, industry is the opposite of nature; from another, industry extracts its raw materials from nature; from yet another, it returns its refuse to nature; and so on. Even within society, this characteristic man-nature, industry-nature, society-nature relationship is responsible for the dis-

---

*As will be seen below, the term Oedipus has many widely varying connotations in this volume. It refers, for instance, not only to the Greek myth of Oedipus and to the Oedipus complex as defined by classical psychoanalysis, but also to Oedipal mechanisms, processes, and structures. The translators follow the authors' use and employ the word "Oedipus" by itself, using the more traditional term "Oedipus complex" only when the authors do so. (*Translators' note.*)

tinction of relatively autonomous spheres that are called production, distribution, consumption. But in general this entire level of distinctions, examined from the point of view of its formal developed structures, presupposes (as Marx has demonstrated) not only the existence of capital and the division of labor, but also the false consciousness that the capitalist being necessarily acquires, both of itself and of the supposedly fixed elements within an over-all process. For the real truth of the matter—the glaring, sober truth that resides in delirium—is that there is no such thing as relatively independent spheres or circuits: production is immediately consumption and a recording process (*enregistrement**), without any sort of mediation, and the recording process and consumption directly determine production, though they do so within the production process itself. Hence everything is production: *production of productions,* of actions and of passions; *productions of recording processes,* of distributions and of co-ordinates that serve as points of reference; *productions of consumptions,* of sensual pleasures, of anxieties, and of pain. Everything is production, since the recording processes are immediately consumed, immediately consummated, and these consumptions directly reproduced.† This is the first meaning of process as we use the term: incorporating recording and consumption within production itself, thus making them the productions of one and the same process.

Second, we make no distinction between man and nature: the human essence of nature and the natural essence of man become one within nature in the form of production or industry, just as they do within the life of man as a species. Industry is then no longer considered from the extrinsic point of view of utility, but rather from the point of view of its fundamental identity with nature as production of man and by man.[4] Not man as the king of creation, but rather as the being who is in intimate contact with the profound life of all forms or all types of beings, who is responsible for even the stars and animal life, and who ceaselessly plugs an organ-machine into an energy-machine, a tree into his body, a breast into his mouth, the sun into his asshole: the eternal custodian of the machines of the universe. This is the second meaning of process as we use the term: man and nature are not like two opposite

*The French term *enregistrement* has a number of meanings, among them the process of making a recording to be played back by a mechanical device (e.g., a phonograph), the recording so made (e.g., a phonograph record or a magnetic tape), and the entering of births, deaths, deeds, marriages, and so on, in an official register. (*Translators' note.*)

†When Georges Bataille speaks of sumptuary, nonproductive expenditures or consumptions in connection with the energy of nature, these are expenditures or consumptions that are not part of the supposedly independent sphere of human production, insofar as the latter is determined by "the useful." They therefore have to do with what we call the production of consumption. See Georges Bataille, *La part maudite, précédé de La notion de dépense* (Paris: Editions de Minuit).

terms confronting each other—not even in the sense of bipolar opposites within a relationship of causation, ideation, or expression (cause and effect, subject and object, etc.); rather, they are one and the same essential reality, the producer-product. Production as process overtakes all idealistic categories and constitutes a cycle whose relationship to desire is that of an immanent principle. That is why desiring-production is the principal concern of a materialist psychiatry, which conceives of and deals with the schizo as *Homo natura*. This will be the case, however, only on one condition, which in fact constitutes the third meaning of process as we use the term: it must not be viewed as a goal or an end in itself, nor must it be confused with an infinite perpetuation of itself. Putting an end to the process or prolonging it indefinitely—which, strictly speaking, is tantamount to ending it abruptly and prematurely— is what creates the artificial schizophrenic found in mental institutions: a limp rag forced into autistic behavior, produced as an entirely separate and independent entity. D. H. Lawrence says of love: "We have pushed a process into a goal. The aim of any process is not the perpetuation of that process, but the completion thereof. . . . The process should work to a completion, not to some horror of intensification and extremity wherein the soul and body ultimately perish."[5] Schizophrenia is like love: there is no specifically schizophrenic phenomenon or entity; schizophrenia is the universe of productive and reproductive desiring-machines, universal primary production as "the essential reality of man and nature."

Desiring-machines are binary machines, obeying a binary law or set of rules governing associations: one machine is always coupled with another. The productive synthesis, the production of production, is inherently connective in nature: "and . . ." "and then . . ." This is because there is always a flow-producing machine, and another machine connected to it that interrupts or draws off part of this flow (the breast—the mouth). And because the first machine is in turn connected to another whose flow it interrupts or partially drains off, the binary series is linear in every direction. Desire constantly couples continuous flows and partial objects that are by nature fragmentary and fragmented. Desire causes the current to flow, itself flows in turn, and breaks the flows. "I love everything that flows, even the menstrual flow that carries away the seed unfecund."* Amniotic fluid spilling out of the sac and kidney stones; flowing hair; a flow of spittle, a flow of sperm, shit, or urine that are produced by partial objects and constantly cut off by other

---

*Henry Miller, *Tropic of Cancer*, Ch. 13. See in this same chapter the celebration of desire-as-flux expressed in the phrase: ". . . and my guts spilled out in a grand schizophrenic rush, an evacuation that leaves me face to face with the Absolute."

partial objects, which in turn produce other flows, interrupted by other partial objects. Every "object" presupposes the continuity of a flow; every flow, the fragmentation of the object. Doubtless each organ-machine interprets the entire world from the perspective of its own flux, from the point of view of the energy that flows from it: the eye interprets everything—speaking, understanding, shitting, fucking—in terms of seeing. But a connection with another machine is always established, along a transverse path, so that one machine interrupts the current of the other or "sees" its own current interrupted.

Hence the coupling that takes place within the partial object–flow connective synthesis also has another form: product/producing. Producing is always something "grafted onto" the product; and for that reason desiring-production is production of production, just as every machine is a machine connected to another machine. We cannot accept the idealist category of "expression" as a satisfactory or sufficient explanation of this phenomenon. We cannot, we must not attempt to describe the schizophrenic object without relating it to the process of production. The *Cahiers de l'art brut** are a striking confirmation of this principle, since by taking such an approach they deny that there is any such thing as a specific, identifiable schizophrenic entity. Or to take another example, Henri Michaux describes a schizophrenic table in terms of a process of production which is that of desire: "Once noticed, it continued to occupy one's mind. It even persisted, as it were, in going about its own business. . . . The striking thing was that it was neither simple nor really complex, initially or intentionally complex, or constructed according to a complicated plan. Instead, it had been desimplified in the course of its carpentering. . . . As it stood, it was a table of additions, much like certain schizophrenics' drawings, described as 'overstuffed,' and if finished it was only in so far as there was no way of adding anything more to it, the table having become more and more an accumulation, less and less a table. . . . It was not intended for any specific purpose, for anything one expects of a table. Heavy, cumbersome, it was virtually immovable. One didn't know how to handle it (mentally or physically). Its top surface, the useful part of the table, having been gradually reduced, was disappearing, with so little relation to the clumsy framework that the thing did not strike one as a table, but as some freak piece of furniture, an unfamiliar instrument . . . for which there was no purpose. A dehumanized table, nothing cozy about it, nothing 'middle-class,' nothing rustic, nothing countrified, not a kitchen table or a work table. A table which lent itself to no function,

---

*A series of monographs, issued periodically, containing reproductions of art works created by inmates of the psychiatric asylums of Europe. *L'Art brut* is edited by Jean Dubuffet.

self-protective, denying itself to service and communication alike. There was something stunned about it, something petrified. Perhaps it suggested a stalled engine."[6]

The schizophrenic is the universal producer. There is no need to distinguish here between producing and its product. We need merely note that the pure "thisness" of the object produced is carried over into a new act of producing. The table continues to "go about its business." The surface of the table, however, is eaten up by the supporting framework. The nontermination of the table is a necessary consequence of its mode of production. When Claude Lévi-Strauss defines *bricolage*,* he does so in terms of a set of closely related characteristics: the possession of a stock of materials or of rules of thumb that are fairly extensive, though more or less a hodgepodge—multiple and at the same time limited; the ability to rearrange fragments continually in new and different patterns or configurations; and as a consequence, an indifference toward the act of producing and toward the product, toward the set of instruments to be used and toward the over-all result to be achieved.† The satisfaction the handyman experiences when he plugs something into an electric socket or diverts a stream of water can scarcely be explained in terms of "playing mommy and daddy," or by the pleasure of violating a taboo. The rule of continually producing production, of grafting producing onto the product, is a characteristic of desiring-machines or of primary production: the production of production. A painting by Richard Lindner, "Boy with Machine," shows a huge, pudgy, bloated boy working one of his little desiring-machines, after having hooked it up to a vast technical social machine—which, as we shall see, is what even the very young child does.

Producing, a product: a producing/product identity. It is this identity that constitutes a third term in the linear series: an enormous undifferentiated object. Everything stops dead for a moment, everything freezes in place—and then the whole process will begin all over again. From a certain point of view it would be much better if nothing worked, if nothing functioned. Never being born, escaping the wheel of continual birth and rebirth, no mouth to suck with, no anus to shit through. Will

---

bricolage: The tinkering about of the *bricoleur*, or amateur handyman. The art of making do with what's at hand. (*Translators' note.*)

†Claude Lévi-Strauss, *The Savage Mind* (Chicago: University of Chicago Press, 1966), p. 17: "The 'bricoleur' is adept at performing a large number of diverse tasks; but unlike the engineer, he does not subordinate each of them to the availability of raw materials and tools conceived and procured for the purpose of the project. His universe of instruments is closed and the rules of his game are always to make do with 'whatever is at hand,' that is to say with a set of tools and materials which is always finite and is also heterogeneous because what it contains bears no relation to the current project, or indeed to any particular project, but is the contingent result of all the occasions there have been to renew or enrich the stock or to maintain it with the remains of previous constructions or destructions."

the machines run so badly, their component pieces fall apart to such a point that they will return to nothingness and thus allow us to return to nothingness? It would seem, however, that the flows of energy are still too closely connected, the partial objects still too organic, for this to happen. What would be required is a pure fluid in a free state, flowing without interruption, streaming over the surface of a full body. Desiring-machines make us an organism; but at the very heart of this production, within the very production of this production, the body suffers from being organized in this way, from not having some other sort of organization, or no organization at all. "An incomprehensible, absolutely rigid stasis" in the very midst of process, as a third stage: "*No mouth. No tongue. No teeth. No larynx. No esophagus. No belly. No anus.*" The automata stop dead and set free the unorganized mass they once served to articulate. The full body without organs is the unproductive, the sterile, the unengendered, the unconsumable. Antonin Artaud discovered this one day, finding himself with no shape or form whatsoever, right there where he was at that moment. The death instinct: that is its name, and death is not without a model. For desire desires death also, because the full body of death is its motor, just as it desires life, because the organs of life are the *working machine.* We shall not inquire how all this fits together so that the machine will run: the question itself is the result of a process of abstraction.

Desiring-machines work only when they break down, and by continually breaking down. Judge Schreber "lived for a long time without a stomach, without intestines, almost without lungs, with a torn oesophagus, without a bladder, and with shattered ribs; he used sometimes to swallow part of his own larynx with his food, etc."[7] The body without organs is nonproductive; nonetheless it is produced, at a certain place and a certain time in the connective synthesis, as the identity of producing and the product: the schizophrenic table is a body without organs. The body without organs is not the proof of an original nothingness, nor is it what remains of a lost totality. Above all, it is not a projection; it has nothing whatsoever to do with the body itself, or with an image of the body. It is the body without an image. This imageless, organless body, the nonproductive, exists right there where it is produced, in the third stage of the binary-linear series. It is perpetually reinserted into the process of production. The catatonic body is produced in the water of the hydrotherapy tub. The full body without organs belongs to the realm of antiproduction; but yet another characteristic of the connective or productive synthesis is the fact that it couples production with antiproduction, with an element of antiproduction.

2 | The Body without Organs

An apparent conflict arises between desiring-machines and the body without organs. Every coupling of machines, every production of a machine, every sound of a machine running, becomes unbearable to the body without organs. Beneath its organs it senses there are larvae and loathsome worms, and a God at work messing it all up or strangling it by organizing it. "The body is the body/it is all by itself/and has no need of organs/the body is never an organism/organisms are the enemies of the body."* Merely so many nails piercing the flesh, so many forms of torture. In order to resist organ-machines, the body without organs presents its smooth, slippery, opaque, taut surface as a barrier. In order to resist linked, connected, and interrupted flows, it sets up a counterflow of amorphous, undifferentiated fluid. In order to resist using words composed of articulated phonetic units, it utters only gasps and cries that are sheer unarticulated blocks of sound. We are of the opinion that what is ordinarily referred to as "primary repression" means precisely that: it is not a "countercathexis," but rather this *repulsion* of desiring-machines by the body without organs. This is the real meaning of the paranoiac machine: the desiring-machines attempt to break into the body without organs, and the body without organs repels them, since it experiences them as an over-all persecution apparatus. Thus we cannot agree with Victor Tausk when he regards the paranoiac machine as a mere projection of "a person's own body" and the genital organs.[8] The genesis of the machine lies precisely here: in the opposition of the process of production of the desiring-machines and the nonproductive stasis of the body without organs. The anonymous nature of the machine and the nondifferentiated nature of its surface are proof of this. Projection enters the picture only secondarily, as does counter-investment,† as the body without organs invests a counterinside or a counteroutside, in the form of a persecuting organ or some exterior agent of persecution. But in and of itself the paranoiac machine is merely an avatar of the desiring-machines: it is a result of the relationship between the desiring-machines and the body without organs, and occurs when the latter can no longer tolerate these machines.

---

*Antonin Artaud, in *84*, nos. 5–6 (1948). The French text reads: "Le corps est le corps/il est seul/et n'a pas besoin d'organe/le corps n'est jamais un organisme/les organismes sont les ennemis du corps." (*Translators' note.*) (Throughout, all English translations of works cited in the text are by the translators, unless otherwise noted.)

†We have adopted this term throughout, except when quoting directly from psychoanalytic literature, because it renders more faithfully the meaning of *investissement*, which in French does service in libidinal as well as political economy. We have likewise chosen to translate *investir* as "to invest" instead of "to cathect." (*Translators' note.*)

If we wish to have some idea of the forces that the body without organs exerts later on in the uninterrupted process, we must first establish a parallel between desiring-production and social production. We intend such a parallel to be regarded as merely phenomenological: we are here drawing no conclusions whatsoever as to the nature and the relationship of the two productions, nor does the parallel we are about to establish provide any sort of a priori answer to the question whether desiring-production and social production are really two separate and distinct productions. Its one purpose is to point out the fact that the forms of social production, like those of desiring-production, involve an unengendered nonproductive attitude, an element of antiproduction coupled with the process, a full body that functions as a *socius*. This socius may be the body of the earth, that of the tyrant, or capital. This is the body that Marx is referring to when he says that it is not the product of labor, but rather appears as its natural or divine presupposition. In fact, it does not restrict itself merely to opposing productive forces in and of themselves. It falls back on (*il se rabat sur*)* all production, constituting a surface over which the forces and agents of production are distributed, thereby appropriating for itself all surplus production and arrogating to itself both the whole and the parts of the process, which now seem to emanate from it as a quasi cause. Forces and agents come to represent a miraculous form of its own power: they appear to be "miraculated" (*miraculés*) by it. In a word, the socius as a full body forms a surface where all production is recorded, whereupon the entire process appears to emanate from this recording surface. Society constructs its own delirium by recording the process of production; but it is not a conscious delirium, or rather is a true consciousness of a false movement, a true perception of an apparent objective movement, a true perception of the movement that is produced on the recording surface.

Capital is indeed the body without organs of the capitalist, or rather of the capitalist being. But as such, it is not only the fluid and petrified substance of money, for it will give to the sterility of money the form whereby money produces money. It produces surplus value, just as the body without organs reproduces itself, puts forth shoots, and branches out to the farthest corners of the universe. It makes the machine responsible for producing a relative surplus value, while embodying itself in the machine as fixed capital. Machines and agents cling so

*The verb *se rabattre sur* (and the noun *rebattement*), used by the authors here and in numerous instances in the text below, has several different connotations, as for instance: in descriptive geometry, to describe the rotation of a plane so as to coincide with another plane, usually followed by a reverse rotation back into its original position; a retreat to a previously held position, as in a battle; and a reduction to a lower level. In the English text below, it will be translated in various ways, depending on the context, followed by the French expression in parentheses. (*Translators' note.*)

closely to capital that their very functioning appears to be miraculated by it. Everything seems objectively to be produced by capital as quasi cause. As Marx observes, *in the beginning* capitalists are necessarily conscious of the opposition between capital and labor, and of the use of capital as a means of extorting surplus labor. But a perverted, bewitched world quickly comes into being, as capital increasingly plays the role of a recording surface that falls back on (*se rabat sur*) all of production. (Furnishing or realizing surplus value is what establishes recording rights.) "With the development of relative surplus-value in the actual specifically capitalist mode of production, whereby the productive powers of social labour are developed, these productive powers and the social interrelations of labour in the direct labour-process seem transferred from labour to capital. Capital thus becomes a very mystic being since all of labour's social productive forces appear to be due to capital, rather than labour as such, and seem to issue from the womb of capital itself."[9] What is specifically capitalist here is the role of money and the use of capital as a full body to constitute the recording or inscribing surface. But some kind of full body, that of the earth or the despot, a recording surface, an apparent objective movement, a fetishistic, perverted, bewitched world are characteristic of all types of society as a constant of social reproduction.

The body without organs now falls back on (*se rabat sur*) desiring-production, attracts it, and appropriates it for its own. The organ-machines now cling to the body without organs as though it were a fencer's padded jacket, or as though these organ-machines were medals pinned onto the jersey of a wrestler who makes them jingle as he starts toward his opponent. An attraction-machine now takes the place, or may take the place, of a repulsion-machine: a miraculating-machine succeeding the paranoiac machine. But what is meant here by "succeeding"? The two coexist, rather, and black humor does not attempt to resolve contradictions, but to make it so that there are none, and never were any. The body without organs, the unproductive, the unconsumable, serves as a surface for the recording of the entire process of production of desire, so that desiring-machines seem to emanate from it in the apparent objective movement that establishes a relationship between the machines and the body without organs. The organs are regenerated, "miraculated" on the body of Judge Schreber, who attracts God's rays to himself. Doubtless the former paranoiac machine continues to exist in the form of mocking voices that attempt to "de-miraculate" (*démiraculer*) the organs, the Judge's anus in particular. But the essential thing is the establishment of an enchanted recording or inscribing surface that arrogates to itself all the productive forces and all the organs of production, and that acts as a quasi cause by communicating the apparent movement (the fetish) to them. So true is it that the schizo practices political economy, and that all sexuality is a matter of economy.

Production is not recorded in the same way it is produced, however. Or rather, it is not reproduced within the apparent objective movement in the same way in which it is produced within the process of constitution. In fact, we have passed imperceptibly into a domain of the production of recording, whose law is not the same as that of the production of production. The law governing the latter was connective synthesis or coupling. But when the productive *connections* pass from machines to the body without organs (as from labor to capital), it would seem that they then come under another law that expresses a *distribution* in relation to the nonproductive element as a "natural or divine presupposition" (the disjunctions of capital). Machines attach themselves to the body without organs as so many points of disjunction, between which an entire network of new syntheses is now woven, marking the surface off into co-ordinates, like a grid. The "either . . . or . . . or" of the schizophrenic takes over from the "and then": no matter what two organs are involved, the way in which they are attached to the body without organs must be such that all the disjunctive syntheses between the two amount to the same on the slippery surface. Whereas the "either/or" claims to mark decisive choices between immutable terms (the alternative: either this or that), the schizophrenic "either . . . or . . . or" refers to the system of possible permutations between differences that always amount to the same as they shift and slide about. As in the case of Beckett's mouth that speaks and feet that walk: "He sometimes halted without saying anything. Either he had finally nothing to say, or while having something to say he finally decided not to say it. . . . Other main examples suggest themselves to the mind. Immediate continuous communication with immediate redeparture. Same thing with delayed redeparture. Delayed continuous communication with immediate redeparture. Same thing with delayed redeparture. Immediate discontinuous communication with immediate redeparture. Same thing with delayed redeparture. Delayed discontinuous communication with immediate redeparture. Same thing with delayed redeparture."[10]

Thus the schizophrenic, the possessor of the most touchingly meager capital—Malone's belongings, for instance—inscribes on his own body the litany of disjunctions, and creates for himself a world of parries where the most minute of permutations is supposed to be a response to the new situation or a reply to the indiscreet questioner. The disjunctive synthesis of recording therefore comes to overlap the connective syntheses of production. The process as process of production extends into the method as method of inscription. Or rather, if what we term libido is the connective "labor" of desiring-production, it should be said that a part of this energy is transformed into the energy of disjunctive inscription (Numen). A transformation of energy. But why call this new form of energy divine, why label it Numen, in view of all the ambiguities caused by a problem of the unconscious that is only apparently religious? The body without organs is not God, quite the contrary. But the energy that sweeps through it is divine, when it attracts to itself the entire process of production and serves as its miraculate, enchanted surface, inscribing it in each and every one of its disjunctions. Hence the strange relationship that Schreber has with God. To anyone who asks: "Do you believe in God?" we should reply in strictly Kantian or Schreberian terms: "Of course, but only as the master of the disjunctive syllogism, or as its a priori principle (God defined as the *Omnitudo realitatis*, from which all secondary realities are derived by a process of division)."

Hence the sole thing that is divine is the nature of an energy of disjunctions. Schreber's divine is inseparable from the disjunctions he employs to divide himself up into parts: earlier empires, later empires; later empires of a superior God, and those of an inferior God. Freud stresses the importance of these disjunctive syntheses in Schreber's delirium in particular, but also in delirium as a general phenomenon. "A process of decomposition of this kind is very characteristic of paranoia. Paranoia decomposes just as hysteria condenses. *Or rather,* paranoia resolves once more into their elements the products of the condensations and identifications which are effected in the unconscious."[11] But why does Freud thus add that, on second thought, hysterical neurosis comes first, and that disjunctions appear only as a result of the projection of a more basic, primordial condensed material? Doubtless this is a way of maintaining intact the rights of Oedipus in the God of delirium and the schizoparanoiac recording process. And for that very reason we must pose the most far-reaching question in this regard: does the recording of desire go by way of the various stages in the formation of the Oedipus complex? Disjunctions are the form that the genealogy of desire assumes; but is this genealogy Oedipal, is it recorded in the Oedipal triangulation? Is it not more likely that Oedipus is a requirement or a consequence of social reproduction, insofar as this latter aims at domesticating a genealogical form and content that are in every way intractable? For there is no doubting the fact that the schizo is constantly subjected to interrogation, constantly cross-examined. Precisely because his relationship with nature does not constitute a specific pole, the questions put to him are formulated in terms of the existing social code: your name, your father, your mother? In the course of his exercises in desiring-production, Beckett's Molloy is cross-examined by a policeman: "Your name is Molloy, said the sergeant. Yes, I said, now I remember. And your mother? said the sergeant. I didn't follow. Is your mother's name Molloy too? said the sergeant. I thought it over. Your mother, said the sergeant, is your mother's— Let me think! I cried. At least I imagine that's how it was. Take your time, said the sergeant. Was mother's name Molloy? Very likely. Her name must be Molloy too, I said. They took me away, to the guardroom I suppose, and there I was told to sit down. I must have tried to explain."[12]

We cannot say that psychoanalysis is very innovative in this respect: it continues to ask its questions and develop its interpretations from the depths of the Oedipal triangle as its basic perspective, even though today it is acutely aware that this frame of reference is not at all adequate to explain so-called psychotic phenomena. The psychoanalyst says that we must *necessarily* discover Schreber's daddy beneath his superior God, and doubtless also his elder brother beneath his inferior God. At times the schizophrenic loses his patience and demands to be left alone. Other times he goes along with the whole game and even invents a few tricks of his own, introducing his own reference points in the model put before him and undermining it from within ("Yes, that's my mother, all right, but my mother's the Virgin Mary, you know"). One can easily imagine Schreber answering Freud: "Yes, I quite agree, naturally the talking birds are young girls, and the superior God is my daddy and the inferior God my brother." But little by little he will surreptitiously "reimpregnate" the series of young girls with all talking birds, his father with the superior God, and his brother with the inferior God, all of them divine forms that become complicated, or rather "desimplified," as they break through the simplistic terms and functions of the Oedipal triangle. As Artaud put it:

> *I don't believe in father*
> > *in mother,*
>
> > *got no*
> > *papamummy*

Desiring-production forms a binary-linear system. The full body is introduced as a third term in the series, without destroying, however, the essential binary-linear nature of this series: 2, 1, 2, 1. . . . The series is completely refractory to a transcription that would transform and mold it into a specifically ternary and triangular schema such as Oedipus. The full body without organs is produced as antiproduction, that is to say it intervenes within the process as such for the sole purpose of rejecting any attempt to impose on it any sort of triangulation implying that it was produced by parents. How could this body have been produced by parents, when by its very nature it is such eloquent witness of its own self-production, of its own engendering of itself? And it is precisely here on this body, right where it is, that the Numen is distributed and disjunctions are established, independent of any sort of projection. *Yes, I have been my father and I have been my son.* "I, Antonin Artaud, am my son, my father, my mother, and myself."[12a] The schizo has his own system of co-ordinates for situating himself at his disposal, because, first of all, he has at his disposal his very own recording code, which does not coincide with the social code, or coincides with it only in order to parody it. The code of delirium or of desire proves to have an extraordinary fluidity. It might be said that the schizophrenic passes from one code to the other, that he deliberately *scrambles all the codes,* by quickly shifting from one to another, according to the questions asked him, never giving the same explanation from one day to the next, never invoking the same genealogy, never recording the same event in the same way. When he is more or less forced into it and is not in a touchy mood, he may even accept the banal Oedipal code, so long as he can stuff it full of all the disjunctions that this code was designed to eliminate.

Adolf Wölfli's drawings reveal the workings of all sorts of clocks, turbines, dynamos, celestial machines, house-machines, and so on. And these machines work in a connective fashion, from the perimeter to the center, in successive layers or segments. But the "explanations" that he provides for them, which he changes as often as the mood strikes him, are based on genealogical series that constitute the recording of each of his drawings. What is even more important, the recording process affects the drawings themselves, showing up in the form of lines standing for "catastrophe" or "collapse" that are so many disjunctions surrounded by spirals.[13] The schizo maintains a shaky balance for the simple reason that the result is always the same, no matter what the disjunctions. Although the organ-machines attach themselves to the body without organs, the latter continues nonetheless to be without organs and does not become an organism in the ordinary sense of the word. It remains fluid and slippery. Agents of production likewise alight on Schreber's body and cling to it—the sunbeams, for instance, that he attracts, which contain thousands of tiny spermatozoids. Sunbeams, birds, voices, nerves enter into changeable and genealogically complex relationships with God and forms of God derived from the godhead by division. But all this happens and is all recorded on the surface of the body without organs: even the copulations of the agents, even the divisions of God, even the genealogies marking it off into squares like a grid, and their permutations. The surface of this uncreated body swarms with them, as a lion's mane swarms with fleas.

3 | The Subject and Enjoyment

Conforming to the meaning of the word "process," recording falls back on (*se rabat sur*) production, but the production of recording itself is produced by the production of production. Similarly, recording is followed by consumption, but the production of consumption is produced in and through the production of recording. This is because something on the order of a *subject* can be discerned on the recording surface. It is a strange subject, however, with no fixed identity, wandering about over the body without organs, but always remaining peripheral to the desiring-machines, being defined by the share of the product it takes for itself, garnering here, there, and everywhere a reward in the form of a becoming or an avatar, being born of the states that it consumes and being reborn with each new state. "It's me, and so it's mine. . . ." Even suffering, as Marx says, is a form of self-enjoyment. Doubtless all desiring-production is, in and of itself, immediately consumption and consummation, and therefore, "sensual pleasure." But this is not yet the case for a subject that can situate itself only in terms of the disjunctions of a recording surface, in what is left after each division. Returning yet again to the case of Judge Schreber, we note that he is vividly aware of this fact: the rate of cosmic sexual pleasure remains constant, so that God will find a way of taking his pleasure with Schreber, even if in order to do so Schreber must transform himself into a woman. But Schreber experiences only a residual share of this pleasure, as a recompense for his suffering or as a reward for his becoming-woman. "On the other hand, God demands a *constant state of enjoyment* . . . and it is my duty to provide him with this . . . in the shape of the greatest possible output of spiritual voluptuousness. And if, in this process, a little sensual pleasure falls to my share, I feel justified in accepting it as some slight compensation for the inordinate measure of suffering and privation that has been mine for so many past years."[14] Just as a part of the libido as energy of production was transformed into energy of recording (Numen), a part of this energy of recording is transformed into energy of consummation (Voluptas).* It is this residual energy that is the motive force behind the third synthesis of the unconscious: the conjunctive synthesis "so it's . . . ," or the production of consumption.

We must examine how this synthesis is formed or how the subject is produced. Our point of departure was the opposition between desiring-machines and the body without organs. The repulsion of these machines, as found in the paranoiac machine of primary repression, gave way to an attraction in the miraculating machine. But the opposition between attraction and repulsion persists. It would seem that a genuine reconciliation of the two can take place only on the level of a new machine, functioning as "the return of the repressed." There are a number of proofs that such a reconciliation does or can exist. With no further details being provided, we are told of Robert Gie, the very talented designer of paranoiac electrical machines: "Since he was unable to free himself of these currents that were tormenting him, he gives every appearance of having finally joined forces with them, taking passionate pride in portraying them in their total victory, in their triumph."[15] Freud is more specific when he stresses the crucial turning point that occurs in Schreber's illness when Schreber becomes reconciled to becoming-woman and embarks upon a process of self-cure that brings him back to the equation Nature = Production (the production of a new humanity). As a matter of fact, Schreber finds himself frozen in the pose and trapped in the paraphernalia of a transvestite, at a moment when he is practically cured and has recovered all his faculties: "I am sometimes to be found, standing before the mirror or elsewhere, with the upper portion of my body partly bared, and wearing sundry feminine adornments, such as ribbons, trumpery necklaces, and the like. This occurs only, I may add, when I am *by myself,* and never, at least so far as I am able to avoid it, in the presence of other people."[16] Let us borrow the term "celibate machine" to designate this machine that succeeds the paranoiac machine and the miraculating machine, forming a new alliance between the desiring-machines and the body without organs so as to give birth to a new humanity or a glorious organism. This is tantamount to saying that the subject is produced as a mere residuum alongside the desiring-machines, or that he confuses himself with this third productive machine and with the residual reconciliation that it brings about: a

*The French term here is *énergie de consommation.* The word *consommation* has a number of meanings in French, among them consummation (as of a marriage); an ultimate fulfillment or perfection; and consumption (as of raw material, fuel, or products). The term has therefore been translated variously below, depending on the context. (*Translators' note.*)

conjunctive synthesis of consummation in the form of a wonderstruck "So *that's* what it was!"

Michel Carrouges has identified a certain number of fantastic machines—"celibate machines"—that he has discovered in works of literature. The examples he points to are of many very different sorts, and at first glance do not seem to belong to a single category: Marcel Duchamp's painting "La mariée mise à nu par ses célibataires, même" ("The Bride Stripped Bare by Her Bachelors, Even"), the machine in Kafka's "In the Penal Colony," Raymond Roussel's machines, those of Jarry's *Surmâle (Supermale)*, certain of Edgar Allan Poe's machines, Villiers's *Eve future (The Future Eve)*, etc.[17] The characteristics that allow us to classify all of them in this one category—though their importance varies according to the example considered—are as follows: the celibate machine first of all reveals the existence of a much older paranoiac machine, with its tortures, its dark shadows, its ancient Law. The celibate machine itself is not a paranoiac machine, however. Everything about it is different: its cogs, its sliding carriage, its shears, needles, magnets, rays. Even when it tortures or kills, it manifests something new and different, a solar force. In the second place, this transfiguration cannot be explained by the "miraculating" powers the machine possesses due to the inscription hidden inside it, though it in fact contains within itself the most impressive sort of inscriptions (cf. the recording supplied by Edison for *Eve future*). A genuine consummation is achieved by the new machine, a pleasure that can rightly be called autoerotic, or rather automatic: the nuptial celebration of a new alliance, a new birth, a radiant ecstasy, as though the eroticism of the machine liberated other unlimited forces.

The question becomes: what does the celibate machine produce? what is produced by means of it? The answer would seem to be: intensive quantities. There is a schizophrenic experience of intensive quantities in their pure state, to a point that is almost unbearable—a celibate misery and glory experienced to the fullest, like a cry suspended between life and death, an intense feeling of transition, states of pure, naked intensity stripped of all shape and form. These are often described as hallucinations and delirium, but the basic phenomenon of hallucination (*I see, I hear*) and the basic phenomenon of delirium (*I think . . .*) presuppose an *I feel* at an even deeper level, which gives hallucinations their object and thought delirium its content—an "I feel that I am becoming a woman," "that I am becoming a god," and so on, which is neither delirious nor hallucinatory, but will project the hallucination or internalize the delirium. Delirium and hallucination are secondary in relation to the really primary emotion, which in the beginning only experiences intensities, becomings, transitions.* Where do these pure intensities come from? They come from the two preceding forces, repulsion and attraction, and from the opposition of these two forces. It must not be thought that the intensities themselves are in opposition to one another, arriving at a state of balance around a neutral state. On the contrary, they are all positive in relationship to the zero intensity that designates the full body without organs. And they undergo relative rises or falls depending on the complex relationship between them and the variations in the relative strength of attraction and repulsion as determining factors. In a word, the opposition of the forces of attraction and repulsion produces an open series of intensive elements, all of them positive, that are never an expression of the final equilibrium of a system, but consist, rather, of an unlimited number of stationary, metastable states through which a subject passes. The Kantian theory according to which intensive quantities fill up, to varying degrees, *matter that has no empty spaces,* is profoundly schizoid.

Further, if we are to believe Judge Schreber's doctrine, *attraction and repulsion* produce intense *nervous states* that fill up the body without organs to varying degrees—states through which Schreber-the-subject passes, becoming a woman and many other things as well, following an endless circle of eternal return. The breasts on the judge's naked torso are neither delirious nor hallucinatory phenomena: they designate, first of all, a band of intensity, a zone of intensity on his body without organs. The body without organs is an egg: it is crisscrossed with axes and thresholds, with latitudes and longitudes and geodesic lines, traversed by *gradients* marking the transitions and the becomings, the destinations of the subject developing along these particular vectors. Nothing here is representative; rather, it is all life and lived experience: the actual, lived emotion of having breasts does not resemble breasts, it does not represent them, any more than a predestined zone in the egg resembles the organ that it is going to be stimulated to produce within itself. Nothing but bands of intensity, potentials, thresholds, and gradients. A harrowing, emotionally overwhelming experience, which brings the schizo as close as possible to matter, to a burning, living center of matter: ". . . this emotion, situated outside of the particular point where the mind is searching for it . . . one's entire soul flows into this emotion that makes the mind aware of the terribly disturbing sound of matter, and passes through its white-hot flame."[18]

How is it possible that the schizo was conceived of as the autistic

*W.R.Bion is the first to have stressed this importance of the *I feel,* but he places it in the realm of fantasy and makes it an affective parallel of the *I think.* See *Elements of Psycho-analysis* (London: Heinemann, 1963), pp. 94ff.

rag—separated from the real and cut off from life—that he is so often thought to be? Worse still: how can psychiatric practice have made him this sort of rag, how can it have reduced him to this state of a body without organs that has become a dead thing—this schizo who sought to remain at that unbearable point where the mind touches matter and lives its every intensity, consumes it? And shouldn't this question immediately compel us to raise another one, which at first glance seems quite different: how does psychoanalysis go about reducing a person, who this time is not a schizophrenic but a neurotic, to a pitiful creature who eternally consumes daddy-and-mommy and nothing else whatsoever? How could the conjunctive synthesis of "So *that's* what it was!" and "So it's *me*!" have been reduced to the endless, dreary discovery of Oedipus: "So it's my father, my mother"? We cannot answer these two questions at this point. We merely see how very little the consumption of pure intensities has to do with family figures, and how very different the connective tissue of the "So it's . . ." is from the Oedipal tissue.

How can we sum up this entire vital progression? Let us trace it along a first path (the shortest route): the points of disjunction on the body without organs form circles that converge on the desiring-machines; then the subject—produced as a residuum alongside the machine, as an appendix, or as a spare part adjacent to the machine—passes through all the degrees of the circle, and passes from one circle to another. This subject itself is not at the center, which is occupied by the machine, but on the periphery, with no fixed identity, forever decentered, *defined* by the states through which it passes. Thus the circles traced by Beckett's Unnamable: "a succession of irregular loops, now sharp and short as in the waltz, now of a parabolic sweep,"[19] with Murphy, Watt, Mercier, etc., as states, without the family having anything whatsoever to do with all of this. Or, to follow a path that is more complex, but leads in the end to the same thing: by means of the paranoiac machine and the miraculating machine, the proportions of attraction and repulsion on the body without organs produce, starting from zero, a series of states in the celibate machine; and the subject is born of each state in the series, is continually reborn of the following state that determines him at a given moment, consuming-consummating all these states that cause him to be born and reborn (the lived state coming first, in relation to the subject that lives it).

This is what Klossowski has admirably demonstrated in his commentary on Nietzsche: the presence of the *Stimmung* as a material emotion, constitutive of the most lofty thought and the most acute perception. "The centrifugal forces do not flee the center forever, but approach it once again, only to retreat from it yet again: such is the nature of the violent oscillations that overwhelm an individual so long as he seeks only his own center and is incapable of seeing the circle of which he himself is a part; for if these oscillations overwhelm him, it is because each one of them corresponds to an individual other than the one he believes himself to be, from the point of view of the unlocatable center. As a result, an identity is essentially fortuitous, and a series of individualities must be undergone by each of these oscillations, so that as a consequence the fortuitousness of this or that particular individuality will render all of them necessary."[20] The forces of attraction and repulsion, of soaring ascents and plunging falls, produce a series of intensive states based on the intensity = 0 that designates the body without organs ("but what is most unusual is that here again a new afflux is necessary, merely to signify this absence"[21]). There is no Nietzsche-the-self, professor of philology, who suddenly loses his mind and supposedly identifies with all sorts of strange people; rather, there is the Nietzschean subject who passes through a series of states, and who identifies these states with the names of history: "*every name in history is I. . . .*"[22] The subject spreads itself out along the entire circumference of the circle, the center of which has been abandoned by the ego. At the center is the desiring-machine, the celibate machine of the Eternal Return. A residual subject of the machine, Nietzsche-as-subject garners a euphoric reward (Voluptas) from everything that this machine turns out, a product that the reader had thought to be no more than the fragmented *oeuvre* by Nietzsche. "Nietzsche believes that he is now pursuing, not the realization of a system, but the application of a program . . . in the form of residues of the Nietzschean discourse, which have now become the repertory, so to speak, of his histrionicism."[23] It is not a matter of identifying with various historical personages, but rather identifying the names of history with zones of intensity on the body without organs; and each time Nietzsche-as-subject exclaims: "They're *me*! So it's *me*!" No one has ever been as deeply involved in history as the schizo, or dealt with it in this way. He consumes all of universal history in one fell swoop. We began by defining him as *Homo natura,* and lo and behold, he has turned out to be *Homo historia.* This long road that leads from the one to the other stretches from Hölderlin to Nietzsche, and the pace becomes faster and faster. "The euphoria could not be prolonged in Nietzsche for as long a time as the contemplative alienation of Hölderlin. . . . The vision of the world granted to Nietzsche does not inaugurate a more or less regular succession of landscapes or still lifes, extending over a period of forty years or so; it is, rather, a parody of the process of recollection of an event: a single actor will play the whole of it in pantomime in the course of a single solemn day—because the whole of it reaches expression and then disappears once again in the space of just one day—even though it may appear to have taken place between December 31 and January 6—in a realm above and beyond the usual rational calendar."[24]

4 | A Materialist Psychiatry

The famous hypothesis put forward by the psychiatrist G. de Clerambault seems well founded: delirium, which is by nature global and systematic, is a secondary phenomenon, a consequence of partial and local automatistic phenomena. Delirium is in fact characteristic of the recording that is made of the process of production of the desiring-machines; and though there are syntheses and disorders (*affections*) that are peculiar to this recording process, as we see in paranoia and even in the paranoid forms of schizophrenia, it does not constitute an autonomous sphere, for it depends on the functioning and the breakdowns of desiring-machines. Nonetheless Clerambault used the term "(mental) automatism" to designate only athematic phenomena— echolalia, the uttering of odd sounds, or sudden irrational outbursts— which he attributed to the mechanical effects of infections or intoxications. Moreover, he explained a large part of delirium in turn as an effect of automatism; as for the rest of it, the "personal" part, in his view it was of the nature of a reaction and had to do with "character," the manifestations of which might well precede the automatism (as in the paranoiac character, for instance).[25] Hence Clerambault regarded automatism as merely a neurological mechanism in the most general sense of the word, rather than a process of economic production involving desiring-machines. As for history, he was content merely to mention its innate or acquired nature. Clerambault is the Feuerbach of psychiatry, in the sense in which Marx remarks: "Whenever Feuerbach looks at things as a materialist, there is no history in his works, and whenever he takes history into account, he no longer is a materialist." A truly materialist psychiatry can be defined, on the contrary, by the twofold task it sets itself: introducing desire into the mechanism, and introducing production into desire.

There is no very great difference between false materialism and typical forms of idealism. The theory of schizophrenia is formulated in terms of three concepts that constitute its trinary schema: dissociation (Kraepelin), autism (Bleuler), and space-time or being-in-the-world (Binswanger). The first of these is an explanatory concept that supposedly locates the specific dysfunction or primary deficiency. The second is an ideational concept indicating the specific nature of the effect of the disorder: the delirium itself or the complete withdrawal from the outside world, "the detachment from reality, accompanied by a relative or an absolute predominance of [the schizophrenic's] inner life." The third concept is a descriptive one, discovering or rediscovering the delirious person in his own specific world. What is common to these three concepts is the fact that they all relate the problem of schizophrenia to the ego through the intermediary of the "body image"—the final avatar of the soul, a vague conjoining of the requirements of spiritualism and positivism.

The ego, however, is like daddy-mommy: the schizo has long since ceased to believe in it. He is somewhere else, beyond or behind or below these problems, rather than immersed in them. And wherever he is, there are problems, insurmountable sufferings, unbearable needs. But why try to bring him back to what he has escaped from, why set him back down amid problems that are no longer problems to him, why mock his truth by believing that we have paid it its due by merely figuratively taking our hats off to it? There are those who will maintain that the schizo is incapable of uttering the word *I,* and that we must restore his ability to pronounce this hallowed word. All of which the schizo sums up by saying: they're fucking me over again. "I won't say *I* any more, I'll never utter the word again; it's just too damn stupid. Every time I hear it, I'll use the third person instead, if I happen to remember to. If it amuses them. And it won't make one bit of difference."[26] And if he does chance to utter the word *I* again, that won't make any difference either. He is too far removed from these problems, too far past them.

Even Freud never went beyond this narrow and limited conception of the ego. And what prevented him from doing so was his own tripartite formula—the Oedipal, neurotic one: daddy-mommy-me. We may well ponder the possibility that the analytic imperialism of the Oedipus complex led Freud to rediscover, and to lend all the weight of his authority to, the unfortunate misapplication of the concept of autism to schizophrenia. For we must not delude ourselves: Freud doesn't like schizophrenics. He doesn't like their resistance to being oedipalized, and tends to treat them more or less as animals. They mistake words for things, he says. They are apathetic, narcissistic, cut off from reality, incapable of achieving transference; they resemble philosophers—"an undesirable resemblance."

The question as to how to deal analytically with the relationship between drives (*pulsions*) and symptoms, between the symbol and what is symbolized, has arisen again and again. Is this relationship to be considered *causal?* Or is it a relationship of *comprehension?* A mode of *expression?* The question, however, has been posed too theoretically. The fact is, from the moment that we are placed within the framework of Oedipus—from the moment that we are measured in terms of Oedipus—the cards are stacked against us, and the only real relationship, that of production, has been done away with. The great discovery of psychoanalysis was that of the production of desire, of the productions of the unconscious. But once Oedipus entered the picture, this discovery was soon buried beneath a new brand of idealism: a classical theater was substituted for the unconscious as a factory; representation was substituted for the units of production of the unconscious; and an unconscious that was capable of nothing but expressing itself—in myth, tragedy, dreams—was substituted for the productive unconscious.

Every time that the problem of schizophrenia is explained in terms of the ego, all we can do is "sample" a supposed essence or a presumed specific nature of the schizo, regardless of whether we do so with love and pity or disgustedly spit out the mouthful we have tasted. We have "sampled" him once as a dissociated ego, another time as an ego cut off from the world, and yet again—most temptingly—as an ego that had not ceased to be, who was there in the most specific way, but in his very own world, though he might reveal himself to a clever psychiatrist, a sympathetic superobserver—in short, a phenomenologist. Let us remember once again one of Marx's caveats: we cannot tell from the mere taste of wheat who grew it; the product gives us no hint as to the system and the relations of production. The product appears to be all the more specific, incredibly specific and readily describable, the more closely the theoretician relates it to *ideal forms of causation, comprehension, or expression,* rather than to *the real process of production on which it depends.* The schizophrenic appears all the more specific and recognizable as a distinct personality if the process is halted, or if it is made an end and a goal in itself, or if it is allowed to go on and on endlessly in a void, so as to provoke that "horror of . . . extremity wherein the soul and body ultimately perish"[27] (the autist). Kraepelin's celebrated terminal state. . . But the moment that one describes, on the contrary, the material process of production, the specificity of the product tends to evaporate, while at the same time the possibility of another outcome, another end result of the process appears. Before being a mental state of the schizophrenic who has made himself into an artificial person through autism, schizophrenia is the process of the production of desire and desiring-machines. How does one get from one to the other, and is this transition inevitable? This remains the crucial question. Karl Jaspers has given us precious insights, on this point as on so many others, because his "idealism" was remarkably atypical. Contrasting the concept of process with those of reaction formation or development of the personality, he views process as a rupture or intrusion, having nothing to do with an imaginary relationship with the ego; rather, it is a relationship with the "demoniacal" in nature. The one thing Jaspers failed to do was to view process as material economic reality, as the process of production wherein Nature = Industry, Nature = History.

To a certain degree, the traditional logic of desire is all wrong from the very outset: from the very first step that the Platonic logic of desire forces us to take, making us choose between *production* and *acquisition*. From the moment that we place desire on the side of acquisition, we make desire an idealistic (dialectical, nihilistic) conception, which causes us to look upon it as primarily a lack: a lack of an object, a lack of the real object. It is true that the other side, the "production" side, has not been entirely ignored. Kant, for instance, must be credited with effecting a critical revolution as regards the theory of desire, by attributing to it "the faculty of being, through its representations, the cause of the reality of the objects of these representations."[28] But it is not by chance that Kant chooses superstitious beliefs, hallucinations, and fantasies as illustrations of this definition of desire: as Kant would have it, we are well aware that the real object can be produced only by an external causality and external mechanisms; nonetheless this knowledge does not prevent us from believing in the intrinsic power of desire to create its own object—if only in an unreal, hallucinatory, or delirious form—or from representing this causality as stemming from within desire itself. The reality of the object, insofar as it is produced by desire, is thus a *psychic reality*. Hence it can be said that Kant's critical revolution changes nothing essential: this way of conceiving of productivity does not question the validity of the classical conception of desire as a lack; rather, it uses this conception as a support and a buttress, and merely examines its implications more carefully.

In point of fact, if desire is the lack of the real object, its very nature as a real entity depends upon an "essence of lack" that produces the fantasized object. Desire thus conceived of as production, though merely the production of fantasies, has been explained perfectly by psychoanalysis. On the very lowest level of interpretation, this means that the real object that desire lacks is related to an extrinsic natural or social production, whereas desire intrinsically produces an imaginary object that functions as a double of reality, as though there were a "dreamed-of object behind every real object," or a mental production behind all real productions. This conception does not necessarily compel psychoanalysis to engage in a study of gadgets and markets, in the form of an utterly dreary and dull psychoanalysis of the object: psychoanalytic studies of packages of noodles, cars, or "thingumajigs." But even when the fantasy is interpreted in depth, not simply as an object, but as a specific machine that brings desire itself front and center, this machine is merely theatrical, and the complementarity of what it sets apart still remains: it is now need that is defined in terms of a relative lack and determined by its own object, whereas desire is regarded as what produces the fantasy and produces itself by detaching itself from the object, though at the same time it intensifies the lack by making it absolute: an "incurable insufficiency of being," an "inability-to-be that is life itself." Hence the presentation of desire as something *supported* by needs, while these needs, and their relationship to the object as something that is lacking or missing, continue to be the basis of the productivity of desire (theory of an underlying support). In a word, when the theoretician reduces desiring-production to a production of fantasy, he is content to exploit to the fullest the idealist principle that defines desire as a lack, rather than a process of production, of "industrial" production. Clément Rosset puts it very well: every time the emphasis is put on a lack that desire supposedly suffers from as a way of defining its object, "the world acquires as its double some other sort of world, in accordance with the following line of argument: there is an object that desire feels the lack of; hence the world does not contain each and every object that exists; there is at least one object missing, the one that desire feels the lack of; hence there exists some other place that contains the key to desire (missing in this world)."[29]

If desire produces, its product is real. If desire is productive, it can be productive only in the real world and can produce only reality. Desire is the set of *passive syntheses* that engineer partial objects, flows, and bodies, and that function as units of production. The real is the end product, the result of the passive syntheses of desire as autoproduction of the unconscious. Desire does not lack anything; it does not lack its object. It is, rather, the *subject* that is missing in desire, or desire that lacks a fixed subject; there is no fixed subject unless there is repression. Desire and its object are one and the same thing: the machine, as a machine of a machine. Desire is a machine, and the object of desire is another machine connected to it. Hence the product is something removed or deducted from the process of producing: between the act of producing and the product, something becomes detached, thus giving the vagabond, nomad subject a residuum. The objective being of desire is the Real in and of itself.* There is no particular form of existence that can be labeled "psychic reality." As Marx notes, what exists in fact is not lack, but passion, as a "natural and sensuous object." Desire is not bolstered by needs, but rather the contrary; needs are derived from desire: they are counterproducts within the real that desire produces. Lack is a countereffect of desire; it is deposited, distributed, vacuolized within a real that is natural and social. Desire always remains in close touch with the conditions of objective existence; it embraces them and follows them, shifts when they shift, and does not outlive them. For that reason it so often becomes the desire to die, whereas need is a measure of the withdrawal of a subject that has lost its desire at the same time that it loses the passive syntheses of these conditions. This is precisely the significance of need as a search in a void: hunting about, trying to capture or become a parasite of passive syntheses in whatever vague world they may happen to exist in. It is no use saying: We are not green plants; we have long since been unable to synthesize chlorophyll, so it's necessary to eat. . . . Desire then becomes this abject fear of lacking something. But it should be noted that this is not a phrase uttered by the poor or the dispossessed. On the contrary, such people know that they are close to grass, almost akin to it, and that desire "needs" very few things—*not those leftovers that chance to come their way, but the very things that are continually taken from them*—and that what is missing is not things a subject feels the lack of somewhere deep down inside himself, but rather the objectivity of man, the objective being of man, for whom to desire is to produce, to produce within the realm of the real.

The real is not impossible; on the contrary, within the real everything is possible, everything becomes possible. Desire does not express a molar lack within the subject; rather, the molar organization deprives desire of its objective being. Revolutionaries, artists, and seers are content to be objective, merely objective: they know that desire clasps life in its powerfully productive embrace, and reproduces it in a way that is all the more intense because it has few needs. And never mind those who believe that this is very easy to say, or that it is the sort of idea to be found in books. "From the little reading I had done I had observed that the men who were most *in* life, who were moulding life, who were life itself, ate little, slept little, owned little or nothing. They had no illusions about duty, or the perpetuation of their kith and kin, or the preservation

*Lacan's admirable theory of desire appears to us to have two poles: one related to "the object small *a*" as a desiring-machine, which defines desire in terms of a real production, thus going beyond both any idea of need and any idea of fantasy; and the other related to the "great Other" as a signifier, which reintroduces a certain notion of lack. In Serge Leclaire's article "La réalité du désir" (Ch. 4, reference note 26), the oscillation between these two poles can be seen quite clearly.

of the State. . . . The phantasmal world is the world which has never been fully conquered over. It is the world of the past, never of the future. To move forward clinging to the past is like dragging a ball and chain."[30] The true visionary is a Spinoza in the garb of a Neapolitan revolutionary. We know very well where lack—and its subjective correlative—come from. Lack (*manque*)* is created, planned, and organized in and through social production. It is counterproduced as a result of the pressure of antiproduction; the latter falls back on (*se rabat sur*) the forces of production and appropriates them. It is never primary; production is never organized on the basis of a pre-existing need or lack (*manque*). It is lack that infiltrates itself, creates empty spaces or vacuoles, and propagates itself in accordance with the organization of an already existing organization of production.† The deliberate creation of lack as a function of market economy is the art of a dominant class. This involves deliberately organizing wants and needs (*manque*) amid an abundance of production; making all of desire teeter and fall victim to the great fear of not having one's needs satisfied; and making the object dependent upon a real production that is supposedly exterior to desire (the demands of rationality), while at the same time the production of desire is categorized as fantasy and nothing but fantasy.

There is no such thing as the social production of reality on the one hand, and a desiring-production that is mere fantasy on the other. The only connections that could be established between these two productions would be secondary ones of introjection and projection, as though all social practices had their precise counterpart in introjected or internal mental practices, or as though mental practices were projected upon social systems, without either of the two sets of practices ever having any real or concrete effect upon the other. As long as we are content to establish a perfect parallel between money, gold, capital, and the capitalist triangle on the one hand, and the libido, the anus, the phallus, and the family triangle on the other, we are engaging in an enjoyable pastime, but the mechanisms of money remain totally unaffected by the anal projections of those who manipulate money. The Marx-Freud parallelism between the two remains utterly sterile and

---

*The French word *manque* may mean both lack and need in a psychological sense, as well as want or privation or scarcity in an economic sense. Depending upon the context, it will hence be translated in various ways below. (*Translators' note.*)

†Maurice Clavel remarks, apropos of Jean-Paul Sartre, that a Marxist philosophy cannot allow itself to introduce the notion of scarcity as its initial premise: "Such a scarcity antedating exploitation makes of the law of supply and demand a reality that will remain forever independent, since it is situated at a primordial level. Hence it is no longer a question of including or deducing this law within Marxism, since it is immediately evident at a prior stage, at a level from which Marxism itself derives. Being a rigorous thinker, Marx refuses to employ the notion of scarcity, and is quite correct to do so, for this category would be his undoing." In *Qui est aliéné?* (Paris: Flammarion, 1970), p. 330.

insignificant as long as it is expressed in terms that make them introjections or projections of each other without ceasing to be utterly alien to each other, as in the famous equation money = shit. The truth of the matter is that *social production is purely and simply desiring-production itself under determinate conditions.* We maintain that the social field is immediately invested by desire, that it is the historically determined product of desire, and that libido has no need of any mediation or sublimation, any psychic operation, any transformation, in order to invade and invest the productive forces and the relations of production. *There is only desire and the social, and nothing else.*

Even the most repressive and the most deadly forms of social reproduction are produced by desire within the organization that is the consequence of such production under various conditions that we must analyze. That is why the fundamental problem of political philosophy is still precisely the one that Spinoza saw so clearly, and that Wilhelm Reich rediscovered: "Why do men fight *for* their servitude as stubbornly as though it were their salvation?" How can people possibly reach the point of shouting: "More taxes! Less bread!"? As Reich remarks, the astonishing thing is not that some people steal or that others occasionally go out on strike, but rather that all those who are starving do not steal as a regular practice, and all those who are exploited are not continually out on strike: after centuries of exploitation, why do people still tolerate being humiliated and enslaved, to such a point, indeed, that they *actually want* humiliation and slavery not only for others but for themselves? Reich is at his profoundest as a thinker when he refuses to accept ignorance or illusion on the part of the masses as an explanation of fascism, and demands an explanation that will take their desires into account, an explanation formulated in terms of desire: no, the masses were not innocent dupes; at a certain point, under a certain set of conditions, they *wanted* fascism, and it is this perversion of the desire of the masses that needs to be accounted for.[31]

Yet Reich himself never manages to provide a satisfactory explanation of this phenomenon, because at a certain point he reintroduces precisely the line of argument that he was in the process of demolishing, by creating a distinction between rationality as it is or ought to be in the process of social production, and the irrational element in desire, and by regarding only this latter as a suitable subject for psychoanalytic investigation. Hence the sole task he assigns psychoanalysis is the explanation of the "negative," the "subjective," the "inhibited" within the social field. He therefore necessarily returns to a dualism between the real object rationally produced on the one hand, and irrational, fantasizing production on the other.* He gives up trying to discover the *common denominator or the coextension of the social field and desire.* In order to establish the basis for a genuinely materialistic psychiatry, there was a category that Reich was sorely in need of: that of desiring-production, which would apply to the real in both its so-called rational and irrational forms.

The fact there is massive social repression that has an enormous effect on desiring-production in no way vitiates our principle: desire produces reality, or stated another way, desiring-production is one and the same thing as social production. It is not possible to attribute a special form of existence to desire, a mental or psychic reality that is presumably different from the material reality of social production. Desiring-machines are not fantasy-machines or dream-machines, which supposedly can be distinguished from technical and social machines. Rather, fantasies are secondary expressions, deriving from the identical nature of the two sorts of machines in any given set of circumstances. Thus fantasy is never individual: it is *group fantasy*—as institutional analysis† has successfully demonstrated. And if there is such a thing as two sorts of group fantasy, it is because two different readings of this identity are possible, depending upon whether the desiring-machines are regarded from the point of view of the great gregarious masses that they form, or whether social machines are considered from the point of view of the elementary forces of desire that serve as a basis for them. Hence in group fantasy the libido may invest all of an existing social field, including the latter's most repressive forms; or on the contrary, it may launch a counterinvestment whereby revolutionary desire is plugged into the existing social field as a source of energy. (The great socialist utopias of the nineteenth century function, for example, not as ideal

*We find in the case of culturalists a distinction between rational systems and projective systems, with psychoanalysis applying only to these latter (as for example in Abram Kardiner). Despite their hostility to culturalism, we find in both Wilhelm Reich and Herbert Marcuse certain traces of this same dualism, even though they define the rational and the irrational in a completely different way and assign them quite different roles.

† *Institutional analysis* is the more political tendency of institutional psychotherapy, begun in the late 1950s as an attempt to collectively deal with what psychoanalysis so hypocritically avoided, namely the psychoses. La Borde Clinic, established in 1955 by Jean Oury of the Ecole Freudienne de Paris, served as the locus for discussions on institutional psychotherapy, and Jacques Lacan's seminars served as the intellectual basis for these discussions "in the beginning." Félix Guattari joined the clinic in 1956, as a militant interested in the notions of desire under discussion—a topic rarely dealt with by militants at that time. Preferring the term "institutional analysis" over "institutional psychotherapy," Guattari sought to push the movement in a more political direction, toward what he later described as a political analysis of desire. In any case this injection of a psychoanalytical discourse (Lacan's version) into a custodial institution led to a collectivization of the analytical concepts. Transference came to be seen as institutional, and fantasies were seen to be collective: *desire was a problem of groups and for groups.* See Jacques Donzelot's excellent article on *Anti-Oedipus*, "Une anti-sociologie" in *Esprit*, December 1972, and Gilles Deleuze's detailed discussion of Guattari's notion of groups and desire, "Trois problèmes de groupe" in Félix Guattari, *Psychanalyse et transversalité* (Paris: Maspero, 1972). (*Translators' note.*)

models but as group fantasies—that is, as agents of the real productivity of desire, making it possible to disinvest the current social field, to "deinstitutionalize" it, to further the revolutionary institution of desire itself.) But there is never any difference in nature between the desiring-machines and the technical social machines. There is a certain distinction between them, but it is merely a distinction of *régime*,* depending on *their* relationships of size. Except for this difference in régime, they are the same machines, as group fantasies clearly prove.

When in the course of our discussion above, we laid down the broad outlines of a parallelism between social production and desiring-production, in order to show that in both cases there is a strong tendency on the part of the forces of antiproduction to operate retroactively on (*se rabattre sur*) productive forms and appropriate them, this parallelism was in no way meant as an exhaustive description of the relationship between the two systems of production. It merely enables us to point to certain phenomena having to do with the difference in régime between them. In the first place, technical machines obviously work only if they are not out of order; they ordinarily stop working not because they break down but because they wear out. Marx makes use of this simple principle to show that the régime of technical machines is characterized by a strict distinction between the means of production and the product; thanks to this distinction, the machine transmits value to the product, but only the value that the machine itself loses as it wears out. Desiring-machines, on the contrary, continually break down as they run, and in fact run only when they are not functioning properly: the product is always an offshoot of production, implanting itself upon it like a graft, and at the same time the parts of the machine are the fuel that makes it run.

Art often takes advantage of this property of desiring-machines by creating veritable group fantasies in which desiring-production is used to short-circuit social production, and to interfere with the reproductive function of technical machines by introducing an element of dysfunction. Arman's charred violins, for instance, or César's compressed car bodies. More generally, Dali's method of critical paranoia assures the explosion of a desiring-machine within an object of social production. But even earlier, Ravel preferred to throw his inventions entirely out of gear rather than let them simply run down, and chose to end his compositions with abrupt breaks, hesitations, tremolos, discordant notes, and unresolved chords, rather than allowing them to slowly wind

*The word *régime* has a number of different meanings in French, including: regimen or form of government; a set of laws, rules, or regulations; rate of flow, as of a current; rate or speed of operation, as of a motor or engine. Since the authors use the word in several senses, the French word *régime* has been retained throughout the English text. (*Translators' note.*)

down to a close or gradually die away into silence.³² The artist is the master of objects; he puts before us shattered, burned, broken-down objects, converting them to the régime of desiring-machines, breaking down is part of the very functioning of desiring-machines; the artist presents paranoiac machines, miraculating-machines, and celibate machines as so many technical machines, so as to cause desiring-machines to undermine technical machines. Even more important, the work of art is itself a desiring-machine. The artist stores up his treasures so as to create an immediate explosion, and that is why, to his way of thinking, destructions can never take place as rapidly as they ought to.

From this, a second difference in régime results: desiring-machines produce antiproduction all by themselves, whereas the antiproduction characteristic of technical machines takes place only within the extrinsic conditions of the reproduction of the process (even though these conditions do not come into being at some "later stage"). That is why technical machines are not an economic category, and always refer back to a socius or a social machine that is quite distinct from these machines, and that conditions this reproduction. A technical machine is therefore not a cause but merely an index of a general form of social production: thus there are manual machines and primitive societies, hydraulic machines and "Asiatic" forms of society, industrial machines and capitalism. Hence when we posited the socius as the analogue of a full body without organs, there was nonetheless one important difference. For desiring-machines are the fundamental category of the economy of desire; they produce a body without organs all by themselves, and make no distinction between agents and their own parts, or between the relations of production and their own relations, or between the social order and technology. Desiring-machines are both technical and social. It is in this sense that desiring-production is the locus of a primal psychic repression,³³ whereas social production is where social repression takes place, and it is between the former and the latter that there occurs something that resembles secondary psychic repression in the "strictest" sense: the situation of the body without organs or its equivalent is the crucial factor here, depending on whether it is the result of an internal process or of an extrinsic condition (and thus affects the role of the death instinct in particular).

But at the same time they are the same machines, despite the fact that they are governed by two different régimes—and despite the fact that it is admittedly a strange adventure for desire to desire repression. There is only one kind of production, the production of the real. And doubtless we can express this identity in two different ways, even though these two ways together constitute the autoproduction of the unconscious as a cycle. We can say that social production, under determinate conditions, derives primarily from desiring-production: which is to say that *Homo natura* comes first. But we must also say, more accurately, that desiring-production is first and foremost social in nature, and tends to free itself only at the end: which is to say that *Homo historia* comes first. The body without organs is not an original primordial entity that later projects itself into different sorts of socius, as though it were a raving paranoiac, the chieftain of the primitive horde, who was initially responsible for social organization. The social machine or socius may be the body of the Earth, the body of the Despot, the body of Money. It is never a projection, however, of the body without organs. On the contrary: the body without organs is the ultimate residuum of a deterritorialized socius. The prime function incumbent upon the socius, has always been to codify the flows of desire, to inscribe them, to record them, to see to it that no flow exists that is not properly dammed up, channeled, regulated. When the primitive *territorial machine* proved inadequate to the task, the *despotic machine* set up a kind of overcoding system. But the *capitalist machine,* insofar as it was built on the ruins of a despotic State more or less far removed in time, finds itself in a totally new situation: it is faced with the task of decoding and deterritorializing the flows. Capitalism does not confront this situation from the outside, since it experiences it as the very fabric of its existence, as both its primary determinant and its fundamental raw material, its form and its function, and deliberately perpetuates it, in all its violence, with all the powers at its command. Its sovereign production and repression can be achieved in no other way. Capitalism is in fact born of the encounter of two sorts of flows: the decoded flows of production in the form of money-capital, and the decoded flows of labor in the form of the "free worker." Hence, unlike previous social machines, the capitalist machine is incapable of providing a code that will apply to the whole of the social field. By substituting money for the very notion of a code, it has created an axiomatic of abstract quantities that keeps moving further and further in the direction of the deterritorialization of the socius. Capitalism tends toward a threshold of decoding that will destroy the socius in order to make it a body without organs and unleash the flows of desire on this body as a deterritorialized field. Is it correct to say that in this sense schizophrenia is the product of the capitalist machine, as manic-depression and paranoia are the product of the despotic machine, and hysteria the product of the territorial machine?*

*On hysteria, schizophrenia, and their relationships with social structures, see the analyses by Georges Devereux in his *Essais d'ethnopsychiatrie générale* (Paris: Gallimard), p. 67ff., and the wonderful pages in Karl Jaspers' *Strindberg und Van Gogh* (Berlin: J. Springer, 1926). (English translation, *Strindberg*

The decoding of flows and the deterritorialization of the socius thus constitutes the most characteristic and the most important tendency of capitalism. It continually draws near to its limit, which is a genuinely schizophrenic limit. It tends, with all the strength at its command, to produce the schizo as the subject of the decoded flows on the body without organs—more capitalist than the capitalist and more proletarian than the proletariat. This tendency is being carried further and further, to the point that capitalism with all its flows may dispatch itself straight to the moon: we really haven't seen anything yet! When we say that schizophrenia is our characteristic malady, the malady of our era, we do not merely mean to say that modern life drives people mad. It is not a question of a way of life, but of a process of production. Nor is it merely a question of a simple parallelism, even though from the point of view of the failure of codes, such a parallelism is a much more precise formulation of the relationship between, for example, the phenomena of shifting of meaning in the case of schizophrenics and the mechanisms of ever increasing disharmony and discord at every level of industrial society.

What we are really trying to say is that capitalism, through its process of production, produces an awesome schizophrenic accumulation of energy or charge, against which it brings all its vast powers of repression to bear, but which nonetheless continues to act as capitalism's limit. For capitalism constantly counteracts, constantly inhibits this inherent tendency while at the same time allowing it free rein; it continually seeks to avoid reaching its limit while simultaneously tending toward that limit. Capitalism institutes or restores all sorts of residual and artificial, imaginary, or symbolic territorialities, thereby attempting, as best it can, to recode, to rechannel persons who have been defined in terms of abstract quantities. Everything returns or recurs: States, nations, families. That is what makes the ideology of capitalism "a motley painting of everything that has ever been believed." The real is not impossible; it is simply more and more artificial. Marx termed the twofold movement of the tendency to a falling rate of profit, and the increase in the absolute quantity of surplus value, the law of the counteracted tendency. As a corollary of this law, there is the twofold movement of decoding or deterritorializing flows on the one hand, and their violent and artificial reterritorialization on the other. The

and Van Gogh, trans. Oskar Grunow [Tucson, Arizona: University of Arizona Press.]) The question has been asked: is madness in our time "a state of total sincerity, in areas where in less chaotic times one would have been capable of honest experience and expression without it?" Jaspers reformulates this question by adding: "We have seen that in former times human beings attempted to drive themselves into hysteria; and we might say that today many human beings attempt to drive themselves into madness in much the same way. But if the former attempt was to a certain extent psychologically possible, the latter is not possible at all, and can lead only to inauthenticity."

more the capitalist machine deterritorializes, decoding and axiomatizing flows in order to extract surplus value from them, the more its ancillary apparatuses, such as government bureaucracies and the forces of law and order, do their utmost to reterritorialize, absorbing in the process a larger and larger share of surplus value.

There is no doubt that at this point in history the neurotic, the pervert, and the psychotic cannot be adequately defined in terms of drives, for drives are simply the desiring-machines themselves. They must be defined in terms of modern territorialities. The neurotic is trapped within the residual or artificial territorialities of our society, and reduces all of them (*les rabat toutes*) to Oedipus as the ultimate territoriality—as reconstructed in the analyst's office and projected upon the full body of the psychoanalyst (yes, my boss is my father, and so is the Chief of State, and so are you, Doctor). The pervert is someone who takes the artifice seriously and plays the game to the hilt: if you want them, you can have them—territorialities infinitely more artificial than the ones that society offers us, totally artificial new families, secret lunar societies. As for the schizo, continually wandering about, migrating here, there, and everywhere as best he can, he plunges further and further into the realm of deterritorialization, reaching the furthest limits of the decomposition of the socius on the surface of his own body without organs. It may well be that these peregrinations are the schizo's own particular way of rediscovering the earth. The schizophrenic deliberately seeks out the very limit of capitalism: he is its inherent tendency brought to fulfillment, its surplus product, its proletariat, and its exterminating angel. He scrambles all the codes and is the transmitter of the decoded flows of desire. The real continues to flow. In the schizo, the two aspects of *process* are conjoined: the metaphysical process that puts us in contact with the "demoniacal" element in nature or within the heart of the earth, and the historical process of social production that restores the autonomy of desiring-machines in relation to the deterritorialized social machine. Schizophrenia is desiring-production as the limit of social production. Desiring-production, and its difference in régime as compared to social production, are thus end points, not points of departure. Between the two there is nothing but an ongoing process of becoming that is the becoming of reality. And if materialist psychiatry may be defined as the psychiatry that introduces the concept of production into consideration of the problem of desire, it cannot avoid posing in eschatological terms the problem of the ultimate relationship between the analytic machine, the revolutionary machine, and desiring-machines.

5 | The Machines

In what respect are desiring-machines really machines, in anything more than a metaphorical sense? A machine may be defined as a *system of interruptions* or breaks (*coupures*). These breaks should in no way be considered as a separation from reality; rather, they operate along lines that vary according to whatever aspect of them we are considering. Every machine, in the first place, is related to a continual material flow (*hylè*) that it cuts into. It functions like a ham-slicing machine, removing portions* from the associative flow: the anus and the flow of shit it cuts off, for instance; the mouth that cuts off not only the flow of milk but also the flow of air and sound; the penis that interrupts not only the flow of urine but also the flow of sperm. Each associative flow must be seen as an ideal thing, an endless flux, flowing from something not unlike the immense thigh of a pig. The term *hylè* in fact designates the pure continuity that any one sort of matter ideally possesses. When Robert Jaulin describes the little balls and pinches of snuff used in a certain initiation ceremony, he shows that they are produced each year as a sample taken from "an infinite series that theoretically has one and only one origin," a single ball that extends to the very limits of the universe.[34] Far from being the opposite of continuity, the break or interruption conditions this continuity: it presupposes or defines what it cuts into as an ideal continuity. This is because, as we have seen, every machine is a machine of a machine. The machine produces an interruption of the flow only insofar as it is connected to another machine that supposedly produces this flow. And doubtless this second machine in turn is really an interruption or break, too. But it is such only in relationship to a third machine that ideally—that is to say, relatively—produces a continuous, infinite flux: for example, the anus-machine and the intestine-machine, the intestine-machine and the stomach-machine, the stomach-machine and the mouth-machine, the mouth-machine and the flow of milk of a herd of dairy cattle ("and then . . . and then . . . and then . . ."). In a word, every machine functions as a break in the flow in relation to the machine to which it is connected, but at the same time is also a flow itself, or the production of a flow, in relation to the machine connected to it. This is the law of the production of production. That is why, at the limit point of

---

*The authors' word for this process is *prélèvement*. The French word has a number of meanings, including: a skimming or a draining off; a removal of a certain quantity as a sample or for purposes of testing; a setting apart of a portion or share of the whole; a deduction from a sum of money on deposit. In the English text that follows, in a number of cases the noun *prélèvement* or the corresponding verb *prélever* will be indicated in parentheses following its translation. (*Translators' note.*)

all the transverse or transfinite connections, the partial object and the continuous flux, the interruption and the connection, fuse into one: everywhere there are breaks-flows out of which desire wells up, thereby constituting its productivity and continually grafting the process of production onto the product. (It is very curious that Melanie Klein, whose discovery of partial objects was so far-reaching, neglects to study flows from this point of view and declares that they are of no importance; she thus short-circuits all the connections.)*

"Connecticut, Connect-I-cut!" cries little Joey. In his study *The Empty Fortress*, Bruno Bettelheim paints the portrait of this young child who can live, eat, defecate, and sleep only if he is plugged into machines provided with motors, wires, lights, carburetors, propellers, and steering wheels: an electrical feeding machine, a car-machine that enables him to breathe, an anal machine that lights up. There are very few examples that cast as much light on the régime of desiring-production, and the way in which breaking down constitutes an integral part of the functioning, or the way in which the cutting off is an integral part of mechanical connections. Doubtless there are those who will object that this mechanical, schizophrenic life expresses the absence and the destruction of desire rather than desire itself, and presupposes certain extremely negative attitudes on the part of his parents to which the child reacts by turning himself into a machine. But even Bettelheim, who has a noticeable bias in favor of Oedipal or pre-oedipal causality, admits that this sort of causality intervenes only in response to autonomous aspects of the productivity or the activity of the child, although he later discerns in him a nonproductive stasis or an attitude of total withdrawal. Hence there is first of all, according to Bettelheim, an autonomous reaction to the total life experience, of which the mother is only a part. Also we must not think that the machines themselves are proof of the loss or repression of desire (which Bettelheim translates in terms of autism). We find ourselves confronted with the same problem once again: How has the process of the production of desire, how have the child's desiring-machines begun to turn endlessly round and round in a total vacuum, so as to produce the child-machine? How has the process turned into an end in itself? Or how has the child become the victim of a premature interruption or a terrible frustration? It is only by means of the body without organs (eyes closed tight, nostrils pinched shut, ears

*"Children of both sexes regard urine in its positive aspect as equivalent to their mother's milk, in accordance with the unconscious, which equates all bodily substances with one another." Melanie Klein, *The Psycho-Analysis of Children*, trans. Alix Strachey, The International Psycho-Analytic Library, no. 22 (London: Hogarth Press and the Institute of Psycho-Analysis, 1954), p. 291. (First edition, 1932.)

stopped up) that something is produced, counterproduced, something that diverts or frustrates the entire process of production, of which it is nonetheless still a part. But the machine remains desire, an investment of desire whose history unfolds, by way of the primary repression and the return of the repressed, in the succession of the states of paranoiac machines, miraculating machines, and celibate machines through which little Joey passes as Bettelheim's therapy progresses.

In the second place, every machine has a sort of code built into it, stored up inside it. This code is inseparable not only from the way in which it is recorded and transmitted to each of the different regions of the body, but also from the way in which the relations of each of the regions with all the others are recorded. An organ may have connections that associate it with several different flows; it may waver between several functions, and even take on the régime of another organ—the anorectic mouth, for instance. All sorts of functional questions thus arise: What flow to break? Where to interrupt it? How and by what means? What place should be left for other producers or antiproducers (the place of one's little brother, for instance)? Should one, or should one not, suffocate from what one eats, swallow air, shit with one's mouth? The data, the bits of information recorded, and their transmission form a grid of disjunctions of a type that differs from the previous connections. We owe to Jacques Lacan the discovery of this fertile domain of a code of the unconscious, incorporating the entire chain—or several chains—of meaning: a discovery thus totally transforming analysis. (The basic text in this connection is his *La lettre volée* [*The Purloined Letter*].) But how very strange this domain seems, simply because of its multiplicity—a multiplicity so complex that we can scarcely speak of *one* chain or even of *one* code of desire. The chains are called "signifying chains" (*chaînes signifiantes*) because they are made up of signs, but these signs are not themselves signifying. The code resembles not so much a language as a jargon, an open-ended, polyvocal formation. The nature of the signs within it is insignificant, as these signs have little or nothing to do with what supports them. Or rather, isn't the support completely immaterial to these signs? The support is the body without organs. These indifferent signs follow no plan, they function at all levels and enter into any and every sort of connection; each one speaks its own language, and establishes syntheses with others that are quite direct along transverse vectors, whereas the vectors between the basic elements that constitute them are quite indirect.

The disjunctions characteristic of these chains still do not involve any exclusion, however, since exclusions can arise only as a function of inhibiters and repressers that eventually determine the support and firmly define a specific, personal subject.* No chain is homogeneous; all of them resemble, rather, a succession of characters from different alphabets in which an ideogram, a pictogram, a tiny image of an elephant passing by, or a rising sun may suddenly make its appearance. In a chain that mixes together phonemes, morphemes, etc., without combining them, papa's mustache, mama's upraised arm, a ribbon, a little girl, a cop, a shoe suddenly turn up. Each chain captures fragments of other chains from which it "extracts" a surplus value, just as the orchid code "attracts" the figure of a wasp: both phenomena demonstrate the surplus value of a code. It is an entire system of shuntings along certain tracks, and of selections by lot, that bring about partially dependent, aleatory phenomena bearing a close resemblance to a Markov chain. The recordings and transmissions that have come from the internal codes, from the outside world, from one region to another of the organism, all intersect, following the endlessly ramified paths of the great disjunctive synthesis. If this constitutes a system of writing, it is a writing inscribed on the very surface of the Real: a strangely polyvocal kind of writing, never a biunivocalized, linearized one; a transcursive system of writing, never a discursive one; a writing that constitutes the entire domain of the "real inorganization" of the passive syntheses, where we would search in vain for something that might be labeled the Signifier—writing that ceaselessly composes and decomposes the chains into signs that have nothing that impels them to become signifying. The one vocation of the sign is to produce desire, engineering it in every direction.

These chains are the locus of continual detachments—schizzes† on every hand that are valuable in and of themselves and above all must not be filled in. This is thus the second characteristic of the machine: breaks that are a detachment (*coupures-détachements*), which must not be confused with breaks that are a slicing off (*coupures-prélèvements*). The latter have to do with continuous fluxes and are related to partial objects. Schizzes have to do with heterogeneous chains, and as their basic unit use detachable segments or mobile stocks resembling building

---

*See Jacques Lacan, "Remarque sur le rapport de Daniel Lagache," in *Ecrits* (reference note 36), of "an exclusion having its source in these signs as such being able to come about only as a condition of consistency within a chain that is to be constituted; let us also add that the one dimension limiting this condition is the translation of which such a chain is capable. Let us consider this game of lotto for just a moment more. We may then discover that it is only because these elements turn up by sheer chance within an ordinal series, in a truly unorganized way, that their appearance makes us draw lots" (p. 658).

†A coined word (French *schize*), based on the Greek verb *schizein*, "to split," "to cleave," "to divide." (*Translators' note.*)

blocks or flying bricks. We must conceive of each brick as having been launched from a distance and as being composed of heterogeneous elements: containing within it not only an inscription with signs from different alphabets, but also various figures, plus one or several straws, and perhaps a corpse. Cutting into the flows (*le prélèvement du flux*) involves detachment of something from a chain; and the partial objects of production presuppose stocks of material or recording bricks within the coexistence and the interaction of all the syntheses.

How could part of a flow be drawn off without a fragmentary detachment taking place within the code that comes to inform the flow? When we noted a moment ago that the schizo is at the very limit of the decoded flows of desire, we meant that he was at the very limit of the social codes, where a despotic Signifier destroys all the chains, linearizes them, biunivocalizes them, and uses the bricks as so many immobile units for the construction of an imperial Great Wall of China. But the schizo continually detaches them, continually works them loose and carries them off in every direction in order to create a new polyvocity that is the code of desire. Every composition, and also every decomposition, uses mobile bricks as the basic unit. *Diaschisis* and *diaspasis,* as Monakow put it: either a lesion spreads along fibers that link it to other regions and thus gives rise *at a distance* to phenomena that are incomprehensible from a purely mechanistic (but not a machinic) point of view; or else a humoral disturbance brings on a shift in nervous energy and creates broken, fragmented paths within the sphere of instincts. These bricks or blocks are the essential parts of desiring-machines from the point of view of the recording process: they are at once component parts and products of the process of decomposition that are spatially localized only at certain moments, by contrast with the nervous system, which is a great chronogeneous machine: a melody-producing machine of the "music box" type, with a nonspatial localization.[35] What makes Monakow and Mourgue's study an unparalleled one, going far beyond the entire Jacksonist philosophy that originally inspired it, is the theory of bricks or blocks, their detachment and fragmentation, and above all what such a theory presupposes: the introduction of desire into neurology.

The third type of interruption or break characteristic of the desiring-machine is the residual break (*coupure-reste*) or residuum, which produces a subject alongside the machine, functioning as a part adjacent to the machine. And if this subject has no specific or personal identity, if it traverses the body without organs without destroying its indifference, it is because it is not only a part that is peripheral to the machine, but also a part that is itself divided into parts that correspond to the detachments from the chain (*détachements de chaîne*) and the removals from the flow (*prélèvements de flux*) brought about by the machine. Thus this subject consumes and consummates each of the states through which it passes, and is born of each of them anew, continuously emerging from them as a part made up of parts, each one of which completely fills up the body without organs in the space of an instant. This is what allows Lacan to postulate and describe in detail an interplay of elements that is more machinic than etymological: *parere:* to procure; *separare:* to separate; *se parere:* to engender oneself. At the same time he points out the intensive nature of this interplay: the part has nothing to do with the whole; "it performs its role all by itself. In this case, only after the subject has partitioned itself does it proceed to its parturition . . . that is why the subject can procure what is of particular concern to it here, a state that we would label a legitimate status within society. Nothing in the life of any subject would sacrifice a very large part of its interests."[36]

Like all the other breaks, the subjective break is not at all an indication of a lack or need (*manque*), but on the contrary a share that falls to the subject as a part of a whole, income that comes its way as something left over. (Here again, how bad a model the Oedipal model of castration is!) That is because breaks or interruptions are not the result of an analysis; rather, in and of themselves, they are syntheses. Syntheses produce divisions. Let us consider, for example, the milk the baby throws up when it burps; it is at one and the same time the restitution of something that has been levied from the associative flux (*restitution de prélèvement sur le flux associatif*); the reproduction of the process of detachment from the signifying chain (*reproduction de détachement sur la chaîne signifiante*); and a residuum (*résidu*) that constitutes the subject's share of the whole. The desiring-machine is not a metaphor; it is what interrupts and is interrupted in accordance with these three modes. The first mode has to do with the connective synthesis, and mobilizes libido as withdrawal energy (*énergie de prélèvement*). The second has to do with the disjunctive synthesis, and mobilizes the Numen as detachment energy (*énergie de détachement*). The third has to do with the conjunctive synthesis, and mobilizes Voluptas as residual energy (*énergie résiduelle*). It is these three aspects that make the process of desiring-production at once the production of production, the production of recording, and the production of consumption. To withdraw a part from the whole, to detach, to "have something left over," is to produce, and to carry out real operations of desire in the material world.

6 | The Whole and Its Parts

In desiring-machines everything functions at the same time, but amid hiatuses and ruptures, breakdowns and failures, stalling and short circuits, distances and fragmentations, within a sum that never succeeds in bringing its various parts together so as to form a whole. That is because the breaks in the process are productive, and are reassemblies in and of themselves. Disjunctions, by the very fact that they are disjunctions, are inclusive. Even consumptions are transitions, processes of becoming, and returns. Maurice Blanchot has found a way to pose the problem in the most rigorous terms, at the level of the literary machine: how to produce, how to think about fragments whose sole relationship is sheer difference—fragments that are related to one another only in that each of them is different—without having recourse either to any sort of original totality (not even one that has been lost), or to a subsequent totality that may not yet have come about?[37] It is only the category of multiplicity, used as a substantive and going beyond both the One and the many, beyond the predicative relation of the One and the many, that can account for desiring-production: desiring-production is pure multiplicity, that is to say, an affirmation that is irreducible to any sort of unity.

We live today in the age of partial objects, bricks that have been shattered to bits, and leftovers. We no longer believe in the myth of the existence of fragments that, like pieces of an antique statue, are merely waiting for the last one to be turned up, so that they may all be glued back together to create a unity that is precisely the same as the original unity. We no longer believe in a primordial totality that once existed, or in a final totality that awaits us at some future date. We no longer believe in the dull gray outlines of a dreary, colorless dialectic of evolution, aimed at forming a harmonious whole out of heterogeneous bits by rounding off their rough edges. We believe only in totalities that are peripheral. And if we discover such a totality alongside various separate parts, it is a whole *of* these particular parts but does not totalize them; it is a unity *of* all of these particular parts but does not unify them; rather, it is added to them as a new part fabricated separately.

"It comes into being, but applying this time to the whole as some inspired fragment composed separately. . . ." So Proust writes of the unity of Balzac's creation, though his remark is also an apt description of his own *oeuvre*.[38] In the literary machine that Proust's *In Search of Lost Time* constitutes, we are struck by the fact that all the parts are produced as asymmetrical sections, paths that suddenly come to an end, hermetically sealed boxes, noncommunicating vessels, watertight compartments, in which there are gaps even between things that are contiguous, gaps that are affirmations, pieces of a puzzle belonging not to any one puzzle but to many, pieces assembled by forcing them into a certain place where they may or may not belong, their unmatched edges violently bent out of shape, forcibly made to fit together, to interlock, with a number of pieces always left over. It is a schizoid work par excellence: it is almost as though the author's guilt, his confessions of guilt are merely a sort of joke. (In Kleinian terms, it might be said that the depressive position is only a cover-up for a more deeply rooted schizoid attitude.) For the rigors of the law are only an apparent expression of the protest of the One, whereas their real object is the absolution of fragmented universes, in which the law never unites anything in a single Whole, but on the contrary measures and maps out the divergences, the dispersions, the exploding into fragments of something that is innocent precisely because its source is madness. This is why in Proust's work the apparent theme of guilt is tightly interwoven with a completely different theme totally contradicting it; the plantlike innocence that results from the total compartmentalization of the sexes, both in Charlus's encounters and in Albertine's slumber, where flowers blossom in profusion and the utter innocence of madness is revealed, whether it be the patent madness of Charlus or the supposed madness of Albertine.

Hence Proust maintained that the Whole itself is a product, produced as nothing more than a part alongside other parts, which it neither unifies nor totalizes, though it has an effect on these other parts simply because it establishes aberrant paths of communication between noncommunicating vessels, transverse unities between elements that retain all their differences within their own particular boundaries. Thus in the trip on the train in *In Search of Lost Time,* there is never a totality of what is seen nor a unity of the points of view, except along the transversal that the frantic passenger traces from one window to the other, "in order to draw together, in order to reweave intermittent and opposite fragments." This drawing together, this reweaving is what Joyce called *re-embodying.* The body without organs is produced as a whole, but in its own particular place within the process of production, alongside the parts that it neither unifies nor totalizes. And when it operates on them, when it turns back upon them (*se rabat sur elles*), it brings about transverse communications, transfinite summarizations, polyvocal and transcursive inscriptions on its own surface, on which the functional breaks of partial objects are continually intersected by breaks in the signifying chains, and by breaks effected by a subject that uses them as reference points in order to locate itself. The whole not only coexists with all the parts; it is contiguous to them, it exists as a product that is produced apart from them and yet at the same time is related to them. Geneticists have noted the same phenomenon in the particular language of their science: ". . . amino acids are assimilated individually into the cell, and then are arranged in the proper sequence by a mechanism analogous to a template onto which the distinctive side chain of each acid keys into its proper position."[39] As a general rule, the problem of the relationships between parts and the whole continues to be rather awkwardly formulated by classic mechanism and vitalism, so long as the whole is considered as a totality derived from the parts, or as an original totality from which the parts emanate, or as a dialectical totalization. Neither mechanism nor vitalism has really understood the nature of desiring-machines, nor the twofold need to consider the role of production in desire and the role of desire in mechanics.

There is no sort of evolution of drives that would cause these drives and their objects to progress in the direction of an integrated whole, any more than there is an original totality from which they can be derived. Melanie Klein was responsible for the marvelous discovery of partial objects, that world of explosions, rotations, vibrations. But how can we explain the fact that she has nonetheless failed to grasp the logic of these objects? It is doubtless because, first of all, she conceives of them as fantasies and judges them from the point of view of consumption, rather than regarding them as genuine production. She explains them in terms of causal mechanisms (introjection and projection, for instance), of mechanisms that produce certain effects (gratification and frustration), and of mechanisms of expression (good or bad)—an approach that forces her to adopt an idealist conception of the partial object. She does not relate these partial objects to a real process of production—of the sort carried out by desiring-machines, for instance. In the second place, she cannot rid herself of the notion that schizoparanoid partial objects are related to a whole, either to an original whole that has existed earlier in a primary phase, or to a whole that will eventually appear in a final depressive stage (the complete Object). Partial objects hence appear to her to be derived from (*prélevés sur*) global persons; not only are they destined to play a role in totalities aimed at integrating the ego, the object, and drives later in life, but they also constitute the original type of object relation between the ego, the mother, and the father. And in the final analysis that is where the crux of the matter lies. Partial objects unquestionably have a sufficient charge in and of themselves to blow up all of Oedipus and totally demolish its ridiculous claim to represent the unconscious, to triangulate the unconscious, to encompass the entire production of desire. The question that thus arises here is not at all that of the relative importance of what might be called the *pre-oedipal* in relation to Oedipus itself, since "pre-oedipal" still has a developmental or structural relationship to Oedipus. The question, rather, is that of the absolutely *anoedipal* nature of the production of desire. But because Melanie Klein insists on considering desire from the point of view of the whole, of global persons, and of complete objects—and also, perhaps, because she is eager to avoid any sort of contretemps with the International Psycho-Analytic Association that bears above its door the inscription "Let no one enter here who does not believe in Oedipus"—she does not make use of partial objects to shatter the iron collar of Oedipus; on the contrary, she uses them—or makes a pretense of using them—to water Oedipus down, to miniaturize it, to find it everywhere, to extend it to the very earliest years of life.

If we here choose the example of the analyst least prone to see everything in terms of Oedipus, we do so only in order to demonstrate what a forcing was necessary for her to make Oedipus the sole measure of desiring-production. And naturally this is all the more true in the case of run-of-the-mill practitioners who no longer have the slightest notion of what the psychoanalytic "movement" is all about. It is no longer a question of suggestion, but of sheer terrorism. Melanie Klein herself writes: "The first time Dick came to me . . . he manifested no sort of affect when his nurse handed him over to me. When I showed him the toys I had put ready, he looked at them without the faintest interest. I took a big train and put it beside a smaller one *and called them* 'Daddy-train' and 'Dick-train.' Thereupon he picked up the train I called 'Dick' and made it roll to the window and said 'Station.' *I explained:* 'The station is mummy; Dick is going into mummy.' He left the train, ran into the space between the outer and inner doors of the room, shutting himself in, saying 'dark,' and ran out again directly. He went through this performance several times. *I explained to him:* 'It is dark inside mummy. Dick is inside dark mummy.' Meantime he picked up the train again, but soon ran back into the space between the doors. While I was saying that he was going into dark mummy, he said twice in a questioning way: 'Nurse?' . . . *As his analysis progressed . . . Dick had also discovered* the wash-basin as symbolizing the mother's body, and he displayed an extraordinary dread of being wetted with water." Say that it's Oedipus, or you'll get a slap in the face. The psychoanalyst no longer says to the patient: "Tell me a little bit about your desiring-machines, won't you?" Instead he screams: "Answer daddy-and-mommy when I speak to you!" Even Melanie Klein. So the entire process of desiring-production is trampled underfoot and reduced to (*rabuttu sur*) parental images, laid out step by step in accordance with supposed pre-oedipal stages, totalized in Oedipus, and the logic of partial objects is thereby reduced to nothing. Oedipus thus becomes at this point the crucial premise in the logic of psychoanalysis. For as we suspected at the very beginning, partial objects are only apparently derived from (*prélevés sur*) global persons; they are really produced by being drawn from (*prélevés sur*) a flow or a nonpersonal *hylè*, with which they re-establish contact by connecting themselves to other partial objects. The unconscious is totally unaware of persons as such. Partial objects are not representations of parental figures or of the basic patterns of family relations; they are parts of desiring-machines, having to do with a process and with relations of production that are both irreducible and prior to anything that may be made to conform to the Oedipal figure.

When the break between Freud and Jung is discussed, the modest and practical point of disagreement that marked the beginning of their differences is too often forgotten: Jung remarked that in the process of transference the psychoanalyst frequently appeared in the guise of a devil, a god, or a sorcerer, and that the roles he assumed in the patient's eyes went far beyond any sort of parental images. They eventually came to a total parting of the ways, yet Jung's initial reservation was a telling one. The same remark holds true of children's games. A child never confines himself to playing house, to playing only at being daddy-and-mommy. He also plays at being a magician, a cowboy, a cop or a robber, a train, a little car. The train is not necessarily daddy, nor is the train station necessarily mommy. The problem has to do not with the sexual nature of desiring-machines, but with the family nature of this sexuality. Admittedly, once the child has grown up, he finds himself deeply involved in social relations that are no longer familial relations. But since these relations supposedly come into being at a later stage in life, there are only two possible ways in which this can be explained: it must be granted either that sexuality is sublimated or neutralized in and through social (*and* metaphysical) relations, in the form of an analytic "afterward"; or else that these relations bring into play a nonsexual energy, for which sexuality has merely served as the symbol of an anagogical "beyond."

It was their disagreement on this particular point that eventually made the break between Freud and Jung irreconcilable. Yet at the same time the two of them continued to share the belief that the libido cannot invest a social or metaphysical field without some sort of mediation. This is not the case, however. Let us consider a child at play, or a child crawling about exploring the various rooms of the house he lives in. He looks intently at an electrical outlet, he moves his body about like a machine, he uses one of his legs as though it were an oar, he goes into the kitchen, into the study, he runs toy cars back and forth. It is obvious that his parents are present all this time, and that the child would have nothing were it not for them. But that is not the real matter at issue. The matter at issue is to find out whether everything he touches is experienced as a representative of his parents. Ever since birth his crib, his mother's breast, her nipple, his bowel movements are desiring-machines connected to parts of his body. It seems to us self-contradictory to maintain, on the one hand, that the child lives among partial objects, and that on the other hand he conceives of these partial objects as being his parents, or even different parts of his parents' bodies. Strictly speaking, it is not true that a baby experiences his mother's breast as a separate part of her body. It exists, rather, as a part of a desiring-machine connected to the baby's mouth, and is experienced as an object providing a nonpersonal flow of milk, be it copious or scanty. A desiring-machine and a partial object do not represent anything. A partial object is not representative, even though it admittedly serves as a basis of relations and as a means of assigning agents a place and a function; but these agents are not persons, any more than these relations are intersubjective. They are relations of production as such, and agents of production and antiproduction. Ray Bradbury demonstrates this very well when he describes the nursery as a place where desiring-production and group fantasy occur, as a place where the only connection is that between partial objects and agents.[41] The small child lives with his family around the clock; but within the bosom of this family, and from the very first days of his life, he immediately begins having an amazing nonfamilial experience that psychoanalysis has completely failed to take into account. Lindner's painting attracts our attention once again.

It is not a question of denying the vital importance of parents or the love attachment of children to their mothers and fathers. It is a question of knowing what the place and the function of parents are within desiring-production, rather than doing the opposite and forcing the entire interplay of desiring-machines to fit within (*rabattre tout le jeu des machines désirantes dans*) the restricted code of Oedipus. How does the child first come to define the places and the functions that the parents are going to occupy as special agents, closely related to other agents? From the very beginning Oedipus exists in one form and one form only: open in all directions to a social field, to a field of production directly invested by libido. It would seem obvious that parents indeed make their appearance on the recording surface of desiring-production. But this is in fact the crux of the entire Oedipal problem: What are the precise forces that cause the Oedipal triangulation to close up? Under what conditions does this triangulation divert desire so that it flows across a surface within a narrow channel that is not a natural conformation of this surface? How does it form a type of inscription for experiences and the workings of mechanisms that extend far beyond it in every direction? It is in this sense and this sense only that the child *relates* the breast as a partial object to the person of his mother, and constantly watches the expression on his mother's face. The word "relate" in this case does not designate a natural productive relationship, but rather a *relation* in the sense of a report or an account, an inscription within the over-all process of inscription, within the Numen. From his very earliest infancy, the child has a wide-ranging life of desire—a whole set of nonfamilial relations with the objects and the machines of desire—that is not related to the parents from the point of view of immediate production, but that is ascribed to them (with either love or hatred) from the point of view of the recording of the process, and in accordance with the very special conditions of this recording, including the effect of these conditions upon the process itself (feedback).

It is amid partial objects and within the nonfamilial relations of desiring-production that the child lives his life and ponders what it means to live, even though the question must be "related" to his parents and the only possible tentative answer must be sought in family relations. "I remember that ever since I was eight years old, and even before that, I always wondered who I was, what I was, and why I was alive; I remember that at the age of six, on a house on the Boulevard de la Blancarde in Marseilles (number 29, to be precise), just as I was eating my afternoon snack—a chocolate bar that a certain woman known as my mother gave me—I asked myself what it meant to exist, to be alive, what it meant to be conscious of oneself breathing, and I remember that I wanted to inhale myself in order to prove that I was alive and to see if I liked being alive, and if so why."[42] That is the crucial point: a question occurs to the child that will perhaps be "related" to the woman known as mommy, but that is not formulated in terms of her, but rather produced within the interplay of desiring-machines—at the level, for example, of the mouth-air machine or the tasting-machine: What does it mean to be alive? What does it mean to breathe? What am I? What sort of thing is this breathing-machine on my body without organs?

The child is a metaphysical being. As in the case of the Cartesian *cogito,* parents have nothing to do with these questions. And we are guilty of an error when we confuse the fact that this question is "related" to the parents, in the sense of being recounted or communicated to them, with the notion that it is "related" to them in the sense of a fundamental connection with them. By boxing the life of the child up within the Oedipus complex, by making familial relations the universal mediation of childhood, we cannot help but fail to understand the production of the unconscious itself, and the collective mechanisms that have an immediate bearing on the unconscious: in particular, the entire interplay between primal psychic repression, the desiring-machines, and the body without organs. For *the unconscious is an orphan,* and produces itself within the identity of nature and man. The autoproduction of the unconscious suddenly became evident when the subject of the Cartesian *cogito* realized that it had no parents, when the socialist thinker discovered the unity of man and nature within the process of production, and when the cycle discovers its independence from an indefinite parental regression. To quote Artaud once again: "I got no/papamummy."

We have seen how a confusion arose between the two meanings of "process": process as the metaphysical production of the demoniacal within nature, and process as social production of desiring-machines within history. Neither social relations nor metaphysical relations constitute an "afterward" or a "beyond." The role of such relations must be recognized in all psychopathological processes, and their importance will be all the greater when we are dealing with psychotic syndromes that would appear to be the most animal-like and the most desocialized. It is in the child's very first days of life, in the most elementary behavior patterns of the suckling babe, that these relations with partial objects, with the agents of production, with the factors of antiproduction are woven, in accordance with the laws of desiring-production as a whole. By failing from the beginning to see what the precise nature of this desiring-production is, and how, under what conditions, and in response to what pressures, the Oedipal triangulation plays a role in the recording of the process, we find ourselves trapped in the net of a diffuse, generalized oedipalism that radically distorts the life of the child and his later development, the neurotic and psychotic problems of the adult, and sexuality as a whole. Let us keep D.H. Lawrence's reaction to psychoanalysis in mind, and never forget it. In Lawrence's case, at least, his reservations with regard to psychoanalysis did not stem from terror at having discovered what real sexuality was. But he had the impression—the purely instinctive impression—that psychoanalysis was shutting sexuality up in a bizarre sort of box painted with bourgeois motifs, in a kind of rather repugnant artifical triangle, thereby stifling the whole of sexuality as production of desire so as to recast it along entirely different lines, making of it a "dirty little secret," the dirty little family secret, a private theater rather than the fantastic factory of Nature and Production. Lawrence had the impression that sexuality possessed more power or more potentiality than that. And though psychoanalysis may perhaps have managed to "disinfect the dirty little secret," the dreary, dirty little secret of Oedipus-the-modern-tyrant benefited very little from having been thus disinfected.

Is it possible that, by taking the path that it has, psychoanalysis is reviving an age-old tendency to humble us, to demean us, and to make us feel guilty? Foucault has noted that the relationship between madness and the family can be traced back in large part to a development that affected the whole of bourgeois society in the nineteenth century: the family was entrusted with functions that became the measuring rod of the responsibility of its members and their possible guilt. Insofar as psychoanalysis cloaks insanity in the mantle of a "parental complex," and regards the patterns of self-punishment resulting from Oedipus as a confession of guilt, its theories are not at all radical or innovative. On the contrary: *it is completing the task begun by nineteenth-century psychology*, namely, to develop a moralized, familial discourse of mental pathology, linking madness to the "half-real, half-imaginary dialectic of the Family," deciphering within it "the unending attempt to murder the father," "the dull thud of instincts hammering at the solidity of the family as an institution and at its most archaic symbols."[43] Hence, instead of participating in an undertaking that will bring about genuine liberation, psychoanalysis is taking part in the work of bourgeois repression at its most far-reaching level, that is to say, keeping European humanity harnessed to the yoke of daddy-mommy and *making no effort to do away with this problem once and for all.*

PSYCHO-ANALYSIS AND FAMILIALISM: THE HOLY FAMILY

Translated by Robert Hurley and Mark Seem

1 | The Imperialism of Oedipus

Oedipus restrained is the figure of the daddy-mommy-me triangle, the familial constellation in person. But when psychoanalysis makes of Oedipus its dogma, it is not unaware of the existence of relations said to be pre-oedipal in the child, exo-oedipal in the psychotic, para-oedipal in others. The function of Oedipus as dogma, or as the "nuclear complex," is inseparable from a forcing by which the psychoanalyst as theoretician elevates himself to the conception of a generalized Oedipus. On the one hand, for each subject of either sex, he takes into consideration an intensive series of instincts, affects, and relations that link the normal and positive form of the complex to its inverse or negative form: a standard model Oedipus, such as Freud presents in *The Ego and the Id,* which makes it possible to connect the pre-Oedipal phases with the negative complex when this seems called for. On the other hand, he takes into consideration the coexistence in extension of the subjects themselves and their multiple interactions: a group Oedipus that brings together relatives, descendants, and ascendants. (It is in this manner that the schizophrenic's visible resistance to oedipalization, the obvious absence of the Oedipal link, can be obscured in a grandparental constellation, either because an accumulation of three generations is deemed necessary in order to produce a psychotic, or because an even more direct mechanism of intervention by the grandparents in the psychosis is discovered, and Oedipuses of Oedipus are constituted, to the second power: neurosis, that's father-mother, but grandma, that's psychosis.) Finally, the distinction between the Imaginary* and the Symbolic* permits the emergence of an Oedipal structure as a system of positions and functions that do not conform to the variable figure of those who come to occupy them in a given social or pathological formation: a structural Oedipus $(3+1)$ that does not conform to a triangle, but performs all the possible triangulations by distributing in a given domain desire, its object, and the law.

It is certain that the two preceding modes of generalization attain their full scope only in structural interpretation. Structural interpretation makes Oedipus into a kind of universal Catholic symbol, beyond all the imaginary modalities. It makes Oedipus into a referential axis not only for the pre-oedipal phases, but also for the para-oedipal varieties, and the exo-oedipal phenomena. The notion of "foreclosure," for example, seems to indicate a specifically structural deficiency, by means of which the schizophrenic is of course repositioned on the Oedipal axis, set back into the Oedipal orbit in the perspective, for example, of the three generations, where the mother was not able to posit her desire toward her own father, nor the son, consequently, toward the mother. One of Lacan's disciples writes: we are going to consider "the means by which the Oedipal organization plays a role in psychoses; next, what the forms of psychotic pregenitality are and how they are able to maintain the Oedipal reference." Our preceding criticism of Oedipus therefore risks being judged totally superficial and petty, as if it applied solely to an imaginary Oedipus and aimed at the role of parental figures, without at all penetrating the structure and its order of symbolic positions and functions.

For us, however, the problem is one of knowing if, indeed, that is where the difference enters in. Wouldn't the real difference be between Oedipus, structural as well as imaginary, and something else that all the Oedipuses crush and repress: desiring-production—the machines of

*In capitalizing these terms, we have followed the suggestion of Jacques Lacan's translator, Anthony Wilden; see *The Language of the Self* (Baltimore: Johns Hopkins University Press, 1968), p. xv.

desire that no longer allow themselves to be reduced to the structure any more than to persons, and that constitute the Real in itself, beyond or beneath the Symbolic as well as the Imaginary? We in no way claim to be taking up an endeavor such as Malinowski's, showing that the figures vary according to the social form under consideration. We even believe what we are told when Oedipus is presented as a kind of invariant. But the question is altogether different: is there an equivalence between the productions of the unconscious and this invariant—between the desiring-machines and the Oedipal structure? Or rather, does not the invariant merely express the history of a long mistake, throughout all its variations and modalities; the strain of an endless repression? What we are calling into question is the frantic Oedipalization to which psychoanalysis devotes itself, practically and theoretically, with the combined resources of image and structure. And despite some fine books by certain disciples of Lacan, we wonder if Lacan's thought really goes in this direction. Is it merely a matter of oedipalizing even the schizo? Or is it a question of something else, and even the contrary?* Wouldn't it be better to schizophrenize—to schizophrenize the domain of the unconscious as well as the sociohistorical domain, so as to shatter the iron collar of Oedipus and rediscover everywhere the force of desiring-production; to renew, on the level of the Real, the tie between the analytic machine, desire, and production? For the unconscious itself is no more structural than personal, it does not symbolize any more than it imagines or represents; it engineers, it is machinic. Neither imaginary nor symbolic, it is the Real in itself, the "impossible real" and its production.

But what is this long history, if we consider it only during the period of psychoanalysis? It does not take place without doubts, detours, and repentances. Laplanche and Pontalis note that Freud "discovers" the Oedipus complex in 1897 in the course of his self-analysis, but that he doesn't give a generalized theoretical form to it until 1923, in *The Ego and the Id,* and that, between these two formulations, Oedipus leads a more or less marginal existence, "confined for example to a separate chapter on object-choice at puberty (*Three Essays*), or to a chapter on typical dreams (*The Interpretation of Dreams*)." They say that this is because a certain abandonment by Freud of the theory of traumatism

*"Nevertheless, it is not because I preach a return to Freud that I am not able to say that *Totem and Taboo* is a twisted story. It is in fact for that reason that we must return to Freud. No one helped me to make this known: *the formations of the unconscious.* . . . I am not saying Oedipus serves no purpose, nor that it (*ça*) bears no relationship with what we do. It serves no purpose for the psychoanalysts, that is indeed true! But since psychoanalysts are assuredly not psychoanalysts, that proves nothing. . . . These are things I set forth in their appropriate time and place; that was a time when I was speaking to people who had to be dealt with tactfully—psychoanalysts. On that level, I spoke of the paternal metaphor, I have never spoken of an Oedipus complex." (Jacques Lacan in a seminar, 1970.)

and seduction leads not to a univocal determination of Oedipus, but to the description as well of a spontaneous infantile sexuality of an endogenous nature. It is as if "Freud never managed to articulate the interrelations of Oedipus and infantile sexuality," the latter referring to a biological reality of development, the former to a psychic fantasy reality. Oedipus is what all but got lost "for the sake of a biological realism."[1]

But is it correct to present things in this way? Did the imperialism of Oedipus require only the renunciation of biological realism? Or wasn't something else sacrificed to Oedipus, something infinitely stronger? For what Freud and the first analysts discover is the domain of free syntheses where everything is possible: endless connections, nonexclusive disjunctions, nonspecific conjunctions, partial objects and flows. The desiring-machines pound away and throb in the depths of the unconscious: Irma's injection, the Wolf Man's ticktock, Anna's coughing machine, and also all the explanatory apparatuses set into motion by Freud, all those neurobiologico-desiring-machines. And the discovery of the productive unconscious has what appear to be two correlates: on the one hand, the direct confrontation between desiring-production and social production, between symptomological and collective formations, given their identical nature and their differing régimes; and on the other hand, the repression that the social machine exercises on desiring-machines, and the relationship of psychic repression with social repression. This will all be lost, or at least singularly compromised, with the establishment of a sovereign Oedipus. Free association, rather than opening onto polyvocal connections, confines itself to a univocal impasse. All the chains of the unconscious are biunivocalized, linearized, suspended from a despotic signifier. The whole of desiring-*production* is crushed, subjected to the requirements of *representation*, and to the dreary games of what is representative and represented in representation. And there is the essential thing: the reproduction of desire gives way to a simple representation, in the process as well as theory of the cure. The productive unconscious makes way for an unconscious that knows only how to express itself—express itself in myth, in tragedy, in dream.

But who says that dream, tragedy, and myth are adequate to the formations of the unconscious, even if the work of transformation is taken into account? Groddeck remained more faithful than Freud to an autoproduction of the unconscious in the coextension of man and Nature. It is as if Freud had drawn back from this world of wild production and explosive desire, wanting at all costs to restore a little order there, an order made classical owing to the ancient Greek theater.

For what does it mean to say that Freud discovered Oedipus in his own self-analysis? Was it in his self-analysis, or rather in his Goethian classical culture? In his self-analysis he discovers something about which he remarks: Well now, that looks like Oedipus! And at first he considers this something as a variant of the "familial romance," a paranoiac recording by which desire causes precisely the familial determinations to explode. It is only little by little that he makes the familial romance, on the contrary, into a mere dependence on Oedipus, and that he neuroticizes everything in the unconscious at the same time as he oedipalizes, and closes the familial triangle over the entire unconscious. The schizo—there is the enemy! Desiring-production is personalized, or rather personologized (*personnologisée*), imaginarized (*imaginarisée*), structuralized. (We have seen that the real difference or frontier did not lie between these terms, which are perhaps complementary.) Production is reduced to mere fantasy production, production of expression. The unconscious ceases to be what it is—a factory, a workshop—to become a theater, a scene and its staging. And not even an avant-garde theater, such as existed in Freud's day (Wedekind), but the classical theater, the classical order of representation. The psychoanalyst becomes a director for a private theater, rather than the engineer or mechanic who sets up units of production, and grapples with collective agents of production and antiproduction.

Psychoanalysis is like the Russian Revolution; we don't know when it started going bad. We have to keep going back further. To the Americans? To the First International? To the secret Committee? To the first ruptures, which signify renunciations by Freud as much as betrayals by those who break with him? To Freud himself, from the moment of the "discovery" of Oedipus? Oedipus is the idealist turning point. Yet it cannot be said that psychoanalysis set to work unaware of desiring-production. The fundamental notions of the *economy* of desire—work and investment—keep their importance, but are subordinated to the forms of an expressive unconscious and no longer to the formations of the productive unconscious. The *anoedipal* nature of desiring-production remains present, but it is fitted over the co-ordinates of Oedipus, which translate it into "pre-oedipal," "para-oedipal," "quasi-oedipal," etc. The desiring-machines are always there, but they no longer function except behind the consulting-room walls. Behind the walls or in the wings, such is the place the primal fantasy concedes to desiring-machines, when it reduces everything to the Oedipal scene.[1a] They continue nevertheless to make a hellish racket. Even the psychoanalyst can't ignore them. He tends therefore to maintain an attitude of denial: all of that is surely true, but it is still daddy-mommy. Over the consulting-room door is written, "Leave your desiring-machines at the door, give up your orphan and celibate machines, your tape recorder and your little bike, enter and allow yourself to be oedipalized." Everything follows from that, beginning with the untellable character of the cure, its interminable and highly contractual nature, flows of speech in exchange for flows of money. All that is needed is what is called a psychotic episode: after a schizophrenic flash, one day we bring our tape recorder into the analyst's office—stop!—with this insertion of a desiring-machine everything is reversed: we have broken the contract, we are not faithful to the major principle of the exclusion of a third party, we have introduced a third element—the desiring-machine in person.* Yet every psychoanalyst should know that, underneath Oedipus, through Oedipus, behind Oedipus, his business is with desiring-machines. At the beginning, psychoanalysts *could not be unaware* of the forcing employed to introduce Oedipus, to inject it into the unconscious. Then Oedipus fell back on and appropriated desiring-production as if all the productive forces emanated from Oedipus itself. The psychoanalyst became the carrier of Oedipus, the great agent of antiproduction in desire. The same history as that of Capital, with its enchanted, "miraculated" world. (Also at the beginning, said Marx, the first capitalists could not be unaware of . . .)

2 | Three Texts of Freud

It is easy to see that the problem is first of all practical, that it concerns above all else the practice of the cure. For the frenzied oedipalization process takes form precisely at the moment when Oedipus has not yet received its full theoretical formulation as the "nuclear complex" and leads a marginal existence. The fact that Schreber's analysis was not *in vivo* detracts nothing from its exemplary value from the point of view of practice. In this text (1911) Freud encounters the most formidable of questions: how does one dare reduce to the paternal theme a delirium so rich, so differentiated, so "divine" as the Judge's— since the Judge in his memoirs makes only very brief references to the

*Jean-Jacques Abrahams, "L'homme au magnétophone, dialogue psychanalytique," *Les Temps modernes*, no. 274 (April 1969): "*A:* You see, it really isn't so serious; I'm not your father, and I can still shout, of course not! There, that's enough.—*Dr. X:* You are imitating your father at this moment?—*A:* Of course not, come off it, I'm imitating *your* father! The one I see in your eyes.—*Dr. X:* You are trying to take the role. . . .—*A:* . . . You can't cure people, you can only palm off your father problems on them—problems you can't get away from. And from session to session you drag along your victims that way with your father problem . . . . *I* was the sick one, *you* were the doctor. You'd finally reversed your childhood problem of being the child to your father. . . .—*Dr. X:* I was just telephoning extension 609 to make you leave—609, the police, to have you thrown out.—*A:* The police? That's it—Daddy! Your father's a policeman! And you were going to call your father to come get me. . . . What insanity! You got all unnerved, excited, just because I brought out a little device that'll let us understand what's going on here."

memory of his father. On several occasions Freud's text marks the extent to which he felt the difficulty: to begin with, it appears difficult to assign as cause of the malady—even if only an occasional cause—an "outburst of homosexual libido" directed at Dr. Flechsig's person.[2] But when we replace the doctor with the father and commission the father to explain the God of delirium, we ourselves have trouble following this ascension; we take liberties that can be justified only by the advantages they afford us in our attempt to understand the delirium.[3] Yet the more Freud states such scruples, the more he thrusts them aside and sweeps them away with a firm and confident response. And this response is double: it is not my fault if psychoanalysis attests to a great monotony and encounters the father everywhere—in Flechsig, in the God, in the sun; it is the fault of sexuality and its stubborn symbolism.[4] Furthermore, it is not surprising that the father returns constantly in current deliriums in the most hidden and least recognizable guises, since he returns in fact everywhere and more visibly in religions and ancient myths, which express forces or mechanisms eternally active in the unconscious.[5] It should be noted that Judge Schreber's destiny was not merely that of being sodomized, while still alive, by the rays from heaven, but also that of being posthumously oedipalized by Freud. From the enormous political, social, and historical content of Schreber's delirium, *not one word is retained,* as though the libido did not bother itself with such things. Freud invokes only a sexual argument, which consists in bringing about the union of sexuality and the familial complex, and a mythological argument, which consists in positing the adequation of the productive force of the unconscious and the "edifying forces of myths and religions."

This latter argument is very important, and it is not by chance that here Freud declares himself in agreement with Jung. In a certain way this agreement subsists after their break. If the unconscious is thought to express itself adequately in myths and religions (taking into account, of course, the work of transformation), there are two ways of reading this adequation, but they have in common the postulate that measures the unconscious against myth, and that from the start substitutes mere expressive forms for the productive formations. The basic question is never asked, but cast aside: *Why return to myth?* Why take it as the model? The supposed adequation can then be interpreted in what is termed anagogical fashion, toward the "higher." Or inversely, in analytical fashion, toward the "lower," relating the myth to the drives. But since the drives are transferred from myth, traced from myth with the transformations taken into account. . . What we mean is that, starting from the same postulate, Jung is led to restore the most diffuse and spiritualized religiosity, whereas Freud is confirmed in his most rigorous atheism. Freud needs to deny the existence of God as much as Jung needs to affirm the essence of the divine, in order to interpret the commonly postulated adequation. But to render religion unconscious, or the unconscious religious, still amounts to injecting something religious into the unconscious. (And what would Freudian analysis be without the celebrated guilt feelings ascribed to the unconscious?)

What came to pass in the history of psychoanalysis? Freud held to his atheism in heroic fashion. But all around him, more and more, they respectfully allowed him to speak, they let the old man speak, ready to prepare behind his back the reconciliation of the churches and psychoanalysis, the moment when the Church would train its own psychoanalysts, and when it would become possible to write in the history of the movement: so even we are still pious! Let us recall Marx's great declaration: he who denies God does only a "secondary thing," for he denies God in order to posit the existence of man, to put man in God's place (the transformation taken into account).[6] But the person who knows that the place of man is entirely elsewhere does not even allow the possibility of a question to subsist concerning "an alien being, a being placed above man and nature": he no longer needs the mediation of myth, he no longer needs to go by way of this mediation—the negation of the existence of God—since he has attained those regions of an autoproduction of the unconscious where the unconscious is no less atheist than orphan—immediately atheist, immediately orphan. And doubtless an examination of the first argument would lead us to a similar conclusion. By joining sexuality to the familial complex, by making Oedipus into the criterion of sexuality in analysis—the test of orthodoxy par excellence—Freud himself posited the whole of social *and* metaphysical relations as an afterward or a beyond that desire was incapable of investing immediately. He then became rather indifferent to the fact that this beyond derives from the familial complex through the analytical transformation of desire, or is signified by it in an anagogical symbolization.

Let us consider another text of Freud's, a later one, where Oedipus is already designated as the "nuclear complex": "A Child Is Being Beaten."[7] The reader cannot escape the impression of a disquieting strangeness. Never was the paternal theme less visible, and yet never was it affirmed with as much passion and resolution. The imperialism of Oedipus is founded here on an absence. After all, of the three supposed phases of the girl's fantasy, the first is such that the father does not yet appear, while in the third the father no longer appears: that leaves the second, then, where the father shines forth in all his brilliance, "clearly without doubt"—but indeed, "this second phase has never had a real existence. It is never remembered, it has never succeeded in becoming conscious. It is a construction of analysis, but it is no less a necessity on that account."[8]

What is at issue in this fantasy? Some boys are beaten by someone—the teacher, for example—in the presence of the little girls. We are present from the start at a double Freudian reduction, which is in no way imposed by the fantasy, but is required by Freud in the manner of a presupposition. On the one hand Freud wants to deliberately reduce the *group* character of the fantasy to a purely individual dimension: the beaten children must in a way be the ego ("substitutes for the subject himself") and the one who does the beating must be the father ("father substitute"). On the other hand it is necessary for the variations of the fantasy to be organized in disjunctions whose use must be strictly exclusive. Hence there will be a girl-series and a boy-series, but dissymmetrical, the female fantasy having three phases, the last of which is "boys are beaten by the teacher," while the male fantasy has only two, the last of which is "my mother beats me." The only common phase—the second for the girls and the first for the boys—affirms without doubt the prevalence of the father in both cases, but this is the famous nonexistent phase.

Such is always the case with Freud. Something common to the two sexes is required, but something that will be lacking in both, and that will distribute the lack in two nonsymmetrical series, establishing the exclusive use of the disjunctions: you are girl *or* boy! Such is the case with Oedipus and its "resolution," different in boys and in girls. Such is the case with castration, and its relationship to Oedipus in both instances. Castration is at once the common lot—that is, the prevalent and transcendent Phallus, and the exclusive distribution that presents itself in girls as desire for the penis, and in boys as fear of losing it or refusal of a passive attitude. This something in common must lay the foundation for the exclusive use of the disjunctions of the unconscious—and teach us resignation. Resignation to Oedipus, to castration: for girls, renunciation of their desire for the penis; for boys, renunciation of male protest—in short, "assumption of one's sex."* This

*Sigmund Freud, "Analysis Terminable and Interminable" (1937), in *Standard Edition of the Complete Psychological Works of Sigmund Freud,* ed. James Strachey (New York: Macmillan; London: Hogarth Press, 1964), Vol. 23, pp. 250–52: "The two corresponding themes are in the female, an *envy for the penis*—a positive striving to possess a male genital—and, in the male, a struggle against his passive or feminine attitude to another male. . . . At no other point . . . does one suffer more from an oppressive feeling that one has been 'preaching to the winds,' than when one is trying to persuade a woman to abandon her wish for a penis on the ground of its being unrealizable or when one is seeking to convince a man that a passive attitude to men does not always signify castration and that it is indispensable in many relationships in life. The rebellious overcompensation of the male produces one of the strongest transference-resistances. He refuses to subject himself to a father-substitute, or to feel indebted to him something in common, the great Phallus, the Lack with two nonsuperimposable sides, is purely mythical; it is like the One in negative theology, it introduces lack into desire and causes exclusive series to emanate, to which it attributes a goal, an origin, and a path of resignation.

The contrary should be said: neither is there anything in common between the two sexes, nor do they cease communicating with each other in a transverse mode where each subject possesses both of them, but with the two of them partitioned off, and where each subject communicates with *one sex or the other in another subject.* Such is the law of partial objects. Nothing is lacking, nothing can be defined as a lack; nor are the disjunctions in the unconscious ever exclusive, but rather the object of a properly inclusive use that we must analyze. Freud had a concept at his disposal for stating this contrary notion: the concept of bisexuality; and it was not by chance that he was never able or never wanted to give this concept the analytical position and extension it required. Without even going that far, a lively controversy developed when certain analysts, following Melanie Klein, tried to define the unconscious forces of the female sexual organ by positive characteristics in terms of partial objects and flows. This slight shift—which did not suppress mythical castration but made it depend secondarily on the organ, instead of the organ's depending on it—met with great opposition from Freud.[9] He maintained that the organ, from the viewpoint of the unconscious, could not be understood except by proceeding from a lack or a primal deprivation, and not the opposite.

Here we have a properly analytical fallacy (which will be found again, to a considerable degree, in the theory of the signifier) that consists in passing from the detachable partial object to the position of a complete object as the thing detached (phallus). This passage implies a subject, defined as a fixed ego of one sex or the other, who necessarily experiences as a lack his subordination to the tyrannical complete object. This is perhaps no longer the case when the partial object is posited for itself on the body without organs, with—as its sole subject—not an "ego," but the drive that forms the desiring-machine along with it, and that enters into relationships of connection, disjunction, and conjunction with other partial objects, at the core of the corresponding multiplicity whose every element can only be defined *positively.* We must speak of "castration" in the same way we speak of oedipalization, whose crowning moment it is: castration designates the operation by which psychoanalysis castrates the unconscious, injects castration into the unconscious. Castration as a practical operation on

for anything, and consequently he refuses to accept his recovery from the doctor." (*Translators' note:* Hereafter this source will be cited as *Standard Edition.*)

the unconscious is achieved when the thousand breaks-flows of desiring-machines—all positive, all productive—are projected into the same mythical space, the unary stroke of the signifier.

We have not finished chanting the litany of the ignorances of the unconscious; it knows nothing of castration or Oedipus, just as it knows nothing of parents, gods, the law, lack. The Women's Liberation movements are correct in saying: We are not castrated, so you get fucked.[10] And far from being able to get by with anything like the wretched maneuver where men answer that this itself is proof that women are castrated—or even console women by saying that men are castrated, too, all the while rejoicing that they are castrated the other way, on the side that is not superimposable—it should be recognized that Women's Liberation movements contain, in a more or less ambiguous state, what belongs to all requirements of liberation: the force of the unconscious itself, the investment by desire of the social field, the disinvestment of repressive structures. Nor are we going to say that the question is not that of knowing if women are castrated, but only if the unconscious "believes it," since all the ambiguity lies there. What does belief applied to the unconscious signify? What is an unconscious that no longer does anything but "believe," rather than produce? What are the operations, the artifices that inject the unconscious with "beliefs" that are not even irrational, but on the contrary only too reasonable and consistent with the established order?

Let us return to the fantasy, "a child is being beaten, children are beaten"—a typical group fantasy where desire invests the social field and its repressive forms. If there is a *mise en scène*, it is directed by a social desiring-machine whose product should not be considered abstractly, separating the girl's and the boy's cases, as if each were a little ego taking up its own business with daddy and mommy. On the contrary, we should consider the complementary emsemble made up of boy-girl and parents-agents of production and antiproduction, this ensemble being present at the same time in each individual and in the socius that presides over the organization of the group fantasy. Simultaneously the boys are beaten-initiated by the teacher on the little girl's erotic stage (seeing-machine), and obtain satisfaction in a masochistic fantasy involving the mother (anal machine). The result is that the boys are able to see only by becoming little girls, and the girls cannot experience the pleasure of punishment except by becoming boys. It is a whole chorus, a montage: back in the village after a raid in Vietnam, in the presence of their weeping sisters, the filthy Marines are beaten by their instructor, on whose knees the mommy is seated, and they have orgasms for having been so evil, for having tortured so well. It's so bad, but also so good!

Perhaps one will recall a sequence from the film *Hearts and Minds:* we see Colonel Patton, the general's son, saying that his guys are great, that they love their mothers, their fathers, and their country, that they cry at the religious services for their dead buddies, fine boys; then the colonel's face changes, grimaces, and reveals a big paranoiac in uniform who shouts in conclusion: but still, they're a bloody good bunch of killers! It is obvious that when traditional psychoanalysis explains that the instructor is the father, and that the colonel too is the father, and that the mother is nonetheless the father too, it reduces all of desire to a familial determination that no longer has anything to do with the social field actually invested by the libido. Of course there is always something from the father or the mother that is taken up in the signifying chain—daddy's mustache, the mother's raised arm—but it comes furtively to occupy a place among the collective agents. The terms of Oedipus do not form a triangle, but exist shattered into all corners of the social field—the mother on the instructor's knees, the father next to the colonel. Group fantasy is plugged into and machined on the socius. Being fucked by the socius, wanting to be fucked by the socius, does not derive from the father and mother, even though the father and mother have their roles there as subordinate agents of transmission or execution.

When the notion of group fantasy was elaborated in the perspective of institutional analysis—in the works of the team at La Borde Clinic, assembled around Jean Oury—the first task was to show how it differed from individual fantasy. It became evident that group fantasy was inseparable from the "symbolic" articulations that define a social field insofar as it is real, whereas the individual fantasy fitted the whole of this field over "imaginary" givens. If this first distinction is drawn out, we see that the individual fantasy is itself plugged into the existing social field, but apprehends it in the form of imaginary qualities that confer on it a kind of transcendence or immortality under the shelter of which the individual, the ego, plays out its pseudo destiny: what does it matter if I die, says the general, since the Army is immortal? The imaginary dimension of the individual fantasy has a decisive importance over the death instinct, insofar as the immortality conferred on the existing social order carried into the ego all the investments of repression, the phenomena of identification, of "superegoization" and castration, all the resignation-desires (becoming a general; acquiring low, middle, or high rank), including the resignation to dying in the service of this order, whereas the drive itself is projected onto the outside and turned against the others (death to the foreigner, to those who are not of our own ranks!). The revolutionary pole of group fantasy becomes visible, on the contrary, in the power to experience institutions themselves as mortal, to destroy them or change them according to the articulations of desire and the social field, by making the death instinct into a veritable institutional creativity. For that is precisely the criterion—at least the formal criterion—that distinguishes the revolutionary institution from the enormous inertia which the law communicates to institutions in an established order. As Nietzsche says; churches, armies, States—which of all these dogs wants to die?

There results a third difference between group fantasy and the so-called individual fantasy. The latter has as subject the ego, insofar as it is determined by the legal and legalized institutions in which it "imagines itself," to the point where, even in its perversions, the ego conforms to the exclusive use of the disjunctions imposed by the law (for example, Oedipal homosexuality). But group fantasy no longer has anything but the drives themselves as subject, and the desiring-machines formed by them with the revolutionary institutions. The group fantasy *includes* the disjunctions, in the sense that each subject, discharged of his personal identity but not of his singularities, enters into relations with others following the communication proper to partial objects: everyone passes into the body of the other on the body without organs.

In this respect Klossowski has convincingly shown the inverse relationship that pulls the fantasy in two directions, as the economic law establishes perversion in the "psychic exchanges," or as the psychic exchanges on the contrary promote a subversion of the law: "Anachronistic, relative to the institutional level of gregariousness, the singular state can, according to its more or less forceful intensity, bring about a deactualization of the institution itself and denounce it in turn as anachronistic."[11] The two kinds of fantasy, or rather the two régimes, are therefore distinguished according to whether the social production of "goods" imposes its rule on desire through the intermediary of an ego whose fictional unity is guaranteed by the goods themselves, or whether the desiring-production of affects imposes its rule on institutions whose elements are no longer anything but drives. If we must still speak of utopia in this sense, à la Fourier, it is most assuredly not as an ideal model, but as revolutionary action and passion. In his recent works Klossowski indicates to us the only means of bypassing the sterile parallelism where we flounder between Freud and Marx: by discovering how social production and relations of production are an institution of desire, and how affects or drives form part of the infrastructure itself. For *they are part of it, they are present there in every way* while creating within the economic forms their own repression, as well as the means for breaking this repression.

The development of distinctions between group and individual fantasy shows sufficiently well, at last, that there is no individual fantasy. Instead there are two types of groups, subject-groups and subjugated groups, with Oedipus and castration forming the imaginary structure under which members of the subjugated groups are induced to live or fantasize individually their membership in the group. It must still be said that the two types of groups are perpetually shifting, a subject-group always being threatened with subjugation, a subjugated group capable in certain cases of being forced to take on a revolutionary role. It is therefore all the more disturbing to see to what extent Freudian analysis retains from the fantasy only its lines of exclusive disjunction, and flattens it into its individual or pseudoindividual dimensions, which by their very nature refer the fantasy to subjugated groups, rather than carrying out the opposite operation and disengaging in the fantasy the underlying element of a revolutionary group potential. When we learn that the instructor, the teacher, is daddy, and the colonel too, and also the mother—*when all the agents of social production and antiproduction are in this way reduced to the figures of familial reproduction*—we can understand why the panicked libido no longer risks abandoning Oedipus, and internalizes it. The libido internalizes it in the form of a castrating duality between the subject of the statement (*l'énoncé*) and the subject of the enunciation, as is characteristic of the pseudoindividual fantasy ("I, as a man, understand you, but as judge, as boss, as colonel or general, *that is to say as the father,* I condemn you"). But this duality is artificial, derived, and supposes a direct relationship proceeding from the statement to the collective agents of enunciation in the group fantasy.

Institutional analysis tries to trace its difficult path between the repressive asylum and the legalistic hospital on the one hand, and contractual psychoanalysis on the other. From the outset, the psychoanalytic relationship modeled itself after the contractual relationship of the most traditional bourgeois medicine: the feigned exclusion of a third party; the hypocritical role of money, to which psychoanalysis brought farcical new justifications; the pretended time limitation that contradicts itself by reproducing a debt to infinity, by feeding an inexhaustible transference, and by always nursing new "conflicts." We are astonished when we hear that a terminated analysis is by that very fact a failure, even if this proposition is accompanied by the analyst's little smile. We are surprised when we hear a knowledgeable analyst mention, in passing, that one of his "patients" still dreams of being invited to eat or have a drink at his place, after several years of analysis, as if this were not a tiny sign of the abject dependence to which analysis reduced the patients. How can we ward off, in the practice of the cure, this abject desire that makes us bend our knees, lays us on the couch, and makes us remain there?

Let us consider a third and final text of Freud's, "Analysis Terminable and Interminable" (1937).[12] We prefer not to follow a recent suggestion that it would be better to translate "Analysis Finite, Analysis Infinite," since finite-infinite is almost mathematics or logic, whereas the problem is particularly practical and concrete. Does this story have an ending? Can an analysis be ended, can the process of analysis be terminated, yes or no? Can it be completed, or is it condemned to a constant self-perpetuation? As Freud says, can a currently given "conflict" be exhausted, can the one who is sick be forewarned against ulterior conflicts, can even new conflicts be awakened for a preventive purpose? A great beauty animates this text of Freud's: an undefined something that is hopeless, disenchanted, tired, and at the same time a serenity, a certitude in the finished work. It is Freud's testament. He is going to die, and knows it. He knows something is wrong in psychoanalysis. The cure tends to be more and more interminable! He knows that soon he will no longer be there to see how things are going. So he takes stock of the obstacles to treatment, with the serenity of the person who senses what a treasure his work is, but senses too the poisons that have already filtered in. Everything would be fine if the economic problem of desire were merely quantitative; it would be a matter of reinforcing the ego against the drives. The celebrated strong, mature ego, the "contract," the "pact" between the analyst and an ego that is normal in spite of everything . . . Except that there are *qualitative factors* in the desiring-economy that indeed present an obstacle to treatment, and Freud reproaches himself for not having taken them sufficiently into account.

The first of these factors is the "rock" of castration, the rock with two nonsymmetrical faces, which creates in us an incurable alveolus, and against which the analyst stumbles. The second is a qualitative aptitude for conflict, which means that the quantity of libido does not branch into two variable forces corresponding to heterosexuality and homosexuality, but creates in most people irreducible oppositions between the two forces. Finally, the third factor—of such economic importance that it outweighs the dynamic and topical considerations—concerns a type of resistance that is nonlocalizable. It would seem that certain subjects have such a *viscous* libido, or on the contrary such a *liquid* one, that nothing succeeds in "taking hold." It would be a mistake to see in this remark of Freud's nothing more than an observation of detail, a mere anecdote. In fact, it concerns what is most essential in the phenomenon of desire: the qualitative flows of the libido.

In some fine pages, André Green recently took up the question again by making up a list of three types of "sessions," the first two of which comprise counterindications, the third alone constituting the ideal session in analysis. According to Type I (viscosity, resistance of a hysterical form), "the session is dominated by a heavy, weighty, boggy climate. The silences are leaden, the discourse is dominated by the events of the day, . . . is uniform, it is a descriptive narration where no reference to the past is disclosable, it unfolds along a continuous thread, unable to allow itself any break. . . . Dreams are narrated, . . . the enigma of dream is taken up in the secondary elaboration that makes dream as narration and as event take precedence over dream as a working over of thoughts. . . . Sticky transference. . . ."[13] According to Type II (liquidity, resistance of an obsessional form), "here the session is dominated by an extreme mobility of representations of all sorts, . . . the language is unfettered, rapid, almost torrential, . . . everything enters here, . . . the patient could just as easily say the opposite of everything he is uttering without changing anything fundamental to the analytic situation. . . . All of this is without consequence, since the analysis slides off the couch like water off a duck's back. The unconscious does not cause anything to 'stick,' there is no anchoring in the transference. Here the transference is volatile. . . ." Only the third type remains, whose characteristics define a *good* analysis. The patient "speaks in order to constitute the process of a chain of signifiers. The meaning is not attached to the signified to which each of the enunciated signifiers refers, but is constituted by process, suture, the concatenation of bound elements. . . . Every interpretation furnished by [the patient] can offer itself as an already-signified awaiting its meaning. For this reason interpretation is always retrospective, as the perceived meaning. *So that was what this meant. . . .*"

What is serious is that Freud never questions the process of the cure. Of course it is too late for him, but is it too late for those who come after him? He interprets these things as obstacles to the cure, and not as shortcomings of the treatment itself, or as effects or countereffects of his method. For castration as an analyzable state—or nonanalyzable; the ultimate rock—is the effect of castration as a psychoanalytic act. And Oedipal homosexuality—the qualitative aptitude for conflict—is rather the effect of oedipalization, which the treatment does not invent, but precipitates and accentuates within the artificial conditions of its exercise (transference). And inversely, when flows of libido resist therapeutic practice, rather than being a resistance of the ego, this is the intense outcry of all of desiring-production. We already knew that the pervert resisted oedipalization: why should he surrender, since he has invented for himself other territorialities, more artificial still and more lunar than that of Oedipus? We knew the schizo was not oedipalizable, because he is beyond territoriality, because he has carried his flows right into the desert. But what remains, once we learn that "resistances" of an hysterical or an obsessional form bear witness to the anoedipal quality of the flows of desire on the very terrain of Oedipus? That is precisely what qualitative economy shows: flows ooze, they traverse the triangle, breaking apart its vertices. The Oedipal wad does not absorb these flows, any more than it could seal off a jar of jam or plug a dike. Against the walls of the triangle, toward the outside, flows exert the irresistible pressure of lava or the invincible oozing of water.

What are the most favorable conditions for the cure, it is asked? A *flow* that lets itself be plugged by Oedipus; *partial objects* that let themselves be subsumed under the category of a complete object, even if absent—the phallus of castration; *breaks-flows* that let themselves be projected onto a mythical space; polyvocal chains that let themselves be biunivocalized, linearized, suspended from a signifier; an unconscious that lets itself be expressed; connective syntheses that let themselves be taken in a global and specific use; disjunctive syntheses that let themselves be taken in an exclusive, restrictive use; conjunctive synthe-ses that let themselves be taken in a personal and segregative use. For what is the meaning of "so *that* was what *this* meant"? The crushing of the "so" onto Oedipus and castration. The sigh of relief: you see, the colonel, the instructor, the teacher, the boss, all of *this* meant *that*: Oedipus and castration, "all history in a new version."

We are not saying that Oedipus and castration do not amount to anything. We are oedipalized, we are castrated; psychoanalysis didn't invent these operations, to which it merely lends the new resources and methods of its genius. But is this sufficient to silence the outcry of desiring-production: We are all schizos! We are all perverts! We are all libidos that are too viscous and too fluid—and not by preference, but wherever we have been carried by the deterritorialized flows. What neurotic, provided he is somewhat serious, is not leaning against the rock of schizophrenia, a rock in this case mobile, aerolitic? Who does not haunt the perverse territorialities, beyond the kindergartens of Oedipus? Who does not feel in the flows of his desire both the lava and the water? And above all, what brings about our sickness? Schizophre-nia itself, as a process? Or is it brought about by the frantic neuroticiza-tion to which we have been delivered, and for which psychoanalysis has invented new means—Oedipus and castration? Is it schizophrenia as a process that makes us sick, or is it the self-perpetuation of the process in the void—a horrible exasperation (the production of the schizophrenic-as-entity)? Or is it the confusion of the process with a goal (the production of the pervert-artifice), or the premature interruption of the process (the production of the neurotic analysis)? We are forcibly confronted with Oedipus and castration, we are reduced to them: either so as to measure us against that cross, or to establish that we cannot measure up to it. But in any case the harm has been done, the treatment has chosen the path of oedipalization, all cluttered with refuse, instead of the schizophrenization that must cure us of the cure.

3 | The Connective Synthesis of Production

Given the syntheses of the unconscious, the practical problem is that of their use, legitimate or not, and of the conditions that define a use of synthesis as legitimate or not. Take the example of homosexuality—though it is something more than an example. We noted how, in Proust, the famous pages of *Sodom and Gomorrah (Cities of the Plain)* interlaced two openly contradictory themes; the fundamental guilt of the "accursed races" and the radical innocence of flowers. The diagnosis of Oedipal homosexuality with a mother fixation, of a dominant depressive nature and a sadomasochistic guilt, was quickly applied to Proust. In a more general way still, some critics were too quick in discovering contradictions, either in order to declare them irreducible, or to resolve them, or to show that they were merely apparent, according to preference. In truth, there are never contradictions, apparent or real, but only degrees of humor. And inasmuch as reading itself has its degrees of humor, from black to white, with which it evaluates the coexisting degrees of what it reads, the sole problem is always one of allocation on a scale of intensities that assigns the position and use of each thing, each being, or each scene: there is this and then that, and let's make do with it, too bad if it doesn't suit us.

In this regard it is possible that Charlus's coarse admonition is prophetic: "A lot we care about our old grandmother, you little shit!" For what does in fact take place in *In Search of Lost Time,* one and the same story with infinite variations? It is clear that the narrator sees nothing, hears nothing, and that he is a body without organs, or like a spider poised in its web, observing nothing, but responding to the slightest sign, to the slightest vibration by springing on its prey. Everything begins with nebulae, statistical wholes whose outlines are blurred, *molar* or collective formations comprising singularities distributed haphazardly (a living room, a group of girls, a landscape). Then, within these nebulae or these collectives, "sides" take shape, series are arranged, *persons* figure in these series, under strange laws of lack, absence, asymmetry, exclusion, noncommunication, vice, and guilt. Next, everything becomes blurred again, everything comes apart, but this time in a *molecular* and pure multiplicity, where the partial objects, the "boxes," the "vessels" all have their positive determinations, and enter into aberrant communication following a transversal that runs through the whole work; an immense flow that each partial object produces and cuts again, reproduces and cuts at the same time. More than vice, says Proust, it is madness and its innocence that disturb us. If schizophrenia is the universal, the great artist is indeed the one who scales the schizophrenic wall and reaches the land of the unknown, where he no longer belongs to any time, any milieu, any school.

Such is the case in an illustrative passage, the first kiss given Albertine. Albertine's face is at first a nebula, barely extracted from the collective of girls. Then her person disengages itself, through a series of views that are like distinct personalities, with Albertine's face jumping from one plane to another as the narrator's lips draw nearer her cheek. At last, within the magnified proximity, everything falls apart like a face drawn in sand, Albertine's face shatters into molecular partial objects, while those on the narrator's face rejoin the body without organs, eyes closed, nosrils pinched shut, mouth filled. What is more, their entire love tells the same story. From the statistical nebula, from the molar entirety of men-women loves, there emerge the two accursed and guilty series that bear witness to the same castration with two nonsuperimposable sides, the Sodom series and the Gomorrah series, each one excluding the other.

This is not all, however, since the vegetal theme—the innocence of flowers—brings us yet another message and another code: everyone is bisexual, everyone has two sexes, but partitioned, noncommunicating; the man is merely the one in whom the male part, and the woman the one in whom the female part, dominates statistically. So that at the level of elementary combinations, at least two men and two women must be made to intervene to constitute the multiplicity in which transverse communications are established—connections of partial objects and flows[14]: the male part of a man can communicate with the female part of a woman, but also with the male part of a woman, or with the female part of another man, or yet again with the male part of the other man, etc. Here all guilt ceases, for it cannot cling to such flowers as these. In contrast to the alternative of the "either/or" exclusions, there is the "either . . . or . . . or" of the combinations and permutations where the differences amount to the same without ceasing to be differences.

We are statistically or molarly heterosexual, but personally homosexual, without knowing it or being fully aware of it, and finally we are transsexual in an elemental, molecular sense. That is why Proust, the first to deny all oedipalizing interpretations of his own interpretations, contrasts two kinds of homosexuality, or rather two regions only one of which is Oedipal, exclusive, and depressive, the other being anoedipal schizoid, included, and inclusive: "For some, doubtless those *whose childhoods were timid,* the material kind of pleasure they take does not matter, so long as they can *relate it to a male countenance.* While others, whose sensuality is doubtless more violent, give their material pleasure certain imperious localizations. The second group would shock most people by their avowals. They live perhaps less exclusively under Saturn's satellite, for in their case women are not entirely excluded. . . . But those in the second group seek out women who prefer women, women who suggest young men . . . *indeed,* they can take, *with such women,* the same pleasure as with a man. . . . For in their relations with women, they play—for the woman who prefers women—the role of *another woman,* and at the same time a woman offers them approximately what they find *in a man."*[15]

The opposition here is between two uses of the connective syntheses: a global and specific use, and a partial and nonspecific use. In the first, desire at the same time receives a fixed subject, an ego specified according to a given sex, and complete objects defined as global persons. The complexity and the foundations of such an operation appear more distinctly if we consider the mutual reactions between the different syntheses of the unconscious following a given use. It is first of all the synthesis of recording that in effect situates, on its surface of inscription within the conditions of Oedipus, a definable and differentiable ego in relation to parental images serving as co-ordinates (mother, father). There we have a triangulation that implies in its essence a constituent prohibition, and that conditions the differentiation between persons: prohibition of incest with the mother, prohibition against taking the father's place. But a strange sort of reasoning leads one to conclude that, since *it* is forbidden, *that very thing* was desired. In reality, global persons—even the very form of persons—do not exist prior to the prohibitions that weigh on them and constitute them, any more than they exist prior to the triangulation into which they enter: desire receives its first complete objects and is forbidden them at one and the same time. Therefore it is indeed the same Oedipal operation that lays the foundations for the possibility of its own "resolution," by way of a differentiation of persons in conformity with the prohibition, as well as the possibility for its own failure or stagnation, by falling into the undifferentiated as the reverse side of the differentiation created by the prohibitions (incest by identification with the father, homosexuality by identification with the mother). The personal material of transgression does not exist prior to the prohibition, any more than does the form of persons.

We can therefore see the property the prohibition has of displacing itself, since from the start it displaces desire. It displaces itself in the sense that the Oedipal inscription does not force its way into the synthesis of recording without reacting on the synthesis of production, and profoundly changing the connections of this synthesis by introducing new global persons. These new images of persons are the sister and the spouse, after the father and the mother. It has often been remarked in fact that the prohibition existed in two forms, the one negative, having to do above all with the mother and imposing differentiation, the other positive, concerning the sister and requiring exchange: I have a moral obligation to take as wife someone other than my sister, and an obligation to keep my sister for someone else; I must give up my sister to a brother-in-law, receive my wife from a father-in-law.[16] And although new stases or relapses are produced at this level, such as new forms of incest and homosexuality, it is certain that the Oedipal triangle would have no way of transmitting and reproducing itself without this second step: the first step elaborates the form of the triangle, but it is only the second step that ensures the transmission of this figure. I take a woman other than my sister in order to constitute the differentiated base of a new triangle whose inverted vertex will be my child—which is called surmounting Oedipus, but reproducing it as well, transmitting it rather than dying all alone, incestuous, homosexual, and a zombie.

Thus the parental or familial use of the synthesis of recording extends into a conjugal use, or an alliance use, of the connective syntheses of production: a régime for the pairing of people replaces the connection of partial objects. On the whole, the connections of organmachines suited to desiring-production give way to a pairing of people under the rules of familial reproduction. Partial objects now seem to be taken from people, rather than from the nonpersonal flows that pass from one person to another. The reason is that persons are derived from abstract quantities, instead of from flows. Instead of a connective appropriation, partial objects become the possessions of a person and, when required, the property of another person. Just as he draws upon centuries of scholastic reflection in defining God as the principle of the disjunctive syllogism, Kant draws upon centuries of Roman juridical reflection when he defines marriage as the tie that makes a person the owner of the sexual organs of another person.[17] One need only consult a religious manual of sexual casuistry to see with what restrictions the organ-desiring machine connections remain tolerated within the régime for the pairing of people, which legally determines what may be appropriated from the body of the wife.

Clearer still, the difference in régime becomes apparent each time a society permits an infantile stage of sexual promiscuity to subsist, where everything is permitted until the age when the young man in turn submits to the principle of pairing that regulates the social production of children. It is true that the connections of desiring-production were found to comply with a binary rule; and we have even seen that a third term intervened in this binarity, the body without organs that reinjects producing into the product, extends the connections of machines, and serves as a surface of recording. But here no biunivocal process is in fact produced that would fit production into the mold of representatives; no triangulation appears at this level that would refer the objects of desire to global persons, or desire to a specific subject. The only subject is desire itself on the body without organs, inasmuch as it machines partial objects and flows, selecting and cutting the one with the other, passing from one body to another, following connections and appropriations that each time destroy the factitious unity of a possessive or proprietary ego (anoedipal sexuality).

The triangle takes form in the parental use, and reproduces itself in the conjugal use. We do not yet know what forces bring about this triangulation that interferes with the recording of desire in order to transform all its productive connections. But we are able at least to follow, abstractly, the manner in which these forces proceed. We are told that partial objects are caught up in an intuition of precocious totality, just as the ego is caught up in an intuition of unity that precedes its fulfillment. (Even in Melanie Klein, the schizoid partial object is related to a whole that prepares for the advent of the complete object in the depressive phase.) It is clear that such a totality-unity is posited only in terms of a certain mode of absence, as that which partial objects and subjects of desire "lack." Consequently, everything is played out from the start: everywhere we encounter the analytic process that consists in extrapolating a transcendent and common something, but that is a common-universal for the sole purpose of introducing lack into desire, in situating and specifying persons and an ego under one aspect or another of its absence, and imposing an exclusive direction on the disjunction of the sexes.

Such is the case in Freud: for Oedipus, for castration, for the second phase of the fantasy "A Child Is Being Beaten," or again for the famous latency period where the analytical mystification culminates. This common, transcendent, absent something will be called phallus or law, in order to designate "the" signifier that distributes the effects of meaning throughout the chain and introduces exclusions there (whence the oedipalizing interpretations of Lacanism). This signifier acts as the formal cause of the triangulation—that is to say, makes possible both the form of the triangle and its reproduction: Oedipus has as its formula $3+1$, the One of the transcendent phallus without which the terms considered would not take the form of a triangle.* It is as if the so-called signifying chain, made up of elements that are themselves nonsignifying—of polyvocal writing and detachable fragments—were the object of a special treatment, a crushing operation that extracted a detached object from the chain, a despotic signifier from whose law the entire chain seems consequently to be suspended, each link triangulated. There we have a curious paralogism implying a transcendent use of the syntheses of the unconscious: *we pass from detachable partial objects to the detached complete object, from which global persons derive by an assigning of lack.* For example, in the capitalist code and its trinitary expression, money as detachable chain is converted into capital as detached object, which exists only in the fetishist view of stocks and lacks.

The same is true of the Oedipal code: the libido as energy of selection and detachment is converted into the phallus as detached object, the latter existing only in the transcendent form of stock and lack (something common and absent that is just as lacking in men as in women). It is this conversion that makes the whole of sexuality shift into the Oedipal framework: this projection of all the breaks-flows onto the same mythical locale, and all the nonsignifying signs into the same major signifier. "The effective triangulation makes it possible to assign sexuality to one of the sexes. The partial objects have lost nothing of their virulence and efficacy. Yet the reference to the penis gives its full meaning to castration. Through it, all the external experiences linked to deprivation, to frustration, to the *lack* of partial objects take on meaning after the fact. All previous history is recast in a new version in the light of castration."[18]

That is indeed what disturbs us, this recasting of history and this "lack" attributed to partial objects. And how could partial objects not have lost their virulence and efficacy, once they had been introduced

*M. C. and Edmond Ortigues, *Oedipe africain* (Ch. 3, reference note 22), p. 83: "In order that the necessary conditions for the existence of a structure in the familial institution or in the Oedipus complex be fulfilled, at least four terms are required—that is, one term more than is naturally necessary."

into a use of synthesis that remains fundamentally illegitimate with regard to them? We do not deny that there is an Oedipal sexuality, an Oedipal heterosexuality and homosexuality, an Oedipal castration, as well as complete objects, global images, and specific egos. We deny that these are productions of the unconscious. What is more, castration and oedipalization beget a basic illusion that makes us believe that real desiring-production is answerable to higher formations that integrate it, subject it to transcendent laws, and make it serve a higher social and cultural production; there then appears a kind of "unsticking" of the social field with regard to the production of desire, in whose name all resignations are justified in advance. Psychoanalysis, at the most concrete level of therapy, reinforces this apparent movement with its combined forces. Psychoanalysis itself ensures this conversion of the unconscious. In what it calls the pre-oedipal, it sees a stage that must be surmounted in the direction of an evolutive integration (toward the depressive position under the reign of the complete object), or organized in the direction of a structural integration (toward the position of a despotic signifier, under the reign of the phallus). The aptitude for conflict of which Freud spoke, the qualitative opposition between homosexuality and heterosexuality, is in fact a consequence of Oedipus: far from being an obstacle to treatment encountered from without, it is a product of oedipalization, and a countereffect of the treatment that reinforces it.

In reality the problem has nothing to do with pre-oedipal stages that would still revolve around an Oedipal axis, but rather with the existence and the nature of an anoedipal sexuality, an anoedipal heterosexuality and homosexuality, an anoedipal castration: the breaks-flows of desiring-production do not let themselves be projected onto a mythical locale; the signs of desire do not let themselves be extrapolated from a signifier; transsexuality does not let any qualitative opposition between a *local and nonspecific* heterosexuality and a *local and nonspecific* homosexuality arise. Everywhere, in this reversion, the innocence of flowers instead of the guilt of conversion. But rather than ensuring, or tending to ensure, the reversion of the entire unconscious according to the anoedipal form and within the anoedipal content of desiring-production, analytic theory and practice never cease to promote the conversion of the unconscious to Oedipus, form and content. (We shall see in effect what psychoanalysis calls "resolving" Oedipus.) This conversion is therefore promoted by psychoanalysis first of all by making a global and specific use of the connective syntheses. This use can be defined as transcendent, and implies a first paralogism in the psychoanalytic process. For a simple reason, we again make use of

Kantian terminology. In what he termed the critical revolution, Kant intended to discover criteria immanent to understanding so as to distinguish the legitimate and the illegitimate uses of the syntheses of consciousness. In the name of *transcendental* philosophy (immanence of criteria), he therefore denounced the transcendent use of syntheses such as appeared in metaphysics. In like fashion we are compelled to say that psychoanalysis has its metaphysics—its name is Oedipus. And that a revolution—this time materialist—can proceed only by way of a critique of Oedipus, by denouncing the illegitimate use of the syntheses of the unconscious as found in Oedipal psychoanalysis, so as to rediscover a transcendental unconscious defined by the immanence of its criteria, and a corresponding practice that we shall call schizoanalysis.

4 | The Disjunctive Synthesis of Recording

When Oedipus slips into the disjunctive syntheses of desiring-recording, it imposes the ideal of a certain restrictive or exclusive use on them that becomes identical with the form of triangulation: being daddy, mommy, or child. This is the reign of the "either/or" in the differentiating function of the prohibition of incest: here is where mommy begins, there daddy, and there you are—stay in your place. Oedipus's misfortune is indeed that it no longer knows who begins where, nor who is who. And "being parent or child" is also accompanied by two other differentiations on the other sides of the triangle; "being man or woman," "being dead or alive." Oedipus must not know whether it is alive or dead, man or woman, any more than it knows whether it is parent or child. Commit incest and you'll be a zombie and a hermaphrodite. In this sense, indeed, the three major neuroses that are termed familial seem to correspond to Oedipal lapses in the differentiating function or in the disjunctive synthesis: the phobic person can no longer be sure whether he is parent or child; the obsessed person, whether he is dead or alive; the hysterical person, whether he is man or woman.[19] In short, the familial triangulation represents the minimum condition under which an "ego" takes on the co-ordinates that differentiate it at one and the same time with regard to generation, sex, and vital state. And the religious triangulation confirms this result in another mode: thus in the trinity, the obliteration of the feminine image in favor of a phallic symbol demonstrates how the triangle displaces itself toward its own cause and attempts to integrate it. This time it is a matter of the maximum conditions under which persons are differentiated. Hence the importance of the Kantian definition that posits God as the a priori principle of the disjunctive syllogism, so that all things derive from it by a restriction of a larger reality (*omnitudo realitatis*): Kant's humor makes God into the master of *a* syllogism.

The action characteristic of Oedipal recording is the introduction of an exclusive, restrictive, and negative use of the disjunctive synthesis. We are so molded by Oedipus that we find it hard to imagine another use, and even the three familial neuroses do not escape this use, although they suffer from no longer being capable of applying it. Everywhere in psychoanalysis, in Freud, we have seen this taste for exclusive disjunctions assert itself. It becomes nevertheless apparent that schizophrenia teaches us a singular extra-Oedipal lesson, and reveals to us an unknown force of the disjunctive synthesis, an immanent use that would no longer be exclusive or restrictive, but fully affirmative, nonrestrictive, inclusive. A disjunction that remains disjunctive, and that still affirms the disjoined terms, that affirms them throughout their entire distance, *without restricting one by the other or excluding the other from the one,* is perhaps the greatest paradox. "Either . . . or . . . or," instead of "either/or."

The schizophrenic is not man and woman. He is man or woman, but he belongs precisely to both sides, man on the side of men, woman on the side of women. Likable Jayet (Albert Désiré, matriculation number 54161001) intones the litany of the parallel series of the masculine and the feminine, and places himself on both sides: "Mat Albert 5416 ricu-le sultan romain vesin," "Mat Désiré 1001 ricu-la sultane romaine vesine" ("Mat Albert 5416 ricu-the insane Roman sultan," Mat Désiré 1001 ricu-the insane Roman sultaness").[20] The schizophrenic is dead *or* alive, not both at once, but each of the two as the terminal point of a distance over which he glides. He is child *or* parent, not both, but the one at the end of the other, like the two ends of a stick in a nondecomposable space. This is the meaning of the disjunctions where Beckett records his characters and the events that befall them: *everything divides, but into itself.* Even the distances are positive, at the same time as the included disjunctions.

It would be a total misunderstanding of this order of thought if we concluded that the schizophrenic substituted vague syntheses of identification of contradictory elements for disjunctions, like the last of the Hegelian philosophers. He does not substitute syntheses of contradictory elements for disjunctive syntheses; rather, for the exclusive and restrictive use of the disjunctive synthesis, he substitutes an affirmative use. He is and remains in disjunction: he does not abolish disjunction by identifying the contradictory elements by means of elaboration; instead, he affirms it through a continuous overflight spanning an indivisible distance. He is not simply bisexual, or between the two, or intersexual. He is transsexual. He is trans-alivedead, trans-parentchild. He does not reduce two contraries to an identity of the same; he affirms their distance as that which relates the two as different. He does not confine himself inside contradictions; on the contrary, he opens out and, like a spore case inflated with spores, releases them as so many singularities that he had improperly shut off, some of which he intended to exclude, while retaining others, but which now become points-signs (*points-signes*),[21] all affirmed by their new distance. The disjunction, being now inclusive, does not closet itself inside its own terms. On the contrary it is nonrestrictive. "I was then no longer this closed box to which I owed being so well preserved, but a partition came crashing down"—an event that will liberate a space where Molloy and Moran no longer designate persons, but singularities flocking from all sides, evanescent agents of production. This is free disjunction; the differential positions persist in their entirety, they even take on a free quality, but they are all inhabited by a faceless and transpositional subject. Schreber is man and woman, parent and child, dead and alive: which is to say, he is situated wherever there is a singularity, in all the series and in all the branches marked by a singular point, because he is himself this distance that transforms him into a woman, and at its terminal point he is already the mother of a new humanity and can finally die.

That is why the schizophrenic God has so little to do with the God of religion, even though they are related to the same syllogism. In *Le Baphomet* Klossowski contrasts God as the master of the exclusions and restrictions that derive from the disjunctive syllogism, with an antichrist who is the prince of modifications, determining instead the passage of a subject through all possible predicates. I am God I am not God, I am God I am Man: it is not a matter of a synthesis that would go beyond the negative disjunctions of the derived reality, in an original reality of Man-God, but rather of an inclusive disjunction that carries out the synthesis itself in drifting from one term to another and following the distance between terms. Nothing is primal. It is like the famous conclusion to *Molloy:* "It is midnight. The rain is beating on the windows. It was not midnight. It was not raining."[22] Nijinsky wrote: "I am God I was not God I am a clown of God; I am Apis. I am an Egyptian. I am a red Indian. I am a Negro. I am a Chinaman. I am a Japanese. I am a foreigner, a stranger. I am a sea bird. I am a land bird. I am the tree of Tolstoy. I am the roots of Tolstoy. . . . I am husband and wife in one. I love my wife. I love my husband."[23]

What counts is not parental designations, nor racial or divine designations, but merely the use made of them. No problem of meaning, but only of usage. Nothing original or derived, but a generalized drift. It would seem that the schizo liberates a raw genealogical material, nonrestrictive, where he can situate himself, record himself, and take his bearings in all the branches at once, on all sides. He explodes the Oedipal genealogy. Through graduated relationships he performs absolute overflights spanning indivisible distances. The genealogist-madman lays out a disjunctive network on the body without organs. And God, who designates none other than the energy of recording, can be the greatest enemy in the paranoiac inscription, but also the greatest friend in the miraculating inscription. In any case, the question of a being superior to man and to nature does not arise here at all. Everything is on the body without organs, both what is inscribed and the energy that inscribes it. On the unengendered body, the nondecomposable distances are necessarily surveyed, while the disjoined terms are all affirmed. I am the letter and the pen and the paper. It was in this fashion that Nijinsky kept his diary: yes, I was my father and I was my son.

The disjunctive synthesis of recording therefore leads us to the same result as the connective synthesis: it too is capable of two uses, the one immanent, the other transcendent. And here again, why does psychoanalysis reinforce the transcendent use that introduces exclusions and restrictions everywhere in the disjunctive network, and that makes the unconscious swing over into Oedipus? And why is oedipalization precisely that? It is because the exclusive relation introduced by Oedipus comes into play not only between the various disjunctions conceived as differentiations, *but between the whole of the differentiations that it imposes and an undifferentiated (un indifférencié) that it presupposes.* Oedipus informs us: if you don't follow the lines of differentiation daddy-mommy-me, and the exclusive alternatives that delineate them, you will fall into the black night of the undifferentiated. It should be made clear that the exclusive disjunctions are not at all the same as the inclusive disjunctions; neither God nor the parental designations play the same role in the two. In exclusive disjunctions, parental appellations no longer designate intensive states through which the subject passes on the body without organs and in the unconscious that remains an orphan (yes, I was . . .); rather, they designate global persons who do not exist prior to the prohibitions that found them, and they differentiate among these global persons and in relation to the ego. So that the transgression of the prohibition becomes correlatively a confusion of persons, where the ego identifies with the global persons, with the loss of differentiating rules or differential functions.

But we should stress the fact that Oedipus creates both *the differentiations that it orders and the undifferentiated with which it threatens us.* With the same movement the Oedipus complex inserts desire into triangulation, and prohibits desire from satisfying itself with the terms of the triangulation. It forces desire to take as its object the differentiated parental persons, and, brandishing the threats of the undifferentiated, prohibits the correlative ego from satisfying its desires with these persons, in the name of the same requirements of differentiation. But it is this undifferentiated *that Oedipus creates as the reverse of the differentiations that it creates.* Oedipus says to us: either you will internalize the differential functions that rule over the exclusive disjunctions, and thereby "resolve" Oedipus, or you will fall into the neurotic night of imaginary identifications. Either you will follow the lines of the triangle—lines that structure and differentiate the three terms—or you will always bring one term into play as if it were one too many in relation to the other two, and you will reproduce in every sense the dual relations of identification in the undifferentiated. But there is Oedipus on either side. And everybody knows what psychoanalysis means by *resolving* Oedipus: internalizing it so as to better rediscover it on the outside, in social authority, where it will be made to proliferate and be passed on to the children. "The child becomes a man only by resolving the Oedipus complex, whose resolution introduces him into society, where he finds, within the figure of Authority, the obligation to relive it, this time with no way out. Nor is it by any means certain that, between the impossible return to that which precedes the stage of culture and the growing malaise that this stage provokes, a point of equilibrium can be found."[24] Oedipus is like the labyrinth, you only get out by re-entering it—or by making someone else enter it. Oedipus as either problem *or* solution is the two ends of a ligature that cuts off all desiring-production. The screws are tightened, nothing relating to production can make its way through any longer, except for a far-distant murmur. The unconscious has been crushed, triangulated, and confronted with a choice that is not its own. With all of the exits now blocked, there is no longer any possible use for the inclusive, nonrestrictive disjunctions. Parents have been found for the (orphan) unconscious!

Double bind is the term used by Gregory Bateson to describe the simultaneous transmission of two kinds of messages, one of which contradicts the other, as for example the father who says to his son: go ahead, criticize me, but strongly hints that all effective criticism—at least a certain type of criticism—will be very unwelcome. Bateson sees in this phenomenon a particularly schizophrenizing situation, which he interprets as a "contrary" from the viewpoint of Russell's theory of types.[25] It seems to us that the double bind, the double impasse, is instead a common situation, oedipalizing par excellence. And although it would require formalization, the other type of non-sense spoken of by Russell is brought to mind by the double-bind situation: an alternative, an exclusive disjunction is defined in terms of a principle which, however, constitutes its two terms or underlying wholes, and where the principle itself enters into the alternative (a completely different case from what happens when the disjunction is inclusive). Here we have the second paralogism of psychoanalysis. In short, *the "double bind" is none other than the whole of Oedipus.* It is in this sense that Oedipus should be presented as a series, or an oscillation between two poles: the neurotic identification, and the internalization that is said to be normative. On either side is Oedipus, the double impasse. And if a schizo is produced here as an entity, this occurs for the simple reason that there is no other means of escaping this double path, where normality is no less blocked than neurosis, and where the solution offers no more of a way out than does the problem. Hence the schizo's withdrawal to the body without organs.

It seems that Freud himself was acutely aware of Oedipus's inseparability from a double impasse into which he was precipitating the unconscious. Thus in the 1936 letter to Romain Rolland, Freud writes: "Everything unfolds as if the essential were to go beyond the father, as if going beyond the father were always forbidden." This becomes even more clear when Freud elaborates the entire historico-mythical series: at one end the Oedipal bond is established by the murderous identification, at the other end it is reinforced by the restoration and internalization of paternal authority ("revival of the old state of things at a new level").[26] Between the two there is latency—the celebrated latency—which is without doubt the greatest psychoanalytic mystification: this society of "brothers" who forbid themselves the fruits of the crime, and spend all the time necessary for internalizing. But we are warned: the society of brothers is very dejected, unstable, and dangerous, it must prepare the way for the rediscovery of an equivalent to parental authority, it must cause us to pass over to the other pole. In accord with a suggestion of Freud's, American society—the industrial society with anonymous management and vanishing personal power, etc.—is presented to us as a resurgence of the "society without the father." Not surprisingly, the industrial society is burdened with the search for original modes for the restoration of the equivalent—for example, the astonishing discovery by Mitscherlich that the British Royal Family, after all, is not such a bad thing.[27]

It is therefore understood that we leave one pole of Oedipus only to pass on to the other. No way of getting out, neurosis or normality. The society of brothers rediscovers nothing of production and desiring-machines; on the contrary, it spreads the veil of latency. As to those who refuse to be oedipalized in one form or another, at one end or the other in the treatment, the psychoanalyst is there to call the asylum or the police for help. The police on our side!—never did psychoanalysis better display its taste for supporting the movement of social repression, and for participating in it with enthusiasm. Let it not be thought that we are alluding to the folkloric aspects of psychoanalysis. The fact that there are some, around Lacan, who are developing another conception of psychoanalysis, does not mean that we should take no notice of the dominant tone in the most respected associations: consider Dr. Mendel and the Drs. Stéphane, the state of fury that is theirs, and their literally police-like appeal at the thought that someone might claim to escape the Oedipal dragnet. Oedipus is one of those things that becomes all the more dangerous the less people believe in it; then the cops are there to replace the high priests. The first profound example of an analysis of double bind, in this sense, can be found in Marx's *On the Jewish Question:* between the family and the State—the Oedipus of familial authority and the Oedipus of social authority.

Oedipus is completely useless, except for tying off the unconscious on both sides. We shall see in what sense Oedipus is strictly "undecidable" (*indécidable*), as the mathematicians would put it. We are extremely tired of those stories where one is said to be in good health because of Oedipus, sick from Oedipus, and suffering from various illnesses under the influence of Oedipus. It sometimes happens that an analyst becomes fed up with this myth that is the bed and board of psychoanalysis, and goes back to the sources: Freud never managed to escape the world of the father, or of guilt. . . . While offering the possibility of constructing a *logic* of the relation to the father, he was the first to open the way for a release from the father's hold on man. The possibility of living *beyond* the father's law, beyond all law, is perhaps the most essential possibility brought forth by Freudian psychoanalysis. But paradoxically, and perhaps because of Freud, everything leads us to conclude that this release, made possible by psychoanalysis, will be achieved, is already being achieved, outside it.[28]

We cannot, however, share either this pessimism or this optimism. For there is much optimism in thinking psychoanalysis makes possible a veritable solution to Oedipus: Oedipus is like God; the father is like God; the problem is not resolved until we do away with *both the problem and the solution.* It is not the purpose of schizoanalysis to resolve Oedipus, it does not intend to resolve it better than Oedipal psychoanalysis does. Its aim is to de-oedipalize the unconscious in order to reach the real problems. Schizoanalysis proposes to reach those regions of the orphan unconscious—indeed "beyond all law"—where the problem of Oedipus can no longer even be raised. By the same token, we do not share the pessimism that consists in thinking that this change, this release, can be achieved only outside psychoanalysis. We believe, on the contrary, in the possibility of an internal reversal that would make the analytic machine into an indispensable part of the revolutionary machinery. What is more, the objective conditions for such a practice appear to be already present.

Everything takes place as if Oedipus of itself had two poles: one pole characterized by imaginary figures that lend themselves to a process of identification, and a second pole characterized by symbolic functions that lend themselves to a process of differentiation. But in any case we are oedipalized: if we don't have Oedipus as a crisis, we have it as a structure. Then the crisis is passed on to others, and the whole movement starts all over again. Such is the Oedipal disjunction, the swing of the pendulum, the exclusive inverse reasoning. That is why, when we are invited to go beyond a simplistic conception of Oedipus based on parental images, in order to define symbolic functions within a structure, it is in vain that the traditional daddy-mommy are replaced by a mother-function, a father-function; we don't quite see what there is to gain by this, except for the founding of the universality of Oedipus beyond the variability of images; the fusing of desire even more strongly to law and prohibitions; and the pushing of the process of oedipalization of the unconscious to its limits. Here Oedipus encounters its two extremes, *its minimum and its maximum,* depending on whether it is regarded as tending toward an undifferentiated value of its variable images, or toward the force of differentiation of its symbolic functions. "When one draws nearer to the material imagination, the differential function diminishes, one tends toward equivalences; when one draws nearer to the formative elements, the differential function increases, one tends toward distinctive valences."[29] It will hardly come as a surprise to learn that Oedipus as a structure is the Christian Trinity, whereas Oedipus as a crisis is a familial trinity insufficiently structured by faith: always the two poles in inverse proportion, Oedipus forever!*

How many interpretations of Lacanism, overtly or secretly pious as the case may be, have in this manner invoked a structural Oedipus to create and shut the double impasse, to lead us back to the question of the

*See J. M. Pohier, "La paternité de Dieu," *L'Inconscient,* no. 5 (January 1968). This article contains a perfect formulation of Oedipus as double bind: "The psychic life of man unfolds in a sort of dialectical tension between two ways of living the Oedipus complex: one that consists in living it, and the other that consists in living according to the structures that might be called Oedipal. Experience also shows us that these structures are not foreign to the most critical phase of this complex. For Freud, man is definitively marked by this complex: it constitutes both his grandeur and his misery," etc. (pp. 57–58).

father, to oedipalize even the schizo, and to show that a gap in the Symbolic would bring us back to the Imaginary, and inversely that imaginary drivel or confusions would lead us to the structure! As a famous predecessor said to these creatures, you've already made this into an old refrain. As for us, that is why we were unable to posit any difference in nature, any border line, any limit at all between the Imaginary and the Symbolic, or between Oedipus-as-crisis and Oedipus-as-structure, or between the problem and its solution. It is solely a question of a correlative double impasse, a swing of a pendulum responsible for sweeping away the entire unconscious, and that continuously carries us from one pole to the other. A double pincer action that crushes the unconscious caught in its exclusive disjunction.

The true difference in nature is not between the Symbolic and the Imaginary, but between the real machinic (*machinique*) element, which constitutes desiring-production, and the structural whole of the Imaginary and the Symbolic, which merely forms a myth and its variants. The difference is not between two uses of Oedipus, but between the anoedipal use of the inclusive, nonrestrictive disjunctions, and the Oedipal use of exclusive disjunctions, whether this last use borrows from the paths of the Imaginary *or* the values of the Symbolic. It would also be necessary to heed Lacan's word of caution concerning the Freudian myth of Oedipus, which "has no way of holding its own indefinitely in the forms of society where the tragic sense is increasingly lost . . . : a myth cannot sustain itself when it supports no ritual, and psychoanalysis is not the Oedipus ritual."[30] Even if we go back from the images to the structure, from imaginary figures to symbolic functions, from the father to the law, from the mother to the great Other, in truth *the question merely retreats.* And if we try to envisage the time put into this retreat, Lacan goes on to say, the sole foundation for the society of brothers, for fraternity, is "segregation" (what does he mean here?).

In any case, it was inopportune to tighten the nuts and bolts where Lacan had just loosened them; or to oedipalize the schizo where on the contrary he had just schizophrenized even neurosis, injecting a schizophrenic flow capable of subverting the field of psychoanalysis. The object (small o) erupts at the heart of the structural equilibrium in the manner of an infernal machine, the desiring-machine. Then a second generation of disciples of Lacan supervenes, less and less sensitive to the false problems of Oedipus. But if the first disciples were tempted to reclose the Oedipus yoke, didn't they do so to the extent that Lacan seemed to maintain a kind of projection of the signifying chains onto a despotic signifier, lacking unto itself and reintroducing lack into the series of desire on which it imposed an exclusive use? Was it possible to denounce Oedipus-as-myth, and nevertheless maintain that the castration complex itself was not a myth but in fact something real? (Wasn't this tantamount to taking up the cry of Aristotle: "We really must come to a halt," in the face of this Freudian *Anankè*, this Rock?)

5 | The Conjunctive Synthesis of Consumption-Consummation

In the third synthesis, the conjunctive synthesis of consumption, we have seen how the body without organs was in fact an egg, crisscrossed with axes, banded with zones, localized with areas and fields, measured off by gradients, traversed by potentials, marked by thresholds. In this sense, we believe in a biochemistry of schizophrenia (in conjunction with the biochemistry of drugs), that will be progressively more capable of determining the nature of this egg and the distribution of field-gradient-threshold. It is a matter of relationships of intensities through which the subject passes on the body without organs, a process that engages him in becomings, rises and falls, migrations and displacements. R. D. Laing is entirely right in defining the schizophrenic process as a voyage of initiation, a transcendental experience of the loss of the Ego, which causes a subject to remark: "I had existed since the very beginning . . . from the lowest form of life [the body without organs] to the present time, . . . I was looking . . . —not looking so much as just *feeling*—ahead of me was lying the most horrific journey."[31] When we speak here of a voyage, this is no more a metaphor than before when we spoke of an egg, and of what takes place in and on it—morphogenetic movements, displacements of cellular groups, stretchings, folds, migrations, and local variations of potentials. There is no reason to oppose an interior voyage to exterior ones: Lenz's stroll, Nijinsky's stroll, the promenades of Beckett's creatures are effective realities, but where the reality of matter has abandoned all extension, just as the interior voyage has abandoned all form and quality, henceforth causing pure intensities—coupled together, almost unbearable—to radiate within and without, intensities through which a nomadic subject passes. Here it is not a case of an hallucinatory experience nor of a delirious mode of thought, but a feeling, a series of emotions and feelings as a consummation and a consumption of intensive quantities, that form the material for subsequent hallucinations and deliriums. The intensive emotion, the affect, is both the common root and the principle of differentiation of deliriums and hallucinations.

We are also of a mind to believe that everything commingles in these intense becomings, passages, and migrations—all this drift that ascends and descends the flows of time: countries, races, families, parental appellations, divine appellations, geographical and historical designations, and even miscellaneous news items. (*I feel that*) I am becoming God, I am becoming woman, I was Joan of Arc and I am Heliogabalus and the Great Mongol, I am a Chinaman, a redskin, a Templar, I was my father and I was my son. And all the criminals, the whole list of criminals, the decent criminals and the scoundrels: Szondi rather than Freud and his Oedipus. "Perhaps it's by trying to be Worm that I'll finally succeed in being Mahood. . . . Then all I'll have to do is be Worm. Which no doubt I shall achieve by trying to be Jones. Then all I'll have to do is be Jones." But if everything commingles in this fashion it does so in intensity, with no confusion of spaces and forms, since these have indeed been undone on behalf of a new order: the intense and intensive order.

What is the nature of this order? The first things to be distributed on the body without organs are races, cultures, and their gods. The fact has often been overlooked that the schizo indeed participates in history; he hallucinates and raves universal history, and proliferates the races. All delirium is racial, which does not necessarily mean racist. It is not a matter of the regions of the body without organs "representing" races and cultures. The full body does not represent anything at all. On the contrary, the races and cultures designate regions on this body—that is, zones of intensities, fields of potentials. Phenomena of individualization and sexualization are produced within these fields. We pass from one field to another by crossing thresholds: we never stop migrating, we become other individuals as well as other sexes, and departing becomes as easy as being born or dying. Along the way we struggle against other races, we destroy civilizations, in the manner of the great migrants in whose wake nothing is left standing once they have passed through—although these destructions can be brought about, as we shall see, in two very different ways.

The crossing of a threshold entails ravages elsewhere—how could it be otherwise? The body without organs closes round the deserted places. The theater of cruelty cannot be separated from the struggle against our culture, from the confrontation of the "races," and from Artaud's great migration toward Mexico, its forces, and its religions: individuations are produced only within fields of forces expressly defined by intensive vibrations, and that animate cruel personages only in so far as they are induced organs, parts of desiring-machines (mannequins).[32] A season in hell—how could it be separated from denunciations of European families, from the call for destructions that don't come quickly enough, from the admiration for the convict, from the intense crossing of the thresholds of history, and from this prodigious migration, this becoming-woman, this becoming-Scandinavian or Mongol, this "displacement of races and of continents," this feeling of raw intensity that presides over delirium as well as over hallucinations, and especially this deliberate, stubborn, material will to be "of a race inferior for all eternity": "I have known every son of good birth, I have never been of this people, I have never been Christian, . . . yes my eyes are closed to your light. I am a beast, a Negro."[33]

And can Zarathustra be separated from the "grand politics," and from the bringing to life of the races that leads Nietzsche to say, I'm not a German, I'm Polish. Here again individuations are brought about solely within complexes of forces that determine persons as so many intensive states embodied in a "criminal," ceaselessly passing beyond a threshold while destroying the factitious unity of a family and an ego: "I am Prado, I am also Prado's father. I venture to say that I am also Lesseps. . . . I wanted to give my Parisians, whom I love, a new idea—that of a decent criminal. I am also Chambige—also a decent criminal. . . . The unpleasant thing, and one that nags at my modesty, is that at root *every name in history is I.*"[34] Yet it was never a question of identifying oneself with personages, as when it is erroneously maintained that a madman "takes himself for so-and-so. . . ." It is a question of something quite different: identifying races, cultures, and gods with fields of intensity on the body without organs, identifying personages with states that fill these fields, and with effects that fulgurate within and traverse these fields. Whence the role of names, with a magic all their own: there is no ego that identifies with races, peoples, and persons in a theater of representation, but proper names that identify races, peoples, and persons with regions, thresholds, or effects in a production of intensive quantities. The theory of proper names should not be conceived of in terms of representation; it refers instead to the class of "effects": effects that are not a mere dependence on causes, but the occupation of a domain, and the operation of a system of signs. This can be clearly seen in physics, where proper names designate such effects within fields of potentials: the Joule effect, the Seebeck effect, the Kelvin effect. History is like physics: a Joan of Arc effect, a Heliogabalus effect—all the *names* of history, and not the name of the father.

Everything has been said about the paucity of reality, the loss of reality, the lack of contact with life, autism and athymia. Schizophrenics themselves have said everything there is to say about this, and have been quick to slip into the expected clinical mold. Dark world, growing desert: a solitary machine hums on the beach, an atomic factory installed in the desert. But if the body without organs is indeed this desert, it is as an indivisible, nondecomposable distance over which the schizo glides in order to be everywhere something real is produced, everywhere something real has been and will be produced. It is true that reality has ceased to be a principle. According to such a principle, the reality of the real was posed as a divisible abstract quantity, whereas the real was divided up into qualified unities, into distinct qualitative forms. But now the real is a product that envelops the distances within intensive quantities. The indivisible is enveloped, and signifies that what envelops it does not divide without changing its nature or form. The schizo has no principles: he is something only by being something else. He is Mahood only by being Worm, and Worm only by being Jones. He is a girl only by being an old man who is miming or simulating the girl. Or rather, by being someone who is simulating an old man simulating a girl. Or rather, by simulating someone . . . , etc. This was already true of the completely oriental art of the Roman Emperors, the twelve paranoiacs of Suetonius. In a great book by Jacques Besse, we encounter once again the double stroll of the schizo, the geographic exterior voyage following nondecomposable distances, and the interior historical voyage enveloping intensities: Christopher Columbus calms his mutinous crew and becomes admiral again only by simulating a (false) admiral who is simulating a whore who is dancing.[35]

But simulation must be understood in the same way as we spoke of identification. It expresses those nondecomposable distances always enveloped in the intensities that divide into one another while changing their form. If identification is a nomination, a designation, then simulation is the writing corresponding to it, a writing that is strangely polyvocal, flush with the real. It carries the real beyond its principle to the point where it is effectively produced by the desiring-machine. The point where the copy ceases to be a copy in order to become the Real *and its artifice.* To seize an intensive real as produced in the coextension of nature and history, to ransack the Roman Empire, the Mexican cities, the Greek gods, and the discovered continents so as to extract from them this always-surplus reality, and to form the treasure of the paranoiac tortures and the celibate glories—all the pogroms of history, that's what I am, and all the triumphs, too, as if a few simple univocal events could be extricated from this extreme polyvocity: such is the "histrionism" of the schizophrenic, according to Klossowski's formula, the true program for a theater of cruelty, the *mise-en-scène* of a machine to produce the real. Far from having lost who knows what contact with life, the schizophrenic is closest to the beating heart of reality, to an intense point identical with the production of the real, and that leads Reich to say: "What belongs specifically to the schizophrenic patient is that . . . he experiences the vital biology of the body. . . . With respect to their experiencing of life, the neurotic patient and the perverted individual are to the schizophrenic as the petty thief is to the daring safecracker."[36] So the question returns: what reduces the schizophrenic to his autistic, hospitalized profile, cut off from reality? Is it the process, or is it rather the interruption of the process, its aggravation, its continuation in the void? What forces the schizophrenic to withdraw to a body without organs that has become deaf, dumb, and blind?

We often hear it said: he thinks he's Louis XVII. Not true. In the Louis XVII affair, or rather in the finest case, that of the pretender Richemont, there is a desiring-machine or a celibate machine in the center: the horse with short, jointed paws, inside which they supposedly put the Dauphin so he could flee. And then, all around, there are agents of production and antiproduction, the organizers of the escape, the accomplices, the allied sovereigns, the revolutionary enemies, the jealous and hostile uncles, who are not persons but so many states of rising and falling through which the pretender passes. Moreover, the pretender Richemont's stroke of genius is not simply that he "takes into account" Louis XVII, or that he takes other pretenders into account by denouncing them as fake. What is so ingenious is that he takes other pretenders into account by assuming them, by authenticating them—that is to say, by making them too into states through which he passes: I am Louis XVII, but I am also Hervagault and Mathurin Bruneau, who claimed to be Louis XVII.[37] Richemont doesn't identify with Louis XVII, he lays claim to the premium due the person who traverses all the singularities of the series converging around the machine for kidnapping Louis XVII. There is no ego at the center, any more than there are persons distributed on the periphery. Nothing but a series of singularities in the disjunctive network, or intensive states in the conjunctive tissue, and a transpositional subject moving full circle, passing through all the states, triumphing over some as over his enemies, relishing others as his allies, collecting everywhere the fraudulent premium of his avatars. Partial object: a well situated scar—ambiguous besides—is better proof than all the memories of childhood that the pretender lacks. The conjunctive synthesis can therefore be expressed: "So *I* am the king! So the kingdom belongs to *me!*" But this *me* is merely the residual subject that sweeps the circle and concludes a self from its oscillations on the circle.

All delirium possesses a world-historical, political, and racial content, mixing and sweeping along races, cultures, continents, and kingdoms; some wonder whether this long drift merely constitutes a derivative of Oedipus. The familial order explodes, families are challenged, son, father, mother, sister—"I mean those families like my own, that owe all to the Declaration of the Rights of Man!"; "When I seek out my most profound opposite, I always encounter my mother and my sister; to see myself related to such German rabble is, as it were, a blasphemy with respect to my doctrine of the Eternal Return!" It is a question of knowing if the historico-political, the racial, and the cultural are merely part of a manifest content and formally depend on a work of elaboration, or if, on the contrary, this content should be followed as the thread of latency that the order of families hides from us. Should the rupture with families be taken as a sort of "familial romance" that would indeed bring us back again to families and refer us to an event or a structural determination inside the family itself? Or is this rather the sign that the problem must be raised in a completely different manner, because it is already raised elsewhere for the schizo himself, outside the family? Are "the names of history" derivatives of the name of the father, and are the races, cultures, and continents substitutes for daddy-mommy, dependent on the Oedipal genealogy? Is history's signifier the dead father?

Once again let us consider Judge Schreber's delirium. To be sure, the use of races and the mobilization or notion of history are developed there in a manner totally different from that employed by the authors we have previously mentioned. The fact remains that Schreber's memoirs are filled with a theory of God's chosen peoples, and with the dangers that face the currently chosen people, the Germans, who are threatened by the Jews, the Catholics, and the Slavs. In his intense metamorphoses and passages, Schreber becomes a pupil of the Jesuits, the burgomaster of a city where the Germans are fighting against the Slavs, and a girl defending Alsace against the French. At last he crosses the Aryan gradient or threshold to become a Mongol prince. What does this becoming-pupil, burgomaster, girl, and Mongol signify? All paranoiac deliriums stir up similar historical, geographic, and racial masses. The error would lie in concluding, for example, that fascists are mere paranoiacs. This would be an error precisely because, in the current state of affairs, this would still amount to leading the historical and political content of the delirium back to an internal familial determination. And what is even more disturbing to us is the fact that the entirety of this enormous content disappears completely from Freud's analysis: not one trace of it remains; everything is ground, squashed, triangulated into Oedipus; everything is reduced to the father, in such a way as to reveal in the crudest fashion the inadequacies of an Oedipal psychoanalysis.

Let us consider another paranoiac delirium as related by Maud

Mannoni, a delirium whose political nature is especially vivid. This example appears all the more striking to us, given our great admiration for Maud Mannoni's work and for the manner in which she poses antipsychiatric and institutional problems. Here then we see a man from Martinique who, in the process of his delirium, situates himself in relation to the Arabs and the Algerian War, in relation to the whites and the May '68 events, and so on: "I fell sick from the Algerian problem. I had partaken in the same foolishness as they (sexual pleasure). They adopted me as one of their own race. Mongol blood flows through my veins. Every time I attempted to put something into effect, the Algerians argued against it. I had racist notions. . . . I descend from the Gallic dynasty. By this right I am a man of noble lineage. . . . Let my name be determined, let it be determined scientifically, and then I shall be able to set up a harem."[38] Though aware of the character of "revolt" and of "truth for all" implied in the psychosis, Maud Mannoni argues that the origin of the breakup of familial relations in favor of themes that the subject himself declares to be racist, metaphysical, and political, is to be found in the familial structure serving as a matrix. This origin would exist therefore in the symbolic void or in "the initial foreclosure (*forclusion*) of the signifier of the father."[39] The name to be determined scientifically, the name that haunts all history, is simply the paternal name.

In this case as in many others, the utilization of the Lacanian concept of foreclosure leads to the forced oedipalization of the rebel: the absence of Oedipus is interpreted as a *lack* with regard to the father, a gaping hole in the structure; next, in the name of this lack, we are referred to the other Oedipal pole, the pole of imaginary identifications within the maternal undifferentiated. The law of the double bind operates relentlessly, ruthlessly, flinging us from one pole to the other, in such a way that what is foreclosed in the Symbolic must reappear in the Real in a hallucinatory form. But in this fashion *the entire historico-political theme gets interpreted as a constellation of imaginary identifications* depending on Oedipus, or on that which the subject "lacks" in order to become oedipalized.* And to be sure, it is not a question of knowing whether or not the familial determinations or indeterminations play a role. It is obvious that they do. But is this an initial role as

---

*"The Oedipal personages are all in their places, but in the play of permutations brought about, there is something like an empty place. . . . What appears as rejected is everything referring to the phallus and the father. . . . Each time Georges tries to take hold of himself as a desiring-person, he is driven back to a form of dissolution of identities. He is another, enthralled by a maternal image. . . . He remains trapped within an imaginary position in which he is captivated by the maternal imago; he situates himself within the Oedipal triangle in terms of this locale, which implies an impossible process of identification, involving forever after, in the mode of a pure imaginary dialectic, the destruction of one or the other of the partners."—Mannoni (reference note 38), pp. 104–107.

symbolic organizer (or symbolic disorganizer) from which the floating contents of the historical delirium would derive, as so many glittering reflections in an imaginary mirror? Is the trinitary formula for the schizo—which leads him, forced and constrained, back to Oedipus—this void left by the absence of the father and this cancerous development of the mother and the sister? And yet, as we have seen, if there is one problem that does not exist in schizophrenia, it is the problem of identifications. And if getting well amounts to getting oedipalized, we can easily understand the outbursts of the patient who "does not want to be cured," and who treats the analyst as one of the family, then as an ally of the police. Is the schizophrenic sick and cut off from reality because he lacks Oedipus, because he "is lacking" in something only to be found in Oedipus—or on the contrary is he sick by virtue of the oedipalization he is unable to bear, and around which everything combines in order to force him to submit (social repression even before psychoanalysis)?

The schizophrenic egg is like the biological egg: they have a similar history, and our knowledge of them has run up against the same sort of difficulties and illusions. During the development of the differentiation of the egg, it was first believed that veritable "organizers" decided the destiny of the parts. But it was soon noticed that on the one hand, all kinds of other variable substances had the same action as the envisaged organizing stimulus, and that on the other hand, the parts themselves had specific abilities and potentials for development that did not exist for the stimulus (experiments with grafting). Whence the idea that the stimuli are not organizers, but mere inductors: ultimately, the nature of these inductors is a matter of indifference. Many different kinds of substances and materials, when killed, boiled, and pulverized, have the same effect. It was the *beginnings* of the development that favored the illusion: the simplicity of the beginning—consisting, for example, of cellular divisions—could lead one to believe in some sort of adequation between the inductor and what is induced. But we are well aware that, when considered in terms of its beginnings, a thing is always poorly judged because, in order to become apparent, it is forced to simulate structural states and to slip into states of forces that serve it as masks. What is more, *from the beginning* we can see that it makes use of masks in an entirely different manner, and that underneath the mask and by means of it, it already invests the terminal forms and the specific higher states whose integrity it will subsequently establish.

Such is the history of Oedipus: the parental figures are in no way organizers, but rather inductors or stimuli of varying, vague import that trigger processes of an entirely different nature, processes that are endowed with what amounts to an indifference with regard to the stimulus. Doubtless one can *believe* that, in the beginning (?), the stimulus—the Oedipal inductor—is a real organizer. But believing is an operation of a conscious or preconscious nature, an extrinsic perception rather than an operation of the unconscious upon itself. From the beginning of the life of the child, it is already an altogether different undertaking that pierces the mask of Oedipus, a different flow running through the openings in the mask, a different adventure—that of desiring-production. Yet it cannot be said that psychoanalysis was unaware of this in a certain respect. In his theory of the primal fantasy, of the traces of an archaic heredity, and the endogenous sources of the superego, Freud constantly asserts that the active factors are not the real parents, nor even the parents as the child imagines them. Such is also the case, and all the more so, for Lacan's disciples, when they take up the distinction between the Imaginary and the Symbolic, when they oppose the name of the father to the imago, and the foreclosure concerning the signifier to a real deficiency or absence of the paternal personage. There is no better example than this to show that the parental figures are indifferent inductors and that the true organizer is elsewhere—on the side of what is induced, not on that of the inductor.

But that is just the beginning of the question, the same question as in the case of the biological egg. For under these conditions is there no solution but to revive the notion of a "terrain," whether in the form of a phylogenetic innateness of preformation, or a cultural symbolic a priori linked to prematuration? Worse yet: it is clear that by invoking such an a priori one does not by any means abandon familialism in the strictest sense, which burdens all of psychoanalysis; on the contrary, one thereby plunges deeper into familialism and generalizes it. Parents have been put in their true places within the workings of the unconscious, as inductors of an indifferent nature, yet the role of organizer continues to be entrusted to symbolic or structural elements that are still part of the family and its Oedipal matrix. Once again one is caught, without a way out: it is simply that the means have been found to render the family transcendent.

There we have it—the incurable familialism of psychoanalysis, enclosing the unconscious within Oedipus, cutting off all vital flows, crushing desiring-production, conditioning the patient to respond daddy-mommy, and to always consume daddy-mommy. Thus Foucault was entirely right in saying that, in a certain sense, the psychoanalyst completed and perfected what the psychiatry of nineteenth-century asylums, with Pinel and Tuke, had set out to do: to fuse madness with a parental complex, to link it to "the half-real, half-imaginary dialectic of the Family"; to constitute for the madman a microcosm symbolizing "the massive structures of bourgeois society and its values," relations of Family-Child, Transgression-Punishment, Madness-Disorder; to arrange things so that disalienation goes the same route as alienation, with Oedipus at both ends; to establish the moral authority of the doctor as Father and Judge, Family and Law; and finally to culminate in the following paradox: "While the victim of mental illness is entirely alienated in the real person of his doctor, the doctor dissipates the reality of the mental illness in the critical concept of madness."* Luminous pages.

Let us add that by *enveloping* the illness in a familial complex internal to the patient, and then the familial complex itself in the transference or the doctor-patient relationship, Freudian psychoanalysis made a somewhat intensive use of the family. Granted, this use distorted the nature of the intensive quantities in the unconscious. Nevertheless it still respected in part the general principle of a production of these quantities. When it became necessary once again to confront psychosis directly, however, the family was immediately reopened in extension, and was in itself considered as the indicator for measuring the forces of alienation and disalienation. In this manner the study of the families of schizophrenics has breathed new life into Oedipus by making it reign over the extensive order of an expanded family, where not only each person would combine to a greater or lesser extent his or her triangle with the triangle of others, but where the entirety of the extended family also would oscillate between the two poles of a "healthy" triangulation, structuring and differentiating, and forms of perverted triangles, bringing about their fusion in the realm of the undifferentiated.

Jacques Hochman analyzes some interesting varieties of psychotic families under the same "fusionist postulate": the properly fusionist family, where differentiations are no longer made except between the inside and the outside (those who are outside the family); the divisive (*scissionnelle*) family that establishes blocks, clans, or coalitions within itself; the tubular family, where the triangle multiplies endlessly, each

---

*Foucault (Ch. 1, reference note 43). "And it is to this degree that all nineteenth-century psychiatry really converges on Freud, the first man to accept in all its seriousness the reality of the physician-patient couple. . . . To the doctor, Freud transferred all the structures Pinel and Tuke had set up within confinement. He did deliver the patient from the existence of the asylum within which his 'liberators' had alienated him; but he did not deliver him from what was essential in this existence; he regrouped its powers, extending them to the maximum by uniting them in the doctor's hands; he created the psychoanalytical situation where, by an inspired short circuit, alienation becomes disalienating because, in the doctor, it becomes a subject.

"The doctor, as an alienating figure, remains the key to psychoanalysis. Perhaps because it did not suppress this ultimate structure, and because it referred all the others to it, psychoanalysis has not been able, will not be able, to hear the voices of unreason, nor to decipher in themselves the signs of the madman. Psychoanalysis can unravel some of the forms of madness; it remains a stranger to the sovereign enterprise of unreason" (pp. 254, 274, 276–78).

member having his own triangle that interlocks with others without one's being able to discern the limits of a nuclear family; the foreclosing family, where differentiation is both included and warded off in the person of one of its members who has been eliminated, rendered null, and foreclosed.[40]

We can understand how such a concept as foreclosure operates within this extensive framework of a family where several generations—at least three—form the condition of fabrication of a psychotic: as for example when the troubles a mother has with regard to her own father lead to the son's inability, in turn, to even "posit his desire" toward his mother. Whence the strange notion that if a psychotic escapes the Oedipal apparatus, this is solely due to the fact that he is doubly embedded there, to the second power, in a field of extension that includes the grandparents. The problem of the cure then becomes rather similar to an operation of differential calculus, where one proceeds by way of depotentialization in order to rediscover the primary functions and reestablish the characteristic or nuclear triangle—always a holy trinity, the means of access to a three-sided situation. It is clear that this extended familialism, wherein the family receives the very forces of alienation and disalienation, carries with it a renunciation of the fundamental positions of psychoanalysis concerning sexuality, despite the formal conservation of an analytic vocabulary. A veritable regression in favor of a taxonomy of families. This is clearly visible in the projects of community psychiatry or of so-called familial psychotherapy, which effectively break apart asylum existence while nonetheless still maintaining all the presuppositions of the asylum, and basically renewing the thrust of nineteenth-century psychiatry according to the slogan put forward by Hochman: "From the family to the institution of the hospital, from the institution of the hospital to the familial institution, . . . a therapeutic return to the family"!

But even within the progressive or revolutionary sectors of institutional analysis on the one hand, and antipsychiatry on the other, the danger of this familialism in extension is ever present, conforming to the double impasse of an extended Oedipus, just as much in the diagnostic of pathogenic families in themselves as in the constitution of therapeutic quasi families. Once it has been said that it is no longer a matter of re-forming cadres of familial and social adaptation or integration, but rather of instituting original forms of active groups, the question arises as to what extent these core groups resemble artificial families, and to what extent they still lend themselves to oedipalization. These questions have been analyzed in depth by Jean Oury. They demonstrate how revolutionary psychiatry broke in vain with the ideals of community adaptation, with everything that Maud Mannoni calls the adaptation police force, since at every moment it still risks being thrust back into the framework of a structural Oedipus whose deficiencies are diagnosed but whose integrity is restored; a holy trinity that continues to strangle desiring-production and suffocate its problems. The political, cultural, world-historical, and racial content is left behind, crushed in the Oedipal treadmill. This is because psychiatrists persist in treating the family as a matrix, or better still as a microcosm, an *expressive* milieu that provides its own justifications, and that—however capable of expressing the action of the alienating forces*—"mediates" them precisely by suppressing the true categories of *production* in the machines of desire.

It seems to us that such a viewpoint is present even in Cooper. (In this respect Laing is better able to disengage himself from familialism, thanks to the resources of a flux from the Orient.) Cooper writes: "Families mediate social reality to their children. If the social reality in question is rife with alienated social forms, then this alienation will be mediated to the individual child and will be experienced as estrangement in the family relationships . . . for example he may say that his mind is controlled by an electrical machine or by men from outer space. These constructions, however, are largely embodiments of the family process, which has the illusion of substantiality but which is none other than the alienated form of the action of praxis of the family members that literally dominates the mind of the psychotic member. *These metaphysical men from outer space* are the literal mother, father, and sibling who sit around the breakfast table with the so-called psychotic patient."[41] Even the essential hypothesis of antipsychiatry, which ultimately posits an identity in nature between social alienation and mental alienation, must be understood in terms of a maintained familialism, and not in terms of a refutation of this familialism. For it is to the extent that the family-microcosm, the family–social-indicator, expresses social alienation that it is believed to "organize" mental alienation in the mind of its own members or its psychotic member. (And among all the members, who is the real psychotic?)

With his general conception of microcosm-macrocosm relationships, Bergson brought about a discreet revolution that deserves further consideration. Likening the living to a microcosm is an ancient platitude. But if the living organism was thought to be similar to the world, this was attributed to the fact that it was or tended to be an isolated system, naturally closed: the comparison between microcosm and macrocosm

---

des forces aliénantes: The French word *aliénation* means both social alienation and what we English-speakers call "mental derangement." Obviously, the authors aim at discrediting the distinction between the two terms. (*Translators' note.*)

was thus a comparison between two closed figures, one of which expressed the other and was inscribed within the other. At the beginning of *Creative Evolution,* Bergson completely alters the scope of the comparison by opening up both ends. If the living being resembles the world, this is true, on the contrary, insofar as it opens itself to the opening of the world; if it is a whole, this is true to the extent that the whole, of the world as of the living being, is always in the process of becoming, developing, coming into being or advancing, and inscribing itself within a temporal dimension that is irreducible and nonclosed.

We believe that this is also true in the case of the family-society relationship. There is no Oedipal triangle: Oedipus is always open in an open social field. Oedipus opens to the four winds, to the four corners of the social field (not even 3+1, but 4+n). A poorly closed triangle, a porous or seeping triangle, an exploded triangle from which the flows of desire escape in the direction of other territories. It is strange that we had to wait for the dreams of colonized peoples in order to see that, on the vertices of the pseudo triangle, mommy was dancing with the missionary, daddy was being fucked by the tax collector, while the self was being beaten by a white man. It is precisely this pairing of the parental figures with agents of another nature, their locking embrace similar to that of wrestlers, that keeps the triangle from closing up again, from being valid in itself, and from claiming to express or represent this different nature of the agents that are in question in the unconscious itself. When Frantz Fanon encounters a case of persecution psychosis linked to the death of the mother, he first asks himself if he has "to deal with an unconscious guilt complex following on the death of the mother, as Freud had described in *Mourning and Melancholia.*" But he soon learns that the mother has been killed by a French soldier, and that the subject himself has murdered the wife of a colonist whose disembow-eled ghost perpetually appears before him, carrying along with it and tearing apart the memory of the mother.[42] It could always be said that these extreme situations of war trauma, of colonization, of dire poverty, and so on, are unfavorable to the construction of the Oedipal apparatus—and that it is precisely because of this that these situations favor a psychotic development or explosion—but we have a strong feeling that the problem lies elsewhere. Apart from the fact that a certain degree of comfort found in the bourgeois family is admittedly necessary to turn out oedipalized subjects, the question of knowing *what is actually invested* in the comfortable conditions of a supposedly normal or normative Oedipus is pushed still further into the background.

The revolutionary is the first to have the right to say: "Oedipus? Never heard of it." For the disjointed fragments of Oedipus remain stuck to all the corners of the historical social field, as a battlefield and not a scene from bourgeois theater. Too bad if the psychoanalysts roar their disapproval at this point. Fanon pointed out that troubled ime times had unconscious effects not only on the active militants, but also on those claiming to be neutral and to remain outside the affair, uninvolved in politics. The same could also be said with respect to apparently peaceful times: what a grotesque error to think that the unconscious-as-child is acquainted only with daddy-mommy, and that it doesn't know "in its own way" that its father has a boss who is not a father's father, or moreover that its father himself is a boss who is not a father. Therefore we formulate the following rule, which we feel to be applicable in all cases: the father and the mother exist only as fragments, and are never organized into a figure or a structure able both to represent the unconscious, and to represent in it the various agents of the collectivity; rather, they always shatter into fragments that come into contact with these agents, meet them face to face, square off with them, or settle the differences with them as in hand-to-hand combat.

The father, the mother, and the self are at grips with, and directly coupled to, the elements of the political and historical situation—the soldier, the cop, the occupier, the collaborator, the radical, the resister, the boss, the boss's wife—who constantly break all triangulations, and who prevent the entire situation from falling back on the familial complex and becoming internalized in it. In a word, the family is never a microcosm in the sense of an autonomous figure, even when inscribed in a larger circle that it is said to mediate and express. The family is by nature eccentric, decentered. We are told of fusional, divisive, tubular, and foreclosing families. But what produces the hiatuses (*coupures*) and their d1stribution that indeed keep the family from being an "interior"? There is always an uncle from America; a brother who went bad; an aunt who took off with a military man; a cousin out of work, bankrupt, or a victim of the Crash; an anarchist grandfather; a grandmother in the hospital, crazy or senile. The family does not engender its own ruptures. Families are filled with gaps and transected by breaks that are not familial: the Commune, the Dreyfus Affair, religion and atheism, the Spanish Civil War, the rise of fascism, Stalinism, the Vietnam war, May '68—all these things form complexes of the unconscious, more effective than everlasting Oedipus. And the unconscious is indeed at issue here. If in fact there are structures, they do not exist in the mind, in the shadow of a fantastic phallus distributing the lacunae, the passages, and the articulations. Structures exist in the immediate impossible real. As Witold Grombrowicz says, the structuralists "search for their structures in culture. As for myself, I look for them in the immediate reality. My way of seeing things was in direct relationship to the events of the times: Hitlerism, Stalinism, fascism. . . . I was fascinated by the grotesque and terrifying forms that surfaced in the sphere of the interhuman, destroying all that was held dear until then."[43]

Hellenists were right to remind us that, even in the case of worthy Oedipus, it was already a matter of "politics." They are simply wrong in concluding from this that the libido has nothing to do with any of it. Quite the contrary: what is invested by the libido throughout the disjoined elements of Oedipus—especially given the fact that these elements never form a mental structure that is autonomous and expressive—are these extrafamilial, subfamilial gaps and breaks (*coupures*), *these forms of social production in conjunction with desiring-production*. Schizoanalysis therefore does not hide the fact that it is a political and social psychoanalysis, a militant analysis: not because it would go about generalizing Oedipus in culture, under the ridiculous conditions that have been the norm until now. It is a militant analysis, on the contrary, because it proposes to demonstrate the existence of an unconscious libidinal investment of sociohistorical production, distinct from the conscious investments coexisting with it. Proust is not wrong in saying that, far from being the author of an "intimate" work, he goes further than the proponents of a populist or proletarian art who are content to describe the social and the political in "willfully" expressive works. For his part, he is interested in the manner in which the Dreyfus Affair and then World War I cut across families, introducing into them new breaks and new connections resulting in a modification of the heterosexual and homosexual libido (in the decomposed milieu of the Guermantes, for example).

It is the function of the libido to invest the social field in unconscious forms, thereby hallucinating all history, reproducing in delirium entire civilizations, races, and continents, and intensely "feeling" the becoming of the world. There is no signifying chain without a Chinaman, an Arab, and a black who drop in to trouble the night of a white paranoiac. Schizoanalysis sets out to undo the expressive Oedipal unconscious, always artificial, repressive and repressed, mediated by the family, in order to attain the immediate productive unconscious. Yes, the family is a *stimulus*—but a stimulus that is qualitatively indifferent, an inductor that is neither an organizer nor a disorganizer. As for the *response,* it always comes from another direction. If there is indeed language (*langage*), it is on the side of the response, not the stimulus. Even Oedipal psychoanalysis recognized the indifference of the effective parental images, the irreducibility of the response to the stimulation performed by these images. But it contented itself with understanding the response by starting from an expressive symbolism that was still familial, instead of interpreting it in an unconscious system of production as such (analytical economy).

The great argument of familialism is: "at least in the beginning . . ." This argument may be explicitly formulated, but it also persists implicitly in theories that nevertheless refuse the viewpoint of genesis. *At least in the beginning,* this argument runs, the unconscious is expressed in a state of familial relations and constellations where the Real, the Imaginary, and the Symbolic intermingle. In this conception, the metaphysical and social relations arise *afterward,* in the manner of a beyond. And since the beginning always proceeds by twos—this is even the necessary condition for rendering escape impossible—a first pre-oedipal beginning is invoked, "the primitive nondifferentiation of the most precocious stages of the personality" in the relationship with the mother; then a second beginning is invoked; Oedipus itself with the law of the father and the exclusive differentiations that this law prescribes at the heart of the family; and finally latency, the celebrated latency, *after which* the beyond begins. But since this beyond consists in duping others into taking the same path (the children to come), and also since the first beginning is said to be "pre-oedipal" only to indicate that it already belongs to Oedipus as a referential axis, it is quite clear that the two ends of Oedipus have simply been closed, and that the beyond and the afterward will always be interpreted in terms of Oedipus, in relation to Oedipus, within the framework of Oedipus. Everything will be reduced to Oedipus, as the discussions on the comparative role of childhood factors and actual factors in neurosis bear out: how could it be otherwise, so long as the "actual" factor is conceived of in this form of the afterward?

But we know in point of fact that the actual factors are there from childhood, and that they determine the libidinal investments in terms of breaks and connections that they introduce into the family. Over the heads of the members of the family, and underneath, it is desiring-production and social production that manifest, through the childhood experience, their identical natures and their differing régimes. In this regard let us consider three important works about children: *L'Enfant* by Jules Vallès, *Bas les coeurs* by Georges Darien, *Mort à crédit* by L.-F. Céline. In them we see how bread, money, dwelling place, social promotion, bourgeois and revolutionary values, wealth and poverty, oppression and revolt, social classes, political events, metaphysical and collective problems—what does it mean to be able to breathe? why be poor? why are there rich people?—form the object of investments in which the parents merely have a role as agents of a special production or antiproduction, always grappling with other agents that they express all the less as they are increasingly at grips with them in the heaven and hell of the child. And the child says: Why? Freud's Rat Man does not wait until he is a man to invest the rich woman and the poor woman who constitute the actual factor of his obsession. For inadmissible reasons, the existence of an infantile sexuality is denied; but for hardly more admissible reasons, this sexuality is reduced to desiring mommy and wanting the place of the father. The Freudian blackmail is this: either you recognize the Oedipal character of infantile sexuality, or you abandon all positions of sexuality.

And yet, not even in the shadow of a transcendent phallus are the unconscious effects of a "signified" established throughout the determinations of a social field; on the contrary, it is the libidinal investment of these determinations that situates their particular use in desiring-production, and the comparative operation of this production with social production, whence derive the state of desire and its repression, the distribution of the agents, and the degree of oedipalization of sexuality. Lacan explains well how, in terms of the crises and the ruptures (*coupures*) within science, there is a drama for the scientist that at times goes as far as madness, and that "would have no way of including itself in the Oedipal apparatus, unless by calling it into question" by way of a consequence.[44] In this sense every child is a little scientist, a little Cantor.* Go back through the course of the ages, you will never find a child caught in a familial order that is autonomous, expressive, or signifying. Even the nursing child, in his games as in his feedings, his chains, and his meditations, is already caught up in an immediate desiring-production where the parents play the role of partial objects, witnesses, reporters, and agents, in a process that outflanks them on all sides, and places desire in an immediate relationship with a historical and social reality. It is true that nothing is pre-oedipal, and that we must take Oedipus back to the earliest age, but within the order of a repression of the unconscious. It is equally true that everything within the order of production is anoedipal, and that there are non-oedipal, anoedipal currents that begin as early as Oedipus and continue just as long, with another rhythm, in a different mode of operation, in another dimension, with other uses of syntheses that feed the autoproduction of the unconscious—the unconscious-as-orphan, the playful unconscious, the meditative and social unconscious.

The Oedipal operation consists in establishing a constellation of biunivocal relations between the agents of social production, reproduc-

*Georg Cantor (1845–1918), a German mathematician known for his theory of transfinite numbers. (*Translators' note.*)

tion, and antiproduction on the one hand, and the agents of the so-called natural reproduction of the family on the other. This operation is called an *application*. It is as if a tablecloth were being folded, as if its 4 (+*n*) corners were reduced to 3 (+1, to designate the transcendent factor performing the operation). From that moment it is a foregone conclusion that the collective agents will be interpreted as derivatives of, or substitutes for, parental figures, in a system of equivalence that rediscovers everywhere the father, the mother, and the ego. (And one merely pushes the difficulty into the background when one considers the system as a whole and then makes it depend on the transcendent term, the phallus). There we have a faulty use of the conjunctive synthesis, leading to the statement, "So it was your father, so it was your mother . . ." It is not at all surprising that only afterward is it discovered that all of this was the father and the mother, since this is assumed to be the case from the beginning, but is subsequently forgotten-repressed, though still subject to a later rediscovery in relation to more recent developments.* Whence the magical formula that characterizes biunivocalization—the flattening of the polyvocal real in favor of a symbolic relationship between two articulations: so *that* is what *this* meant. Everything is made to begin with Oedipus, by means of explanation, with all the more certainty as one has reduced everything to Oedipus by means of application.

Only in appearance is Oedipus a beginning, either as a historical or prehistorical origin, or as a structural foundation. In reality it is a completely ideological beginning, for the sake of ideology. Oedipus is always and solely an aggregate of destination fabricated to meet the requirements of an aggregate of departure constituted by a social formation. It can be applied to everything, in that the agents and relations of social production, and the libidinal investments corresponding to them, are made to conform to the figures of familial reproduction. In the aggregate of departure there is the social formation, or rather the social formations: the races, the classes, the continents, the peoples, the kingdoms, the sovereignties; Joan of Arc and the Great Mongol, Luther and the Aztec Serpent. In the aggregate of destination, there remains only daddy, mommy, and me.

Thus it must be said *of Oedipus as well as of desiring-production:* it is at the end, not at the beginning. But not at all in the same fashion. We have seen that desiring-production was the limit of social production, always thwarted in the capitalist formation: the body without organs at

*Perhaps the reader would enjoy this parody of psychoanalytic logic in the authors' French: "Et qu'on découvre seulement par après que tout ça c'était le père et la mère, n'a rien d'étonnant, puisqu'on suppose que ça l'est dès le début, mais que c'est ensuite oublié-refoulé, quitte à le retrouver après par rapport à l'ensuite." (*Translators' note.*)

the edge of the deterritorialized socius, the desert at the gates of the city. But it is urgent, it is essential that the limit be displaced, rendered inoffensive, and that it pass or seem to pass into the social formation itself. Schizophrenia or desiring-production is the boundary between the molar organization and the molecular multiplicity of desire; this limit of deterritorialization must now pass into the interior of the molar organization, and it must be applied to a factitious and subjugated territoriality. We are now able to surmise what Oedipus signifies: it displaces the limit, it internalizes the limit. Rather a society of neurotics than one successful schizophrenic who has not been made autistic. Oedipus, the incomparable instrument of gregariousness, is the ultimate private and subjugated territoriality of European man. (Moreover the displaced, exorcised limit or border shifts to the interior of Oedipus, between its two poles.)

One word here on the disgrace of psychoanalysis in history and politics. The procedure is well known: two figures are made to appear, the Great Man and the Crowd. One then claims to make history with these two entities, these two puppets, the Great Crustacean and the Crazy Invertebrate. Oedipus is placed at the beginning. On the one side there is the great man defined oedipally: so he killed the father, in a murder without end, either to annihilate him and identify with the mother, or to internalize him, to take his place or reach a reconciliation (with a host of variations in detail that correspond to neurotic, psychotic, perverse, or "normal" solutions, that is to say solutions of sublimation). In any case the great man is already great because, for good or for evil, he has found a certain original solution to the Oedipal conflict. Hitler annihilates the father and unleashes in him the forces of the Bad Mother; Luther internalizes the father and reaches a compromise with the superego. On the other side there is the crowd, also defined oedipally, by means of parental images of a second order, this time collective; the encounter can therefore take place between Luther and the sixteenth-century Christians, or between Hitler and the German people, with corresponding elements that do not necessarily imply identity: Hitler plays the role of father through "homosexual transfusion" and in relation to the female crowd; Luther plays the role of woman in relation to the God of the Christians. Naturally, to ensure against the historian's justified anger, the psychoanalyst specifies that he is concerned only with a certain causal order, that one must take "other" causes into account, but that he alone cannot do everything. Besides, he deals just enough with other causes so as to give us a foretaste: he takes into account the institutions of a particular period (from the sixteenth-century Church to twentieth-century capitalist power), if only to see in them parental images of yet another order, associating the father and the mother, who will then be dissociated and otherwise regrouped within the action of the great man and the crowd. It hardly matters whether the tone of these books is orthodox Freudian, culturalist, or Jungian.

Books like those are nauseating. Let's not dismiss them by saying that they belong to the distant past of psychoanalysis: similar books—a lot of them—are still written today. Let's not say that it is merely a question of a careless use of Oedipus: what other use could be made of Oedipus? Nor is it a case of an ambiguous dimension of "applied psychoanalysis"; for all Oedipus—Oedipus in and of itself—is already an application, in the strictest sense of the word. And when the best psychoanalysts forbid themselves historico-political applications, we can't say things are much better, since the analysts *retreat* to the rock of castration presented as the locus of an "untenable truth" that is irreducible: they closet themselves in a phallocentrism that leads them to think of the analytic activity as always having to evolve within a familial microcosm, and they continue to treat the libido's direct investments of the social field as simple imaginary dependencies on Oedipus, where it becomes necessary to denounce "a fusional dream," "a fantasy of a-return-to-Oneness." "Castration," they say, "is what separates us from politics, is what makes for our originality as analysts—we who do not forget that society too is triangular and symbolic!"

If it is true that Oedipus is obtained by reduction or application, it presupposes in itself a certain kind of libidinal investment of the social field, of the production and the formation of this field. There is no more an individual Oedipus than there is an individual fantasy. Oedipus is a means of integration into the group, in both the adaptive form of its own reproduction that makes it pass from one generation to the next, and in its unadapted neurotic stases that block desire at prearranged impasses. Oedipus also flourishes in subjugated groups, where an established order is invested through the group's own repressive forms. And it is not the forms of the subjugated group that depend on Oedipal projections and identifications, but the reverse: it is Oedipal applications that depend on the determinations of the subjugated group as an aggregate of departure and on their libidinal investment (from the age of thirteen I've worked hard, rising on the social ladder, getting promotions, being a part of the exploiters). There is therefore a *segregative use* of the conjunctive syntheses of the unconscious, a use that does not coincide with divisions between classes, although it is an incomparable weapon in the service of a dominating class: it is this use that brings about the feeling of "indeed being one of us," of being part of a superior race threatened by enemies from outside. Thus the Little White pioneers' son, the Irish Protestant who commemorates the victory of his ancestors, the fascist who belongs to the master race.

Oedipus depends on this sort of nationalistic, religious, racist sentiment, and not the reverse: it is not the father who is projected onto the boss, but the boss who is applied to the father, either in order to tell us "you will not surpass your father," or "you will surpass him to find our forefathers." Lacan has demonstrated in a profound way the link between Oedipus and segregation. Not, however, in the sense where segregation would be a consequence of Oedipus, subjacent to the fraternity of the brothers once the father is dead. On the contrary, the segregative use is a precondition of Oedipus, to the extent that the social field is not reduced to the familial tie except by presupposing an enormous archaism, an incarnation of the race in person or in spirit: yes, I am one of you.

It is not a question of ideology. There is an unconscious libidinal investment of the social field that coexists, but does not necessarily coincide, with the preconscious investments, or with what the preconscious investments "ought to be." That is why, when subjects, individuals, or groups act manifestly counter to their class interests—when they rally to the interests and ideals of a class that their own objective situation should lead them to combat—it is not enough to say: they were fooled, the masses have been fooled. It is not an ideological problem, a problem of failing to recognize, or of being subject to, an illusion. It is a problem of desire, *and desire is part of the infrastructure.* Preconscious investments are made, or should be made, according to the interests of the opposing classes. But unconscious investments are made according to positions of *desire* and uses of synthesis, very different from the interests of the subject, individual or collective, who desires.

These investments of an unconscious nature can ensure the general submission to a dominant class by making cuts (*coupures*) and segregations pass over into a social field, insofar as it is effectively invested by desire and no longer by interests. A form of social production and reproduction, along with its economic and financial mechanisms, its political formations, and so on, can be desired as such, in whole or in part, independently of the interests of the desiring-subject. It was not by means of a metaphor, even a paternal metaphor, that Hitler was able to sexually arouse the fascists. It is not by means of a metaphor that a banking or stock-market transaction, a claim, a coupon, a credit, is able to arouse people who are not necessarily bankers. And what about the effects of money that grows, money that produces more money? There are socioeconomic "complexes" that are also veritable complexes of the unconscious, and that communicate a voluptuous wave from the top to the bottom of their hierarchy (the military-industrial complex). And ideology, Oedipus, and the phallus have nothing to do with this, because they depend on it rather than being its impetus. For it is a matter of flows, of stocks, of breaks in and fluctuations of flows; desire is present wherever something flows and runs, carrying along with it interested subjects—but also drunken or slumbering subjects—toward lethal destinations.

Hence the goal of schizoanalysis: to analyze the specific nature of the libidinal investments in the economic and political spheres, and thereby to show how, in the subject who desires, desire can be made to desire its own repression—whence the role of the death instinct in the circuit connecting desire to the social sphere. All this happens, not in ideology, but well beneath it. An unconscious investment of a fascist or reactionary type can exist alongside a conscious revolutionary investment. Inversely, it can happen—rarely—that a revolutionary investment on the level of desire coexists with a reactionary investment conforming to a conscious interest. In any case conscious and unconscious investments are not of the same type, even when they coincide or are superimposed on each other. We define the reactionary unconscious investment as the investment that conforms to the interest of the dominant class, but operates on its own account, according to the terms of desire, through the segregative use of the conjunctive syntheses from which Oedipus is derived: I am of the superior race. The revolutionary unconscious investment is such that desire, still in its own mode, cuts across the interest of the dominated, exploited classes, and causes flows to move that are capable of breaking apart both the segregations and their Oedipal applications—flows capable of hallucinating history, of reanimating the races in delirium, of setting continents ablaze. No, I am not of your kind, I am the outsider and the deterritorialized, "I am of a race inferior for all eternity. . . . I am a beast, a Negro."[45]

There again it is a question of an intense potential for investment and counterinvestment in the unconscious. Oedipus disintegrates because its very conditions have disintegrated. *The nomadic and polyvocal use* of the conjunctive syntheses is in opposition to *the segregative and biunivocal use.* Delirium has something like two poles, racist and racial, paranoiac-segregative and schizonomadic. And between the two, ever so many subtle, uncertain shiftings where the unconscious itself oscillates between its reactionary charge and its revolutionary potential. Even Schreber finds himself to be the Great Mongol when he breaks through the Aryan segregation. Whence the ambiguity in the texts of great authors, when they develop the theme of races, as rich in ambiguity as destiny itself. Here schizoanalysis must unravel the thread.

For reading a text is never a scholarly exercise in search of what is signified, still less a highly textual exercise in search of a signifier. Rather it is a productive use of the literary machine, a montage of desiring-machines, a schizoid exercise that extracts from the text its revolutionary force. The exclamation "So it's . . . !", or the meditation of *Igitur* on race, in an essential relationship with madness.

6 | A Recapitulation of the Three Syntheses

Stupefying Oedipus, inexhaustible and ever present. We are told that the father died "over a period of thousands of years" (well, well!) and that the "internalization" corresponding to the paternal image was produced during the Paleolithic right up until the start of the Neolithic, "approximately 8,000 years ago."[46] One analyzes historically or one doesn't. But honestly, as to the death of the father, news doesn't travel very fast: it would be a mistake to embark Nietzsche on that particular voyage through history. For Nietzsche is not the kind to ruminate over the death of the father, and spend all his Paleolithic period internalizing him. On the contrary, Nietzsche is exceedingly tired of all these stories revolving around the death of the father, the death of God, and wants to put an end to the interminable discourses of this nature, discourses already in vogue in his Hegelian epoch. Alas, he was wrong, the discourses have continued. But Nietzsche wanted us finally to pass on to serious things. He gives us twelve or thirteen versions of the death of God, for good measure and to be done with it, so as to render the event comical. And he explains that strictly speaking this event has no importance whatever, that it merely concerns the latest Pope: God dead or not dead, the father dead or not dead, it amounts to the same thing, since the same psychic repression (*refoulement*) and the same social repression (*répression*) continue unabated, here in the name of God or a living father, there in the name of man or the dead father.

Nietzsche says that what is important is not the news that God is dead, but the time this news takes to bear fruit. Here the psychoanalyst perks up his ears, believing he has heard a familiar chord: it is well known that the unconscious takes a lot of time to digest a bit of news; one can even quote some texts of Freud on the unconscious being ignorant of time, conserving its objects like an Egyptian tomb. But that is not at all what Nietzsche is saying: he does not mean that the death of God spends a long time plodding around in the unconscious. He means that what takes so long in coming *to consciousness* is the news that the death of God makes no difference *to the unconscious*. The fruits of this news are not the consequences brought about by the death of God, but this other news that the death of God is of no consequence. In other terms: that God and the father never existed (or if they did, it was so long ago, perhaps during the Paleolithic). All they did was kill a dead man, from time immemorial. The fruits of the news of the death of God do away with the flower of His death as well as the bud of His life. For, alive or dead, it is still a question of belief: the element of belief has not been abandoned. The announcement of the father's death constitutes a last belief, "a belief by virtue of nonbelief" about which Nietzsche says: "This violence always manifests the need for a belief, for a prop, for a *structure.*" Oedipus-as-structure.

Engels paid homage to the genius of Bachofen, for having recognized in myth the figures of a maternal and a paternal law, their struggles and their relationships. But Engels slips in a reproach that changes everything: it really seems as if Bachofen believes all this, that he believes in myths, in the Furies, Apollo, and Athena.[47] The same reproach applies even better to psychoanalysts: it would seem that they believe in all of this—in myth, in Oedipus and castration. They reply: the question is not one of knowing whether we believe in this, but whether or not the unconscious itself believes in it. But what is this unconscious when reduced to the state of belief? Who injects it with belief? Psychoanalysis cannot become a rigorous discipline unless it accepts putting belief in parentheses, which is to say a *materialist reduction* of Oedipus as an ideological form. It is not a matter of saying that Oedipus is a false belief, but rather that belief is necessarily something false that diverts and suffocates effective production. That is why seers are the least believing of men. When we relate desire to Oedipus, we are condemned to ignore the productive nature of desire: we condemn desire to vague dreams or imaginations that are merely conscious expressions of it; we relate it to independent existences—the father, the mother, the begetters—that do not yet comprise their elements as internal elements of desire. The question of the father is like that of God: born of an abstraction, it assumes the link to be already broken between man and nature, man and the world, so that man must be produced as man by something exterior to nature and to man. On this point Nietzsche makes a remark completely akin to those of Marx or Engels: "We now laugh when we find 'Man *and* World' placed beside one another, separated by the sublime presumption of the little word 'and.' "[48]

Coextensiveness is another matter entirely, the coextension of man and nature; a circular movement by which the unconscious, always remaining subject, produces and reproduces itself. The unconscious does not follow the paths of a generation progressing (or regressing) from one body to another: your father, your father's father, and so on. The organized body is the object of reproduction by generation; it is not its subject. The sole subject of reproduction is the unconscious itself, which holds to the circular form of production. Sexuality is not a means in the service of generation; rather, the generation of bodies is in the service of sexuality as an autoproduction of the unconscious. Sexuality does not represent a premium for the ego, in exchange for its subordination to the process of generation; on the contrary, generation is the ego's solace, its prolongation, the passage from one body to another through which the unconscious does no more than reproduce itself in itself. Indeed, in this sense we must say the unconscious has always been an orphan—that is, it has engendered itself in the identity of nature and man, of the world and man. The question of the father, the question of God, is what has become impossible, a matter of indifference, so true is it that to affirm or deny such a being amounts to the same thing, or to live it or kill it: one and the same misconception (*contresens*) concerning the nature of the unconscious.

But psychoanalysts are bent on producing man abstractly, that is to say ideologically, for culture. It is Oedipus who produces man in this fashion, and who gives a structure to the false movement of infinite progression and regression: your father, and your father's father, a snowball gathering speed as it moves from Oedipus all the way to the father of the primal horde, to God and the Paleolithic age. It is Oedipus who makes us man, for better or for worse, say those who would make fools of us all. The tone may vary, but the message remains basically the same: you will not escape Oedipus, your sole choice is between the "neurotic outlet" and the "nonneurotic outlet." The tone may be that of the scandalized psychoanalyst, the psychoanalyst-as-cop: those who do not bow to the imperialism of Oedipus are dangerous deviants, leftists who ought to be handed over to social and police repression; they talk too much and are lacking in anality (Dr. Gérard Mendel, Doctors Stéphane). What kind of disquieting play on words is it that can make the analyst a promoter of anality? Or there is the psychoanalyst-as-priest, the pious psychoanalyst who is forever chanting the incurable insufficiency of being: don't you see that Oedipus saves us from Oedipus, it is our agony but also our ecstasy, depending on whether we live it neurotically or live its structure; it is the mother of the holy faith (J. M. Pohier). Or the technopsychoanalyst, the reform psychoanalyst obsessed with the triangle, who wraps the splendid gifts of civilization in Oedipus—identity, manic-depression, and liberty in an infinite progression: "Through Oedipus the individual learns to live the triangular situation, the token of his identity, and at the same time he discovers—sometimes in a depressive mode, sometimes in a mode of exaltation—his fundamental alienation, his irremediable solitude, the price of his liberty. The basic structure of the Oedipal apparatus must not only be generalized in time so as to account for all the triangular experiences of the child and his parents, it must be generalized in space to include those triangular relations other than the parent-child relations."[49]

The unconscious poses no problem of meaning, solely problems of use. The question posed by desire is not "What does it mean?" but rather "*How does it work?*" How do these machines, these desiring-machines, work—yours and mine? With what sort of breakdowns as a part of their functioning? How do they pass from one body to another? How are they attached to the body without organs? What occurs when their mode of operation confronts the social machines? A tractable gear is greased, or on the contrary an infernal machine is made ready. What are the connections, what are the disjunctions, the conjunctions, what use is made of the syntheses? It represents nothing, but it produces. It means nothing, but it works. Desire makes its entry with the general collapse of the question "What does it mean?" No one has been able to pose the problem of language except to the extent that linguists and logicians have first eliminated meaning; and the greatest force of language was only discovered once a *work* was viewed as a machine, producing certain effects, amenable to a certain use. Malcolm Lowry says of his work: it's anything you want it to be, so long as it works—"It works too, believe me, as I have found out"—a machinery.[50] But on condition that meaning be nothing other than use, that it become a firm principle only if we have at our disposal *immanent criteria* capable of determining the legitimate uses, as opposed to the illegitimate ones that relate use instead to a hypothetical meaning and re-establish a kind of transcendence.

Analysis termed transcendental is precisely the determination of these criteria, immanent to the field of the unconscious, insofar as they are *opposed* to the transcendent exercises of a "What does it mean?" Schizoanalysis is at once a transcendental and a materialist analysis. It is critical in the sense that it leads the criticism of Oedipus, or leads Oedipus, to the point of its own self-criticism. It sets out to explore a transcendental unconscious, rather than a metaphysical one; an unconscious that is material rather than ideological; schizophrenic rather than Oedipal; nonfigurative rather than imaginary; real rather than symbolic; machinic rather than structural—an unconscious, finally, that is molecular, microphysical, and micrological rather than molar or gregarious; productive rather than expressive. And it is a matter here of practical principles as directions for the "cure."

Thus we have already seen how the immanent criteria of desiring-production permitted a definition of legitimate uses of syntheses, uses completely distinct from Oedipal uses. And in relation to this desiring-production, the Oedipal illegitimate uses seemed to us to be multiform, but always to revolve around the same error, and to envelop theoretical and practical paralogisms. In the first place, a partial and nonspecific use of the connective syntheses was found to be in opposition to the Oedipal use, itself global and specific. This global-specific use was found to have two aspects, parental and conjugal, to which the triangular form of Oedipus and the reproduction of this form corresponded. This use rested upon a paralogism of extrapolation that in fact constituted Oedipus's formal cause—an extrapolation whose illegitimate nature weighed on the whole operation: the extraction of a transcendent complete object from the signifying chain, which served as a despotic signifier on which the entire chain thereafter seemed to depend, assigning an element of lack to each position of desire, fusing desire to a law, and engendering the illusion that this loosened up and freed the elements of the chain.

In the second place, an inclusive or nonrestrictive use of the disjunctive syntheses is in opposition to their Oedipal, exclusive, restrictive use. This restrictive use in its turn has two poles, imaginary and symbolic, since the only choice it permits is between the exclusive symbolic differentiations and the undifferentiated Imaginary, correlatively determined by Oedipus. This use demonstrates this time how Oedipus proceeds, it demonstrates Oedipus's method: a paralogism of the double bind, the double impasse. (Or, in line with a suggestion made by Henri Gobard, would it be better to translate this as "double hold," like a full nelson hold in wrestling, so as to better describe the treatment forced on the unconscious when it is bound at both ends, leaving it no other choice than to respond Oedipus, to cry Oedipus, in sickness as in health, in its crises as in their outcome, in its resolution as in its problem. In any case, the double bind is not the schizophrenic process; on the contrary, the double bind is Oedipus insofar as it arrests the motion of the process, or forces it to spin around in the void.)

In the third place, a nomadic and polyvocal use of the conjunctive syntheses is opposed to the segregative and biunivocal use made of them. There again this biunivocal use, illegitimate from the point of view of the unconscious itself, has what appear to be two moments: first, a moment that is racist, nationalistic, religious, etc., and that, by means of a segregation, constitutes an aggregate of departure that is always presupposed by Oedipus, even if in a totally implicit fashion; next, a familial moment that constitutes the aggregate of destination by means of an application. Whence the third paralogism, the paralogism of application, which fixes the precondition for Oedipus by establishing a set of biunivocal relations between the determinations of the social field and the familial determinations, thereby making possible and inevitable the reduction of libidinal investments to the eternal daddy-mommy. We still have not exhausted all the paralogisms that lead the practice of the cure in the direction of a frenzied oedipalization, a betrayal of desire, the unconscious closeted in a day nursery, a narcissistic machine for arrogant and mouthy little egos, a perpetual absorption of capitalist surplus value, flows of words against flows of money, the interminable story—psychoanalysis.

The three errors concerning desire are called lack, law, and signifier. It is one and the same error, an idealism that forms a pious conception of the unconscious. And it is futile to interpret these notions in terms of a combinative apparatus (*une combinatoire*) that makes of lack an empty position and no longer a deprivation, that turns the law into a rule of the game and no longer a commandment, and the signifier into a distributor and no longer a meaning, for these notions cannot be prevented from dragging their theological cortege behind—insufficiency of being, guilt, signification. Structural interpretation challenges all beliefs, rises above all images, and from the realm of the mother and the father retains only functions, defines *the prohibition and the transgression* as structural operations. But what water will cleanse these concepts of their background, their previous existences—religiosity? Scientific knowledge as nonbelief is truly the last refuge of belief, and as Nietzsche put it, there never was but one psychology, that of the priest.

From the moment lack is reintroduced into desire, all of desiring-production is crushed, reduced to being no more than the production of fantasy; but the sign does not produce fantasies, it is a production of the real and a position of desire within reality. From the moment desire is welded again to the law—we needn't point out what is known since time began: that there is no desire without law—the eternal operation of eternal repression recommences, the operation that closes around the unconscious the circle of prohibition and transgression, white mass and black mass; but the sign of desire is never a sign of the law, it is a sign of strength (*puissance*). And who would dare use the term "law" for the fact that desire situates and develops its strength, and that wherever it is, it causes flows to move and substances to be intersected ("I am careful not to speak of chemical laws, the word has a moral aftertaste")? From the moment desire is made to depend on the signifier, it is put back under the yoke of a despotism whose effect is castration, there where one recognizes the stroke of the signifier itself; but the sign of desire is never signifying, it exists in the thousands of productive breaks-flows that never allow themselves to be signified within the unary stroke of castration. It is always a point-sign of many dimensions, polyvocity as the basis for a punctual semiology.

It is said that the unconscious is dark and somber. Reich and Marcuse are often reproached for their "Rousseauism," their naturalism: a conception of the unconscious that is thought to be too idyllic. But doesn't one indeed lend to the unconscious horrors that could only be those of consciousness, and of a belief too sure of itself? Would it be an exaggeration to say that in the unconscious there is necessarily less cruelty and terror, and of a different type, than in the consciousness of an heir, a soldier, or a Chief of State? The unconscious has its horrors, but they are not anthropomorphic. It is not the slumber of reason that engenders monsters, but vigilant and insomniac rationality. The unconscious is Rousseauistic, being man-nature. And how much malice and ruse there are in Rousseau! Transgression, guilt, castration: are these determinations of the unconscious, or is this *the way a priest sees things?* Doubtless there are many other forces besides psychoanalysis for oedipalizing the unconscious, rendering it guilty, castrating it. But psychoanalysis reinforces the movement, it invents a last priest. Oedipal analysis imposes a transcendent use on all the syntheses of the unconscious, ensuring their *conversion.*

The practical problem of schizoanalysis is, then, to ensure the contrasting *reversion:* restoring the syntheses of the unconscious to their immanent use. De-oedipalizing, undoing the daddy-mommy spider web, undoing the beliefs so as to attain the production of desiring-machines, and to reach the level of economic and social investments where the militant analysis comes into play. Nothing is accomplished as long as machines are not touched upon. This implies interventions that are in fact very concrete; in place of the benevolent pseudo neutrality of the Oedipal analyst, who wants and understands only daddy and mommy, we must substitute a malevolent, an openly malevolent activity: your Oedipus is a fucking drag, keep it up and the analysis will be stopped, or else we'll apply a shock treatment to you; stop saying daddy-mommy; of course "Hamlet lives in you as Werther lives in you," and Oedipus too, and anything you want, *but* "you grow uterine arms and legs, uterine lips, uterine mustache. In tracing back the 'memory deaths' your ego becomes a sort of mineral theorem which constantly proves the futility of living . . . . Were *you* born Hamlet? *Or did you not rather create the type in yourself?* Whether this be so or not, what seems infinitely more important is—*why revert to myth?*"[51]

If myth is given up, a little joy, a little discovery, is restored to psychoanalysis. For it has become very dismal, very sad, quite interminable, with everything decided in advance. Will it be retorted that the schizo is not joyous either? But doesn't his sadness come from the fact that he can no longer bear the forces of oedipalization and hamletization that hem him in on all sides? Better to flee to the body without organs and hide out there, closing himself up in it. The little joy lies in schizophrenization as a process, not in the schizo as a clinical entity. "You have pushed a process into a goal. . . ." If we made a psychoanalyst enter into the domains of the productive unconscious, he would feel as out of place with his theater as an actress from the Comédie-Française in a factory, a *priest* from the Middle Ages on an assembly line. We must set up units of production, plug in desiring-machines. What takes place in this factory, what this process is, its spasms and its glories, its labors and its joys, still remain unknown.

7 | Social Repression and Psychic Repression

We have attempted to analyze the form, the reproduction, the (formal) cause, the method, and the condition of the Oedipal triangle. But we have postponed the analysis of the real forces, the real causes on which the triangulation depends. The general line of the response is simple, it has been sketched out by Reich: it is social repression, the forces of social repression. This response, however, leaves two problems untouched and makes them even more urgent: on the one hand, the specific relationship between psychic repression and social repression; on the other hand, the particular situation of Oedipus in this social repression–psychic repression system. The two problems are obviously linked because, *if psychic repression did bear on incestuous desires,* it would thereby gain a certain independence and primacy, as a condition for constituting a system of exchange or any society, in relation to social repression, which would then concern only the returns of the psychically repressed in a constituted society. Therefore we should first of all consider the second question: does psychic repression bear upon the Oedipus complex as an adequate expression of the unconscious? Must we even follow Freud in saying that the Oedipus complex, according to one or the other of its two poles, is either repressed (not without leaving behind traces and returns that will be confronted by the prohibitions), or suppressed (not without being passed on to the children, with whom the same story begins all over again)?[52]

We wonder if Oedipus in fact expresses desire; if Oedipus is desired, then it is indeed on it that psychic repression comes to bear. Now the Freudian argument is of a nature to leave us wondering: Freud quotes a remark by Sir J. G. Frazer according to which "the law only forbids men to do what their instincts incline them to do; . . . Instead of assuming, therefore, from the legal prohibition of incest that there is a natural aversion to incest, we ought rather to assume that there is a natural instinct in favor of it."[53] In other words: if it is prohibited, this is because it is desired—there would be no need to prohibit what is not desired. Once again, it is this confidence in the law, the unawareness of the ruses and the procedures of the law, that leaves us wondering.

The immortal father of Céline's *Death on the Installment Plan (Mort à credit)* cries out: So you want to see me die, eh, is that what you want, speak up? We didn't want anything of the sort, however. We didn't want the train to be daddy, or the station mommy. We only wanted peace and innocence, and to be left alone to machine our little machines, O desiring-production. Of course pieces from the bodies of the mother and the father are taken up in the connections, parental appellations crop up in the disjunctions of the chain, the parents are there as ordinary stimuli of an indifferent nature that trigger the becoming of adventures, of races, and of continents. But what a bizarre Freudian mania—to relate to Oedipus what overflows it on every side and from all angles, beginning with the hallucination of books and the delirium of apprenticeships (the teacher as father-substitute, and the book as family romance). Freud couldn't abide a simple humorous remark by Jung, to the effect that Oedipus must not really exist, since even the primitive prefers a pretty young woman to his mother or his grandmother. If Jung betrayed everything, it was nevertheless not by way of this remark, which can only suggest that the mother functions as a pretty girl as much as the pretty girl functions as mother, since the main thing for the primitive or the child is to form and put into motion their desiring-machines, to make flows circulate and to perform breaks in these flows.

The law tells us: You will not marry your mother, and you will not kill your father. And we docile subjects say to ourselves: so *that*'s what I wanted! Will it ever be suspected that the law discredits—and has an interest in discrediting and disgracing—the person it presumes to be guilty, the person the law wants to be guilty and wants to be made to feel guilty? One acts as if it were possible to conclude directly from psychic repression the nature of the repressed, and from the prohibition the nature of what is prohibited. There we have a typical paralogism—yet another, a fourth paralogism that we shall have to call *displacement*. For what really takes place is that the law prohibits something that is perfectly fictitious in the order of desire or of the "instincts," so as to persuade its subjects that they had the intention corresponding to this fiction. This is indeed the only way the law has of getting a grip on intention, of making the unconscious guilty. In short, we are not witness here to a system of two terms where we could conclude from the formal prohibition what is really prohibited. Instead we have before us a system of three terms, where this conclusion becomes completely illegitimate. Distinctions must be made: the repressing representation which performs the repression; the repressed representative, on which the repression actually comes to bear; the displaced represented, which gives a falsified apparent image that is meant to trap desire.

Such is the nature of Oedipus—the sham image. Repression does not operate through Oedipus, nor is it directed at Oedipus. It is not a question of the return of the repressed. Oedipus is a factitious product of psychic repression. It is only the represented, insofar as it is induced by repression. Repression cannot act without displacing desire, without giving rise to a *consequent desire,* all ready, all warm for punishment, and without putting this desire in the place of the *antecedent desire* on which repression comes to bear in principle or in reality ("Ah, so *that*'s what it was!").

D. H. Lawrence—who does not struggle against Freud in the name of the rights of the Ideal, but who speaks by virtue of the flows of sexuality and the intensities of the unconscious, and who is incensed and bewildered by what Freud is doing when he closets sexuality in the Oedipal nursery—has a foreboding of this operation of displacement, and protests with all his might: no, Oedipus is not a state of desire and the drives, it is an *idea,* nothing but an idea that repression inspires in us concerning desire; not even a compromise, but an idea in the service of repression, its propaganda, or its propagation. "The incest motive is a logical deduction of the human reason, which has recourse to this last extremity, to save itself . . . which first and foremost is a logical deduction made by the human reason, even if unconsciously made, and secondly is introduced into the affective passional sphere, where it now proceeds to serve as a principle for action. . . .This has nothing to do with the active unconscious [which] sparkles, vibrates, travels . . . we realize that the unconscious contains nothing ideal, nothing in the least conceptual, and hence nothing in the least personal, since personality, like the ego, belongs to the conscious or mental-subjective self. So the first analyses are, or should be, so impersonal that the so-called *human* relations are not involved. The first relationship is neither personal nor biological—a fact which psychoanalysis has not succeeded in grasping."[54]

Oedipal desires are not at all repressed, nor do they have any reason to be. They are nevertheless in an intimate relationship with psychic repression, but in a different manner. Oedipal desires are the bait, the disfigured image by means of which repression catches desire in the trap. If desire is repressed, this is not because it is desire for the mother and for the death of the father; on the contrary, desire becomes that only because it is repressed, it takes on that mask only under the reign of the repression that models the mask for it and plasters it on its face. Besides, it is doubtful that incest was a real obstacle to the establishment of society, as the partisans of an *exchangist* conception claim. We have seen that there were other obstacles. The real danger is elsewhere. If desire is repressed, it is because every position of desire, no matter how small, is capable of calling into question the established order of a society: not that desire is asocial, on the contrary. But it is explosive; there is no desiring-machine capable of being assembled without demolishing entire social sectors. Despite what some revolutionaries think about this, desire is revolutionary in its essence—desire, not left-wing holidays!—and no society can tolerate a position of real desire without its structures of exploitation, servitude, and hierarchy being compromised.

If a society is identical with its structures—an amusing hypothesis—then yes, desire threatens its very being. It is therefore of vital importance for a society to repress desire, and even to find something more efficient than repression, so that repression, hierarchy, exploitation, and servitude are themselves desired. It is quite troublesome to have to say such rudimentary things: desire does not threaten a society because it is a desire to sleep with the mother, but because it is revolutionary. And that does not at all mean that desire is something other than sexuality, but that sexuality and love do not live in the bedroom of Oedipus, they dream instead of wide-open spaces, and cause strange flows to circulate that do not let themselves be stocked within an established order. Desire does not "want" revolution, it is revolutionary in its own right, as though involuntarily, by wanting what it wants. From the beginning of this study we have maintained both that social production and desiring-production are one and the same, and that they have differing régimes, with the result that a social form of production exercises an essential repression of desiring-production, and also that desiring-production—a "real" desire—is potentially capable of demolishing the social form. But what is a "real" desire, since repression is also desired? How can we tell them apart? We demand the right to a very deliberate analysis. For even in their contrary uses, let us make no mistake about it, *the same syntheses are at issue.*

It is clear what psychoanalysis expects to gain from claiming a link, where Oedipus would be the object of repression, and even its subject through the intermediary of the superego. From this it expects a cultural justification for psychic repression—a justification that makes psychic repression move into the foreground and no longer considers the problem of social repression as anything more than secondary from the point of view of the unconscious. That is why critics have been able to observe a conservative or reactionary turning point in Freud, from the moment that he gave an autonomous value to psychic repression as a condition of culture acting against the incestuous drives: Reich goes so far as to say that the crucial turning point of Freudianism, *the abandonment of sexuality,* comes when Freud accepts the idea of a primary anxiety that supposedly touches off psychic repression in an endogenous fashion. Consider the 1908 article on "civilized sexual morality": Oedipus is not yet named here; psychic repression is considered in terms of social repression, which gives rise to a *displacement* and acts on the partial drives insofar as they represent in their own fashion a sort of desiring-production, before being exercised against the incestuous or other drives threatening legitimate marriage. But it then becomes evident that, the more the problem of Oedipus and incest comes to occupy center stage, the more psychic repression and its correlates, suppression and sublimation, will be founded on supposedly transcendent requirements of civilization, at the same time that the psychoanalyst plunges deeper into a familialist and ideological vision.

We do not need to relate again the reactionary compromises of Freudianism, and even its "theoretical surrender": this work has been accomplished several times, in a profound way, rigorously, and with nuances.[55] We see no special problem in the possibility of a coexistence of revolutionary, reformist, and reactionary elements at the heart of the same theoretical and practical doctrine. We refuse to play "take it or leave it," under the pretext that theory justifies practice, being born from it, or that one cannot challenge the process of "cure" except by starting from elements drawn from this very cure. As if every great doctrine were not a *combined formation,* constructed from bits and pieces, various intermingled codes and flux, partial elements and derivatives, that constitute its very life or its becoming. As if we could reproach someone for having an ambiguous relationship with psychoanalysis, without first mentioning that psychoanalysis owes its existence to a relationship, theoretically and practically ambiguous, with what it discovers and the forces that it wields.

While the critical study of Freudian ideology has been done, and done well, on the other hand the history of the movement has never even been sketched out: the structure of the psychoanalytic group, its politics, its tendencies and its focal points, its self-applications, its suicides and its follies, the enormous group superego—everything that took place on the body of the master. What has come to be called the monumental work of Ernest Jones does not penetrate censorship, it codifies it. And the way the three elements coexisted: the exploratory, pioneering, revolutionary element, whereby desiring-production was discovered; the classical cultural element, which reduces everything to a scene from Oedipal theatrical representation (the return to myth!); and finally the third element, the most disturbing, a sort of racket thirsting after respectability, which will never have done with getting itself recognized and institutionalized—a formidable enterprise of absorption of surplus value, with its codification of the interminable cure, its cynical justification of the role of money, and all the pledges it makes to the established order. All these elements were present in Freud, a fantastic Christopher Columbus, a brilliant bourgeois reader of Goethe, Shakespeare, and Sophocles, a masked Al Capone.

The strength of Reich consists in having shown how psychic repression depended on social repression. Which in no way implies a confusion of the two concepts, since social repression needs psychic repression precisely in order to form docile subjects and to ensure the reproduction of the social formation, including its repressive structures. But social repression should not be understood by using as a starting point a familial repression coextensive with civilization—far from it; it is civilization that must be understood in terms of a social repression inherent to a given form of social production. Social repression bears on desire—and not solely on needs or interests—only by means of sexual repression. The family is indeed the delegated agent of this psychic repression, insofar as it ensures "a mass psychological reproduction of the economic system of a society." Of course it should not be concluded from this that desire is Oedipal. On the contrary, it is the social repression of desire or sexual repression—that is, the *stasis* of libidinal energy—that actualizes Oedipus and engages desire in this requisite impasse, organized by the repressive society.

Reich was the first to raise the problem of the relationship between desire and the social field (and went further than Marcuse, who treats the problem lightly). He is the true founder of a materialist psychiatry. Situating the problem in terms of desire, he is the first to reject the explanations of a summary Marxism too quick to say the masses were fooled, mystified. But since he had not sufficiently formulated the concept of desiring-production, he did not succeed in determining the insertion of desire into the economic infrastructure itself, the insertion of the drives into social production. Consequently, revolutionary investment seemed to him such that the desire moving within it simply coincided with an economic rationality; as to the reactionary mass investments, they seemed to him to derive from ideology, so that psychoanalysis merely had the role of explaining the subjective, the negative, and the inhibited, without participating directly as psychoanalysis in the positivity of the revolutionary movement or in the desiring-creativity. (To a certain extent, didn't this amount to a reintroduction of the error or the illusion?) The fact remains that Reich, in the name of desire, caused a song of life to pass into psychoanalysis. He denounced, in the final resignation of Freudianism, a fear of life, a resurgence of the ascetic ideal, a cultural broth of bad consciousness. Better to depart in search of the Orgone, he said to himself, in search of the vital and cosmic element of desire, than to continue being a psychoanalyst under those conditions. No one forgave him this, whereas Freud got full pardon. Reich was the first to attempt to make the analytic machine and the revolutionary machine function together. In the end, he only had his own desiring-machines, his paranoiac, miraculous, and celibate boxes, with metallic inner walls lined with cotton and wool.

Psychic repression distinguishes itself from social repression by the unconscious nature of the operation and by its result ("even the inhibition of revolt has become unconscious"), a distinction that expresses clearly the difference in nature between the two repressions. But a real independence cannot be concluded from this. Psychic repression is such that social repression becomes desired; it induces a consequent desire, a faked image of its object, on which it bestows the appearance of independence. Strictly speaking, psychic repression is a means in the service of social repression. What it bears on is also the object of social repression: desiring-production. But it in fact implies an original double operation: the repressive social formation delegates its power to an agent of psychic repression, and correlatively the repressed desire is as though masked by the faked displaced image to which the repression gives rise. Psychic repression is delegated by the social formation, while the desiring-formation is disfigured, displaced by psychic repression.

The family is the delegated agent of psychic repression, or rather the agent delegated to psychic repression; the incestuous drives are the disfigured image of the repressed. The Oedipus complex, the process of oedipalization, is therefore the result of this double operation. *It is in one and the same movement that the repressive social production is replaced by the repressing family, and that the latter offers a displaced image of desiring-production that represents the repressed as incestuous familial drives.* In this way the family/drives relationship is substituted for the relationship between the two orders of production, in a diversion where the whole of psychoanalysis goes astray. And the interest of such an operation, from the point of view of social production, becomes evident, for the latter could not otherwise ward off desire's potential for revolt and revolution. By placing the distorting mirror of incest before desire (that's what you wanted, isn't it?), desire is shamed, stupefied, it is placed in a situation without exit, it is easily persuaded to deny "itself" in the name of the more important interests of civilization (what if everyone did the same, what if everyone married his mother or kept his sister for himself? there would no longer be any differentiation, any exchanges possible). We must act quickly and soon. Incest, *a slandered shallow stream.*

Although we can see social production's interest in such an operation, it is less clear what makes this operation possible from the point of view of desiring-production itself. We do have, however, the elements of a response. Social production would need at its disposal, on the recording surface of the socius, an agent that is also capable of acting on, of inscribing the recording surface of desire. Such an agent exists: the family. It belongs essentially to the recording of social production, as a system of reproduction of the producers. And doubtless, at the other pole, the recording of desiring-production on the body without organs is brought about through a genealogical network *that is not familial:* parents only intervene here as partial objects, flows, signs, and agents of a process that outflanks them on all sides. At most, the child innocently "relates" to his parents some part of the astonishing productive experience he is undergoing with his desire; but this experience is not related to them as such. Yet this is precisely where the operation arises. Under the precocious action of social repression, the family slips into and interferes with the network of desiring-genealogy; it assumes the task of alienating the entire genealogy; it confiscates the Numen (but see here, God is daddy). The desiring-experience is treated as if it were intrinsically related to the parents, and as if the family were its supreme law. Partial objects are subjected to the notorious law of totality-unity acting as "lacking." The disjunctions are subjected to the alternative of the undifferentiated or exclusion.

The family is therefore introduced into the production of desire and will perform a displacement, an unparalleled repression of desire commencing with the earliest age of the child. Social production delegates the family to psychic repression. And if the family is able in this manner to slip into the recording of desire, it is because the body without organs on which this recording is accomplished already exercises on its own account, as we have seen, a *primal repression* of desiring-production. It falls to the family to profit from this, and to superimpose *the repression that is properly termed secondary,* this being a function delegated to the family or one to which the family is delegated. (Psychoanalysis has clearly demonstrated the difference between these two repressions, but has not shown the scope of this difference or the distinction between their respective régimes.) That is why psychic repression in the strict sense does not content itself with repressing real desiring-production, but offers a displaced apparent image of the repressed, by substituting a familial recording for the recording of desire. Desiring-production taken as a whole does not assume the well-known Oedipal figure except in the familial translation of its recording. Translation-betrayal.

At times we say that Oedipus is nothing, almost nothing (within the order of desiring-production, even in the child); at other times we say that it is everywhere (in the enterprise of domesticating the unconscious, of representing desire and the unconscious). To be sure, we have never dreamed of saying that psychoanalysis invented Oedipus. Everything points in the opposite direction: the subjects of psychoanalysis arrive already oedipalized, they demand it, they want more. News flash: Stravinsky declares before dying: "My misfortune, I am sure of it, came from my father's being so distant with me and from the small amount of affection shown me by my mother. So I decided that one day I would show them." If even artists give in to this, it would be a mistake to stand on ceremony and hold to the ordinary scruples of a diligent psychoanalyst. If a musician tells us that music does not attest to active and conquering forces, but to reactive forces, to reactions to daddy-mommy, we have only to play again on a paradox dear to Nietzsche, while barely modifying it: Freud-as-musician.

No, psychoanalysts invent nothing, though they have invented much in another way, and have legislated a lot, reinforced a lot, injected a lot. All that psychoanalysts do is to reinforce the movement; they add a last burst of energy to the displacement of the entire unconscious. What they do is merely to make the unconscious speak according to the transcendent uses of synthesis imposed on it by other forces: Global Persons, the Complete Object, the Great Phallus, the Terrible Undifferentiated of the Imaginary, Symbolic Differentiations, Segregation. What psychoanalysts invent is only the transference, a transference Oedipus, a consulting-room Oedipus of Oedipus, especially noxious and virulent, but where the subject finally has what he wants, and sucks away at his Oedipus on the full body of the analyst. And that's already too much. But Oedipus takes shape in the family, not in the analyst's office, which merely acts as the last territoriality. And Oedipus is not made by the family. The Oedipal uses of synthesis, oedipalization, triangulation, castration, all refer to forces a bit more powerful, a bit more subterranean than psychoanalysis, than the family, than ideology, even joined together. There we have all the forces of social production, reproduction, and repression. This can be explained by the simple truth that very powerful forces are required to defeat the forces of desire, lead them to resignation, and substitute everywhere reactions of the daddy-mommy type for what is essentially active, aggressive, artistic, productive, and triumphant in the unconscious itself. It is in this sense, as we have seen, that Oedipus is an application, and the family a delegated agent. Even by application it is hard, it is difficult for a child to live and experience himself as an angle,

> Cet enfant
> il n'est pas là,
> il n'est qu'un angle,
> un angle à venir,
> et il n'y a pas d'angle. . . .
> or ce monde du père-mère est justement ce qui doit s'en aller,
> c'est ce monde dédoublé-double,
> en état de désunion constante,
> en volonté d'unification constante aussi. . . .
> autour duquel tourne tout le système de ce monde
> malignement soutenu par la plus sombre organisation.*

8 | Neurosis and Psychosis

In 1924 Freud proposed a simple criterion for distinguishing between neurosis and psychosis: in neurosis the ego obeys the requirements of reality and stands ready to repress the drives of the id, whereas in psychosis the ego is under the sway of the id, ready to break with reality. Freud's ideas often took quite some time before making their way into France. Not this one, however; that same year Capgras and Carrette presented a case of schizophrenia with a delusion of doubles, where the patient manifested a strong hatred for her mother and an incestuous desire for her father, but under conditions of reality loss where the parents were lived as false parents or "doubles." From this they drew the illustration of the inverse relationship: in neurosis the object function of reality is preserved, but on condition that the causal

*Antonin Artaud, "Ainsi donc la question. . .," in *Tel Quel*, No. 30 (1967). "This child/he is not there,/he is but an angle,/an angle to come,/and there is no angle. . . . /and yet it is precisely this world of father-mother which must go away,/it is this world, split in two—doubled/in a state of constant disunion, also willing a constant unification. . . . /around which turns the entire system of this world/maliciously sustained by the most somber organization."

complex be repressed; in psychosis the complex invades consciousness and becomes its object, at the price of a "repression" that now bears on reality itself or the function of the real. Doubtless Freud was merely insisting on the schematic character of the distinction, for the rupture is also found in neurosis with the return of the repressed (hysterical amnesia, obsessional cancellation), while in psychosis a regaining of reality appears along with the delirious reconstruction. The fact remains that Freud never dropped this simple distinction.[56] And it seems important that, following an original path, Freud encounters again an idea dear to traditional psychiatry: that madness is fundamentally linked to a loss of reality. Thus there is a convergence with the psychiatric elaboration of the notions of dissociation and autism. Hence the reason, perhaps, for the rapid diffusion that the Freudian account enjoyed.

What interests us is the precise role of the Oedipus complex in this convergence. For if it is true that the familial themes often erupt into the psychotic consciousness, we would be all the more surprised—in line with a remark by Lacan—if Oedipus were in fact "discovered" in neurosis where it is supposed to be latent, rather than in psychosis where it is held to be patent.[57] But isn't it true instead that, in psychosis, the familial complex appears precisely as a stimulus whose quality is a matter of indifference, a simple inductor not playing the role of organizer, where the intensive investments of reality bear on something totally different (the social, historical, and cultural fields)? Oedipus simultaneously invades consciousness and dissolves into itself, testifying to its incapacity to be an "organizer."

Once this is admitted, it is enough to measure psychosis against this fake standard—enough to lead it to this false criterion, Oedipus—to obtain the loss-of-reality effect. This is not an abstract operation: an Oedipal "organization" is imposed on the psychotic, though for the sole purpose of assigning the *lack* of this organization in the psychotic, in his very body. It is an exercise in naked flesh, in the depths of the soul. The psychotic reacts with autism and the loss of reality. Could it be that the loss of reality is not the effect of the schizophrenic process, but the effect of its forced oedipalization, that is to say, its interruption? Must we correct what we were saying a little earlier, and suppose that some tolerate oedipalization less well than others? Thus the schizo would not be ill within the Oedipus complex, from an Oedipus arising all the more in his hallucinated consciousness as he lacked it in the symbolic organization of "his" unconscious. On the contrary, he is ill because of the oedipalization to which he is made to submit—the most somber organization—and which he can no longer tolerate: he who has gone on a distant journey. As though one were constantly bringing back home the person capable of setting whole continents and cultures adrift. He is not suffering from a divided self or a shattered Oedipus, but on the contrary, from having been brought back to everything he had left. A drop in intensity to the body without organs = 0, autism: the schizo has no other means of reacting to this blocking of all his investments of reality, the barriers placed before him by the Oedipal system of social and psychic repression. As Laing says, they are interrupted in their journey. They have lost reality But when did they lose it? During the journey, or during the interruption of the journey?

Hence another possible formulation of an inverse relationship: there would be something like two groups, the psychotics and neurotics, those who do not tolerate oedipalization, and those who tolerate it and are even content with it and evolve within it. Those on whom the Oedipal imprint does not take, and those on whom it does. "I believe my friends cast off in a group at the start of the New Age, with forces for a practical explosion that thrust them into a paternalistic deviation that I find depraved. . . . *A second group of loners,* of which I am a part, doubtless constituted by centers of collarbones, was deprived of any possibility of individual success at the moment they were engaged in laborious studies in innate science. With regard to them, my rebellion against *the paternalism of the first group* placed me from the second year in a socially difficult position that was growing more and more suffocating. So, *do you believe these two groups are capable of being joined?* I am not too angry with these bastards of virile paternalism, I am not vindictive. . . . In any case, if I have won, there will be no more struggles between the Father and the Son! . . . I am speaking of God's people, naturally, not of those close to Him who take themselves for his people."[58] It is the recording of desire on the increate body without organs, and the familial recording on the socius, that are in opposition throughout the two groups. The innate science in psychosis and the neurotic experimental sciences. The schizoid excentric circle and the neurosis triangle.

On a more general level, it is the two kinds of use made of synthesis that are in opposition. On the one hand there are the desiring-machines, and on the other the Oedipal-narcissistic machine. In order to understand the details of this struggle, it must be borne in mind that the family relentlessly operates on desiring-production. Inscribing itself into the recording process of desire, clutching at everything, the family performs a vast appropriation of the productive forces; it displaces and reorganizes in its own fashion the entirety of the connections and the hiatuses that characterize the machines of desire. It reorganizes them all along the lines of the universal castration that conditions the family itself ("a dead rat's ass," said Artaud, "suspended from the ceiling of the sky"), but it also redistributes these breaks in accordance with its own laws and the requirements of social production. The inscription performed by the family follows the pattern of its triangle, by distinguishing what belongs to the family from what does not. It also cuts inwardly, along the lines of differentiation that form global persons: there's daddy, there's mommy, there you are, and then there's your sister. Cut into the flow of milk here, it's your brother's turn, don't take a crap here, cut into the stream of shit over there. Retention is the primary function of the family: it is a matter of learning what elements of desiring-production the family is going to reject, what it is going to retain, what it is going to direct along the dead-end roads leading to its own undifferentiated (the miasma), and what on the contrary it is going to lead down the paths of a contagious and reproduceable differentiation. For the family creates at the same time its disgraces and its honors, the nondifferentiation of its neurosis and the differentiation of its ideal, which are distinguishable only in appearance.

While this is taking place, what is desiring-production doing? The retained elements do not enter into the new use of synthesis that imposes such a profound change on them without causing the whole triangle to reverberate. The desiring-machines are at the door, they make everything shake when they enter. Moreover, what does not enter causes perhaps even more vibrations to be felt. The desiring-machines reintroduce or attempt to reintroduce their deviant cuts and breaks. The child feels the task required of him. But what is to be put into the triangle, how are selections to be made? The father's nose or the mother's ear—will that do, can that be retained, will that constitute a good Oedipal incision? And the bicycle horn? What is part of the family? It is the triangle's job to vibrate, to resonate, under the pressure of what it retains as much as what it thrusts aside. Resonance—here again, either muffled or public, disgraceful or proud—is the family's second function. The family is at the same time an anus that retains, a voice that resounds, and a mouth that consumes: its very own three syntheses, since it is a matter of connecting desire to the ready-made objects of social production. Go buy madeleines in Combray if you really want to feel the vibrations.

We now come to the realization that the simple opposition between the two groups is inadequate, an opposition that would allow one to define neurosis as an intra-oedipal disorder, and psychosis as an extra-oedipal escape. It is not even enough to state that the two groups are "capable of being joined." Rather it is the possibility of discriminating directly between the two that creates the difficulty. How can we distinguish between the pressure that familial reproduction exercises on desiring-production, and the pressure that desiring-production exercises on familial reproduction? The Oedipal triangle vibrates and trembles, but is this in terms of the hold over the machines of desire that it constantly guarantees itself, or in terms of these machines that escape the Oedipal imprint and cause the triangle to release its grip? Where does the resonance of the triangle reach its limit? A familial romance expresses an effort to save the Oedipal genealogy, but it also expresses a free thrust of non-oedipal genealogy. Fantasies are never pregnant forms, but border or frontier phenomena ready to cross over to one side or the other. In short, *Oedipus is strictly undecidable.* It can be found everywhere all the more readily for being undecidable, and in this sense it is correct to say that Oedipus is strictly good for nothing.

Let us turn to the beautiful story of Gérard de Nerval: he wants Aurélie, his fondest love, to be the same as Adrienne, the little girl of his childhood; he "perceives" them as identical.[59] And Aurélie and Adrienne, both in one, are his mother. Will it be said that the identification as "a perceptual identity" is here a sign of psychosis? One then encounters the criterion of reality: the complex invades the psychotic consciousness only at the price of a rupture with the real, whereas in neurosis the identity remains that of unconscious representations and does not compromise perception. But what is there to gain from inscribing everything in Oedipus, even psychosis? One step further and Aurélie, Adrienne, *and* the mother are the Virgin. Nerval seeks the point where the vibration of the triangle is at its limit. "You are simply seeking for drama," says Aurélie. Everything is not inscribed in Oedipus without everything at its extreme fleeing beyond the reach of Oedipus. These identifications were not identifications with persons from the viewpoint of perception, but identifications of names with regions of intensity that provide the impetus toward other still more intense regions, stimuli of one sort or another that set in motion another journey altogether, stases that prepare for other breakthroughs, other movements where the mother is no longer encountered, but the Virgin and God: "*And twice I have crossed and conquered the Acheron.*"[60] Thus the schizo will accept the reduction of everything to the mother, since it is of no importance whatsoever: he is sure of being able to make everything rise again from the mother, and to keep for his own secret use all the Virgins that had been placed there.

Everything can be converted into neurosis, or warped out of shape into psychosis: it is therefore not in this fashion that the question must be posed. It would be inaccurate to maintain an Oedipal interpretation for the neuroses, and to reserve an extra-oedipal explanation for the psychoses. There are not two groups, there is no difference in nature between neuroses and psychoses. *For in any case desiring-production is the cause,* the ultimate cause of both the psychotic subversions that shatter Oedipus or overwhelm it, and of the neurotic reverberations that constitute it. Such a principle takes on its full meaning if it is related to the problem of "actual factors." One of the most important points of psychoanalysis was the evaluation of the role of these actual factors, even in neurosis, insofar as they are distinguishable from the familial infantile factors; all the major dissensions were linked to this evaluation. The difficulties bore on several aspects. First, the nature of these factors: were they somatic, social, metaphysical? Were they the famous "problems of living," through which a very pure desexualized idealism was reintroduced into psychoanalysis? In the second place, the modality of these factors: did they act in a negative, privative fashion, by mere frustration? Finally, their moment, their own time: was it not self-evident that the actual factor arose *afterward,* and signified "recent," in opposition to the infantile or the oldest factor that could be sufficiently explained by the familial complex? Even a writer like Reich—so careful to situate desire in relation to the forms of social production, demonstrating thereby that there is no psychoneurosis that is not also an actual neurosis—continues to present the actual factors as acting by means of a repressive deprivation (the "sexual stasis") and as arising afterward. Which leads him to maintain a kind of diffuse oedipalism, since the stasis or the actual privative factor only defines the energy of the neurosis, but not the content that for its own part refers to the infantile Oedipal conflict, this old conflict becoming reactivated by the actual stasis.*

But the oedipalists are not saying anything different from this when they remark that an actual deprivation or frustration cannot be experienced except in the midst of an older internal qualitative conflict, which blocks not merely the roads prohibited by reality, but also those that reality leaves open and that the ego forbids itself in its turn (the double-impasse formula): "Could one find examples [illustrating the diagram of actual neuroses] in the prisoner or the concentration-camp victim or the worker harassed by work? It is not certain that they would furnish a large quota. . . . Our systematic tendency is not to accept the evident iniquities of reality without taking stock of them, without trying to disclose in what sense the disorder of the world is manifested in the subjective disorder, even if it is, *with the passing of time,* inscribed

*Reich, *The Function of the Orgasm,* p. 112: "All neurotic fantasies can be traced back to the child's early sexual relationship to the parents. However, if it were not continually nourished by the contemporary stasis of excitation which it initially produced, the child-parent conflict could not by itself cause a permanent disturbance of the psychic equilibrium."

within more or less irreversible structures."[61] We understand this sentence, but can't help finding its tone disturbing. The following choice is imposed on us: either the actual factor is conceived in a totally exterior privative fashion (which is an impossibility), or it descends into an internal qualitative conflict that is necessarily understood in relation to Oedipus. (Oedipus, the fountainhead where the psychoanalyst washes his hands of the world's iniquities.)

In an altogether different direction, if we consider the idealist deviations of psychoanalysis, we see in them an interesting attempt at giving the actual factors a status other than ulterior or privative. This came about as two concerns were found to be linked in an apparent paradox, for example in Jung: the concern for curtailing the interminable cure by addressing oneself to the present or actual state of the disorder, and the concern for going further than Oedipus, even further than the pre-oedipal, for going much further back—as if what was most actual was also the most primary, the shortest, the furthest removed.* Jung presents his archetypes as actual factors that extend in fact beyond the familial images in the transference, as well as being archaic factors infinitely older and from an order of time which is not that of the infantile factors themselves. But nothing has been gained thereby, since the actual factor ceases to be privative only provided it enjoys the rights of the Ideal, and does not cease to be an afterward except by becoming a beyond, which must be signified anagogically by Oedipus instead of depending on it analytically. This necessarily results in the reintroduction of the afterward in the temporal difference, as the astonishing distribution proposed by Jung attests: for the young, whose problems concern the family and love, Freud's method! For those less young, whose problems have to do with social adaptation, Adler! And Jung for the adults and the old people, whose problems have to do with the Ideal.[62] And we have seen what remains common to Freud and Jung: the unconscious always measured against myths (and not against the units of production), although the measuring is done in two contrary directions. But what does it matter, after all, if morality or religion find an analytical and regressive meaning in Oedipus, or if Oedipus finds an anagogical and prospective meaning in morality or religion?

We maintain that the cause of the disorder, neurosis or psychosis, is always in desiring-production, in its relation to social production, in their

---

*The same remark applies to Otto Rank: the birth trauma not only implies going further back than Oedipus, and the pre-oedipal phase, but should also be a means for shortening the cure. Freud notes with bitterness in the beginning of "Analysis Terminable and Interminable": "Rank hoped that if this primal trauma were dealt with by a subsequent analysis the whole neurosis would be got rid of. Thus this one small piece of analytic work would save the necessity for all the rest."

different or conflicting régimes, and the modes of investment that desiring-production performs in the system of social production. *The actual factor is desiring-production* insofar as it is caught up in this relationship, this conflict, and these modalities. Nor is this factor either ulterior or privative. Being constitutive of the full life of desire, it is contemporary with the most tender age, and it accompanies this life with every step. It does not arise after Oedipus, it in no way presupposes an Oedipal organization, nor a pre-oedipal preorganization. On the contrary, *it is Oedipus that depends on desiring-production, either as a stimulus of one form or another, a simple inductor through which the anoedipal organization of desiring-production is formed, beginning with early childhood, or as an effect of the psychic and social repression imposed on desiring-production by social reproduction by means of the family.* The term "actual" is not used because it designates what is most recent, and because it would be opposed to "former" or "infantile"; it is used in terms of its difference with respect to "virtual." *And it is the Oedipus complex that is virtual, either inasmuch as it must be actualized in a neurotic formation as a derived effect of the actual factor, or inasmuch as it is dismembered and dissolved in a psychotic formation as the direct effect of this same factor.* It is indeed in this sense that the idea of the afterward seemed to us to be a final paralogism in psychoanalytic theory and practice; active desiring-production, in its very process, invests from the beginning a constellation of somatic, social, and metaphysical relations that do not follow after Oedipal psychological relations, but that on the contrary will *be applied* to the underlying Oedipal constellation defined by reaction, or else will exclude this constellation from the field of investment constituting their activity. *Undecidable, virtual, reactive or reactional (réactionnel),* such is Oedipus. It is only a reactional formation, a formation that results from a reaction to desiring-production. It is a serious mistake to consider this formation in isolation, abstractly, independently of the actual factor that coexists with it and to which it reacts.

Yet this is what psychoanalysis does when it closets itself in Oedipus, and determines its progressions and regressions in terms of Oedipus, or even in relationship to it: thus the idea of pre-oedipal regression, by means of which one sometimes attempts to characterize psychosis. It is like a Cartesian devil;* the regressions and progressions are made only within the artificially closed vessel of Oedipus, and in

*A Cartesian devil, or bottle imp, is a small hollow glass figure used in physics. Immersed in a closed vessel of water, it can be made to rise or sink by varying the pressure, and hence the amount of water in the figure. (*Translators' note.*)

reality depend on a state of forces that is changing, yet always actual and contemporary, within *anoedipal* desiring-production. Desiring-production has solely an actual existence; progressions and regressions are merely the effectuations of a virtuality that is always fulfilled as perfectly as it can be by virtue of the states of desire. Rarely have psychiatrists and psychoanalysts been able to establish a really inspired direct relationship with either child or adult schizophrenics; Gisela Pankow and Bruno Bettelheim break new ground in this area by the force of their theory and the efficacy of their therapy. It is not by chance that both of them call into question the notion of regression. Taking the example of the bodily cares administered to a schizophrenic—massages, baths, swathings—Gisela Pankow asks if it is a matter of reaching the invalid at the point of his regression, in order to give him indirect symbolic satisfactions that would allow him to resume a progression, to take up a progressive pace. It is not at all a question, she says, "of administering care that the schizophrenic presumably did not receive when he was a baby. It is a question of giving the patient tactile and other bodily sensations that lead him to a recognition of the limits of his body. . . . It is a question of the *recognition* of an unconscious desire, and not of this desire's satisfaction."[63] Recognizing the desire is tantamount to setting desiring-production back into motion on the body without organs, in the very place to which the schizo had retreated in order to silence and suffocate this production. This recognition of desire, this position of desire, this *Sign* refers to an order of real and actual productivity that is not to be confused with an indirect or symbolic satisfaction, and that, in its stops as in its starts, is as distinct from a pre-oedipal regression as from a progressive restoration of Oedipus.

9 | The Process

Between neurosis and psychosis there is no difference in nature, species, or group. Neurosis can no more be explained oedipally than can psychosis. It is rather the contrary; neurosis explains Oedipus. Then how do we conceive of the relationship between psychosis and neurosis? Everything changes depending on whether we call psychosis the process itself, or on the contrary, an interruption of the process (and what type of interruption?). Schizophrenia as a process is desiring-production, but it is this production as it functions at the end, as the limit of social production determined by the conditions of capitalism. It is our very own "malady," modern man's sickness. The end of history has no other meaning. In it the two meanings of process meet, as the movement of social production that goes to the very extremes of its deterritorialization, and as the movement of metaphysical production that carries desire along with it and reproduces it in a new Earth. "The desert grows . . . the sign is near." The schizo carries along the decoded flows, makes them traverse the desert of the body without organs, where he installs his desiring-machines and produces a perpetual outflow of acting forces. He has crossed over the limit, the schiz, which maintained the production of desire always at the margins of social production, tangential and always repelled.

The schizo knows how to leave: he has made departure into something as simple as being born or dying. But at the same time his journey is strangely stationary, in place. He does not speak of another world, he is not from another world: even when he is displacing himself in space, his is a journey in intensity, around the desiring-machine that is erected here and remains here. For here is the desert propagated by our world, and also the new earth, and the machine that hums, around which the schizos revolve, planets for a new sun. These men of desire—or do they not yet exist?—are like Zarathustra. They know incredible sufferings, vertigos, and sicknesses. They have their specters. They must reinvent each gesture. But such a man produces himself as a free man, irresponsible, solitary, and joyous, finally able to say and do something simple in his own name, without asking permission; a desire lacking nothing, a flux that overcomes barriers and codes, a name that no longer designates any ego whatever. He has simply ceased being afraid of becoming mad. He experiences and lives himself as the sublime sickness that will no longer affect him. Here, what is, what would a psychiatrist be worth?

In the whole of psychiatry only Jaspers, then Laing have grasped what process signified, and its fulfillment—and so escaped the familialism that is the ordinary bed and board of psychoanalysis and psychiatry. "If the human race survives, future men will, I suspect, look back on our enlightened epoch as a veritable age of Darkness. They will presumably be able to savor the irony of this situation with more amusement than we can extract from it. The laugh's on us. They will see that what we call 'schizophrenia' was one of the forms in which, often through quite ordinary people, the light began to break through the cracks in our all-too-closed minds. . . . Madness need not be all breakdown. It may also be breakthrough. . . . The person going through ego-loss or transcendental experiences may or may not become in different ways confused. Then he might legitimately be regarded as mad. But to be mad is not necessarily to be ill, notwithstanding that in our culture the two categories have become confused. . . . From the alienated starting point of our pseudo-sanity, everything is equivocal. Our sanity is not 'true' sanity. Their madness is not 'true' madness. The madness of our patients is an artifact of the destruction wreaked on them by us and by them on themselves. Let no one suppose that we meet 'true' madness any more than that we are truly sane. The madness that we encounter in 'patients' is a gross travesty, a mockery, a grotesque caricature of what the natural healing of that estranged integration we call sanity might be. True sanity entails in one way or another the dissolution of the normal ego."*

The visit to London is our visit to Pythia. Turner is there. Looking at his paintings, one understands what it means to scale the wall, and yet to remain behind; to cause flows to pass through, without knowing any longer whether they are carrying us elsewhere or flowing back over us already. The paintings range over three periods. If the psychiatrist were allowed to speak here, he could talk about the first two, although they are in fact the most reasonable. The first canvases are of end-of-the-world catastrophes, avalanches, and storms. That's where Turner begins. The paintings of the second period are somewhat like the delirious reconstruction, where the delirium hides, or rather where it is on a par with a lofty technique inherited from Poussin, Lorrain, or the Dutch tradition: the world is reconstructed through archaisms having a modern function. But something incomparable happens at the level of the paintings of the third period, in the series Turner does not exhibit, but keeps secret. It cannot even be said that he is far ahead of his time: there is here something ageless, and that comes to us from an eternal future, or flees toward it. The canvas turns in on itself, it is pierced by a hole, a lake, a flame, a tornado, an explosion. The themes of the preceding paintings are to be found again here, their meaning changed. The canvas is truly broken, sundered by what penetrates it. All that remains is a background of gold and fog, intense, intensive, traversed in depth by what has just sundered its breadth: the schiz. Everything becomes mixed and confused, and it is here that the breakthrough—not the breakdown—occurs.

Strange Anglo-American literature: from Thomas Hardy, from D. H. Lawrence to Malcolm Lowry, from Henry Miller to Allen Ginsberg and Jack Kerouac, men who know how to leave, to scramble the codes,

---

*Laing, *The Politics of Experience*, pp. 129, 133, 138, 144. In a closely connected sense Michel Foucault announced: "Perhaps one day one will no longer know clearly what madness really was. . . . Artaud will belong to the ground of our language, and not to its rupture. . . . Everything that we experience today in the mode of the limit, or of strangeness, or of the unbearable, will have joined again with the serenity of the positive. And what for us currently designates this Exterior stands a chance, one day of designating us. . . . Madness is breaking its kinship ties with mental illness, . . . madness and mental illness are ceasing to belong to the same anthropological entity" ("La folie, l'absence d'oeuvre," *La Table ronde*, May 1964).

to cause flows to circulate, to traverse the desert of the body without organs. They overcome a limit, they shatter a wall, the capitalist barrier. And of course they fail to complete the process, they never cease failing to do so. The neurotic impasse again closes—the daddy-mommy of oedipalization, America, the return to the native land—or else the perversion of the exotic territorialities, then drugs, alcohol—or worse still, an old fascist dream. Never has delirium oscillated more between its two poles. But through the impasses and the triangles a schizophrenic flow moves, irresistibly; sperm, river, drainage, inflamed genital mucus, or a stream of words that do not let themselves be coded, a libido that is too fluid, too viscous: a violence against syntax, a concerted destruction of the signifier, non-sense erected as a flow, polyvocity that returns to haunt all relations. How poorly the problem of literature is put, starting from the ideology that it bears, or from the co-option of it by a social order. People are co-opted, not works, which will always come to awake a sleeping youth, and which never cease extending their flame. As for ideology, it is the most confused notion because it keeps us from seizing the relationship of the literary machine with a field of production, and the moment when the emitted sign breaks through this "form of the content" that was attempting to maintain the sign within the order of the signifier. Yet it has been a long time since Engels demonstrated, already apropos of Balzac, how an author is great because he cannot prevent himself from tracing flows and causing them to circulate, flows that split asunder the catholic and despotic signifier of his work, and that necessarily nourish a revolutionary machine on the horizon. That is what style is, or rather the absence of style—asyntactic, agrammatical: the moment when language is no longer defined by what it says, even less by what makes it a signifying thing, but by what causes it to move, to flow, and to explode—desire. For literature is like schizophrenia: a process and not a goal, a production and not an expression.

Here again, oedipalization is one of the most important factors in the reduction of literature to an object of consumption conforming to the established order, and incapable of causing anyone harm. It is not a question here of the personal oedipalization of the author and his readers, but of the *Oedipal form* to which one attempts to enslave the work itself, to make of it this minor expressive activity that secretes ideology according to the dominant codes. The work of art is supposed to inscribe itself in this fashion between the two poles of Oedipus, problem and solution, neurosis and sublimation, desire and truth—the one regressive, where the work hashes out and redistributes the nonresolved conflicts of childhood, and the other prospective, by which the work invents the paths leading toward a new solution concerning the future of man. It is said that the work is constituted by a conversion interior to itself as "cultural object." From this point of view, there is no longer even any need for applying psychoanalysis to the work of art, since the work itself constitutes a successful psychoanalysis, a sublime "transference" with exemplary collective virtualities. The hypocritical warning resounds: a little neurosis is good for the work of art, good material, but not psychosis, especially not psychosis; we draw a line between the eventually creative neurotic aspect, and the psychotic aspect, alienating and destructive. As if the great voices, which were capable of performing a breakthrough in grammar and syntax, and of making all language a desire, were not speaking from the depths of psychosis, and as if they were not demonstrating for our benefit an eminently psychotic and revolutionary means of escape.

It is correct to measure established literature against an Oedipal psychoanalysis, for this literature deploys a form of superego proper to it, even more noxious than the nonwritten superego. Oedipus is in fact literary before being psychoanalytic. There will always be a Breton against Artaud, a Goethe against Lenz, a Schiller against Hölderlin, in order to superegoize literature and tell us: Careful, go no further! No "errors for lack of tact"! Werther yes, Lenz no! The Oedipal form of literature is its commodity form. We are free to think that there is finally even less dishonesty in psychoanalysis than in the established literature, since the neurotic pure and simple produces a solitary work, irresponsible, illegible, and nonmarketable, which on the contrary must pay not only to be read, but to be translated and reduced. He makes at least an economic error, an error in tact, and does not spread his values. Artaud puts it well: all writing is so much pig shit—that is to say, any literature that takes itself as an end or sets ends for itself, instead of being a process that "ploughs the crap of being and its language," transports the weak, the aphasiacs, the illiterate. At least spare us sublimation. Every writer is a sellout. The only literature is that which places an explosive device in its package, fabricating a counterfeit currency, causing the superego and its form of expression to explode, as well as the market value of its form of content.

But some reply: Artaud does not belong to the realm of literature, he is outside it because he is schizophrenic. Others retort: he is not schizophrenic, since he belongs to literature, and the most important literature at that, the textual. Both groups hold at least one thing in common; they subscribe to the same puerile and reactionary conception of schizophrenia, and the same marketable neurotic conception of literature. A shrewd critic writes: one need understand nothing of the concept of the signifier "in order to declare absolutely that Artaud's language is that of a schizophrenic; the psychotic produces an involuntary discourse, fettered, subjugated: *therefore* in all respects the contrary of textual writing." But what is this enormous textual archaism, the signifier, that subjects literature to the mark of castration and sanctifies the two aspects of its Oedipal form? And who told this shrewd critic that the discourse of the psychotic was "involuntary, fettered, subjugated"? Not that it is more nearly the opposite, thank God. But these very oppositions are singularly lacking in relevance. *Artaud makes a shambles of psychiatry, precisely because he is schizophrenic and not because he is not.* Artaud is the fulfillment of literature, precisely because he is schizophrenic and not because he is not. It has been a long time since he broke down the wall of the signifier: Artaud the Schizo. From the depths of his suffering and his glory, he has the right to denounce what society makes of the psychotic in the process of decoding the flows of desire (*Van Gogh, the Man Suicided by Society*), but also what it makes of literature when it opposes literature to psychosis in the name of a neurotic or perverse recoding (Lewis Carroll, or the coward of belles-lettres).

Very few accomplish what Laing calls the breakthrough of this schizophrenic wall or limit: "quite ordinary people," nevertheless. But the majority draw near the wall and back away horrified. Better to fall back under the law of the signifier, marked by castration, triangulated in Oedipus. So they displace the limit, they make it pass into the interior of the social formation, between the social production and reproduction that they invest, and the familial reproduction that they fall back on, to which they apply all the investments. They make the limit pass into the interior of the domain thus described by Oedipus, between the two poles of Oedipus. They never stop involuting and evolving between these two poles. Oedipus as the last rock, and castration as the cavern: the ultimate territoriality, although reduced to the analyst's couch, rather than the decoded flows of desire that flee, slip away, and take us where? Such is neurosis, the displacement of the limit, in order to create a little colonial world of one's own. But others want virgin lands, more truly exotic, families more artificial, societies more secret that they design and institute along the length of the wall, in the locales of perversion. Still others, sickened by the utensility (*l'ustensilité*) of Oedipus, but also by the shoddiness and aestheticism of perversions, reach the wall and rebound against it, sometimes with an extreme violence. Then they become immobile, silent, they retreat to the body without organs, still a territoriality, but this time totally desert-like, where all desiring-production is arrested, or where it becomes rigid, feigning stoppage: psychosis.

These catatonic bodies have fallen into the river like lead weights, immense transfixed hippopotamuses who will not come back up to the surface. They have entrusted all their forces to primal repression, in order to escape the system of social and psychic repression that fabricates neurotics. But a more naked repression befalls them that declares them identical with the hospital schizo, the great autistic one, the clinical entity that "lacks" Oedipus. Why the same word, schizo, to designate both the process insofar as it goes beyond the limit, and the result of the process insofar as it runs up against the limit and pounds endlessly away there? Why the same word to designate both the eventual breakthrough and the possible breakdown, and all the transitions, the intrications of the two extremes? In point of fact, of the three preceding adventures, the adventure of psychosis is the most intimately related to the process: in the sense of Jaspers' demonstration, when he shows that the "demonic"—ordinarily repressed—erupts by means of such a state, or gives rise to such states, which endlessly run the risk of making it topple into breakdown and disintegration.

We no longer know if it is the process that must truly be called madness, the sickness being only disguise or caricature, or if the sickness is our only madness and the process our only cure. But in any case, the intimate nature of the relationship appears directly in inverse ratio: the more the process of production is led off course, brutally interrupted, the more the schizo-as-entity arises as a specific product. That is why, on the other hand, we were unable to establish any direct relationship between neurosis and psychosis. The relationships of neurosis, psychosis, and also perversion depend on the situation of each one with regard to the process, and on the manner in which each one represents a mode of interruption of the process, a residual bit of ground to which one still clings so as not to be carried off by the deterritorialized flows of desire. Neurotic territoriality of Oedipus, perverse territorialities of the artifice, psychotic territoriality of the body without organs: sometimes the process is caught in the trap and made to turn about within the triangle, sometimes it takes itself as an end-in-itself, other times it continues on in the void and substitutes a horrible exasperation for its fulfillment. Each of these forms has schizophrenia as a foundation; schizophrenia as a process is the only universal. Schizophrenia is at once the wall, the breaking through this wall, and the failures of this breakthrough: "How does one get through this wall, for it is useless to hit it hard, it has to be undermined and penetrated with a file, slowly and with patience, as I see it".[64] What is at stake is not merely art or literature. For either the artistic machine, the analytical machine, and the revolutionary machine will remain in extrinsic relationships that make them function in the deadening framework of the system of social and psychic repression, or they will become parts and cogs of one another in the flow that feeds one and the same desiring-machine, so many local fires patiently kindled for a generalized explosion—the schiz and not the signifier.

SAVAGES, BARBARIANS, CIVILIZED MEN

3

Translated by Robert Hurley and Mark Seem

1 | The Inscribing Socius

If the universal comes at the end—the body without organs and desiring-production—under the conditions determined by an apparently victorious capitalism, where do we find enough innocence for generating universal history? Desiring-production also exists from the beginning: there is desiring-production from the moment there is social production and reproduction. But in a very precise sense it is true that precapitalist social machines are inherent in desire: they code it, they code the flows of desire. To code desire—and the fear, the anguish of decoded flows—is the business of the socius. As we shall see, capitalism is the only social machine that is constructed on the basis of decoded flows, substituting for intrinsic codes an axiomatic of abstract quantities in the form of money. Capitalism therefore liberates the flows of desire, but under the social conditions that define its limit and the possibility of its own dissolution, so that it is constantly opposing with all its exasperated strength the movement that drives it toward this limit. At capitalism's limit the deterritorialized socius gives way to the body without organs, and the decoded flows throw themselves into desiring-production. Hence it is correct to retrospectively understand all history in the light of capitalism, provided that the rules formulated by Marx are followed exactly.

First of all, universal history is the history of contingencies, and not the history of necessity. Ruptures and limits, and not continuity. For great accidents were necessary, and amazing encounters that could have happened elsewhere, or before, or might never have happened, in order for the flows to escape coding and, escaping, to nonetheless fashion a new machine bearing the determinations of the capitalist socius. Thus the encounter between private property and commodity production, which presents itself, however, as two quite distinct forms of decoding, by privatization and by abstraction. Or, from the viewpoint of private property itself, the encounter between flows of convertible wealth owned by capitalists and a flow of workers possessing nothing more than their labor capacity* (here again, two distinct forms of deterritorialization). In a sense, capitalism has haunted all forms of society, but it haunts them as their terrifying nightmare, it is the dread they feel of a flow that would elude their codes. Then again, if we say that capitalism determines the conditions and the possibility of a universal history, this is true only insofar as capitalism has to deal essentially with its own limit, its own destruction—as Marx says, insofar as it is capable of self-criticism (at least to a certain point: the point where the limit appears, in the very movement that counteracts the tendency).* In a word, universal history is not only retrospective, it is also contingent, singular, ironic, and critical.

The earth is the primitive, savage unity of desire and production. For the earth is not merely the multiple and divided object of labor, it is also the unique, indivisible entity, the full body that falls back on the forces of production and appropriates them for its own as the natural or divine precondition. While the ground can be the productive element

---

*force de travail. Here we have followed Martin Nicolaus's translation of Marx's Grundrisse in translating this Marxian term as "labor capacity" instead of "labor power." (Translators' note.)

*Marx, Grundrisse (see reference note 63), pp. 104–108. Maurice Godelier comments: "The West's line of development, far from being universal because it will recur everywhere, appears universal because it recurs nowhere else. . . . It is typical therefore because, in its singular progress, it has obtained a universal result. It has furnished a practical base (industrial economy) and a theoretical conception (socialism) that permit it to leave behind, and to cause all other societies to leave behind, the most ancient and the most recent forms of exploitation of man by man. . . . The authentic universality of the West's line of development lies therefore in its singularity, in its difference, not in its resemblance to the other lines of evolution." (Godelier [see reference note 47], pp. 92–96.)

and the result of appropriation, the Earth is the great unengendered stasis, the element superior to production that conditions the common appropriation and utilization of the ground. It is the surface on which the whole process of production is inscribed, on which the forces and means of labor are recorded, and the agents and the products distributed. It appears here as the quasi cause of production and the object of desire (it is on the earth that desire becomes bound to its own repression). The *territorial machine* is therefore the first form of socius, the machine of primitive inscription, the "megamachine" that covers a social field. It is not to be confused with technical machines. In its simplest, so-called manual forms, the technical machine already implies an acting, a transmitting, or even a driving element that is nonhuman, and that extends man's strength and allows for a certain disengagement from it. The social machine, in contrast, has men for its parts, even if we view them *with* their machines, and integrate them, internalize them in an institutional model at every stage of action, transmission, and motricity. Hence the social machine fashions a memory without which there would be no synergy of man and his (technical) machines. The latter do not in fact contain the conditions for the reproduction of their process; they point to the social machines that condition and organize them, but also limit and inhibit their development. It will be necessary to await capitalism to find a semiautonomous organization of technical production that tends to appropriate memory and reproduction, and thereby modifies the forms of the exploitation of man; but as a matter of fact, this organization presupposes a dismantling of the great social machines that preceded it.

The same machine can be both technical and social, but only when viewed from different perspectives: for example, the clock as a technical machine for measuring uniform time, and as a social machine for reproducing canonic hours and for assuring order in the city. When Lewis Mumford coins the word "megamachine" to designate the social machine as a collective entity, he is literally correct (although he limits its application to the barbarian despotic institution): "If, more or less in agreement with Reuleaux's classic definition, one can consider the machine to be the combination of solid elements, each having its specialized function and operating under human control in order to transmit a movement and perform a task, then the human machine was indeed a true machine."[1] The social machine is literally a machine, irrespective of any metaphor, inasmuch as it exhibits an immobile motor and undertakes a variety of interventions: flows are set apart, elements are detached from a chain, and portions of the tasks to be performed are distributed. Coding the flows implies all these operations. This is the social machine's supreme task, inasmuch as the apportioning of production corresponds to extractions from the chain, resulting in a residual share for each member, in a global system of desire and destiny that organizes the productions of production, the productions of recording, and the productions of consumption. Flows of women and children, flows of herds and of seed, sperm flows, flows of shit, menstrual flows: nothing must escape coding. The primitive territorial machine, with its immobile motor, the earth, is already a social machine, a megamachine, that codes the flows of production, the flows of means of production, of producers and consumers: the full body of the goddess Earth gathers to itself the cultivable species, the agricultural implements, and the human organs.

Meyer Fortes makes a passing remark that is joyous and refreshingly sound: "The circulation of women is not the problem. . . . A woman circulates of herself. She is not at one's disposal, but the juridical rights governing progeniture are determined for the profit of a specific person."[2] We see no reason in fact for accepting the postulate that underlies exchangist notions of society; society is not first of all a milieu for exchange where the essential would be to circulate or to cause to circulate, but rather a socius of inscription where the essential thing is to mark and to be marked. There is circulation only if inscription requires or permits it. The method of the primitive territorial machine is in this sense the collective investment of the organs; for flows are coded only to the extent that the organs capable respectively of producing and breaking them are themselves encircled, instituted as partial objects, distributed on the socius and attached to it. A mask is such an institution of organs. Initiation societies compose the pieces of a body, which are at the same time sensory organs, anatomical parts, and joints. Prohibitions (see not, speak not) apply to those who, in a given state or on a given occasion, are deprived of the right to enjoy a collectively invested organ. The mythologies sing of organs–partial objects and their relations with a full body that repels or attracts them: vaginas riveted on the woman's body, an immense penis shared by the men, an independent anus that assigns itself a body without anus. A Gourma story begins: "When the mouth was dead, the other parts of the body were consulted to see which of them would take charge of the burial. . . ." The unities in question are never found in persons, but rather in *series* which determine the connections, disjunctions, and conjunctions of organs. That is why fantasies are group fantasies. It is the collective investment of the organs that plugs desire into the socius and assembles social production and desiring-production into a whole on the earth.

Our modern societies have instead undertaken a vast privatization of the organs, which corresponds to the decoding of flows that have become abstract. The first organ to suffer privatization, removal from the social field, was the anus. It was the anus that offered itself as a model for privatization, at the same time as money came to express the flows' new state of abstraction. Hence the relative truth of psychoanalytic remarks concerning the anal nature of monetary economy. But the "logical" order is the following: the substitution of abstract quantity for the coded flows; the resulting collective disinvestment of the organs, on the model of the anus; the constitution of private persons as individual centers of organs and functions derived from the abstract quantity. One is even compelled to say that, while in our societies the penis has occupied the position of a detached object distributing lack to the persons of both sexes and organizing the Oedipal triangle, it is the anus that in this manner detaches it, it is the anus that removes and sublimates the penis in a kind of *Aufhebung* that will constitute the phallus. Sublimation is profoundly linked to anality, but this is not to say that the latter furnishes a material to be sublimated, for want of another use. Anality does not represent a lower requiring conversion to a higher. It is the anus itself that ascends on high, under the conditions (which we must analyze) of its removal from the field, conditions that do not presuppose sublimation, since on the contrary sublimation results from them. It is not the anal that presents itself for sublimation, it is sublimation in its entirety that is anal; moreover, the simplest critique of sublimation is the fact that it does not by any means rescue us from the shit (only the mind is capable of shitting). Anality is all the greater once the anus is disinvested. The libido is indeed the essence of desire; but when the libido becomes abstract quantity, the elevated and disinvested anus produces the global persons and the specific egos that serve this same quantity as units of measure. Artaud expresses it well: this "dead rat's ass suspended from the ceiling of the sky," whence issues the daddy-mommy-me triangle, "the uterine mother-father of a frantic anality," whose child is only an angle, this "kind of covering eternally hanging on something that is the self."

The whole of Oedipus is anal and implies an individual overinvestment of the organ to compensate for its collective disinvestment. That is why the commentators most favorable to the universality of Oedipus recognize nonetheless that one does not encounter in primitive societies any of the mechanisms or any of the attitudes that make it a reality in our society. No superego, no guilt. No identification of a specific ego with global persons—but group identifications that are always partial, following the compact, agglutinated series of ancestors, and the fragmented series of companions and cousins. No anality—although, or rather because, there is a collectively invested anus. What remains then for the making of Oedipus?* The structure—that is to say, an unrealized potentiality? Are we to believe that a universal Oedipus haunts all societies, but exactly as capitalism haunts them, *that is to say,* as the nightmare and the anxious foreboding of what might result from the decoding of flows and the collective disinvestment of organs, the becoming-abstract of the flows of desire, and the becoming-private of the organs?

The primitive territorial machine codes flows, invests organs, and marks bodies. To such a degree that circulating—exchanging—is a secondary activity in comparison with the task that sums up all the others: marking bodies, which are the earth's products. The essence of the recording, inscribing socius, insofar as it lays claim to the productive forces and distributes the agents of production, resides in these operations: tattooing, excising, incising, carving, scarifying, mutilating, encircling, and initiating. Nietzsche thus defined the *"morality of mores* (. . .)—the labor performed by man upon himself during the greater part of the existence of the human race, his entire *prehistoric* labor";[3] a system of evaluations possessing the force of law concerning the various members and parts of the body. Not only is the criminal deprived of organs according to a regime (*ordre*) of collective investments; not only is the one who has to be eaten, eaten according to social rules as exact as those followed in carving up and apportioning a steer; but the man who enjoys the full exercise of his rights and duties has his whole body marked under a régime that consigns his organs and their exercise to the collectivity (the privatization of the organs will only begin with "the shame felt by man *at the sight of* man"[4]). For it is a founding act—that the organs be hewn into the socius, and that the flows run over its surface—through which man ceases to be a biological organism and becomes a full body, an earth, to which his organs become attached, where they are attracted, repelled, miraculated, following the requirements of a socius. Nietzsche says: it is a matter of creating a memory for man; and man, who was constituted by means of an active faculty of forgetting (*oubli*), by means of a repression of biological memory, must create an *other* memory, one that is collective, a memory of words (*paroles*) and no longer a memory of things, a memory of signs and no longer of effects. This organization, which traces its signs

*Paul Parin et al., *Les blancs pensent trop* (Paris: Payot, 1963): "The pre-object relations with the mothers pass over and are divided into relations of identification with the group of companions of the same age. The conflict with the fathers finds itself neutralized in relations of identification with the group of older brothers . . ." (pp. 428–36). Similar analysis and results in M. C. and Edmond Ortigues, *Oedipe africain* (reference note 22), pp. 302–305. But these authors indulge in a strange gymnastics to maintain the existence of an Oedipal problem or complex, despite all the reasons they advance to the contrary, and although they say this complex is not "clinically accessible."

directly on the body, constitutes a system of cruelty, a terrible alphabet: "Perhaps indeed there was nothing more fearful and uncanny in the whole prehistory of man than his *mnemotechnics* (. . .) Man could never do without blood, torture, and sacrifices when he felt the need to create a memory for himself; the most dreadful sacrifices and pledges (. . .), the most repulsive mutilations (. . .), the cruelist rites of all the religious cults . . . one has only to look at our former codes of punishments to understand what effort it costs on this earth to breed a 'nation of thinkers'!"[5]

Cruelty has nothing to do with some ill-defined or natural violence that might be commissioned to explain the history of mankind; cruelty is the movement of culture that is realized in bodies and inscribed on them, belaboring them. That is what cruelty means. This culture is not the movement of ideology: on the contrary, it forcibly injects production into desire, and conversely, it forcibly inserts desire into social production and reproduction. For even death, punishment, and torture are desired, and are instances of production (compare the history of fatalism). It makes men or their organs into the parts and wheels of the social machine. The sign is a position of desire; but the first signs are the territorial signs that plant their flags in bodies. And if one wants to call this inscription in naked flesh "writing," then it must be said that speech in fact presupposes writing, and that it is this cruel system of inscribed signs that renders man capable of language, and gives him a memory of the spoken word.

2 | The Primitive Territorial Machine

The notion of territoriality merely appears ambiguous. For if it is taken to mean a principle of residence or of geographic distribution, it is obvious that the primitive social machine is not territorial. Only the apparatus of the State will be territorial in this sense because, following Engel's formula, it "subdivides not the people but the territory," and substitutes a geographic organization for the organization of *gens*. Yet even where kinship seems to predominate over the earth, it is not difficult to show the importance of local ties. This is because the primitive machine subdivides the people, but does so on an indivisible earth where the connective, disjunctive, and conjunctive relations of each section are inscribed along with the other relations (thus, for example, the coexistence or complementarity of the section chief and the guardian of the earth). When the division extends to the earth itself, by virtue of an administration that is landed and residential, this cannot be regarded as a promotion of territoriality; on the contrary, it is rather the effect of the first great movement of deterritorialization on the primitive communes. The immanent unity of the earth as the immobile motor gives way to a transcendent unity of an altogether different nature—the unity of the State; the full body is no longer that of the earth, it is the full body of the Despot, the Unengendered, which now takes charge of the fertility of the soil as well as the rain from the sky and the general appropriation of the productive forces. Hence the savage, primitive socius was indeed the only territorial machine in the strict sense of the term. And the functioning of such a machine consists in the following: *the declension of alliance and filiation*—declining the lineages on the body of the earth, before there is a State.

If declension characterizes the primitive machine, it is because it is not possible simply to deduce alliance from filiation, the alliances from the filiative lines. It would be erroneous to ascribe to alliance no more than an individuating power over the persons of a lineage; it produces instead a generalized distinguishability. E. R. Leach cites cases of very diverse matrimonial régimes where no difference in filiation can be inferred among the corresponding groups. In many analyses, "the stress has been upon ties within the unilineal corporation or between different corporations linked by ties of common descent. The structural ties deriving from marriage between members of different corporations have been largely ignored or else assimilated into the all-important descent concept. Thus Fortes (1953), while recognizing that ties of affinity have comparable importance to ties of descent, disguises the former under his expression *complementary filiation.* The essence of this concept, which resembles the Roman distinction between agnation and cognation, is that any Ego is related to the kinsman of his two parents because he is the descendant of both parents and not because his parents were married. . . . [However] the cross ties linking the different patrilineages laterally are *not* felt by the peoples themselves to be of the nature of descent. The continuity of the structure vertically through time is adequately expressed through the agnatic transmission of a patrilineage name. But the continuity of the structure laterally is not so expressed. Instead, it is maintained by a continuing chain of debt relationships of an economic kind. . . . It is the existence of these outstanding debts which assert the continuance of the affinal relationship."[6]

Filiation is administrative and hierarchical, but alliance is political and economic, and expresses power insofar as it is not fused with the hierarchy and cannot be deduced from it, and the economy insofar as it is not identical with administration. Filiation and alliance are like the two forms of a primitive capital: fixed capital or filiative stock, and circulating capital or mobile blocks of debts. There are two memories that correspond to them, the one biofiliative, the other a memory of alliance and of words. While production is recorded in the network of filiative disjunctions on the socius, the connections of labor still must detach themselves from the productive process and pass into the element of recording that appropriates them for itself as quasi cause. But it can accomplish this only by reclaiming the connective régime for its own, in the form of an affinal tie or a pairing of persons that is compatible with the disjunctions of filiation. It is in this sense that the economy goes by way of alliance. In the production of children, the child is inscribed in relation to the disjunctive lines of its father or mother, but inversely, the disjunctive lines inscribe it only through a connection represented by the marriage of the father and the mother. At no time, therefore, does alliance derive from filiation, but both form an essentially open cycle where the socius acts on production, but also where production reacts on the socius.

Marxists are right to remind us that if kinship is dominant in primitive society, it is determined as dominant by economic and political factors. And if filiation expresses what is dominant while being itself determined, alliance expresses what is determinant, or rather the return of the determinant in the determinate system of dominance. That is why it is essential to take into consideration how ties of alliance combine concretely with relations of filiation on a given territorial surface. Leach has specifically underscored the importance of *local lineages* insofar as they are differentiated from lineages of filiation, and insofar as they operate at the level of small segments: it is these groups of men residing in the same area, or in neighboring areas, who arrange marriages and shape concrete reality to a much greater extent than do the systems of filiation and the abstract matrimonial classes. A kinship system is not a structure but a practice, a praxis, a method, and even a strategy. Louis Berthe, analyzing a relationship of alliance and hierarchy, shows convincingly that a village intervenes as a third party to permit matrimonial connections between elements that the disjunction of two moieties would forbid from the strict viewpoint of structure: "The third term must be interpreted much more as a method than as a true structural element."* Every time one interprets kinship relations in the primitive commune in terms of a structure unfolding in the mind, one relapses into an ideology of large segments that makes alliance depend on the major filiations, and that finds itself contradicted by *practice*. "It is necessary to ask if there exists in the asymmetrical systems of alliance a

*Louis Berthe, "Aînés et cadets, l'alliance et la hiérarchie chez les Baduj," *L'Homme,* July 1965. See Luc de Heusch's statement, in "Lévi-Strauss," *L'Arc,* no. 26: "A kinship system is also and first of all a praxis" (p. 11).

fundamental tendency toward generalized exchange, that is to say, toward the closing of the cycle. I have been unable to find anything of that nature among the Mru. . . . Everyone behaves as if he were ignorant of the compensation that would result from the closing of the cycle, and everyone stresses the relationship of asymmetry, emphasizing the creditor-debtor behavior."[7] A kinship system only appears closed to the extent that it is severed from the political and economic references that keep it open, and that make alliance something other than an arrangement of matrimonial classes and filiative lineages.

It is the same for the whole project of coding the flows. How does one ensure reciprocal adaptation, the respective embrace of a signifying chain and flows of production? The great nomad hunter follows the flows, exhausts them in place, and moves on with them to another place. He reproduces in an accelerated fashion his entire filiation, and contracts it into a point that keeps him in a direct relationship with the ancestor or the god. Pierre Clastres describes the solitary hunter who becomes identical with his force and his destiny, and delivers his song in a language that becomes increasingly rapid and distorted: Me, me, me, "I am a powerful nature, a nature incensed and aggressive!"[8] Such are the two characteristics of the hunter, the great paranoiac of the bush or the forest: real displacement with the flows and direct filiation with the god. It has to do with the nature of nomadic space, where the full body of the socius is as if adjacent to production; it has not yet brought production under its sway. The space of the encampment remains adjacent to that of the forest; it is constantly reproduced in the process of production, but has not yet appropriated this process. The apparent objective movement of inscription has not suppressed the real movement of nomadism. But a pure nomad does not exist; there is always and already an encampment where it is a matter of stocking—however little—and where it is a matter of inscribing and allocating, of marrying, and of feeding oneself. (Clastres shows well how, among the Guayaki, the *connection* between the hunters and the living animals is succeeded in the encampment by a *disjunction* between the dead animals and the hunters—a disjunction similar to an incest prohibition, since the hunter cannot consume his own kill.) In short, as we shall see elsewhere, there is always a pervert who succeeds the paranoiac or accompanies him—sometimes the same man in two situations: the bush paranoiac and the village pervert.

Once the socius becomes fixed, falling back on the productive forces and appropriating them for its own, the problem of coding can no longer be resolved by the simultaneity of a displacement from the standpoint of the flows, and an accelerated reproduction from the standpoint of the chain. The flows must be the object of *deductions* (*prélèvements*) that constitute a minimum of stock, and the signifying chain must be the object of *detachments* (*détachements*) that constitute a minimum of mediations. A flow is coded insofar as detachments from the chain and deductions from the flows are effected in correspondence, united in a mutual embrace. And this is already the highly perverse activity of local groups who arrange marriages on the surface of the primitive territoriality: a normal or nonpathological perversity, as Henry Ey would say, referring to other cases where "a psychic work of selection, refinement, and calculation" was manifested. And this is the case from the start, since there does not exist a pure nomad who can be afforded the satisfaction of drifting with the flows and singing direct filiation, but always a socius waiting to bear down, already deducting and detaching.

The flow deductions constitute a filiative stock in the signifying chain; but inversely, the detachments from the chain constitute mobile debts of alliance that guide and direct the flows. On the blanket that serves as a familial stock, affinal stones or cowries are made to circulate. There is a sort of vast cycle of flows of production and chains of inscription, and a lesser cycle, between the stocks of filiation that connect or encaste (*encastent*) the flows, and the blocks of alliance that cause the chains to flow. Descent is at the same time flow of production and chain of inscription, stock of filiation and fluxion of alliance. Everything takes place as though the stock constituted a surface energy of inscription or recording, the potential energy of the apparent movement; but debt is the actual direction of this movement, a kinetic energy that is determined by the respective paths of the gifts and countergifts on the surface. Among the Kula, the circulation of necklaces and bracelets comes to a standstill in certain places, on certain occasions, so that a stock may be re-formed. There are no productive connections without disjunctions of filiation that appropriate them, but there are no disjunctions of filiation that do not reconstitute lateral connections across the alliances and pairings of persons. Not only the flows and the chains, but the fixed stocks and the mobile debts—insofar as they in turn imply relations between chains and flows in both directions—are in a state of perpetual relativity: their elements vary—women, consumer goods, ritual objects, rights, prestige, status.

If one postulates that somewhere there has to be a kind of equilibrium of prices, one is compelled to see in the manifest disequilibrium of the relations a pathological consequence, which one explains by saying that the supposedly closed system extends in one direction and opens as the prestations become wider and more complex. But such a conception is in contradiction with the primitive "cold economy," which is without net investment, without money or market, and without exchangist commodity relations. The mainspring of such an economy is a veritable *surplus value of code:* each detachment from the chain produces, on one side or the other in the flows of production, phenomena of excess and deficiency, phenomena of lack and accumulation, which will be compensated for by nonexchangeable elements of the acquired-prestige or distributed-consumption type. ("The chief converts this perishable wealth into imperishable prestige through the medium of spectacular feasting. The ultimate consumers are in this way the original producers.")* Surplus value of code is the primitive form of surplus value, inasmuch as it corresponds to Mauss's celebrated formula: the spirit of the thing given, or the force of circumstance that requires that gifts be reciprocated with interest, being territorial signs of desire and power (*puissance*), and principles of abundance and the fructification of wealth. Far from being a pathological consequence, the disequilibrium is functional and fundamental. Far from being the extension of a system that is at first closed, the opening is primary, founded in the heterogeneity of the elements that compose the prestations and that compensate for the disequilibrium by displacing it. In short, the detachments from the signifying chain, in accordance with the relations of alliance, engender surplus values of code at the level of the flows, whence are derived differences in status between the filiative lines (for example, the superior or inferior ranks of the givers and receivers of wives). The surplus value of code carries out the diverse operations of the primitive territorial machine: detaching segments from the chain, organizing selections from the flows, and allocating the portions due each person.

The idea that primitive societies have no history, that they are dominated by archetypes and their repetition, is especially weak and inadequate. This idea was not conceived by ethnologists, but by ideologists in the service of a tragic Judaeo-Christian consciousness that they wished to credit with the "invention" of history. If what is called history is a dynamic and open social reality, in a state of functional disequilibrium, or an oscillating equilibrium, unstable and always compensated, comprising not only institutionlized conflicts but conflicts that

*Leach, *Rethinking Anthropology*, p. 89. Also the criticism Leach addresses to Lévi-Strauss: "Lévi-Strauss rightly argues that the structural implications of a marriage can only be understood if we think of it as one item in a whole series of transactions between kin groups. So far, so good. But in none of the examples which he provides in his book does he carry this principle far enough. . . . Fundamentally he is not really interested in the nature and significance of the counter-prestations that serve as equivalents for women in the systems he is discussing. . . . We cannot predict from first principles how the different categories of prestation will be evaluated in any particular society. . . . It is very important to distinguish between consumable and non-consumable materials; it is also very important to appreciate that quite intangible elements such as 'rights' and 'prestige' form part of the total inventory of 'things' exchanged" (pp. 90, 100).

generate changes, revolts, ruptures, and scissions, then primitive societies are fully inside history, and far distant from the stability, or even
from the harmony, attributed to them in the name of a primacy of a
unanimous group. The presence of history in every social machine
plainly appears in the disharmonies that, as Lévi-Strauss says, "bear the
unmistakable stamp of time elapsed."* It is true that there are several
ways to interpret such disharmonies: ideally, by the gap between the real
institution and the assumed ideal model; morally, by invoking a structural bond between law and transgression; physically, as though it were a
question of attrition that would cause the social machine to lose its
capacity to wield its materials. But here too it seems that the correct
interpretation would be, above all, actual and functional: it is *in order to
function* that a social machine must *not function well.* This has been
shown precisely with regard to the segmentary system, which is always
destined to reconstitute itself on its own ruins; and likewise for the
organization of the political function in these systems, which in effect is
exercised only by indicating its own impotence.[9] Ethnologists are
constantly saying that kinship rules are neither applied nor applicable to
real marriages: not because these rules are ideal but rather because they
determine critical points where the apparatus starts up again—provided
it is blocked, and where it necessarily places itself in a negative relation
to the group. Here it becomes apparent that the social machine is
identical with the desiring-machine. The social machine's limit is not
attrition, but rather its misfirings; it can operate only by fits and starts,
by grinding and breaking down, in spasms of minor explosions. The
dysfunctions are an essential element of its very ability to function,
which is not the least important aspect of the system of cruelty. The
death of a social machine has never been heralded by a disharmony or a
dysfunction; on the contrary, social machines make a habit of feeding on
the contradictions they give rise to, on the crises they provoke, on the
anxieties they *engender,* and on the infernal operations they regenerate.
Capitalism has learned this, and has ceased doubting itself, while even
socialists have abandoned belief in the possibility of capitalism's natural
death by attrition. No one has ever died from contradictions. And the
more it breaks down, the more it schizophrenizes, the better it works, the
American way.

But this is already the point of view required—given a change of
perspective—for examining the primitive socius, the territorial machine

*Claude Lévi-Strauss, *Structural Anthropology,* trans. Claire Jacobs and Brooke Grundfest Schoepf
(New York: Basic Books, Harper Torchbooks, 1963), p. 117. (*Translators' note:* The French reads: "la
marque, impossible à méconnaître, de l'événement." The above translation misses the impact of
marque [mark] and *événement* [event].)

for declining alliances and filiations. This machine is *segmentary* because, through its double apparatus of tribe and lineage, it cuts up segments of varying lengths: genealogical filiative units of major, minor, and minimal lineages, with their hierarchy, their respective chiefs, their elders who guard the stocks and organize marriages; territorial tribal units of primary, secondary, and tertiary sections, also having their dominant roles and their alliances. "The point of separation between the tribal sections becomes the point of divergence in the clan structure of the lineages associated with each section. For, as we have seen, clans and their lineages are not distinct corporate groups, but are embodied in local communities, through which they function structurally."[10] The two systems intersect, each segment being associated with the flows and the chains, with the stocked flows and the passing flows, with selections from the flows and detachments from the chains (certain production projects are executed in the framework of the tribal system, others in the framework of the lineage system). The variability and relativity of the segments are responsible for all sorts of penetrations between the inalienable elements of filiation and the mobile elements of alliance. This is explained by the fact that the length of each segment—or even its existence as such—is determined only by its opposition to other segments in a series of interrelated stages. The segmentary machine mixes rivalries, conflicts, and ruptures throughout the variations of filiation and the fluctuations of alliance. The whole system evolves between two poles: that of fusion through opposition to other groups, and that of scission through the constant formation of new lineages aspiring to independence, with capitalization of alliances and filiation. From one pole to the other, all the misfirings and failures in a system that is constantly reborn of its own disharmonies. What does Jeanne Favret mean when she shows, along with other ethnologists, that "the persistence of a segmentary organization requires paradoxically that its mechanisms be ineffectual enough so that fear remains the motor of the whole"? And what is this fear? It would appear that social formations experienced a morbid and mournful foreboding of things to come, although what comes to them always comes from without, rushing in through their opening. Perhaps it is even for this reason that it arrives from without; they suffocate its inner potentiality, at the cost of the dysfunctions that constitute an integral part of the functioning of their system.

The segmentary territorial machine makes use of scission to exorcise fusion, and impedes the concentration of power by maintaining the organs of chieftainry in a relationship of impotence with the group:

as though the savages themselves sensed the rise of the imperial Barbarian, who will come nonetheless from without and will overcode all their codes. But the greatest danger would be yet another dispersion, a scission such that all the possibilities of coding would be suppressed: decoded flows, flowing on a blind, mute, deterritorialized socius—such is the nightmare that the primitive social machine exorcises with all its forces, and all its segmentary articulations. The primitive machine is not ignorant of exchange, commerce, and industry; it exorcises them, localizes them, cordons them off, encastes them, and maintains the merchant and the blacksmith in a subordinate position, so that the flows of exchange and the flows of production do not manage to break the codes in favor of their abstract or fictional quantities. And isn't that also what Oedipus, the fear of incest, is about: the fear of a decoded flow? If capitalism is the universal truth, it is so in the sense that makes capitalism *the negative* of all social formations. It is the thing, the unnamable, the generalized decoding of flows that reveals *a contrario* the secret of all these formations, coding the flows, and even overcoding them, rather than letting anything escape coding. Primitive societies are not outside history; rather, it is capitalism that is at the end of history, it is capitalism that results from a long history of contingencies and accidents, and that brings on this end. It cannot be said that the previous formations did not foresee this Thing that only came from without by rising from within, and that at all costs had to be prevented from rising. Whence the possibility of a retrospective reading of all history in terms of capitalism. It is already possible to see signs of classes in precapitalist societies. But ethnologists observe how difficult it is to distinguish those protoclasses from the castes organized by the imperial machine and from the rankings distributed by the segmentary primitive machine. The criteria that distinguish classes, castes, and ranks must not be sought in a fixity or a permeability, nor in a relative closing or opening; these criteria always reveal themselves to be deceptive, eminently misleading. But the ranks are inseparable from the primitive territorial coding process, just as castes are inseparable from the overcoding practiced by the imperial State, while classes are relative to the process of an industrial and commodity production decoded under the conditions of capitalism. All history can therefore be read under the sign of classes, but by observing the rules set forth by Marx, and bearing in mind that classes are the "negative" of castes and ranks. For it is certain that the régime of decoding does not signify the absence of organization, but rather the most somber organization, the harshest compatibility, with the axiomatic replacing the codes and incorporating them, always *a contrario*.

3 | The Problem of Oedipus

The full body of the earth is not without distinguishing characteristics. Suffering and dangerous, unique, universal, it falls back on production, on the agents and connections of production. But on it, too, everything is attached and inscribed, everything is attracted, miraculated. It is the basis of the disjunctive synthesis and its reproduction: a pure force of filiation or genealogy, Numen. The full body is the unengendered, but filiation is the first character of inscription marked on this body. And we know the nature of this intensive filiation, this inclusive disjunction where everything divides, but into itself, and where the same being is everywhere, on every side, at every level, *differing only in intensity.* The same included being traverses indivisible distances on the full body, and passes through all the singularities, all the intensities of a synthesis that shifts and reproduces itself. It serves no purpose to recall that genealogical filiation is social rather than biological, for it is necessarily biosocial inasmuch as it is inscribed on the cosmic egg of the full body of the earth. It has a mythical origin that is the One, or rather the primitive one-two. Should one say the twins or the twin? Which divides and unites into itself—the Nommo, or the Nommos? The disjunctive synthesis distributes the primordial ancestors, but each member of the primitive community is himself a complete full body, male and female, binding to itself all the partial objects, with variations that are solely intensive, and that correspond to the internal zigzag of the Dogon egg. Each one intensively repeats the entire genealogy for himself. And everywhere it is the same, at both ends of the indivisible distance and on every side, a litany of twins, an intense filiation. At the beginning of *Le renard pâle,* Marcel Griaule and Germaine Dieterlen sketch out a splendid theory of the sign: the signs of filiation, guide-signs and master-signs, signs of desire, intensive at first, which fall in a spiral and traverse a series of explosions before extending into images, figures, and drawings.

If the full body falls back on the productive connections and inscribes them in a network of intensive and inclusive disjunctions, it still has to find again and reanimate lateral connections in the network itself, and it must attribute them to itself as though it were their cause. These are the two aspects of the full body: an enchanted surface of inscription, the fantastic law, or the apparent objective movement; but also a magical agent or fetish, the quasi cause. It is not content to inscribe all things, it must act as if it produced them. It is necessary that the connections reappear in a form compatible with the inscribed disjunctions, even if they react in turn on the form of these disjunctions.

Such is alliance, the second characteristic of inscription: alliance imposes on the productive connections the extensive form of a pairing of persons, compatible with the disjunctions of inscription, but inversely reacts on inscription by determining an exclusive and restrictive use of these same disjunctions. It is therefore inevitable that alliance be mythically represented as supervening at a certain moment in the filiative lines (although in another sense it is already there from time immemorial). Marcel Griaule describes how, among the Dogons, something is produced at a certain moment, at the level and on the side of the eighth ancestor: a derailment of the disjunctions, which cease to be inclusive and become exclusive. Once this occurs, there is a dismembering of the full body, a canceling of twinness (*la gémelléité*), a separation of the sexes marked by circumcision, but also a recomposition of the body according to a new model of connection or conjugation, an articulation of bodies for and between themselves, a lateral inscription with articulatory stones of alliance, in short, a whole *ark* of alliance.[11] Alliances never derive from filiations, nor can they be deduced from them. But, this principle once established, we must distinguish between two points of view: the one economic and political, where alliance is there from time immemorial, combining and declining itself with the extended filiative lineages that do not exist prior to alliances in a system assumed to be given in extended form; the other mythical, which shows how the extension of a system takes form and delimits itself, proceeding from intense and primordial filiative lineages that necessarily lose their inclusive or nonrestrictive use. From this viewpoint the extended system is like a memory of alliance and of words, implying an active repression of the intense memory of filiation. For if genealogy and filiations are the object of an ever vigilant memory, it is to the degree that they are already apprehended in an extensive sense that they certainly did not possess before the determinations of alliances conferred it on them. On the contrary, as intensive filiations they become the object of a separate memory, nocturnal and biocosmic—the memory that indeed must suffer repression in order for the new extended memory to be established.

We can better understand why the problem does not in the least consist of going from filiations to alliances, or of deducing the latter from the former. The problem is one of passing from an intensive energetic order to an extensive system, which comprises both qualitative alliances and extended filiations. Nothing is changed by the fact that the primary energy of the intensive order—the Numen—is an energy of filiation, for this intense filiation is not yet extended, and does not as yet comprise any distinction of persons, nor even a distinction of sexes, but only prepersonal variations in intensity, taking on the same twinness or bisexuality in differing degrees. The signs belonging to this order are therefore fundamentally neuter or ambiguous (according to an expression employed by Leibnitz to designate a sign that can be + as well as −). It is a question of knowing how, starting from this primary intensity, it will be possible to pass to a system in extension where (1) the filiations will be filiations extended in the form of lineages, comprising distinctions of persons and of parental appellations; (2) the alliances will be at the same time qualitative relations, which the filiations presuppose as much as vice versa; (3) in short, the ambiguous intense signs will cease to be ambiguous and will become positive or negative.

This may be seen clearly in a passage from Lévi-Strauss, explaining for the simple forms of marriage the prohibition of parallel cousins and the approbation of cross-cousins: each marriage between two lines A and B bears a (+) or (−) sign, according to whether this couple results from a woman being lost to or acquired by line A or B. In this regard it is not important whether the régime of filiation is patrilineal or matrilineal. In a patrilineal or patrilocal régime, for example, "related women are women lost; women brought in by marriage are women gained. Each family descended from these marriages thus bears a sign, which is determined, for the initial group, by whether the children's mother is a daughter or a daughter-in-law. . . . The sign changes in passing from the brother to the sister, since the brother gains a wife, while the sister is lost to her own family." But, as Lévi-Strauss remarks, one also changes signs *in passing from one generation to the next:* "It depends upon whether, from the initial group's point of view, the father has received a wife, or the mother has been transferred outside, whether the sons have the right to a woman or owe a sister. Certainly, in real life this difference does not mean that half the male cousins are destined to remain bachelors. However, at all events, it does express the law that a man cannot receive a wife except from the group from which a woman can be claimed, because in the previous generation a sister or a daughter was lost, while a brother owes a sister (or a father, a daughter) to the outside world if a woman was gained in the previous generation. . . . The pivot-couple, formed by an A man married to a B woman, obviously has two signs, according to whether it is envisaged from the viewpoint of A, or that of B, and the same is true for children. It is now only necessary to look at the cousins' generation to establish that all those in the relationship (+ +) or (− −) are parallel to one another, while all those in the relationship (+ −) or (− +) are cross."[12]

But once the problem is put in this way, it is less a question of applying a logical combinative apparatus governing an interplay of exchanges, as Lévi-Strauss would have it, than one of establishing a physical system that will express itself naturally in terms of debts. It seems to us very significant that Lévi-Strauss himself invokes the co-ordinates of a physical system, although he sees this as nothing more than a metaphor. In the physical system in extension, *something passes through* that is of the nature of an energy flow ($+-$ or $-+$), *something does not pass or remains blocked* ($++$ or $--$), and something blocks, or on the contrary causes, passage. Something or someone. In this system in extension there is no primary filiation, nor is there a first generation or an initial exchange, but there are always and already alliances, at the same time as the filiations are extended, expressing both what must remain blocked in the filiation and what must pass through in the alliance.

The essential is not that the signs change according to the sexes and the generations, but that one passes from the intensive to the extensive, that is to say, from an order of ambiguous signs to an order of signs that are changing but determined. It is here that resorting to myth is indispensable, not because the myth would be a transposed or even an inverse representation of real relations in extension, but because only the myth can determine the intensive conditions of the system (the system of production included) in conformity with indigenous thought and practice. That is why a text of Marcel Griaule's, which looks to myth for a principle that would explain the avunculate, seems decisive to us, and seems to avoid the reproach of idealism that usually greets this kind of attempt. We have a similar view of the recent article in which Adler and Cartry return to the question.[13] These authors are right in remarking that Lévi-Strauss's kinship atom—with its four relationships: brother-sister, husband-wife, father-son, maternal uncle–sister's son—presents itself as a ready-made whole from which the mother as such is strangely excluded, although, depending on the circumstances, she can be more or less a "kinswoman" or more or less an "affine" in relation to her children. Now this is indeed where the myth takes root, the myth that does not express but conditions. As Griaule relates it, the Yourougou, breaking into the piece of placenta he has stolen, is like the brother of his mother, with whom he is united by that fact: "This individual went away into the distance carrying with him a part of the nourishing placenta, which is to say a part of his own mother. He saw this organ as his own and as forming a part of his own person, in such a way that he identified himself with the one who gave birth to him. She was the matrix of the world, and he considered himself to be placed *on the same plane as she from the viewpoint of the generations.* . . . He senses unconsciously his symbolic membership in his mother's generation and his detachment from the real generation of which he is a member. . . . Being, according to him, *of the same substance and generation as his mother,* he likens himself to a male twin of his genetrix, and the mythical rule of the union of two paired members proposes him as the ideal husband. Hence, in his capacity as pseudo brother to his genetrix, he should be in the position of his maternal uncle, the designated husband of this woman."[14]

Doubtless all the dramatis personae will be found to come into play from this point on: mother, father, son, mother's brother, son's sister. But it is evident and striking that these are not persons. Their names do not designate persons, but rather the intensive variations of a "vibratory spiraling movement," inclusive disjunctions, necessarily twin states through which a subject passes on the cosmic egg. Everything must be interpreted in intensity. The egg and the placenta itself, swept by an unconscious life energy "susceptible to augmentation and diminution." The father is in no way absent. But Amma, the father and genitor, is himself a high intensive part, immanent to the placenta, inseparable from the twinness, which relates him to his feminine part. And if the Yourougou son carries away a part of the placenta in his turn, it is in an intensive relationship with another part that contains his own sister or twin sister. But, aiming too high, the part he carries away makes him the sister of his mother, who eminently replaces the sister, and to whom he becomes united by replacing Amma. In short, a whole world of ambiguous signs, included divisions and bisexual states. I am the son, and also my mother's brother and my sister's husband and my own father. Everything rests on the placenta, which has become the earth, the unengendered, the full body of antiproduction where the organs—partial objects of a sacrificed Nommo are attached. It is because the placenta, as a substance common to the mother and the child, a common part of their bodies, makes it such that these bodies are not like cause and effect, but are both products derived from this same substance, in relation to which the son is his mother's twin: such is indeed the axis of the Dogon myth related by Griaule. Yes, I have been my mother and I have been my son. It is rare that one sees myth and science saying the same thing from such a great distance: the Dogon narrative develops a mythical Weismannism, where the germinative plasma forms an immortal and continuous lineage that does not depend on bodies; on the contrary, the bodies of the parents as well as the children depend on it. Whence the distinction between two lines, the one continuous and germinal, but the other discontinuous and somatic, it alone being subjected to a succession of generations. (T. D. Lysenko employed a naturally Dogon tone, turning it back against Weismann, to reproach him for making the son the genetic or germinal brother of the mother: "The

Morganists-Mendelians, following Weismann, start from the idea that the parents are not genetically the parents of their children; if we are to believe their doctrine, parents and children are brothers and sisters."[15])

But the son is not somatically his mother's brother and twin. That is why he cannot marry her (bearing in mind what we said earlier to be the meaning of "that is why"). The one who should have married the mother was therefore the maternal uncle. The first consequence of this is that incest with the sister is not a substitute for incest with the mother, but on the contrary the intensive model of incest as a manifestation of the germinal lineage. Then again, Hamlet is not an extension of Oedipus, an Oedipus to the second degree; on the contrary, a negative or inverse Hamlet is primary in relation to Oedipus. The subject does not reproach the uncle for having done what he himself wanted to do; he reproaches him for *not* having done what he the son could not do. And why didn't the uncle marry the mother, his somatic sister? Because he *must* not, except in the name of this germinal filiation, marked by ambiguous signs of twinness and bisexuality, according to which the son *could have* done it as well, and could have been himself this uncle in an intense relationship with the mother-twin. The vicious circle of the germinal lineage closes (the primitive double bind): neither can the uncle marry his sister, the mother, nor from that moment can the son marry his own sister—the Yourougou female twin will be delivered over to the Nommos as a potential affine. The somatic order causes the whole intensive scale to collapse again. Actually, if the son cannot marry his mother, it is not because he is somatically from a different generation. Arguing against Malinowski, Lévi-Strauss has demonstrated convincingly that the mixing of generations was not in the least feared as such, and that the incest prohibition could not be explained in this manner.[16] This is because the mixing of the generations in the son-mother case has the same effect as their correspondence in the case of the uncle-sister, that is, it testifies to one and the same intensive germinal filiation that must be repressed in both cases. In short, a somatic system in extension can constitute itself only insofar as the filiations become extended, correlatively to lateral alliances that become established. It is through the prohibition of incest with the sister that the lateral alliance is sealed; it is through the prohibition of incest with the mother that the filiation becomes extended. There we find no repression of the father, no foreclosure of the name of the father. The respective position of the mother or father as kin or affine, the patrilineal or matrilineal character of the filiation, and the patrilateral or matrilateral character of the marriage, are active elements of the repression, and not objects at which the repression is directed. It is not even the memory of filiation in general that is repressed by a memory of alliance. It is the great nocturnal memory of the intensive germinal filiation that is repressed for the sake of an extensive somatic memory, created from filiations that have become extended (patrilineal *or* matrilineal) and from the alliances that they imply. The entire Dogon mythology is a patrilineal version of the opposition between the two genealogies and the two filiations: in intensity and in extension, the intense germinal order and the extensive régime of the somatic generations.

The system in extension is born of the intensive conditions that make it possible, but it reacts on them, cancels them, represses them, and allows them no more than a mythical expression. The signs cease to be ambiguous at the same time as they are determined in relation to the extended filiations and the lateral alliances: the disjunctions become exclusive, restrictive (the "either/or else" replaces the intense "either . . . or . . . or . . ."); the names, the appellations no longer designate intensive states, but discernible persons. Discernibility settles on the sister and the mother as prohibited spouses. The reason is that persons, with the names that now designate them, do not exist prior to the prohibitions that constitute them as such. Mother and sister do not exist prior to their prohibition as spouses. Robert Jaulin says it well: "The mythical discourse has as its theme the passage from indifference to incest to its prohibition. Implicit or explicit, this theme underlies all the myths; it is therefore a formal property of this language."[17] We must conclude that, strictly speaking, incest does not and cannot exist. We are always on this side of incest, in a series of intensities that is ignorant of discernible persons; or else beyond incest, in an extension that recognizes them, that constitutes them, but that does not constitute them without rendering them impossible as sexual partners. One can commit incest only after a series of substitutions that always moves us away from it, that is to say, with a person who is equivalent to the mother or the sister only by virtue of not being either: she who is discernible as a possible spouse. Such is the meaning of preferential marriage: the first incest that is permitted. But it is not by chance that this kind of marriage rarely occurs, as though it were still too close to the nonexistent impossible (for example, the preferential Dogon marriage with the uncle's daughter, she being equivalent to the aunt, who is herself equivalent to the mother).

Griaule's article is without doubt the text most profoundly inspired by psychoanalysis in the whole of anthropology. Yet it leads to conclusions that cause the whole of Oedipus to shatter, because it is not content to pose the problem in extension, thereby assuming its solution. These are the conclusions drawn by Adler and Cartry: "It is customary to consider incestuous relations in myth either as the expression of the desire or the nostalgia for a world where such relations would be possible or would meet with indifference, or as the expression of a structural function of the inversion of the social rule, a function destined to found the prohibition and its transgression. . . . In both instances, one takes as something already constituted what is in fact the emergence of an order that the myth narrates and explains. In other words, one reasons as if the myth placed on the stage persons defined as father, mother, brother, and sister, whereas these roles belong to the order constituted by the prohibition . . . : *incest does not exist.*"* Incest is a pure limit. Provided that two false beliefs concerning the limit are avoided: one that makes the limit a matrix or an origin, as though the prohibition proved that the thing was "first" desired as such; another that makes the limit a structural function, as though the supposedly "fundamental" relationship between desire and law were manifested in transgression. It is necessary to recall once more that the law proves nothing about an original reality of desire because it essentially disfigures the desired; and that the transgression proves nothing about a functional reality of the law because, far from being a mockery of the law, it is itself derisory in relation to what the law prohibits in reality (the reason why revolutions have nothing to do with transgressions). In short, the limit is neither a this-side-of nor a beyond: it is the boundary line between the two— *Incest, that slandered shallow stream*—always crossed already or not yet crossed. For incest is like this motion, it is impossible. And it is not impossible in the same sense that the Real would be impossible, but quite the contrary, in the sense that the Symbolic is.

But what does it mean to say that incest is impossible? Isn't it possible to go to bed with one's sister or mother? And how do we dispense with the old argument: it must be possible since it is prohibited? The problem lies elsewhere. The possibility of incest would require *both persons and names*—son, sister, mother, brother, father. Now in the incestuous act we can have persons at our disposal, but they lose their names inasmuch as these names are inseparable from the prohibition that proscribes them as partners; or else the names subsist, and designate nothing more than prepersonal intensive states that could just as well "extend" to other persons, as when one calls his legitimate wife "mama," or one's sister his wife. It is in this sense that we said we are always on this side of it or beyond. Our mothers and our sisters melt in

---

*Adler and Cartry (see reference note 13). Jacques Derrida wrote, in a commentary of Rousseau: "Before the feast there was no incest because there was no prohibition of incest. After the feast there is no longer any incest because it is prohibited. . . . The feast *itself* would be the incest *itself* if any such thing—*itself*—could take place" (*De la grammatologie* [see reference note 53], pp. 372–77).

our arms; their names slide on their persons like a stamp that is too wet. This is because one can never enjoy the person and the name at the same time—yet this would be the condition for incest. Granted, incest is a lure, it is impossible. But the problem is only deferred. Is that not the nature of desire, that one desires the impossible? At least in this instance, the platitude is not even true. We are reminded how illegitimate it is to conclude from the prohibition anything regarding the nature of what is prohibited; for the prohibition proceeds by dishonoring the guilty, that is to say, by inducing a disfigured or displaced image of the thing that is really prohibited or desired. Indeed, this is how social repression prolongs itself by means of a psychic repression without which it would have no grip on desire. What is desired is the intense germinal or germinative flow, where one would look in vain for persons or even functions discernible as father, mother, son, sister, etc., since these names only designate intensive variations on the full body of the earth determined as the germen. It is always possible to use the term incest, as well as indifference to incest, for this régime composed of one and the same being or flow, varying in intensity according to inclusive disjunctions. But that is precisely the problem; one cannot confound incest as it would be in this intensive nonpersonal régime that would institute it, with incest as represented in extension in the state that prohibits it, and that defines it as a transgression against persons. Jung is therefore entirely correct in saying that the Oedipus complex signifies something altogether different from itself, and that in the Oedipal relation the mother is also the earth, and incest is an infinite renaissance. (He is wrong only in thinking that he has thus "transcended" sexuality.) The *somatic complex* refers to a *germinal implex.* Incest refers to a this-side-of that cannot be represented as such in the complex, since the complex is an element derived from this this-side-of. Incest as it is prohibited (the form of discernible persons) is employed to repress incest as it is desired (the substance of the intense earth). The intensive germinal flow is the representative of desire; it is against this flow that the repression is directed. The extensive Oedipal figure is its displaced represented (*le représenté déplacé*), the lure or fake image, born of repression, that comes to conceal desire. It matters little that this image is "impossible": it does its work from the moment that desire lets itself be caught as though by the impossible itself. You see, *that* is what you wanted! However it is this conclusion, going directly from the repression to the repressed, and from the prohibition to the prohibited, that already implies the whole paralogism of social repression.

But why is the germinal implex or influx repressed, since it is nevertheless the territorial representative of desire? Because the thing it refers to, in its capacity as representative, is a flow that would not be codable, that would not let itself be coded—specifically, the terror of the primitive socius. No chain could be detached, nothing could be selected; nothing would pass from filiation to descent, but descent would be perpetually reduced to filiation in the act of re-engendering oneself; the signifying chain would not form any code, it would only emit ambiguous signs and be perpetually eroded by its own energetic support; what would flow on the full body of the earth would be as unfettered as the noncoded flows that shift and slide on the desert of a body without organs. For it is less a question of abundance or scarcity, of a spring or the exhaustion of a spring (even the drying up of a spring is a flow), than of what is codable or noncodable. The germinal flow is such that it amounts to the same to say that everything would pass or flow with it, or on the contrary, that everything would be blocked. For the flows to be codable, their energy must allow itself to be quantified and qualified; it is necessary that selections from the flows be made in relation to detachments from the chain: something must pass through but something must also be blocked, and something must block and cause to pass through. Now this is possible only in the system in extension that renders persons discernible, that makes a determinate use of signs, an exclusive use of the disjunctive syntheses, and a conjugal use of the connective syntheses. Such is indeed the meaning of the incest prohibition conceived as the establishment of a physical system in extension: one must look in each case for the part of the flow of intensity that passes through, for what does not pass, and for what causes passage or prevents it, according to the patrilateral or matrilateral nature of the marriages, according to the patrilineal or matrilineal nature of the lineages, according to the general régime of the extended filiations and the lateral alliances.

Let us return to the Dogon preferential marriage as analyzed by Griaule: what is blocked is the relationship with the aunt as a substitute for the mother, in the form of a make-believe parent; what passes through is the relationship with the aunt's daughter as a substitute for the aunt, as the first possible or permitted incest; what does the blocking or causes passage is the maternal uncle. What passes through leads to—as compensation for what is blocked—a veritable *surplus value of code,* which falls to the uncle insofar as he causes passage, while he suffers a kind of "minus value" insofar as he does the blocking (thus the ritual thefts perpetrated by the nephews in the uncle's house, but also, as Griaule says, "the augmentation and fructification" of the uncle's possessions when the oldest of the nephews comes to live with him). The fundamental problem—who has the right to the matrimonial prestations in a given system?—cannot be resolved independently of the lines of passage and the lines of blockage, as if what was blocked or prohibited reappeared "in marriages in spectral form,"[18] coming to demand its due. Löffler writes of a specific case: "Among the Mru, the patrilineal model predominates over the matrilineal tradition: the brother-sister relationship, which is transmitted from father to son and from mother to daughter, can be transmitted indefinitely through the father-son relationship, but not through the mother-daughter relationship, which terminates with the daughter's marriage. A married daughter transmits to her own daughter a new relationship, namely that which joins her to her own brother. At the same time, a daughter who marries becomes detached not from her brother's line, but solely from that of her mother's brother. The significance of the payments to the mother's brother upon the marriage of his niece can be understood only in the following way: the girl leaves the previous family group, to which her mother belongs. The niece becomes herself a mother and the point of departure for a new brother-sister relationship, on which a new alliance is founded."[19] What is prolonged, what comes to a halt, what is detached, and the different relationships according to which these actions and passions are distributed, help us to understand the formation mechanism of the surplus value of code as an indispensable element of any coding of flows.

We are now able to outline the various instances of *territorial representation* in the primitive socius. In the first place, the germinal influx of intensity conditions all representation: it is the *representative* of desire. But if it is termed representative, this is because it is equivalent to the noncodable, noncoded, or decoded flows. In this sense it implies, in its own way, the socius's limit, the limit or the negative of every socius; the repression of this limit is possible only to the extent that the representative itself undergoes a repression. This repression determines what part of the influx will pass through and what will not in the system in extension, what will remain blocked or stocked in the extended filiations, and on the contrary, what will move and flow following the relations of alliance, in such a way that the systematic coding of the flows will be carried out. We call this second instance—the *repressing representation* itself—alliance, since the filiations become extended only in terms of lateral alliances that measure their variable segments. Whence the importance of these "local lines" that Leach has identified—and which, two by two, organize the alliances and arrange (*machine*) the marriages. When we ascribed to them a perverse-normal activity, we meant that these local groups were the agents of repression, the great coders. Wherever men meet and assemble to take wives for themselves, to negotiate for them, to share them, etc., one recognizes the perverse tie of a primary homosexuality between local groups, between brothers-in-law, co-husbands, childhood partners.

Underlining the universal fact that marriage is not an alliance between a man and a woman, but "an alliance between two families," "a transaction between men concerning women," Georges Devereux drew the correct conclusion of a basic homosexual motivation of a group character.[20] Through women, men establish their own connections; through the man-woman disjunction, which is always the outcome of filiation, alliance places in connection men from different filiations. The question why a female homosexuality hasn't given rise to Amazon groups capable of negotiating for men perhaps finds its reply in women's affinity with the germinal influx, resulting in the enclosed position of women in the midst of extended filiations (filiation hysteria as opposed to alliance paranoia). Male homosexuality is therefore the representation of alliance that represses the ambiguous signs of intense bisexual filiation. However, Devereux seems to us to be wrong on two occasions. First, when he admits having recoiled too long before this—so serious (he says)—discovery of a homosexual representation (there we merely see a primitive version of the formula "All men are homosexuals," and to be sure, they are never more so than when they arrange marriages). Then again—and this is his most serious error— when he wants to make of this homosexuality of alliance a product of the Oedipus complex as something repressed. Alliance can never be deduced from the lines of filiation through the intermediary of Oedipus; on the contrary, alliance articulates them, impelled by the action of the local lines and their non-oedipal primary homosexuality. And if it is true that there exists an Oedipal or filiative homosexuality, this should be understood merely as a secondary reaction to this group homosexuality, non-oedipal at first.

As for Oedipus in general, it is not the repressed—that is, the representative of desire, which is on this side of and completely ignorant of daddy-mommy. Nor is it the repressing representation, which is beyond, and which renders the persons discernible only by subjecting them to the homosexual rules of alliance. Incest is only the retroactive effect of the repressing representation *on* the repressed representative: the representation disfigures or displaces this representative against which it is directed; it projects onto the representative, categories, rendered discernible, that it has itself established; it applies to the representative terms that did not exist before the alliance organized the positive and the negative into a system in extension—the representation reduces the representative to what is blocked in this system. Hence

Oedipus is indeed the limit, but the displaced limit that now passes into the interior of the socius. Oedipus is the baited image with which desire allows itself to be caught (*That*'s what you wanted! The decoded flows were incest!). Then a long story begins, the story of oedipalization. But to be exact, everything begins in the mind of Laius, the old group homosexual, the pervert, who sets a trap for desire. For desire is that, too: a trap. Territorial representation comprises these three instances: the *repressed representative,* the *repressing representation,* and the *displaced represented.*

4 | Psychoanalysis and Ethnology

We are moving too fast, acting as if Oedipus were already installed within the savage territorial machine. However, as Nietzsche says with regard to bad conscience, such a plant does not grow on that kind of terrain. This is explained by the fact that the necessary conditions for Oedipus as a "familial complex," existing in the framework of the familialism suited to psychiatry and psychoanalysis, are obviously not present. Primitive families constitute a praxis, a politics, a strategy of alliances and filiations; formally, they are the driving elements of social reproduction; they have nothing to do with an expressive microcosm; in these families the father, the mother, and the sister always also function as something other than father, mother, or sister. And in addition to the father, the mother, etc., there is the affine, who constitutes the active, concrete reality and makes the relations between families coextensive with the social field. It would not even be exact to say that the family determinations burst apart at every corner of this field and remain attached to strictly social determinations, since both kinds of determinations form one and the same component in the territorial machine. Since familial reproduction is not yet a simple means, or a material at the service of a social reproduction of another nature, there is no possibility of reducing (*rabattre sur*) social reproduction to familial reproduction, nor is it possible to establish one-to-one relations between the two that would confer on any familial complex whatever an expressive value and an apparent autonomous form. On the contrary, it is evident that the individual in the family, however young, directly invests a social, historical, economic, and political field that is not reducible to any mental structure or affective constellation. That is why, when one considers pathological cases and processes of cure in primitive societies, it seems to us entirely insufficient to compare them with psychoanalytic procedure by relating them to criteria borrowed from the latter: for example, a familial complex, even if it differs from our own, or cultural material (*des contenus culturels*), even if it is brought into relation with an ethnic unconscious—as seen in attempted parallelisms between the psychoanalytic cure and the shamanistic cure (Devereux, Lévi-Strauss). Our definition of schizoanalysis focused on two aspects: the destruction of the expressive pseudo forms of the unconscious, and the discovery of desire's unconscious investments of the social field. It is from this point of view that we must consider many primitive cures; they are schizoanalysis in action.

Victor Turner gives a remarkable example of such a cure among the Ndembu.[21] The example is the more striking—to our perverted eyes— for the fact that, at first glance, everything appears Oedipal. Effeminate, insufferable, vain, failing at everything he tries, the sick K is preyed upon by the ghost of his maternal grandfather, who cruelly reproaches him. Although the Ndembu are matrilineal and must live with their maternal kin, K has stayed an exceptionally long time in the matrilineage of his father, whose favorite he was, and has entered into marriage with paternal cousins. But with the death of his father he is driven away, and returns to the maternal village. There his house expresses his situation well, being wedged between two sectors, the houses of the members of the paternal group and those belonging to his own matrilineage. How does the divination, responsible for indicating the cause of the illness, proceed, and the medical cure responsible for treating it? The teeth are the cause, the two top incisors of the ancestor hunter, contained in a sacred pouch, but which can escape from the pouch and penetrate the body of the sick man. In order to diagnose and ward off the effects of the incisor, the soothsayer and the medicine man launch into a social analysis concerning the territory and its environs, the chieftainship and its subchieftainships, the lineages and their segments, the alliances and the filiations: they constantly bring to light desire in its relations with political and economic units—the very point on which, moreover, the witnesses try to mislead them. "Divination becomes a form of social analysis in the course of which hidden struggles between individuals and factions are brought to light, in such a way that they can be treated by traditional ritual methods . . . , the vague nature of mystical beliefs allowing them to be manipulated in relation to a great number of social situations." It seems that the pathological incisor is indeed mainly that of the maternal grandfather. But the latter was a great chief; his successor, the "real chief," had had to relinquish the throne for fear of being bewitched, and his would-be heir, intelligent and ambitious, does not exercise the power; the actual chief is not the real chief; as for the sick K, he has not been able to assume the role of mediator that could have made him a candidate for chief. Everything becomes complicated because of the colonizer-colonized relations: the English have not recognized the chieftainship; the impoverished village is falling into decrepitude (the two sectors of the village result from a fusion of two groups that have fled the English; the elders bemoan the current decadence). The medicine man does not organize a sociodrama, but a veritable group analysis centering on the sick individual. Giving him potions, attaching horns to his body for drawing up the incisor, making the drums beat, the medicine man proceeds with a ceremony interrupted by halts and fresh departures, flows of all sorts, flows of words and breaks: the members of the village come to talk, the sick subject talks, the ghost is invoked, the medicine man explains, everything recommences, drums, chants, trances. It is not only a question of discovering the preconscious investments of a social field by interests, but—more profoundly—its unconscious investments by desire, such as they pass by way of the sick person's marriages, his position in the village, and all the positions of a chief lived in intensity within the group.

We said that the point of departure seemed Oedipal. It was only the point of departure *for us,* conditioned to say Oedipus every time someone speaks to us of father, mother, grandfather. In fact, the Ndembu analysis was never Oedipal: it was directly plugged into social organization and disorganization; sexuality itself, through the women and the marriages, was just such an investment of desire; the parents played the role of stimuli in it, and not the role of group organizers (or disorganizers)—the role held by the chief and his personages. Rather than everything being reduced to the name of the father, or that of the maternal grandfather, the latter opened onto all the names of history. Instead of everything being projected onto a grotesque hiatus of castration, everything was scattered in the thousand breaks-flows of the chieftainships, the lineages, the relations of colonization. The whole interplay of races, clans, alliances, and filiations, this entire historical and collective drift: exactly the opposite of the Oedipal analysis, when it stubbornly crushes the content of a delirium, when it stuffs it with all its might into "the symbolic void of the father." Or rather, if it is true that the analysis doesn't even begin as Oedipal, except to our way of seeing, doesn't it become Oedipal nevertheless, in a certain way—and in what way? Yes, it becomes Oedipal in part, under the effect of colonization. The colonizer, for example, abolishes the chieftainship, or uses it to further his own ends (and he uses many other things besides: the chieftainship is only a beginning). The colonizer says: your father is your father and nothing else, or your maternal grandfather—don't mistake them for chiefs; you can go have yourself triangulated in your corner, and place your house between those of your paternal and

maternal kin; your family is your family and nothing else; sexual reproduction no longer passes through those points, although we rightly need your family to furnish a material that will be subjected to a new order of reproduction. Yes, then, an Oedipal framework is outlined for the dispossessed primitives: a shantytown Oedipus. We have seen, however, that the colonized remained a typical example of resistance to Oedipus: in fact, that's where the Oedipal structure does not manage to close itself, and where the terms of the structure remained stuck to the agents of oppressive social reproduction, either in a struggle or in a complicity: the White Man, the missionary, the tax collector, the exporter of goods, the person with standing in the village who becomes the agent of the administration, the elders who curse the White Man, the young people who enter into a political struggle, etc. Both are true: the colonized resists oedipalization, and oedipalization tends to close around him again. To the degree that there is oedipalization, it is due to colonization, and it is necessary to add oedipalization to all the methods that Jaulin was able to describe in *La paix blanche*. "The condition of the colonized can lead to a reduction in the humanization of the universe, so that any solution that is sought will be a solution on the scale of the individual and the restricted family, with, by way of consequence, an extreme anarchy or disorder at the level of the collective: an anarchy whose victim will always be the individual—with the exception of those who occupy the key positions in such a system, namely the colonizers, who, during this same period when the colonized reduce the universe, will tend to extend it."* Oedipus is something like euthanasia within ethnocide. The more social reproduction escapes the members of the group, in nature and in extension, the more it falls back on them, or reduces them to a restricted and neuroticized familial reproduction whose agent is Oedipus.

After all, how are we to understand those who claim to have discovered an Indian Oedipus or an African Oedipus? They are the first to admit that they re-encounter *none* of the mechanisms or attitudes that constitute our own Oedipus (our own presumed Oedipus). No matter, they say that the structure is there, although it has no existence whatever that is "accessible to clinical practice"; or that the problem,

---

*Robert Jaulin, *La paix blanche: introduction à l'ethnocide* (Paris: Editions du Seuil, 1970), p. 309. Jaulin analyzes the situation of those Indians whom the Capucines "persuaded" to abandon the collective house in favor of "small personal houses" (pp. 391–400). In the collective house the familial apartment and personal intimacy were based on a relationship with the neighbor defined as an *ally*, so that interfamilial relations were coextensive with the social field. In the new situation, on the contrary, "there occurred an excessive ferment of the elements of the couple affecting the couple itself" and the children, so that the restrictive family closes into an expressive microcosm where each person reflects his own lineage, while the social and productive destiny (*devenir*) escapes him more and more. For Oedipus is not only an ideological process, but the result of a destruction of the environment, the habitat, etc.

the point of departure, is indeed Oedipal, although the developments and the solutions are completely different from ours (Parin, Ortigues). They say that "there is no end to the existence of this Oedipus," when in fact it does not even have (apart from colonization) the necessary conditions to begin to exist. If it is true that thought can be evaluated in terms of the degree of oedipalization, then yes, whites think too much. The competence, the honesty, and the talent of these authors—psychoanalysts specializing in Africa—are beyond question. But the same applies to them as to certain psychotherapists here: it would seem that they don't know what they are doing. We have psychotherapists who sincerely believe they are engaged in progressive work when they apply new methods for triangulating the child: but watch out—a structural Oedipus, and this time it isn't imaginary! The same is true of the psychoanalysts in Africa who apply the yoke of a structural or "problematical" Oedipus, in the service of their progressive intentions. There or here, it's the same thing: Oedipus is always colonization pursued by other means, it is the interior colony, and we shall see that even here at home, where we Europeans are concerned, it is our intimate colonial education.

How are we to understand the phrases with which M. C. and Edmond Ortigues conclude their book? "Illness is considered as a sign of an election, of a special attention coming from supernatural powers, or as a sign of an aggression of a magical nature, an idea that is difficult to express in profane terms. Analytic psychotherapy can intervene only starting from the moment a demand can be formulated by the subject. Our entire research was therefore conditioned by the possibility of establishing a psychoanalytic domain. When a subject adhered fully to the traditional norms and had nothing to say in his own name, he allowed himself to be taken into the care of the traditional therapists and the familial group, or into that of the medical practice of 'medicines.' At times, the fact that he wanted to speak to us about traditional treatments corresponded to a beginning of psychotherapy and became for him a means of situating himself personally in his own society. . . . At other times, the analytic dialogue was able to unfold to a greater extent, and in this case the Oedipal problem tended to assume its diachronic dimension, causing the generation gap to appear."[22] Why think that supernatural powers and magical aggressions constitute a myth that is inferior to Oedipus? On the contrary, is it not true that they move desire in the direction of more intense and more adequate investments of the social field, in its organization as well as its disorganizations? Meyer Fortes at least showed Job's place beside Oedipus. And what entitles one to determine that the subject has nothing to say in his own name so long as he adheres to the traditional norms? Doesn't the Ndembu cure demonstrate just the opposite? Could it not be said that Oedipus is also a traditional norm—our own, to be exact? How can one say that Oedipus makes us speak in our own name, when one also goes on to say that its resolution teaches us "the incurable inadequacy of being" and universal castration? And what is this "demand" that is invoked to justify Oedipus? It goes without saying, the subject demands and redemands daddy-mommy: but which subject, and in what state? Is that the means "to situate oneself personally in one's own society"? And which society? The neocolonized society that is constructed for the subject, and that finally succeeds in what colonization was only able to outline: an effective reduction of the forces of desire to Oedipus, to a father's name, in the grotesque triangle?

Let us return to the well-known and inexhaustible debate between culturalists and orthodox psychoanalysts: Is Oedipus universal? Is Oedipus the great paternal catholic symbol, the meeting place of all the churches? The debate began between Malinowski and Jones, it continued between Kardiner and Fromm on one side, and Roheim on the other. It is still pursued between certain ethnologists and certain disciples of Lacan—those who offered not only an oedipalizing interpretation of Lacan's doctrine, but also an ethnographic extension to this interpretation. On the side of the universal there are two poles: one—outdated, it would seem—that makes of Oedipus an original affective constellation, and that constitutes an extreme position arguing that Oedipus was a real event whose effects were transmitted through phylogenetic heredity. And the other pole, which makes Oedipus into a structure, a pole whose extreme position argues the possibility of discovering the structure in fantasy, in relation to biological prematuration and neoteny. Two very different conceptions of the limit, one as original matrix, the other as structural function. But in both these senses of the universal, we are invited to "interpret," since the latent presence of Oedipus appears only through its patent absence, understood as an effect of psychic repression—or, better still, since the structural constant is discovered only through its imaginary variations, attesting to the need for a symbolic foreclosure (the father as an empty position). Oedipus-as-universal recommences the old metaphysical operation that consists in interpreting negation as a deprivation, as a lack: the symbolic lack of the dead father, or the Great Signifier. Interpretation is our modern way of believing and of being pious. Already Geza Roheim proposed organizing primitives into a series of variables converging toward the structural neotenic constant.[23] It was he who said in all seriousness that the Oedipus complex was not to be found if it wasn't looked for. And that one wasn't looking if one hadn't had oneself analyzed. And that is why your daughter is mute, which is to say: the tribes, daughters of the ethnologist, do not say Oedipus, although it is Oedipus who makes them speak. Roheim added that it was ridiculous to think that the Freudian theory of censorship depended on the repressive régime in the empire of Franz Joseph. He did not seem to see that Franz Joseph was not a pertinent historical break (*coupure*), but that perhaps the oral, the written, or even the "capitalist" civilizations were such breaks with which the nature of social repression (*répression*), and the meaning and scope of psychic repression (*refoulement*), would vary.

This story of psychic repression is quite complicated. Things would be simpler if the libido or the affect were repressed, in the most general sense of the word (suppressed, inhibited, or transformed)—at the same time as the supposed Oedipal representation. But such is not the case: most ethnologists have clearly noted the sexual nature of affects in the public symbols of primitive societies, and this nature remains integrally lived by the members of these societies, even though they have not been psychoanalyzed, and in spite of the displacement of the representation. As Leach says apropos of the sex/hair relationship, "displaced phallic symbolism is very common, but the phallic origin of the symbolism is not repressed".[24] Must it be said that primitives repress the representation and keep the affect intact? And would the contrary be true in our case, in the patriarchal organization where the representation would remain clear, but with the affects suppressed, inhibited, or transformed? No, in fact: psychoanalysis tells us that we too repress the representation. And everything tells us that we too often keep the full sexuality of the affect; we know perfectly well what it is about, without having been psychoanalyzed. But what enables one to speak of an Oedipal representation that would be the object of repression? Is it because incest is prohibited? We always fall back on this pale rationale: incest is desired because it is prohibited. The prohibition of incest would therefore imply an Oedipal representation, and it would be born of the repression of this representation and of the latter's return. Now the opposite is clearly the case; not only does the Oedipal representation presuppose the prohibition of incest, but it is not even possible to say that the representation is born of the prohibition or results from it.

Adopting Malinowski's arguments, Reich added a profound remark: desire is all the more Oedipal as the prohibitions are aimed, not simply at incest, but "at *all other types* of sexual relations," blocking the other paths.[25] In a word, the repression of incest is not born of a repressed Oedipal representation any more than it provokes this repression. But—and this is something altogether different—the general social repression–psychic repression system gives rise to an Oedipal image as a disfiguration of the repressed. The fact that this image in turn finally suffers a repression, that it comes to take the place of the repressed or of the thing that is effectively desired, insofar as sexual repression is directed at *something other* than incest—such is the long history of our society. But the repressed is not first of all the Oedipal representation. What is repressed is desiring-production. It is the part of this production that does not enter into social production or reproduction. It is what would introduce disorder and revolution into the socius, the noncoded flows of desire. The part that passes, on the contrary, from desiring-production to social production forms a direct sexual investment men of this social production, without any repression of a sexual nature of the symbolism and the corresponding affects, and above all, without any reference to an Oedipal representation that could be held to be originally repressed or structurally foreclosed. The animal in us is not merely the object of a preconscious investment determined by interest, but the object of a libidinal investment of desire that only secondarily derives an image of the father from desiring-production. The same holds true for the libidinal investment of food, wherever a fear of going hungry is evident, or a pleasure at not being hungry, and this investment refers only secondarily to an image of the mother.* We have already seen how the prohibition of incest referred, not to Oedipus, but to the noncoded flows that constitute desire, and to their representative, the intense prepersonal flow. As for Oedipus, it is another way of coding the uncodable, of codifying what eludes the codes, or of displacing desire and its object, a way of entrapping them.

Culturalists and ethnologists have demonstrated that institutions are primary in relation to affects and structures. For structures are not mental, they are present in things (*elles sont dans les choses*), in the forms of social production and reproduction. Even an author like Marcuse, whom one would not suspect of complaisance in this regard, acknowledges that culturalism started on the right track: introducing desire into production, strengthening the link "between instinctual and economic structure; and at the same time [indicating] the possibility of progress beyond the 'patricentric-acquisitive' culture."[26] Then what caused culturalism to go wrong? And here again there is no contradiction in the fact that it started on the right track, and that it went wrong from the start. Perhaps the answer lies in the postulate common to Oedipal relativism and Oedipal absolutism—i.e., the stubborn mainte-

*In his study of the Marquesa Islands, Abram Kardiner has convincingly demonstrated the role of a collective or economic alimentary anxiety that, even from the viewpoint of the unconscious, does not allow itself to be reduced to the familial relationship with the mother: *The Individual and His Society* (See reference note 28), pp. 223ff.

nance of a familialist perspective, which wreaks havoc everywhere. For if the institution is first understood as a familial institution, it matters little to say that the familial complex varies with the institutions, or that Oedipus is to the contrary a nuclear constant around which families and institutions turn. The culturalists invoke other triangles—maternal uncle–aunt–nephew, for example; but the oedipalists have no difficulty in demonstrating that these are imaginary variations of one and the same structural constant, different figures of one and the same symbolic triangulation, which are not identical either with the personages who come to realize the triangulation, or with the attitudes that come to place these personages in relation to each other. But inversely, the invocation of such a transcendent symbolism does not rescue the structuralists from the narrowest familial point of view. The same holds for the endless debates on "Is it daddy? Is it mommy?" (You are neglecting the mother! No, *you*'re the one who fails to see the father off to the side, as the empty position!)

The conflict between culturalists and orthodox psychoanalysts has often been reduced to these evaluations of the respective roles of the mother and the father, or of the pre-oedipal and the Oedipal, without allowing either side to leave the family or even Oedipus, always oscillating between the famous two poles, the pre-oedipal maternal pole of the Imaginary, and the Oedipal paternal pole of the structural, both on the same axis, both speaking the same language of a familialized social realm, where one pole designates the customary maternal dialects, while the other designates the imperative law of the language of the father. The ambiguity of what Kardiner called the "primary institution" has been clearly shown. In certain cases it can be a question of the way desire invests the social field from childhood, and under the familial stimuli coming from the adult: all the conditions would then be given for an adequate (extrafamilial) understanding of the libido. But more often it is solely a question of the familial organization in itself, which is thought to be lived first by the child as a microcosm, then projected into the adult and social development (*devenir*).* From this point of view, the discussion can only go round in circles between the holders of a cultural interpretation and the holders of a symbolic or structural interpretation of this same organization.

A second postulate common to the culturalists and the symbolists should be added. They all agree that, in our patriarchal and capitalist

---

*Mikel Dufrenne, analyzing the concepts of Kardiner, raises these essential questions: Is it the family that is "primary," while the political, the economic, and the social are merely secondary? Which comes first from the viewpoint of the libido, the familial investment or the social investment? And methodologically is it necessary to go from the child to the adult, or from the adult to the child? (Mikel Dufrenne, *La personnalité de base* [Paris: Presses Universitaires de France, 1953], pp. 287ff.)

society at least, Oedipus is a sure thing (even if they underline, as does Fromm, the elements of a new matriarchy). They all agree that our society is the stronghold of Oedipus: the starting point for re-encountering an Oedipal structure everywhere; or on the contrary, they hold that the terms and the relations should be made to vary within non-oedipal complexes that are no less "familial" on that account. That is why our preceding criticism was directed at Oedipus as it is meant to command our respect and to function for us: it is not at the weakest point—the primitives—that Oedipus must be attacked, but at the strongest point, at the level of the strongest link, by revealing the degree of disfiguration it implies and brings to bear on desiring-production, on the syntheses of the unconscious, and on libidinal investments *in our cultural and social milieu.* Not that Oedipus counts for nothing in our society: we have said repeatedly that Oedipus is demanded, and demanded again and again; and even an attempt as profound as Lacan's at shaking loose from the yoke of Oedipus has been interpreted as an unhoped-for means of making it heavier still and of resecuring it on the baby and the schizo. To be sure, it is not only legitimate but indispensable that the ethnological or historical explanation not be in contradiction with our social organization, or that this organization contain in its own way the basic elements of the ethnological hypothesis. This is what Marx was saying as he recalled the requirements of a universal history—but, as he went on to say, provided that the current organization be capable of conducting its own criticism. And yet Oedipus's autocritique is something rarely seen in our organization, of which psychoanalysis forms a part. In certain respects it is correct to question all social formations starting from Oedipus. But not because Oedipus might be a truth of the unconscious that is especially visible where we are concerned; on the contrary, because it is a mystification of the unconscious that has only succeeded with us by assembling the parts and wheels of its apparatus from elements of the previous social formations. It is universal in that sense. Thus it is indeed within capitalist society that the critique of Oedipus must always resume its point of departure and find again its point of arrival.

Oedipus is a limit. But "limit" has many different meanings, since it can be at the beginning as an inaugural event, in the role of a matrix; or in the middle as a structural function ensuring the mediation of personages and the ground of their relations; or at the end as an eschatological determination. Now we have seen that it is only in this last sense that Oedipus is a limit. This is also the case for desiring-production. But in fact this last sense itself can be understood in many different ways. In the first place, desiring-production is situated at the limits of social production; the decoded flows, at the limits of the codes and the territorialities; the body without organs, at the limits of the socius. We shall speak of an *absolute limit* every time the schizo-flows pass through the wall, scramble all the codes, and deterritorialize the socius: the body without organs is the deterritorialized socius, the wilderness where the decoded flows run free, the end of the world, the apocalypse. Secondly, however, the *relative limit* is no more nor less than the capitalist social formation, because the latter engineers (*machine*) and mobilizes flows that are effectively decoded, but does so by substituting for the codes a quantifying axiomatic (*une axiomatique comptable*) that is even more oppressive. With the result that capitalism—in conformity with the movement by which it counteracts its own tendency—is continually drawing near the wall, while at the same time pushing the wall further way. Schizophrenia is the absolute limit, but capitalism is the relative limit. Thirdly, there is no social formation that does not foresee, or experience a foreboding of, the real form in which the limit threatens to arrive, and which it wards off with all the strength it can command. Whence the obstinacy with which the formations preceding capitalism encaste the merchant and the technician, preventing flows of money and flows of production from assuming an autonomy that would destroy their codes. Such is the *real limit.*

When such societies are confronted with this real limit, repressed from within, but which returns to them from without, they regard this event with melancholy as the sign of their approaching death. For example, the Bohannans describe the Tiv economy, which codes three kinds of flows: consumer goods, prestige goods, and women and children. When money supervenes, it can only be coded as an object of prestige, yet merchants use it to lay hold of sectors of consumer goods traditionally held by the women: all the codes vacillate. Doubtless, to begin with money and to finish with money is an operation that cannot be expressed in terms of a code; seeing the trucks that leave loaded with export goods, "the Tiv elders deplore this situation, and know what is happening, but do not know where to place their blame"[27]—a harsh reality. But, fourthly, this limit inhibited from the interior was already projected onto a primordial beginning, a mythical matrix as the *imaginary limit.* How can this nightmare be imagined: the invasion of the socius by noncoded flows that move like lava? An irrepressible wave of shit, as in the Fourbe myth; or the intense germinal influx, the this-side-of incest, as in the Yourougou myth, which introduces disorder into the world by acting as the representative of desire. Whence, in the fifth and last instance, the importance of the task of displacing the limit: causing it to pass into the interior of the socius, in the middle, between a beyond of alliance and a filiative this-side-of, between a representation of alliance and the representative of filiation, as one attempts to tame the dreaded forces of a river by digging an artificial river bed, or by diverting it into a thousand shallow little streams. Oedipus is this *displaced limit*. Yes, Oedipus is universal. But the error lies in having believed in the following alternative: either Oedipus is the product of the social repression–psychic repression system, in which case it is not universal; or it is universal, and a position of desire. In reality, it is universal because it is the displacement of the limit that haunts all societies, the displaced represented (*le représenté déplacé*) that disfigures what all societies dread absolutely as their most profound negative: namely, the decoded flows of desire.

This is not to say that the universal Oedipal limit is "occupied," strategically occupied in all social formations. We must take Kardiner's remark seriously: a Hindu or an Eskimo can dream of Oedipus, without however being subjected to the complex, without "having the complex."[28] For Oedipus to be occupied, a certain number of conditions are indispensable: the field of social production and reproduction must become independent of familial reproduction, that is, independent of the territorial machine that declines alliances and filiations; the detachable fragments of the chain must be converted, by virtue of this independence, into a transcendent detached object that crushes their polyvocal character; the detached object (phallus) must perform a kind of folding operation—a kind of application or reduction (*rabattement*): a reduction of the social field, defined as the aggregate of departure, to the familial field, now defined as the aggregate of destination—and it must establish a network of one-to-one relations between the two. For Oedipus to be occupied, it is not enough that it be a limit or a displaced represented in the system of representation; it must *migrate* to the heart of this system and itself come to occupy the position of the representative of desire. These conditions, inseparable from the paralogisms of the unconscious, are realized in the capitalist formation; furthermore, they imply certain archaisms borrowed from the imperial barbarian formations—in particular, the position of the transcendent object. The capitalist style has been described by D. H. Lawrence: "our democratic, industrial order of things whose style is my-dear-little-lamb-I-want-to-see-mommy."

Now on the one hand, it is evident that the primitive formations do not come close to fulfilling these conditions. Precisely because the family, when opened to alliances, is coextensive with and adequate to the social historical field; because it animates social reproduction itself; because it mobilizes or causes passage of the detachable fragments without ever converting them into a detached object—no reduction whatever, no application is possible that would answer to the formula 3+1 (the four corners of the field folded into three, like a tablecloth, plus the transcendent term that performs the folding operation). "Speaking, dancing, exchanging, and allowing to flow, and even urinating, in the midst of the community of men," as Parin himself puts it, to express the fluidity of the flows and the primitive codes.* At the heart of primitive production one always finds oneself at 4+*n,* in the system of ancestors and affines. Far from being able to claim that here there is no end to Oedipus, one sees that it never manages to begin; one is always brought to a halt well before 3+1, and if there is a primitive Oedipus, it is a neg-Oedipus, in the sense of a neg-entropy. Oedipus is indeed a limit or a displaced represented, but precisely in such a way that each member of the group is always on this side of or beyond, without ever occupying the position (Kardiner has understood this very well in the formula we cited). It is colonization that causes Oedipus to exist, but an Oedipus that is taken for what it is, a pure oppression, inasmuch as it assumes that these Savages are deprived of the control over their own social production, that they are ripe for being reduced to the only thing they have left, the familial reproduction imposed on them being no less oedipalized by force than it is alcoholic or sickly.

On the other hand, when the requisite conditions are realized in capitalist society, it should not be thought on that account that Oedipus ceases to be what it is, the simple displaced represented that comes to usurp the place of the representative of desire, snaring the unconscious in the trap of its paralogisms, crushing the whole of desiring-production, replacing it with a system of beliefs. Oedipus is never a cause: it depends on a previous social investment of a certain type, capable of falling back on (*se rabattre sur*) family determinations. It will be objected that such a principle is perhaps valid for the adult, but surely not for the child. But in effect, Oedipus begins in the mind of the father. And the beginning is not absolute: it is only constituted starting from investments of the social historical field that are effected by the father. And if it passes over to the son, this is not by virtue of a familial heredity, but by virtue of a much more complex relationship that depends on the communication of the unconsciouses. With the result that, even in the child, what is

<hr/>

*Paul Parin et al., *Les blancs pensent trop*, p. 432. Regarding the coextensivity of marriages with the primitive social field, see Jaulin's remarks, *La paix blanche*, p. 256: "Marriages are not governed by kinship laws, they obey a dynamic that is infinitely more complex, less rigid, whose invention at each moment utilizes a number of co-ordinates of another order of importance. . . . Marriages are more apt to be a speculation on the future than on the past, and in any case these marriages and their speculation derive from what is complex, not from what is elementary, and never from what is rigidly fixed. The reason for this is not by any means that man knows laws only so that he may violate them. . . ." Whence the stupidity of the concept of transgression.

invested through the familial stimuli is still the social field, and a whole system of breaks and extrafamilial flows. The fact that the father is first in relation to the child can only be understood analytically in terms of another primacy, that of social investments and counterinvestments in relation to familial investments: this will be seen later, at the level of an analysis of deliriums. But already, if it appears that Oedipus is an effect, this is because it forms an aggregate of destination (the family become microcosm) on which capitalist production and reproduction fall back. The organs and the agents of the latter no longer pass through a coding of flows of alliance and filiation, but through an axiomatic of decoded flows. Consequently, the capitalist formation of sovereignty will need an intimate colonial formation that corresponds to it, to which it will be applied, and without which it would have no hold on the productions of the unconscious.

Given these conditions, what is there to say about the relationship between ethnology and psychoanalysis? Must we be content with an uncertain parallelism where each contemplates the other with perplexity, placing in opposition two irreducible sectors of symbolism? A social sector of symbols, and a sexual sector that would constitute a kind of private universal, a kind of individual-universal? (Transversals between the two, since social symbolism can become a sexual material, and sexuality, a ritual of social aggregation.) But the problem is too theoretical when posed this way. Practically speaking, the psychoanalyst often claims to explain to the ethnologist the meaning of the symbol: it means phallus, castration, Oedipus. But the ethnologist asks other questions, and sincerely asks himself *of what use can psychoanalytic interpretations be to me?* Hence the duality is displaced, it is no longer between two sectors, but between two kinds of questions, "What does it mean?" and "What purpose does it serve?" Of what use is it not only to the ethnologist, but what purpose does it serve and how does it work in the very formation that makes use of the symbol?* Whatever may be the meaning of a thing, it is not certain that the thing serves any useful purpose whatever. It is possible, for example, that Oedipus serves no useful purpose, either for psychoanalysts or for the unconscious. And to what use could the phallus be put, since it is inseparable from the castration that deprives us of its use? Of course we are told not to confuse the signified with the signifier. But does the signifier take us

*Roger Bastide has systematically developed the theory of the two symbolic sectors, in *Sociologie et psychanalyse* (Paris: Presses Universitaires de France, 1950). But, starting from a viewpoint that is analogous at first, E. R. Leach is led to displace the duality, causing it to pass between the question of meaning and that of use, thereby changing the scope of the problem: see "Magical Hair" (reference note 24).

beyond the question, "What does it mean?" Is it anything other than this same question, only this time barred? This is still the domain of representation.

The true misunderstandings, the misunderstandings between ethnologists (or Hellenists) and psychoanalysts, do not come from a faulty knowledge or recognition of the unconscious, of sexuality, of the phallic nature of symbolism. In theory, everyone could reach an agreement on this point: everything is sexual or sex-influenced (*sexué*) from one end to the other. Everyone knows this, beginning with the users. The practical misunderstandings come rather from the profound difference between the two sorts of questions. Without always formulating it clearly, the ethnologists and the Hellenists think that a symbol is not defined by what it means, but by what it does and by what is done with it. It always means the phallus or something similar, except that what it means does not tell what purpose it serves. In a word, there is no ethnological interpretation for the simple reason that there is no ethnographic material: there are only uses and functionings (*des fonctionnements*). On this point, it could be that psychoanalysts have much to learn from ethnologists: about the unimportance of "What does it mean?" When Hellenists place themselves in opposition to the Freudian Oedipus, it should not be thought that they put forward other interpretations to replace the psychoanalytic interpretation. It could be that ethnologists and Hellenists will compel psychoanalysts for their part to make a similar discovery: namely, that there is no unconscious material either, nor is there a psychoanalytic interpretation, but only uses, analytic uses of the syntheses of the unconscious, which do not allow themselves to be defined by an assignment of a signifier any more than by the determination of signifieds. How it works is the sole question. Schizoanalysis foregoes all interpretation because it foregoes discovering an unconscious material: the unconscious does not mean anything. On the other hand the unconscious constructs machines, which are machines of desire, whose use and functioning schizoanalysis discovers in their immanent relationship with social machines. The unconscious does not speak, it engineers. It is not expressive or representative, but productive. A symbol is nothing other than a social machine that functions as a desiring-machine, a desiring-machine that functions within the social machine, an investment of the social machine by desire.

It has often been said and demonstrated that an institution cannot be explained by its use, any more than an organ can. Biological formations and social formations are not formed in the same way in which they function. Nor is there a biological, sociological, linguistic, etc., functionalism at the level of large determinate aggregates (*des grands ensembles spécifiés*). But the same does not hold true in the case of desiring-machines as molecular elements: there, use, functioning, production, and formation are one and the same process. And it is this synthesis of desire that, under certain determinate conditions, explains the molar aggregates (*les ensembles molaires*) *with* their specific use in a biological, social, or linguistic field. This is because the large molar machines presuppose pre-established connections that are not explained by their functioning, since the latter results from them. Only desiring-machines produce connections according to which they function, and function by improvising and forming the connections. A molar functionalism is therefore a functionalism that did not go far enough, that did not reach those regions where desire engineers, independently of the macroscopic nature of what it is engineering: organic, social, linguistic, etc., elements, all tossed into the same pot to stew. The only unities-multiplicities that functionalism must know are the desiring-machines themselves and the configurations they form in all the sectors of a field of production (the "total fact"). A magical chain brings together plant life, pieces of organs, a shred of clothing, an image of daddy, formulas and words: we shall not ask what it means, but what kind of machine is assembled in this manner—what kind of flows and breaks in the flows, in relation to other breaks and other flows.

Analyzing the symbolism of the forked branch among the Ndembu, Victor Turner shows that the names given to them form a part of a chain that mobilizes the species and the properties of the trees from which the branches are taken, as well as the names of these species in turn, and the technical procedures with which they are treated. Selections are made from signifying chains no less than from material flows. The exegetical meaning (what is said about the thing) is only one element among others, and is less important than the operative use (what is done with the thing) or the positional functioning (the relationship with other things in one and the same complex), according to which the symbol is never in a one-to-one relationship with what it means, but always has a multiplicity of referents, being "always multivocal and polysemous."[29] Analyzing the magical object *buti* among the Kukuya of the Congo, Pierre Bonnafé shows how it is inseparable from the practical syntheses that produce, record, and consume it: the partial and nonspecific connection that combines fragments from the body of the subject with those of an animal; the inclusive disjunction that inscribes the object in the body of the subject, and transforms the latter into a man-animal; the residual conjunction that causes the "residue" to submit to a long voyage before burying or immersing it.* If present-day ethnologists are again evincing a lively interest in the hypothetical concept of the fetish, this is unquestionably due to the influence of psychoanalysis. But it would seem that psychoanalysis offers them just as many reasons for doubting the notion as it offers for attracting their interest. For psychoanalysis has never said Phallus-Oedipus-Castration more often than apropos of the fetish. While for his part, the ethnologist senses that there is a problem of political power and economic and religious force inseparable from the fetish, even when its use is individual and private. Hair, for example—the rituals of hair-cutting and coiffure: is there any interest in referring these rituals to the phallus entity as signifying the "separate thing," and in everywhere re-encountering the father as the symbolic representative of the separation? Wouldn't this be tantamount to remaining at the level of what it means? The ethnologist finds himself before a flow of hair, with the breaks in such a flow, and with what passes from one state into another through the break. As Leach says, hair as a partial object or as a separable part of the body does not represent an aggressive and separate phallus; hair *is* a thing in its own right, a material part in an aggressing apparatus, in a separating machine.

Once again, it is not a question of knowing if the essence of a ritual is sexual, or if it is necessary to take into account political, economic, and religious dimensions that would go beyond sexuality. So long as the problem is put in this manner, so long as a choice is imposed between libido and numen, the misunderstanding between ethnologists and psychoanalysts can only be aggravated—just as it continues to grow between Hellenists and psychoanalysts apropos of Oedipus. Oedipus, the clubfooted despot, who clearly invokes an entire political history that brings into conflict the despotic machine and the old primitive territorial machine—whence derive both the negation and the persistence of autochthony, brought into clear relief by Lévi-Strauss. But this is not enough to desexualize the drama. On the contrary. In reality, it is a question of knowing how one conceives of sexuality and libidinal investment. Must they be referred to an event or to something that is

*Pierre Bonnafé, "Objet magique, sorcellerie et fétichisme?", *Nouvelle revue de psychanalyse*, no. 2 (1970): "The Kukuya affirm that the nature of the object matters little: the essential thing is that it acts." See also Alfred Adler, "L'ethnologue et les fétiches." The interest of this issue of the *N.R.P.*, devoted to "objects of fetishism," is that in its pages ethnologists do not place one theory in opposition to another, but reflect on the bearing of psychoanalytic interpretations on their own ethnological practice, and on the social practices they study. In a paper entitled "Les interprétations de Turner" (Faculté de Nanterre), Eric Laurent was able to make explicit in a profound way the problems of method in this regard: the necessity for performing a series of reversals, for privileging use over exegesis or justification; productivity over expressivity; the actual state of the social field over the cosmological myths; the exact ritual over structural models; the "social drama," the political tactic, and strategy over kinship diagrams.

"felt," which remains familial and intimate in spite of everything, an intimate Oedipal feeling, even when it is interpreted structurally, on behalf of the pure signifier? Or rather is it necessary to open sexuality and libidinal investment onto the determinations of a sociohistorical field, where the economic, the political, and the religious are things that are invested by the libido for themselves, and not the derivatives of a daddy-mommy? In the first instance one studies large molar aggregates, large social machines—the economic, the political, etc.—and this entails searching for *what they mean* by applying them to an abstract familial whole that is thought to contain the secret of the libido: in this way, one remains in the framework of representation.

In the second instance one goes beyond these large aggregates, including the family, toward the molecular elements that form the parts and wheels of desiring-machines. One searches for the way in which these machines *function,* for how they invest and underdetermine (*subdéterminent*) the social machines that they constitute on a large scale. One then reaches the regions of a productive, molecular, micrological, or microphysical unconscious that no longer means or represents anything. Sexuality is no longer regarded as a specific energy that unites persons derived from the large aggregates, but as the molecular energy that places molecules–partial objects (libido) in connection, that organizes inclusive disjunctions on the giant molecule of the body without organs (numen), and that distributes states of being and becoming according to domains of presence or zones of intensity (voluptas). For desiring-machines are precisely that: the microphysics of the unconscious, the elements of the microunconscious. But as such they never exist independently of the historical molar aggregates, of the macroscopic social formations that they constitute statistically. In this sense, there is only desire and the social. Beneath the conscious investments of economic, political, religious, etc., formations, there are unconscious sexual investments, microinvestments that attest to the way in which desire is present in a social field, and joins this field to itself as the statistically determined domain that is bound to it. Desiring-machines function within social machines, as though they maintained their own régime in the molar aggregates that they form at the level of large numbers. Symbols and fetishes are manifestations of desiring-machines. Sexuality is by no means a molar determination that is representable in a familial whole; it is the molecular underdetermination functioning within social and secondarily familial aggregates that trace desire's field of presence and its field of production: an entire non-Oedipal unconscious that will only produce Oedipus as one of its secondary statistical formations ("complexes"), at the end of a history bringing into play the destiny of social machines, their régime compared to that of desiring-machines.

5 | Territorial Representation

While representation is always a social and psychic repression of desiring-production, it should be borne in mind that this repression is exercised in very diverse ways, according to the social formation considered. The system of representation comprises three elements that vary in depth: the repressed representative, the repressing representation, and the displaced represented. But the agents (*les instances*) that come to carry them into effect are themselves variable; there are migrations in the system. We see no reason for believing in the universality of one and the same apparatus of sociocultural repression (*refoulement*). One can speak instead of a coefficient of affinity that varies in degree between social machines and desiring-machines, according to whether their respective régimes are more or less similar; according to whether the desiring-machines have a greater or lesser chance of causing their connections and interactions to pass into the régime of the social machines; according to whether the social machines execute more or less of a movement of detachment (*décollement*) in relation to the desiring-machines; and whether the death-carrying elements remain caught in the machinery of desire, encasted in the social machine, or on the contrary join together to form a death instinct that extends throughout the social machine, crushing desire.

The principal factor in each of these respects is the type or genus of social inscription, its alphabet, its characteristics: the inscription on the socius is in fact the agent of a secondary psychic repression, or repression "in the proper sense of the term," that is necessarily situated in relation to the desiring-inscription of the body without organs, and in relation to the primary repression that the latter already performs in the domain of desire—a relation that is essentially variable. There is always social repression (*refoulement*), but the apparatus of repression varies, depending in particular on what plays the role of the representative on which the repression is brought to bear. In this sense it is possible that the primitive codes, at the moment they are acting on the flows of desire with a maximum of vigilance and extension, binding them in a *system of cruelty*, maintain an infinitely greater affinity with desiring-machines than does the capitalist axiomatic, which nonetheless liberates the decoded flows. This is because in the primitive socius desire is not yet trapped, not yet introduced into a set of impasses, the flows have lost none of their polyvocity, and the simple represented in representation has not yet taken the place of the representative. In order to evaluate in every instance the nature of the apparatus and its effects on desiring-production, it is therefore necessary to take into account not only the elements of representation as they are organized in depth, but the manner in which representation itself is organized at the surface, on the inscription surface of the socius.

Society is not exchangist, the socius is inscriptive: not exchanging but marking bodies, which are part of the earth. We have seen that the régime of debt directly resulted from this savage inscription. For debt is the unit of alliance, and alliance is representation itself. It is alliance that codes the flows of desire and that, by means of debt, creates for man a memory of words (*paroles*). It is alliance that represses the great, intense, mute filiative memory, the germinal influx as the representative of the noncoded flows of desire capable of submerging everything. It is debt that articulates the alliances with the filiations that have become extended, in order to form and to forge a system in extension (representation) based on the repression of nocturnal intensities. The alliance-debt answers to what Nietzsche described as humanity's prehistoric labor: the use of the cruelist mnemotechnics, in naked flesh, to impose a memory of words founded on the ancient biocosmic memory. That is why it is so important to see debt as a direct consequence of the primitive inscription process, instead of making it—and the inscriptions themselves—into an indirect means of universal exchange.

There is a question that Marcel Mauss at least left open: is debt primary in relation to exchange, or is it merely a mode of exchange, a means in the service of exchange? But Lévi-Strauss seems to have closed the question again with a categorical reply: debt is no more than a superstructure, a conscious form whereby the unconscious social reality of exchange is converted into cash.* What is involved is not a theoretical discussion of the first principles of anthropology: the whole notion of social practice, and the postulates conveyed by this practice, are at issue here—and the whole problem of the unconscious. For if exchange underlies everything, why is it that what takes place looks like anything but an exchange? Why must it be a gift, or a countergift, and not an exchange? And why is it necessary that the giver also be in the position

*Claude Lévi-Strauss, "Introduction à l'oeuvre de Marcel Mauss," in Marcel Mauss, *Sociologie et anthropologie* (Paris: Presses Universitaires de France), pp. 38–39. And Lé vi-Strauss, *The Elementary Structures of Kinship,* p. 181: ". . . to explain why the system of generalized exchange has remained subjacent and why the explicit system is formulated in very different terms." To see how, starting from this principle, Lévi-Strauss arrives at a conception of the unconscious as an empty form, indifferent to the drives of desire, see his *Structural Anthropology,* p. 203. It is true that Lévi-Strauss's *Mythologiques* series elaborates a theory of primitive codes, and of codings of flows and of organs, that goes beyond the exchangist conception on all sides.

of someone who has been robbed, so as to demonstrate clearly that he does not expect an exchange, not even a deferred exchange? It is theft that prevents the gift and the countergift from entering into an exchangist relation. Desire knows nothing of exchange, *it knows only theft and gift,* at times the one within the other under the effect of a primary homosexuality. Thus the antiexchangist amorous machine encountered by Joyce in *Exiles,* and by Klossowski in *Roberte.* "In Gourma ideology, it is as though a wife could only be given (the lityuatieli), or carried away, kidnapped, hence in a certain sense stolen (the lipwotali); every union that could too manifestly appear to be the result of a direct exchange between two lineages or lineage segments is, in this society, if not prohibited, at least widely disapproved of."[30]

Will it be said that, if desire knows nothing of exchange, it is because exchange is desire's unconscious? Will this be explained by the exigencies of generalized exchange? But what entitles one to declare that shares of debt are secondary compared with a totality that is "more real"? Yet exchange is known, well known in the primitive socius—but as that which must be exorcised, encasted, severely restricted, so that no corresponding value can develop as an exchange value that would introduce the nightmare of a commodity economy. The primitive market operates through bargaining rather than by fixing an equivalent that would lead to a decoding of flows and a collapse of the mode of inscription on the socius. We are brought back to our point of departure: the fact that exchange is inhibited and exorcised by no means attests to its primary reality, but demonstrates on the contrary that the essential process is not exchanging, but inscribing or marking. And when exchange is made into an unconscious reality, structural rights are invoked in vain—along with the necessary inadequation of attitudes and ideologies in relation to this structure—for one does nothing more than hypostatize the principles of an exchangist psychology to account for institutions that on the other hand are recognized to be nonexchangist. And above all, what is made of the unconscious itself, if not its explicit reduction to an *empty form,* from which desire itself is absent and expelled? Such a form can serve to define a preconscious, but certainly not the unconscious. For if it is true that the unconscious has no material or content, this is assuredly not because it is an empty form, but rather because it is always and already a functioning machine, a desiring-machine and not an anorexic structure.

The difference between machine and structure appears in the postulates that implicitly animate the structural and exchangist conception of the socius, with the correctives that must be introduced into this conception so that the structure is able to function. First of all, when considering kinship structures, it is difficult not to proceed as though the alliances derived from the lines of filiation and their relationships, although the lateral alliances and the blocks of debt condition the extended filiations in the system in extension, and not the opposite. Secondly, there is a tendency to make the system in extension into a logical combinative arrangement, instead of taking it for what it is: a physical system where intensities are distributed, where some cancel out and block a current, where others cause the current to circulate, etc. The objection according to which the qualities developed in the system are not only physical objects, "but also honors, responsibilities, privileges," seems to indicate a misunderstanding of the role of the incommensurable elements and the inequalities in the conditions of the system. More precisely, in the third place, the structural exchangist conception tends to postulate a kind of primary equilibrium of prices, a primary equivalence or equality in the underlying principles, which allows it to explain that the inequalities are necessarily introduced in the consequences.

Nothing is more significant in this regard than the controversy between Lévi-Strauss and Leach concerning the Kachin marriage system. Invoking a "conflict between the egalitarian conditions of generalized exchange, and its aristocratic consequences," Lévi-Strauss acts as though he thought the system were in a state of equilibrium. However, the problem is altogether different: it is a question of knowing if the disequilibrium is pathological and a manifestation of consequences, as Lévi-Strauss maintains, or functional and fundamental, as Leach argues.[31] Is the instability derived in relation to an ideal of exchange, or is it already given in the preconditions, included in the heterogeneity of the terms that compose the prestations and counterprestations? The more one directs one's attention to the economic and political compromises conveyed by the alliances, to the nature of the counterprestations that come to compensate the disequilibrium of the prestations of wives, and generally the original manner in which the aggregate of prestations is evaluated in a particular society, the more clearly the necessarily open nature of the system in extension appears, as in the case of the primitive mechanism of surplus value as a surplus value of code. But—and this is the fourth point—the exchangist conception finds it necessary to postulate a closed system, statistically closed, and to shore up the structure with a psychological conviction ("confidence that the cycle will reclose"). Thus not only the essential opening of the blocks of debts according to the lateral alliances and the successive generations, but above all the relationship of the statistical formations to their molecular elements, find themselves brought back to the simple empirical reality, insofar as it is not adequate to the structural model.[32]

All this depends, finally, on a postulate that burdens ethnology to the same extent that it has determined bourgeois political economy: the reduction of social reproduction to the sphere of circulation. One retains the apparent objective movement as it is described on the socius, without taking into account the real instance that inscribes it, and the forces—economic and political—with which it is inscribed; one fails to see that alliance is the form in which the socius appropriates the connections of labor in the disjunctive order of its inscriptions. "From the viewpoint of the relations of production, in fact, the circulation of women appears as a distribution of labor capacity, but in the ideological representation that the society gives itself of its economic base, this aspect fades before the relations of exchange, which are, however, merely the form this distribution takes within the sphere of circulation: by isolating the moment of circulation in the reproduction process, ethnology ratifies this representation," and grants bourgeois economy its whole colonial extension.[33] In this sense the essential thing seemed to us to be, not exchange and circulation, which closely depend on the requirements of inscription, but inscription itself, with its imprint of fire, its alphabet inscribed in bodies, and its blocks of debts. The soft structure would never function, would never cause a circulation, without the hard machinic element that presides over inscriptions.

Savage formations are oral, are vocal, but not because they lack a graphic system: a dance on the earth, a drawing on a wall, a mark on the body are a graphic system, a geo-graphism, a geography. These formations are oral precisely because they possess a graphic system that is independent of the voice, a system that is not aligned on the voice and not subordinate to it, but connected to it, co-ordinated "in an organization that is radiating, as it were," and multidimensional. (And it must be said that this graphic system is linear writing's contrary: civilizations cease being oral only through losing the independence and the particular dimensions of the graphic system; by aligning itself on the voice, graphism supplants the voice and induces a fictitious voice.) André Leroi-Gourhan has admirably described these two heterogeneous poles of the savage inscription process or territorial representation: the couple voice-audition and hand-graphics.[34] How does such a machine work? For it *does* work: the voice is like a voice of alliance to which, on the side of the extended filiation, a graphics is co-ordinated that bears no resemblance. The calabash of the excision is placed on the body of the young woman. Furnished by the husband's lineage, the calabash serves as a conductor for the voice of alliance; but the graphism must be traced by a member of the young woman's clan. The articulation of the two elements takes place on the body itself, and constitutes the sign, which is not a resemblance or imitation, nor an effect of a signifier, but rather a position and a production of desire: "In order for the young woman's transformation to be fully effective, a direct contact must take place between her stomach, on the one hand, and the calabash and the signs inscribed on her, on the other hand. The young woman must become physically saturated with the signs of procreation and she must incorporate them. The young women are never taught the meaning of the ideograms during their initiation. The sign acts through its inscription in the body. . . . The inscription of a mark on the body does not merely possess a message value here, but is an instrument of action that acts on the body itself. . . . The signs command the things they signify, and far from being a mere imitator, the artisan of the signs accomplishes a work that calls to mind the divine creation."[35]

But how does one explain the role played by sight, indicated by Leroi-Gourhan, in the contemplation of the face that is speaking, as well as in the reading of the manual graphism? Or more precisely, what enables the eye to grasp a terrible equivalence between the voice of alliance that inflicts and constrains, and the body afflicted by the sign that a hand is carving in it? Isn't it necessary to add a third element of the sign: eye-pain, in addition to voice-audition and hand-graphics? In the rituals of affliction the patient does not speak, but receives the spoken word. He does not act, but is passive under the graphic action; he receives the stamp of the sign. And what is his pain if not a pleasure for the eye that regards it, the collective or divine eye that is not motivated by any idea of revenge, but is alone capable of grasping the subtle relationship between the sign engraved in the body and the voice issuing from a face—between the mark and the mask. Between these two elements of the code, pain is like the surplus value that the eye extracts, taking hold of the effect of active speech on the body, but also of the reaction of the body insofar as it is acted upon. This is indeed what must be called a debt system or territorial representation: a voice that speaks or intones, a sign marked in bare flesh, an eye that extracts enjoyment from the pain; these are the three sides of a savage triangle forming a territory of resonance and retention, a *theater of cruelty* that implies the triple independence of the articulated voice, the graphic hand, and the appreciative eye. Such is the manner in which territorial representation organizes itself at the surface, still quite close to a desiring-machine of eye-hand-voice. A magic triangle. Everything in this system is active, acted upon, or reacted to: the action of the voice of alliance, the passion of the body of filiation, the reaction of the eye evaluating the declension of the two. To choose the stone that will make a man of the young Guayaki, with *enough* pain and suffering, by cleaving the length of his back: "It must have a good cutting edge"—says Clastres in an admirable text—"but not like a sliver of bamboo, which cuts too easily. Choosing the right stone therefore requires *a practiced eye.* The whole apparatus of this new ceremony is reduced to that: a rock. . . . Furrowed skin, scarified earth, one and the same mark."[36]

The great book of modern ethnology is not so much Mauss's *The Gift* as Nietzsche's *On the Genealogy of Morals.* At least it should be. For the *Genealogy,* the second essay, is an attempt—and a success without equal—at interpretating primitive economy in terms of debt, in the debtor-creditor relationship, by eliminating every consideration of exchange or interest "à l'anglaise." And if they are eliminated from psychology, it is not in order to place them in structure. Nietzsche has only a meager set of tools at his disposal—some ancient Germanic law, a little Hindu law. But he does not hesitate, as does Mauss, between exchange and debt. (Georges Bataille, motivated by a Nietzschean inspiration, will not hesitate either.) The fundamental problem of the primitive socius, which is the problem of inscription, of coding, of marking, has never been raised in such an incisive fashion. Man must constitute himself through the repression of the intense germinal influx, the great biocosmic memory that threatens to deluge every attempt at collectivity. But at the same time, how is a new memory to be created for man—a collective memory of the spoken word and of alliances that declines the alliances with the extended filiations, that endows him with faculties of resonance and retention, of selection (*prélèvement*) and detachment, and that effects in this way the coding of the flows of desire as a condition of the socius? The answer is simple, it is debt—open, mobile, and finite blocks of debt: this extraordinary composite of the speaking voice, the marked body, and the enjoying eye. All the stupidity and the arbitrariness of the laws, all the pain of the initiations, the whole perverse apparatus of repression and education, the red-hot irons, and the atrocious procedures have only this meaning: *to breed* man,* to mark him in his flesh, to render him capable of alliance, to form him within the debtor-creditor relation, which on both sides turns out to be a matter of memory—a memory straining toward the future.

Far from being an appearance assumed by exchange, debt is the immediate effect or the direct means of the territorial and corporal inscription process. Debt is the direct result of inscription. Once again

---

*"*dresser* l'homme" in the French. See Friedrich Nietzsche, *Will to Power,* Book IV, for his discussion of this notion. (*Translators' note.*)

no revenge, no *ressentiment* will be invoked here—that is not the ground they grow on, any more than does Oedipus. The fact that innocent men suffer all the marks on their bodies derives from the respective autonomy of the voice and the graphic action, and also from the autonomous eye that extracts pleasure from the event. It is not because everyone is suspected, in advance, of being a future bad debtor; the contrary would be closer to the truth. It is the bad debtor who must be understood as if the marks had not sufficiently "taken" on him, as if he were or had been unmarked. He has merely widened, beyond the limits allowed, the gap that separated the voice of alliance and the body of filiation, to such a degree that it is necessary to re-establish the equilibrium through an increase in pain. Nietzsche doesn't say this, but what does it matter? For it is indeed here that he encounters the terrible equation of debt: injury done = pain to be suffered. How does one explain, he asks, that the criminal's pain can serve as an "equivalent" of the harm he has done? How can one "pay back" with suffering? An eye must be invoked that extracts pleasure from the event (this has nothing to do with vengeance): something that Nietzsche himself calls the evaluating eye, or the eye of the gods who enjoy cruel spectacles, "and in punishment there is so much that is festive!"[37] So much is pain part of an active life and an obliging gaze. The equation injury = pain has nothing exchangist about it, and it shows in this extreme case that the debt itself had nothing to do with exchange. Simply stated, the eye extracts from the pain it is contemplating a surplus value of code that compensates the broken relationship between the voice of alliance that the criminal has wronged, and the mark that had not sufficiently penetrated his body. The crime, a rupture of the phonographic connection, re-established by the spectacle of the punishment: as primitive justice, territorial representation has *foreseen* everything.

Coding pain and death, it has foreseen everything—except for the way *its own* death would come to it from without. "*They* come like fate, without reason, consideration, or pretext; they appear as lightning appears, too terrible, too convincing, too sudden, too *different* even to be hated. Their work is an instinctive creation and imposition of forms; they are the most involuntary, unconscious artists there are—wherever they appear something new arises, a ruling structure that *lives,* in which parts and functions are delimited and coordinated, in which nothing whatever finds a place that has not first been assigned a 'meaning' in relation to the whole. They do not know what guilt, responsibility, or consideration are, these born organizers; they exemplify that terrible artist's egoism that has the look of bronze and knows itself justified to all eternity in its 'work,' like a mother in her child. It is not in *them* that the 'bad conscience' developed, that goes without saying—but it would not have developed if a tremendous quantity of freedom had not been expelled from the world, or at least from the visible world, and made as it were *latent* under their hammer blows and artist's violence."[38] It is here that Nietzsche speaks of a break, a rupture, a leap. Who are these beings, *they* who come like fate? ("Some pack of blond beasts of prey, a conqueror and master race which, organized for war and with the ability to organize, unhesitatingly lays its terrible claws upon a populace perhaps tremendously superior in numbers but still formless. . . ."[39]) Even the most ancient African myths speak to us of these blond men. They are the *founders of the State.* Nietzsche will come to establish the existence of other breaks: those of the Greek city-state, Christianity, democratic and bourgeois humanism, industrial society, capitalism, and socialism. But it could be that all these—in various ways—presuppose this first great hiatus, although they all claim to repel and to fill it. It could be that, spiritual or temporal, tyrannical or democratic, capitalist or socialist, *there has never been but a single State,* the State-as-dog that "speaks with flaming roars."[40] And Nietzsche suggests how this new socius proceeds: a terror without precedent, in comparison with which the ancient system of cruelty, the forms of primitive regimentation and punishment, are nothing. A concerted destruction of all the primitive codings, or worse yet, their derisory preservation, their reduction to the condition of secondary parts in the new machine, and the new apparatus of repression (*refoulement*). All that constituted the essential element of the primitive inscription machine—the blocks of mobile, open, finite debts, "the parcels of destiny"—finds itself taken into an immense machinery *that renders the debt infinite* and no longer forms anything but one and the same crushing fate: "the *aim* now is to preclude pessimistically, once and for all, the prospect of a final discharge; the *aim* now is to make the glance recoil disconsolately from an iron impossibility."[41] The earth becomes a madhouse.

6 | The Barbarian Despotic Machine

The founding of the despotic machine or the barbarian socius can be summarized in the following way: a new alliance and direct filiation. The despot challenges the lateral alliances and the extended filiations of the old community. He imposes a new alliance system and places himself in direct filiation with the deity: the people must follow. A leap into a new alliance, a break with the ancient filiation—this is expressed in a strange machine, or rather a machine of the strange whose locus is the desert, imposing the harshest and the most barren of ordeals, and attesting to the resistance of an old order as well as to the validation of the new order. The machine of the strange is both a great paranoiac machine, since it expresses the struggle with the old system, and already a glorious celibate machine, insofar as it exalts the triumph of the new alliance. The despot is the paranoiac: there is no longer any reason to forego such a statement, once one has freed oneself from the characteristic familialism of the concept of paranoia in psychoanalysis and psychiatry, and provided one sees in paranoia a type of investment of a social formation. And new perverse groups spread the despot's invention (perhaps they even fabricated it for him), broadcast his fame, and impose his power in the towns they found or conquer. Wherever a despot and his army pass, doctors, priests, scribes, and officials are part of the procession. It might be said that the ancient complementarity has shifted to form a new socius: no longer the bush paranoiac and the encampment or village perverts, but the desert paranoiac and the town perverts.

In theory the despotic barbarian formation has to be conceived of in terms of an opposition between it and the primitive territorial machine: the birth of an empire. But in reality one can perceive the movement of this formation just as well when one empire breaks away from a preceding empire; or even when there arises the dream of a spiritual empire, wherever temporal empires fall into decadence. It may be that the enterprise is primarily military and motivated by conquest, or that it is primarily religious, the military discipline being converted into internal asceticism and cohesion. It may be that the paranoiac himself is either a gentle creature or a raging beast. But we always rediscover the figures of this paranoiac and his perverts, the conqueror and his elite troops, the despot and his bureaucrats, the holy man and his disciples, the anchorite and his monks, Christ and his Saint Paul. Moses flees from the Egyptian machine into the wilderness and installs his new machine there, a holy ark and a portable temple, and gives his people a new religious-military organization. In order to summarize Saint John the Baptist's enterprise, one author declares: "John attacks at its foundation the central doctrine of Judaeism, the doctrine of the alliance with God through a filiation that goes back to Abraham."[42] There is the essential: every time the categories of new alliance and direct filiation are mobilized, we are talking about the imperial barbarian formation or the despotic machine. And this holds true whatever the context of this mobilization, whether in a relationship with preceding empires or not, since throughout these vicissitudes the imperial formation is always defined by a certain type of code and inscription that is in direct opposition to the primitive territorial codings. The number of elements in the alliance makes little difference: new alliance and direct filiation are specific categories that testify to the existence of a new socius, irreducible to the lateral alliances and the extended filiations that declined the primitive machine. It is this force of projection that defines paranoia, this strength to start again from zero, to objectify a complete transformation: the subject leaps outside the intersections of alliance-filiation, installs himself at the limit, at the horizon, in the desert, the subject of a deterritorialized knowledge that links him directly to God and connects him to the people. For the first time, something has been withdrawn from life and from the earth that will make it possible to judge life and to survey the earth from above: a first principle of paranoiac knowledge. The whole relative play of alliances and filiations is carried to the absolute in this new alliance and this direct filiation.

It remains to be said that, in order to understand the barbarian formation, it is necessary to relate it not to other formations in competition with it temporally and spiritually, according to relationships that obscure the essential, but to the savage primitive formation that it supplants by imposing its own rule of law, but that continues to haunt it. It is exactly in this way that Marx defines Asiatic production: a higher unity of the State establishes itself on the foundations of the primitive rural communities, which keep their ownership of the soil, while the State becomes the true owner in conformity with the apparent objective movement that attributes the surplus product to the State, assigns the productive forces to it in the great projects undertaken, and makes it appear as the cause of the collective conditions of appropriation.[43] The full body as socius has ceased to be the earth, it has become the body of the despot, the despot himself or his god. The prescriptions and prohibitions that often render him almost incapable of acting make of him a body without organs. *He* is the sole quasi cause, the source and fountainhead and estuary of the apparent objective movement. In place of mobile detachments from the signifying chain, a detached object has jumped outside the chain; in place of flow selections, all the flows converge into a great river that constitutes the sovereign's consumption: a radical change of régimes in the fetish or the symbol. What counts is not the person of the sovereign, nor even his function, which can be limited. It is the social machine that has profoundly changed: in place of the territorial machine, there is the "megamachine" of the State, a functional pyramid that has the despot at its apex, an immobile motor, with the bureaucratic apparatus as its lateral surface and its transmission gear, and the villagers at its base, serving as its working parts. The stocks form the object of an accumulation, the blocks of debt become an infinite relation in the form of the tribute. The entire surplus value of code is an object of appropriation. This conversion crosses through all the syntheses: the synthesis of production, with the hydraulic machine and the mining machine; the synthesis of inscription, with the accounting machine, the writing machine, and the monument machine; and finally the synthesis of consumption, with the upkeep of the despot, his court, and the bureaucratic caste. Far from seeing in the State the principle of a territorialization that would inscribe people according to their residence, we should see in the principle of residence the effect of a movement of deterritorialization that divides the earth as an object and subjects men to the new imperial inscription, to the new full body, to the new socius. "They come like fate, . . . they appear as lightning appears, too terrible, too sudden."[44]

The death of the primitive system always comes from without; history is the history of contingencies and encounters. Like a cloud blown in from the desert, the conquerors are there: "In some way that is incomprehensible to me they have pushed right into the capital, although it is a long way from the frontier. At any rate, here they are; it seems that every morning there are more of them. . . . Speech with the nomads is impossible. They do not know our own language."[45] But this death that comes from without is also that which was rising from within: the general irreducibility of alliance to filiation, the independence of the alliance groups, the way in which they serve as a conducting element for the political and economic relations, the system of primitive rankings, the mechanism of surplus value—all this already prefigured despotic formations and caste hierarchies. And how does one distinguish the way in which the primitive community remains on its guard with respect to its own institutions of chieftainship, and exorcises or strait-jackets the image of the possible despot whom it threatens to secrete from within, from the way in which it binds up the symbol—a symbol that has become derisory—of a former despot who thrust himself upon the community from the outside long ago? It is not always easy to know if one is considering a primitive community that is repressing an endogenous tendency, or one that is regaining its cohesion as best it can after a terrible exogenous adventure. The game of alliances is ambiguous: are we still on this side of the new alliance, or already beyond it, having fallen back, as it were, into a this-side-of that is residual and transformed? (Related question: what is the feudal system?) We are only able to fix the precise moment of the imperial formation as that of the new exogenous alliance, not only in the place of former alliances, but *in relation to them*.

This new alliance is something altogether different from a treaty or a contract. What is suppressed is not the former régime of lateral alliances and extended filiations, but merely their determining character. They subsist, more or less modified, more or less harnessed by the great paranoiac, since they furnish the material of surplus value. In point of fact, that is what forms the specific character of Asiatic production: the autochthonous rural communities subsist, and continue to produce, inscribe, and consume; in effect, they are the State's sole concern. The wheels of the territorial lineage machine subsist, but are no longer anything more than the working parts of the State machine. The objects, the organs, the persons, and the groups retain at least a part of their intrinsic coding, but these coded flows of the former régime find themselves overcoded by the transcendent unity that appropriates surplus value. The old inscription remains, but is bricked over by and in the inscription of the State. The blocks subsist, but have become encasted and embedded bricks, having only a controlled mobility. The territorial alliances are not replaced, but are merely allied with the new alliance; the territorial filiations are not replaced, but are merely affiliated with the direct filiation. It is like an immense right of the first-born over all filiations, an immense right of the wedding night over all alliances. The filiative stock becomes the object of an accumulation in the other filiation, while the alliance debt becomes an infinite relation in the other alliance. It is the entire primitive system that finds itself mobilized, requisitioned by a superior power, subjugated by new exterior forces, put in the service of other ends; so true is it, said Nietzsche, that what is called the evolution of a thing is "a succession of more or less profound, more or less mutually independent processes of subduing, plus the resistances they encounter, the attempts at transformation for the purpose of defense and reaction, and the results of successful counteractions."[46]

It has often been remarked that the State commences (or recommences) with two fundamental acts, one of which is said to be an act of territoriality through the fixing of residence, and the other, an act of liberation through the abolition of small debts. But the State operates by means of euphemisms. The pseudo territoriality is the product of an effective deterritorialization that substitutes abstract signs for the signs of the earth, and that makes the earth itself into the object of a State ownership of property, or an ownership held by the State's richest servants and officials. (There is no great change, *from this point of view*, when the State no longer does anything more than guarantee the private property of a ruling class that becomes distinct from the State.) The abolition of debts, when it takes place, is a means of maintaining the distribution of land, and a means of preventing the entry on stage of a new territorial machine, possibly revolutionary and capable of raising and dealing with the agrarian problem in a comprehensive way. In other cases where a redistribution occurs, the cycle of credits is maintained, in the new form established by the State—money. For without question, money does not begin by serving the needs of commerce, or at least it has no autonomous mercantile model. The despotic machine holds the following in common with the primitive machine, it confirms the latter in this respect: the dread of decoded flows—flows of production, but also mercantile flows (*flux marchands*) of exchange and commerce that might escape the State monopoly, with its tight restrictions and its plugging of flows. When Etienne Balazs asks why capitalism wasn't born in China in the thirteenth century, when all the necessary scientific and technical conditions nevertheless seemed to be present, the answer lies in the State, which closed the mines as soon as the reserves of metal were judged sufficient, and which retained a monopoly or a narrow control over commerce (the merchant as functionary).[47]

The role of money in commerce hinges less on commerce itself than on its control by the State. Commerce's relationship with money is synthetic, not analytical. And money is fundamentally inseparable, not from commerce, but from taxes as the maintenance of the apparatus of the State. Even where dominant classes set themselves apart from this apparatus and make use of it for the benefit of private property, the despotic tie between money and taxes remains visible. Basing himself on the research of Edouard Will, Michel Foucault shows how, in certain Greek tyrannies, the tax on aristocrats and the distribution of money to the poor are a means of bringing the money back to the rich and a means of remarkably widening the régime of debts, making it even stronger, by anticipating and repressing any reterritorialization that might be produced by the economic givens of the agrarian problem.[48] (As if the Greeks had discovered in their own way what the Americans rediscovered after the New Deal: that heavy taxes are good for business.) In a word, money—the circulation of money—*is the means for rendering the debt infinite.* And that is what is concealed in the two acts of the State: the residence or territoriality of the State inaugurates the great movement of deterritorialization that subordinates all the primitive filiations to the despotic machine (the agrarian problem); the abolition of debts or their accountable transformation initiates the duty of an interminable service to the State that subordinates all the primitive alliances to itself (the problem of debts). The infinite creditor and infinite credit have replaced the blocks of mobile and finite debts. There is always a monotheism on the horizon of despotism: the debt becomes a *debt of existence,* a debt of the existence of the subjects themselves. A time will come when the creditor has not yet lent while the debtor never quits repaying, for repaying is a duty but lending is an option—as in Lewis Carroll's song, the long song about the infinite debt:

A man may surely claim his dues:
But, when there's money to be lent,
A man must be allowed to choose
Such times as are convenient.[49]

The despotic State, such as it appears in the purest conditions of "Asiatic" production, has two correlative aspects: on the one hand it replaces the territorial machine, it forms a new deterritorialized full body; on the other hand it maintains the old territorialities, integrates them as parts or organs of production in the new machine. It is perfected all at once because it functions on the basis of dispersed rural communities, which are like pre-existing autonomous or semiautonomous machines from the viewpoint of production; but from this same viewpoint, it reacts on them in producing the conditions for major work projects that exceed the capacities of the separate communities. What is produced on the body of the despot is a connective synthesis of the old alliances with the new, and a disjunctive synthesis that entails an overflowing of the old filiations into the direct filiation, gathering all the subjects into the new machine. The essential action of the State, therefore, is the creation of a second inscription by which the new full body—immobile, monumental, immutable—appropriates all the forces and agents of production; but this inscription of the State allows the old territorial inscriptions to subsist, as "bricks" on the new surface. And finally, from this appropriation there results the way in which the conjunction of the two parts is implemented and the respective portions are distributed to the higher proprietary unity and to the propertied communities, to the overcoding process and to the intrinsic codes, to the appropriated surplus value and to the usufruct put into use, to the State machine and to the territorial machines. As in Kafka's "The Great Wall of China," the State is the transcendent higher unity that integrates relatively isolated subaggregates, functioning separately, to which it assigns a development in bricks and a labor of construction by fragments. Scattered partial objects hanging on the body without organs. No one has equaled Kafka in demonstrating that the law had nothing to do with a natural, harmonious, and immanent totality, but that it acted as an eminent formal unity, and *reigned accordingly over pieces and fragments* (the wall and the tower). Hence the State is not primeval, it is an origin or an abstraction, it is the original abstract essence that is not to be confused with a beginning. "We think only about the Emperor. But not about the present one; or rather we would think about the present one if we knew who he was or knew anything definite about him. . . . [The people] do not know what emperor is reigning, and there exist doubts regarding even the name of the dynasty. . . . Long-dead emperors are set on the throne in our villages, and one that only lives in song recently had a proclamation of his read out by the priest before the altar."[50]

As for the subaggregates themselves, the primitive territorial machines, they are the concrete itself, the concrete base and beginning, but their segments here enter into relationships corresponding to the essence, they assume precisely this form of bricks that ensures their integration into the higher unity, and their distributive operation, consonant with the great collective designs of this same unity: major work projects, extortion of surplus value, tributes, generalized servitude. Two inscriptions coexist in the imperial formation, and mutually adjust insofar as the one is imbricated into the other, but the new inscription cements the whole and brings producers and products into relations with itself (they do not need to speak the same language). The imperial inscription countersects all the alliances and filiations, prolongs them, makes them converge into the direct filiation of the despot with the deity, and the new alliance of the despot with the people. All the coded flows of the primitive machine are now forced into a bottleneck, where the despotic machine overcodes them. *Overcoding* is the operation that constitutes the essence of the State, and that measures both its continuity and its break with the previous formations: the dread of flows of desire that would resist coding, but also the establishment of a new inscription that overcodes, and that makes desire into the property of the sovereign, even though he be the death instinct itself. The castes are inseparable from this overcoding, and imply the existence of dominant "classes" that do not yet manifest themselves as classes, but are merged with a State apparatus. Who is able to touch the full body of the sovereign? Here we have a problem of castes. It is overcoding that impoverishes the earth for the benefit of the deterritorialized full body, and that on this full body renders the movement of debt infinite. It is a measure of Nietzsche's force to have stressed the importance of such a movement that begins with the founders of States, these artists with a look of bronze, creating "an oppressive and remorseless machine,"[51] erecting before any perspective of liberation an ironclad impossibility. This "infinitivation" (*infinitivation*) cannot be understood exactly as Nietzsche would have it—that is, as a consequence of the interplay of ancestors, profound genealogies, and extended filiations; rather, when these are short-circuited, abducted by the new alliance and direct filiation, *then* the ancestor—the master of the mobile and finite blocks—finds himself dismissed by the deity, the immobile organizer of the bricks and of their infinite circuit.

7 | Barbarian or Imperial Representation

Incest with the sister and incest with the mother are very different things. The sister is not a substitute for the mother: the one belongs to the connective category of alliance, the other to the disjunctive category of filiation. Incest with the sister is prohibited insofar as the conditions of territorial coding require that alliance not be confounded with filiation; and incest with the mother, insofar as descent within filiation must not be allowed to interfere with ascending lines. That is why the despot's incest is twofold, by virtue of the new alliance and direct filiation. He begins by marrying *the* sister. But he enters into this forbidden endogamous marriage outside the tribe, inasmuch as he is himself outside his tribe, on the outside or at the outer limits of the territory. This is what Pierre Gordon showed in his strange book: the same rule that proscribes incest must prescribe it for certain persons. Exogamy must result in the position of men outside the tribe who for their part are entitled to an endogamous marriage and are able, by virtue of this formidable right, to serve as initiators to exogamous subjects of both sexes: the "sacred deflowerer," the "ritual initiator" on the mountain or across the waters.* The wilderness, land of betrothal. All the flows converge on a man such as this, all the alliances find themselves countersected by this new alliance that overcodes them. Endogamous marriage outside the tribe places the hero in a position to overcode all the endogamous marriages in the tribe.

It is clear that incest with *the* mother has a completely different meaning: this time it is a question of the mother of the tribe, as she exists in the tribe, as the hero finds her in penetrating into the tribe, or finds her again in returning to the tribe after his first marriage. He countersects the extended filiations with a direct filiation. The initiated or initiating hero becomes king. The second marriage develops the consequences of the first, it draws out the effects of the first. The hero begins by marrying the sister, than he marries the mother. The fact that the two acts can, to varying degrees, be bound together, assimilated, does not rule out the

---

*Pierre Gordon, *L'initiation sexuelle et l'évolutuion religieuse* (Paris: Presses Universitaires de France, 1946), p. 164: "The sacred personage . . . did not live in the little agricultural village, but in the woods, like the hero Enkidu of the Chaldean epic, or on the mountain, in the sacred enclosure. His occupations were those of a herdsman or a hunter, not those of a cultivator. The obligation to resort to him for sacred marriages, the only kind of marriage that enhanced the woman's position, therefore entailed *ipso facto* an exogamy. Under these conditions only the young women belonging to the same group as the ritual deflowerer could be *endogamous*."

existence of two sequences in the phenomenon: the union with the princess-sister and the union with the mother-queen. Incest goes by twos. The hero is always sitting astride two groups, the one where he leaves to find his sister, the other where he returns to find his mother again. The purpose of this double incest is not to produce a flow, not even a magic flow, but to overcode all the existing flows, and to ensure that no intrinsic code, no underlying flow escapes the overcoding of the despotic machine; hence it is by virtue of his sterility that he guarantees the general fecundity.[52] The marriage with the sister is on the outside, it is the wilderness ordeal, it expresses the spatial divergence from the primitive machine; it provides the old alliances with an outcome; it founds the new alliance by effecting a generalized appropriation of all the alliance debts. The marriage with the mother is the return to the tribe; it expresses the temporal divergence from the primitive machine (the difference between the generations); it constitutes the direct filiation that results from the new alliance, by effecting a generalized accumulation of filiative stock. Both marriages are essential to the overcoding, as the two ends of a tie for the despotic knot.

A pause seems in order here while we ask how such a thing is possible. How is it that incest has become "possible," and not only possible, but the manifest property and seal of the despot? Who is this sister, this mother? The sister and mother of the despot himself? Or should the question be framed in a different way? For it concerns the whole system of representation when it ceases to be territorial and becomes imperial. First of all, we have the impression that the elements of the in-depth system of representation have begun to move: the cellular migration has begun that will carry the Oedipal cell from one locus of representation to another. In the imperial formation, *incest has ceased being the displaced represented of desire to become the repressing representation itself.* For there can be no doubt: this way the despot has of committing incest, and of making it possible, in no way involves removing the apparatus of social and psychic repression (*l'appareil répression-refoulement*). On the contrary, the despot's intervention forms part of the apparatus, it changes only the parts of the machine; yet it is still as the displaced represented that incest now comes to occupy the position of the repressing representation. Another gain in the sum of repression, a new economy in the repressive, repressing apparatus (*l'appareil refoulant répressif*), a new mark, a new severity. It would be easy, too easy, if it were enough to make incest possible, and to implement this in sovereign fashion, so that the exercise of psychic repression and the service of social repression would be made to end. The royal barbarian incest is merely the means to overcode the flows of desire, certainly not a means to liberate them. O Caligula, O Heliogabalus, O mad memory of vanished emperors! Incest never having been the desire, but merely its displaced represented as it results from psychic repression, social repression has everything to gain when incest comes to take the place of the representation itself, and in this capacity take charge of the repressing function (*la fonction refoulante*). (That is what we have already seen in psychosis, where the intrusion of the complex into consciousness, according to the traditional criterion, did not, to be sure, alleviate the repression of desire.) With incest's new position in the imperial formation, we are therefore speaking only of a migration in the in-depth elements of *representation,* which will render the latter more foreign, more ruthless, more definitive, or more "infinite" with respect to desiring-*production.* But this migration would never be possible if there did not occur correlatively a considerable change in the other elements of representation, those elements that operate on the surface of the inscribing socius.

What changes singularly in the surface organization of representation is the relationship between the voice and graphism: it is the despot who establishes the practice of writing (the most ancient authors saw this clearly); it is the imperial formation that makes graphism into a system of writing in the proper sense of the term. Legislation, bureaucracy, accounting, the collection of taxes, the State monopoly, imperial justice, the functionaries' activity, historiography: everything is written in the despot's procession. Let us return to the paradox that emerges from the analyses of Leroi-Gourhan: primitive societies are oral not because they lack a graphic system but because, on the contrary, the graphic system in these societies is independent of the voice; it marks signs on the body that respond to the voice, react to the voice, but that are autonomous and do not align themselves on it. In return, barbarian civilizations are written, not because the voice has been lost, *but* because the graphic system has lost its independence and its particular dimensions, has aligned itself on the voice and has become subordinated to the voice, enabling it to extract from the voice a deterritorialized abstract flux that it retains and makes reverberate in the linear code of writing. In short, graphism in one and the same movement begins to depend on the voice, and induces a mute voice from on high or from the beyond, a voice that begins to depend on graphism. It is by subordinating itself to the voice that writing supplants it.

Jacques Derrida is correct in saying that every language presupposes a writing system from which it originates, if by that he means the existence and the connection of some sort of graphism—writing in the largest sense of the term. He is also right in saying that, within writing in the narrow sense, hardly any breaks can be established between pictographic, ideogrammic, and phonetic procedures: there is always and already an alignment on the voice, at the same time as a substitution for the voice (supplementarity), and "phonetism is never all-powerful, but has also always-already begun to labor and elaborate the mute signifier." He is again correct in linking writing to incest in a mysterious fashion. But we see nothing in this link that would lead us to conclude in favor of the constancy of an apparatus of psychic repression, operating in the manner of a graphic machine capable of performing as well by means of hieroglyphs as by phonemes.[53] For there is indeed a break that changes everything in the world of representation, between this writing in the narrow sense and writing in the broad sense—that is, between two completely different orders of inscription: a graphism that leaves the voice dominant by being independent of the voice while connecting with it, and a graphism that dominates or supplants the voice by depending on it in various ways and by subordinating itself to the voice. The primitive territorial sign is self-validating; it is a position of desire in a state of multiple connections. It is not a sign of a sign nor a desire of a desire. It knows nothing of linear subordination and its reciprocity: neither pictogram nor ideogram, it is rhythm and not form, zigzag and not line, artifact and not idea, production and not expression. Let us try to summarize the differences between these two forms of representation, territorial and imperial.

In the first place, territorial representation is made up of two heterogeneous elements, voice and graphism: the former is like the representation of words constituted in lateral alliance, while the latter is like the representation of things—of *bodies*—established in extended filiation. The former acts on the latter, while the latter reacts on the former, each element having its own particular force that is connoted along with that of the other, so as to perform the great task of germinal intense repression. What is repressed, in fact, is the full body as the foundation of the intense earth, which must yield its place to the socius in extension, into which the intensities in question pass or fail to pass. The full body of the earth must assume an extension in the socius and as the socius. The primitive socius covers itself in this manner with a network wherein one is continually jumping from words to things, and from bodies to appellations, according to the extensive requirements of the system in its length and its width. What we call the order of connotation is an order in which the word (*le mot*) as a vocal sign designates something, but where the thing designated is no less a sign, because it is furrowed by a graphism that is connoted in conjunction with the voice. The heterogeneity, the divergence, the disequilibrium of the two elements—vocal and graphic—is resolved by a third element: the visual, the eye. It might be said of this eye that it *sees the word*—it sees it, it does not read it—insofar as it evaluates the suffering caused by the graphism. Jean-François Lyotard has attempted to describe such a system in another context, where the word has only a designating function but does not of itself constitute the sign; what becomes a sign is rather the thing or body designated as such, insofar as it reveals an unknown facet described on it, traced by the graphism that responds to the word. The gap between the two elements is bridged by the eye, which "sees" the word without reading it, inasmuch as it appraises the pain emanating from the graphism applied to the flesh itself: the eye jumps.*

The magic triangle with its three sides—voice-audition, graphism-body, eye-pain—thus seems to us to be an order of connotation, a system of cruelty where the word has an essentially designating function, but where the graphism itself constitutes a sign in conjunction with the thing designated, and where the eye goes from one to the other, extracting and measuring the visibility of the one against the pain of the other. Everything in the system is active, en-acted (*agi*), or reacting; everything is a matter of use and function. So that when one considers the whole of territorial representation, one is struck by the complexity of the networks with which it covers the socius: the chain of territorial signs is continually jumping from one element to another; radiating in all directions; emitting detachments wherever there are flows to be selected; including disjunctions; consuming remains; extracting surplus values; connecting words, bodies, and sufferings, and formulas, things, and affects; connoting voices, graphic traces, and eyes, always in a polyvocal usage—*a way of jumping* that cannot be contained within an order of meaning, still less within a signifier. And if incest seemed impossible to us from this point of view, it is because incest is nothing other than a jump that necessarily fails, this jump that goes from appellations to persons, from names to bodies: on the one hand, the repressed this-side-of of appellations that do not yet designate persons, but only intensive germinal states; on the other hand, the repressing beyond that only applies appellations to persons by prohibiting persons who answer

*Lyotard re-establishes the overly neglected rights of a theory of pure designation. He shows the irreducible gap between the word and the thing in the relationship of designation that connotes them. By virtue of this gap, it is the thing designated that becomes the sign by revealing an unknown facet as a hidden content. (Words are not themselves signs, but they transform into signs the things or bodies they designate.) At the same time it is the designating word that becomes *visible*, independently of any writing-reading, by revealing a strange ability to be seen, not read. See Lyotard, *Discours, figure* (see reference note 85), pp. 41–82: "Words are not things, but as soon as there is a word, the object designated becomes a sign, which means precisely that it conceals a hidden content within its manifest identity, and that it reserves another face for another view focused on it, . . . which perhaps will never be seen"—but which in return will be viewed in the word itself.

to the names of sister, mother, father. Between the two, the shallow stream *where nothing passes,* where the appellations do not adhere to the persons, where the persons elude the graphic action, and where the eye no longer has anything to see or evaluate: incest, the simple displaced limit, neither repressed nor repressing, but merely the displaced represented of desire. From this moment on it appears indeed that the two dimensions of representation—its surface organization with the elements voice-graphy-eye, and its in-depth organization with the representing instances of desire–repressing representation/displaced represented—share the same fate, like a system of correspondences in the heart of a given social machine.

All this finds itself overwhelmed in a new destiny, with the despotic machine and imperial representation. In the first place, graphism aligns itself on the voice, falls back on the voice, and becomes writing. At the same time it induces the voice no longer as the voice of alliance, but as that of the *new alliance,* a fictitious voice from beyond that expresses itself in the flow of writing as *direct filiation.* These two fundamental despotic categories are also the movement of graphism that, at one and the same time, subordinates itself to the voice in order to subordinate the voice and supplant it. Then there occurs a crushing of the magic triangle: the voice no longer sings but dictates, decrees; the graphy no longer dances, it ceases to animate bodies, but is set into writing on tablets, stones, and books; the eye sets itself to reading. (Writing does not entail but implies a kind of blindness, a loss of vision *and* of the ability to appraise; it is now the eye that suffers, although it also acquires other functions.) Or rather, we are unable to say that the magic triangle is completely crushed: it subsists as a base and as a brick, insofar as the territorial machine continues to function in the framework of the new machine. The triangle has become the base for a pyramid, all of whose sides cause the vocal, the graphic, and the visual to converge toward the eminent unity of the despot. If we call the order of representation in a social system a plane of consistency (*plan de consistance*), it is evident that this plane has changed, that it has become a plane of subordination and no longer one of connotation. And here, in the second place, is the essential: the flattening of the graphy onto the voice has made a transcendent object jump outside the chain—a mute voice on which the whole chain now seems to depend, and in relation to which it becomes linearized. The subordination of graphism to the voice induces a fictitious voice from on high which, inversely, no longer expresses itself except through the writing signs that it emits (revelation). This is perhaps the first assembling of formal operations that will lead to Oedipus (the paralogism of extrapolation): a flattening out or a set of biunivocal relations that leads to the breakaway and elevation of a detached object, and the linearization of the chain that derives from this object.

It is perhaps at this juncture that the question "What does it mean?" begins to be heard, and that problems of exegesis prevail over problems of use and efficacy. The emperor, the god—what did he mean? In place of segments of the chain that are always detachable, a detached partial object on which the whole chain depends; in place of a polyvocal graphism flush with the real, a biunivocalization forming the transcendent dimension that gives rise to a linearity; in place of nonsignifying signs that compose the networks of a territorial chain, a despotic signifier from which all the signs uniformly flow in a deterritorialized flow of writing. Men have even been seen drinking this flow. Andras Zempléni shows how, in certain regions of Senegal, Islam superimposes a plane of subordination on the old plane of connotation of animist values: "The divine or prophetic word, written or recited, is the foundation of this universe; the transparence of the animist prayer yields to the opacity of the rigid Arab verse; speech (*le verbe*) rigidifies into formulas whose power is ensured by the truth of the Revelation and not by a symbolic or incantatory efficacy. . . . The Moslem holy man's learning refers to a hierarchy of names, verses, numbers, and corresponding beings"—and if necessary, the verse will be placed in a bottle filled with pure water, *the verse water will be drunk,* one's body will be rubbed with it, and one's hands will be washed with it."[54] Writing—the first deterritorialized flow, drinkable on this account: it flows from the despotic signifier. For what is the signifier in the first instance? What is it in relation to the nonsignifying territorial signs, when it jumps outside their chains and imposes—superimposes—a plane of subordination on their plane of immanent connotation? The signifier is the sign that has become a sign of the sign, the despotic sign having replaced the territorial sign, having crossed the threshold of deterritorialization; *the signifier is merely the deterritorialized sign itself.* The sign made *letter.* Desire no longer dares to desire, having become a desire of desire, a desire of the despot's desire. The mouth no longer speaks, it drinks the letter. The eye no longer sees, it reads. The body no longer allows itself to be engraved like the earth, but prostrates itself before the engravings of the despot, the region beyond the earth, the new full body.

No water will ever cleanse the signifier of its imperial origin: the signifying master or "the master signifier." In vain will the signifier be immersed in the immanent system of language (*la langue*), or be used to clear away problems of meaning and signification, or be resolved into the coexistence of phonematic elements, where the signified is no more than the summary of the respective differential values of these elements in the relationships among themselves. In vain will the comparison of language (*langage*) to exchange and money be pushed to its furthest point, subjecting language to the paradigms of an active capitalism, for one will never prevent the signifier from reintroducing its transcendence, and from bearing witness for a vanished despot who still functions in modern imperialism. Even when it speaks Swiss or American, linguistics manipulates the shadow of Oriental despotism. Ferdinand de Saussure does not merely emphasize the following: that the arbitrariness of language establishes its sovereignty, as a servitude or a generalized slavery visited upon the "masses." It has also been shown that two dimensions exist side by side in Saussure: the one horizontal, where the signified is reduced to the value of coexisting minimal terms into which the signifier decomposes; but the other vertical, where the signifier is elevated to the concept corresponding to the acoustic image—that is, to the voice, taken in its maximum extension, which recomposes the signifier ("value" as the opposite of the coexisting terms, but also the "concept" as the opposite of the acoustic image). In short, the signifier appears twice, once in the chain of elements in relation to which the signified is always a signifier for another signifier, and a second time in the detached object on which the whole of the chain depends, and that spreads over the chain the effects of signification. There is no phonological or even phonetic code operating on the signifier in the first sense, without an overcoding effected by the signifier itself in the second sense.

There is no linguistic field without biunivocal relations—whether between ideographic and phonetic values, or between articulations of different levels, monemes and phonemes—that finally ensure the independence and the linearity of the deterritorialized signs. But such a field remains defined by a transcendence, even when one considers this transcendence as an absence or an empty locus, performing the necessary foldings, levelings (*rabattements*), and subordinations—a transcendence whence issues throughout the system the inarticulate material flux in which this transcendence operates, opposes, selects, and combines: *the* signifier. It is curious, therefore, that one can show so well the servitude of the masses with respect to the minimal elements of the sign within the immanence of language, without showing how the domination is exercised through and in the transcendence of the signifier.* There, however, as elsewhere, an irreducible exteriority of

*Bernard Pautrat tries to establish a rapprochement between Nietzsche and Saussure, starting from problems of domination and servitude: *Versions du soleil: figures et système de Nietzsche* (Paris: Editions du Seuil, 1971), pp. 207ff. He does well to remark that Nietzsche, in contrast to Hegel, causes the master-slave relationship to go by way of language and not by way of labor. But when he proceeds

conquest asserts itself. For if language itself does not presuppose conquest, the leveling operations (*les opérations de rabattement*) that constitute written language indeed presuppose two inscriptions that do not speak the same language: two languages (*langages*), one of masters, the other of slaves. Jean Nougayrol describes just such a situation: "For the Sumerians, [a given sign] is water; the Sumerians read this sign *a*, which signifies water in Sumerian. An Akkadian comes along and asks his Sumerian master: what is this sign? The Sumerian replies: that's *a*. The Akkadian takes this sign for *a*, and on this point there is no longer any relationship between the sign and water, which in Akkadian is called *mû*. . . . I believe that the presence of the Akkadians determined the phoneticization of the writing system . . . and that the contact of two peoples is almost necessary before the spark of a new writing can spring forth."[55]

One cannot better show how an operation of biunivocalization organizes itself around a despotic signifier, so that a phonetic and alphabetical chain flows from it. Alphabetical writing is not for illiterates, but by illiterates. It goes by way of illiterates, those unconscious workers. The signifier implies a language that overcodes another language, while the other language is completely coded into phonetic elements. And if the unconscious in fact includes the topical order of a double inscription, it is not structured like one language, but like two. The signifier does not appear to keep its promise, which is to give us access to a modern and functional understanding of language. The imperialism of the signifier does not take us beyond the question, "What does it mean?"; it is content to bar the question in advance, to render all the answers insufficient by relegating them to the status of a simple signified. It challenges exegesis in the name of recitation, pure textuality, and superior "scientificity" (*scientificité*). Like the young palace dogs too quick to drink the verse water, and who never tire of crying: The signifier, you have not reached the signifier, you are still at the level of the signifieds! The signifier is the only thing that gladdens their hearts. But this master signifier remains what it was in ages past, a transcendent stock that distributes lack to all the elements of the chain, something in common for a common absence, the authority that channels all the breaks-flows into one and the same locus of one and the same cleavage: the detached object, the phallus-and-castration, the bar that delivers over all the depressive subjects to the great paranoiac king. O signifier, terrible archaism of the despot where they still look for the empty tomb,

---

to the comparison with Saussure, he retains language as a system to which the masses are enslaved, and consigns to fiction the Nietzschean idea of a language of masters through which this enslavement is accomplished.

the dead father, and the mystery of the name! And perhaps that is what incites the anger of certain linguists against Lacan, no less than the enthusiasm of his followers: the vigor and the serenity with which Lacan accompanies the signifier back to its source, to its veritable origin, the despotic age, and erects an infernal machine that welds desire to the Law, because, everything considered—so Lacan thinks—this is indeed the form in which the signifier is in agreement with the unconscious, and the form in which it produces effects of the signified in the unconscious.* The signifier as the repressing representation, and the new displaced represented that it induces, the famous metaphors and metonymy—all of that constitutes the overcoding and deterritorialized despotic machine.

The despotic signifier has the effect of overcoding the territorial chain. The signified is precisely the effect of the signifier, and not what it represents or what it designates. The signified is the sister of the borders and the mother of the interior. Sister and mother are the concepts that correspond to the great acoustic image, to the voice of the new alliance and direct filiation. Incest is the very operation of overcoding at the two ends of the chain in all the territory ruled by the despot, from the borders to the center: all the debts of alliance are converted into the infinite debt of the new alliance, and all the extended filiations are subsumed by direct filiation. Incest or the royal trinity is therefore the whole of the repressing representation insofar as it initiates the overcoding. The system of subordination or signification has replaced the system of connotation. To the extent that graphism is flattened onto the voice—the graphism that, not so long ago, was inscribed flush with the body—body representation subordinates itself to word representation: sister and mother are the voice's signifieds. But to the extent that this flattening induces a fictitious voice from on high that no longer expresses itself except in the linear flux, the despot himself is the signifier of the voice that, along with the two signifieds, effects the overcoding of the whole chain. What made incest impossible—namely, that at times we had the appellations (mother, sister) but not the persons or the bodies, while at other times we had the bodies, but the appellations disappeared from view as soon as we broke through the prohibitions they bore—has ceased to exist. Incest has become possible in the wedding of the kinship bodies and family appellations, in the union of the signifier with its signifieds.

*See Elisabeth Roudinesco's excellent article on Lacan, where she analyzes the twofold aspect of the analytic signifying chain and the transcendent signifier on which the chain depends. She shows that, in this sense, Lacan's theory should be interpreted less as a linguistic conception of the unconscious than as a critique of linguistics in the name of the unconscious. (Elisabeth Roudinesco, "L'action d'une métaphore," *La Pensée*, February 1972.)

Hence it is by no means a question of knowing if the despot marries his "true" sister and his true mother. For in any case his true sister is the sister of the wilderness, just as his true mother is the mother of the tribe. Once incest is *possible,* it matters little whether it is simulated or not, since in any case something else again is simulated through incest. And in accordance with the complementarity of simulation and identity that we encountered earlier, if the identification is that of the object on high, the simulation is indeed the writing that corresponds to it, the flux that flows from this object, the graphic flux that flows from the voice. Simulation does not replace reality, it is not an equivalent that stands for reality, but rather it appropriates reality in the operation of despotic overcoding, it produces reality on the new full body that replaces the earth. It expresses the appropriation and production of the real by a quasi cause. In incest it is the signifier that makes love with its signifieds. System of simulation is the other name for signification and subordination. And what is simulated and therefore produced, through the incest that is itself simulated and therefore produced—all the more real for being simulated, *and vice versa*—is something very much like the extreme states of a reconstituted, re-created intensity. With his sister the despot simulates "a zero state from which the phallic force will arise," like a promise "whose hidden presence in the very interior of the body must be situated at the extreme limit"; and with his mother the despot simulates a superforce where the two sexes would be "at the maximum [degree of externalization] of their specific natures": the B-A Ba of the phallus as voice.[56]

Hence something else is always at issue in royal incest: bisexuality, homosexuality, castration, transvestism, as so many gradients and passages in the cycle of intensities. This is because the despotic signifier aims at the reconstitution of the full body of the intense earth that the primitive machine had repressed, but on new foundations or under new conditions present in the deterritorialized full body of the despot himself. This is the reason that incest changes its meaning or locus, and becomes the repressing representation. For what is at stake in the overcoding effected by incest is the following: that all the organs of all the subjects, all the eyes, all the mouths, all the penises, all the vaginas, all the ears, and all the anuses become attached to the full body of the despot, as though to the peacock's tail of a royal train, and that they have in this body their own intensive representatives. Royal incest is inseparable from the intense multiplication of organs and their inscription on the new full body. (Sade saw clearly this always royal role of incest.) The apparatus of social repression–psychic repression—i.e., the repressing representation—now finds itself defined in terms of a supreme danger that expresses the representative on which it bears: the danger that a single organ might flow outside the despotic body, that it might break away or escape. Suddenly the despot sees rising up before him, against him, the enemy who brings death—an eye with too steady a look, a mouth with too unfamiliar a smile; each organ is a possible protest. It is at one and the same time that a half-deaf Caesar complains of an ear that no longer hears, and sees weighing on him the look of Cassius, "lean and hungry," and the smile of Cassius, who "smiles in such a sort as if he mock'd himself." A long chronicle that will carry the assassinated, dismembered, dis-organ-ized, filed-down body of the despot into the latrines of the city. Wasn't it already the anus that detached the object on high and produced the eminent voice? Didn't the transcendence of the phallus depend on the anus? But the latter is revealed only at the end, as the last vestige of the vanished despot, the underside of his voice: the despot is nothing more than this "dead rat's ass suspended from the ceiling of the sky." The organs begin by detaching themselves from the despotic body, the organs of the citizen risen up against the tyrant. Then they will become those of private man, they will become privatized after the model and memory of the disgraced anus, ejected from the social field—the obsessive fear of smelling bad. The entire history of primitive coding, of despotic overcoding, and of the decoding of private man turns on these movements of flows: the intense germinal influx, the surflux of royal incest, and the reflux of excrement that conducts the dead despot to the latrines, and conducts us all to today's "private man"—the history sketched out by Artaud in his masterpiece *Héliogabale*. The entire history of the graphic flux goes from the flood of sperm in the tyrant's cradle, to the wave of shit in his sewer tomb—"all writing is so much pig shit," all writing is this simulation, sperm and excrement.

One might think that the system of imperial representation was, in spite of everything, milder than that of territorial representation. The signs are no longer inscribed in the flesh itself but on stones, parchments, pieces of currency, and lists. According to Wittfogel's law of "diminishing administrative returns," wide sectors are left semiautonomous insofar as they do not compromise the power of the State. The eye no longer extracts a surplus value from the spectacle of suffering, it has ceased to evaluate; it has begun rather to "forewarn" and keep watch, to see that no surplus value escapes the overcoding of the despotic machine. For all the organs and their functions experience a detachment and elevation that relates them to, and makes them converge on, the full body of the despot. In point of fact the régime is not milder; the system of terror has replaced the system of cruelty. The old cruelty persists, especially in the autonomous or quasi-autonomous sectors; but it is now bricked into the State apparatus, which at times organizes it and at other times tolerates or limits it, in order to make it serve the ends of the State, and to subsume it under the higher superimposed unity of a Law that is more terrible. As a matter of fact, the law's opposition or apparent opposition to despotism comes late—when the State presents itself as an apparent peacemaker between classes that become distinct from the State, making it necessary for the latter to reshape its form of sovereignty.*

The law does not begin by being what it will become or seek to become later: a guarantee against despotism, an immanent principle that unites the parts into a whole, that makes of this whole the object of a general knowledge and will whose sanctions are merely derivative of a judgment and an application directed at the rebellious parts. The imperial barbarian law possesses instead two features that are in opposition to those just mentioned—the two features that Kafka so forcefully developed: first, the paranoiac-schizoid trait of the law (metonymy) according to which the law governs nontotalizable and nontotalized parts, partitioning them off, organizing them as bricks, measuring their distance and forbidding their communication, henceforth acting in the name of a formidable but formal and empty Unity, eminent, distributive, and not collective; and second, the maniacal depressive trait (metaphor) according to which the law reveals nothing and has no knowable object, the verdict having no existence prior to the penalty, and the statement of the law having no existence prior to the verdict. The trial by ordeal presents these two traits in a raw state. As in the machine of "In the Penal Colony," it is the penalty that writes both the verdict and the rule that has been broken. In vain did the body liberate itself from its characteristic graphism in the system of connotation, for it now becomes the stone and the paper, the tablet and the currency on which the new writing is able to mark its figures, its phonetism, and its alphabet. Overcoding is the essence of the law, and the origin of the new sufferings of the body. Punishment has ceased to be a festive occasion, from which the eye extracts a surplus value in the magic triangle of alliance and filiations. *Punishment becomes a vengeance,* the vengeance of the voice, the hand, and the eye now joined together on the despot—the vengeance of the new alliance, whose public character does not spoil the *secret:* "I will bring down upon you the

*Regarding the transition from a royal system of justice based on magico-religious speech to a city-state system of justice based on a speech-as-dialogue, and regarding the change in "sovereignty" that corresponds to this transition, see L. Gernet, "Droit et prédroit en Grèce ancienne," *L'année sociologique 1948–49;* M. Détienne, *Les maîtres de vérité dans la Grèce archaïque* (Paris: Maspero, 1967); and Michel Foucault, "La volonté de savoir" (see reference note 48).

avenging sword of the vengeance of alliance." For once again, before it becomes a feigned guarantee against despotism, the law is the invention of the despot himself: *it is the juridical form assumed by the infinite debt.* The jurist will be seen in the despot's procession up to the time of the late Roman emperors, and the juridical form will accompany the imperial formation, the legislator alongside the monster, Gaius and Commodus, Papinian and Caracalla, Ulpian and Heliogabalus, "the delirium of the twelve Caesars and the Golden Age of Roman Law"— taking the debtor's side against the creditor when necessary, so as to consolidate the infinite debt.

As vengeance, and a vengeance exercised in advance, the imperial barbarian law crushes the whole primitive interplay of action, the en-acted (*l'agi*), and reaction. Passivity must now become the virtue of the subjects attached to the despotic body. As Nietzsche says when he shows precisely how punishment becomes a vengeance in the imperial formations, a "tremendous quantity of freedom" must have "been expelled from the world, or at least from the *visible* world, and made as it were *latent* under their hammer blows and artists' violence."[57] There occurs a detachment and elevation of the death instinct, which ceases to be coded in the interplay of savage actions and reactions where fatalism was still something en-acted, in order to become the somber agent of overcoding, the detached object that hovers over each subject, as though the social machine had come unstuck from its desiring-machines: death, the desire of desire, the desire of the despot's desire, a latency inscribed in the bowels of the State apparatus. Better not a sole survivor than for a single organ to flow outside this apparatus or slip away from the body of the despot. This is because there is no other necessity (no other fatum) than that of the signifier in its relationships with its signifieds: such is the régime of terror. What the law is supposed to signify will only be revealed later, when it has evolved and assumed the new figure that appears to place it in opposition to despotism. But from the beginning it expresses the imperialism of the signifier that produces its signifieds as effects that are the more effective and necessary as they escape knowing, and as they owe all to their eminent cause. Occasionally it still happens that the young dogs will call for a return to the despotic signifier, without exegesis or interpretation, while the law, however, wants to explain what it signifies, to assert an independence of its signified—against the despot, says the law. For the dogs, according to Kafka's observations, want desire to be firmly wedded to the law in the pure detachment and elevation of the death instinct, rather than to hear, it is true, hypocritical doctors explain what it all means. But all that—the development of the democratic signified or the wrapping of the despotic signifier—nevertheless forms part of the same question, sometimes open and sometimes barred, the same extended abstraction, a repressive machinery that always moves us away from the desiring-machines. For there has never been but one State. The question "What is the use of that?" fades more and more, and disappears in the fog of pessimism, of nihilism, Nada, Nada!

The order of law as it appears in the imperial formation, and as it will evolve later, indeed have something in common: the indifference to designation. It is in the nature of the law to signify without designating anything. The law does not designate anything or anybody (the democratic conception of law will make this into a criterion). The complex relationship of designation, as we have seen it elaborated in the system of primitive connotation with its interplay of voice, graphism, and eye, here disappears in the new relationship of barbarian subordination. How could designation subsist when the sign has ceased to be a position of desire, in order to become this imperial sign, a universal castration that welds desire to the law? It is the crushing of the old code, it is the new relationship of signification, it is the *necessity* of this new relationship established in the overcoding process, that refers designations to the *arbitrary* (or that lets them subsist in the form of bricks held over from the old system). Why is it that linguists are constantly rediscovering the truths of the despotic age? And finally, could it be that this arbitrariness of designations, as the reverse side of a necessity of signification, does not bear only on the despot's subjects, nor even on his servants, but on the despot himself, his dynasty, and his name ("[The people] do not know what emperor is reigning, and there exist doubts regarding even the name of the dynasty"[58])? This would mean that the death instinct is even more deeply rooted in the State than thought, and that latency not only befalls the subjects of the State, but is also at work in the highest machinery of the apparatus. The revenge becomes that of the subjects against the despot. In the latency system of terror, what is no longer active, en-acted, or reacted to, "this *instinct for freedom* forcibly made latent (. . .) pushed back and repressed, incarcerated within and finally able to discharge and vent itself only on itself,"[59]—that very thing is now *ressenti:** The eternal *ressentiment* of the subjects answers to the

ressenti(e) is the past participle of the French verb, ressentir, and *ressentiment* is the noun form. Nietzsche makes use of *ressentiment* constantly, in his own singular fashion, to describe the phenomenon whereby an active force is deprived of its normal conditions of existence, where it directs itself inward and turns against itself. "Pushed back and repressed, incarcerated within and finally able to discharge and vent itself only on itself" is a perfect definition of what is meant for something to be *ressenti* according to Nietzsche's concept of *ressentiment*. In his *Nietzsche et la philosophie* (Paris: Presses Universitaires de France, 1970), Deleuze defines *ressentiment* as the becoming-reactive of force in general: "separated from what it is capable of, the active force does not however cease to exist. Turning against itself, it produces suffering" (p. 147). Hence, Deleuze concludes, with *ressentiment* a new meaning and depth is created for suffering, *an intimate, internal meaning. (Translators' note.)*

eternal vengeance of the despots. The inscription is *"ressentie"* when it is no longer en-acted or reacted to. When the deterritorialized sign becomes a signifier, a formidable quantity of reaction passes into a latent state; all the resonance and all the retention change in volume and time (the "after-the-event"). Vengeance and *ressentiment*: not the beginning of justice, to be sure, but its becoming and its destiny in the imperial formation as Nietzsche analyzes it. And according to his prophecy, wouldn't the State itself be that dog which wants to die? But that is also reborn from its ashes. For it is this whole constellation of the new alliance—the imperialism of the signifier, the metaphoric or metonymic necessity of the signifieds, *with* the arbitrary of the designations—that ensures the maintenance of the system, and sees to it that the name is succeeded by another name, one dynasty by another, without changing the signifieds, and without a collapse of the wall of the signifier. This is why the order of latency in the African, Chinese, Egyptian, and other empires was that of rebellions and constant secessions, and not that of revolution. Here again, death will have to be felt from within, but it will have to come from without.

The founders of empires caused everything to pass into a latent state; they invented vengeance and incited *ressentiment,* that counter-vengeance. And yet Nietzsche says about them what he has already said about the primitive system: it was not in their midst that "bad con-science," this ugly growth—i.e., Oedipus—took root and began to grow. It is simply that one more step has been taken in that direction: Oedipus, bad conscience, interiority, they made it possible.[60] What does Nietzsche mean, this man who dragged Caesar along with him as a despotic signifier, along with its two signifieds, his sister and his mother, and who felt their weight grow heavier as he drew nearer to madness? It is true that Oedipus begins its cellular, ovular migration in the system of imperial representation: from being at first the displaced represented of desire, it becomes the repressing representation itself. The impossible has become possible; the unoccupied limit now finds itself occupied by the despot. Oedipus has received its name, the clubfooted despot committing double incest through overcoding, with his sister and his mother as body representations subjected to verbal representation. Moreover, Oedipus is in the process of establishing each of the formal operations that will make it all possible: the extrapolation of a detached object; the double bind of overcoding or royal incest; the biuni-vocalization, application, and linearization of the chain between masters and slaves; the introduction of the law into desire, and of desire into the law; the terrible latency with its afterward or its after-the-event. All the parts of the five paralogisms thus seem to be ready.

But we are still very far from the psychoanalytic Oedipus, and the Hellenists are right to not grasp clearly the story that psychoanalysis is trying at all costs to tell them. It is indeed the story of desire and its sexual history (there is no other). But here all the parts figure as cogs and wheels in the State machine. Desire is by no means an interplay between a son, a mother, and a father. Desire institutes a libidinal investment of a State machine that overcodes the territorial machine and, with an additional turn of the screw, represses the desiring-machines. Incest derives from this investment and not the reverse. At first it brings into play only the despot, the sister, and the mother: it is the overcoding and repressing representation. The father intervenes only as the representative of the old territorial machine, but the sister is the representative of the new alliance, and the mother is the representative of direct filiation. Father and son are not yet born. All sexuality functions in terms of the conjoined operations of machines, their internecine struggle, their superposition, their interlocking arrangements. Let us marvel once again at Freud's account of Oedipus. In *Moses and Monotheism* he indeed surmises that latency is a State affair. But then latency must not succeed the "Oedipus complex," marking the complex's repression or even its suppression. It must result from the repressing action of the incestuous representation, which is not yet by any means a complex in the sense of repressed desire, since on the contrary the representation exercises its repressive action on desire itself. The Oedipus complex, as it is called by psychoanalysis, will be born of latency, after latency, and it signifies the return of the repressed under conditions that disfigure, displace, and even decode desire. The Oedipus complex appears only after latency; and when Freud recognizes two phases separated by latency, it is only the second phase that merits the complex's name, while the first expresses only its parts and wheels functioning from a completely different viewpoint, in a completely different organization. There we see the mania of psychoanalysis with all its paralogisms: it presents as a resolution, or an attempted resolution, of the complex what is rather the latter's definitive establishment or its interior installation, and it presents as the complex what is still the complex's opposite. What will be necessary in order for Oedipus to become *the* Oedipus, the Oedipus complex? Many things, in fact—those things that Nietzsche partially grasped in the evolution of the infinite debt.

The Oedipal cell will have to complete its migration; it must no longer be content to pass from the state of the displaced represented to that of repressing representation; rather, from being the repressing representation, it will have to finally become the representative of desire itself. And it must become the latter by virtue of being the displaced represented. The debt must not only become an infinite debt, it will have to be internalized and spiritualized as an infinite debt (Christianity and what follows). The father and the son will have to take form—that is, the royal triad must "masculinize" itself—and this must occur as a direct consequence of the infinite debt that is now internalized.* Oedipus-the-despot will have to be replaced by Oedipuses-as-subjects, Oedipuses-as-subjugated individuals, Oedipuses-as-fathers, and Oedipuses-as-sons. All the formal operations will have to be resumed within a decoded social field, and must reverberate in the pure and private element of interiority, of interior reproduction. The apparatus of social repression-psychic repression will have to undergo a complete reorganization. Hence desire, having completed its migration, will have to experience this extreme affliction of being turned against itself: the turning back against itself, bad conscience, the guilt that attaches it to the most decoded of social fields as well as to the sickest interiority, the trap for desire, its ugly growth. So long as the history of desire does not experience this outcome, Oedipus haunts all societies, but as the nightmare of something that has still not happened to them—its hour has not come. (And isn't this the strength of Lacan, to have saved psycho-analysis from the frenzied oedipalization to which it was linking its fate—to have brought about this salvation even at the price of a regression, and even though it meant the unconscious would be kept under the weight of the despotic apparatus, that it would be reinterpreted starting from this apparatus, the Law, and the signifier—phallus and castration, yes! Oedipus, no!—the despotic age of the unconscious.)

8 | The Urstaat

The city of Ur, the point of departure of Abraham or the new alliance. The State was not formed in progressive stages; it appears fully armed, a master stroke executed all at once; the primordial *Urstaat*, the eternal model of everything the State wants to be and desires. "Asiatic" production, with the State that expresses or consti-tutes its objective movement, is not a distinct formation; it is the basic formation, on the horizon throughout history. There comes back to us from all quarters the discovery of imperial machines that preceded the traditional historical forms, machines characterized by State ownership

*Historians of religions and psychoanalysts are very familiar with this problem of the masculinization of the imperial triad, in terms of the father-son relationship that is brought into it. Nietzsche sees in this problem an essential moment in the development of the infinite debt: "that stroke of genius on the part of Christianity: God himself sacrifices himself for the guilt of Mankind, God himself makes payment to himself, God as the only being who can redeem man from what has become unredeemable for man himself—the creditor sacrifices himself for his debtor, out of *love* (can one credit that?), out of love for his debtor!" (*On the Genealogy of Morals*, II, 21.)

of property, with communal possession bricked into it, and collective dependence. Every form that is more "evolved" is like a palimpsest: it covers a despotic inscription, a Mycenaean manuscript. Under every Black and every Jew there is an Egyptian, and a Mycenaean under the Greeks, an Etruscan under the Romans. And yet their origin sinks into oblivion, a latency that lays hold of the State itself, and where the writing system sometimes disappears. It is beneath the blows of private property, then of commodity production, that the State witnesses its decline. Land enters into the sphere of private property and into that of commodities. *Classes* appear, inasmuch as the dominant classes are no longer merged with the State apparatus, but are distinct determinations that make use of this transformed apparatus. At first situated adjacent to communal property, then entering into the latter's composition or conditioning it, then becoming more and more a determining force, private property brings about an internalization of the creditor-debtor relation in the relations of opposed classes.[61]

But how does one explain both this latency into which the despotic State enters, and this power with which it re-forms itself on modified foundations, in order to spring back more "mendacious," "colder," and more "hypocritical" than ever? This oblivion and this return. On the one hand, the ancient city-state, the Germanic commune, and feudalism presuppose the great empires, and cannot be understood except in terms of the Urstaat that serves as their horizon. On the other hand, the problem confronting these forms is to reconstitute the Urstaat insofar as possible, given the requirements of their new distinct determinations. For what do private property, wealth, commodities, and classes signify? *The breakdown of codes.* The appearance, the surging forth of now decoded flows that pour over the socius, crossing it from one end to the other. The State can no longer be content to overcode territorial elements that are already coded, it must invent specific codes for flows that are increasingly deterritorialized, which means: putting despotism in the service of the new class relations; integrating the relations of wealth and poverty, of commodity and labor; reconciling market money and money from revenues; everywhere stamping the mark of the Urstaat on the new state of things. And everywhere, the presence of the latent model that can no longer be equaled, but that one cannot help but imitate. The Egyptian's melancholy warning to the Greeks echoes through history: "You Greeks will never be anything but children!"

This special situation of the State as a category—oblivion and return—has to be explained. To begin with, it should be said that the primordial despotic state is not a historical break like any other. Of all the institutions, it is perhaps the only one to appear fully armed in the brain of those who institute it, "the artists with a look of bronze." That is why Marxism didn't quite know what to make of it: it has no place in the famous five stages: primitive communism, ancient city-states, feudalism, capitalism, and socialism.* *It is not one formation among others, nor is it the transition from one formation to another.* It appears to be set back at a remove from what it transects and from what it resects, as though it were giving evidence of another dimension, a cerebral ideality that is added to, superimposed on the material evolution of societies, a regulating idea or principle of reflection (terror) that organizes the parts and the flows into a whole. What is transected, supersected, or over-coded by the despotic State is what comes before—the territorial machine, which it reduces to the state of bricks, of working parts henceforth subjected to the cerebral idea. In this sense the despotic State is indeed the origin, but the origin as an abstraction that must include its differences with respect to the concrete beginning. We know that myth always expresses a passage and a divergence (*un écart*). The primitive territorial myth of the beginning expressed the divergence of a characteristically intense energy—what Marcel Griaule called "the metaphysical part of mythology," the vibratory spiral—in relation to the social system in extension that it conditioned, passing back and forth between alliance and filiation. But the imperial myth of the origin expresses something else: the divergence of this beginning from the origin itself, the divergence of the extension from the idea, of the genesis from the order and the power (the new alliance), and also what repasses from filiation to alliance, what is taken up again by filiation. Jean-Pierre Vernant shows in this way that the imperial myths are not able to conceive a law of organization that is immanent in the universe: they need to posit and internalize this difference between the origin and the beginnings, between the sovereign power and the genesis of the world; "the myth constitutes itself within this distance, it makes it into the very object of its narrative, retracing the avatars of sovereignty down through the succession of generations to the moment when a supremacy, this time definitive, puts an end to the dramatic elaboration of the *dunesteia.*"[62] So that in the end one no longer really knows what comes first, and whether the territorial machine does not in fact presuppose a despotic machine from which it extracts the bricks or that it segments in its turn.

*Regarding whether it is possible to bring "Asiatic" production into agreement with the five stages, and regarding the reasons behind Engel's renunciation of this category in *Origins of the Family,* and the Russian and Chinese Marxists' resistance to this category, see Godelier, *Sur le mode de production asiatique* (reference note 47). One may recall the insults addressed to Wittfogel for having raised this simple question: wasn't the category of the Oriental despotic State challenged for reasons having to do with its special paradigmatic status as a horizon for modern socialist States?

In a certain sense it is necessary to say as much in regard to what comes after the primal State, in regard to what is resected by this State. It supersects what comes before, but resects the formations that follow. There too it is like an abstraction that belongs to another dimension, always at a remove and struck by latency, but that springs back and returns stronger than before in the later forms that lend it a concrete existence. A protean State, yet there has never been but one State. Whence the variations, all the variants of the new alliance, falling nevertheless under the same category. For example, feudalism not only presupposes an abstract despotic State that it divides into segments according to the régime of its private property and the rise of its commodity production, but the latter induce in return the concrete existence of a *feudal state in the proper sense of the term,* where the despot returns as the absolute monarch. For it is a double error to think that the development of commodity production is enough to bring about feudalism's collapse—on the contrary, this development reinforces feudalism in many respects, offering the latter new conditions of existence and survival—and that feudalism of itself is in opposition to the State, which on the contrary, as the feudal State, is capable of preventing commodities from introducing the decoding of flows that *alone* would be ruinous to the system under consideration.* And in more recent examples, we have to go along with Wittfogel when he shows the degree to which modern capitalist and socialist States take on the characteristic features of the primordial despotic State. As for democracies, how could one fail to recognize in them the despot who has become colder and more hypocritical, more calculating, since he must himself count and code instead of overcoding the accounts? It is useless to compose the list of differences after the manner of conscientious historians: village communes here, industrial societies there, and so on. The differences could be determining only if the despotic State were one concrete formation among others, to be treated comparatively. But the despotic State is the abstraction that is realized—in imperial formations, to be sure—only as an abstraction (the overcoding eminent unity). It assumes its immanent concrete existence only in the subsequent forms that cause it to return under other guises and conditions. Being the common horizon for what comes before and what comes after, it conditions universal history on;y proied itis ot on the outside, but always

*Maurice Dobb has shown how the development of commerce, of the market, and of money had very diverse effects on feudalism, at times reinforcing serfdom and the whole array of feudal structures: *Studies in the Development of Capitalism* (reference note 70), pp. 33–83. François Hincker has elaborated the concept of "State feudalism" to show how the French absolute monarchy, in particular, maintained the productive forces and commodity production in the framework of a feudalism that did not end until the eighteenth century (*Sur le féodalisme* [Paris: Editions Sociales, 1971], pp. 61–66).

off to the side, the cold monster that represents the way in which history is in the "head," in the "brain"—the Urstaat.

Marx recognized that there was indeed a way in which history proceeded from the abstract to the concrete: "the simple categories are the expression of relations within which the less developed concrete may have already realized itself before having posited the more many-sided connection or relation which is mentally expressed in the more concrete category; while the more developed concrete preserves the same category as a subordinate relation."[63] The State was first this abstract unity that integrated subaggregates functioning separately; it is now subordinated to a field of forces whose flows it co-ordinates and whose autonomous relations of domination and subordination it expresses. It is no longer content to overcode maintained and imbricated territorialities; it must constitute, invent codes for the decoded flows of money, commodities, and private property. It no longer of itself forms a ruling class or classes; it is itself formed by these classes, which have become independent and delegate it to serve their power and their contradictions, their struggles and their compromises with the dominated classes. It is no longer the transcendent law that governs fragments; it must fashion as best it can a whole to which it will render its law immanent. It is no longer the pure signifier that regulates its signifieds; it now appears behind them, depending on the things it signifies. It no longer produces an overcoding unity; it is itself produced inside the field of decoded flows. As a machine it no longer determines a social system; it is itself determined by the social system into which it is incorporated in the exercise of its functions. In brief, it does not cease being artificial, but it becomes concrete, it "tends to concretization" while subordinating itself to the dominant forces. The existence of an analogous evolution has been demonstrated for the technical machine, when it ceases to be an abstract unity or intellectual system reigning over separate subaggregates to become a relation that is subordinated to a field of forces operating as a concrete physical system.[64]

But isn't this tendency to concretization in the social or technical machine precisely the movement of desire? Again and again we come upon the monstrous paradox: the State is desire that passes from the head of the despot to the hearts of his subjects, and from the intellectual law to the entire physical system that disengages or liberates itself from the law. A State desire, the most fantastic machine for repression, is still desire—the subject that desires and the object of desire. Desire—such is the operation that consists in always stamping the mark of the primordial Urstaat on the new state of things, rendering it immanent to the new system insofar as possible, making it interior to this system. As for the rest, it will be a question of starting again from zero: the founding of a spiritual empire there where forms exist under which the State can no longer function as such in the physical system. When the Christians took possession of the Empire, this complementary duality reappeared between those who wanted to do everything possible to reconstruct the Urstaat from the elements they found in the immanence of the objective Roman world, and the purists, who wanted a fresh start in the wilderness, a new beginning for a new alliance, a rediscovery of the Egyptian and Syriac inspiration that would provide the impetus for a transcendent Urstaat. What strange machines those were that cropped up on columns and in tree trunks! In this sense, Christianity was able to develop a whole set of paranoiac and celibate machines, a whole string of paranoiacs and perverts who also form part of our history's horizon and people our calendar.* These are the two aspects of a becoming of the State: its internalization in a field of increasingly decoded social forces forming a physical system; its spiritualization in a supraterrestrial field that increasingly overcodes, forming a metaphysical system. The infinite debt must become internalized at the same time as it becomes spiritualized. The hour of bad conscience draws nigh; it will also be the hour of the greatest cynicism, "that repressed cruelty of the animal-man made inward and scared back into himself, the creature imprisoned in the 'state' so as to be tamed. . . ."[65]

9 | The Civilized Capitalist Machine

The first great movement of deterritorialization appears with the overcoding performed by the despotic State. But it is nothing compared to the other great movement, the one that will be brought about by the decoding of flows. The action of decoded flows is not enough, however, to cause the new break to traverse and transform the socius—not enough, that is, to induce the birth of capitalism. Decoded flows strike the despotic State with latency; they submerge the tyrant,

*In this regard Jacques Lacarrière hascal;ed attention to the figures and the moments of Christian asceticism Egypt, Palestine, and Syria, starting with the third century: *Les hommes ivres de Dieu* (Grenoble: Arthaud, 1961). First come gentle paranoiacs who install themselves close to a village, then withdraw into the desert where they invent astonishing ascetic machines expressing their struggle against the old alliances and filiations (the Saint Anthony stage); next, communities of disciples are formed, monasteries where one of the main activities is to *write* the life of the founding saint: celibate machines with a military discipline where the monk "reconstructs around him, in the form of ascetic and collective constraints, the aggressive universe of the old persecutions" (the Saint Pachomius stage); and finally, the return to the city or the village; armed groups of perverts who assign themselves the task of struggling against the dying paganism (the Schnoudi stage). More generally, concerning the monastery's relationship with the city, see Lewis Mumford, who talks about an "elaboration of a new form of urban structuration" in terms of monasteries (*The City in History* [New York: Harcourt, Brace, and World, 1961], pp. 246ff., 258–59).

but they also cause him to return in unexpected forms; they democratize him, oligarchize him, segmentalize him, monarchize him, and always internalize and spiritualize him, while on the horizon there is the latent Urstaat, for the loss of which there is no consolation. It is now up to the State to recode as best it can, by means of regular or exceptional operations, the product of the decoded flows. Let us take the example of Rome: the decoding of the landed flows (*des flux fonciers*) through the privatization of property, the decoding of the monetary flows through the formation of great fortunes, the decoding of the commercial flows through the development of commodity production, the decoding of the producers through expropriation and proletarization—all the preconditions are present, everything is given, without producing a capitalism properly spreaking, but rather a régime based on slavery.[66] Or the example of feudalism: there again private property, commodity production, the monetary afflux, the extension of the market, the development of towns, and the appearance of manorial ground rent in money form, or of the contractual hiring of labor, do not by any means produce a capitalist economy, but rather a reinforcing of feudal offices and relations, at times a return to more primitive stages of feudalism, and occasionally even the re-establishment of a kind of slavery (*esclavagisme*). And it is well known that the monopolistic action favoring the guilds and the companies promotes, not the rise of capitalist production, but the insertion of the bourgeoisie into a town and State feudalism that consists in devising codes for flows that are decoded as such, and in keeping the merchants, according to Marx's formula, "in the very pores" of the old full body of the social machine. Hence capitalism does not lead to the dissolution of feudalism, but rather the contrary, and that is why so much time was required between the two. There is a great difference in this respect between the despotic age and the capitalist age. For the founders of the State come like lightning; the despotic machine is synchronic while the capitalist machine's time is diachronic. The capitalists appear in succession in a series that institutes a kind of creativity of history, a strange menagerie: the schizoid time of the new creative break.

The dissolutions are defined by a simple decoding of flows, and they are always compensated by residual forces or transformations of the State. Death is felt rising from within and desire itself becomes the death instinct, latency, but it also passes over into these flows that carry the seeds of a new life. Decoded flows—but who will give a name to this new desire? Flows of property that is sold, flows of money that circulates, flows of production and means of production making ready in the shadows, flows of workers becoming deterritorialized: the encounter of all these flows will be necessary, their conjunction, and their reaction on one another—and the contingent nature of this encounter, this conjunction, and this reaction, which occur one time—in order for capitalism to be born, and for the old system to die this time from without, at the same time as the new life begins and desire receives its name. The only universal history is the history of contingency. Let us return to this eminently contingent question that modern historians know how to ask: why Europe, why not China? Apropos of ocean navigation, Fernand Braudel asks: why not Chinese, Japanese, or even Moslem ships? Why not Sinbad the Sailor? It is not the technique, the technical machine, that is lacking. Isn't it rather that desire remains caught in the nets of the despotic State, entirely invested in the despot's machine? "Perhaps then the merit of the West, confined as it was on its narrow 'Cape of Asia,' was to have needed the world, to have needed to venture outside its own front door."[67] The schizophrenic voyage is the only kind there is. (Later this will be the American meaning of frontiers: something to go beyond, limits to cross over, flows to set in motion, noncoded spaces to enter.)

Decoded desires and desires for decoding have always existed; history is full of them. But we have just seen that only through their encounter in a place, and their conjunction in a space that takes time, do decoded flows constitute a desire—a desire that, instead of just dreaming or lacking it, actually produces a desiring-machine that is at the same time social and technical. That is why capitalism and its break are defined not solely by decoded flows, but by the generalized decoding of flows, the new massive deterritorialization, the conjunction of deterritorialized flows. It is the singular nature of this conjunction that ensured the universality of capitalism. By simplifying a lot, we can say that the savage territorial machine operated on the basis of connections of production, and that the barbarian despotic machine was based on disjunctions of inscription derived from the eminent unity. But the capitalist machine, the civilized machine, will first establish itself on the conjunction. When this occurs, the conjunction no longer merely designates remnants that have escaped coding, or consummations-consumptions as in the primitive feasts, or even the "maximum consumption" in the extravagance of the despot and his agents. When the conjunction moves to the fore in the social machine, it seems on the contrary that it ceases to be tied to enjoyment or to the excess consumption of a class, that it makes luxury itself into a means of investment, and reduces all the decoded flows to production, in a "production for production's sake" that rediscovers the primitive connections of labor, on condition—on the sole condition—that they be linked to capital and to the new deterritorialized full body, the true consumer from whence they seem to emanate (as in the pact with the devil that Marx describes—the "industrial eunuch": so it's *your* fault if . . .)[68]

At the heart of *Capital*, Marx points to the encounter of two "principal" elements: on one side, the deterritorialized worker who has become free and naked, having to sell his labor capacity; and on the other, decoded money that has become capital and is capable of buying it. The fact that these two elements result from the segmentation of the despotic State in feudalism, and from the decomposition of the feudal system itself and that of its State, still does not give us the extrinsic conjunction of these two flows: flows of producers and flows of money. The encounter might not have taken place, with the free workers and the money-capital existing "virtually" side by side. One of the elements depends on a transformation of the agrarian structures that constitute the old social body, while the other depends on a completely different series going by way of the merchant and the usurer, as they exist marginally in the pores of this old social body.[69] What is more, each of these elements brings into play several processes of decoding and deterritorialization having very different origins. For the free worker: the deterritorialization of the soil through privatization; the decoding of the instruments of production through appropriation; the loss of the means of consumption through the dissolution of the family and the corporation; and finally, the decoding of the worker in favor of the work itself or of the machine. And for capital: the deterritorialization of wealth through monetary abstraction; the decoding of the flows of production through merchant capital; the decoding of States through financial capital and public debts; the decoding of the means of production through the formation of industrial capital; and so on.

Let us consider more in detail how the elements come together, with the conjunction of all their processes. It is no longer the age of cruelty or the age of terror, but the age of cynicism, accompanied by a strange piety. (The two taken together constitute humanism: cynicism is the physical immanence of the social field, and piety is the maintenance of a spiritualized Urstaat; cynicism is capital as the means of extorting surplus labor, but piety is this same capital as God-capital, whence all the forces of labor seem to emanate.) This age of cynicism is that of the accumulation of capital—an age that implies a period of time, precisely for the conjunction of all the decoded and deterritorialized flows. As Maurice Dobb has shown, an accumulation of property title deeds—in land, for example—will be necessary in a first period of time, in a favorable conjuncture, at a time when this property costs little (the disintegration of the feudal system); and a second period is required when the property is sold during a rise in prices and under conditions that make industrial investment especially advantageous (the "price-revolution," an abundant reserve supply of labor, the formation of a proletariat, an easy access to sources of raw materials, favorable conditions for the production of tools and machinery).[70] All sorts of contingent factors favor these conjunctions. So many encounters for the formation of the thing, the unnamable! But the effect of the conjunction is indeed capital's tighter and tighter control over production: capitalism or its break, the conjunction of all the decoded and deterritorialized flows, cannot be defined by commercial capital or by financial capital—these being merely flows among other flows and elements among other elements—but rather by industrial capital. Doubtless the merchant was very early an active factor in production, either by turning into an industrialist himself in occupations based on commerce, or by making artisans into his own intermediaries or employees (the struggles against the guilds and the monopolies). But capitalism doesn't begin, the capitalist machine is not assembled, until capital directly appropriates production, and until financial capital and merchant capital are no longer anything but specific functions corresponding to a division of labor in the capitalist mode of production in general. One then re-encounters the production of productions, the production of recordings, and the production of consumptions—but precisely in this conjunction of de-coded flows that makes of capital the new social full body, whereas commercial and financial capitalism in its primitive forms merely installed itself in the pores of the old socius without changing the old mode of production.

Even before the capitalist production-machine is assembled, commodities and money effect a decoding of flows through abstraction. But this does not occur in the same way for both instances. First, simple exchange inscribes commercial products as particular *quanta* of a unit of abstract labor. It is abstract labor, posited in the exchange relation, that forms the disjunctive synthesis of the apparent movement of commodities, since the abstract labor is divided into qualified pieces of labor to which a given determinate quantum corresponds. But it is only when a "general equivalent" appears as money that one enters into the reign of the *quantitas,* which can have all sorts of particular values or be worth all sorts of quanta. This abstract quantity nonetheless must have some particular value, so that it still appears only as a relation of magnitude between quanta. It is in this sense that the exchange relation formally unites partial objects that are produced and even inscribed independently of it. The commercial and monetary inscription remains overcoded and even repressed by the previous characteristics and modes of inscription of a socius considered in its specific mode of production, which knows nothing of and does not recognize abstract labor. As Marx says, the latter is indeed the simplest and most ancient relation of productive activity, but it does not appear as such and only becomes a true practical relation in the modern capitalist machine.[71] That is why, before, the monetary and commercial inscription does not have a body of its own at its disposal, and why it is inserted into the interstices of the pre-existing social body. The merchant is continually speculating with the maintained territorialities, so as to buy where prices are low and sell where they are high. Before the capitalist machine, merchant or financial capital is merely in a relationship of alliance with noncapitalist production; it enters into the new alliance that characterizes precapitalist States—whence the alliance of the merchant and banking bourgeoisie with feudalism. In brief, the capitalist machine begins when capital ceases to be a capital of alliance to become a filiative capital. Capital becomes filiative when money begets money, or value a surplus value—"value in process, money in process, and, as such, capital. . . . Value . . . suddenly presents itself as an independent substance, endowed with a motion of its own, in which money and commodities are mere forms which it assumes and casts off in turn. Nay more: instead of simply representing the relations of commodities, it enters now, so to say, into relations with itself. It differentiates itself as original value from itself as surplus-value; as the father differentiates himself qua the son, yet both are one and of one age: for only by the surplus-value of £10 does the £100 originally advanced become capital."[72]

It is solely under these conditions that capital becomes the full body, the new socius or the quasi cause that appropriates all the productive forces. We are no longer in the domain of the quantum or of the quantitas, but in that of the differential relation as a conjunction that defines the immanent social field particular to capitalism, and confers on the abstraction as such its effectively concrete value, its tendency to concretization. The abstraction has not ceased to be what it is, but it no longer appears in the simple quantity as a variable relation between independent terms; it has taken upon itself the independence, the quality of the terms and the quantity of the relations. The abstract itself posits the more complex relation within which it will develop "like" something concrete. This is the differential relation $\frac{Dy}{Dx}$, where Dy derives from labor power and constitutes the fluctuation of variable capital, and where Dx derives from capital itself and constitutes the fluctuation of constant capital ("the definition of constant capital by no means excludes the possibility of a change in the value of its constituent parts"). It is from the fluxion of decoded flows, from their conjunction, that the filiative form of capital, $x+dx$, results. The differential relation expresses the fundamental capitalist phenomenon of *the transformation of the surplus value of code into a surplus value of flux*. The fact that a mathematical appearance here replaces the old code simply signifies that one is witnessing a breakdown of the subsisting codes and territorialities for the benefit of a machine of another species, functioning in an entirely different way. This is no longer the cruelty of life, the terror of one life brought to bear against another life, but a *post-mortem* despotism, the despot become anus and vampire: "Capital is dead labour, that vampire-like, only lives by sucking living labour, and lives the more, the more labour it sucks." Industrial capital thus offers a new new filiation that is a constituent part of the capitalist machine, in relation to which commercial capital and financial capital will now take the form of a new alliance by assuming specific functions.

The celebrated problem of the tendency to a falling rate of profit, that is, of surplus value in relation to total capital, can be understood only from the viewpoint of capitalism's entire field of immanence, and by taking into account the conditions under which a surplus value of code is transformed into a surplus value of flux. First of all, it appears that—in keeping with Balibar's remarks—this tendency to a falling rate of profit has no end, but reproduces itself while reproducing the factors that counteract it. But why does it have no end? Doubtless for the same reasons that provoke the laughter of the capitalists and their economists when they ascertain that surplus value cannot be determined mathematically. Yet they have little cause to rejoice. They would be better off concluding in favor of the very thing they are bent on hiding: that it is not the same money that goes into the pocket of the wage earner and is entered on the balance sheet of a commercial enterprise. In the one case, there are impotent money signs of exchange value, a flow of means of payment relative to consumer goods and use values, and a one-to-one relation between money and an imposed range of products ("which I have a right to, which are my due, so they're mine"); in the other case, signs of the power of capital, flows of financing, a system of differential quotients of production that bear witness to a prospective force or to a long-term evaluation, not realizable *hic et nunc*, and functioning as an axiomatic of abstract quantities. In the one case, money represents a potential break-deduction in a flow of consumption; in the other case, it represents a break-detachment and a rearticulation of economic chains directed toward the adaptation of flows of production to the disjunctions of capital. The extreme importance in the capitalist system of the dualism that exists in banking has been demonstrated, the dualism between the formation of means of payment and the structure of financing, between the management of money and the financing of capitalist accumulation, between exchange money and credit money.[73] The fact that banks participate in both, that they are situated at the pivotal point between financing and payment, merely shows the multiple interactions of these two operations. Thus in credit money, which comprises all the commercial and bank credits, purely commercial credit has its roots in simple circulation where money develops as means of payment (bills of exchange falling due on a fixed date, which constitute a monetary form of finite debt). Inversely, bank credit effects a demonetization or dematerialization of money, and is based on the circulation of drafts instead of the circulation of money. This credit money traverses a particular circuit where it assumes, then loses, its value as an instrument of exchange, and where the conditions of flux imply conditions of reflux, giving to the infinite debt its capitalist form; but the State as a regulator ensures a principle of convertibility of this credit money, either directly by tying it to gold, or indirectly through a mode of centralization that comprises a guarantor of the credit, a uniform interest rate, a unity of capital markets, etc.

Hence one is correct in speaking of a profound *dissimulation* of the dualism of these two forms of money, payment and financing—the two aspects of banking practice. But this dissimulation does not depend on a faulty understanding so much as it expresses the capitalist field of immanence, the apparent objective movement where the lower or subordinate form is no less necessary than the other (it is necessary for money to play on both boards), and where no integration of the dominated classes could occur without the shadow of this unapplied principle of convertibility—which is enough, however, to ensure that the Desire of the most disadvantaged creature will invest with all its strength, irrespective of any economic understanding or lack of it, the capitalist social field as a whole. Flows, who doesn't desire flows, and relationships between flows, and breaks in flows?—all of which capitalism was able to mobilize and break under these hitherto unknown conditions of money. While it is true that capitalism is industrial in its essence or mode of production, it functions only as merchant capitalism. While it is true that it is filiative industrial capital in its essence, it functions only through its alliance with commercial and financial capital.

In a sense, it is the bank that controls the whole system and the investment of desire.* One of Keynes's contributions was the reintroduction of desire into the problem of money; it is this that must be subjected to the requirements of Marxist analysis. That is why it is unfortunate that Marxist economists too often dwell on considerations concerning the mode of production, and on the theory of money as the general equivalent as found in the first section of *Capital*, without attaching enough importance to banking practice, to financial operations, and to the specific circulation of credit money—which would be the meaning of a return to Marx, to the Marxist theory of money.

Let us return to the dualism of money, to the two boards, the two inscriptions, the one going into the account of the wage earner, the other into the balance sheet of the enterprise. Measuring the two orders of magnitude in terms of the same analytical unit is a pure fiction, a cosmic swindle, as if one were to measure intergalactic or intra-atomic distances in meters and centimeters. There is no common measure between the value of the enterprises and that of the labor capacity of wage earners. That is why the falling tendency has no conclusion. A quotient of differentials is indeed calculable if it is a matter of the limit of variation of the production flows from the viewpoint of a full output, but it is not calculable if it is a matter of the production flow and the labor flow on which surplus value depends. Thus the difference is not canceled in the relationship that constitutes it as a difference in nature; the "tendency" has no end, it has no exterior limit that it could reach or even approximate. The tendency's only limit is internal, and it is continually going beyond it, but by displacing this limit—that is, by reconstituting it, by rediscovering it as an internal limit to be surpassed again by means of a displacement; thus the continuity of the capitalist process engenders itself in this break of a break that is always displaced, in this unity of the schiz and the flow. In this respect already the field of social immanence, as revealed under the withdrawal and the transformation of the Urstaat, is continually expanding, and acquires a consistency entirely its own, which shows the manner in which capitalism for its part was able to interpret the general principle according to which things work well only providing they break down, crises being "the means immanent to the capitalist mode of production." If capitalism is the exterior limit of all societies, this is because capitalism for its part has no exterior limit, but

*Brunhoff, *L'offre de monnaie* (reference note 73), p. 124: "The very notion of a monetary mass can have a meaning only relative to the workings of a system of credit where the different kinds of money combine. Without such a system, one would have only a sum of means of payment that would have no access to the social nature of the general equivalent and that could serve only in local private circuits. There would be no general monetary circulation. Only in the centralized system can the different kinds of money become homogeneous and appear as the components of an articulated whole." And with regard to the objective *dissimulation* in the system, see pp. 110, 114.

only an interior limit that is capital itself and that it does not encounter, but reproduces by always displacing it.* Jean-Joseph Goux rigorously analyzes the mathematical phenomenon of the curve without a tangent, and the direction it is apt to take in economy as well as linguistics: "If the movement does not tend toward any limit, if the quotient of differentials is not calculable, the present no longer has any meaning. . . . The quotient of differentials is not resolved, the differences no longer cancel one another in their relationship. No limit opposes the break (*la brisure*), or the breaking of this break. The tendency finds no end, the thing in motion never quite reaches what the immediate future has in store for it; it is endlessly delayed by accidents and deviations. . . . Such is the complex notion of a continuity within the absolute break."[74] In the expanded immanence of the system, the limit tends to reconstitute in its displacement the thing it tended to diminish in its primitive emplacement.

Now this movement of displacement belongs essentially to the deterritorialization of capitalism. As Samir Amin has shown, the process of deterritorialization here goes from the center to the periphery, that is, from the developed countries to the undereveloped countries, which do not constitute a separate world, but rather an essential component of the world-wide capitalist machine. It must be added, however, that the center itself has its organized enclaves of underdevelopment, its reservations and its ghettos as interior peripheries. (Pierre Moussa has defined the United States as a fragment of the Third World that has succeeded and has preserved its immense zones of underdevelopment.) And if it is true that the tendency to a falling rate of profit or to its equalization asserts itself at least partially at the center, carrying the economy toward the most progressive and the most automated sectors, a veritable "development of underdevelopment" on the periphery ensures a rise in the rate of surplus value, in the form of an increasing exploitation of the peripheral proletariat in relation to that of the center. For it would be a great error to think that exports from the periphery originate primarily in traditional sectors or archaic territorialities: on the contrary, they come from modern industries and plantations that generate an immense surplus value, to a point where it is no longer the developed countries that supply the underdeveloped countries with capital, but quite the opposite. So true is it that primitive accumulation is not produced just once at the dawn of capitalism, but is continually reproducing itself. Capitalism exports filiative capital. At the same time

*Marx, *Capital* (see reference note 72), Vol. 3, p. 250: "Capitalist production seeks continually to overcome these immanent barriers, but overcomes them only by means which again place these barriers in its way and on a more formidable scale. The real barrier of capitalist production is capital itself."

as capitalist deterritorialization is developing from the center to the periphery, the decoding of flows on the periphery develops by means of a "disarticulation" that ensures the ruin of traditional sectors, the development of extraverted economic circuits, a specific hypertrophy of the tertiary sector, and an extreme inequality in the different areas of productivity and in incomes.[75] Each passage of a flux is a deterritorialization, and each displaced limit, a decoding. Capitalism schizophrenizes more and more on the periphery. It will be said that, even so, at the center the falling tendency retains its restricted sense, i.e., the relative diminution of surplus value in relation to total capital—a diminution that is ensured by the development of productivity, automation, and constant capital.

This problem was raised again recently by Maurice Clavel in a series of decisive and willfully incompetent questions—that is, questions addressed to Marxist economists by someone who doesn't quite understand how one can maintain human surplus value as the basis for capitalist production, while recognizing that machines too "work" or produce value, that they have always worked, and that they work more and more in proportion to man, who thus ceases to be a constituent part of the production process, in order to become adjacent to this process.[76] Hence there is a machinic surplus value produced by constant capital, which develops along with automation and productivity, and which cannot be explained by factors that counteract the falling tendency—the increasing intensity of the exploitation of human labor, the diminution of the price of the elements of constant capital, etc.—since, on the contrary, these factors depend on it. It seems to us, with the same indispensable incompetence, that these problems can only be viewed under the conditions of the transformation of the surplus value of code into a surplus value of flux. In defining precapitalist régimes by a surplus value of code, and capitalism by a generalized decoding that converted this surplus value of code into a surplus value of flux, we were presenting things in a summary fashion, we were still acting as though the matter were settled once and for all, at the dawn of a capitalism that had lost all code value. This is not the case, however. On the one hand, codes continue to exist—even as an archaism—but they assume a function that is perfectly contemporary and adapted to the situation within personified capital (the capitalist, the worker, the merchant, the banker). But on the other hand, and more profoundly, every technical machine presupposes flows of a particular type: *flows of code* that are both interior and exterior to the machine, forming the elements of a technology and even a science. It is these flows of code that find themselves encasted, coded, or overcoded in the precapitalist societies in such a way that they never achieve any independence (the blacksmith, the astronomer). But the decoding of flows in capitalism has freed, deterritorialized, and decoded the flows of code just as it has the others—to such a degree that the automatic machine has always increasingly internalized them in its body or its structure as a field of forces, while depending on a science and a technology, on a so-called intellectual labor distinct from the manual labor of the worker (the evolution of the technical object). In this sense, it is not machines that have created capitalism, but capitalism that creates machines, and that is constantly introducing breaks and cleavages through which it revolutionizes its technical modes of production.

But several correctives must be introduced in this regard. These breaks and cleavages take time, and their extension is very wide-ranging. By no means does the diachronic capitalist machine allow itself to be revolutionized by one or more of its synchronous technical machines, and by no means does it confer on its scientists and its technicians an independence that was unknown in the previous régimes. Doubtless it can let a certain number of scientists—mathematicians, for example—"schizophrenize" in their corner, and it can allow the passage of socially decoded flows of code that these scientists organize into axiomatics of research that is said to be basic. But *the true axiomatic* is elsewhere. (Leave the scientists alone to a certain point, let them create their own axiomatic, but when the time comes for serious things . . . For example, nondeterminist physics, with its corpuscular flows, will have to be brought into line with "determinism.") The true axiomatic is that of the social machine itself, which takes the place of the old codings and organizes all the decoded flows, including the flows of scientific and technical code, for the benefit of the capitalist system and in the service of its ends. That is why it has often been remarked that the Industrial Revolution combined an elevated rate of technical progress with the maintenance of a great quantity of "obsolescent" equipment, along with a great suspicion concerning machines and science. An innovation is adopted only from the perspective of the rate of profit its investment will offer by the lowering of production costs; without this prospect, the capitalist will keep the existing equipment, and stand ready to make a parallel investment in equipment in another area.[77]

Thus the importance of human surplus value remains decisive, even at the center and in highly industrialized sectors. What determines the lowering of costs and the elevation of the rate of profit through machinic surplus value is not innovation itself, whose value is no more measurable than that of human surplus value. It is not even the profitability of the new technique considered in isolation, but its effect on the over-all profitability of the firm in its relationships with the market and with commercial and financial capital. This implies diachronic encounters and countersectings such as one already sees for example in the early part of the nineteenth century, between the steam engine and textile machines or techniques for the production of iron. In general, the introduction of innovations always tends to be delayed beyond the time scientifically necessary, until the moment when the market forecasts justify their exploitation on a large scale. Here again, alliance capital exerts a strong selective pressure on machinic innovations within industrial capital. In brief, there where the flows are decoded, the specific flows of code that have taken a technical and scientific form are subjected to a properly social axiomatic that is much severer than all the scientific axiomatics, much severer too than all the old codes and overcodes that have disappeared: the axiomatic of the world capitalist market. In brief, the flows of code that are "liberated" in science and technics by the capitalist régime engender a machinic surplus value that does not directly depend on science and technics themselves, but on capital—a surplus value that is added to human surplus value and that comes to correct the relative diminution of the latter, *both of them constituting the whole of the surplus value of flux that characterizes the system.* Knowledge, information, and specialized education are just as much parts of capital ("knowledge capital") as is the most elementary labor of the worker. And just as we found, on the side of human surplus value insofar as it resulted from decoded flows, an incommensurability or a fundamental asymmetry (no assignable exterior limit) between manual labor and capital, or between two forms of money, here too, on the side of the machinic surplus value resulting from scientific and technical flows of code, we find no commensurability or exterior limit between scientific or technical labor—even when highly remunerated—and the profit of capital that inscribes itself with another sort of writing. In this respect the knowledge flow and the labor flow find themselves in the same situation, determined by capitalist decoding or deterritorialization.

But if it is true that innovations are adopted only insofar as they entail a rise in profits through a lowering of costs of production, and if there exists a sufficiently high volume of production to justify them, the corollary that derives from this proposition is that investment in innovations is never sufficient to realize or absorb the surplus value of flux that is produced on the one side as on the other.[78] Marx has clearly demonstrated the importance of the problem: the ever widening circle of capitalism is completed, while reproducing its immanent limits on an ever larger scale, only if the surplus value is not merely produced or extorted, but absorbed or realized.[79] If the capitalist is not defined in terms of enjoyment, the reason is not merely that his aim is the "production for production's sake" that generates surplus value, it also includes the realization of this surplus value: an unrealized surplus value of flux is as if not produced, and becomes embodied in unemployment and stagnation. It is easy to list the principal modes of absorption of surplus value outside the spheres of consumption and investment: advertising, civil government, militarism, and imperialism. The role of the State in this regard, within the capitalist axiomatic, is the more manifest in that what it absorbs is not sliced from the surplus value of the firms, but added to their surplus value by bringing the capitalist economy closer to full output within the given limits, and by widening these limits in turn—especially within an order of military expenditures that are in no way competitive with private enterprise, quite the contrary (it took a war to accomplish what the New Deal had failed to accomplish). The role of a politico-military-economic complex is the more manifest in that it guarantees the extraction of human surplus value on the periphery and in the appropriated zones of the center, but also because it engenders for its own part an enormous machinic surplus value by mobilizing the resources of knowledge and information capital, and finally because it absorbs the greater part of the surplus value produced.

The State, its police, and its army form a gigantic enterprise of antiproduction, but at the heart of production itself, and conditioning this production. Here we discover a new determination of the properly capitalist field of immanence: not only the interplay of the relations and differential coefficients of decoded flows, not only the nature of the limits that capitalism reproduces on an ever wider scale as interior limits, but the presence of antiproduction within production itself. The apparatus of antiproduction is no longer a transcendent instance that opposes production, limits it, or checks it; on the contrary, it insinuates itself everywhere in the productive machine and becomes firmly wedded to it in order to regulate its productivity and realize surplus value— which explains, for example, the difference between the despotic bureaucracy and the capitalist bureaucracy. This effusion from the apparatus of antiproduction is characteristic of the entire capitalist system; the capitalist effusion is that of antiproduction within production at all levels of the process. On the one hand, it alone is capable of realizing capitalism's supreme goal, which is to produce lack in the large aggregates, to introduce lack where there is always too much, by effecting the absorption of overabundant resources. On the other hand, it alone doubles the capital and the flow of knowledge with a capital and an equivalent flow of *stupidity* that also effects an absorption and a realization, and that ensures the integration of groups and individuals into the system. Not only lack amid overabundance, but stupidity in the midst of knowledge and science; it will be seen in particular how it is at the level of the State and the military that the most progressive sectors of scientific or technical knowledge combine with those feeble archaisms bearing the greatest burden of current functions.

Here André Gorz's double portrait of the "scientific and technical worker" takes on its full meaning. Although he has mastered a flow of knowledge, information, and training, he is so absorbed in capital that the reflux of organized, axiomatized stupidity coincides with him, so that, when he goes home in the evening, he rediscovers his little desiring-machines by tinkering with a television set—O despair.[80] Of course the scientist as such has no revolutionary potential; he is the first integrated agent of integration, a refuge for bad conscience, and the *forced* destroyer of his own creativity. Let us consider the more striking example of a career *à l'américaine,* with abrupt mutations, just as we imagine such a career to be: Gregory Bateson begins by fleeing the civilized world, by becoming an ethnologist and following the primitive codes and the savage flows; then he turns in the direction of flows that are more and more decoded, those of schizophrenia, from which he extracts an interesting psychoanalytic theory; then, still in search of a beyond, of another wall to break through, he turns to dolphins, to the language of dolphins, to flows that are even stranger and more deterritorialized. But where does the dolphin flux end, if not with the basic research projects of the American army, which brings us back to preparations for war and to the absorption of surplus value.

In comparison to the capitalist State, the socialist States are children—but children who learned something from their father concerning the axiomatizing role of the State. But the socialist States have more trouble stopping unexpected flow leakage except by direct violence. What on the contrary is called the co-opting power of capitalism can be explained by the fact that its axiomatic is not more flexible, but wider and more englobing. In such a system no one escapes participation in the activity of antiproduction that drives the entire productive system. "But it is not only those who man and supply the military machine who are engaged in an anti-human enterprise. The same can be said in varying degrees of many millions of other workers who produce, and create wants for, goods and services which no one needs. And so interdependent are the various sectors and branches of the economy that nearly everyone is involved in one way or another in these anti-human activities: the farmer supplying food to troops fighting in

Vietnam, the tool and die makers turning out the intricate machinery needed for a new automobile model, the manufacturers of paper and ink and TV sets whose products are used to control the minds of the people, and so on and so on."[81] Thus the three segments of the ever widening capitalist reproduction process are joined, three segments that also define the three aspects of its immanence: (1) the one that extracts human surplus value on the basis of the differential relation between decoded flows of labor and production, and that moves from the center to the periphery while nevertheless maintaining vast residual zones at the center; (2) the one that extracts machinic surplus value, on the basis of an axiomatic of the flows of scientific and technical code, in the "core" areas of the center; (3) and the one that absorbs or realizes these two forms of surplus value of flux by guaranteeing the emission of both, and by constantly injecting antiproduction into the producing apparatus. Schizophrenization occurs on the periphery, but it occurs at the center and at the core as well.

The definition of surplus value must be modified in terms of the machinic surplus value of constant capital, which distinguishes itself from the human surplus value of variable capital and from the nonmeasurable nature of this aggregate of surplus value of flux. It cannot be defined by the difference between the value of labor capacity and the value created by labor capacity, but by the incommensurability between two flows that are nonetheless immanent to each other, by the disparity between the two aspects of money that express them, and by the absence of a limit exterior to their relationship—the one measuring the true economic force, the other measuring a purchasing power determined as "income." The first is the immense deterritorialized flow that constitutes the full body of capital. An economist of the caliber of Bernard Schmitt finds strange lyrical words to characterize this flow of infinite debt: an instantaneous creative flow that the banks create spontaneously as a debt owing to themselves, a creation *ex nihilo* that, instead of transferring a pre-existing currency as means of payment, hollows out at one extreme of the full body a negative money (a debt entered as a liability of the banks), and projects at the other extreme a positive money (a credit granted the productive economy by the banks)—"a flow possessing a power of mutation" *that does not enter into income and is not assigned to purchases,* a pure availability, nonpossession and nonwealth.[82] The other aspect of money represents the reflux, that is, the relationship that it assumes with goods as soon as it acquires a purchasing power through its distribution to workers or production factors, through its allotment in the form of incomes—a relationship that it loses as soon as the latter are converted into real goods (at which point everything recommences by means of a new production that will first come under the sway of the first aspect). The incommensurability of the two aspects—the flux and the reflux—shows that nominal wages fail to embrace the totality of the national income, since the wage earners allow a great quantity of revenues to escape. These revenues are tapped by the firms and in turn form an afflux by means of a conjunction; a flow—this time uninterrupted—of raw *profit*, constituting "at one go" an undivided quantity flowing over the full body, however diverse the uses for which it is allocated (interest, dividends, management salaries, purchase of production goods, etc.).[83]

The incompetent observer has the impression that this whole economic schema, this whole story is profoundly schizo. The aim of the theory is clear—a theory that refrains, however, from employing any moral reference. "Who is robbed?" is the serious implied question that echoes Clavel's ironic question, "Who is alienated?" Yet no one is or can be robbed—just as, according to Clavel, one no longer knows who is alienated or who does the alienating. Who steals? Certainly not the finance capitalist as the representative of the great instantaneous creative flow, which is not even a possession and has no purchasing power. Who is robbed? Certainly not the worker who is not even bought, since the reflux or salary distribution creates the purchasing power, instead of presupposing it. Who would be capable of stealing? Certainly not the industrial capitalist as the representative of the afflux of profit, since "profits do not flow in the reflux, but side by side with, deviating from rather than penalizing the flow that creates incomes." How much flexibility there is in the axiomatic of capitalism, always ready to widen its own limits so as to add a new axiom to a previously saturated system! You say you want an axiom for wage earners, for the working class and the unions? Well then, let's see what we can do—and thereafter profit will flow alongside wages, side by side, reflux and afflux. An axiom will be found even for the language of dolphins. Marx often alluded to the Golden Age of the capitalist, when the latter didn't hide his own cynicism: in the beginning, at least, he could not be unaware of what he was doing, extorting surplus value. But how this cynicism has grown—to the point where he is able to declare: no, nobody is being robbed! For everything is then based on the disparity between two kinds of flows, as in the fathomless abyss where profit and surplus value are engendered: the flow of merchant capital's economic force and the flow that is derisively named "purchasing power"—a flow made truly *impotent* that represents the absolute impotence of the wage earner as well as the relative dependence of the industrial capitalist. This is money and the market, capitalism's true police.

In a certain sense, capitalist economists are not mistaken when they present the economy as being perpetually "in need of monetarization," as if it were always necessary to inject money into the economy from the outside according to a supply and a demand. In this manner the system indeed holds together and functions, and perpetually fulfills its own immanence. In this manner it is indeed the global object of an investment of desire. The wage earner's desire, the capitalist's desire, everything moves to the rhythm of one and the same desire, founded *on the differential relation of flows having no assignable exterior limit, and where capitalism reproduces its immanent limits on an ever widening and more comprehensive scale.* Hence it is at the level of a generalized theory of flows that one is able to reply to the question: how does one come to desire strength while also desiring one's own impotence? How was such a social field able to be invested by desire? And how far does desire go beyond so-called objective interests, when it is a question of flows to set in motion and to break? Doubtless Marxists will remind us that the formation of money as a specific relation within capitalism depends on the mode of production that makes the economy a monetary economy. The fact remains that the apparent objective movement of capital—which is by no means a failure to recognize or an illusion of consciousness—shows that the productive essence of capitalism can itself function only in this necessarily monetary or commodity form that controls it, and whose flows and relations between flows contain the secret of the investment of desire. It is at the level of flows, the monetary flows included, and not at the level of ideology, that the integration of desire is achieved.

So what is the solution? Which is the revolutionary path? Psychoanalysis is of little help, entertaining as it does the most intimate of relations with money, and recording—while refusing to recognize it—an entire system of economic-monetary dependences at the heart of the *desire* of every subject it treats. Psychoanalysis constitutes for its part a gigantic enterprise of absorption of surplus value. But which is the revolutionary path? Is there one?—To withdraw from the world market, as Samir Amin advises Third World countries to do, in a curious revival of the fascist "economic solution"? Or might it be to go in the opposite direction? To go still further, that is, in the movement of the market, of decoding and deterritorialization? For perhaps the flows are not yet deterritorialized enough, not decoded enough, from the viewpoint of a theory and a practice of a highly schizophrenic character. Not to withdraw from the process, but to go further, to "accelerate the process," as Nietzsche put it: in this matter, the truth is that we haven't seen anything yet.

10 | Capitalist Representation

Writing has never been capitalism's thing. Capitalism is profoundly illiterate. The death of writing is like the death of God or the death of the father: the thing was settled a long time ago, although the news of the event is slow to reach us, and there survives in us the memory of extinct signs with which we still write. The reason for this is simple: writing implies a use of language in general according to which graphism becomes aligned on the voice, but also overcodes it and induces a fictitious voice from on high that functions as a signifier. The arbitrary nature of the thing designated, the subordination of the signified, the transcendence of the despotic signifier, and finally, its consecutive decomposition into minimal elements within a field of immanence uncovered by the withdrawal of the despot—all this is evidence that writing belongs to imperial despotic representation. Once this is said, what exactly is meant when someone announces the collapse of the "Gutenberg galaxy"? Of course capitalism has made and continues to make use of writing; not only is writing adapted to money as the general equivalent, but the specific functions of money in capitalism went by way of writing and printing, and in some measure continue to do so. The fact nonetheless remains that writing typically plays the role of an archaism in capitalism, the Gutenberg press being the element that confers on the archaism a *current function*. But the capitalist use of language is different in nature; it is realized or becomes concrete within the field of immanence peculiar to capitalism itself, with the appearance of the technical means of expression that correspond to the generalized decoding of flows, instead of still referring, in a direct or indirect form, to despotic overcoding.

This seems to us to be the significance of McLuhan's analyses: to have shown what a language of decoded flows is, as opposed to a signifier that strangles and overcodes the flows. In the first place, for nonsignifying language anything will do: whether it be phonic, graphic, gestural, etc., no flow is privileged in this language, which remains indifferent to its substance or its support, inasmuch as the latter is an amorphous continuum. The electric flow can be considered as the realization of such a flow that is indeterminate as such. But a substance is said to be formed when a flow enters into a relationship with another flow, such that the first defines a content and the second, an expression.* The deterritorialized flows of content and expression are in a state of conjunction or reciprocal precondition that constitutes figures as the ultimate units of both content and expression. These figures do not derive from a signifier nor are they even signs as minimal elements of the signifier; they are nonsigns, or rather nonsignifying signs, points-signs having several dimensions, flows-breaks or schizzes that form images through their coming together in a whole, but that do not maintain any identity when they pass from one whole to another. Hence the figures, that is, the schizzes or breaks-flows are in no way "figurative"; they become figurative only in a particular constellation that dissolves in order to be replaced by another one. Three million points per second transmitted by television, only a few of which are retained. Electric language does not go by way of the voice or writing; data processing does without them both, as does that discipline appropriately named fluidics, which operates by means of streams of gas; the computer is a machine for instantaneous and generalized decoding. Michel Serres defines in this sense the correlation of the break and the flow in the signs of the new technical language machines, where production is narrowly determined by information: "Take for example a cloverleaf highway interchange. . . . It is a quasi point that analyses, through multiple overlappings, along a dimension that is normal to the network space, the lines of flow for which it serves as a receiver. On it one can go from any afferent direction to any efferent direction, and in whatever order, without ever encountering any of the other directions. . . . If I like, *I will never come back to the same point*, although it will be the same. . . . A topological knot where everything is connected without confusion, where everything flows together and is distributed. . . . Thus a knot may be seen as a point having several dimensions"—which, far from cancelling the flows, contains them and sets them in motion.[84] This cordoning off of production through information shows once again that the productive essence of capitalism functions or "speaks" only in the language of signs imposed on it by merchant capital or the axiomatic of the market.

There are great differences between such a linguistics of flows and linguistics of the signifier. Saussurian linguistics, for example, in effect discovers a field of immanence constituted by "value"—i.e., by the

*Marshall McLuhan, *Understanding Media* (New York: McGraw-Hill, Signet, 1964), p. 23: "The electric light is pure information. It is a medium without a message, as it were, unless it is used to spell out some verbal ad or name. This fact, characteristic of all media, means that the content of any medium is always another medium. The content of writing is speech, just as the written word is the content of print, and print is the content of the telegraph."

system of relations among ultimate elements of the signifier; but apart from the fact that this field of immanence still presupposes the transcendence of the signifier, which uncovers the field if only through the signifier's own withdrawal, the elements populating this field have for a criterion a minimal identity that they owe to their relations of opposition, and that they keep throughout all the types of variations affecting them. The elements of the signifier as distinguishing units are regulated by "coded gaps" that the signifier overcodes in its turn. There result diverse but always convergent consequences: the comparison of language to a game; the signified-signifier relationship, where the signified finds itself by nature subordinated to the signifier; figures defined as effects of the signifier itself; the formal elements of the signifier determined in relation to a phonic substance on which writing even confers a secret privilege. We believe that, from all points of view and despite certain appearances, Louis Hjelmslev's linguistics stands in profound opposition to the Saussurian and post-Saussurian undertaking. Because it abandons all privileged reference. Because it describes a pure field of algebraic immanence that no longer allows any surveillance on the part of a transcendent instance, even one that has withdrawn. Because within this field it sets in motion its flows of form and substance, content and expression. Because it substitutes the relationship of reciprocal precondition between expression and content for the relationship of subordination between signifier and signified. Because there no longer occurs a double articulation between two hierarchized levels of language, but between two convertible deterritorialized planes, constituted by the relation between the form of content and the form of expression. Because in this relation one reaches figures that are no longer effects of a signifier, but schizzes, points-signs, or flows-breaks that collapse the wall of the signifier, pass through, and continue on beyond. Because these signs have crossed a new threshold of deterritorialization. Because these figures have definitively lost the minimum conditions of identity that defined the elements of the signifier itself. Because in Hjelmslev's linguistics the order of the elements is secondary in relation to the axiomatic of flows and figures. Because the money model in the point-sign, or in the figure-break stripped of its identity, having now only a floating identity, tends to replace the model of the game. In short, Hjelmslev's very special position in linguistics, and the reactions he provokes, seem to be explained by the following: that he tends to fashion a purely immanent theory of language that shatters the double game of the voice-graphism domination; that causes form and substance, content and expression to flow according to the flows of desire; and that breaks these flows according to points-signs and figures-schizzes.* Far from being an overdetermination of structuralism and of its fondness for the signifier, Hjelmslev's linguistics implies the concerted destruction of the signifier, and constitutes a decoded theory of language about which one can also say—an ambiguous tribute—that it is the only linguistics adapted to the nature of *both* the capitalist *and* the schizophrenic flows: until now, the only modern—and not archaic— theory of language.

The extreme importance of J.-F. Lyotard's recent book is due to its position as the first generalized critique of the signifier. In his most general proposition, in fact, he shows that the signifier is overtaken toward the outside by figurative images, just as it is ovvertaken toward the inside by the pure figures that compose it—or, more decisively, by "the figural" that comes to short-circuit the signifier's coded gaps, inserting itself between them, and working under the conditions of identity of their elements. In language and in writing itself, sometimes the letters as breaks, as shattered partial objects—and sometimes the words as undivided flows, as nondecomposable blocks, or full bodies having a tonic value—constitute assignifying signs that deliver themselves over to the order of desire: rushes of breath and cries. (In particular, formal investigations concerning manual or printed writing change their meaning according to whether the characteristics of the letters and the qualities of the words are in the service of a signifier, whose effects they express following exegetical rules; or whether, on the contrary, they break through this wall so as to set flows in motion, and establish breaks that overflow or rupture the sign's conditions of identity, and that cause books within "the book" to flow and to disintegrate, entering into multiple configurations whose possibilities were already the object of the typographical exercises of Mallarmé— always passing underneath the signifier, filing through the wall: which again shows that the death of writing is infinite, so long as it arises and arrives from within.)

Similarly, in the plastic arts there is the pure figural dimension formed by the active line and the multidimensional point, and on the other hand, the multiple configurations formed by the passive line and the surface it engenders, so as to reveal—as in Paul Klee—those "intermundia that perhaps are visible only to children, madmen, and primitives."[85] Or in dreams: in some very beautiful pages, Lyotard shows that what is *at work* in dreams is not the signifier but a figural

*Nicolas Ruwet, for example, takes Hjelmslev to task for having elaborated a theory whose applications are on the order of *Jabberwocky* or *Finnegans Wake: Introduction à la grammaire générative* (Paris: Plon, 1967), p. 54. (Regarding Hjelmslev's indifference to the "order of the elements," see p. 345.) André Martinet stresses the loss of the conditions of identity in Hjelmslev's theory: *Au sujet des fondements de la théorie linguistique de Louis Hjelmslev,* 2nd ed. (Paris: Paulet, 1946).

dimension underneath, which gives rise to configurations of images that make use of words, making them flow and cutting them according to flows and points that are not linguistic and do not depend on the signifier or its regulated elements. Thus Lyotard everywhere reverses the order of the signifier and the figure. It is not the figures that depend on the signifier and its effects, but the signifying chain that depends on the figural effects—this chain itself being composed of asignifying signs—crushing the signifiers as well as the signifieds, treating words as things, fabricating new unities, creating from nonfigurative figures configurations of images that form and then disintegrate. And these constellations are like flows that imply the breaks effected by points, just as the points imply the fluxion of the material they cause to flow or leak: the sole unity without identity is that of the flux-schiz or the break-flow. The pure figural element—the "figure-matrix"—Lyotard correctly names desire, which carries us to the gates of schizophrenia as a process.[86]

But what explains the reader's impression that Lyotard is continually arresting the process, and steering the schizzes toward shores he has so recently left behind: toward coded or overcoded territories, spaces, and structures, to which they bring only "transgressions," disorders, and deformations that are secondary in spite of everything, instead of forming and transporting further the desiring-machines that are in opposition to the structures, and the intensities that are in opposition to the spaces? The explanation is that, despite his attempt at linking desire to a fundamental *yes*, Lyotard reintroduces lack and absence into desire; maintains desire under the law of castration, at the risk of restoring the entire signifier along with the law; and discovers the matrix of the figure in fantasy, the simple fantasy that comes to veil desiring-production, the whole of desire as effective production. But at least for an instant the mortgage of the signifier was raised: that enormous archaism that causes so many of us to groan and bow under its weight, and that others use to establish a new terrorism, diverting Lacan's imperial discourse into a university discourse characterized by a pure scientificity, that "scientificity" perfectly suited for resupplying our neuroses, for strangling the process once again, and for overcoding Oedipus with castration, while chaining us to the current structural functions of a vanished archaic despot. For it is certain that, even and especially in their manifestations of extreme force, neither capitalism nor revolution nor schizophrenia follows the paths of the signifier.

Civilization is defined by the decoding and the deterritorialization of flows in capitalist production. Any method will do for ensuring this universal decoding: the privatization brought to bear on property, goods, and the means of production, but also on the organs of "private man" himself; the abstraction of monetary quantities, but also the abstraction of the quantity of labor; the limitless nature of the relationship between capital and labor capacity, and between the flows of financing and the flows of incomes or means of payment; the scientific and technical form assumed by flows of code themselves; the formation of floating configurations starting from lines and points without a discernible identity. The route taken by the decoded flows is traced by recent monetary history: the role of the dollar, short-term migrating capital, the floating of currencies, the new means of financing and credit, the special drawing rights, and the new form of crises and speculations. Our societies exhibit a marked taste for all codes—codes foreign or exotic—but this taste is destructive and morbid. While decoding doubtless means understanding and translating a code, it also means destroying the code as such, assigning it an archaic, folkloric, or residual function, which makes of psychoanalysis and ethnology two disciplines highly regarded in our modern societies. Yet it would be a serious error to consider *the capitalist flows and the schizophrenic flows* as identical, under the general theme of a decoding of the flows of desire. Their affinity is great, to be sure: everywhere capitalism sets in motion schizo-flows that animate "our" arts and "our" sciences, just as they congeal into the production of "our own" sick, the schizophrenics. We have seen that the relationship of schizophrenia to capitalism went far beyond problems of modes of living, environment, ideology, etc., and that it should be examined at the deepest level of one and the same economy, one and the same production process. Our society produces schizos the same way it produces Prell shampoo or Ford cars, the only difference being that the schizos are not salable. How then does one explain the fact that capitalist production is constantly arresting the schizophrenic process and transforming the subject of the process into a confined clinical entity, as though it saw in this process the image of its own death coming from within? Why does it make the schizophrenic into a sick person—not only nominally but in reality? Why does it confine its madmen and madwomen instead of seeing in them its own heros and heroines, its own fulfillment? And where it can no longer recognize the figure of a simple illness, why does it keep its artists and even its scientists under such close surveillance—as though they risked unleashing flows that would be dangerous for capitalist production and charged with a revolutionary potential, so long as these flows are not co-opted or absorbed by the laws of the market? Why does it form in turn a gigantic machine for social repression–psychic repression, aimed at what nevertheless constitutes its own reality—the decoded flows?

The answer—as we have seen—is that capitalism is indeed the limit of all societies, insofar as it brings about the decoding of the flows that the other social formations coded and overcoded. But it is the *relative* limit of every society; it effects *relative* breaks, because it substitutes for the codes an extremely rigorous axiomatic that maintains the energy of the flows in a bound state on the body of capital as a socius that is deterritorialized, but also a socius that is even more pitiless than any other. Schizophrenia, on the contrary, is indeed the *absolute* limit that causes the flows to travel in a free state on a desocialized body without organs. Hence one can say that schizophrenia is the *exterior* limit of capitalism itself or the conclusion of its deepest tendency, but that capitalism only functions on condition that it inhibit this tendency, or that it push back or displace this limit, by substituting for it its own *immanent* relative limits, which it continually reproduces on a widened scale. It axiomatizes with one hand what it decodes with the other. Such is the way one must reinterpret the Marxist law of the counteracting tendency. With the result that schizophrenia pervades the entire capitalist field from one end to the other. But for capitalism it is a question of binding the schizophrenic charges and energies into a world axiomatic that always opposes the revolutionary potential of decoded flows with new interior limits. And it is impossible in such a régime to distinguish, even in two phases, between decoding and the axiomatization that comes to replace the vanished codes. The flows are decoded *and* axiomatized by capitalism at the same time. Hence schizophrenia is not the identity of capitalism, but on the contrary its difference, its divergence, and its death. Monetary flows are perfectly schizophrenic realities, but they exist and function only within the immanent axiomatic that exorcises and repels this reality. The language of a banker, a general, an industrialist, a middle or high-level manager, or a government minister is a perfectly schizophrenic language, but that functions only statistically within the flattening axiomatic of connections that puts it in the service of the capitalist order.[87] (At the highest level of linguistics as a science, Hjelmslev is able to effect a vast decoding of language only by setting in motion from the start an axiomatic machine based on the supposed finite number of the figures considered.) Then what becomes of the "truly" schizophrenic language and the "truly" decoded and unbound flows that manage to break through the wall or absolute limit? The capitalist axiomatic is so rich that one more axiom is added—for the books of a great writer whose lexical and stylistic characteristics can always be computed by means of an electronic machine, or for the discourse of madmen that can always be heard within the framework of a hospital, administrative, and psychiatric axiomatic. In brief, the notion of break-flow has seemed to us to define both capitalism and schizophrenia. But not in the same way; they are not at all the same thing, depending on whether the decodings are caught up in an axiomatic or not; on whether one remains at the level of the large aggregates functioning statistically, or crosses the barrier that separates them from the unbound molecular positions; on whether the flows of desire reach this absolute limit or are content to displace a relative immanent limit that will reconstitute itself further along; on whether controlling reterritorializations are added to the processes of deterritorialization; and on whether money burns or bursts into flames.

Why not merely say that capitalism replaces one code with another, that it carries into effect a new type of coding? For two reasons, one of which represents a kind of moral impossibility, the other a logical impossibility. All the cruelties and terrors meet in the precapitalist formations; some fragments of the signifying chain are struck by secrecy—secret societies or initiation groups— but there is never anything in these societies that is, strictly speaking, unavowable. It is with the thing, capitalism, that the unavowable begins: there is not a single economic or financial operation that, assuming it is translated in terms of a code, would not lay bare its own unavowable nature, that is, its intrinsic perversion or essential cynicism (the age of bad conscience is also the age of pure cynicism). But in point of fact it is impossible to code such operations: in the first place, a code determines the respective qualities of the flows passing through the socius (for example, the three circuits of consumer goods, prestige goods, and women and children); the characteristic object of codes is therefore to establish necessarily indirect relations among these qualified and therefore incommensurable codes. Such relations indeed imply a quantitative siphoning off of portions of the different sorts of flows, but these quantities do not enter into equivalences that would presuppose an unlimited "something"; they simply form composites that are themselves qualitative, essentially mobile and limited, where differences between the elements compensate the disequilibrium (whence the relationship of prestige and consumption in the block of finite debt).

All these code characteristics—indirect, qualitative, and limited— are sufficient to show that a code is not, and can never be, economic: on the contrary, it expresses the apparent objective movement according to which the economic forces or productive connections are attributed to an extraeconomic instance as though they emanated from it, an instance that serves as a support and an agent of inscription. That is what Althusser and Balibar show so well: how juridical and political relations are *determined as dominant*—in the case of feudalism, for example— because surplus labor as a form of surplus value constitutes a flux that is

qualitatively and temporally distinct from that of labor, and consequently must enter into a composite that is itself qualitative and implies
noneconomic factors.* Or the way the autochthonous relations of
alliance and filiation are determined as dominant in the so-called
primitive societies, where the economic forces and flows are inscribed
on the full body of the earth and are attributed to it. In short, there is a
code where a full body as an instance of antiproduction falls back on the
economy that it appropriates. That is why the sign of desire, as an
economic sign that consists in producing and breaking flows, is accompanied by a sign of necessarily extraeconomic power, although its
causes and effects lie within the economy (for example, the sign of
alliance in relation to the power of the creditor). Or—what amounts to
the same thing—surplus value here is determined as a surplus value of
code. Hence the code relation is not only indirect, qualitative, and
limited; because of these very characteristics, it is also extraeconomic,
and by virtue of this fact engineers the couplings between qualified
flows. Consequently it implies a system of collective appraisal and
evaluation, and a set of organs of perception, or more precisely of belief,
as a condition of existence and survival of the society in question—thus
the collective investment of organs that causes men to be directly coded,
and the appraising eye as we have analyzed it in the primitive system. It
should be noted that these general traits characterizing a code are
rediscovered precisely in what today is called a genetic code; not
because it depends on an effect of a signifier, but on the contrary
because the chain it constitutes is only signifying in a secondary way,
insofar as it calls into play couplings between qualified flows, interactions that are exclusively indirect, qualitative composites that are
essentially limited, and organs of perception and *extrachemical* factors
that select and appropriate the cellular connections.

So many reasons for defining capitalism by a social axiomatic that
stands opposed to codes in every respect. First of all, money as a general
equivalent represents an abstract quantity that is indifferent to the
qualified nature of the flows. But the equivalence itself points to the
position of a relation without limitation: in the formula M-C-M, "the
circulation of money as capital has therefore no limits."[88] The studies of
Bohannan concerning the Tiv of the Niger River, or those of Salisbury
concerning the Siane of New Guinea, have shown how the introduction
of money as an equivalent—which makes it possible to begin and end
with money, therefore never to end at all—is enough to disturb the

*See Marx, *Capital*, Vol. 3, p. 791: "Under such conditions the surplus-labour for the nominal owner of
the land can only be extorted from them by other than economic pressure, whatever the form assumed
may be."

circuits of qualified flows, to decompose the finite blocks of debt, and to destroy the very basis of codes. Secondly, the fact remains that money as an unlimited abstract quantity cannot be divorced from a becoming-concrete without which it would not become capital and would not appropriate production. We have seen that this becoming-concrete appeared in the differential relation; but it must be borne in mind that the differential relation is not an indirect relation between qualified or coded flows, it is a direct relation between decoded flows whose respective qualities have no existence prior to the differential relation itself. The quality of the flows results solely from their conjunction as decoded flows; outside this conjunction they would remain purely virtual; this conjunction is also the disjunction of the abstract quantity through which it becomes something concrete. Dx and dy are nothing independent of their relation, which determines the one as a pure quality of the flow of labor and the other as a pure quality of the flow of capital. The progression is therefore the opposite of that of a code; it expresses the capitalist transformation of the surplus value of code into a surplus value of flux. Whence the fundamental change in the order of powers. For if one of the flows finds itself subordinated and enslaved to the other, the reason is precisely that they are not to the same power (x and y^2 for example), and that the relation is established between a power and a given magnitude. This is something that became evident as we pursued the analysis of capital and labor at the level of the differential relation between flows of financing, and flows of means of payment or income. Such an extension merely signifies that capital has no industrial essence functioning other than as merchant, financial, and commercial capital, where money would take on functions other than those deriving from its form as the equivalent. But in this way the signs of power completely cease being what they were from the viewpoint of a code: they become coefficients that are directly economic, instead of being doubles to the economic signs of desire and expressing for their part noneconomic factors determined as dominant. That the flow of financing is raised to an entirely different power from the flow of means of payment signifies that the power has become directly economic. And yet, as regards paid labor, it is evident that there is no longer any need for a code in order to ensure surplus labor, when the latter is merged qualitatively and temporally with labor itself into one and the same simple magnitude (the condition characterized by surplus value of flux).

Hence capital differentiates itself from any other socius or full body, inasmuch as capital itself figures as a directly economic instance, and falls back on production without interposing extraeconomic factors that would be inscribed in the form of a code. With the advent of capitalism the full body becomes truly naked, as does the worker himself who is attached to this full body. In this sense the antiproduction apparatus ceases to be transcendent, and pervades all production and becomes coextensive with it. Thirdly, as a result of these developed conditions involving the destruction of all codes within a becoming-concrete, the absence of limits takes on a new meaning. This absence no longer simply designates the unlimited abstract quantity, but the effective absence of any limit or end for the differential relation where the abstract becomes something concrete. Concerning capitalism, we maintain that it both does and does not have an exterior limit: it has an exterior limit that is schizophrenia, that is, the absolute decoding of flows, but it functions only by pushing back and exorcising this limit. And it also has, yet does not have, interior limits: it has interior limits under the specific conditions of capitalist production and circulation, that is, in capital itself, but it functions only by reproducing and widening these limits on an always vaster scale. The strength of capitalism indeed resides in the fact that its axiomatic is never saturated, that it is always capable of adding a new axiom to the previous ones. Capitalism defines a field of immanence and never ceases to fully occupy this field. But this deterritorialized field finds itself determined by an axiomatic, in contrast to the territorial field determined by primitive codes. Differential relations of such a nature as to be filled by surplus value; an absence of exterior limits that it is "filled" by the widening of internal limits; and the effusion of antiproduction within production so as to be filled by the absorption of surplus value—these constitute the three aspects of capitalism's immanent axiomatic. And monetarization everywhere comes to fill the abyss of capitalist immanence, introducing there, as Schmitt says, "a deformation, a convulsion, an explosion—in a word, a movement of extreme violence."[89]

There results, finally, a fourth characteristic that places the axiomatic in opposition to codes. The axiomatic does not need to write in bare flesh, to mark bodies and organs, nor does it need to fashion a memory for man. In contrast to codes, the axiomatic finds in its different aspects its own organs of execution, perception, and memorization. Memory has become a bad thing. Above all, there is no longer any need of belief, and the capitalist is merely striking a pose when he bemoans the fact that nowadays no one believes in anything any more. Language no longer signifies something that must be believed, it indicates rather what is going to be done, something that the shrewd or the competent are able to decode, to half understand. Moreover, despite the abundance of identity cards, files, and other means of control, capitalism does not even need to write in books to make up for the vanished body markings.

Those are only relics, archaisms with a current function. The person has become "private" in reality, insofar as he derives from abstract quantities and becomes concrete in the becoming-concrete of these same quantities. It is these quantities that are marked, no longer the persons themselves: *your capital or your labor capacity,* the rest is not important, we'll always find a place for you within the expanded limits of the system, even if an axiom has to be created just for you. There is no longer any need of a collective investment of organs, as they are sufficiently filled with the floating images constantly produced by capitalism. To pursue a remark of Henri Lefebvre's, these images do not initiate a making public of the private so much as a privatization of the public: the whole world unfolds right at home, without one's having to leave the TV screen. This gives private persons a very special role in the system: a role of *application,* and no longer of implication, in a code. The hour of Oedipus draws nigh.

While capitalism thus proceeds by means of an axiomatic and not by means of a code, one must not think that it replaces the socius, the social machine, with an aggregate of technical machines. The difference in nature between the two types of machines persists, although they are both machines in the strict sense, without metaphor. Capitalism's originality resides rather in the fact that the social machine has for its parts technical machines as constant capital attached to the full body of the socius, and no longer men, the latter having become adjacent to the technical machines—whence the fact that inscription no longer bears directly, or at least in theory has no need of bearing directly, on men. But an axiomatic of itself is by no means a simple technical machine, not even an automatic or cybernetic machine. Bourbaki* says as much concerning scientific axiomatics: they do not form a Taylor system, nor a mechanical game of isolated formulas, but rather imply "intuitions" that are linked to resonances and conjunctions of structures, and that are merely aided by the "powerful levers" of technique. This holds even truer of the social axiomatic: the way in which this axiomatic fulfills its own immanence; pushes back or enlarges its limits; adds still more axioms while preventing the system from becoming saturated; and functions well only by grinding, sputtering, and starting up again—all this implies social organs of decision, administration, reaction, inscrip-

---

*Nicolas Bourbaki is the pseudonym of a group of French mathematicians who are known for their work in the theory of sets and for their advocacy of an "axiomatic method" which "allows us, when we are concerned with complex mathematical objects, to separate their properties and regroup them around a small number of concepts: that is to say, using a word which will receive a precise definition later, to classify them according to the *structures* to which they belong" (Nicolas Bourbaki, *Elements of Mathematics* Vol. 3: *Theory of Sets* [Reading, Mass.: Addison-Wesley, 1968], p. 9). In this way they propose to elaborate a language of mathematical formalization capable of integrating the different branches of mathematics. (*Translators' note.*)

tion; a technocracy and a bureaucracy that cannot be reduced to the operation of technical machines. In short, the conjunction of the decoded flows, their differential relations, and their multiple schizzes or breaks require a whole apparatus of regulation whose principal organ is the State. The capitalist State is the regulator of decoded flows as such, insofar as they are caught up in the axiomatic of capital. In this sense it indeed completes the becoming-concrete that seemed to us to preside over the evolution of the abstract despotic Urstaat: from being at first the transcendent unity, it becomes immanent to the field of social forces, enters into their service, and serves as a regulator of the decoded and axiomatized flows. The capitalist State completes the becoming-concrete so fully that, in another sense, it alone represents a veritable rupture with this becoming, a break with it, in contrast to the other forms that were established on the ruins of the Urstaat. For the Urstaat was defined by overcoding, and its derivatives, from the ancient City-State to the monarchic State, already found themselves in the presence of flows that were decoded or in the process of being decoded. These flows doubtless had the effect of making the State more and more immanent and subordinate to the actual field of forces; but precisely because the circumstances were not right for these flows to enter into a conjunction, the State could be content to save fragments of overcoding and of codes, to invent others, and by marshaling all its forces, was even able to prevent the conjunction from taking place (as for the rest, its project was to resuscitate the Urstaat insofar as possible).

The capitalist State is in a different situation: it is produced by the conjunction of the decoded or deterritorialized flows, and is able to carry the becoming-immanent to its highest point only to the extent that it is party to the generalized breakdown of codes and overcodings, and evolves entirely within this new axiomatic that results from a hitherto unknown conjunction. Once again, this axiomatic is not the invention of capitalism, since it is identical with capital itself. On the contrary, capitalism is its offspring, its result. Capitalism merely ensures the regulation of the axiomatic; it regulates or even organizes the failures of the axiomatic as conditions of the latter's operation; it watches over or directs progress toward a saturation of the axiomatic and the corresponding widenings of the limits. Never before has a State lost so much of its power in order to enter with so much force into the service of the signs of economic power. And capitalism, despite what is said to the contrary, assumed this role very early, in fact from the start, from its gestation in forms still semifeudal or monarchic—from the standpoint of the flow of "free" workers: the control of manual labor and of wages; from the standpoint of the flow of industrial and commercial production:

the granting of monopolies, favorable conditions for accumulation, and the struggle against overproduction. There has never been a liberal capitalism: action against monopolies goes back first of all to a time when commercial and financial capital is still allied with the old system of production, and when nascent industrial capitalism can secure its production and its market only by obtaining the abolition of such privileges. That the struggle against monopolistic privileges does not imply any struggle against the very principle of State control—providing the State sees fit—can be seen clearly in mercantilism, inasmuch as it expresses the new commercial functions of a capital that has secured for itself direct interests in production. As a general rule, State controls and regulations tend to disappear or diminish only in situations where there is an abundant labor supply and an unusual expansion of markets.[90] That is, *when capitalism functions with a very small number of axioms within relative limits that are sufficiently wide.* This situation ceased to exist long ago, and one must regard as a decisive factor in this evolution the organization of a powerful working class that required a high and stable level of employment, and forced capitalism to multiply its axioms while having at the same time to reproduce its limits on an ever expanding scale (the axiom of displacement from the center to the periphery). Capitalism was able to digest the Russian Revolution only by continually adding new axioms to the old ones: an axiom for the working class, for the unions, and so on. But it is always prepared to add more axioms, it adds axioms for many other things besides, things that are much smaller, tiny even, absurdly insignificant; it has a peculiar passion for such things that leaves the essential unchanged. The State is thus induced to play an increasingly important role in the regulation of the axiomatized flows, with regard to production and its planning, the economy and its "monetarization," and surplus value and its absorption (by the State apparatus itself).

The regulative functions of the State do not imply any sort of arbitration between social classes. That the State is entirely in the service of the so-called ruling class is an obvious practical fact, but a fact that does not reveal its theoretical foundation. The latter is simple to explain: from the viewpoint of the capitalist axiomatic there is only one class, a class with a universalist vocation, the bourgeosie. Plekhanov notes that the French School of the nineteenth century, under the influence of Saint-Simon, should be credited with the discovery of class struggle and its role in history—precisely the same men who praise the struggle of the bourgeois class against the nobility and feudalism, and who come to a halt before the proletariat and deny that there can be any difference in class between the industrialist or banker and the worker, but only a fusion into one and the same flow as with profits and wages.[91] This proposition contains something other than an ideological blindness or denial. Classes are *the* negative of castes and statuses; classes are orders, castes, and statuses that have been decoded. To reread history through the class struggle is to read it in terms of the bourgeoisie as the decoding and decoded class. It is the *only* class as such, inasmuch as it leads the struggle against codes, and merges with the generalized decoding of flows. In this capacity it is sufficient to fill the capitalist field of immanence. And in point of fact, something new occurs with the rise of the bourgeoisie: the disappearance of enjoyment as an end, the new conception of the conjunction according to which the sole end is abstract wealth and its realization in forms other than consumption. The generalized slavery of the despotic State at least implied the existence of masters, and an apparatus of antiproduction distinct from the sphere of production. But the bourgeois field of immanence—as delimited by the conjunction of the decoded flows, the negation of any transcendence or exterior limit, and the effusion of antiproduction inside production itself—institutes an unrivaled slavery, an unprecedented subjugation: there are no longer even any masters, but only slaves commanding other slaves; there is no longer any need to burden the animal from the outside, it shoulders its own burden. Not that man is ever the slave of technical machines; he is rather the slave of the social machine. The bourgeois sets the example, he absorbs surplus value for ends that, taken as a whole, have nothing to do with his own enjoyment: more utterly enslaved than the lowest of slaves, he is the first servant of the ravenous machine, the beast of the reproduction of capital, internalization of the infinite debt. "I too am a slave"—these are the new words spoken by the master. "Only as personified capital is the capitalist respectable. As such, he shares with the miser the passion for wealth as wealth. But that which in the miser is a mere idiosyncrasy, is, in the capitalist, the effect of the social mechanism, of which he is but one of the wheels."[92]

It will be said that there is nonetheless a class that rules and a class that is ruled, both defined by surplus value, the distinction between the flow of financing and the flow of income in wages. But this is only partially true, since capitalism is born of the conjunction of the two in the differential relations, and integrates them both in the continually expanded reproduction of its limits. So that the bourgeois is justified in saying, not in terms of ideology, but in the very organization of his axiomatic: there is only one machine, that of the great mutant decoded flow—cut off from goods—and one class of servants, the decoding bourgeosie, the class that decodes the castes and the statuses, and that draws from the machine an undivided flow of income convertible into consumer and production goods, a flow on which profits and wages are based. In short, the theoretical opposition is not between two classes, for it is the very notion of class, insofar as it designates the "negative" of codes, that implies there is only one class. The theoretical opposition lies elsewhere: it is between, on the one hand, the decoded flows that enter into a class axiomatic on the full body of capital, and on the other hand, the decoded flows that free themselves from this axiomatic just as they free themselves from the despotic signifier, that break through this wall, and this wall of a wall, and begin flowing on the full body without organs. The opposition is between the class and those who are outside the class.* Between the servants of the machine, and those who sabotage it or its cogs and wheels. Between the social machine's régime and that of the desiring-machines. Between the relative interior limits and the absolute exterior limit. If you will: between the capitalists and the schizos in their basic intimacy at the level of decoding, in their basic antagonism at the level of the axiomatic—whence the resemblance, in the nineteenth-century socialists' portrait of the proletariat, between the latter and a perfect schizo.

That is why the problem of a proletarian class belongs first of all to praxis. The task of the revolutionary socialist movement was to organize a bipolarity of the social field, a bipolarity of classes. Of course it is possible to conceive a theoretical determination of the proletarian class at the level of production (those from whom surplus value is extorted), or at the level of money (income in wages). But not only are these determinations sometimes too narrow and sometimes too wide, but the objective being they define as *class interest* remains purely virtual so long as it is not embodied in a consciousness that, to be sure, does not create it, but actualizes it in an organized party suited to the task of conquering the State apparatus. If the movement of capitalism, in the interplay of its differential relations, is to dodge any assignable fixed limit, to exceed and displace its interior limits, and to always effect breaks of breaks, then the socialist movement seems necessarily led to fix or assign a limit that differentiates the proletariat from the bourgeoisie—a great cleavage that will animate a struggle not only economic and financial, but political as well. Now the meaning of just such a conquest of the State apparatus has always been and remains problematical. A supposedly socialist State implies a transformation of production, of the units of production and the economic rationale. But this transformation can only take place starting from an already

*les hors-classe: This term shares an affinity with hors-caste (outcaste) and hors-la-loi (outlaw). (Translators' note.)

conquered State that finds itself confronted by the same axiomatic problems of extraction of a surplus or surplus value, of accumulation and absorption, of the market and monetary reckoning. Consequently, either the proletariat prevails and transforms the apparatus in conformity with its objective interest—but these operations are carried out under the domination of its consciousness or party vanguard, that is, for the benefit of a bureaucracy or technocracy that stands in for the bourgeoisie as the "great-absent" class—or the bourgeoisie keeps its control of the State and is free to secrete its own technobureaucracy, and above all to add a few more axioms for the recognition of the proletariat as a second class. It is correct to say that the alternative is not between the market and economic planning, since planning is necessarily introduced in the capitalist State, and the market subsists in the socialist State, if only as a monopolistic market of the State itself. And in effect, how does one define the true alternative without assuming all these problems resolved beforehand?

The immense accomplishment of Lenin and the Russian Revolution was to have forged a class consciousness consonant with the objective being or interest of the class, and as a consequence, to have imposed on the capitalist countries a recognition of class bipolarity. But this great Leninist break did not prevent the resurrection of a State capitalism inside socialism itself, any more than it prevented classical capitalism from getting round the break by continuing its veritable mole work, always effecting breaks of breaks that allowed it to integrate into its axiomatic sections of the newly recognized class, while throwing the uncontrolled revolutionary elements—no more controlled by official socialism than by capitalism itself—further into the distance, to the periphery or into enclaves. Thus the only choice left was between the new terroristic and rigid axiomatic—quickly saturated—of the socialist State, and the old cynical axiomatic—all the more dangerous for being flexible and never saturated—of the capitalist State. But in reality, the most direct question is not that of knowing whether an industrial society can do without a surplus, without the absorption of a surplus, without a commodity-exchanging and planner State, and even without an equivalent of the bourgeoisie: it is evident both that the answer is no, and that in these terms the question is poorly put. Nor is it a question of knowing whether or not class consciousness, embodied in a party or a State, betrays the objective class interest, to which a kind of potential spontaneity would be ascribed, suffocated by the agents claiming to represent that interest. Sartre's analysis in *Critique de la raison dialectique* appears to us profoundly correct where he concludes that there does not exist any class spontaneity, but only a "group" spontaneity:

whence the necessity for distinguishing "groups-in-fusion" from the class, which remains "serial," represented by the party or the State.[99] And the two do not exist on the same scale. This is because class interest remains a function of the large molar aggregates; it merely defines a collective preconscious that is necessarily represented in a distinct consciousness that, at this level, does not even present any grounds for asking whether it betrays or not, alienates or not, deforms or not. The problem is situated there, between unconscious group desires and preconscious class interests. It is only starting from this point, as we shall see, that one is able to pose the questions issuing indirectly therefrom, concerning the class preconscious and the representative forms of class consciousness, and the nature of the interests and the process of their realization. Reich always comes back to us with his innocent standards, claiming the rights of a prior distinction between desire and interest: "The leadership has no task more urgent, besides that of acquiring a precise understanding of the objective historical process, than to understand : (a) what are the progressive desires, ideas and thoughts which are latent in people of different social strata, occupations, age groups and sexes, and (b) what are the desires, fears, thoughts and ideas ('traditional bonds') which prevent the progressive desires, ideas, etc., from developing."[93] (The leadership has a tendency rather to reply: when I hear the word "desire," I pull out my gun.)

Desire can never be deceived. Interests can be deceived, unrecognized, or betrayed, but not desire. Whence Reich's cry: no, the masses were not deceived, they desired fascism, and that is what has to be explained. It happens that one desires against one's own interests: capitalism profits from this, but so does socialism, the party, and the party leadership. How does one explain that desire devotes itself to operations that are not failures of recognition, but rather perfectly reactionary unconscious investments? And what does Reich mean when he speaks of "traditional bonds"? The latter also belong to the historical process and bring us back to the modern functions of the State. Civilized modern societies are defined by processes of decoding and deterritorialization. But *what they deterritorialize with one hand, they reterritorialize with the other.* These neoterritorialities are often artificial, residual, archaic; but they are archaisms having a perfectly current function, our modern way of "imbricating," of sectioning off, of reintroducing code fragments, resuscitating old codes, inventing pseudo codes or jargons. Neoarchaisms, as Edgar Morin puts it. These modern archaisms are extremely complex and varied. Some are mainly folkloric, but they nonetheless represent social and potentially political forces (from domino players to home brewers via the Veterans of Foreign Wars).

Others are enclaves whose archaism is just as capable of nourishing a modern fascism as of freeing a revolutionary charge (the ethnic minorities, the Basque problem, the Irish Catholics, the Indian reservations). Some of these archaisms take form as if spontaneously, in the very current of the movement of deterritorialization (neighborhood territorialities, territorialities of the large aggregates, "gangs"). Others are organized or promoted by the State, even though they might turn against the State and cause it serious problems (regionalism, nationalism). The fascist State has been without doubt capitalism's most fantastic attempt at economic and political reterritorialization. But the socialist State also has its own minorities, its own territorialities, which re-form themselves against the State, or which the State instigates and organizes. (Russian nationalism, the territoriality of the party: the proletariat was only able to constitute itself as a class on the basis of artificial neoterritorialities; in parallel fashion, the bourgeoisie reterritorializes itself in forms that are at times the most archaic.)

The famous personalization of power is like a territoriality that accompanies the deterritorialization of the machine, as its other side. If it is true that the function of the modern State is the regulation of the decoded, deterritorialized flows, one of the principal aspects of this function consists in reterritorializing, so as to prevent the decoded flows from breaking loose at all the edges of the social axiomatic. One sometimes has the impression that the flows of capital would willingly dispatch themselves to the moon if the capitalist State were not there to bring them back to earth. For example: deterritorialization of the flows of financing, but reterritorialization of purchasing power and the means of payment (the role of the central banks). Or the movement of deterritorialization that goes from the center to the periphery is accompanied by a peripheral reterritorialization, a kind of economic and political self-centering of the periphery, either in the modernistic forms of a State socialism or capitalism, or in the archaic form of local despots. It may be all but impossible to distinguish deterritorialization from reterritorialization, since they are mutually enmeshed, or like opposite faces of one and the same process.

This essential aspect of the regulation performed by the State is even more readily understood if one sees that it is directly based on the social and economic axiomatic of capitalism as such. It is the very conjunction of the deterritorialized flows that delineates archaic or artificial neoterritorialities. Marx has shown what was the foundation of political economy properly speaking: the discovery of an abstract subjective essence of wealth, in labor or production—and in desire as well, it would seem. ("It was an immense step forward for Adam Smith to throw out every limiting specification of wealth-creating activity—not only manufacturing, or commercial, or agricultural labour; but one as well as others, labour in general . . . the abstract universality of wealth-creating activity."[95] Here we have the great movement of decoding or deterritorialization: the nature of wealth is no longer to be sought on the side of the object, under exterior conditions, in the territorial or despotic machine. But Marx is quick to add that this essentially "cynical" discovery finds itself rectified by a new territorialization, in the form of a new fetishism or a new "hypocrisy." Production as the abstract subjective essence is discovered only in the forms of property that objectifies it all over again, that alienates it by reterritorializing it. Although they had a presentiment of the subjective nature of wealth, the mercantilists had determined it as a special activity still tied to a "money-creating" despotic machine; the physiocrats, pushing this presentiment still further, had tied subjective activity to a territorial or reterritorialized machine, in the form of agriculture and landed property. And even Adam Smith discovers the great essence of wealth, abstract and subjective, industrial and deterritorialized, only by immediately reterritorializing it in the private ownership of the means of production. (Nor can one say in this regard that so-called common ownership changes the direction of this movement.) Moreover, if it is not a question of writing the history of political economy, but the real history of the corresponding society, one is better able to understand why capitalism is continually reterritorializing with one hand what it was deterritorializing with the other.

In *Capital* Marx analyzes the true reason for the double movement: on the one hand, capitalism can proceed only by continually developing the subjective essence of abstract wealth or production for the sake of production, that is, "production as an end in itself, the absolute development of the social productivity of labor"; but on the other hand and at the same time, it can do so only in the framework of its own limited purpose, as a determinate mode of production, "production of capital," "the self-expansion of existing capital."[96] Under the first aspect capitalism is continually surpassing its own limits, always deterritorializing further, "displaying a cosmopolitan, universal energy which overthrows every restriction and bond"; but under the second, strictly complementary, aspect, capitalism is continually confronting limits and barriers that are interior and immanent to itself, and that, precisely because they are immanent, let themselves be overcome only provided they are reproduced on a wider scale (always more reterritorialization—local, world-wide, planetary). That is why the law of the falling tendency—that is, limits never reached because they are always surpassed and always reproduced—has seemed to us to have as a corollary and even as a direct manifestation, the simultaneity of the two movements of deterritorialization and reterritorialization.

An important consequence emerges from the above considerations. The social axiomatic of modern societies is caught between two poles, and is constantly oscillating from one pole to the other. Born of decoding and deterritorialization, on the ruins of the despotic machine, these societies are caught between the Urstaat that they would like to resuscitate as an overcoding and reterritorializing unity, and the unfettered flows that carry them toward an absolute threshold. They recode with all their might, with world-wide dictatorship, local dictators, and an all-powerful police, while decoding—or allowing the decoding of—the fluent quantities of their capital and their populations. They are torn in two directions: archaism and futurism, neoarchaism and ex-futurism, paranoia and schizophrenia. They vacillate between two poles: the paranoiac despotic sign, the sign-signifier of the despot that they try to revive as a unit of code; and the sign-figure of the schizo as a unit of decoded flux, a schiz, a point-sign or flow-break. They try to hold on to the one, but they pour or flow out through the other. They are continually behind or ahead of themselves.*

How can the nostalgia for, and the necessity of, the Urstaat be reconciled with the insistence and the inevitability of the fluxion of the flows? What can be done so that the decoding and the deterritorialization constitutive of the system do not make it flee through one end or another that would escape the axiomatic and throw the machine into a panic (a Chinese on the horizon, a Cuban missile-launcher, an Arab highjacker, a consul kidnapper, a Black Panther, a May '68, or even stoned hippies, angry gays, etc.)? There is an oscillation between the reactionary paranoiac overcharges and the subterranean, schizophrenic, and revolutionary charges. Moreover, one no longer quite knows how it goes on one side or the other: the two ambiguous poles of delirium, their transformations, the way in which an archaism or folklore in a given set of circumstances can suddenly become charged with a dangerous progressive value. How things turn fascist or revolutionary is the problem of the universal delirium about which everyone is silent, first of all and especially the psychiatrists (they have no ideas on the subject—why would they?). Capitalism, and socialism as well, are as though torn between the despotic signifier that they adore, and the schizophrenic

*Suzanne de Brunhoff, *La monnaie chez Marx* (reference note 73), p. 147: "That is why in capitalism even credit, formed into a system, brings together composite elements that are both *ante-capitalist* (money, money commerce) and *post-capitalist* (the credit circuit being a higher circulation . . .). Adapted to the needs of capitalism, credit is never really contemporary with capital. The system of financing born of the capitalist mode of production remains a bastard."

figure that sweeps them along. We are thus entitled to maintain two conclusions that we have already put forward and that seemed to stand mutually opposed. On the one hand, the modern State forms a break that represents a genuine advance in comparison with the despotic State, in terms of its fulfillment of a becoming-immanent, its generalized decoding of flows, and its axiomatic that comes to replace the codes and overcodings. But on the other hand there has never been but one State, the Urstaat, the Asiatic despotic formation, which constitutes in its shadow existence history's only break, since even the modern social axiomatic can function only by resuscitating it as one of the poles between which it produces its own break. Democracy, fascism, or socialism, which of these is not haunted by the Urstaat as a model without equal? The name of the local dictator Duvalier's chief of police was Desyr.

But the events that restore a thing to life are not the same as those that gave rise to it in the first place. We have distinguished among three social machines corresponding to the savage, the barbarian, and the civilized societies. The first is the underlying territorial machine, which consists in coding the flows on the full body of the earth. The second is the transcendent imperial machine, which consists in overcoding the flows on the full body of the despot or his apparatus, the Urstaat: it effects the first great movement of deterritorialization, but does so by adding its eminent unity to the territorial communes that it conserves by bringing them together, overcoding them and appropriating their surplus labor. The third is the modern immanent machine, which consists in decoding the flows on the full body of capital-money: it has realized the immanence, it has rendered concrete the abstract as such and has naturalized the artificial, replacing the territorial codes and the despotic overcoding with an axiomatic of decoded flows, and a regulation of these flows; it effects the second great movement of deterritorialization, but this time because it doesn't allow any part of the codes and overcodes to subsist. However, what it doesn't allow to subsist it rediscovers through its own original means; it reterritorializes where it has lost the territorialities, it creates new archaisms where it has destroyed the old ones—and the two become as one. The historian says no, the Modern State, its bureaucracy and its technocracy, do not resemble the ancient despotic State. Of course not, since it is a matter in the one case of reterritorializing decoded flows, but in the other case of overcoding the territorial flows. The paradox is that capitalism makes use of the Urstaat for effecting its reterritorializations. But the imperturbable modern axiomatic, from the depths of its immanence, reproduces the transcendence of the Urstaat as its internalized limit, or one of the poles between which it is determined to oscillate. And in its imperturbable and cynical existence, it is prey to great forces that form the other pole of the axiomatic, its accidents, its breakdowns, its chances of being blown to pieces, of causing what it decodes to pass beyond the wall of its immanent regulations and beyond its transcendental resurrections.

Each type of social machine produces a particular kind of *representation* whose elements are organized at the surface of the socius: the system of connotation-connection in the savage territorial machine, corresponding to the coding of the flows; the system of subordination-disjunction in the barbarian despotic machine, corresponding to over-coding; the system of co-ordination-conjunction in the civilized capitalist machine, corresponding to the decoding of the flows. Deterritorialization, the axiomatic, and reterritorialization are the three surface elements of the representation of desire in the modern socius. So we come back to the question: in each case what is the relationship between social production and desiring-production, once it is said that they have identical natures and differing régimes? Could it be that the identity in nature is at its highest point in the order of modern capitalist representation, because this identity is "universally" realized in the immanence of this order and in the fluxion of the decoded flows? But also that the difference in régime is greatest in the capitalist order of representation, and that this representation subjects desire to an operation of social repression–psychic repression that is stronger than any other, because, by means of the immanence and the decoding, antiproduction has spread throughout all of production, instead of remaining localized in the system, and has freed a fantastic death instinct that now permeates and crushes desire? And what is this death that always rises from within, but that must arrive from without—and that, in the case of capitalism, rises with all the more power as one still fails to see exactly what this outside is that will cause it to arrive? In short, the general theory of society is a generalized theory of flows; it is in terms of the latter that one must consider the relationship of social production to desiring-production, the variations of this relationship in each case, and the limits of this relationship in the capitalist system.

11 | Oedipus at Last

In the territorial or even the despotic machine, social economic reproduction is never independent of human reproduction, of the social form of this reproduction. The family is therefore an open praxis, a strategy that is coextensive with the social field; the relations of filiation and alliance are determinant, or rather "determined as domi-nant." As a matter of fact, what is marked or inscribed on the socius—directly—is the producers (or nonproducers) according to the standing of their family or their standing inside the family. The reproduction process is not directly economic, but passes by way of the noneconomic factors of kinship. This is true not only with respect to the territorial machine, and to local groups that determine the place of each member in social economic reproduction, according to one's status from the standpoint of the alliances and the filiations, but also with respect to the despotic machine, which adds the relations of the new alliance and direct filiation to the old alliance and filiations (whence the role of the sovereign's family in despotic overcoding, and that of the "dynasty"—whatever its mutations, its indecisions—which are inscribed under the same category of new alliance). The process by no means remains the same in the capitalist system.[97] Representation no longer relates to a distinct object, but to productive activity itself. The socius as full body has become directly economic as capital-money; it does not tolerate any other preconditions. What is inscribed or marked is no longer the producers or nonproducers, but the forces and means of production as abstract quantities that become effectively concrete in their becoming related or their conjunction: labor capacity or capital, constant capital or variable capital, capital of filiation or capital of alliance. Capital has taken upon itself the relations of alliance and filiation. There ensues a privatization of the family according to which the family ceases to give its social form to economic reproduction: it is as though disinvested, placed outside the field; in the language of Aristotle, the family is now simply the form of human matter or material that finds itself subordinat-ed to the autonomous social form of economic reproduction, and that comes to take the place assigned it by the latter. That is to say that the elements of production and antiproduction are not reproduced in the same way as humans themselves, but find in them a simple material that the form of economic reproduction preorganizes in a mode that is entirely distinct from the form this material has as human reproduction. Precisely because it is privatized, placed outside the field, the form of the material or the form of human reproduction begets people whom one can readily assume to be all equal in relation to one another; but inside the field itself, the form of social economic reproduction has already preformed the form of the material so as to engender, there where they are needed, *the* capitalist as a function derived from capital, and *the* worker as a function derived from labor capacity, etc., in such a way that the family finds itself countersected by the order of classes. (In this sense, indeed, segregation is the only origin of equality.[98])

This placing of the family outside the social field is also its greatest social fortune. For it is the condition under which the entire social field can be *applied* to the family. Individual persons are social persons first of all, i.e., functions derived from the abstract quantities; they become concrete in the becoming-related or the axiomatic of these quantities, in their conjunction. They are nothing more nor less than configurations or images produced by the points-signs, the breaks-flows, the pure "figures" of capitalism; the capitalist as personified capital—i.e., as a function derived from the flow of capital; and the worker as personified labor capacity—i.e., a function derived from the flow of labor. In this way capitalism fills its field of immanence with images: even destitution, despair, revolt—and on the other side, the violence and the oppression of capital—become images of destitution, despair, revolt, violence, or oppression. But starting from nonfigurative figures or from the breaks-flows that produce them, these images will themselves be capable of figuring and reproducing only by shaping a human material whose specific form of reproduction falls outside the social field that nonetheless determines this form. Private persons are therefore images of the second order, images of images—that is, *simulacra* that are thus endowed with an aptitude for representing the first-order images of social persons. These private persons are formally delimited in the locus of the restricted family as father, mother, child. But instead of being a strategy that, through the action of alliances and filiations, opens onto the entire social field, is coextensive with it, and countersects its co-ordinates, it would appear that the family is now merely a simple tactic around which the social field recloses, to which it applies its autonomous requirements of reproduction, and that it counteracts with all its dimensions. The alliances and filiations no longer pass through people but through money; so the family becomes a microcosm, suited to expressing what it no longer dominates. In a certain sense the situation has not changed; for what is invested through the family is still the economic, political, and cultural social field, its breaks and flows. Private persons are an illusion, images of images or derivatives of derivatives. But in another sense everything has changed, because the family, instead of constituting and developing the dominant factors of social reproduction, is content to apply and envelop these factors in its own mode of reproduction. Father, mother, and child thus become the simulacrum of the images of capital ("Mister Capital, Madame Earth," and their child the Worker), with the result that these images are no longer recognized at all in the desire that is determined to invest only their simulacrum. The familial determinations become the application of the social axiomatic.

The family becomes the subaggregate to which the whole of the social field is applied. Since *each person* has his own private father and mother, it is a distributive subaggregate that simulates for each person the collective whole of social persons and that closes off his domain and scrambles his images. Everything is reduced to the father-mother-child triangle, which reverberates the answer "daddy-mommy" every time it is stimulated by the images of capital. In short, Oedipus arrives: it is born in the capitalist system of the application of first-order social images to the private familial images of the second order. It is the aggregate of destination that corresponds to an aggregate of departure that is socially determined. It is our intimate colonial formation that corresponds to the form of social sovereignty. We are all little colonies and it is Oedipus that colonizes us. When the family ceases to be a unit of production and of reproduction, when the conjunction again finds in the family the meaning of a simple unit of consumption, it is father-mother that we consume. In the aggregate of departure there is the boss, the foreman, the priest, the tax collector, the cop, the soldier, the worker, all the machines and territorialities, all the social images of our society; but in the aggregate of destination, in the end, there is no longer anyone but daddy, mommy, and me, the despotic sign inherited by daddy, the residual territoriality assumed by mommy, and the divided, split, castrated ego. Isn't this operation of flattening, folding, or application what leads Lacan to say, willingly betraying the secret of psycho-analysis as an applied axiomatic: what appears to "come most freely into play in what is called the analytic dialogue, in fact depends on a subfoundation that is perfectly reducible to a few essential and formaliz-able articulations."[99] Everything is pre-formed, arranged in advance. The social field, where everyone acts and is acted upon (*patit*) as a collective agent of enunciation, an agent of production and antiproduc-tion, is reduced to Oedipus, where everyone now finds himself cornered and cut along the line that divides him into an individual subject of the statement and an individual subject of enunciation. The subject of the statement is the social person, and the subject of enunciation, the private person. "So" it's your father, so it's your mother, so it's you: the familial conjunction results from the capitalist conjunctions, insofar as they are applied to private persons. Daddy-mommy-me—one is sure to re-encounter them everywhere, since everything has been applied to them. The reign of images is the new way in which capitalism utilizes the schizzes and diverts the flows: composite images, images flattened onto other images, so that when this operation reaches its outcome the little ego of each person, related to its father-mother, is truly the center of the world. Much more underhanded than the subterranean reign of the fetishes of the earth, or the celestial reign of the despot's idols, is the advent of the Oedipal-narcissistic machine: "No more glyphs and hieroglyphs, we'll have the real objective reality . . . our Kodak-vision. . . . To every man, to every woman, the universe is just a setting to the absolute little picture of himself, herself. . . . A picture! A Kodak snap, in a universal film of snaps."[100] Each person as a little triangulated microcosm—the narcissistic ego is identical with the Oedipal subject.

Oedipus at last: in the end it is a very simple operation, one that indeed readily lends itself to formalization, although it involves universal history. We have seen in what sense schizophrenia was the *absolute limit* of every society, inasmuch as it sets in motion decoded and deterritorialized flows that it restores to desiring-production, "at the bounds" of all social production. And capitalism, the *relative limit* of every society, inasmuch as it axiomatizes the decoded flows and reterritorializes the deterritorialized flows. We have also seen that capitalism finds in schizophrenia its own *exterior limit,* which it is continually repelling and exorcising, while capitalism itself produces its *immanent limits,* which it never ceases to displace and enlarge. But capitalism still needs a displaced *interior limit* in another way: precisely in order to neutralize or repel the absolute exterior limit, the schizophrenic limit; it needs to internalize this limit, this time by restricting it, by causing it to pass no longer between social production and the desiring-production that breaks away from social reproduction, but inside social production, between the form of social reproduction and the form of a familial reproduction to which social production is reduced, between the social aggregate and the private subaggregate to which the social aggregate is applied.

Oedipus is this displaced or internalized limit where desire lets itself be caught. The Oedipal triangle is the personal and private territoriality that corresponds to all of capitalism's efforts at social reterritorialization. Oedipus was always the displaced limit for every social formation, since it is the displaced represented of desire. But in the primitive formations this limit remains vacant, precisely insofar as the flows are coded and as the interplay of alliances and filiations keeps families extended according to the scale of the determinations of the social field, preventing any secondary reduction of the latter to the former. In the despotic formations the Oedipal limit is occupied, symbolically occupied but not lived or inhabited, inasmuch as the imperial incest effects an overcoding that in turn surveys the entire social field from above (the repressing representation): the formal operations of flattening, extrapolation, and so on, that later belong to Oedipus, are already sketched out, but within a symbolic space where the object from on high is formed. It is only in the capitalist formation that the Oedipal limit finds itself not only occupied, but inhabited and lived, in the sense in which the social images produced by the decoded flows actually fall back on restricted familial images invested by desire. It is at this point in the Imaginary that Oedipus is constituted, at the same time as it *completes its migration* in the in-depth elements of representation: *the displaced represented has become, as such, the representation of desire.* Hence it goes without saying that this becoming or this constitution does not develop under the categories imagined in the earlier social formation, since the imaginary Oedipus results from such a becoming and not the inverse. It is not via a flow of shit or a wave of incest that Oedipus arrives, but via the decoded flows of capital-money. The waves of incest and shit are only secondary derivates of the latter, insofar as they transport the private persons to which the flows of capital are reduced or applied. (Which explains the complex origin of the relation that is completely distorted in the psychoanalytic equation, shit=money; in reality, it is a question of encounters or conjunctions, of derivatives and resultants between decoded flows.)

In Oedipus there is a recapitulation of the three states, or the three machines. For Oedipus makes ready in the territorial machine, as an empty unoccupied limit. It takes form in the despotic machine as a symbolically occupied limit. But it is filled and carried to completion only by becoming the imaginary Oedipus of the capitalist machine. The despotic machine preserved the primitive territorialities, and the capitalist machine resuscitates the Urstaat as one of the poles of its axiomatic, it makes the despot into one of its images. That is why Oedipus gathers up everything, everything is found again in Oedipus, which is indeed the result of universal history, but in the singular sense in which capital is already this result. *Fetishes, idols, images, and simulacra*—here we have the whole series: territorial fetishes, despotic idols or symbols, then everything is recapitulated in the images of capitalism, which shapes and reduces them to the Oedipal simulacrum. The representative of the local group with Laius, the territoriality with Jocasta, the despot with Oedipus himself: "a motley painting of everything that has ever been believed." It comes as no surprise that Freud looks to Sophocles for the central image of Oedipus-the-despot, the myth become tragedy, in order to make the image radiate in two contrary directions: the ritual primitive direction of *Totem and Taboo,* and the private direction of modern man the dreamer. (Oedipus can be a myth, a tragedy, or a dream: it always expresses the displacement of the limit.)

Oedipus would be nothing if the symbolic position of an object from on high, in the despotic machine, did not first make possible the folding and flattening operations that will constitute Oedipus in the modern social field: the triangulation's *cause*. Whence the extreme importance—but also the indeterminate nature, the nondecidability—of the argument advanced by psychoanalysis's most profound innovator, which makes the displaced limit pass between the Symbolic and the Imaginary, between symbolic castration and imaginary Oedipus. For castration in the order of the despotic signifier, as the law of the despot or the effect of the object from on high, is in reality the formal condition of the Oedipal images that will be deployed in the field of immanence left uncovered by the withdrawal of the signifier. I reach desire when I arrive at castration! What does the desire-castration equation signify, if not in fact a prodigious operation that consists in replacing desire under the law of the despot, in introducing lack there at the deepest levels, and in rescuing us from Oedipus by means of a fantastic regression. A fantastic and brilliant regression: someone had to do it, "no one helped me," as Lacan says, to shake loose the yoke of Oedipus and carry it to the point of its autocritique. But it is like the story of the Resistance fighters who, wanting to destroy a pylon, balanced the plastic charges so well that the pylon blew up and fell back into its hole. From the Symbolic to the Imaginary, from castration to Oedipus, and from the despotic age to capitalism, inversely there is the progress leading to the withdrawal of the overseeing and overcoding object from on high, which gives way to a social field of immanence where the decoded flows produce images and level them down. Whence the two aspects of the signifier: a barred transcendent signifier taken in a maximum that distributes lack, and an immanent system of relations between minimal elements that come to fill the uncovered field (somewhat similar, in traditional terms, to the way one goes from the Parmenidean Being to the atoms of Democritus).

A transcendent object that is more and more spiritualized, for a field of forces that is more and more immanent, more and more internalized: this describes the evolution of the infinite debt—through Catholicism, then the Reformation. The extreme spiritualization of the despotic State, and the extreme internalization of the capitalist field, define bad conscience. The latter is not cynicism's contrary; it is, in private persons, the correlate of the cynicism of social persons. All the cynical tactics of bad conscience, just as Nietzsche and then Lawrence and Miller analyzed them to arrive at a definition of civilized European man: the hypnosis and the reign of images, the torpor they spread; the hatred of life and of all that is free, of all that passes and flows; the universal effusion of the death instinct; depression and guilt used as a means of contagion, the kiss of the Vampire: aren't you ashamed to be happy? follow my example, I won't let go before you say, "It's my fault," O ignoble contagion of the depressives, neurosis as the only illness consisting in making others ill; the permissive structure: let me deceive, rob, slaughter, kill! but in the name of the social order, and so daddy-mommy will be proud of me; the double direction given to *ressentiment,* the turning back against oneself, and the projection against the Other: the father is dead, it's my fault, who killed him? it's your fault, it's the Jews, the Arabs, the Chinese, all the resources of racism and segregation; the abject desire to be loved, the whimpering at not being loved enough, at not being "understood," concurrent with the reduction of sexuality to the "dirty little secret," this whole *priest's psychology*—there is not a single one of these tactics that does not find in Oedipus its land of milk and honey, its good provider. Nor is there a single one of these tactics that does not serve and develop in psychoanalysis, with the latter as the new avatar of the "ascetic ideal."

Once again, psychoanalysis does not invent Oedipus; it merely provides the latter a last territoriality, the couch, and a last Law, the analyst as despot and money collector. But the mother as the simulacrum of territoriality, and the father as the simulacrum of the despotic Law, with the slashed, split, castrated ego, are the products of capitalism insofar as it engineers an operation that has no equivalent in the other social formations. Everywhere else the familial position is merely a stimulus to the investment of the social field by desire: the familial images function only by opening onto social images to which they become coupled or which they confront in the course of struggles and compromises; so that what is invested through the breaks and segments of families is the economic, political, and cultural breaks of the field into which they are plunged (cf. Ndembu schizophrenia). This is the case even in the peripheral zones of capitalism, where the colonizer's efforts at oedipalizing the indigenous population—African Oedipus—find themselves contradicted by the breakup of the family along the lines of social exploitation and oppression. But it is at the soft center of capitalism, in the temperate zones of the bourgeoisie, that the colony becomes intimate and private, interior to each person: it is there that the flow of the investment of desire, which travels from the familial stimulus to the social organization (or disorganization), is as it were *covered over by a reflux* that flattens the social investment onto the familial investment serving as a pseudo organizer. The family has become the locus of retention and resonance of all the social determinations. It falls to the reactionary investment of the capitalist field to apply all the social images to the simulcra of the restricted family, with the result that, wherever one turns, one no longer finds anything but father-mother—this Oedipal filth that sticks to our skin. Yes, I desired my mother and wanted to kill my father; a single subject of enunciation—Oedipus—for all the capitalist statements, and between the two, the leveling cleavage of castration.

Marx said that Luther's merit was to have determined the essence of religion, no longer on the side of the object, but as an interior religiosity; that the merit of Adam Smith and Ricardo was to have determined the essence or nature of wealth no longer as an objective nature, but as an abstract and deterritorialized subjective essence, *the activity of production in general.* But as this determination develops under the condition of capitalism, they objectify the essence all over again, they alienate and reterritorialize it, this time in the form of the private ownership of the means of production. So that capitalism is without doubt the universal of every society, but only insofar as it is capable of carrying to a certain point its own critique—that is, the critique of the processes by which it re-enslaves what within it tends to free itself or to appear freely.[101] The same thing must be said of Freud: his greatness lies in having determined the essence or nature of desire, no longer in relation to objects, aims, or even sources (territories), but as an abstract subjective essence—libido or sexuality. But he still relates this essence to the family as the last territoriality of private man— whence the position of Oedipus, marginal at first in the *Three Essays,* then centering more and more around desire. It is as though Freud were asking to be forgiven his profound discovery of sexuality by saying to us: at least it won't go any further than the family! The dirty little secret, in place of the wide open spaces glimpsed for a moment. The familialist reduction, in place of the drift of desire. In place of the great decoded flows, little streams recoded in mommy's bed. Interiority in place of a new relationship with the outside. Throughout psychoanalysis, the discourse of bad conscience and guilt always rises up and finds its nourishment—what is called being cured.

On two points at least, Freud exonerates the real exterior family of any wrongs, the better to internalize the family and the wrongs in the person of the family's smallest member, the child. The way in which he posits an autonomous repression independent of social repression; the way in which he abandons the theme of the seduction of the child by the adult, in order to substitute the individual fantasy that makes the real parents into so many innocents or even victims.* For the family must appear in two forms: one where doubtless it is guilty, but only in the manner in which the child lives it intensely, internally, and where it is

---

*Erich Fromm, apropos of the analysis of Little Hans in particular, has pointed to the increasingly clear evolution of Freud, who comes to posit the child's guilt and exonerate parental authority: *The Crisis of Psychoanalysis* (New York: Fawcett, 1970), pp. 55–59, 90–100.

confounded with the child's own guilt; the other where it is a tribunal of responsibility, before which one stands as a guilty child, and in relation to which one becomes a responsible adult (Oedipus as sickness *and* sanity, the family as an alienating factor *and* as an agent of dealienation, if only through the way in which it is reconstituted in the transference). This is what Foucault has shown in his very fine analysis: the familialism inherent in psychoanalysis doesn't so much destroy classical psychiatry as shine forth as the latter's crowning achievement. After the madman of the earth and the madman of the despot comes the madman of the family; what nineteenth-century psychiatry had wanted to organize in the asylum—"the imperative fiction of the family," Reason-the-father and madness-the-child or minor, the parents who are ill only from their own childhood—all this finds its fulfillment outside the asylum, in psychoanalysis and in the consulting room of the analyst. Freud is the Luther and the Adam Smith of psychiatry. He mobilizes all the resources of myth, of tragedy, of dreams, in order to re-enslave desire, this time from within: an intimate theater. Yes, Oedipus is nevertheless the universal of desire, the product of universal history—but on one condition, which is not met by Freud: that Oedipus be capable, at least to a certain point, of conducting its autocritique. Universal history is nothing more than a theology if it does not seize control of the conditions of its contingent, singular existence, its irony, and its own critique. And what are these conditions, this point where the autocritique is possible and necessary? To discover beneath the familial reduction the nature of the social investments of the unconscious. To discover beneath the individual fantasy the nature of group fantasies. Or, what amounts to the same thing, to push the simulacrum to the point where it ceases to be the image of an image, so as to discover the abstract figures, the schizzes-flows that it harbors and conceals. To substitute, for the private subject of castration, split into a subject of enunciation and a subject of the statement relating only to the two orders of personal images, the collective agents of enunciation that for their part refer to machinic arrangements. To overturn the theater of representation into the order of desiring-production: this is the whole task of schizoanalysis.

INTRO-
DUCTION TO
SCHIZOANALYSIS

Translated by Robert Hurley and Mark Seem

1 | The Social Field

Which comes first, the chicken or the egg—but also the father and the mother, or the child? Psychoanalysis acts as if it were the child (the father is sick only from his own childhood), but at the same time is forced to postulate a parental pre-existence (the child is sick only in relation to a father and a mother). This is clearly evident in the primal position of the father of the horde. Oedipus itself would be nothing without the identifications of the parents with the children; and the fact cannot be hidden that everything begins in the mind of the father: isn't that what you want, to kill me, to sleep with your mother? It is first of all a father's idea: thus Laius. It is the father who raises hell, and who brandishes the law (the mother tends to be obliging: we musn't make this into a scene, it's only a dream, a territoriality). Lévi-Strauss puts it very well: "The initial theme of the key myth is the incest committed by the hero with the mother. Yet the idea that he is 'guilty' seems to exist mainly in the mind of the father, who desires his son's death and schemes to bring it about. . . . In the long run it is the father who appears guilty, through having tried to avenge himself, and it is he who is killed. . . . This curious indifference toward incest appears in other myths".[1] *Oedipus is first the idea of an adult paranoiac, before it is the childhood feeling of a neurotic.* So it is that psychoanalysis has much difficulty extracting itself from an infinite regression: the father must have been a child, but was able to be a child only in relation to a father, who was himself a child, in relation to another father.

How does a delirium begin? Perhaps the cinema is able to capture the movement of madness, precisely because it is not analytical and regressive, but explores a global field of coexistence. Witness a film by Nicolas Ray, supposedly representing the formation of a cortisone delirium: an overworked father, a high-school teacher who works overtime for a radio-taxi service and is being treated for heart trouble. He begins to rave about the educational system *in general,* the need to restore a pure *race,* the salvation of the social and moral *order,* then he passes to *religion,* the timeliness of a return to the Bible, Abraham. But what in fact did Abraham do? Well now, he killed or wanted to kill his son, and perhaps God's only error lies in having stayed his hand. But doesn't this man, the film's protagonist, have a son of his own? Hmm . . . What the film shows so well, to the shame of psychiatrists, is that every delirium is first of all the investment of a field that is social, economic, political, cultural, racial and racist, pedagogical, and religious: the delirious person applies a delirium to his family and his son that overreaches them on all sides.

Joseph Gabel, presenting a case of paranoiac delirium with a strong politico-erotic content replete with suggestions for social reform, believes it possible to say that such a case is rare, and that, moreover, its origins are not reconstructible.[2] Yet it is evident that there is never a delirium that does not possess this characteristic to a high degree, and that is not originally economic, political, and so forth, before being crushed in the psychiatric and psychoanalytic treadmill. Judge Schreber would not deny this (nor his father, who invented the Pangymnastikon and a general pedagogical system). Everything changes, then: the infinite regression forced us to postulate a primacy of the father, but an always relative and hypothetical primacy that carried us to infinity, barring a shift into the position of an absolutely primary father; but it is clear that the viewpoint of regression is the result of abstraction. When we say the father is first in relation to the child, this proposition, devoid of meaning in itself, concretely means the following: the social investments are first in relation to the familial investments, which result solely from the application or the reduction (*rabattement*) of the social investments. To say that the father is first in relation to the child really amounts to saying that the investment of desire is in the first instance the investment of a social field into which the father and the child are plunged, simultaneously immersed.

Let us again consider the example of the Marquesans, as analyzed by Kardiner: he distinguishes between an adult alimentary anxiety linked to an endemic famine, and an infantile alimentary anxiety linked to a deficiency of maternal care.[3] Not only is it impossible to derive the first anxiety from the second, but one cannot even consider, as Kardiner does, that the social investment corresponding to the first anxiety comes *after* the infantile familial investment of the second. For a determination of the social field is already invested in the second type of anxiety, namely, the rarity of women that explains how it is that the adults no less than the children "are wary of them." In brief, what the child invests through the infantile experience, the mother's breast, and the familial structure is already a state of the breaks and the flows of the social field in its entirety, flows of women and of food, recordings and distributions. Never is the adult an afterward of the child, but in the family both relate to the determinations of the field in which both the family and they are simultaneously immersed.

Hence we are confronted by three unavoidable conclusions. (1) From the point of view of regression, whose meaning is only *hypothetical,* it is the father who is first in relation to the child. The paranoiac father Oedipalizes the son. Guilt is an idea projected by the father before it is an inner feeling experienced by the son. The first error of psychoanalysis is in acting as if things began with the child. This leads psychoanalysis to develop an absurd theory of fantasy, in terms of which the father, the mother, and their real actions and passions must first be understood as "fantasies" of the child (the Freudian abandonment of the theme of seduction). (2) If regression taken in an absolute sense reveals itself to be inadequate, it is because this regression encloses us in simple reproduction or generation. Furthermore, taking organic bodies and organized persons as its object, the theory of regression merely attains the object of reproduction. The point of view of the cycle alone is *categorical and absolute,* because it attains production as the subject of reproduction, which is to say it attains the process of autoproduction of the unconscious (a unity of history and of nature, from *Homo natura* to *Homo historia*). It is certainly not sexuality that is in the service of generation, but progressive or regressive generation that is in the service of sexuality as a cyclical movement by which the unconscious, always remaining "subject," reproduces itself. There is, then, no longer any call for wondering which is first, the father or the child, because such a question can be raised only within the framework of familialism. The father is first in relation to the child, but only because what is first is the social investment in relation to the familial investment, the investment of the social field in which the father, the child, and the family as a subaggregate are at one and the same time immersed. The primacy of the social field as the terminus of the investment of desire defines the cycle, and the states through which a subject passes. The second error of psychoanalysis, made just as it was completing the separation of sexuality from reproduction, lies in having remained captive to an unrepentant familialism that condemned it to evolve solely within the movement of regression or progression. (Even the psychoanalytic conception of repetition remains captive to such a movement.[4])

(3) Finally, the point of view of the community, which is *disjunctive* or takes account of the disjunctions in the cycle. Not only is generation second in relation to the cycle, but transmission is second in relation to an information or a communication. The genetic revolution occurred when it was discovered that, strictly speaking, there is no transmission of flows, but a communication of a code or an axiomatic, of a combinative apparatus (*combinatoire*) informing the flows. Such is also the case for the social field: its coding or its axiomatic first determine within it a communication of unconsciouses. This phenomenon of communication, which Freud touched on only marginally in his remarks on occultism, constitutes in fact the norm, and pushes into the background the problems of hereditary transmission that animated the Freud-Jung controversy.* It appears that, in the common social field, the first thing that the son represses, or has to repress, or tries to repress, is *the unconscious of the father and the mother.* The failure of that repression is the basis of neuroses. But this communication of unconsciouses does not by any means take the family as its principle; it takes as its principle the commonalty of the social field insofar as it is the object of the investment of desire. In all respects the family is never determining, but is always determined, first as a stimulus of departure, then as an aggregate of destination, and finally as an intermediary or an interception of communication.

If the familial investment is only a dependence or an application of

---

*It is also within the perspective of marginal phenomena that the problem, nevertheless fundamental, of the communication of unconsciouses was posed, first by Spinoza in letter 17 to Balling, then by Myers, James, Bergson, etc.

the unconscious investments of the social field—and if this is just as true of the child as of the adult; if it is true that the child, through the mommy-territoriality and the daddy-law, already aims for the schizzes and the encoded or axiomated flows of the social field—then we must transport the essential difference to the heart of this domain. Delirium is the general matrix of every unconscious social investment. Every unconscious investment mobilizes a delirious interplay of disinvestments, of counterinvestments, of overinvestments. But we have seen in this context that there were two major types of social investment, segregative and nomadic, just as there were two poles of delirium: first, a paranoiac fascisizing (*fascisant*) type or pole that invests the formation of central sovereignty; overinvests it by making it the final eternal cause for all the other social forms of history; counterinvests the enclaves or the periphery; and disinvests every free "figure" of desire—yes, I am your kind, and I belong to the superior race and class. And second, a schizorevolutionary type or pole that follows the *lines of escape* of desire; breaches the wall and causes flows to move; assembles its machines and its groups-in-fusion in the enclaves or at the periphery—proceeding in an inverse fashion from that of the other pole: I am not your kind, I belong eternally to the inferior race, I am a beast, a black. Good people say that we must not flee, that to escape is not good, that it isn't effective, and that one must work for reforms. But the revolutionary knows that escape is revolutionary—*withdrawal, freaks*—provided one sweeps away the social cover on leaving, or causes a piece of the system to get lost in the shuffle. What matters is to break through the wall, even if one has to become black like John Brown. George Jackson. 'I may take flight, but all the while I am fleeing, I will be looking for a weapon!'[5]

Doubtless there are astonishing oscillations of the unconscious, from one pole of delirium to the other: the way in which an expected revolutionary force (*puissance*) breaks free, sometimes even in the midst of the worst archaisms; inversely, the way in which everything turns fascist or envelops itself in fascism, the way in which it falls back into archaisms. Or, staying on the level of literary examples: the case of Céline, the great victim of delirium who evolves while communicating more and more with the paranoia of his father. The case of Jack Kerouac, the artist possessing the soberest of means who took revolutionary "flight," but who later finds himself immersed in dreams of a Great America, and then in search of his Breton ancestors of the superior race. Isn't the destiny of American literature that of crossing limits and frontiers, causing deterritorialized flows of desire to circulate, but also always making these flows transport fascisizing, moralizing, Puritan, and familialist territorialities?

These oscillations of the unconscious, these underground passages from one type of libidinal investment to the other—often the coexistence of the two—form one of the major objects of schizoanalysis. The two poles united by Artaud in the formula: Heliogabalus-the-anarchist, "the image of all human contradictions, and of the contradiction *in principle.*" But no passage impairs or suppresses the difference in nature between the two, nomadism and segregation. If we are able to define this difference as that which separates paranoia and schizophrenia, it is because on the one hand we have distinguished the schizophrenic process ("the breakthrough") from the accidents and relapses that hinder or interrupt it ("the breakdown"), and because on the other hand we have posited paranoia no less than schizophrenia as independent of all familial pseudo etiologies, so as to make them bear directly upon the social field: every name in history, and not the name of the father. On the contrary, the nature of the familial investments depends on the breaks and the flows of the social field as they are invested in one type or another, at one pole or the other. And the child does not wait until he is an adult before grasping—underneath father-mother—the economic, financial, social, and cultural problems that cross through a family: his belonging or his desire to belong to a superior or an inferior "race," the reactionary or the revolutionary tenor of a familial group with which he is already preparing his ruptures and his conformities.

What a muddle, what an emulsion the family is, agitated by backwashes, pulled in one direction or another, in such a way that the Oedipal bacillus takes or doesn't take, imposes its mold or doesn't succeed in imposing it, pursuing directions of an entirely different nature that traverse the family from the exterior. What we mean is that Oedipus is born of an application or a reduction to personalized images, which presupposes a social investment of a paranoiac type—which explains why Freud first discovers the familial romance and Oedipus while reflecting on paranoia. Oedipus is a dependency of the paranoiac territoriality, whereas the schizophrenic investment commands an entirely different determination, a family gasping for breath and stretched out over the dimensions of a social field that does not reclose or withdraw: a family-as-matrix for depersonalized partial objects, which plunge again and again into the torrential or depleted flux of a historic cosmos, a historic chaos. The matrical fissure of schizophrenia, as opposed to paranoiac castration; and the line of escape as opposed to the "blue line," the blues.

O mother
farewell
with a long black shoe
farewell
with Communist Party and a broken stocking. . . .
with your sagging belly
with your fear of Hitler
with your mouth of bad short stories. . . .
with your belly of strikes and smokestacks
with your chin of Trotsky and the Spanish War
with your voice singing for the decaying overbroken workers. . . .

with your eyes
with your eyes of Russia
with your eyes of no money. . . .
with your eyes of starving India. . . .
with your eyes of Czechoslovakia attacked by robots. . . .
with your eyes being led away by policemen to an ambulance
with your eyes with the pancreas removed
with your eyes of appendix operation
with your eyes of abortion
with your eyes of ovaries removed
with your eyes of shock
with your eyes of lobotomy
with your eyes of divorce. . . . [6]

Why these words, paranoia and schizophrenia, which are like talking birds and girls' first names? Why do social investments follow this dividing line that gives them a specifically delirious content (recreating history in delirium)? And what is this line, how can we situate schizophrenia and paranoia on either side of it? Our assumption is that everything happens on the body without organs; but this body has, as it were, two faces. Elias Canetti has clearly shown how the paranoiac organizes masses and "packs." The paranoiac opposes them to one another, maneuvers them.* The paranoiac engineers masses, he is the artist of the large molar aggregates, the statistical formations or gregariousnesses, the phenomena of organized crowds. He invests everything that falls within the province of large numbers. The night of the battle,

*Elias Canetti, *Crowds and Power* (New York: Viking Press, 1960), p. 434: "His mind was dominated by four kinds of crowds: his army, his treasure, his corpses and his court (and, with it, his capital). He juggled with them ceaselessly, but only succeeded in increasing one at the expense of another. . . . Whatever he did there was always *one* crowd which he managed to preserve. In no circumstances did he ever cease to kill. . . . The heaps of corpses piled up in every province of his empire."

Colonel Lawrence lines up the young naked corpses on the full body of the desert. Judge Schreber attaches little men by the thousands to his body. It might be said that, of the two directions in *physics*—the molar direction that goes toward the large numbers and the mass phenomena, and the molecular direction that on the contrary penetrates into singularities, their interactions and connections at a distance or between different orders—the paranoiac has chosen the first: he practices macrophysics. And it could be said that by contrast the schizo goes in the other direction, that of microphysics, of molecules insofar as they no longer obey the statistical laws: waves and corpuscles, flows and partial objects that are no longer dependent upon the large numbers; infinitesimal lines of escape, instead of the perspectives of the large aggregates.

Doubtless it would be a mistake to contrast these two dimensions in terms of the collective and the individual. On the one hand, the microunconscious presents no fewer arrangements, connections, and interactions, although these arrangements are of an original type; on the other hand, the form of individualized persons does not belong to it, since it knows only partial objects and flows, but belongs instead to the laws of statistical distribution of the molar unconscious or the macrounconscious. Freud was Darwinian, neo-Darwinian, when he said that in the unconscious everything was a problem of population (likewise, in the contemplation of multiplicities he saw a sign of psychosis).* It is therefore more a matter of the difference between two kinds of collections or populations: the large aggregates and the micromultiplicities. In both cases the investment is collective, it is an investment of a collective field; even a lone particle has an associated wave as a flow that defines the coexisting space of *its* presences. Every investment is collective, every fantasy is a group fantasy and in this sense a position of reality. But the two kinds of investments are radically different, according as the one bears upon the molar structures that subordinate the molecules, and the other on the contrary bears upon the molecular multiplicities that subordinate the structured crowd phenomena. One is a *subjugated group* investment, as much in its sovereign form as in its colonial formations of the gregarious aggregate, which socially and psychically represses the desire of persons; the other, a *subject-group* investment in the transverse multiplicities that convey desire as a molecular phenomenon, that is, as partial objects and flows, as opposed to aggregates and persons.

It is true that social investments are made on the socius itself as a

*In the article of 1913 on "The Unconscious," Freud shows that psychosis causes small multiplicities to intervene, as opposed to neurosis, which requires a global object: for example, the multiplicity of holes. But Freud explains this psychotic phenomenon solely by invoking the power of verbal representation.

full body, and that their respective poles necessarily relate to the character or the "map" of this socius—earth, despot, or capital-money (for each social machine the two poles, paranoiac and schizophrenic, are distributed in varying ways). Whereas the paranoiac and the schizophrenic, properly speaking, do not operate on the socius, but on the body without organs in a pure state. It might then be said that the paranoiac, in the clinical sense of the term, makes us spectators to the imaginary birth of the mass phenomenon, and does so at a level that is still microscopic. The body without organs is like the cosmic egg, the *giant molecule* swarming with worms, bacilli, Lilliputian figures, animalcules, and homunculi, with their organization and their machines, minute strings, ropes, teeth, fingernails, levers and pulleys, catapults: thus in Schreber the millions of spermatazoids in the sunbeams, or the souls that lead a brief existence as little men on his body. Artaud says: this world of microbes, which is nothing more than coagulated nothingness. The two sides of the body without organs are, therefore, the side on which the mass phenomenon and the paranoiac investment corresponding to it are organized on a microscopic scale, and the other side on which, on a submicroscopic scale, the molecular phenomena and their schizophrenic investment are arranged. It is on the body without organs, as a pivot, as a frontier between the molar and the molecular, that the paranoia-schizophrenia division is made. Are we to believe, then, that social investments are secondary projections, as if a large two-headed schizonoiac, father of the primitive horde, were at the base of the socius in general? We have seen that this is not at all the case. The socius is not a projection of the body without organs; rather, the body without organs is the limit of the socius, its tangent of deterritorialization, the ultimate residue of a deterritorialized socius. The socius—the earth, the body of the despot, capital-money—are clothed full bodies, just as the body without organs is a naked full body; but the latter exists at the limit, at the end, not at the origin. And doubtless the body without organs haunts all forms of socius. But in this very sense, if social investments can be said to be paranoiac or schizophrenic, it is to the extent that they have paranoia and schizophrenia as ultimate products under the determinate conditions of capitalism.

From the standpoint of a universal clinical theory, paranoia and schizophrenia can be presented as the two extreme oscillaions of a pendulum oscillating around the position of a socius as a full body and, at the limit, of a body without organs, one of whose sides is occupied by the molar aggregates, and the other populated by molecular elements. But one can also present this as a single line along which the different forms of socius, their planes and their large aggregates, are arranged; on

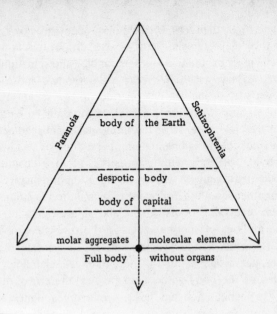

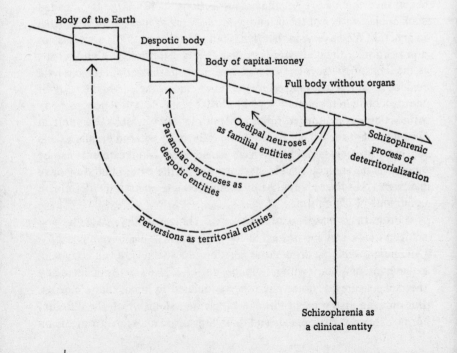

each of these planes there is a paranoiac dimension, another that is perverse, a kind of familial position, and a dotted line of escape or schizoid breakthrough. The major line ends at the body without organs, and there it either passes through the wall, opening onto the molecular elements where it becomes in actual fact what it was from the start: the schizophrenic process, the pure schizophrenic process of deterritorialization. Or it strikes the wall, rebounds off it, and falls back into the most miserably arranged territorialities of the modern world as simulacra of the preceding planes, getting caught up in the asylum aggregate of paranoia and schizophrenia as clinical entities, in the artificial aggregates or societies established by perversion, in the familial aggregate of Oedipal neuroses.

2 | The Molecular Unconscious

What is the meaning of this distinction between two regions: one molecular and the other molar; one micropsychic or micrological, the other statistical and gregarious? Is this anything more than a metaphor lending the unconscious a distinction grounded in physics, when we speak of an opposition between intra-atomic phenomena and the mass phenomena that operate through statistical accumulation, obeying the laws of aggregates? But in reality the unconscious belongs to the realm of physics; the body without organs and its intensities are not metaphors, but matter itself. Nor is it our intention to revive the question of an individual psychology and a collective psychology, and of the priority of the one or the other; this distinction, as it appears in *Group Psychology and the Analysis of the Ego,* remains completely stymied by Oedipus. In the unconscious there are only populations, groups, and machines. When we posit in one case an involuntariness (*un involontaire*) of the social and technical machines, in the other case an unconscious of the desiring-machines, it is a question of a necessary relationship between inextricably linked forces. Some of these are elementary forces by means of which the unconscious is produced; the others, resultants reacting on the first, statistical aggregates through which the unconscious is represented and already suffers psychic and social repression of its elementary productive forces.

But how can we speak of machines in this microphysical or micropsychic region, *there where there is desire*—that is to say, not only its functioning, but formation and autoproduction? A machine works according to the previous intercommunications of its structure and the positioning of its parts, but does not set itself into place any more than it forms or reproduces itself. This is even the point around which the usual polemic between vitalism and mechanism revolves: the machine's ability to account for the workings of the organism, but its fundamental inability to account for its formations. From machines, mechanism abstracts a *structural unity* in terms of which it explains the functioning of the organism. Vitalism invokes an *individual and specific unity* of the living, which every machine presupposes insofar as it is subordinate to organic continuance, and insofar as it extends the latter's autonomous formations on the outside. But it should be noted that, in one way or another, the machine and desire thus remain in an extrinsic relationship, either because desire appears as an effect determined by a system of mechanical causes, or because the machine is itself a system of means in terms of the aims of desire. The link between the two remains secondary and indirect, both in the new means appropriated by desire and in the derived desires produced by the machines.

A profound text by Samuel Butler, "The Book of the Machines," nevertheless allows us to go beyond these points of view.[7] It is true that this text seems at first merely to contrast the two common arguments, the one according to which the organisms are for the moment only more perfect machines ("Whether those things which we deem most purely spiritual are anything but disturbances of equilibrium in an infinite series of levers, beginning with those levers that are too small for microscopic detection"[8]), the other according to which machines are never more than extensions of the organism ("The lower animals keep all their limbs at home in their bodies, but many of man's are loose, and lie about detached, now here and now there, in various parts of the world"[9]). But there is a Butlerian manner for carrying each of the arguments to an extreme point where it can no longer be opposed to the other, a point of nondifference or *dispersion*. For one thing, Butler is not content to say that machines extend the organism, but asserts that they are really limbs and organs lying on the body without organs of a society, which men will appropriate according to their power and their wealth, and whose poverty deprives them as if they were mutilated organisms. For another, he is not content to say that organisms are machines, but asserts that they contain such an abundance of parts that they must be compared to very different parts of distinct machines, each relating to the others, engineered in combination with the others.

What is essential is this double movement whereby Butler drives both arguments beyond their very limits. *He shatters the vitalist argument by calling in question the specific or personal unity of the organism, and the mechanist argument even more decisively, by calling in question the structural unity of the machine.* It is said that machines do not reproduce themselves, or that they only reproduce themselves through the intermediary of man, but "does any one say that the red clover has no reproductive system because the bumble bee (and the bumble bee only) must aid and abet it before it can reproduce? No one. The bumble bee is a part of the reproductive system of the clover. Each one of ourselves has sprung from minute animalcules whose entity was entirely distinct from our own. . . . These creatures are part of our reproductive system; then why not we part of that of the machines? . . . We are misled *by considering any complicated machine as a single thing;* in truth it is a city or a society, each member of which was bred truly after its kind. We see a machine as a whole, we call it by a name and individualize it; we look at our own limbs, and know that the combination forms an individual which springs from a single centre of reproductive action; we therefore assume that there can be no reproductive action which does not arise from a single center; but this assumption is unscientific, and the bare fact that no vapour-engine was ever made entirely by another, or two others, of its own kind, is not sufficient to warrant us in saying that vapour-engines have no reproductive system. The truth is that each part of every vapour-engine is bred by its own special breeders, whose function is to breed that part, and that only, while the combination of the parts into a whole forms another department of the mechanical reproductive system."[10] In passing, Butler encounters the phenomenon of surplus value of code, when a part of a machine captures within its own code a code fragment of another machine, and thus owes its reproduction to a part of another machine: the red clover and the bumble bee; or the orchid and the male wasp that it attracts and intercepts by carrying on its flower the image and the odor of the female wasp.

At *this point of dispersion* of the two arguments, it becomes immaterial whether one says that machines are organs, or organs, machines. The two definitions are exact equivalents: man as a "vertebro-machinate mammal," or as an "aphidian parasite of machines." What is essential is not in the passage to infinity itself—the infinity composed of machine parts or the temporal infinity of the animalcules—but rather in what this passage blossoms into. Once the structural unity of the machine has been undone, once the personal and specific unity of the living has been laid to rest, a direct link is perceived between the machine and desire, the machine passes to the heart of desire, the machine is desiring and desire, machined. Desire is not in the subject, but the machine in desire—with the residual subject off to the side, alongside the machine, around the entire periphery, a parasite of machines, an accessory of vertebro-machinate desire. In a word, the real difference is not between the living and the machine, vitalism and mechanism, but between two states of the machine that are two states of the living as well. The machine taken in its structural unity, the living taken in its specific and even personal unity, are mass phenomena or molar aggregates; for this reason each points to the extrinsic existence of the other. And even if they are differentiated and mutually opposed, it is merely as two paths in the same statistical direction. But in the other more profound or intrinsic direction of multiplicities there is interpenetration, direct communication between the molecular phenomena and the singularities of the living, that is to say, between the small machines scattered in every machine, and the small formations dispersed in every organism: a domain of nondifference between the microphysical and the biological, there being as many living beings in the machine as there are machines in the living. Why speak of machines in this domain, when there would seem to be none, strictly speaking—no structural unity nor any preformed mechanical interconnections? "But there is the possibility of formation of such machines—in indefinitely superimposed relays, in working cycles that mesh with each other—which, once assembled, will obey the laws of thermo-dynamics, but which in the process of assembly do not depend on these laws, since the chain of assembly begins in a domain where by definition there are as yet no statistical laws. . . . *At this level, functioning and formation are still confounded as in the molecule;* and, starting from this level, two diverging paths open up, of which one will lead to the more or less regular accumulations of individuals, the other to the perfectings of the individual organization whose simplest schema is the formation of a pipe."*

The real difference is therefore between on the one hand the molar machines—whether social, technical, or organic—and on the other the desiring-machines, which are of a molecular order. Desiring-machines are the following: formative machines, whose very misfirings are functional, and whose functioning is indiscernible from their formation; chronogeneous machines engaged in their own assembly (*montage*), operating by nonlocalizable intercommunications and dispersed localizations, bringing into play processes of temporalization, fragmented

*Raymond Ruyer, *La genèse des formes vivantes* (Paris: Flammarion, 1958), pp. 80–81. Taking up certain arguments of Bohr, Schrödinger, Jordan, and Lillie, Ruyer shows that the living is directly coupled to the individual phenomena of the atom, beyond the mass effects that appear in the internal mechanical circuits of the organism as well as in the external technical activities: "Classical physics only concerns itself with mass phenomena. In contrast, micro-physics naturally leads to biology. Starting from the individual phenomena of the atom, one can in fact go in two directions. Their statistical accumulation leads to the laws of common physics. But as these individual phenomena become complicated through systematic interactions—all the while keeping their individuality at the core of the molecule, then at the core of the macromolecule, then of the virus, then of the one-celled organism, by subordinating the mass phenomena—one is led all the way to the organism that, no matter how large, remains in this sense microscopic" (p. 54). These themes are developed at length by Ruyer in *Néo-finalisme* (Paris: Presses Universitaires de France, 1952).

formations, and detached parts, with a surplus value of code, and where the whole is itself produced alongside the parts, as a part apart or, as Butler would say, "in another department" that fits the whole over the other parts; machines in the strict sense, because they proceed by breaks and flows, associated waves and particles, associative flows and partial objects, inducing—always at a distance—transverse connections, inclusive disjunctions, and polyvocal conjunctions, thereby producing selections, detachments, and remainders, with a transference of individuality, in a generalized schizogenesis whose elements are the schizzes-flows.

Subsequently—rather, we should say on the other hand—when the machines become unified at the structural level of techniques and institutions that give them an existence as visible as a plate of steel; when the living, too, become structured by the statistical unities of their persons and their species, varieties, and locales; when a machine appears as a single object, and a living organism appears as a single subject; when the connections become global and specific, the disjunctions exclusive, and the conjunctions biunivocal; then desire does not need to project itself into these forms that have become opaque. These forms are immediately molar manifestations, statistical determinations of desire and of *its own* machines. They are the same machines (there is no difference in nature): here, as organic, technical, or social machines apprehended in *their* mass phenomenon, to which they become subordinated; there, as desiring-machines apprehended in their submicroscopic singularities that subordinate the mass phenomena. That is why from the start we have rejected the idea that desiring-machines belong to the domain of dreams or the Imaginary, and that they stand in for the other machines. There is only desire and environments, fields, forms of herd instinct. Stated differently, the molecular desiring-machines are in themselves the investment of the large molar machines or of the configurations that the desiring-machines *form according to the laws of large numbers,** in either or both senses of subordination, in one sense and the other of subordination. Desiring-machines in one sense, but organic, technical, or social machines in the other: these are the same machines under determinate conditions. By "determinate conditions" we mean those statistical forms into which the machines enter as so

---

*Allen Wallis and Harry Roberts, in *Statistics, a New Approach* (New York: Free Press of Glencoe, 1956), define the "law of large numbers" as follows: "the larger the samples, the less will be the variability in the sample proportions . . . the basis of the Law of Large Numbers is that for an improbable event to occur *n* times is improbable to the *n*th degree" (p. 123); "the larger the groups averaged, the less the variation" (p. 159). And the consecutive sequences will be "swamped" by a large number of subsequent observations (see L. H. C. Tippett, *Statistics* [New York: Oxford University Press, 1943], p. 87). (*Translators' note.*)

many stable forms, unifying, structuring, and proceeding by means of large heavy aggregates; the selective pressures that group the parts retain some of them and exclude others, organizing the crowds. These are therefore the same machines, but not at all the same régime, the same relationships of magnitude, or the same uses of syntheses. It is only at the submicroscopic level of desiring-machines that there exists a functionalism—machinic arrangements, an engineering of desire; for it is only there that functioning and formation, use and assembly, product and production merge. All molar functionalism is false, since the organic or social machines are not formed in the same way they function, and the technical machines are not assembled in the same way they are used, but imply precisely the specific conditions that separate their own production from their distinct product. Only what is not produced in the same way it functions has a meaning, and also a purpose, an intention. The desiring-machines on the contrary represent nothing, signify nothing, mean nothing, and are exactly what one makes of them, what is made with them, what they make in themselves.

Desiring-machines work according to régimes of syntheses that have no equivalent in the large aggregates. Jacques Monod has defined the originality of these syntheses, from the standpoint of a molecular biology or of a "microscopic cybernetics" without regard to the traditional opposition between mechanism and vitalism. Here the fundamental traits of synthesis are the indifferent nature of the chemical signals, the indifference to the substrate, and the indirect character of the interactions. Such formulas as these are negative only in appearance, and in relation to the laws of aggregates, but must be understood positively in terms of force (*puissance*). "Between the substrate of an allosteric enzyme and the ligands prompting or inhibiting its activity there exists no chemically necessary relationship of structure or of reactivity. . . . An allosteric protein should be seen as a specialized product of molecular "engineering," enabling an interaction, positive or negative, to come about between compounds without chemical affinity, and thereby eventually subordinating any reaction to the intervention of compounds that are chemically foreign and indifferent to this reaction. The way in which allosteric interactions work hence permits a complete freedom in the "choice" of controls. And these controls, having no chemical requirements to answer to, will be the more responsive to physiological requirements, and will accordingly be selected for the extent to which they confer heightened coherence and efficiency upon the cell or organism. In a word, the very gratuitousness of these systems, giving molecular evolution a practically limitless field for exploration and experiment, enabled it to elaborate the huge network of cybernetic inter-connections."*

How, starting from this domain of chance or of real inorganization, large configurations are organized that necessarily reproduce a structure under the action of DNA and its segments, the genes, performing veritable lottery drawings, creating switching points as *lines of selection or evolution*—this, indeed, is what all the stages of the passage from the molecular to the molar demonstrate, such as this passage appears in the organic machines, but no less so in the social machines with other laws and other figures. In this sense it was possible to insist on a common characteristic of human cultures and of living species, as "Markov chains": aleatory phenomena that are partially dependent. In the genetic code as in the social codes, what is termed a signifying chain is more a jargon than a language (*langage*), composed of nonsignifying elements that have a meaning or an effect of signification only in the large aggregates that they constitute through a linked drawing of elements, a partial dependence, and a superposition of relays.† It is not a matter of biologizing human history, nor of anthropologizing natural history. It is a matter of showing the common participation of the social machines *and* the organic machines in the desiring-machines. At man's most basic stratum, the Id: the schizophrenic cell, the schizo molecules, their chains and their jargons. There is a whole biology of schizophrenia; molecular biology is itself schizophrenic—as is microphysics. But inversely schizophrenia—the theory of schizophrenia—is biological, biocultural, inasmuch as it examines the machinic connections of a molecular order, their distribution into maps of intensity on the giant molecule of the body without organs, and the statistical accumulations that form and select the large aggregates.

Szondi set out on this molecular path, discovering a genic unconscious that he contrasted with the Freudian individual unconscious as well as with Jung's collective unconscious.** He often calls this genic or

*Jacques Monod, *Chance and Necessity* (see reference note 27), pp. 77–78. And pp. 90–98: "With the globular protein we already have, at the molecular level, a veritable machine—a machine in its functional properties, but not, we now see, in its fundamental structure, where nothing but the play of blind combinations can be discerned. Randomness caught on the wing, preserved, reproduced by the machinery of invariance and thus converted into order, rule, necessity."

†On the Markov chains and their applications to the living species as well as to cultural formations, see Ruyer, *La genèse des formes vivantes,* Ch. 8. The phenomena of surplus value of code are clearly explained in this perspective of "semifortuitous sequences." Several times Ruyer compares this with the language of schizophrenia.

**Lipot Szondi, *Experimental Diagnostics of Drives* (New York: Grune & Stratton, 1952). Szondi's work was the first to establish a fundamental relationship between psychoanalysis and genetics. See also the recent attempt by André Green, in terms of the advances made in molecular biology: "Répétition et instinct de mort," *Revue franç aise de psychanalyse,* May 1970.

genealogical unconscious familial; and Szondi himself went on to study schizophrenia using familial aggregates as his units of measure. But the genic unconscious is familial only to a very small degree, much less so than Freud's unconscious, since the diagnosis is carried out by comparing desire to the photographs of hermaphrodites, assassins, etc., instead of reducing it as usual to the images of daddy-mommy. Finally some relation to the outside! A whole alphabet, an entire axiomatic done with photos of mad people; this has to be tried, testing "the need for paternal feeling" against a series of portraits of assassins. It is no use saying this remains within the bounds of Oedipus, the truth is that it throws them open in a remarkable way. The hereditary genes of drives therefore play the role of simple stimuli that enter into variable combinations following vectors that survey an entire social historical field—an analysis of destiny.

In point of fact, the truly molecular unconscious cannot confine itself to genes as its units of reproduction; these units are still expressive, and lead to molar formations. Molecular biology teaches us that it is only the DNA that is reproduced, and not the proteins. Proteins are both products and units of production; they are what constitutes the unconscious as a cycle or as the autoproduction of the unconscious—the ultimate molecular elements in the arrangement of the desiring-machines and the syntheses of desire. We have seen that, *through* reproduction and its objects (defined familially or genetically), it is always the unconscious that produces itself in a cyclical orphan movement, a cycle of destiny where it always remains a subject. It is precisely on this point that the statutory independence of sexuality with regard to generation rests. Szondi senses this direction—according to which one must go beyond the molar to the molecular—so acutely that he takes exception to all statistical interpretations of what is wrongly called his "test." What is more, he calls for going beyond contents toward the realm of *functions*. But he makes this advance, follows this direction, only by going from aggregates or classes toward "categories," of which he establishes a systematically closed list—categories that are still only expressive forms of existence that a subject is meant to choose and combine freely. For this reason Szondi misses the internal or molecular elements of desire, the nature of their machinic choices, arrangements, and combinations. He also misses the real question of schizoanalysis: What drives your own desiring-machines? What is their functioning? What are the syntheses into which they enter and operate? What use do you make of them, in all the transitions that extend from the molecular to the molar and inversely, and that constitute the cycle whereby the unconscious, remaining a subject, produces and reproduces itself?

We use the term *Libido* to designate the specific energy of desiring-machines; and the transformations of this energy—*Numen* and *Voluptas*—are never desexualizations or sublimations. This terminology indeed seems extremely arbitrary. Considering the two ways in which the desiring-machines must be viewed, what they have to do with a properly sexual energy is not immediately clear: either they are assigned to the molecular order that is their own, or they are assigned to the molar order where they form the organic or social machines, and invest organic or social surroundings. It is in fact difficult to present sexual energy as directly cosmic and intra-atomic, and at the same time as directly sociohistorical. It would be futile to say that love has to do with proteins and society. This would amount to reviving yet once more the old attempts at liquidating Freudianism, by substituting for the libido a vague cosmic energy capable of all of the metamorphoses, or a kind of socialized energy capable of all the investments. Or would we do better to review Reich's final attempt, involving a "biogenesis" that not without justification is qualified as a schizoparanoiac mode of reasoning? It will be remembered that Reich concluded in favor of an intra-atomic cosmic energy—the orgone—generative of an electrical flux and carrying submicroscopic particles, the bions. This energy produced differences in potential or intensities distributed on the body considered from a molecular viewpoint, and was associated with a mechanics of fluids in this same body considered from a molar viewpoint. What defined the libido as sexuality was therefore the association of the two modes of operation, mechanical and electrical, in a sequence with two poles, molar and molecular (mechanical tension, electrical charge, electrical discharge, mechanical relaxation). Reich thought he had thus overcome the alternative between mechanism and vitalism, since these functions, mechanical and electrical, existed in matter in general, but were combined in a particular sequence within the living. And above all he upheld the basic psychoanalytic truth, the supreme disavowal of which he was able to denounce in Freud: the independence of sexuality with regard to reproduction, the subordination of progressive or regressive reproduction to sexuality as a cycle.*

*All of Reich's last studies, biocosmic and biogenetic, are summarized at the end of Wilhelm Reich, *The Function of the Orgasm* (reference note 22), Ch. 7. The primacy of sexuality over generation and reproduction comes to be based on the cycle of sexuality (mechanical tension–electrical charge, etc.), which leads to a division of the cell: pp. 282–86. But very early in his work Reich reproached Freud for having abandoned the sexual position. *It was not only the dissidents from Freud who abandoned this position, it was Freud himself, in a certain fashion:* a first time when he introduces the death instinct,

If the details of Reich's final theory are taken into consideration, we admit that its simultaneously schizophrenic and paranoiac nature is no obstacle where we are concerned—on the contrary. We admit that any comparison of sexuality with cosmic phenomena such as "electrical storms," "the blue color of the sky and the blue-gray of atmospheric haze," the blue of the orgone, "St. Elmo's fire, and the bluish formations [of] sunspot activity," fluids and flows, matter and particles, in the end appear to us more adequate than the reduction of sexuality to the pitiful little familialist secret. We think that Lawrence and Miller have a more accurate evaluation of sexuality than Freud, even from the viewpoint of the famous scientificity. It is not the neurotic stretched out on the couch who speaks to us of love, of its force and its despair, but the mute stroll of the schizo, Lenz's outing in the mountains and under the stars, the immobile voyage in intensities on the body without organs. As to the whole of Reichian theory, it possesses the incomparable advantage of showing the double pole of the libido, as a molecular formation on the submicroscopic scale, and as an investment of the molar formations on the scale of social and organic aggregates. All that is missing is the confirmations of common sense: why, in what sense is this sexuality?

Cynicism has said, or claimed to have said, everything there is to say about love: that it is a matter of a copulation of social and organic machines on a large scale (at bottom, love is in the organs; at bottom, love is a matter of economic determinations, money). But what is properly cynical is to claim a scandal where there is none to be found, and to pass for bold while lacking boldness. Better the delirium of common sense than its platitude. For the prime evidence points to the fact that desire does not take as its object persons or things, but the entire surroundings that it traverses, the vibrations and flows of every sort to which it is joined, introducing therein breaks and captures—an always nomadic and migrant desire, characterized first of all by its "gigantism": no one has shown this more clearly than Charles Fourier. In a word, the social as well as biological surroundings are the object of unconscious investments that are necessarily desiring or libidinal, in contrast with the preconscious investments of need or of interest. The libido as sexual energy is the direct investment of masses, of large

and begins to speak of Eros instead of sexuality (Reich, pp. 124–27); next, when he makes anxiety into the cause of sexual repression, and no longer its result (p. 136); and more generally when he comes back to a traditional primacy of procreation over sexuality (p. 283: "Thus, *procreation* is a function of sexuality, and not vice versa, as was hitherto believed. Freud had maintained the same thing with respect to psychosexuality, when he separated the concepts 'sexual' and 'genital.' But for a reason I was not able to understand, he later stated that 'sexuality in puberty' is 'in the service of procreation.'") Here Reich is obviously referring to Freud's Schopenhauerian or Weismannian texts, where sexuality comes under the sway of the species and the germen: for example, "On Narcissism: An Introduction," in *Collected Papers* (London: Hogarth Press), Vol. 4, pp. 36–38.

aggregates, and of social and organic fields. We have difficulty under-standing what principles psychoanalysis uses to support its conception of desire, when it maintains that the libido must be desexualized or even sublimated in order to proceed to the social investments, and inversely that the libido only resexualizes these investments during the course of pathological regression.* Unless the assumption of such a conception is still familialism—that is, an assumption holding that sexuality operates only in the family, and must be transformed in order to invest larger aggregates.

The truth is that sexuality is everywhere: the way a bureaucrat fondles his records, a judge administers justice, a businessman causes money to circulate; the way the bourgeoisie fucks the proletariat; and so on. And there is no need to resort to metaphors, any more than for the libido to go by way of metamorphoses. Hitler got the fascists sexually aroused. Flags, nations, armies, banks get a lot of people aroused. A revolutionary machine is nothing if it does not acquire at least as much force as these coercive machines have for producing breaks and mobilizing flows. It is not through a desexualizing extension that the libido invests the large aggregates. On the contrary, it is through a restriction, a blockage, and a reduction that the libido is made to repress its flows in order to contain them in the narrow cells of the type "couple," "family," "person," "objects." And doubtless such a block-age is necessarily justified: the libido does not come to consciousness except in relation to a given body, a given person that it takes as object. But our "object choice" itself refers to a conjunction of flows of life and of society that this body and this person intercept, receive, and transmit, always within a biological, social, and historical field where we are equally immersed or with which we communicate. The persons to whom our loves are dedicated, including the parental persons, intervene only as points of connection, of disjunction, of conjunction of flows whose libidinal tenor of a properly unconscious investment they translate. Thus no matter how well grounded the love blockage is, it curiously changes its function, depending on whether it engages desire in the Oedipal impasses of the couple and the family in the service of the repressive machines, or whether on the contrary it condenses a free energy capable of fueling a revolutionary machine. (Here again, everything has already

*Freud, *Three Case Histories* (reference note 42), p. 164: "Persons who have not freed themselves completely from the stage of narcissism, who, that is to say, have at that point a fixation which may operate as a disposing factor for a later illness, are exposed to the danger that some unusually intense wave of libido, finding no other outlet, may lead to a sexualization of their social instincts and so undo the work of sublimation which they had achieved in the course of their development. This result may be produced by anything that causes the libido to flow backwards (i.e., that causes a 'regression'): . . . paranoiacs *endeavour to protect themselves against any such sexualization of their social instinctual cathexes.*"

been said by Fourier, when he shows the two contrary directions of the "captivation" or the "mechanization" of the passions.) But we always make love with worlds. And our love addresses itself to this libidinal property of our lover, to either close himself off or open up to more spacious worlds, to masses and large aggregates. There is always something statistical in our loves, and something belonging to the laws of large numbers. And isn't it in this way that we must understand the famous formula of Marx?—the relationship between man and woman is "the direct, natural, and necessary relation of person to person." That is, the relationship between the two sexes (man and woman) is only the measure of the relationship of sexuality in general, insofar as it invests large aggregates (man and man)? Whence what came to be called the species determination of the sexuality of the two sexes. And must it not also be said that the phallus is not one sex, but sexuality in its entirety, which is to say the sign of the large aggregate invested by the libido, whence the two sexes necessarily derive, both in their separation (the two homosexual series of man and man, woman and woman) and in their statistical relations within this aggregate?

But Marx says something even more mysterious: that the true difference is not the difference between the two sexes, but the difference between the human sex and the "nonhuman" sex.[11] It is clearly not a question of animals, nor of animal sexuality. Something quite different is involved. If sexuality is the unconscious investment of the large molar aggregates, it is because on its other side sexuality is identical with the interplay of the molecular elements that constitute these aggregates under determinate conditions. The dwarfism of desire as a correlate to its gigantism. Sexuality and the desiring-machines are one and the same inasmuch as these machines are present and operating in the social machines, in their field, their formation, their functioning. Desiring-machines are the nonhuman sex, the molecular machinic elements, their arrangements and their syntheses, without which there would be neither a human sex specifically determined in the large aggregates, nor a human sexuality capable of investing these aggregates. In a few sentences Marx, who is nonetheless so miserly and reticent where sexuality is concerned, exploded something that will hold Freud and all of psychoanalysis forever captive: *the anthropomorphic representation of sex!*

What we call anthropomorphic representation is just as much the idea that there are two sexes as the idea that there is only one. We know how Freudianism is permeated by this bizarre notion that there is finally only one sex, the masculine, in relation to which the woman, the feminine, is defined as a lack, an absence. It could be thought at first that such a hypothesis founds the omnipotence of a male homosexuality. Yet this is not at all the case; what is founded here is rather the statistical aggregate of intersexual loves. For if the woman is defined as a lack in relation to the man, the man in his turn lacks what is lacking in the woman, simply in another fashion: the idea of a single sex necessarily leads to the erection of a phallus as an object on high, which distributes lack as two nonsuperimposable sides and makes the two sexes communicate in a common absence—*castration*. Women, as psychoanalysts or psychoanalyzed, can then rejoice in showing man the way, and in recuperating equality in difference. Whence the irresistibly comical nature of the formulas according to which one gains access to desire through castration. But the idea that there are two sexes, after all, is no better. This time, like Melanie Klein, one attempts to define the female sex by means of positive characteristics, even if they be terrifying. At least in this way one avoids phallocentrism, if not anthropomorphism. But this time, far from founding the communication between the two sexes, one founds instead their separation into two homosexual series that remain statistical. And one does not by any means escape castration. It is simply that castration, instead of being the principle of sex conceived as the masculine sex (the great castrated soaring Phallus), becomes the result of sex conceived as the feminine sex (the little hidden absorbed penis). We maintain therefore that *castration is the basis for the anthropomorphic and molar representation of sexuality.* Castration is the universal belief that brings together and disperses both men and women under the yoke of one and the same illusion of consciousness, and makes them adore this yoke. Every attempt to determine the nonhuman nature of sex—for example, "the Great Other" in Lacan—while conserving myth and castration, is defeated from the start. And what does Jean-François Lyotard mean, in his commentary—so profound, nevertheless—on Marx's text, when he sees the opening of the nonhuman as having to be "the entry of the subject into desire through castration"?[12] Long live castration, so that desire may be strong? Only fantasies are truly desired? What a perverse, human, all-too-human idea! An idea originating in bad conscience, and not in the unconscious. Anthropomorphic molar representation culminates in the very thing that founds it, the ideology of lack. The molecular unconscious, on the contrary, knows nothing of castration, because partial objects lack nothing and form free multiplicities as such; because the multiple breaks never cease producing flows, instead of repressing them, cutting them at a single stroke—the only break capable of exhausting them; because the syntheses constitute local and nonspecific connections, inclusive disjunctions, nomadic conjunctions: everywhere a microscopic transsexuality, resulting in the woman containing as many men as the man, and the man as many women, all capable of entering—men with women, women with men—into relations of production of desire that overturn the statistical order of the sexes. Making love is not just becoming as one, or even two, but becoming as a hundred thousand. Desiring-machines or the nonhuman sex: not one or even two sexes, but *n* sexes. Schizoanalysis is the variable analysis of the *n* sexes in a subject, beyond the anthropomorphic representation that society imposes on this subject, and with which it represents its own sexuality. The schizoanalytic slogan of the desiring-revolution will be first of all: to each its own sexes.

3 | Psychoanalysis and Capitalism

The schizoanalytic argument is simple: desire is a machine, a synthesis of machines, a machinic arrangement—desiring-machines. The order of desire is the order of *production;* all production is at once desiring-production and social production. We therefore reproach psychoanalysis for having stifled this order of production, for having shunted it into *representation.* Far from showing the boldness of psychoanalysis, this idea of unconscious representation marks from the outset its bankruptcy or its abnegation: an unconscious that no longer produces, but is content to *believe.* The unconscious believes in Oedipus, it believes in castration, in the law. It is doubtless true that the psychoanalyst would be the first to say that, everything considered, belief is not an act of the unconscious; it is always the preconscious that believes. Shouldn't it even be said that it is the psychoanalyst who believes—the psychoanalyst in each of us? Would belief then be an effect on the conscious material that the unconscious representation exerts from a distance? But inversely, who or what reduced the unconscious to this state of representation, if not first of all a system of beliefs put in the place of productions? In reality, social production becomes alienated in allegedly autonomous beliefs at the same time that desiring-production becomes enticed into allegedly unconscious representations. And as we have seen, it is the same agency—the family—that performs this double operation, distorting and disfiguring social desiring-production, leading it into an impasse.

Thus the link between *representation-belief* and the family is not accidental; it is of the essence of representation to be a familial representation. But production is not thereby suppressed, it continues to rumble, to throb beneath the representative agency (*instance représentative*) that suffocates it, and that it in return can make resonate to the breaking point. Thus in order to keep an effective grip on the zones of production, representation must inflate itself with all the power of myth and tragedy, it must give a *mythic and tragic presentation* of the family—and a familial presentation of myth and tragedy. Yet aren't myth and tragedy, too, productions—forms of production? Certainly not; they are production only when brought into connection with real social production, real desiring-production. Otherwise they are ideological forms, which have taken the place of the units of production. *Who believes in all this*—Oedipus, castration, etc.? The Greeks? Then the Greeks did not produce in the same way they believed? The Hellenists? Do the Hellenists believe that the Greeks produced according to their beliefs? This is true at least of the nineteenth-century Hellenists, about whom Engels said: you'd think they really believed in all that—in myth, in tragedy. Is it the unconscious that represents itself through Oedipus and castration? Or is it the psychoanalyst—the psychoanalyst in us all, who represents the unconscious in this way? For never has Engels's remark regained so much meaning: you'd think the psychoanalysts really believed in all this—in myth, in tragedy. (They go on believing, whereas the Hellenists have long since stopped.)

The Schreber case again applies: Schreber's father invented and fabricated astonishing little machines, sadistico-paranoiac machines— for example head straps with a metallic shank and leather bands, for restrictive use on children, for making them straighten up and behave.* These machines play no role whatever in the Freudian analysis. Perhaps it would have been more difficult to crush the entire sociopolitical content of Schreber's delirium of these desiring-machines of the father had been taken into account, as well as their obvious participation in a pedagogical social machine in general. For the real question is this: of course the father acts on the child's unconscious—but does he act as a head of a family in an expressive familial transmission, or rather as the agent of a machine, in a machinic information or communication? Schreber's desiring-machines communicate with those of his father; but it is in this very way that they are from early childhood the libidinal investment of a social field. *In this field the father has a role only as an agent of production and antiproduction.* Freud, on the contrary, chooses the first path: it is not the father who indicates the action of machines, but just the opposite; thereafter there is no longer even any reason for considering machines, whether as desiring-machines or as social machines. In return, the father will be inflated with all the "forces of myth

---

*W. G. Niederland discovered and reproduced Schreber's father's machines: see especially, "Schreber, Father and Son," *Psychoanalytic Quarterly,* Vol. 28 (1959), pp. 151–69. Quite similar instruments of pedagogical torture are to be found in the Contesse de Ségur: thus "the good behavior belt," "with an iron plate for the back and an iron rod to hold the chin in place" (*Comédies et proverbes, On ne prend pas les mouches*).

and religion" and with phylogenesis, so as to ensure that the little familial representation has the appearance of being coextensive with the field of delirium. The production couple—the desiring-machines and the social field—gives way to a representative couple of an entirely different nature: family-myth. Once again, have you ever seen a child at play: how he already populates the technical social machines with his own desiring-machines, O sexuality—while the father or mother remains in the background, from whom the child borrows parts and gears according to his need, and who are there as agents of transmission, reception, and interception: kindly agents of production or suspicious agents of anti-production.

Why was mythic and tragic representation accorded such a sense-less privilege? Why were expressive forms and a whole *theater* installed there where there were fields, workshops, factories, units of production? The psychoanalyst parks his circus in the dumbfounded unconscious, a real P. T. Barnum in the fields and in the factory. That is what Miller, and already Lawrence, have to say against psychoanalysis (the living are not believers, the seers do not believe in myth and tragedy): "By retracing the paths to the earlier heroic life . . . you defeat the very element and quality of the heroic, for the hero never looks backward, nor does he ever doubt his powers. Hamlet was undoubtedly a hero to himself, and for every Hamlet born the only true course to pursue is the very course which Shakespeare describes. But the question, it seems to me, is this: are we *born* Hamlets? Were *you* born Hamlet? *Or did you not rather create the type in yourself?* Whether this be so or not, what seems infinitely more important is—*why revert to myth? . . .* This ideational rubbish out of which our world has erected its cultural edifice is now, by a critical irony, being given its poetic immolation, its mythos, *through a kind of writing which,* because it is *of* the disease and therefore *beyond,* clears the ground for fresh superstructures. (In my own mind the thought of 'fresh superstructures' is abhorrent, but this is merely the awareness of a process and not the process itself.) Actually, in process, I believe with each line I write that I am scouring the womb, giving it the *curette,* as it were. Behind this process lies the idea not of 'edifice' and 'superstructure,' which is culture and hence false, but of continuous birth, renewal, *life, life.* . . . In the myth there is no life for us. Only the myth lives in the myth. . . . *This ability to produce the myth is born out of awareness, out of ever-increasing consciousness.* That is why, speaking of the *schizophrenic nature* of our age, I said—'until the process is completed the belly of the world shall be the Third Eye.' Now, Brother Ambrose, just what did I mean by that? What could I mean except that from this intellectual world in which we are swimming there must body forth a new world; but this new world can only be bodied forth in so far as it is *conceived*. And to conceive there must first be desire, . . . Desire is instinctual and holy: it is only through desire that we bring about the immaculate conception."[13]

Everything is said in these pages from Miller: Oedipus (or Hamlet) led to the point of autocritique; the expressive forms—myth and tragedy—denounced as conscious beliefs or illusions, nothing more than ideas; the necessity of a scouring of the unconscious, schizoanalysis as a curettage of the unconscious; the matrical fissure in opposition to the line of castration; the splendid affirmation of the orphan- and producer-unconscious; the exaltation of the process as a schizophrenic process of deterritorialization that must produce a new earth; and even the functioning of the desiring-machines against tragedy, against "the fatal drama of the personality," against "the inevitable confusion between mask and actor." It is obvious that Miller's correspondent, Michael Fraenkel, does not understand. He talks like a psychoanalyst, or like a nineteenth-century Hellenist: yes, myth, tragedy, Oedipus, and Hamlet are good expressions, pregnant forms; they express the true permanent drama of desire and knowledge. Fraenkel calls to his aid all the commonplaces, Schopenhauer, and the Nietzsche of *The Birth of Tragedy*. He thinks Miller is unaware of these things, and never wonders for a second why Nietzsche himself broke with *The Birth of Tragedy*, why he stopped believing in tragic representation.

Michel Foucault has convincingly shown what break (*coupure*) introduced the irruption of production into the world of representation. Production can be that of labor or that of desire, it can be social or desiring, it calls forth forces that no longer permit themselves to be contained in representation, and it calls forth flows and breaks that break through representation, traversing it through and through: "an immense expanse of shade" extended beneath the level of representation.[14] And this collapse or sinking of the classical world of representation is assigned a date by Foucault; the end of the eighteenth and the beginning of the nineteenth century. So it seems that the situation is far more complex than we made it out to be, since psychoanalysis participates to the highest degree in this discovery of the units of production, which subjugate all possible representations rather than being subordinated to them. Just as Ricardo founds political or social economy by discovering quantitative labor as the principle of every representable value, Freud founds desiring-economy by discovering the quantitative libido as the principle of every representation of the objects and aims of desire. Freud discovers the subjective nature or abstract essence of desire, just as Ricardo discovers the subjective nature or abstract essence of labor, beyond all representations that would bind it to objects, to aims, or even to particular sources. Freud is thus the first to disengage desire itself (*le désir tout court*), as Ricardo disengages labor itself (*le travail tout court*), and thereby the sphere of production that effectively eclipses representation. And subjective abstract desire, like subjective abstract labor, is inseparable from a movement of deterritorialization that discovers the interplay of machines and their agents underneath all the specific determinations that still linked desire or labor to a given person, to a given object in the framework of representation.

Desiring-production and machines, psychic apparatuses and machines of desire, desiring-machines and the assembling of an analytic machine suited to decode them: the domain of free syntheses where everything is possible; partial connections, included disjunctions, nomadic conjunctions, polyvocal flows and chains, transductive* breaks; the relation of desiring-machines as formations of the unconscious with the molar formations that they constitute statistically in organized crowds; and the apparatus of social and psychic repression resulting from these formations—such is the composition of the analytic field. And this subrepresentative field will continue to survive and work, even through Oedipus, even through myth and tragedy, which nevertheless mark the reconciliation of psychoanalysis with representation. The fact remains that a conflict cuts across the whole of psychoanalysis, the conflict between mythic and tragic familial representation and social and desiring-production. For myth and tragedy are systems of symbolic representations that still refer desire to determinate exterior conditions as well as to particular objective codes—the body of the Earth, the despotic body—and that in this way confound the discovery of the abstract or subjective essence. It has been remarked in this context that each time Freud brings to the fore the study of the psychic apparatuses, the social and desiring-machines, the mechanisms of the drives, and the institutional mechanisms, his interest in myth and tragedy tends to diminish, while at the same time he denounces in Jung, then in Rank, the re-establishment of an exterior representation of the essence of desire as an objective desire, alienated in myth or tragedy.†

*For a definition of transduction with respect to production and representation, see "Interview/*Félix Guattari*" in *Diacritics: a review of contemporary criticism,* Fall 1974, p. 39: "Signs work as much as matter. Matter expresses as much as signs. . . . Transduction is the idea that, in essence, something is conducted, something happens between chains of semiotic expression, and material chains." (*Translators' note.*)

†Didier Anzieu distinguishes between two periods in particular: 1906–1920, which "constitutes the great period of mythological works in the history of psychoanalysis"; then a period of relative discredit, as Freud turns toward the problems of the second topography [*Translators' note:* the id, ego, and super ego], and the relationships between desire and institutions, and takes less and less of an interest in a systematic exploration of myths ("Freud et la mythologie," *Incidences de la psychanalyse,* no. 1 [1970], pp. 126–29).

How can this very complex ambivalence of psychoanalysis be explained? Several different things must be distinguished. In the first place, symbolic representation indeed grasps the essence of desire, but by referring it to large "objectities" (*objectités*)* as to the specific elements that determine its objects, aims, and sources. It is in this way that myth ascribes desire to the element of the earth as a full body, and to the territorial code that distributes prescriptions and prohibitions. Likewise tragedy ascribes desire to the full body of the despot and to the corresponding imperial code. Consequently, the understanding of symbolic representations may consist in a systematic phenomenology of these elements and objectities (as in the old Hellenists or even Jung); or else these representations may be understood by historical study that assigns them to their real and objective social conditions (as with recent Hellenists). Viewed in the latter fashion, representation implies a certain lag, and expresses less a stable element than the conditioned passage from one element to another: mythic representation does not express the element of the earth, but rather the conditions under which this element fades before the despotic element; and tragic representation does not express the despotic element properly speaking, but the conditions under which—in fifth-century Greece, for example—this element diminishes in favor of the new order of the city-state.[15] It is obvious that neither one of these ways of treating myth or tragedy is suited to the psychoanalytic approach. The psychoanalytic method is quite different: rather than referring symbolic representation to determinate objectities and to objective social conditions, psychoanalysis refers them to the subjective and universal essence of desire as libido. Thus the operation of *decoding* in psychoanalysis can no longer signify what it signifies in the sciences of man; the discovery of the secret of such and such a code. Psychoanalysis must undo the codes so as to attain the quantitative and qualitative flows of libido that traverse dreams, fantasies, and pathological formations as well as myth, tragedy, and the social formations. Psychoanalytic interpretation does not consist in competing with codes, adding a code to the codes already recognized, but in decoding in an absolute way, in eliciting something that is uncodable by virtue of its polymorphism and its polyvocity.† It appears then that the

objectités: This term corresponds to the German *objektität*. The following definition appears in *Vocabulaire technique et critique de la philosophie* (Paris: Presses Universitaires de France, 1968): "the form in which the thing-in-itself, the real, appears as an object." (*Translators' note.*)

†It cannot be said, therefore, that psychoanalysis adds a code—a psychological one—to the social codes through which histories and mythologists explain myths. Freud pointed this out apropos dreams: it is not a question of a deciphering process according to a code. In this regard see Jacques Derrida's comments in *L'écriture et la différence* (Paris: Editions du Seuil, 1967), pp. 310ff.: "It is doubtless true that [dream writing] works with a mass of elements codified in the course of an individual or collective history. But in its operations, its lexicon, and its syntax, a purely idiomatic residue remains

interest psychoanalysis has in myth (or in tragedy) is an essentially critical interest, since the specificity of myth, understood objectively, must melt under the rays of the subjective libido: it is indeed the world of representation that crumbles, or tends to crumble.

It follows that, in the second place, the link between psychoanalysis and capitalism is no less profound than that between political economy and capitalism. This discovery of the decoded and deterritorialized flows is the same as that which takes place for political economy and in social production, in the form of subjective abstract labor, and for psychoanalysis and in desiring-production, in the form of subjective abstract libido. As Marx says, in capitalism the essence becomes subjective—*the activity of production in general*—and abstract labor becomes something real from which all the preceding social formations can be reinterpreted from the point of view of a generalized decoding or a generalized process of deterritorialization: "The simplest abstraction, then, which modern economics places at the head of its discussions, and which expresses an immeasurably ancient relation valid in all forms of society, nevertheless achieves practical truth as an abstraction only as a category of the most modern society." This is also the case for desire as abstract libido and as subjective essence. Not that a simple parallelism should be drawn between capitalist social production and desiring-production, or between the flows of money-capital and the shit-flows of desire. The relationship is much closer: desiring-machines are in social machines and nowhere else, so that the conjunction of the decoded flows in the capitalist machine tends to liberate the free figures of a universal subjective libido. In short, the discovery of an activity of production *in general and without distinction,* as it appears in capitalism, is the identical discovery of *both* political economy *and* psychoanalysis, beyond the determinate systems of representation.

Obviously this does not mean that the capitalist being, or the being in capitalism, desires to work or that he works according to his desire. But the identity of desire and labor is not a myth, it is rather the active utopia par excellence that designates the capitalist limit to be overcome through desiring-production. But why, precisely, is desiring-production situated at the always counteracted limit of capitalism? Why, at the same time as it discovers the subjective essence of desire and labor—a common essence, inasmuch as it is the activity of production in general—is capitalism continually realienating this essence, and without interruption, in a repressive machine that divides the essence in two, and maintains it divided—abstract labor on the one hand, abstract desire on

irreducible, that must carry the whole weight of the interpretation, in the communication among unconsciouses. The dreamer invents his own grammar."

the other: political economy *and* psychoanalysis, political economy *and* libidinal economy? Here we are able to appreciate the full extent to which psychoanalysis belongs to capitalism. For as we have seen, capitalism indeed has as its limit the decoded flows of desiring-production, but it never stops repelling them by binding them in an axiomatic that takes the place of the codes. Capitalism is inseparable from the movement of deterritorialization, but this movement is exorcised through factitious and artificial reterritorializations. Capitalism is constructed on the ruins of the territorial and the despotic, the mythic and the tragic representations, but it re-establishes them in its own service and in another form, as images of capital.

Marx summarizes the entire matter by saying that the subjective abstract essence is discovered by capitalism only to be put in chains all over again, to be subjugated and alienated—no longer, it is true, in an exterior and independent element as objectity, but in the element, itself subjective, of private property: "What was previously being external to oneself—man's externalization in the thing—has merely become the act of externalizing—the process of alienating." It is, in fact, the form of private property that conditions the conjunction of the decoded flows, which is to say their axiomatization in a system where the flows of the means of production, as the property of the capitalists, is directly related to the flow of so-called free labor, as the "property" of the workers (so that the State restrictions on the substance or the content of private property do not at all affect this form). It is also the form of private property that constitutes the center of the factitious reterritorializations of capitalism. And finally, it is this form that produces the images filling the capitalist field of immanence, "the" capitalist, "the" worker, etc. In other terms, capitalism indeed implies the collapse of the great objective determinate representations, for the benefit of production as the universal interior essence, but it does not thereby escape the world of representation. It merely performs a vast conversion of this world, by attributing to it the new form of an infinite subjective representation.*

We seem to be straying from the main concern of psychoanalysis, yet never have we been so close. For here again, as we have seen previously, it is in the interiority of its movement that capitalism requires and institutes not only a social axiomatic, but an application of this axiomatic to the privatized family. Representation would never be able to ensure its own conversion without this application that furrows deep into it, cleaves it, and forces it back upon itself. Thus subjective

*Michel Foucault shows that "the human sciences" found their principle in production and were constituted on the collapse of representation, but that they immediately re-establish a new type of representation, as unconscious representation (*The Order of Things* [see reference note 14], pp. 352–67).

abstract Labor as represented in private property has, as its correlate, subjective abstract Desire as represented in the privatized family. Psychoanalysis undertakes the analysis of this second term, as political economy analyzes the first. Psychoanalysis is the technique of application, for which political economy is the axiomatic. In a word, psychoanalysis disengages the second pole in the very movement of capitalism, which substitutes the infinite subjective representation for the large determinate objective representations. It is in fact essential that the limit of the decoded flows of desiring-production be doubly exorcised, doubly displaced, once by the position of immanent limits that capitalism does not cease to reproduce on an ever expanding scale, and again by the marking out of an interior limit that reduces this social reproduction to restricted familial reproduction.

Consequently, the ambiguity of psychoanalysis in relation to myth or tragedy has the following explanation: psychoanalysis undoes them as objective representations, and discovers in them the figures of a subjective universal libido; but it reanimates them, and promotes them as subjective representations that extend the mythic and tragic contents to infinity. Psychoanalysis does treat myth and tragedy, but it treats them *as* the dreams and the fantasies of private man, *Homo familia*— and in fact dream and fantasy are to myth and tragedy as private property is to public property. What acts in myth and tragedy at the level of objective elements is therefore reappropriated and raised to a higher level by psychoanalysis, but as an unconscious dimension of subjective representation (myth as humanity's *dream*). What acts as an objective and public element—the Earth, the Despot—is now taken up again, but as the expression of a subjective and private reterritorialization: Oedipus is the fallen despot—banished, deterritorialized—but a reterritorialization is engineered, using the Oedipus complex conceived of as the daddy-mommy-me of today's everyman. Psychoanalysis and the Oedipus complex gather up all beliefs, all that has ever been believed by humanity, but only in order to raise it to the condition of a *denial* that preserves belief without believing in it (it's only a dream: the strictest piety today asks for nothing more). Whence this double impression, that psychoanalysis is opposed to mythology no less than to mythologists, but at the same time extends myth and tragedy to the dimensions of the subjective universal: if Oedipus himself "has no complex," the Oedipus complex has no Oedipus, just as narcissism has no Narcissus.* Such is

*Didier Anzieu, "Freud et la mythologie," pp. 124, 128: "Freud grants myth no specificity. This is one of the points that have most seriously encumbered the subsequent relations between psychoanalysts and anthropologists. . . . Freud undertakes a veritable leveling. . . . The article 'On Narcissism: An Introduction,' which constitutes an important step toward the revision of the theory of the drives, contains no allusion to the myth of Narcissus."

the ambivalence that traverses psychoanalysis, and that extends beyond the specific problem of myth and tragedy: with one hand psychoanalysis undoes the system of objective representations (myth, tragedy) for the benefit of the subjective essence conceived as desiring-production, while with the other hand it reverses this production in a system of subjective representations (dream and fantasy, with myth and tragedy posited as their developments or projections). Images, nothing but images. What is left in the end is an intimate familial theater, the theater of private man, which is no longer either desiring-production or objective representation. The unconscious as a stage. A whole theater put in the place of production, a theater that disfigures this production even more than could tragedy and myth when reduced to their meager ancient resources.

Myth, tragedy, dream, and fantasy—and myth and tragedy reinterpreted in terms of dream and fantasy—are the representative series that psychoanalysis substitutes for the line of production: social and desiring-production. A theater series, instead of a production series. But why in fact does representation, having become subjective representation, assume this theatrical form ("There is a mysterious tie between psychoanalysis and the theater")? We are familiar with the eminently modern reply of certain recent authors: the theater elicits the finite structure of the infinite subjective representation. What is meant by "elicit" is very complex, since the structure can never present more than its own absence, or represent something not represented in the representation: but it is claimed that the theater's privilege is that of staging this metaphoric and metonymic causality that marks both the presence and the absence of the structures in its effects. While André Green expresses reservations about the adequacy of the structure, he does so only in the name of a theater necessary for the actualization of this structure, playing the role of revealer, a place by which the structure becomes visible.* In her fine analysis of the phenomenon of belief, Octave Mannoni likewise uses the theater model to show how the denial of belief in fact implies a transformation of belief, under the effect of a structure that the theater embodies or places on stage.[16] We should understand that representation, when it ceases to be objective, when it becomes subjective infinite—that is to say, imaginary—effectively loses all consistency, unless it is supported by a structure that determines the

*André Green goes very far in the analysis of the representation-theater-structure-unconscious relations: *Un oeil en trop* (Paris: Editions de Minuit, 1969), Prologue (especially p. 43, concerning "the representation of the nonrepresented in representation"). However, the criticism that Green makes of the structure is not conducted in the name of production, but in the name of representation, and invokes the necessity for extrastructural factors that must do nothing more than reveal the structure, and reveal it as Oedipal.

place and the functions of the subject of representation, as well as the objects represented as images, and the formal relations between them all. "Symbolic" thus no longer designates the relation of representation to an objectity as an element; it designates the ultimate elements of subjective representation, pure signifiers, pure nonrepresented representatives whence the subjects, the objects, and their relationships all derive. In this way the structure designates the unconscious of subjective representation. The series of this representation now presents itself: (imaginary) infinite subjective representation–theatrical representation–structural representation. And precisely because the theater is thought to stage the latent structure, as well as to embody its elements and relations, it is in a position to reveal the universality of this structure, even in the objective representations that it salvages and reinterprets in terms of hidden representatives, their migrations and variable relations. All former beliefs are gathered up and revived in the name of a structure of the unconscious: we are still pious. Everywhere, the great game of the symbolic signifier that is embodied in the signifieds of the Imaginary—Oedipus as a universal metaphor.

Why the theater? How bizarre, this theatrical and pasteboard unconscious: the theater taken as the model of production. Even in Louis Althusser we are witness to the following operation: the discovery of social production as "machine" or "machinery," irreducible to the world of objective representation (*Vorstellung*); but immediately the reduction of the machine to structure, the identification of production with a structural and theatrical representation (*Darstellung*).[17] Now the same is true of both desiring-production and social production: every time that production, rather than being apprehended in its originality, in its reality, becomes *reduced (rabattue)* in this manner to a representational space, it can no longer have value except by its own absence, and it appears as a lack within this space. In search of the structure in psychoanalysis, Moustafa Safouan is able to present it as a "contribution to a theory of lack." It is in the structure that the fusion of desire with the impossible is performed, with lack defined as castration. From the structure there arises the most austere song in honor of castration— yes, yes, we enter the order of desire through the gates of castration— once desiring-production has spread out in the space of a representation that allows it to go on living only as an absence and a lack unto itself. For a *structural unity* is imposed on the desiring-machines that joins them together in a molar aggregate; the partial objects are referred to a totality that can appear only as that which the partial objects lack, and as that which is lacking unto itself while being lacking in them (the Great Signifier "symbolizable by the inherency of a -1 in the ensemble of signifiers"). Just how far will one go in the development of a lack of lack traversing the structure? Such is the structural operation: it distributes lack in the molar aggregate. The limit of desiring-production—the border line separating the molar aggregates and their molecular elements, the objective representations and the machines of desire—is now completely displaced. The limit now passes only within the molar aggregate itself, inasmuch as the latter is furrowed by the line of castration. The formal operations of the structure are those of extrapolation, application, and biunivocalization, which reduce the social aggregate of departure to a familial aggregate of destination, with the familial relation becoming "metaphorical for all the others" and hindering the molecular productive elements from following their own line of escape.

When André Green looks for the reasons that establish the affinity of psychoanalysis with the theatrical and structural representation it makes visible, he offers two that are especially striking: the theater raises the familial relation to the condition of a universal metaphoric structural relation, whence the imaginary place and interplay of persons derives; and inversely, the theater forces the play and the working of machines into the wings, behind a limit that has become impassible (exactly as in fantasy the machines are there, but *behind the wall*). In short, the displaced limit no longer passes between objective representation and desiring-production, but between the two poles of subjective representation, as infinite imaginary representation, and as finite structural representation. Thereafter it is possible to oppose these two aspects to each other, the imaginary variations that tend toward the night of the indeterminate or the nondifferentiated, and the symbolic invariant that traces the path of the differentiations: the same thing is found all over, following a rule of inverse relation, or double bind. All of production is conducted into the double impasse of subjective representation. Oedipus can always be consigned to the Imaginary, but no matter, it will be encountered again, stronger and more whole, more lacking and triumphant by the very fact that it is lacking, it will be encountered again in its entirety in symbolic castration. And it's a sure thing that structure affords us no means for escaping familialism; on the contrary, it adds another turn, it attributes a universal metaphoric value to the family at the very moment it has lost its objective literal values. Psychoanalysis makes its ambition clear: to relieve the waning family, to replace the broken-down familial bed with the psychoanalyst's couch, to make it so that the "analytic situation" is *incestuous in its essence,* so that it is its own proof or voucher, on a par with Reality.[18]

In the final analysis that is indeed what is at issue, as Octave Mannoni shows: how can belief continue after repudiation, how can we continue to be pious? We have repudiated and lost all our beliefs that proceeded by way of objective representations. The earth is dead, the desert is growing: the old father is dead, the territorial father, and the son too, the despot Oedipus. We are alone with our bad conscience and our boredom, our life where nothing happens; nothing left but images that revolve within the infinite subjective representation. We will muster all our strength so as to believe in these images, from the depths of a structure that governs our relationships with them and our identifications as so many effects of a symbolic signifier. The "good identification." We are all Archie Bunker at the theater, shouting out before Oedipus: there's my kind of guy, there's my kind of guy! Everything, the myth of the earth, the tragedy of the despot, is taken up again as shadows projected on a stage. The great territorialities have fallen into ruin, but the structure proceeds with all the subjective and private reterritorializations. What a perverse operation psychoanalysis is, where this neoidealism, this rehabilitated cult of castration, this ideology of lack culminates: *the anthropomorphic representation of sex!* In truth, they don't know what they are doing, nor what mechanism of repression they are fostering, for their intentions are often progressive. But no one today can enter an analyst's consulting room without at least being aware that everything has been *played out* in advance: Oedipus and castration, the Imaginary and the Symbolic, the great lesson of the inadequacy of being or of dispossession. Psychoanalysis as a gadget, Oedipus as a reterritorialization, a retimbering of modern man on the "rock" of castration.

The path marked out by Lacan led in a completely different direction. He is not content to turn, like the analytic squirrel, inside the wheel of the Imaginary and the Symbolic; he refuses to be caught up in the Oedipal Imaginary and the oedipalizing structure, the imaginary identity of persons and the structural unity of machines, everywhere knocking against the impasses of a molar representation that the family closes round itself. What is the use of going from the imaginary dual order to the symbolic third (or fourth), if the latter is biunivocalizing whereas the first is biunivocalized? As partial objects the desiring-machines undergo two totalizations, one when the socius confers on them a structural unity under a symbolic signifier acting as absence and lack in an aggregate of departure, the other when the family imposes on them a personal unity with imaginary signifieds that distribute, that "vacuolize" lack in an aggregate of destination: a double abduction of the orphan machines, inasmuch as the structure applies its articulation to them, inasmuch as the parents lay their fingers on them. To trace back from images to the structure would have little significance and would not rescue us from representation, *if the structure did not have a reverse side* that is like the real production of desire.

This reverse side is the "real inorganization" of the molecular elements: partial objects that enter into indirect syntheses or interactions, since they are not partial (*partiels*) in the sense of extensive parts, but rather partial ("*partiaux*")* like the intensities under which a unit of matter always fills space in varying degrees (the eye, the mouth, the anus as degrees of matter); pure positive multiplicities where everything is possible, without exclusiveness or negation, syntheses operating without a plan, where the connections are transverse, the disjunctions included, the conjunctions polyvocal, indifferent to their underlying support, since this matter that serves them precisely as a support receives no specificity from any structural or personal unity, but appears as the body without organs that fills the space each time an intensity fills it; signs of desire that compose a signifying chain but that are not themselves signifying, and do not answer to the rules of a linguistic game of chess, but instead to the lottery drawings that sometimes cause a word to be chosen, sometimes a design, sometimes a thing or a piece of a thing, depending on one another only by the order of the random drawings, and holding together only by the absence of a link (nonlocalizable connections), having no other statutory condition than that of being dispersed elements of desiring-machines that are themselves dispersed.† It is this entire reverse side of the structure that Lacan discovers, with the "o" as machine, and the "O" as nonhuman sex: schizophrenizing the analytic field, instead of oedipalizing the psychotic field.

Everything hinges on the way in which the structure is elicited from the machines, according to planes of consistency or of structuration, and

---

*partiel: partial, incomplete; *partial (pl. partiaux):* partial, biased, as a biased judge. We have chosen to translate *objets partiels* throughout as "partial objects" rather than as "part-objects" (as in Melanie Klein), in anticipation of this point in the book where Deleuze and Guattari shift from Klein's concept of the partial objects as "part of," hence as an incomplete part of a lost unity or totality (molar), toward a concept of the partial objects as biased, evaluating intensities that know no lack and are capable of selecting organs (molecular). (*Translators' note.*)

†Lacan, *Ecrits* (see reference note 19), pp. 657–59. Serge Leclaire has made a profound attempt to define within this perspective the reverse side of the structure as the "pure being of desire" ("La réalité du désir" [reference note 26], pp. 242–49). In desire he sees a multiplicity of prepersonal singularities, or indifferent elements that are defined precisely by the absence of a link. But this absence of a link—and of a meaning—is positive, "it constitutes the specific force of coherence of this constellation." Of course, meaning and link can always be re-established, if only by inserting fragments assumed to be forgotten: this is even the very function of Oedipus. But "*if the analysis again discovers the link between two elements, this is a sign that they are not the ultimate, irreducible terms of the unconscious.*" It will be noticed here that Leclaire uses the exact criterion of real distinction in Spinoza and Leibniz: the ultimate elements (the infinite attributes) are attributable to God, because they do not depend on one another and do not tolerate any relation of opposition or contradiction among themselves. The absence of all direct links guarantees their common participation in the divine substance. Likewise for the partial objects and the body without organs: the body without organs is substance itself, and the partial objects, the ultimate attributes or elements of substance.

lines of selection that correspond to the large statistical aggregates or molar formations, and that determine the links and reduce production to representation—*that* is where the disjunctions become exclusive (and the connections global, and the conjunctions, biunivocal), at the same time that the support gains a specificity under a structural unity, and the signs themselves become signifying under the action of a despotic symbol that totalizes them in the name of its own absence or withdrawal. Yes, in fact, there the production of desire can be *represented* only in terms of an extrapolated sign that joins together all the elements of production in a constellation of which it is not itself a part. There the absence of a tie necessarily appears as an absence, and no longer as a positive force. There desire is necessarily referred to a missing term, whose very essence is to be lacking. The signs of desire, being nonsignifying, become signifying in representation only in terms of a signifier of absence or lack. The structure is formed and appears only in terms of the symbolic term defined as a lack. The great Other as the nonhuman sex gives way, in representation, to a signifier of the great Other as an always missing term, the all-too-human sex, the phallus of molar castration.*

Here too Lacan's approach appears in all its complexity; for it is certain that he does not enclose the unconscious in an Oedipal structure. He shows on the contrary that Oedipus is imaginary, nothing but an image, a myth; that this or these images are produced by an oedipalizing structure; that this structure acts only insofar as it reproduces the element of castration, which itself is not imaginary but symbolic. There we have the three major planes of structuration, which correspond to the molar aggregates: Oedipus as the imaginary reterritorialization of private man, produced under the structural conditions of capitalism, inasmuch as capitalism reproduces and revives the archaism of the imperial symbol or the vanished despot. All three are necessary—precisely in order to lead Oedipus to the point of its self-critique. The task undertaken by Lacan is to lead Oedipus to such a point. (Likewise, Elisabeth Roudinesco has clearly seen that, in Lacan, the hypothesis of an unconscious-as-language does not closet the unconscious in a linguistic structure, but leads linguistics to the point of its autocritique, by showing how the structural organization of signifiers still depends on a despotic Great Signifier acting as an archaism.)[19]

*Lacan, *Ecrits* (see reference note 19), p. 819: "For want of this signifier, all the others would represent nothing." Serge Leclaire shows how the structure is organized around a missing term, or rather a signifier of lack: "It is the elective signifier of the absence of a link, the phallus, that we find again in the unique privilege of its relation to the essence of lack—an emblem of difference par excellence—the irreducible difference, the difference between the sexes. . . . If man can talk, this is because at one point in the language system there is a guarantor of the irreducibility of lack: the phallic signifier" ("La réalité du désir" [see reference note 26], p. 251). How strange all this is!

What is this point of self-criticism? It is the point where the structure, beyond the images that fill it and the Symbolic that conditions it within representation, reveals its reverse side as a positive principle of nonconsistency that dissolves it: where desire is shifted into the order of production, related to its molecular elements, and where it lacks nothing, because it is defined as *the natural and sensuous objective being,* at the same time as the Real is defined as *the objective being of desire.* For the unconscious of schizoanalysis is unaware of persons, aggregates, and laws, and of images, structures, and symbols. It is an orphan, just as it is an anarchist and an atheist. It is not an orphan in the sense that the father's name would designate an absence, but in the sense that the unconscious reproduces itself wherever the names of history designate present intensities ("the sea of proper names"). The unconscious is not figurative, since its *figural* is abstract, the figure-schiz. It is not structural, nor is it symbolic, for its reality is that of the Real in its very production, in its very inorganization. It is not representative, but solely machinic, and productive.

Destroy, destroy. The task of schizoanalysis goes by way of destruction—a whole scouring of the unconscious, a complete curettage. Destroy Oedipus, the illusion of the ego, the puppet of the superego, guilt, the law, castration. It is not a matter of pious destructions, such as those performed by psychoanalysis under the benevolent neutral eye of the analyst. For these are Hegel-style destructions, ways of conserving. How is it that the celebrated neutrality, and what psychoanalysis calls—dares to call—the disappearance or the dissolution of the Oedipus complex, do not make us burst into laughter? We are told that Oedipus is indispensable, that it is the source of every possible differentiation, and that it saves us from the terrible nondifferentiated mother. But this terrible mother, the sphinx, is herself part of Oedipus; her nondifferentiation is merely the reverse of the exclusive differentiations created by Oedipus, she is herself created by Oedipus: Oedipus necessarily operates in the form of this double impasse. We are told that Oedipus in its turn must be overcome, and that this is achieved through castration, latency, desexualization, and sublimation. But what is castration if not still Oedipus, to the nth power, now symbolic, and therefore all the more virulent? And what is latency, this pure fable, if not the silence imposed on desiring-machines so that Oedipus can develop, be fortified in us, so that it can accumulate its poisonous sperm and gain the time necessary for propagating itself, and for passing on to our future children? And what is the elimination of castration anxiety in its turn—desexualization and sublimation—if not divine acceptance of, and infinite resignation to, bad conscience, which consists for the woman of "the appeased wish for a penis . . . destined to be converted into a wish for a baby and for a husband," and for the man in assuming his passive attitude and in "[subjecting] himself to a father substitute"?[20]

We are all the more "extricated" from Oedipus as we become a living example, an advertisement, a theorem in action, so as to attract our children to Oedipus: we have evolved in Oedipus, we have been structured in Oedipus, and under the neutral and benevolent eye of the substitute, we have learned the song of castration, the lack-of-being-that-is-life; "yes it is through castration/that we gain access/to Deeeeesire." What one calls the disappearance of Oedipus is Oedipus become an idea. Only the idea can inject the venom. Oedipus has to become an idea so that it sprouts each time a new set of arms and legs, lips and mustache: "In tracing back the 'memory deaths' your ego becomes a sort of mineral theorem which constantly proves the futility of living."[21] We have been triangulated in Oedipus, and will triangulate in it in turn. From the family to the couple, from the couple to the family. In actuality, the benevolent neutrality of the analyst is very limited: it ceases the instant one stops responding daddy-mommy. It ceases the instant one introduces a little desiring-machine—the tape-recorder—into the analyst's office; it ceases as soon as a flow is made to circulate that does not let itself be stopped by Oedipus, the mark of the triangle (they tell you you have a libido that is too viscous, or too liquid, contraindications for analysis).

When Fromm denounces the existence of a psychoanalytic bureaucracy, he still doesn't go far enough, because he doesn't see what the stamp of this bureaucracy is, and that an appeal to the pre-oedipal is not enough to escape this stamp: the pre-oedipal, like the post-oedipal, is still a way of bringing all of desiring-production—the anoedipal—back to Oedipus. When Reich denounces the way in which psychoanalysis joins forces with social repression, he still doesn't go far enough, because he doesn't see that the tie linking psychoanalysis with capitalism is not merely ideological, that it is infinitely closer, infinitely tighter; and that psychoanalysis depends directly on an economic mechanism (whence its relations with money) through which the decoded flows of desire, as taken up in the axiomatic of capitalism, must necessarily be reduced to a familial field where the application of this axiomatic is carried out: Oedipus as the last word of capitalist consumption—sucking away at daddy-mommy, being blocked and triangulated on the couch; "So it's . . ." Psychoanalysis, no less than the bureaucratic or military apparatus, is a mechanism for the absorption of surplus value, nor is this true from the outside, extrinsically; rather, its very form and its finality are marked by this social function. It is not the pervert, nor even the autistic person, who escapes psychoanalysis; the whole of psychoanalysis is an immense perversion, a drug, a radical break with reality, starting with the reality of desire; it is a narcissism, a monstrous autism: the characteristic autism and the intrinsic perversion of the machine of capital. At its most autistic, psychoanalysis is no longer measured against any reality, it no longer opens to any outside, but becomes itself the test of reality and the guarantor of its own test: reality as the lack to which the inside and the outside, departure and arrival, are reduced. Psychoanalysis *index sui,* with no other *reference* than itself or "the analytic situation."

Psychoanalysis states clearly that unconscious representation can never be apprehended independently of the deformations, disguises, or displacements it undergoes. Unconscious representation therefore comprises essentially, by virtue of its own *law,* a represented that is displaced in relation to an agency in a constant state of displacement. But from this, two unwarranted conclusions are drawn: that this agency can be discovered by way of the displaced represented; and this, precisely because this agency itself belongs to representation, as a nonrepresented representative, or as a lack "that juts out into the overfull (*trop-plein*) of a representation." This results from the fact that displacement refers to very different movements: at times, the movement through which desiring-production is continually overcoming the limit, becoming deterritorialized, causing its flows to escape, going beyond the threshold of representation; at times, on the contrary, the movement through which the limit itself is displaced, and now passes to the interior of the representation that performs the artificial reterritorializations of desire. If the displacing agency can be concluded from the displaced, this is only true in the second sense, where molar representation is organized around a representative that displaces the represented. But this is certainly not true in the first sense, where the molecular elements are continually passing through the links in the chain. We have seen in this perspective how the law of representation perverted the productive forces of the unconscious, and induced in its very structure a false image that caught desire in its trap (the impossibility of concluding from the prohibition as to what is actually prohibited). Yes, Oedipus is indeed the displaced represented; yes, castration is indeed the representative, the displacing agency (*le déplaçant*), the signifier—but none of that constitutes an unconscious material, nor does any of it concern the productions of the unconscious. Oedipus, castration, the signifier, etc., exist at the crossroads of two operations of capture: one where repressive social production becomes replaced by beliefs, the other where repressed desiring-production finds itself replaced by representations. To be sure, it is not psychoanalysis that makes us believe: Oedipus and castration are demanded, then demanded again, and these demands come from elsewhere and from deeper down. But psychoanalysis did find the following means, and fills the following function: causing beliefs to survive even after repudiation; causing those who no longer believe in anything to continue believing; reconstituting a private territory for them, a private Urstaat, a private capital (dreams as capital, said Freud).

That is why, inversely, schizoanalysis must devote itself with all its strength to the necessary destructions. Destroying beliefs and representations, theatrical scenes. And when engaged in this task no activity will be too malevolent. Causing Oedipus and castration to explode, brutally intervening each time the subject strikes up the song of myth or intones tragic lines, carrying him back *to the factory.* As Charlus says, "A lot we care about your grandmother, you little shit!" Oedipus and castration are no more than reactional formations, resistances, blockages, and armorings whose destruction can't come fast enough. Reich intuits a fundamental principle of schizoanalysis when he says that the destruction of resistances must not wait upon the discovery of the material.[22] But the reason for this is even more radical than he thought: there is no unconscious material, so that schizoanalysis has nothing to interpret. There are only resistances, and then machines desiring-machines. Oedipus is a resistance; if we have been able to speak of the intrinsically perverted nature of psychoanalysis, this is due to the fact that perversion in general is the artificial reterritorialization of the flows of desire, whose machines on the contrary are indices of deterritorialized production. The psychoanalyst reterritorializes on the couch, in the representation of Oedipus and castration. Schizoanalysis on the contrary must disengage the deterritorialized flows of desire, in the molecular elements of desiring-production. We should again call to mind the practical rule laid down by Leclaire, following Lacan, the rule of the right to non-sense as well as to the absence of a link: you will not have reached the ultimate and irreducible terms of the unconscious so long as you find or restore a link between two elements. (But how then can one see in this extreme dispersion—machines dispersed in every machine—nothing more than a pure "fiction" that must give way to Reality defined as a lack, with Oedipus and castration back at a gallop, at the same time that one reduces the absence of a link to a "signifier" of absence charged with representing the absence, with linking this absence itself, and with moving us back and forth from one pole of displacement to the other? One falls back into the molar hole while claiming to unmask the real.)

What complicates everything is that there is indeed a necessity for desiring-production to be induced from representation, to be discovered through its lines of escape. But this is true in a way altogether different from what psychoanalysis believes it to be. The decoded flows of desire form the free energy (libido) of the desiring-machines. The desiring-machines take form and train their sights along a tangent of deterritorialization that traverses the representative spheres, and that runs along the body without organs. Leaving, escaping, but while causing more escapes. The desiring-machines themselves are the flows-schizzes or the breaks-flows that break and flow at the same time on the body without organs: not the gaping wound represented in castration, but the myriad little connections, disjunctions, and conjunctions by which every machine produces a flow in relation to another that breaks it, and breaks a flow that another produces. But how would these decoded and deterritorialized flows of desiring-production keep from being reduced to some representative territoriality, how would they keep from forming for themselves yet another such territory, even if on the body without organs as the indifferent support for a last representation? Even those who are best at "leaving," those who make leaving into something as natural as being born or dying, those who set out in search of nonhuman sex—Lawrence, Miller—stake out a far-off territoriality that still forms an anthropomorphic and phallic representation: the Orient, Mexico, or Peru. Even the schizo's stroll or voyage does not effect great deterritorializations without borrowing from territorial circuits: the tottering walk of Molloy and his bicycle preserves the mother's room as the vestige of a goal; the vacillating spirals of *The Unnamable* keep the familial tower as an uncertain center where it continues to turn while treading its own underfoot; the infinite series of juxtaposed and unlocalized parks in *Watt* still contains a reference to Mr. Knott's house, the only one capable of "pushing the soul out-of-doors," but also of summoning it back to its place. We are all little dogs, we need circuits, and we need to be taken for walks. Even those best able to disconnect, to unplug themselves, enter into connections of desiring-machines that re-form little earths. Even Gisela Pankow's great deterritorialized subjects are led to discover the image of a family castle under the roots of the uprooted tree that crosses through their body without organs.[23]

Previously we distinguished two poles of delirium, one as the molecular schizophrenic line of escape, and the other as the paranoiac molar investment. But the perverted pole is equally opposed to the schizophrenic pole, just as the reconstitution of territorialities is opposed to the movement of deterritorialization. And if perversion in the narrowest sense of the word performs a certain very specific type of reterritorialization within the artifice, perversion in the broad sense comprises all the types of reterritorializations, not merely artificial, but also exotic, archaic, residual, private, etc.: thus Oedipus and psychoanalysis as perversion. Even Raymond Roussel's schizophrenic machines turn into perverse machines in a theater representing Africa. In short, there is no deterritorialization of the flows of schizophrenic desire that is not accompanied by global or local reterritorializations, reterritorializations that always reconstitute shores of representation. What is more, the force and the obstinacy of a deterritorialization can only be evaluated through the types of reterritorialization that represent it; the one is the reverse side of the other. Our loves are complexes of deterritorialization and reterritorialization. What we love is always a certain mulatto—male or female. The movement of deterritorialization can never be grasped in itself, one can only grasp its indices in relation to the territorial representations. Take the example of dreams: yes, dreams are Oedipal, and this comes as no surprise, since dreams are a perverse reterritorialization in relation to the deterritorialization of sleep and nightmares. But *why return to dreams,* why turn them into the royal road of desire and the unconscious, when they are in fact the manifestation of a superego, a superpowerful and superarchaized ego (the Urszene of the Urstaat)? Yet at the heart of dreams themselves—as with fantasy and delirium—machines function as indices of deterritorialization. In dreams there are always machines endowed with the strange property of passing from hand to hand, of escaping and causing circulations, of carrying and being carried away. The airplane of parental coitus, the father's car, the grandmother's sewing machine, the little brother's bicycle, all objects of flight and theft, stealing and stealing away—the machine is always infernal in the family dream. The machine introduces breaks and flows that prevent the dream from being reconfined in its scene and systematized within its representation. It makes the most of an irreducible factor of non-sense, which will develop elsewhere and from without, in the conjunctions of the real as such. Psychoanalysis, with its Oedipal stubbornness, has only a dim understanding of this; for one reterritorializes on persons and surroundings, but one deterritorializes on machines. Is it Schreber's father who acts through machines, or on the contrary is it the machines themselves that function through the father? *Psychoanalysis settles on the imaginary and structural representatives of reterritorialization, while schizoanalysis follows the machinic indices of deterritorialization.* The opposition still holds between the neurotic on the couch—as an ultimate and sterile land, the last exhausted colony—and the schizo out for a walk in a deterritorialized circuit.

The following excerpt from an article by Michel Cournot on Chaplin helps us understand what schizophrenic laughter is, as well as the schizophrenic line of escape or breakthrough, and the process as deterritorialization, with its machinic indices: "The moment Charlie Chaplin makes the board fall a second time on his head—a psychotic gesture—he provokes the spectator's laughter. Yes, but what laughter is this? And what spectator? For example, the question no longer applies at all, at this point in the film, of knowing whether the spectator must see the accident coming or be surprised by it. It is as though the spectator, at that very moment, were no longer in his seat, were no longer in a position to observe things. A kind of perceptive gymnastics has lead him, progressively, not to identify with the character of *Modern Times,* but to experience so directly the resistance of the events that he accompanies this character, has the same surprises, the same premonitions, the same habits as he. Thus it is that the famous *eating machine,* which in a sense, by its excess, is foreign to the film (Chaplin had invented it twenty-two years before the film), is merely the formal, absolute exercise that prepares for the conduct—also psychotic—of the worker trapped in the machine, with only his upside-down head sticking out, and who has Chaplin feed him his lunch, since it is lunch time. If laughter is a reaction that takes certain circuits, it can be said that Charlie Chaplin, as the film's sequences unfold, progressively *displaces* the reactions, causes them to recede, level by level, until the moment when the spectator is no longer master of his own circuits, and tends to spontaneously take either a shorter path, which is not passable, which is barred, or else a path that is very explicitly posted as leading nowhere. After having suppressed the spectator as such, Chaplin perverts the laughter, which comes to be like so many *short-circuits of a disconnected piece of machinery.* Critics have occasionally spoken of the pessimism of *Modern Times* and of the optimism of the final image. Neither term suits the film. Charles Chaplin in *Modern Times* sketches rather, *on a very small scale,* with a precise stroke, the finished design of several oppressive and fundamental manifestations. The leading character, played by Chaplin, has to be neither active nor passive, neither consenting nor insubordinate, since he is the pencil point that traces the design, he is the stroke itself. . . . That is why the final image is without optimism. One does not see what optimism would be doing at the conclusion of this statement. This man and this woman seen from the back, all black, whose shadows are not projected by any sun, advance toward nothing. The wireless telegraph poles that run along the left side of the road, the barren trees that dot the right side, do not meet at the horizon. There is no horizon. The bald hills facing the spectator only form a line that merges with the void hanging over them. Anyone can see that this man and this woman are no longer alive. There is no pessimism here either. What had to happen happened. They did not kill each other.

They were not brought down by the police. And it will not be necessary to go looking for the alibi of an accident. Charles Chaplin did not dwell on this. He went quickly, as usual. He traced the finished design."[24]

In its destructive task, schizoanalysis must proceed as quickly as possible, but it can also proceed only with great patience, great care, by successively undoing the representative territorialities and reterritorializations through which a subject passes in his individual history. For there are several layers, several planes of resistance that come from within or are imposed from without. Schizophrenia as a process, deterritorialization as a process, is inseparable from the stases that interrupt it, or aggravate it, or make it turn in circles, and reterritorialize it into neurosis, perversion, and psychosis. To a point where the process cannot extricate itself, continue on, and reach fulfillment, except insofar as it is capable of creating—what exactly?—a new land. In each case we must go back by way of old lands, study their nature, their density; we must seek to discover how the machinic indices are grouped on each of these lands that permit going beyond them. How can we reconquer the process each time, constantly resuming the journey on these lands— Oedipal familial lands of neurosis, artificial lands of perversion, clinical lands of psychosis? *In Search of Lost Time* as a great enterprise of schizoanalysis: all the planes are traversed until their molecular line of escape is reached, their schizophrenic breakthrough; thus in the kiss where Albertine's face jumps from one plane of consistency to another, in order to finally come undone in a nebula of molecules. The reader always risks stopping at a given plane and saying yes, *that* is where Proust is explaining himself. But the narrator-spider never ceases undoing webs and planes, resuming the journey, watching for the signs or the indices that operate like machines and that will cause him to go on further. This very movement is humor, black humor. Oh, the narrator does not homestead in the familial and neurotic lands of Oedipus, there where the global and personal connections are established; he does not remain there, he crosses these lands, he desecrates them, he penetrates them, he liquidates even his grandmother with a machine for tying shoes. The perverse lands of homosexuality, where the exclusive disjunctions of women with women, and men with men, are established, likewise break apart in terms of the machinic indices that undermine them. The psychotic earths, with their conjunctions in place (Charlus is therefore surely mad, and Albertine too, perhaps!), are traversed in their turn to a point where the problem is no longer posed, no longer posed in this way. The narrator continues his own affair, until he reaches the *unknown country,* his own, the *unknown land,* which alone is created by his own work in progress, the *Search of Lost Time* "*in progress,*" functioning as a desiring-machine capable of collecting and dealing with all the indices. He goes toward these new regions where the connections are always partial and nonpersonal, the conjunctions nomadic and polyvocal, the disjunctions included, where homosexuality and hetero-sexuality cannot be distinguished any longer: the world of transverse communications, where the finally conquered nonhuman sex mingles with the flowers, a new earth where desire functions according to its molecular elements and flows. Such a voyage does not necessarily imply great movements in extension; it becomes immobile, in a room and on a body without organs—an intensive voyage that undoes all the lands for the benefit of the one it is creating.

The patient resumption of the process, or on the contrary its interruption—the two are so closely interrelated that they can only be evaluated each within the other. How would the schizo's voyage be possible independent of certain circuits, how could it exist without a land? But inversely, how can we be certain that these circuits don't reconstitute the lands—only too well known—of the asylum, the arti-fice, or the family? We always return to the same question: from what does the schizo suffer, he whose sufferings are unspeakable? Does he suffer from the process itself, or rather from its interruptions, when he is neuroticized in the family, in the land of Oedipus; when the one who does not allow himself to be Oedipalized is psychoticized in the land of the asylum; when the one who escapes the family and the asylum is perverted in the artificial locales? Perhaps there is only one illness, neurosis, the Oedipal decay against which all the pathogenic interrup-tions of the process should be measured. Most of the modern endeavors—outpatient centers, inpatient hospitals, social clubs for the sick, family care, institutions, and even antipsychiatry—remain threat-ened by a common danger, a danger which Jean Oury has been able to analyze in depth: how does one avoid the institution's re-forming an asylum structure, or constituting perverse and reformist artificial socie-ties, or residual paternalistic or mothering pseudo families? We do not have in mind the so-called community psychiatry endeavors, whose admitted purpose is to triangulate, to Oedipalize everyone—people, animals, and things—to a point where we will witness a new race of sick people implore by reaction that they be given back an asylum, or a little Beckettian land, a garbage can, so they can become catatonic in a corner. But in a less openly repressive manner, who says that the family is a good place, a good circuit for the deterritorialized schizo? Such a thing would be very surprising, to say the least: "the therapeutic potentialities of the familial surroundings." The whole town, then, the whole neighborhood? What molar unit will constitute a sufficiently nomadic circuit? How does one prevent the unit chosen, even if a specific institution, from constituting a perverted society of tolerance, a mutual-aid society that hides the real problems? Will the structure of the institution save it? But how will the structure break its relationship with neuroticizing, perverting, psychoticizing castration? How will this structure produce anything but a subjugated group? How will it give free play to the process, when its entire molar organization has the function of binding the molecular process? Even antipsychiatry—especially sensitive to the schizophrenic breakthrough and the intense voyage—tires out and proposes the image of a subject-group that would become immediately reperverted, with former schizos guiding the most recent ones, and, as relays, little chapels, or better yet, a convent in Ceylon.

The only thing that can save us from these impasses is an effective politicization of psychiatry. And doubtless, with R. D. Laing and David Cooper antipsychiatry went very far in this direction. But it seems to us that they still conceive of this politicization in terms of the structure and the event, rather than the process itself. Furthermore, they localize social and mental alienation on a single line, and tend to consider them as identical by showing how the familial agent extends the one into the other.* Between the two, however, the relationship is rather that of an *included disjunction*. This is because the decoding and the deterritorialization of flows define the very process of capitalism—that is, its essence, its tendency, and its external limit. But we know that the process is continually interrupted, or the tendency counteracted, or the limit displaced, by subjective reterritorializations and representations that operate as much at the level of capital as a subject (the axiomatic), as at the level of the persons serving as capital's agents (application of the axiomatic). But we seek in vain to assign social alienation and mental alienation to one side or the other, as long as we establish a relation of exclusion between the two. The deterritorialization of flows in general effectively merges with mental alienation, inasmuch as it *includes* the reterritorializations that permit it to subsist only as the state of a particular flow, a flow of madness that is defined thus because it is charged with representing whatever escapes the axiomatics and the applications of reterritorialization in other flows. Inversely, one can find the form of social alienation in action in all the reterritorializations of capitalism, inasmuch as they keep the flows from escaping the system,

*David Cooper, "Aliénation mentale et aliénation sociale," *Recherches*, December 1968, pp. 48–49: "Social alienation comes for the most part to overlap the diverse forms of mental alienation. . . . Those admitted into a psychiatric hospital are admitted not so much because they are sick, as because they are protesting in a more or less adequate way against the social order. The social system in which they are caught thereby comes to reinforce the damages wrought by the familial system in which they grew up. This autonomy that they seek to affirm with regard to a microsociety acts as an indicator of a massive alienation performed by society as a whole."

and maintain labor in the axiomatic framework of property, and desire in the applied framework of the family; but this social alienation includes in its turn mental alienation, which finds itself represented or reterritorialized in neurosis, perversion, and psychosis (the mental illnesses).

A true politics of psychiatry, or antipsychiatry, would consist therefore in the following praxis: (1) undoing all the reterritorializations that transform madness into mental illness; (2) liberating the schizoid movement of deterritorialization in all the flows, in such a way that this characteristic can no longer qualify a particular residue as a flow of madness, but affects just as well the flows of labor and desire, of production, knowledge, and creation in their most profound tendency. Here, madness would no longer exist as madness, not because it would have been transformed into "mental illness," but on the contrary because it would receive the support of all the other flows, including science and art—once it is said that madness is called madness and appears as such only because it is deprived of this support, and finds itself reduced to testifying all alone for deterritorialization as a universal process. It is merely its unwarranted privilege, a privilege beyond its capacities, that renders it mad. In this perspective Foucault announced an age when madness would disappear, not because it would be lodged within the controlled space of mental illness ("great tepid aquariums"), but on the contrary because the exterior limit designated by madness would be overcome by means of other flows escaping control on all sides, and carrying us along.*

It should therefore be said that one can never go far enough in the direction of deterritorialization: you haven't seen anything yet—an irreversible process. And when we consider what there is of a profoundly artificial nature in the perverted reterritorializations, but also in the psychotic reterritorializations of the hospital, or even the familial neurotic reterritorializations, we cry out, "More perversion! More artifice!"—to a point where the earth becomes so artificial that the movement of deterritorialization creates of necessity and by itself a new earth. Psychoanalysis is especially satisfying in this regard: its entire perverted practice of the cure consists in transforming familial neurosis into artificial neurosis (of transference), and in exalting the couch, a little island with its commander, the psychoanalyst, as an autonomous territoriality of the ultimate artifice. A little additional effort is enough to overturn everything, and to lead us finally toward other far-off places. The schizoanalytic flick of the finger, which restarts the movement, links

---

*Michel Foucault, "La folie, l'absence d'oeuvre," *La Table ronde,* May 1964: "Everything that we experience today in the mode of the *limit,* or of strangeness, or of the unbearable, will have joined again with the serenity of the positive."

up again with the tendency, and pushes the simulacra to a point where they cease being artificial images to become indices of the new world. That is what the completion of the process is: not a promised and a pre-existing land, but a world created in the process of its tendency, its coming undone, its deterritorialization. The movement of the theater of cruelty; for it is the only theater of production, there where the flows cross the threshold of deterritorialization and produce the new land—not at all a hope, but a simple "finding," a "finished design," where the person who escapes causes other escapes, and marks out the land while deterritorializing himself. An active point of escape where the revolutionary machine, the artistic machine, the scientific machine, and the (schizo) analytic machine become parts and pieces of one another.

4 | The First Positive Task of Schizoanalysis

The negative or destructive task of schizoanalysis is in no way separable from its positive tasks—all these tasks are necessarily undertaken at the same time. The first positive task consists of discovering in a subject the nature, the formation, or the functioning of *his* desiring-machines, independently of any interpretations. What are your desiring-machines, what do you put into these machines, what is the output, how does it work, what are your nonhuman sexes? The schizoanalyst is a mechanic, and schizoanalysis is solely functional. In this respect it cannot remain at the level of a still interpretative examination—interpretative from the point of view of the unconscious—of the social machines in which the subject is caught as a cog or as a user; nor of the technical machines that are his prized possession, or that he perfects or even produces through handiwork; nor of the subject's use of his machines in his dreams and his fantasies. These machines are still too representative, and represent units that are too large—even the perverted machines of the sadist or the masochist, even the influencing machines of the paranoiac. We have seen in general that the pseudo analyses of the "object" were really the lowest level of analytic activity, even and especially when they claim to double the real object with an imaginary object; and better a how-to-interpret-your-dreams book than a psychoanalysis of the market place.

The consideration of all these machines, however, whether they be real, symbolic, or imaginary, must indeed intervene in a specific way—but as functional indices to point us in the direction of the desiring-machines, to which these indices are more or less close and affinal. The desiring-machines in fact are only reached starting from a certain threshold of dispersion that no longer permits either their imaginary identity or their structural unity to subsist. (These instances still belong to the order of interpretation, that is to say the order of the signified *or* the signifier.) Partial objects are what make up the parts of the desiring-machines; partial objects define the working machine or the working parts, but in a state of dispersion such that one part is continually referring to a part from an entirely different machine, like the red clover and the bumble bee, the wasp and the orchid, the bicycle horn and the dead rat's ass. Let's not rush to introduce a term that would be like a phallus structuring the whole and personifying the parts, unifying and totalizing everything. Everywhere there is libido as machine energy, and neither the horn nor the bumble bee have the privilege of being a phallus: the phallus intervenes only in the structural organization and the personal relations deriving from it, where everyone, like the worker called to war, abandons his machines and sets to fighting for a war trophy that is nothing but a great absence, with one and the same penalty, one and the same ridiculous wound for all—castration. This entire struggle for the phallus, this poorly understood will to power, this anthropomorphic representation of sex, this whole conception of sexuality that horrifies Lawrence precisely because it is no more than a conception, because it is an idea that "reason" imposes on the unconscious and introduces into the passional sphere, and is not by any means a formation of this sphere—here is where desire finds itself trapped, specifically limited to human sex, unified and identified in the molar constellation. But the desiring-machines live on the contrary under the order of dispersion of the molecular elements. And one fails to understand the nature and function of partial objects if one does not see therein such elements, rather than parts of even a fragmented whole. As Lawrence said, analysis does not have to do with anything that resembles a concept or a person, "the so-called human relations are not involved."[25] Analysis should deal solely (except in its negative task) with the machinic arrangements grasped in the context of their molecular dispersion.

Let us therefore return to the rule so clearly stated by Serge Leclaire, even if he sees this only as a fiction instead of the real-desire (*réel-désir*): the elements or parts of the desiring-machines are recognized by their mutual independence, such that nothing in the one depends or should depend on something in the other. They must not be opposed determinations of a same entity, nor the differentiations of a single being, such as the masculine and the feminine in the human sex, but different or really-distinct things (*des réellement-distincts*), distinct "beings," as found in the dispersion of the nonhuman sex (the clover and the bee). As long as schizoanalysis has not arrived at these *disparate* elements, it has not yet discovered the partial objects as the ultimate elements of the unconscious. It is in this sense that Leclaire used the term "erogenous body" not to designate a fragmented organism, but an emission of preindividual and prepersonal singularities, a pure dispersed and anarchic multiplicity, without unity or totality, and whose elements are welded, pasted together by the real distinction or the very absence of a link. Such is the case in the schizoid sequences of Beckett: stones, pockets, mouth; a shoe, a pipe bowl, a small limp bundle that is undefined, a cover for a bicycle bell, half a crutch ("if one indefinitely runs up against the same set of pure singularities, one can feel confident that he has drawn near the singularity of the subject's desire").[26] To be sure, one can always establish or re-establish some sort of link between these elements: organic links between organs or fragments of organs that eventually form part of the multiplicity; psychological and axiological links—the good, the bad—that finally refer to the persons or to the scenes from which these elements are borrowed; structural links between the ideas or the concepts apt to correspond to them. But it is not in this respect that the partial objects are elements of the unconscious, and we cannot even go along with the image of the partial objects that their inventor, Melanie Klein, proposes. This is because, whether organs or fragments of organs, the partial objects do not refer in the least to an organism that would function phantasmatically as a lost unity or a totality to come. Their dispersion has nothing to do with a lack, and constitutes their mode of presence in the multiplicity they form without unification or totalization. With every structure dislodged, every memory abolished, every organism set aside, every link undone, they function as raw partial objects, dispersed working parts of a machine that is itself dispersed. In short, *partial objects are the molecular functions of the unconscious.* That is why, when we insisted earlier on the difference between desiring-machines and all the figures of molar machines, we were fully aware that they were both contained in, and did not exist without, one another, but we had to stress the difference in régime and in scale between these two machinic species.

It is true that one might instead wonder how these conditions of dispersion, of real distinction, and of the absence of a link permit any machinic régime to exist—how the partial objects thus defined are able to form machines and arrangements of machines. The answer lies in the passive nature of the syntheses, or—what amounts to the same thing—in the indirect nature of the interactions under consideration. If it is true that every partial object emits a flow, it is also the case that this flow is associated with another partial object and defines the other's potential field of presence, which is itself multiple (a multiplicity of anuses for the flows of shit). The synthesis of connection of the partial objects is indirect, since one of the partial objects, in each point of its presence within the field, always breaks the flow that another object emits or produces relatively, itself ready to emit a flow that other partial objects will break. The flows are two-headed, so to speak, and it is by means of these flows that every productive connection is made, such as we have tried to account for with the notion of flow-schiz or break-flow. So that the true activities of the unconscious, causing to flow and breaking flows, consist of the passive synthesis itself insofar as it ensures the relative coexistence and displacement of the two different functions.

Now let us assume that the respective flows associated with two partial objects at least partially overlap: their production remains distinct in relation to the objects x and y that emit them, but not the fields of presence in relation to the objects a and b that inhabit and interrupt them, such that the partial a and the partial b become in this regard indiscernible (thus the mouth and the anus, the mouth-anus of the anorexic). And they are not indiscernible solely in the mixed region, since one can always assume that, having exchanged their function within this region, they cannot be further distinguished by exclusion there where the two flows no longer overlap: one then finds oneself before a new passive synthesis where a and b are in a paradoxical relationship of included disjunction. Finally there remains the possibility, not of an overlapping of the flows, but of a permutation of the objects that emit them: one discovers fringes of interference on the edge of each field of presence, fringes that testify to the remainder of a flow in the other, and form residual conjunctive syntheses guiding the passage or the heartfelt becoming from the one to the other. A permutation involving 2, 3, n organs; deformable abstract polygons that make game of the figurative Oedipal triangle, and never cease to undo it. Through binarity, overlapping, or permutation, all these indirect passive syntheses are one and the same engineering of desire. But who will be able to describe the desiring-machines of each subject, what analysis will be exacting enough for this? Mozart's desiring-machine? "Raise your ass to your mouth, . . . ah, my ass burns like fire, but *what can be the meaning of that? Perhaps a turd wants to come out. . . . Yes, yes, turd, I know you, I see you, I feel you. What is this—is such a thing possible?"*

These syntheses necessarily imply the position of a body without organs. This is due to the fact that the body without organs is in no way the contrary of the organs–partial objects. It is itself produced in the

---

*From a letter by Mozart, cited by Marcel Moré, *Le Dieu Mozart et le monde des oiseaux* (Paris: Gallimard, 1971), p. 124: "Having come of age, he found the means of concealing his divine essence, by indulging in scatological amusements." Moré shows convincingly how the scatological machine works underneath and against the Oedipal "cage."

first passive synthesis of connection, as that which is going to neutralize—or on the contrary put into motion—the two activities, the two heads of desire. For as we have seen, it can be produced as the amorphous fluid of antiproduction, just as it can be produced as the support that appropriates for itself the flow production. It can as well *repel* the organs-objects as *attract* them, and appropriate them for itself. But in repulsion as in attraction, the body without organs is not in opposition to these organs-objects; it merely ensures its own opposition, and their opposition, with regard to an organism. The body without organs and the organs–partial objects are opposed conjointly to the organism. The body without organs is in fact produced as a whole, but a whole alongside the parts—a whole that does not unify or totalize them, but that is added to them like a new, really distinct part.

When it repels the organs, as in the mounting of the paranoiac machine, the body without organs marks the external limit of the pure multiplicity formed by these organs themselves insofar as they constitute a nonorganic and nonorganized multiplicity. And when it attracts them and fits itself over them, in the process of a miraculating fetishistic machine, it still does not totalize them, unify them in the manner of an organism: the organs–partial objects cling to the body without organs, and enter into the new syntheses of included disjunction and nomadic conjunction, of overlapping and permutation, on this body—syntheses that continue to repudiate the organism and its organization. Desire indeed passes through the body, and through the organs, but not through the organism. That is why the partial objects are not the expression of a fragmented, shattered organism, which would presuppose a destroyed totality or the freed parts of a whole; nor is the body without organs the expression of a "de-differentiated" ("*dé-différencié*") organism stuck back together that would surmount its own parts. The organs–partial objects and the body without organs are at bottom one and the same thing, one and the same multiplicity that must be conceived as such by schizoanalysis. *Partial objects are the direct powers of the body without organs, and the body without organs, the raw material of the partial objects.** The body without organs is the matter that always fills space to

*In his study on "Objet magique, sorcellerie et fétichisme" in *Nouvelle revue de psychanalyse*, no. 2 (1970), Pierre Bonnafé clearly demonstrates in this respect the inadequacy of a notion like that of a fragmented body: "There is indeed a fragmenting of the body, but not at all with a feeling of loss or degradation. Quite to the contrary, as much for the holder as for the others, the body is fragmented by multiplication: the others no longer have to do with a simple person, but with a *man to the $x + y + z$ power* whose life has been immeasurably increased, dispersed while being united with other natural forces . . . , since its existence no longer rests at the center of its person, but has hidden itself in several far-off and impregnable locations" (pp. 166–67). Bonnafé recognizes in the magic object the existence of the three desiring syntheses: the connective synthesis, which combines the fragments of the person with those of animals or plants; the included disjunctive synthesis, which records the man-animal composite; the conjunctive synthesis, which implies a veritable migration of the remainder or residue.

given degrees of intensity, and the partial objects are these degrees, these intensive parts that produce the real in space starting from matter as intensity=0. The body without organs is the immanent substance, in the most Spinozist sense of the word; and the partial objects are like its ultimate attributes, which belong to it precisely insofar as they are really distinct and cannot on this account exclude or oppose one another. The partial objects and the body without organs are the two material elements of the schizophrenic desiring-machines: the one as the immobile motor, the others as the working parts; the one as the giant molecule, the others as the micromolecules—the two together in a relationship of continuity from one end to the other of the molecular chain of desire.

The chain is like the apparatus of transmission or of reproduction in the desiring-machine. Insofar as it brings together—without unifying or uniting them—the body without organs and the partial objects, the desiring-machine is inseparable both from the distribution of the partial objects on the body without organs, and from the leveling effect exerted on the partial objects by the body without organs, which results in appropriation. The chain also implies another type of synthesis than the flows: it is no longer the lines of connection that traverse the productive parts of the machine, but an entire network of disjunction on the recording surface of the body without organs. And we have doubtless been able to present things in a logical order where the disjunctive synthesis of recording seemed to follow after the connective synthesis of production, with a part of the energy of production (Libido) being converted into a recording energy (Numen). But in fact, from the standpoint of the machine itself, there is no succession that ensures the strict coexistence of the chains and the flows, as well as of the body without organs and the partial objects. The conversion of a portion of the energy does not occur at a given moment, but is a preliminary and constant condition of the system. The chain is the network of included disjunctions on the body without organs, inasmuch as these disjunctions resect the productive connections; the chain causes them to pass over to the body without organs itself, thereby channeling or "codifying" the flows. However, the whole question is in knowing whether one can speak of a *code* at the level of this molecular chain of desire. We have seen that a code implied two things—one or the other, or the two together: on the one hand, the specific determination of the full body as a territoriality of support; on the other hand, the erection of a despotic signifier on which the entire chain depends. In this regard, in vain is the axiomatic in profound opposition to codes; since it works on the decoded flows, it cannot itself proceed except by effecting reterritorializations and by reviving the signifying unity. The very notions of code and axiomatic therefore seem to be valid only for the molar aggregates, where the signifying chain forms a given determinate configuration on a support that is itself specifically determined, and in terms of a detached signifier. These conditions are not fulfilled without exclusions forming and appearing in the disjunctive network—at the same time as the connective lines take on a global and specific meaning.

But it is another case altogether with the properly molecular chain: insofar as the body without organs is a nonspecific and nonspecified support that marks the molecular limit of the molar aggregates, the chain no longer has any other function than that of deterritorializing the flows and causing them to pass through the signifying wall, thereby undoing the codes. The function of the chain is no longer that of coding the flows on a full body of the earth, the despot, or capital, but on the contrary that of decoding them on the full body without organs. It is a chain of escape, and no longer a code. The signifying chain has become a chain of decoding and deterritorialization, which must be apprehended—and can only be apprehended—as the reverse of the codes and the territorialities. This molecular chain is still signifying because it is composed of signs of desire; but these signs are no longer signifying, given the fact that they are under the order of the included disjunctions where *everything is possible.* These signs are points whose nature is a matter of indifference, abstract machinic figures that play freely on the body without organs and as yet form no structured configuration—or rather, they form one no longer. As Jacques Monod says, we must conceive of a machine that is such by its functional properties but not by its structure, "where nothing but the play of blind combinations can be discerned."[27] It is precisely the ambiguity of what the biologists call a genetic code that enables us to understand this kind of situation: for if the corresponding chain effectively forms codes, inasmuch as it folds into exclusive molar configurations, it undoes the codes by unfolding along a molecular fiber that includes all the possible figures. Similarly, in Lacan, the symbolic organization of the structure, with its exclusions that come from the function of the signifier, has as its reverse side the real inorganization of desire.

It would seem that the genetic code points to a genic decoding: one need only grasp the decoding and deterritorialization functions in their own positivity, inasmuch as they imply a particular chain state that is metastable and distinct both from any axiomatic and from any code. The molecular chain is the form in which the genic unconscious, always remaining subject, reproduces itself. And as we have seen, that is the primary inspiration of psychoanalysis: it does not add a code to all those that are already known. The signifying chain of the unconscious, Numen, is not used to discover or decipher codes of desire, but to cause absolutely decoded flows of desire, Libido, to circulate, and to discover in desire that which scrambles all the codes and undoes all the territorialities. It is true that Oedipus will restore psychoanalysis to the status of a simple code, with the familial territoriality and the signifier of castration. Worse yet, it will happen that psychoanalysis itself wants to act as an axiomatic, which is the famous turning point where it no longer even relates to the familial scene, but solely to the psychoanalytic scene that supposedly answers for its own truth, and to the psychoanalytic operation that supposedly answers for its own success—the couch as an axiomatized earth, the axiomatic of the "cure" as a *successful* castration! But by recoding or axiomatizing the flows of desire in this way, psychoanalysis makes a molar use of the signifying chain that results in a misappreciation of all the syntheses of the unconscious.

The body without organs is the model of death. As the authors of horror stories have understood so well, it is not death that serves as the model for catatonia, it is catatonic schizophrenia that gives its model to death. Zero intensity. The death model appears when the body without organs repels the organs and lays them aside: no mouth, no tongue, no teeth—to the point of self-mutilation, to the point of suicide. Yet there is no real opposition between the body without organs and the organs as partial objects; the only real opposition is to the molar organism that is their common enemy. In the desiring-machine, one sees the same catatonic inspired by the immobile motor that forces him to put aside his organs, to immobilize them, to silence them, but also, impelled by the working parts that work in an autonomous or stereotyped fashion, to reactivate the organs, to reanimate them with local movements. It is a question of different parts of the machine, different and coexisting, different in their very coexistence. Hence it is absurd to speak of a death desire that would presumably be in qualitative opposition to the life desires. Death is not desired, there is only death that desires, by virtue of the body without organs or the immobile motor, and there is also life that desires, by virtue of the working organs. There we do not have two desires but two parts, two kinds of desiring-machine parts, in the dispersion of the machine itself. And yet the problem persists: how can all that function together? For it is not yet a functioning, but solely the (nonstructural) condition of a molecular functioning. The functioning appears when the motor, under the preceding conditions—ie., without ceasing to be immobile and without forming an organism—attracts the organs to the body without organs, and appropriates them for itself in the apparent objective movement. Repulsion is the condition of the machine's functioning, but attraction is the functioning itself. That the functioning depends on repulsion is clear to us, inasmuch as it all works only by breaking down. One is then able to say what this running or this functioning consists of: in the cycle of the desiring-machine it is a matter of constantly translating, constantly converting the death model into something else altogether, which is the experience of death. Converting the death that rises from within (in the body without organs) into the death that comes from without (on the body without organs).

But it seems that things are becoming very obscure, for what is this distinction between the experience of death and the model of death? Here again, is it a death desire? A being-for-death? Or rather an investment of death, even if speculative? None of the above. The experience of death is the most common of occurrences in the unconscious, precisely because it occurs in life and for life, in every passage or becoming, in every intensity as passage or becoming. It is in the very nature of every intensity to invest within itself the zero intensity starting from which it is produced, in one moment, as that which grows or diminishes according to an infinity of degrees (as Klossowski noted, "an afflux is necessary merely to signify the absence of intensity"). We have attempted to show in this respect how the relations of attraction and repulsion produced such states, sensations, and emotions, which imply a new energetic conversion and form the third kind of synthesis, the synthesis of conjunction. One might say that the unconscious as a real subject has scattered an apparent residual and nomadic subject around the entire compass of its cycle, a subject that passes by way of all the becomings corresponding to the included disjunctions: the last part of the desiring-machine, the adjacent part. These intense becomings and feelings, these intensive emotions, feed deliriums and hallucinations. But in themselves, these intensive emotions are closest to the matter whose zero degree they invest in itself. They control the unconscious experience of death, insofar as death is what is felt in every feeling, *what never ceases and never finishes happening in every becoming*—in the becoming-another-sex, the becoming-god, the becoming-a-race, etc., forming zones of intensity on the body without organs. Every intensity controls within its own life the experience of death, and envelops it. And it is doubtless the case that every intensity is extinguished at the end, that every becoming itself becomes a becoming-death! Death, then, does actually happen. Maurice Blanchot distinguishes this twofold nature clearly, these two irreducible aspects of death; the one, according to which the apparent subject never ceases to live and travel as a *One*—"*one* never stops and never has done with dying"; and the other, according to which this same subject, fixed as *I,* actually dies—which is to say it finally ceases to die since it ends up dying, in the reality of a last instant that fixes it in this way as an *I*, all the while undoing the intensity, carrying it back to the zero that envelops it.[28]

From one aspect to the other, there is not at all a personal deepening, but something quite different: there is a return from the experience of death to the model of death, in the cycle of the desiring-machines. The cycle is closed. For a new departure, since this *I* is another? The experience of death must have given us exactly enough broadened experience, in order to live and know that the desiring-machines do not die. And that the subject as an adjacent part is always a "one" who conducts the experience, not an *I* who receives the model. For the model itself is not the *I* either, but the body without organs. And *I* does not rejoin the model without the model starting out again in the direction of another experience. Always going from the model to the experience, and starting out again, returning from the model to the experience, is what *schizophrenizing death* amounts to, the exercise of the desiring-machines (which is their very secret, well understood by the terrifying authors). The machines tell us this, and make us live it, feel it, deeper than delirium and further than hallucination: yes, the return to repulsion will condition other attractions, other functionings, the setting in motion of other working parts on the body without organs, the putting to work of other adjacent parts on the periphery that have as much a right to say *One* as we ourselves do. "Let him die in his leaping through unheard-of and unnamable things: other horrible workers will come; they will begin on the horizons where the other collapsed!"[29] The Eternal Return as experience, and as the deterritorialized circuit of all the cycles of desire.

How odd the psychoanalytic venture is. Psychoanalysis ought to be a song of life, or else be worth nothing at all. It ought, *practically,* to teach us to sing life. And see how the most defeated, sad song of death emanates from it: *eiapopeia.* From the start, and because of his stubborn dualism of the drives, Freud never stopped trying to limit the discovery of a subjective or vital essence of desire as libido. But when the dualism passed into a death instinct against Eros, this was no longer a simple limitation, it was a liquidation of the libido. Reich did not go wrong here, and was perhaps the only one to maintain that the product of analysis should be a free and joyous person, a carrier of the life flows, capable of carrying them all the way into the desert and decoding them—even if this idea necessarily took on the appearance of a crazy idea, given what had become of analysis. He demonstrated that Freud, no less than Jung and Adler, had repudiated the sexual position: the fixing of the death instinct in fact deprives sexuality of its generative role on at least one essential point, which is the genesis of anxiety, since this genesis becomes the autonomous cause of sexual repression instead of its result; it follows that sexuality as desire no longer animates a social critique of civilization, but that civilization on the contrary finds itself sanctified as the sole agency capable of opposing the death desire. And how does it do this? By in principle turning death against death, by making this turned-back death (*la mort retournée*) into a force of desire, by putting it in the service of a pseudo life through an entire culture of guilt feeling.

There is no need to tell all over how psychoanalysis culminates in a theory of culture that takes up again the age-old task of the ascetic ideal, Nirvana, the cultural extract, judging life, belittling life, measuring life against death, and only retaining from life what the death of death wants very much to leave us with—a sublime resignation. As Reich says, when psychoanalysis began to speak of Eros, the whole world breathed a sigh of relief: one knew what this meant, and that everything was going to unfold within a mortified life, since Thanatos was now the partner of Eros, for worse but also *for better*.[30] Psychoanalysis becomes the training ground of a new kind of priest, the director of bad conscience: bad conscience has made us sick, but that is what will cure us! Freud did not hide what was really at issue with the introduction of the death instinct: it is not a question of any fact whatever, but merely of a principle, a question of principle. The death instinct is pure silence, pure transcendence, not givable and not given in experience. This very point is remarkable: it is because death, according to Freud, has neither a model nor an experience, that he makes of it a transcendent principle.[31] So that the psychoanalysts who refused the death instinct did so for the same reasons as those who accepted it: some said that there was no death instinct *since* there was no model or experience in the unconscious; others, that there was a death instinct precisely *because* there was no model or experience. We say, to the contrary, that there is no death instinct because there is both the model and the experience of death in the unconscious. Death then is a part of the desiring-machine, a part that must itself be judged, evaluated in the functioning of the machine and the system of its energetic conversions, and not as an abstract principle.

If Freud needs death as a principle, this is by virtue of the requirements of the dualism that maintains a qualitative opposition between the drives (you will not escape the conflict): once the dualism of the sexual drives and the ego drives has only a topological scope, the qualitative or dynamic dualism passes between Eros and Thanatos. But the same enterprise is continued and reinforced—eliminating the machinic element of desire, the desiring-machines. It is a matter of eliminating the libido, insofar as it implies the possibility of energetic conversions in the machine (Libido-Numen-Voluptas). It is a matter of imposing the idea of an energetic duality rendering the machinic transformations impossible, with everything obliged to pass by way of an indifferent neutral energy, that energy emanating from Oedipus and capable of being added to either of the two irreducible forms—neutralizing, mortifying life.* The purpose of the topological and dynamic dualities is to thrust aside the point of view of *functional multiplicity* that alone is economic. (Szondi situates the problem clearly: why two kinds of drives qualified as molar, functioning mysteriously, which is to say oedipally, rather than *n* genes of drives—eight molecular genes, for example—functioning machinically?)

If one looks in this direction for the ultimate reason why Freud erects a transcendent death instinct as a principle, the reason will be found in Freud's practice itself. For if the principle has nothing to do with the facts, it has a lot to do with the psychoanalyst's conception of psychoanalytic practice, a conception the psychoanalyst wishes to impose. Freud made the most profound discovery of the abstract subjective essence of desire—Libido. But since he realienated this essence, reinvesting it in a subjective system of representation of the ego, and since he recoded this essence on the residual territoriality of Oedipus and under the despotic signifier of castration, he could no longer conceive the essence of life except in a form turned back against itself, in the form of death itself. And this neutralization, this turning against life, is also the last way in which a depressive and exhausted libido can go on surviving, and dream that it is surviving: "The ascetic ideal is an artifice for the *preservation* of life . . . even when he *wounds* himself, this master of destruction, of self-destructing—the very wound itself compels him *to live. . . .*"[32] It is Oedipus, the marshy earth, that gives off a powerful odor of decay and death; and it is castration, the pious ascetic wound, the signifier, that makes of this death a conservatory for the Oedipal life. Desire is in itself not a desire to love, but a force to love, a virtue that gives and produces, that engineers. (For how could what is in life still desire life? Who would want to call that a desire?) But desire must turn back against itself in the name of a horrible Ananke, the Ananke of the weak and the depressed, the contagious neurotic Ananke;

---

*On the impossibility of immediate qualitative conversions, and the necessity for going by way of neutral energy, see Sigmund Freud, *The Ego and the Id,* trans. Joan Riviere (New York: Norton, 1961). This impossibility, this necessity is no longer understandable, it seems to us, if one agrees with Jean Laplanche that "the death drive has no energy of its own" (*Vie et mort en psychanalyse* [Paris: Flammarion, 1970], p. 211). Therefore the death drive could not enter into a veritable dualism, or would have to be confused with the neutral energy itself, which Freud denies.

desire must produce its shadow or its monkey, and find a strange artificial force for vegetating in the void, at the heart of its own lack. For better days to come? It must—but who talks in this way? what abjectness—become a desire to be loved, and worse, a sniveling desire to have been loved, a desire that is reborn of its own frustration: no, daddy-mommy didn't love me enough. Sick desire stretches out on the couch, an artificial swamp, a little earth, a little mother. "Look at you, stumbling and staggering with no use in your legs. . . . And it's nothing but your wanting to be loved which does it. A maudlin crying to be loved, which makes your knees go all ricky."[33] Just as there are two stomachs for the ruminant, there must also exist two abortions, two castrations for sick desire: once in the family, in the familial scene, with the knitting mother; another time in an aseptizied clinic, in the psychoanalytic scene, with specialist artists who know how to handle the death instinct and "bring off" castration, "bring off" frustration.

Is this really the right way to bring on better days? And aren't all the destructions performed by schizoanalysis worth more than this psycho-analytic conservatory, aren't they more a part of an affirmative task? "Lie down, then, on the soft couch which the analyst provides and try to think up something different . . . if you realize that he is not a god but a human being like yourself, with worries, defects, ambitions, frailties, that he is not the repository of an all-encompassing wisdom [=code] but a wanderer, along the [deterritorialized] path, perhaps you will cease pouring it out like a sewer, however melodious it may sound to your ears, and rise up on your own two legs and sing with your own God-given voice [Numen]. To confess, to whine, to complain, to commiserate, always demands a toll. To sing it doesn't cost you a penny. Not only does it cost nothing—you actually enrich others (instead of infecting them). . . . The phantasmal world is the world which has not been fully conquered over. It is the world of the past, never of the future. To move forward clinging to the past is like dragging a ball and chain. . . . We are all guilty of crime, the great crime of not living life to the full."[34] You weren't born Oedipus, you caused it to grow in yourself; and you aim to get out of it through fantasy, through castration, but this in turn you have caused to grow in Oedipus—namely, in yourself: the horrible circle. Shit on your whole mortifying, imaginary, and symbolic theater. What does schizoanalysis ask? Nothing more than a bit of a *relation to the outside,* a little real reality. And we claim the right to a radical laxity, a radical incompetence—the right to enter the analyst's office and say it smells bad there. It reeks of the great death and the little ego.

Freud himself indeed spoke of the link between his "discovery" of the death instinct and World War I, which remains the model of capitalist war. More generally, the death instinct celebrates the wedding of psychoanalysis and capitalism; their engagement had been full of hesitation. What we have tried to show apropos of capitalism is how it inherited much from a transcendent death-carrying agency, the despotic signifier, but also how it brought about this agency's effusion in the full immanence of its own system: the full body, having become that of capital-money, suppresses the distinction between production and anti-production; everywhere it mixes antiproduction with the productive forces in the immanent reproduction of its own always widened limits (the axiomatic). The death enterprise is one of the principal and specific forms of the absorption of surplus value in capitalism. It is this itinerary that psychoanalysis rediscovers and retraces with the death instinct: the death instinct is now only pure silence in its transcendent distinction from life, but it effuses all the more, throughout all the immanent combinations it forms with this same life. Absorbed, diffuse, immanent death is the condition formed by the signifier in capitalism, the empty locus that is everywhere displaced in order to block the schizophrenic escapes and place restraints on the flights.

The only modern myth is the myth of zombies—mortified schizos, good for work, brought back to reason. In this sense the primitive and the barbarian, with their ways of coding death, are children in comparison to modern man and his axiomatic (so many unemployed are needed, so many deaths, the Algerian War doesn't kill more people than weekend automobile accidents, planned death in Bengal, etc.). Modern man "raves to a far greater extent. His delirium is a switchboard with thirteen telephones. He gives his orders to the world. He doesn't care for the ladies. He is brave, too. He is decorated like crazy. In man's game of chance the death instinct, the silent instinct is decidedly well placed, perhaps next to egoism. It takes the place of zero in roulette. The house always wins. So too does death. The law of large numbers works for death."[35] It is now or never that we must take up a problem we had left hanging. Once it is said that capitalism works on the basis of decoded flows as such, how is it that it is infinitely further removed from desiring-production than were the primitive or even the barbarian systems, which nonetheless code and overcode the flows? Once it is said that desiring-production is itself a decoded and deterritorialized production, how do we explain that capitalism, with its axiomatic, its statistics, performs an infinitely vaster repression of this production than do the preceding régimes, which nonetheless did not lack the necessary repressive means? We have seen that the molar statistical aggregates of social production were in a variable relationship of affinity with the molecular formations of desiring-production. What must be explained is that the capitalist aggregate is the least affinal, at the very moment it decodes and deterritorializes with all its might.

The answer is the death instinct, if we call instinct in general the conditions of life that are historically and socially determined by the relations of production and antiproduction in a system. We know that molar social production and molecular desiring-production must be evaluated both from the viewpoint of their identity in nature and from the viewpoint of their difference in régime. But it could be that these two aspects, nature and régime, are in a sense potential and are actualized only in inverse proportion. Which means that where the régimes are the closest, the identity in nature is on the contrary at its minimum; and where the identity in nature appears to be at its maximum, the régimes differ to the highest degree. If we examine the primitive or the barbarian constellations, we see that the subjective essence of desire as production is referred to large objectities, to the territorial or the despotic body, which act as natural or divine preconditions that thus ensure the coding or the overcoding of the flows of desire by introducing them into systems of representation that are themselves objective. Hence it can be said that the identity in nature between the two productions is completely hidden there: as much by the difference between the objective socius and the subjective full body of desiring-production, as by the difference between the qualified codes and overcodings of social production and the chains of decoding or of deterritorialization belonging to desiring-production, and by the entire repressive apparatus represented in the savage prohibitions, the barbarian law, and the rights of antiproduction. And yet the difference in régime, far from being accentuated and deepened, is on the contrary reduced to a minimum, because desiring-production as an absolute limit remains an exterior limit, or else stays unoccupied as an internalized and displaced limit, with the result that the machines of desire operate on this side of their limit within the framework of the socius and its codes. That is why the primitive codes and even the despotic overcodings testify to a polyvocity that functionally draws them nearer to a chain of decoding of desire: the parts of the desiring-machine function in the very workings of the social machine; the flows of desire enter and exit through the codes that continue, however, to inform the model and experience of death that are elaborated in the unity of the sociodesiring-apparatus. And it is even less a question of the death instinct to the extent that the model and the experience are better coded in a circuit that never stops grafting the desiring-machines onto the social machine and implanting the social machine in the desiring-machines. Death comes all the more from without as it is coded from within. This is especially true of the system of cruelty, where death is inscribed in the primitive mechanism of surplus value as well as in the movement of the finite blocks of debt. But even in the system of despotic terror, where debt becomes infinite and where death experiences an elevation that tends to make of it a *latent* instinct, there nonetheless subsists a model in the overcoding law, and an experience for the overcoded subjects, at the same time as antiproduction remains separate as the share owing to the overlord.

Things are very different in capitalism. Precisely because the flows of capital are decoded and deterritorialized flows; precisely because the subjective essence of production is revealed in capitalism; precisely because the limit becomes internal to capitalism, which continually reproduces it, and also continually occupies it as an internalized and displaced limit; precisely for these reasons, the identity in nature must appear for itself between social production and desiring-production. But in its turn, this identity in nature, far from favoring an affinity in régime between the two modes of production, increases the difference in régime in a catastrophic fashion, and assembles an apparatus of repression the mere idea of which neither savagery nor barbarism could provide us. This is because, on the basis of a general collapse of the large objectities, the decoded and deterritorialized flows of capitalism are not recaptured or co-opted, but directly apprehended in a codeless axiomatic that consigns them to the universe of subjective representation. Now this universe has as its function the splitting of the subjective essence (the identity in nature) into two functions, that of abstract labor alienated in private property that reproduces the ever wider interior limits, and that of abstract desire alienated in the privatized family that displaces the ever narrower internalized limits. The double alienation—labor-desire—is constantly increasing and deepening the difference in régime at the heart of the identity in nature. At the same time that death is decoded, it loses its relationship with a model and an experience, and becomes an instinct; that is, it effuses in the immanent system where each act of production is inextricably linked to the process of antiproduction as capital. There where the codes are undone, the death instinct lays hold of the repressive apparatus and begins to direct the circulation of the libido. A mortuary axiomatic. One might then believe in liberated desires, but ones that, like cadavers, feed on images. Death is not desired, but what is desired is dead, already dead: images. Everything labors in death, everything wishes for death. In truth, capitalism has nothing to co-opt; or rather, its powers of co-option coexist more often than not with what is to be co-opted, and even anticipate it. (How many revolutionary groups *as such* are already in place for a co-option that will be carried out only in the future, and form an apparatus for the absorption of a surplus value not even produced yet—which gives them precisely an apparent revolutionary position.) In a world such as this, there is no living desire that could not of itself cause the system to explode, or that would not make the system dissolve at one end where everything would end up following behind and being swallowed up—a question of régime.

Here are the desiring-machines, with their three parts: the working parts, the immobile motor, the adjacent part; their three forms of energy: Libido, Numen, and Voluptas; and their three syntheses: the connective syntheses of partial objects and flows, the disjunctive syntheses of singularities and chains, and the conjunctive syntheses of intensities and becomings. The schizoanalyst is not an interpreter, even less a theater director; he is a mechanic, a micromechanic. There are no excavations to be undertaken, no archaeology, no statues in the unconscious: there are only stones to be sucked, à la Beckett, and other machinic elements belonging to deterritorialized constellations. The task of schizoanalysis is that of learning what a subject's desiring-machines are, how they work, with what syntheses, what bursts of energy in the machine, what constituent misfires, with what flows, what chains, and what becomings in each case. Moreover, this positive task cannot be separated from indispensable destructions, the destruction of the molar aggregates, the structures and representations that prevent the machine from functioning. It is not easy to rediscover the molecules—even the giant molecule—their paths, their zones of presence, and their own syntheses, amid the large accumulations that fill the preconscious, and that delegate their representatives in the unconscious itself, thereby immobilizing the machines, silencing them, trapping them, sabotaging them, cornering them, holding them fast. *In the unconscious it is not the lines of pressure that matter, but on the contrary the lines of escape.* The unconscious does not apply pressure to consciousness; rather, consciousness applies pressure and strait-jackets the unconscious, to prevent its escape. As to the unconscious, it is like the Platonic opposite whose opposite draws near: it flees or it perishes. What we have tried to show from the outset is how the unconscious productions and formations were not merely repelled by an agency of psychic repression that would enter into compromises with them, but actually covered over by antiformations that disfigure the unconscious in itself, and impose on it causations, comprehensions, and expressions that no longer have anything to do with its real functioning: thus all the *statues,* the Oedipal images, the phantasmal *mises en scène,* the Symbolic of castration, the effusion of the death instinct, the perverse reterritorializations. So that one can never, as in an interpretation, read the repressed through and in the repression, since the latter is constantly inducing a false image of the thing it represses: illegitimate and transcendent uses of the syntheses according to which the unconscious can no longer operate in accordance with its own constituent machines, but merely "represent" what a repressive apparatus gives it to represent. It is the very form of interpretation that shows itself to be incapable of attaining the unconscious, since it gives rise to the inevitable illusions (including the structure and the signifier) by means of which the conscious makes of the unconscious an image consonant with its wishes: we are still pious, psychoanalysis remains in the precritical age.

Doubtless these illusions would not take hold if they did not benefit from a coincidence and a support in the unconscious itself that ensures the "hold." We have seen what this support was: primal repression, as exerted by the body without organs at the moment of repulsion, at the heart of molecular desiring-production. Without this primal repression, a psychic repression in the proper sense of the word could not be delegated in the unconscious by the molar forces and thus crush desiring-production. Repression properly speaking profits from an occasion without which it could not interfere in the machinery of desire.[36] In contrast to psychoanalysis, which itself falls into the trap while causing the unconscious to fall into its trap, schizoanalysis follows the lines of escape and the machinic indices all the way to the desiring-machines. If the essential aspect of the destructive task is to undo the Oedipal trap of repression properly speaking, and all its dependencies, each time in a way adapted to the "case" in question, the essential aspect of the first positive task is to ensure the machinic conversion of primal repression, there too in an adapted variable manner. Which is to say: undoing the blockage or the coincidence on which the repression properly speaking relies; transforming the apparent opposition of repulsion (the body without organs/the machines–partial objects) into a condition of real functioning; ensuring this functioning in the forms of attraction and production of intensities; thereafter integrating the failures in the attractive functioning, as well as enveloping the zero degree in the intensities produced; and thereby causing the desiring-machines to start up again. Such is the delicate and focal point that fills the function of transference in schizoanalysis—dispersing, schizophrenizing the perverse transference of psychoanalysis.

5 | The Second Positive Task

We cannot however allow the difference in régime to make us forget the identity in nature. There are fundamentally two poles; but we would not be satisfied if we had to present them merely as the duality of the molar formations and the molecular formations, since there is not one molecular formation that is not by itself an investment of a molar formation. There are no desiring-machines that exist outside the social machines that they form on a large scale; and no social machines without the desiring-machines that inhabit them on a small scale. Nor is there any molecular chain that does not intercept and reproduce whole blocks of molar code or axiomatic, nor any such blocks that do not contain or seal off fragments of molecular chain. A sequence of desire is extended by a social series, or a social machine contains desiring-machine parts within its workings. The desiring micromultiplicities are no less collective than the large social aggregates; they are strictly inseparable and constitute one and the same process of production. From this point of view, the duality of the poles passes less between the molar and the molecular than to the interior of the molar social investments, since *in any case* the molecular formations are such investments. That is why our terminology concerning the two poles has necessarily varied. At times we contrasted the molar and the molecular as the paranoiac, signifying, and structured lines of integration, and the schizophrenic, machinic, and dispersed lines of escape; or again as the staking out of the perverse reterritorializations, and as the movement of the schizophrenic deterritorializations. At other times, on the contrary, we contrasted them as the two major types of equally social investments: the one sedentary and biunivocalizing, and of a reactionary or fascist tendency; the other nomadic and polyvocal, and of a revolutionary tendency. In fact, in the schizoid declaration—"I am of a race inferior for all eternity," "I am a beast, a black," "We are all German Jews"—the historico-social field is no less invested than in the paranoiac formula: "I am one of your kind, from the same place as you, I am a pure Aryan, of a superior race for all time."

From the viewpoint of the unconscious libidinal investment, all the oscillations from one formula to the other are possible. How can this be? How can the schizophrenic escape, with its molecular dispersion, form an investment that is as strong and determined as the other? And why are there two types of social investment that correspond to the two poles? The answer is that everywhere there exist the molecular *and* the molar: their disjunction is a relation of included disjunction, which varies only according to the two directions of subordination, according as the molecular phenomena are subordinated to the large aggregates, or on the contrary subordinate them to themselves. At one of the poles the large aggregates, the large forms of gregariousness, do not prevent the flight that carries them along, and they oppose to it the paranoiac investment only as an "escape in advance of the escape." But at the other pole, the schizophrenic escape itself does not merely consist in withdrawing from the social, in living on the fringe: it causes the social to take flight through the multiplicity of holes that eat away at it and penetrate it, always coupled directly to it, everywhere setting the molecular charges that will explode what must explode, make fall what must fall, make escape what must escape, at each point ensuring the conversion of schizophrenia as a process into an effectively revolutionary force. For what is the schizo, if not first of all the one who can no longer bear "all that": money, the stock market, the death forces, Nijinsky said—values, morals, homelands, religions, and private certitudes? There is a whole world of difference between the schizo and the revolutionary: the difference between the one who escapes, and the one who knows how to make what he is escaping escape, collapsing a filthy drainage pipe, causing a deluge to break loose, liberating a flow, resecting a schiz. The schizo is not revolutionary, but the schizophrenic process—in terms of which the schizo is merely the interruption, or the continuation in the void—is the potential for revolution. To those who say that escaping is not courageous, we answer: what is not escape *and social investment at the same time?* The choice is between one of two poles, the paranoiac counterescape that motivates all the conformist, reactionary, and fascisizing investments, and the schizophrenic escape convertible into a revolutionary investment. Maurice Blanchot speaks admirably of this revolutionary escape, this fall that must be thought and carried out as the most positive of events: "What is this escape? The word is poorly chosen to please. Courage consists, however, in agreeing to flee rather than live tranquilly and hypocritically in false refuges. Values, morals, homelands, religions, and these private certitudes that our vanity and our complacency bestow generously on us, have as many deceptive sojourns as the world arranges for those who think they are standing straight and at ease, among stable things. They know nothing of this immense flight that transports them, ignorant of themselves, in the monotonous buzzing of their ever quickening steps that lead them impersonally in a great immobile movement. An escape in advance of the escape. [Consider the example of one of these men] who, having had the revelation of the mysterious drift, is no longer able to stand living in the false pretences of residence. First he tries to take this movement as his own. He would like to personally withdraw. He lives on the fringe. . . . [But] perhaps that is what the fall is, that it can no longer be a personal destiny, but the common lot."[37] In this regard, the first thesis of schizoanalysis is this: every investment is social, and in any case bears upon a sociohistorical field.

Let us recall the major traits of a molar formation or of a form of gregariousness (*herd instinct*). They effect a unification, a totalization of the molecular forces through a statistical accumulation obeying the laws of large numbers. This unity can be the biological unity of a *species* or the structural unity of a socius: an organism, social or living, is composed as a whole, as a global or complete object. It is in relation to this new order that the partial objects of a molecular order appear as a lack, at the same time that the whole itself is said to be lacked by the partial objects. In this way desire will be fused to lack. The myriad breaks-flows that determine the positive dispersion in a molecular multiplicity are fitted over vacuoles of lack that perform this fusion in a statistical constellation of a molar order. Freud demonstrated clearly in this respect how one went from psychotic multiplicities of dispersion, founded on the breaks or schizzes, to large vacuoles determined globally, of the neurosis and castration type: the neurotic needs a global object in relation to which the partial objects can be determined as a lack, and inversely.[38] But on a more general level, the statistical transformation of molecular multiplicity into a molar constellation is what organizes lack on a large scale. Such an organization belongs essentially to the biological or social organism—species or socius. There is no society that does not arrange lack in its midst, by variable means peculiar to it. (These means are not the same, for example, in a despotic type of society, or in a capitalist society where the market economy raises them to a degree of perfection unknown before capitalism.) This welding of desire to lack is precisely what gives desire collective and personal ends, goals or intentions—instead of desire taken in the real order of its production, which behaves as a molecular phenomenon devoid of any goal or intention.

Nor must it be thought that the statistical accumulation results from chance, or that it is a random result. This accumulation is on the contrary the fruit of a selection exerting its force on the elements of chance. When Nietzsche says that the selection is most often exerted *in favor of the large number,* he inaugurates a fundamental intuition that will inspire modern thought. For what he means is that the large numbers or the large aggregates do not exist prior to a selective pressure that might elicit singular lines from them, but that, quite on the contrary, these large numbers and aggregates are born of this selective pressure that crushes, eliminates, or regularizes the singularities. Selection does not presuppose a primary gregariousness; gregariousness presupposes the selection and is born of it. "Culture" as a selective process of marking or inscription invents the large numbers in whose favor it is exerted. That is why statistics is not functional but structural, and concerns chains of phenomena that selection has already placed in a state of partial dependence (the Markov chains). This can even be seen in the genetic code. In other terms, forms of gregariousness are never indifferent: they refer back to the qualified forms that produce them by creative selection. The order is not: gregariousness → selection, but on the contrary, molecular multiplicity → forms of selection performing the selection → molar or gregarious aggregates that result from this selection.

What are these qualified forms—"formations of sovereignty," as Nietzsche said—that play the role of totalizing, unifying, signifying objectivities, that assign organizations, lacks, and goals? The full bodies determine the different modes of the socius, veritable heavy aggregates of the earth, the despot, and capital. Full bodies or clothed substances, which are distinguished from the full body without organs or the naked matter of molecular desiring-production.[39] If we wonder where these forms of *force* come from, it is evident that they are not to be explained in terms of any goal or end, since they are what determines goals and ends. The form or quality of a given socius—the body of the earth, the body of the despot, the body of capital-money—depends on a state or degree of intensive development of the productive forces, insofar as these forces define a man-nature independent of all the social formations, or rather common to them all (what the Marxists term "the givens of useful labor"). The form or quality of the socius is therefore itself produced, but as the unengendered—that is, as the natural or divine precondition of production corresponding to a given degree to which it affixes a structural unity and apparent goals, to which it falls back, and whose forces it appropriates, thereby determining the selections, the accumulations, and the attractions without which these forces would not assume a social character. It is indeed in this sense that social production is desiring-production itself *under determinate conditions*. These determinate conditions are thus the forms of gregariousness as a socius or full body, under whose effect the molecular formations constitute molar aggregates.

Now we can present the second thesis of schizoanalysis: within the social investments we will distinguish the unconscious libidinal investment of group or desire, and the preconscious investment of class or interest. The latter passes by way of the large social goals, and concerns the organism and the collective organs, including the arranged vacuoles of lack. A class is defined by a régime of syntheses, a state of global connections, exclusive disjunctions, and residual conjunctions that characterize the aggregate being considered. Membership in a class refers to the role in production or antiproduction, to the place in the inscription, to the portion that is due the subjects. The preconscious class interest itself thus refers to the selections of flows, to the detachments of codes, to the subjective remains or revenues. And from this viewpoint it is indeed true that an aggregate comprises *practically* only a single class, that class which has an interest in a given régime. The other class can constitute itself only by a counterinvestment that creates its own interest in terms of new social aims, new organs and means, a new possible state of social syntheses. Whence the necessity for the other class to be represented by a party apparatus that assigns these aims and means, and effects a revolutionary break in the preconscious domain—the Leninist break, for example. In this domain of preconscious investments of class or interest it is therefore easy to distinguish what is reactionary or reformist, or what is revolutionary. But those who have an interest, in this sense, are always of a smaller number than those whose interest, in some fashion, "is had" or represented: the class from the standpoint of praxis is infinitely less numerous or less extensive than the class taken in its theoretical determination. Whence the subsisting contradictions within the dominant class, i.e., the class pure and simple. This is obvious in the capitalist régime where, for example, primitive accumulation can take place only for the benefit of a restricted fraction of the whole of the dominant class.* But it is just as obvious for the Russian Revolution, with its formation of a party apparatus.

This situation is not at all adequate, however, for resolving the following problem: why do many of those who have or should have an objective revolutionary interest maintain a preconscious investment of a reactionary type? And more rarely, how do certain people whose interest is objectively reactionary come to effect a preconscious revolutionary investment? Must we invoke in the one case a thirst for justice, a just ideological position, as well as a correct and just view; and in the other case a blindness, the result of an ideological deception or mystification? Revolutionaries often forget, or do not like to recognize, that one wants and makes revolution out of desire, not duty. Here as elsewhere, the concept of ideology is an execrable concept that hides the real problems, which are always of an organizational nature. If Reich, at

*Maurice Dobb, *Studies in the Development of Capitalism* (see Ch. 3, reference note 70), p. 178: "There are reasons why the full flowering of industrial capitalism demands, not only a transfer of titles to wealth into the hands of the bourgeois class, but a concentration of the ownership of wealth into much fewer hands."

the very moment he raised the most profound of questions—"Why did the masses desire fascism?"—was content to answer by invoking the ideological, the subjective, the irrational, the negative, and the inhibited, it was because he remained the prisoner of derived concepts that made him fall short of the materialist psychiatry he dreamed of, that prevented him from seeing how desire was part of the infrastructure, and that confined him in the duality of the objective and the subjective. (Consequently, psychoanalysis was consigned to the analysis of the subjective, as defined by ideology.) But everything is objective or subjective, as one wishes. That is not the distinction: the distinction to be made passes into the economic infrastructure itself *and into its investments.* Libidinal economy is no less objective than political economy, and the political no less subjective than the libidinal, even though the two correspond to two modes of different investments of the same reality as social reality. There is an unconscious libidinal investment of desire that does not necessarily coincide with the preconscious investments of interest, and that explains how the latter can be perturbed and perverted in "the most somber organization," below all ideology.

Libidinal investment does not bear upon the régime of the social syntheses, but upon the degree of development of the forces or the energies on which these syntheses depend. It does not bear upon the selections, detachments, and remainders effected by these syntheses, but upon the nature of the codes and the flows that condition them. It does not bear upon the social means and ends, but upon the full body as socius, the formation of sovereignty, or the form of power for itself, devoid of meaning and purpose, since the meanings and the purposes derive from it, and not the contrary. It is doubtless true that interests predispose us to a given libidinal investment, but they are not identical with this investment. Moreover, the unconscious libidinal investment is what causes us to look for our interest in one place rather than another, to fix our aims on a given path, convinced that this is where our chances lie—since love drives us on. The manifest syntheses are merely the preconscious indicators of a degree of development; the apparent interests and aims are merely the preconscious exponents of a social full body. As Klossowski says in his profound commentary on Nietzsche, a form of power is identical with the violence it exerts by its very absurdity, but it can exert this violence only by assigning itself aims and meanings in which even the most enslaved elements participate: "The sovereign formations will have no other purpose than that of masking the absence of a purpose or a meaning of their sovereignty by means of the organic purpose of their creation," and the purpose of thereby converting the absurdity into spirituality. That is why it is so futile to attempt to distinguish what is rational and what is irrational in a society. To be sure, the role, the place, and the part one has in a society, and from which one inherits in terms of the laws of social reproduction, impel the libido to invest a given socius as a full body—a given absurd power in which we participate, or have the chance to participate, under the cover of aims and interests. The fact remains that there exists a disinterested love of the social machine, of the form of power, and of the degree of development in and for themselves. Even in the person who has an interest—and loves them besides with a form of love other than that of his interest. This is also the case for the person who has no interest, and who substitutes the force of a strange love for this counterinvestment. Flows that run on the porous full body of a socius—these are the object of desire, higher than all the aims. It will never flow too much, it will never break or code enough—and in that very way! Oh how beautiful the machine is! The officer of "In the Penal Colony" demonstrates what an intense libidinal investment of a machine can be, a machine that is not only technical but social, and through which desire desires its own repression.

We have seen how the capitalist machine constituted a system of immanence bordered by a great mutant flow, nonpossessive and non-possessed, flowing over the full body of capital and forming an absurd power. Everyone in his class and his person receives something from this power, or is excluded from it, insofar as the great flow is converted into incomes, incomes of wages or of enterprises that define aims or spheres of interest, selections, detachments, and portions. But the investment of the flow itself and its axiomatic, which to be sure requires no precise knowledge of political economy, is the business of the unconscious libido, inasmuch as it is presupposed by the aims. We see the most disadvantaged, the most excluded members of society invest with passion the system that oppresses them, and where they always *find* an interest, since it is here that they search for and measure it. Interest always comes after. Antiproduction effuses in the system: antiproduction is loved for itself, as is the way in which desire represses itself in the great capitalist aggregate. Repressing desire, not only for others but in oneself, being the cop for others and for oneself—that is what arouses, and it is not ideology, it is economy. Capitalism garners and possesses the force of the aim and the interest (*power*), but it feels a disinterested love for the absurd and nonpossessed force of the machine. Oh, to be sure, it is not for himself or his children that the capitalist works, but for the immortality of the system. A violence without purpose, a joy, a pure joy in feeling oneself a wheel in the machine, traversed by flows, broken by schizzes. Placing oneself in a position where one is thus traversed, broken, fucked by the socius, looking for the right place where, according to the aims and the interests assigned to us, one feels something moving that has neither an interest nor a purpose. A sort of art for art's sake in the libido, a taste for a job well done, each one in his own place, the banker, the cop, the soldier, the technocrat, the bureaucrat, and why not the worker, the trade-unionist. Desire is agape.

Not only can the libidinal investment of the social field interfere with the investment of interest, and constrain the most disadvantaged, the most exploited, to seek their ends in an oppressive machine, but what is reactionary or revolutionary in the preconscious investment of interest does not necessarily coincide with what is reactionary or revolutionary in the unconscious libidinal investment. A revolutionary preconscious investment bears upon new aims, new social syntheses, a new power. But it could be that a part at least of the unconscious libido continues to invest the former body, the old form of power, its codes, and its flows. It is all the easier, and the contradiction is all the better masked, as a state of forces does not prevail over the former state without preserving or reviving the old full body as a residual and subordinated territoriality (witness how the capitalist machine revives the despotic Urstaat, or how the socialist machine preserves a State and market monopoly capitalism). But there is something more serious: even when the libido embraces the new body—the new force that corresponds to the effectively revolutionary goals and syntheses from the viewpoint of the preconscious—it is not certain that the unconscious libidinal investment is itself revolutionary. For the same breaks do not pass at the level of the unconscious desires and the preconscious interests. The preconscious revolutionary break is sufficiently well defined by the promotion of a socius as a full body carrying new aims, as a form of power or a formation of sovereignty that subordinates desiring-production under new conditions. But even though the unconscious libido is charged with investing this socius, its investment is not necessarily revolutionary in the same sense as the preconscious investment. In fact, the unconscious revolutionary break implies for its part the body without organs as the limit of the socius that desiring-production subordinates in its turn, under the condition of an overthrown power, an overthrown subordination.

The preconscious revolution refers to a new régime of social production that creates, distributes, and satisfies new aims and interests. But the unconscious revolution does not merely refer to the socius that conditions this change as a form of power; it refers within this socius to the régime of desiring-production as an overthrown power on the body without organs. It is not the same state of flows and schizzes: in one case the break is between two forms of socius, the second of which is measured according to its capacity to introduce the flows of desire into a new code or a new axiomatic of interest; in the other case the break is within the socius itself, in that it has the capacity for causing the flows of desire to circulate following their positive lines of escape, and for breaking them again following breaks of productive breaks. The most general principle of schizoanalysis is that desire is always constitutive of a social field. In any case desire belongs to the infrastructure, not to ideology: desire is in production as social production, just as production is in desire as desiring-production. But these forms can be understood in two ways, depending on whether desire is enslaved to a structured molar aggregate that it constitutes under a given form of power and gregariousness, or whether it subjugates the large aggregate to the functional multiplicities that it itself forms on the molecular scale (it is no more a case of persons or individuals in this instance than in the other). If the preconscious revolutionary break appears at the first level, and is defined by the characteristics of a new aggregate, the unconscious or libidinal break belongs to the second level and is defined by the driving role of desiring-production and the position of its multiplicities. It is understandable, therefore, that a group can be revolutionary from the standpoint of class interest and its preconscious investments, but not be so—and even remain fascist and police-like—from the standpoint of its libidinal investments. Truly revolutionary preconscious interests do not necessarily imply unconscious investments of the same nature; an apparatus of interest never takes the place of a machine of desire.

A revolutionary group at the preconscious level remains a *subjugated group,* even in seizing power, as long as this power itself refers to a form of force that continues to enslave and crush desiring-production. The moment it is preconsciously revolutionary, such a group already presents all the unconscious characteristics of a subjugated group: the subordination to a socius as a fixed support that attributes to itself the productive forces, extracting and absorbing the surplus value therefrom; the effusion of antiproduction and death-carrying elements within the system, which feels and pretends to be all the more immortal; the phenomena of group "superegoization," narcissism, and hierarchy—the mechanisms for the repression of desire. A *subject-group,* on the contrary, is a group whose libidinal investments are themselves revolutionary; it causes desire to penetrate into the social field, and subordinates the socius or the form of power to desiring-production; productive of desire and a desire that produces, the subject-group invents always mortal formations that exorcise the effusion in it of a death instinct; it opposes real coefficients of transversality to the symbolic determinations of subjugation, coefficients without a hierarchy or a group superego. What complicates everything, it is true, is that the same individuals can participate in both kinds of groups in diverse ways (Saint-Juste, Lenin). Or the same group can present both characteristics at the same time, in diverse situations that are nevertheless coexistent. A revolutionary group can already have reassumed the form of a subjugated group, yet be determined under certain conditions to continue to play the role of a subject-group. One is continually passing from one type of group to the other. Subject-groups are continually deriving from subjugated groups through a rupture of the latter: they mobilize desire, and always cut its flows again further on, overcoming the limit, bringing the social machines back to the elementary forces of desire that form them.*

But inversely, they are also continually closing up again, remodeling themselves in the image of subjugated groups: re-establishing interior limits, reforming a great break that the flows will not pass through or overcome, subordinating the desiring-machines to the repressive aggregate that they constitute on a large scale. There is a speed of subjugation that is opposed to the coefficients of transversality. And what revolution is not tempted to turn against its subject-groups, stigmatized as anarchistic or irresponsible, and to liquidate them? How do we combat the deadly inclination that makes a group pass from its revolutionary libidinal investments to revolutionary investments that are simply preconscious investments or investments of interest, then to preconscious investments that are simply reformist? And where do we even situate such and such a group? Did it ever have revolutionary unconscious investments? The surrealist group, for example, with its fantastic subjugation, its narcissism, and its superego? (It can happen that one lone man functions as a flow-schiz, as a subject-group, through a break with the subjugated group from which he excludes himself or is excluded: Artaud-the-schizo). And where do we situate the psychoanalytic group within this complexity of social investments? Every time we wonder when it started going bad, it is always necessary to trace further back in time. Freud as the group superego, an oedipalizing grandfather, establishing Oedipus as an interior limit, with all kinds of little Narcissuses around, and Reich-the-marginal, plotting a tangent of deterritorialization, causing the flows of desire to circulate, smashing the limit,

*On the group and its rupture or schiz, see Jean-Pierre Faye, "Eclats," *Change*, no. 7, p. 217: "What counts, what is effective in our opinion, is not such and such a group, but rather the dispersion or the Diaspora produced by their splinterings (*éclats*)." Also pp. 212–13, on the necessarily polyvocal character of subject-groups and their writing.

breaching the wall. But it is not just a matter of literature or even psychoanalysis. It is a matter of politics—though not, as we shall see, of a *program*.

The task of schizoanalysis is therefore to reach the investments of unconscious desire of the social field, insofar as they are differentiated from the preconscious investments of interest, and insofar as they are not merely capable of counteracting them, but also of coexisting with them in opposite modes. In the generation-gap conflict we hear old people reproach the young, in the most malicious way, for putting their desires (a car, credit, a loan, girl-boy relationships) ahead of their interests (work, savings, a good marriage). But what appears to other people as raw desire still contains complexes of desire and interest, and a mixture of forms of desire and of interest that are specifically reactionary and vaguely revolutionary. The situation is completely muddled. It seems that schizoanalysis can make use only of indices—the machinic indices—in order to discern, at the level of groups or individuals, the libidinal investments of the social field. Now in this respect it is sexuality that constitutes the indices. Not that the revolutionary capacity can be evaluated in terms of the objects, the aims, or the sources of the sexual drives animating an individual or a group; assuredly perversions, and even sexual emancipation, give no privilege as long as sexuality remains confined within the framework of the "dirty little secret." It is in vain that the secret is published, that one demands one's right to be heard; it can even be disinfected, treated in a psychoanalytic or scientific manner, yet thereby one stands a greater chance of killing desire, or of inventing forms of liberation for it drearier than the most repressive prison—as long as one has not succeeded in rescuing sexuality from the category of secrets, even if public, even if disinfected: i.e., as long as it has not been rescued from the Oedipal-narcissistic origin imposed on it as the lie under which it can merely become cynical, shameful, and mortified. It is a lie to claim to liberate sexuality, and to demand its rights to objects, aims, and sources, all the while maintaining the corresponding flows within the limits of an Oedipal code (conflict, regression, resolution, sublimation of Oedipus), and while continuing to impose a familialist and masturbatory form or motivation on it that makes any perspective of liberation futile in advance. For example, no "gay liberation movement" is possible as long as homosexuality is caught up in a relation of exclusive disjunction with heterosexuality, a relation that ascribes them both to a common Oedipal and castrating stock, charged with ensuring only their differentiation in two noncommunicating series, instead of bringing to light their reciprocal inclusion and their transverse communication in the decoded flows of desire (included disjunctions, local connections, nomadic conjunctions). In short, sexual repression, more insistent than ever, will survive all the publications, demonstrations, emancipations, and protests concerning the liberty of sexual objects, sources, and aims, as long as sexuality is kept—consciously or not—within narcissistic, Oedipal, and castrating co-ordinates that are enough to ensure the triumph of the most rigorous censors, the gray gentlemen mentioned by Lawrence.

Lawrence shows in a profound way that sexuality, including chastity, is a matter of flows, an infinity of different and even contrary flows. Everything depends on the way in which these flows—whatever their object, source, and aim—are coded and broken according to uniform figures, or on the contrary taken up in chains of decoding that resect them according to mobile and nonfigurative points (the flows-schizzes). Lawrence attacks the poverty of the immutable identical images, the figurative roles that are so many tourniquets cutting off the flows of sexuality: "fiancée, mistress, wife, mother"—one could just as easily add "homosexuals, heterosexuals," etc.—all these roles are distributed by the Oedipal triangle, father-mother-me, a representative ego thought to be defined in terms of the father-mother representations, by fixation, regression, assumption, sublimation—and all of that according to what rule? The law of the great Phallus that no one possesses, the despotic signifier prompting the most miserable struggle, a common absence for all the reciprocal exclusions where the flows dry up, drained by bad conscience and *ressentiment.* ". . . sticking a woman on a pedestal, or the reverse, sticking her beneath notice; or making a 'model' housewife of her, or a 'model' mother, or a 'model' help-meet. All mere devices for avoiding any contact with her. A woman is not a 'model' anything. She is not even a distinct and definite personality. . . . A woman is a strange soft vibration on the air, going forth unknown and unconscious, and seeking a vibration of response. Or else she is a discordant, jarring, painful vibration, going forth and hurting everyone within range. *And a man the same.*"[41] Let's not be too quick to make light of the pantheism of flows present in such texts as this: it is not easy to de-oedipalize even nature, even landscapes, to the extent that Lawrence could. The fundamental difference between psychoanalysis and schizoanalysis is the following: schizoanalysis attains a nonfigurative and nonsymbolic unconscious, a pure abstract figural dimension ("abstract" in the sense of abstract painting), flows-schizzes or real-desire, apprehended below the minimum conditions of identity.

What does psychoanalysis do, and first of all what does Freud do, if not maintain sexuality under the morbid yoke of the little secret, while finding medical means for rendering it public, for making it into an open secret, the analytic Oedipus? We are told, "See here, it's quite normal, everybody's like that," but one continues to embrace the same humiliating and degrading conception of sexuality, the same figurative conception *as the censors'*. It is certain that psychoanalysis has not made its pictorial revolution. There is a hypothesis dear to Freud: the libido does not invest the social field as such except on condition that it be desexualized and sublimated. If he holds so closely to this hypothesis, it is because he wants above all to keep sexuality in the limited framework of Narcissus and Oedipus, the ego and the family. Consequently, every sexual libidinal investment having a social dimension seems to him to testify to a pathogenic state, a "fixation" in narcissism, or a "regression" to Oedipus and to the pre-oedipal stages, by means of which homosexuality will be explained as a reinforced drive, and paranoia as a means of defense.[42] We have seen on the contrary that what the libido invested, through its loves and sexuality, was the social field itself in its economic, political, historical, racial, and cultural determinations: in delirium the libido is continually re-creating History, continents, kingdoms, races, and cultures. Not that it is advisable to put historical representations in the place of the familial representations of the Freudian unconscious, or even the archetypes of a collective unconscious. It is merely a question of ascertaining that our choices in matters of love are at the crossroads of "vibrations," which is to say that they express connections, disjunctions, and conjunctions of flows that cross through a society, entering and leaving it, linking it up with other societies, ancient or contemporary, remote or vanished, dead or yet to be born. Africas and Orients, always following the underground thread of the libido. Not geohistorical figures or statues, although our apprenticeship is more readily accomplished with these figures, with books, histories, and reproductions, than with our mommy. But flows and codes of socius that do not portray anything, that merely *designate* zones of libidinal intensity on the body without organs, and that are emitted, captured, intercepted by the being that we are then determined to love, like a point-sign, a singular point in the entire network of the intensive body that responds to History, that vibrates with it. Never was Freud more adventurous than in *Gradiva*. In short, our libidinal investments of the social field, reactionary or revolutionary, are so well hidden, so unconscious, so well masked by the preconscious investments, that they appear only in our sexual choices of lovers. A love is not reactionary or revolutionary, but it is the index of the reactionary or revolutionary character of the social investments of the libido. The desiring sexual relationships of man and woman (or of man and man, or woman and woman) are the index of social relationships between people. Love and sexuality are the exponents or the indicators, this time unconscious, of the libidinal investments of the social field. Every loved or desired being serves as a collective agent of enunciation. And it is certainly not, as Freud believed, the libido that must be desexualized and sublimated in order to invest society and its flows; on the contrary, it is love, desire, and their flows that manifest the directly social character of the nonsublimated libido and its sexual investments.

For those looking for a thesis topic on psychoanalysis, one should not suggest vast considerations on analytic epistemology, but modest and rigorous topics such as the theory of maids or domestic servants in Freud's thought. There are some real indices in such areas. On the subject of maids—who are present everywhere in the cases studied by Freud—there occurs an exemplary hesitation in Freudian thought, a hesitation too quickly resolved in favor of what was to become a dogma of psychoanalysis. Philippe Girard, in unpublished remarks that seem to us to have a wide application, situates the problem at several levels. In the first place, Freud discovers "his own" Oedipus in a complex social context that brings into play the older half brother from the rich side of the family, and the thievish maid as the poor woman. Secondly, the familial romance and fantasy activity in general will be presented by Freud as a veritable drift of the social field, where one substitutes persons of a *higher or lower rank* for the parents (the son of a princess kidnapped by gypsies, or the son of a poor man taken in by bourgeois); Oedipus was already doing this when he claimed a low birth of servant parents. Thirdly, the Rat Man not only installs his neurosis in a social field determined from one end to the other as military, he not only makes it revolve around a form of torture originating in the Orient, but also in this very field he causes his neurosis to oscillate between two poles constituted by *the rich woman and the poor woman*, under the effect of a strange unconscious communication with the unconscious of the father. Lacan was the first to emphasize these themes, which were enough to challenge the whole of Oedipus; and he shows the existence of a "social complex" where the subject at times attempts to assume his own role—but at the price of a splitting of the sexual object into a rich woman and a poor woman—and at other times ensures the unity of the object, but this time at the price of a splitting of "his own social function" at the other extremity of the chain. Fourthly, the Wolf Man demonstrates a marked taste for the poor woman: the peasant girl on all fours washing some clothes, or the servant scrubbing the floor.[43]

The fundamental problem with regard to these texts is the following: must we see, in all these *sexual-social* investments of the libido and these object choices, mere dependences of a familial Oedipus? Must we save Oedipus at all costs by interpreting these investments and object choices as defenses against incest? (Thus the familial romance, or Oedipus's own wish to have been born of poor parents who would cleanse him of his crime.) Must these be understood as compromises and substitutes for incest? (Thus in "The Wolf Man," the peasant girl as a substitute for the sister, having the same name as she, or the girl on hands and knees, working, as a substitute for the mother surprised in the coitus scene; and in *The Rat Man*, the disguised repetition of the paternal situation, making it possible to enrich or impregnate Oedipus with a fourth "symbolic" term charged with accounting for the splittings through which the libido invests the social field.) Freud makes a firm choice of this last direction; all the more firm in that, according to his own confession, he wants to set things straight with Jung and Adler. And after having ascertained in the Wolf Man case the existence of an "intention of debasing" the woman as love object, he concludes that it is merely a matter of a "rationalization," and that the "true underlying determination" almost always leads us back to the sister, to the mommy, considered as the only "purely erotic motives"! Taking up the eternal refrain of Oedipus, the eternal lullaby, he writes: "A child pays no regard to social distinctions, which have little meaning for it as yet; and it classes people of inferior rank with its parents if they love it as its parents do."[44]

We always fall back into the false alternative where Freud was led by Oedipus, and then confirmed in this position by his controversy with Adler and Jung: either, he says, you will abandon the sexual position of the libido in favor of an individual and social will to power, or in favor of a prehistoric collective unconscious—or you will recognize Oedipus, making of it the sexual abode of the libido, and you will make daddy-mommy into "the purely erotic motive." Oedipus: the touchstone of the pure psychoanalyst, on which to sharpen the sacred blade of a *successful castration.* Yet what was the other direction, glimpsed for a moment by Freud apropos of the familial romance, before the Oedipal trapdoor slams shut? It is the direction rediscovered, at least hypothetically, by Philippe Girard: there is no family where vacuoles are not arranged, and where extrafamilial breaks are not manifest, by means of which the libido is engulfed in order to sexually invest the nonfamilial— i.e., *the other class* as determined under the empirical rubrics of the "richest and the poorest," and sometimes both at once. Wouldn't the Great Other, indispensable to the position of desire, be the Social Other, social difference apprehended and invested as the nonfamily within the family itself? The other class is by no means grasped by the libido as a magnified or impoverished image of the mother, but as the foreign, the nonmother, the nonfather, the nonfamily, *the index of what is nonhuman in sex,* and without which the libido would not assemble its desiring-machines. Class struggle goes to the heart of the ordeal of desire. The familial romance is not a derivative of Oedipus; Oedipus is a drift of the familial romance, and thereby of the social field. It is not a question of denying the importance of parental coitus, and the position of the mother; but when this position makes the mother resemble a floor-washer, or an animal, what authorizes Freud to say that the animal or the maid stand for the mother, independently of the social or generic differences, instead of concluding that the mother also functions as something other than the mother, and gives rise in the child's libido to an entire differentiated social investment at the same time as she opens the way to a relation with the nonhuman sex? For whether the mother works or not, whether the mother is from a richer or poorer background than the father, etc., has to do with breaks and flows that traverse the family, but that overreach it on all sides and are not familial.

From the start we wonder if the libido knows father-mother, or rather if it makes the parents function as something entirely different, as agents of production in relation to other agents in sociodesiring-production. From the point of view of libidinal investment, parents not only open to the other, they are themselves countersected and divided by the other who defamilializes them according to the laws of social production and desiring-production: the mother herself functions as rich woman or poor woman, maid or princess, pretty girl or old lady, animal or Blessed Virgin, and all at once. Everything passes into the machine that causes the properly familial determinations to disintegrate. What the orphan libido invests is a field of social desire, a field of production and antiproduction with its breaks and flows, where the parents are apprehended in nonparental functions and roles confronting other roles and other functions. Does this amount to saying that the parents have no unconscious role as such? Of course they have an unconscious role, but in two quite specific ways that deprive them even more of their supposed autonomy. In accordance with the distinction made by embry-ologists with regard to the egg between the stimulus and the organizer, parents are *stimuli having an indifferent value* that trigger the allocation of gradients or zones of intensity on the body without organs: it is in relation to the parents that in each case wealth or poverty will be situated, the relative richest or poorest, as empirical forms of social difference—so that within this difference the parents again appear, allocated to such and such a zone, but under a different rubric from that of parents. And the organizer is the social field of desire, which alone *designates* the zones of intensity, with all the beings that populate these zones and determine their libidinal investment. Secondly, the parents as parents are terms of application that express the reduction of the social field invested by the libido to a finite aggregate of destination, where the destination finds nothing but impasses and blockages consonant with the mechanisms of psychic and social repression active in this field: Oedipus, such is Oedipus. In each of these senses, the third thesis of schizoanalysis posits the primacy of the libidinal investments of the social field over the familial investment, both in point of fact and by statute: an indifferent stimulus at the beginning, an extrinsic result at the point of arrival. The relation to the nonfamilial is always primary: in the form of sexuality of the field in social production, and the nonhuman sex in desiring-production (gigantism and dwarfism).

One often has the impression that families have understood the lesson of psychoanalysis only too well, even from far off or by osmosis, in the air of the times: *they play at Oedipus,* a sublime alibi. But behind all this, there is an economic situation: the mother reduced to house-work, or to a difficult and uninteresting job on the outside; children whose future remains uncertain; the father who has had it with feeding all those mouths—in short, a fundamental relation to the outside of which the psychoanalyst washes his hands, too attentive to seeing that his clients play nice games. Now the economic situation, the relation to the outside, is what the libido invests and counterinvests as sexual libido. One gets off on flows and the breaks in these flows. Let us consider for a moment the motivations that lead someone to be psychoanalyzed: it involves a situation of economic dependence that has become unbearable for desire, or full of conflicts for the investment of desire. The psychoanalyst, who says so many things about the necessity for money in the cure, remains supremely indifferent to the question of who is footing the bill. For example, the analysis reveals the unconscious conflicts of a woman with her husband, but the husband is paying for his wife's analysis. This isn't the only time we encounter the duality of money, as a structure of external financing and as a means of internal payment, along with the objective "dissimulation" that it comprises, essential to the capitalist system. But it is interesting to find this essential concealment, miniaturized, occupying a place of honor in the analyst's office. The analyst talks about Oedipus, about castration and the phallus, about the necessity of assuming one's sex, as Freud says, the human sex, and the necessity for the woman to renounce her desire for the penis and for the man to renounce his male protest. We maintain that there is not one woman—more particularly, not one child—who can as such "assume" her or his situation in a capitalist society, precisely because this situation has nothing to do with the phallus and castration, but directly concerns an unbearable economic dependence. And the woman and the children who succeed in "assuming" do so only by detours and determinations completely distinct from their being-woman and their being-child. Nothing to do with the phallus, but much to do with desire, with sexuality as desire. For the phallus has never been either the object or the cause of desire, but is itself the castrating apparatus, the machine for putting lack into desire, for drying up all the flows, and for making all the breaks *from* the outside and *from* the Real into one and the same break *with* the outside, *with* the Real.

Too much always penetrates from the outside, where the analyst is concerned, too much penetrates into his office. Even the closed familial scene appears to him to be an excessive outside. He promotes the pure analytic scene, an office Oedipus and an office castration, that should be its own reality, its own proof, and that, contrary to the movement, proves itself only by not working, by being interminable. Psychoanalysis has become quite a stupefying drug, where the strangest personal dependence allows the clients to forget, during the time spent in sessions on the couch, the economic dependencies that drive them there in the first place (a bit like the way the decoding of flows entails a reinforcement of bondage). Do these psychoanalysts who are oedipalizing women, children, blacks, and animals know what they are doing? We dream of entering their offices, opening the windows and saying, "It smells stuffy in here—some relation with the outside, if you please." For desire does not survive cut off from the outside, cut off from its economic and social investments and counterinvestments. And if there is, to use Freud's terms, a "purely erotic motive," it is certainly not Oedipus that harbors it, nor the phallus that actuates it, nor castration that transmits it. The erotic, the purely erotic motive pervades the social field, wherever desiring-machines are agglutinated or dispersed in social machines, and where love-object choices occur at the meeting place of the two kinds of machine, following lines of escape or integration. Will Aaron leave with his flute, which is not a phallus, but a desiring-machine and a process of deterritorialization?

Let us suppose that we are granted everything: it will only be granted *afterward*. It is only afterward that the libido would invest the social field, and that it would "participate" in the social and the metaphysical. Which permits the preservation of the fundamental Freudian position, according to which the libido must be desexualized in order to perform such investments, but begins with Oedipus, me, father and mother (the pre-oedipal stages relating structurally or eschatologically to the Oedipal organization). We have seen that this conception of the afterward implied a radical misunderstanding with regard to the nature of the actual factors. For either the libido is caught up in molecular desiring-production and knows nothing of persons just as it knows nothing of the ego—even the most undifferentiated ego of narcissism—since its investments are already differentiated, but differentiated according to the prepersonal régime of partial objects, of singularities, of intensities, of gears and parts of machines of desire, where one would have a hard time recognizing mother or father or me (we have seen how contradictory it was to invoke the partial objects, and to make of them representatives of parental persons or the supports of familial relations); or on the other hand the libido invests persons and an ego, but is already caught up in a social production and social machines that do not merely differentiate them as familial beings, but as derivatives of the molar aggregate to which they belong under this other régime.

It is indeed true that the social and the metaphysical arrive at the same time, in accordance with the two simultaneous meanings of *process,* as the historical process of social production and as the metaphysical process of desiring-production. But they do not come afterward. Lindner's painting again asserts its presence, where the turgid little boy has already plugged a desiring-machine into a social machine, short-circuiting the parents, who can only intervene as agents of production and antiproduction in one case as in the other. There is only the social and the metaphysical. If something crops up afterward, it is certainly not the social and metaphysical investments of the libido, the unconscious syntheses; rather, on the contrary, it is Oedipus, narcissism, and the entire series of psychoanalytic concepts. The factors of production are always "actual," and are so from the tenderest age; "actual" does not signify recent as opposed to infantile, but rather in action, as opposed to what is virtual and will come about under certain conditions. Oedipus is virtual and reactional. Let us consider the conditions under which Oedipus arrives: an aggregate of departure—transfinite, constituted by all the objects, agents, and relations of sociodesiring-production—is reduced to a finite familial aggregate as an aggregate of arrival (a minimum of three terms, which one can and even must augment, but not to infinity). Such an *application* in fact presupposes a fourth, extrapolated, mobile term, the symbolic abstract phallus, charged with performing the folding or the correspondence; but this application effectively operates on the three persons who constitute the minimum familial constellation, or on their substitutes—father, mother, child. One does not stop there, since these three terms tend to be reduced to two, either in the scene of castration where the father kills the child, or in the scene of the terrible mother where the mother kills the child or the father. Then from two we pass to one in narcissism, which in no way precedes Oedipus but is its product. That is why we speak of an Oedipal-narcissistic machine, at the end of which the ego encounters its own death, as the zero term of a pure abolition that has haunted oedipalized desire from the start, and that is identified now, at the end, as Thanatos. 4, 3, 2, 1, 0—Oedipus is a race for death.

Since the nineteenth century, the study of mental illnesses and madness has remained the prisoner of the familial postulate and its correlates, the personological correlate and the egoic postulate (*le postulat moïïque*). We have seen, following Foucault, how nineteenth-century psychiatry had conceived of the family as both cause and judge of the illness, and the closed asylum as an artificial family charged with internalizing guilt and with instituting responsibility, enveloping madness no less than its cure in a father-child relationship everywhere present. In this respect, far from breaking with psychiatry, psychoanalysis transported its requirements outside the asylum walls, and first imposed a certain "free," intensive, phantasmal use of the family that seemed particularly suited to what was isolated as the neuroses. But the resistance of the psychoses on the one hand, and the necessity for taking into account a social etiology on the other hand, has led psychiatrists and psychoanalysts to redeploy under open conditions the order of an extended family, which is still believed to possess the secret of the illness as well as its cure. After the family has been internalized in Oedipus, Oedipus is externalized in the symbolic order, in the institutional order, in the community order, the sectorial order, etc. This progression contains a constant of all modern attempts at reform. And if this tendency appears in its most naïve form in community psychiatry aimed at adjustment—"the therapeutic return to the family," to the identity of persons and the integrity of the ego, the whole works being blessed by successful castration in a sacred triangular form—the same tendency in more disguised forms is at work in other trends. It is not by chance that Lacan's symbolic order has been diverted, utilized for grounding a structural Oedipus applicable to psychosis, and for extending the familial co-ordinates beyond their real and even imaginary domain. It is not by chance that institutional analysis has difficulty in maintaining a position against the reconstitution of artificial families where the symbolic order, embodied in the institution, re-forms group Oedipuses, with all the lethal characteristics of the subjugated groups.

What is more, antipsychiatry has sought the secret of a causality at once social and schizophrenic in the redeployed families. This is perhaps where the mystification appears most clearly, because antipsychiatry, by certain of its aspects, was the most suited to break with the traditional familial reference. What does one see, in fact, in the American familial-ist studies pursued by antipsychiatrists? Completely ordinary families are baptized as schizophrenogenic, as well as completely ordinary familial mechanisms, and an ordinary familial logic, i.e., neuroticizing at worst. In so-called schizophrenic familial monographs everyone easily recognizes his own daddy, his own mommy. For example, Bateson's "double impasse" or "double bind": where is there a father who doesn't simultaneously transmit the two contradictory injunctions—"Let's be friends, son, I'm the best friend you've got," and "Watch out, son, don't treat me like one of your buddies"? There is nothing there with which to make a schizophrenic. We have seen in this sense that the double impasse in no way defined a specific schizophrenogenic mechanism, but merely characterized Oedipus in the whole of its extension. If there is a veritable impasse, a veritable contradiction, it is the one into which the researcher himself is led, when he claims to assign schizophrenogenic social mechanisms, and at the same time to discover them within the order of the family, which both social production and the schizophrenic process escape. This contradiction is perhaps especially perceptible in Laing, because he is the most revolutionary of the antipsychiatrists. At the very moment he breaks with psychiatric practice, undertakes assigning a veritable social genesis to psychosis, and calls for a continuation of the "voyage" as a process and for a dissolution of the "normal ego," he falls back into the worst familialist, personological, and egoic postulates, so that the remedies invoked are no more than a "sincere corroboration among parents," a "recognition of the real persons," a discovery of the true ego or self as in Martin Buber.[45] Even more than the hostility of traditional authorities, perhaps this is the source of the actual failure of the antipsychiatric undertakings, of their co-option for the benefit of adaptational forms of familial psychotherapy and of community psychiatry, and of Laing's own retreat to the Orient. And is it not a contradiction on another level, but analogous, when some, attempting to hasten the teaching of Lacan, place it back on a familial and personological axis—whereas Lacan assigns the cause of desire in a nonhuman "object," heterogeneous to the person, below the minimum conditions of identity, escaping the intersubjective co-ordinates as well as the world of meanings?

Long live the Ndembu, for if we follow the detailed account by the ethnologist Turner, the Ndembu doctor alone has been able to treat Oedipus as an appearance, a décor, and to go back to the unconscious libidinal investments of the social field. Oedipal familialism, even and especially in its most modern forms, makes impossible the discovery of what one claims nevertheless to be searching for today: schizophrenogenic social production. In the first place, it is futile to affirm that the family expresses more profound social contradictions, for one confers on it a value as microcosm, gives it the role of a necessary relay for the transformation of social into mental alienation; what is more, one acts as if the libido did not directly invest the social contradictions as such, and in order to awaken, needed these contradictions translated according to the family code. By that very fact, one has already substituted a familial causation or expression for social production, and finds oneself back within the categories of idealist psychiatry. Whatever one's stake in all of this, society is thereby justified: all that remains to contest it with are vague considerations on the sick nature of the family, or more generally still, considerations on the modern way of life. One has therefore glossed over what is essential: that society is schizophrenizing at the level of its infrastructure, its mode of production, its most precise capitalist economic circuits; and that the libido invests this social field, not in a form where it would be expressed and translated by means of a family-microcosm, but in the form where it causes its nonfamilial breaks and flows, invested as such, to enter into the family; hence, that the familial investments are always a result of the sociodesiring libidinal investments, which alone are primary; finally, that mental alienation refers directly to these investments and is no less social than social alienation, which refers for its part to the preconscious investments of interest.

Not only does one thereby fail to correctly evaluate social production in its pathogenic nature, but secondly, one also fails to understand the schizophrenic process in its relationship with the schizophrenic as a sick person. For one attempts to neuroticize everything. And doubtless one thus conforms to the family's mission, which is to produce neurotics by means of its oedipalization, its system of impasses, its delegated psychic repression, without which social repression would never find docile and resigned subjects, and would not succeed in choking off the flows' lines of escape. We don't feel any need to attach the slightest importance to psychoanalysis's claim to cure neurosis, since, for it, curing consists of an infinite maintenance, an infinite resignation, an accession to desire by way of castration—and of the establishment of conditions where the subject is able to spread, to pass the sickness to his offspring, rather than dying celibate, impotent, and masturbatory. Again, perhaps it will be discovered that *the only incurable is the neurotic*— whence interminable psychoanalysis. It is a cause for self-congratulation when one succeeds in transforming a schizo into a paranoiac or a neurotic. Such a transformation perhaps entails many misunderstandings. For the schizo is the one who escapes all Oedipal, familial, and personological references—I'll no longer say me, I'll no longer say daddy-mommy—and he keeps his word. Now the question is, first, if that is what makes him ill, or if on the contrary that is the schizophrenic process, which is not an illness, not a "breakdown" but a "breakthrough," however distressing and adventurous: breaking through the wall or the limit separating us from desiring-production, causing the flows of desire to circulate. Laing's importance lies in the fact that, starting from certain intuitions that remained ambiguous in Jaspers, he was able to indicate the incredible scope of this voyage. With the result that schizoanalysis would come to nothing if it did not add to its positive tasks the constant destructive task of disintegrating the normal ego. Lawrence, Miller, and then Laing were able to demonstrate this in a profound way: it is certain that neither men nor women are clearly defined personalities, but rather vibrations, flows, schizzes, and "knots." The ego refers to personological co-ordinates from which it results, persons in their turn refer to familial co-ordinates, and we shall see what the familial constellation refers to in order to produce individuals in its turn. The task of schizoanalysis is that of tirelessly taking apart egos and their presuppositions; liberating the prepersonal singularities they enclose and repress; mobilizing the flows they would be capable of transmitting, receiving, or intercepting; establishing always further and more sharply the schizzes and the breaks well below conditions of identity; and assembling the desiring-machines that countersect everyone and group everyone with others. For everyone is a little group (*un groupuscule*) and must live as such—or rather, like the Zen tea box broken in a hundred places, whose every crack is repaired with cement made of gold, or like the church tile whose every fissure is accentuated by the layers of paint or lime covering it (the contrary of castration, which is unified, molarized, hidden, scarred, unproductive). Schizoanalysis is so named because throughout its entire process of treatment it schizophrenizes, instead of neuroticizing like psychoanalysis.

What makes the schizophrenic ill, since the cause of the illness is not schizophrenia as a process? What transforms the breakthrough into a breakdown? It is the constrained arrest of the process, or its continuation in the void, or the way in which it is forced to take itself as a goal. We have seen in this sense how social production produced the sick schizo: constructed on decoded flows that constitute its profound tendency or its absolute limit, capitalism is constantly counteracting this tendency, exorcizing this limit by substituting internal relative limits for it that it can reproduce on an ever expanding scale, or an axiomatic of flows that subjects this tendency to the harshest forms of despotism and repression. It is in this sense that contradiction installs itself not only at the level of the flows that traverse the social field, but at the level of their libidinal investments, which form the flows' constituent parts—between the paranoiac reconstruction of the Urstaat and the positive schizophrenic lines of escape. Thereafter three possibilities emerge. First, the process is arrested, the limit of desiring-production is displaced, travestied, and now passes over into the Oedipal subaggregate. So the schizo is effectively neuroticized, and it is this neuroticization that constitutes his illness, for in any case neuroticization precedes neurosis, the latter being the result of the former. Or, second, the schizo resists neuroticization and oedipalization. Even the use of modern resources, the pure analytic scene, the symbolic phallus, structural foreclosure, and the name of the father do not succeed in "taking" on him. (Here again, in these modern resources, what a strange use is made of Lacan's discoveries—Lacan, who was the first on the contrary to schizophrenize the analytic field!) In this second case the process, confronted with a neuroticization that it resists, but that suffices to block it on all sides, is led to take itself as an end: a psychotic is produced who escapes the delegated repression properly speaking only to take refuge in primal repression, closing the body without organs around itself and silencing his desiring-machines. Catatonia rather than neurosis, catatonia rather than Oedipus and castration—but it is still an effect of neuroticization, a countereffect of one and the same illness. Or—the third case—the process sets to turning round in the void. Since it is now a process of deterritorialization, it can no longer search for and create its new land. Confronted with Oedipal reterritorialization—an archaic, residual, ludicrously restricted sphere—it will form still more artificial lands that, barring an accident, accommodate themselves in one way or another to the established order: the pervert. After all, Oedipus was already an artificial sphere, O family! And the resistance to Oedipus, the return to the body without organs was still an artificial sphere, O asylum! So that everything is perversion. But everything is psychosis and paranoia as well, since everything is set in motion by the counterinvestment of the social field that produces the psychotic. Again, everything is neurosis, since it is an outcome of the neuroticization that runs counter to the process. Finally, everything is process, schizophrenia as process, since it is against schizophrenia that everything is measured; its peculiar trajectory, its neurotic arrests, its perverse continuations in the void, its psychotic finalizations.

Inasmuch as Oedipus arises out of an application of the entire social field to the finite familial figure, it does not imply just any investment of this field by the libido, but a very particular investment that renders this application possible and necessary. That is why Oedipus seemed to us a paranoiac's idea before being a neurotic's feeling. In fact, the paranoiac investment consists in subordinating molecular desiring-production to the molar aggregate it forms on one surface of the full body without organs, enslaving it by that very fact to a form of socius that exercises the function of a full body under determinate conditions. The paranoiac engineers masses, and is continually forming large aggregates, inventing heavy apparatuses for the regimentation and the repression of the desiring-machines. Doubtless it is not hard for him to appear reasonable, by appealing to collective interests and goals, reforms to be brought about, sometimes even revolutions to be made. But madness breaks through, beneath the reformist investments, or the reactionary and fascist investments, which assume a reasonable appearance only in the light of the preconscious, and which animate the strange discourse of an organization of society. Even its language is demented. Listen to a Secretary of State, a general, the boss of a firm, a technician. Listen to the great paranoiac din beneath the discourse of reason that speaks for others, in the name of the silent majority. The explanation is that, beneath preconscious goals and interests, a uniquely unconscious investment rises up that embraces a full body for itself, independently of all aims, and a degree of development for itself, independently of all reason: that very degree and no other, don't take another step; that very socius and no other, hands off. A disinterested love of the molar machine, a veritable enjoyment, with all the hatred it contains for those who do not submit to the molar machine: the entire libido is at stake. From the point of view of libidinal investment, it is clear that there are few differences between a reformist, a fascist, and sometimes even certain revolutionaries, who are distinguished from one another only in a preconscious fashion, but whose unconscious investments are of the same type, even when they do not adopt the same body. We can't go along with Maud Mannoni when she sees the first historical act of antipsychiatry in the 1902 decision granting Judge Schreber his liberty and responsibility, despite the recognized continuation of his delirious ideas.[46] There is room for doubting that the decision would have been the same if Schreber had been schizophrenic rather than paranoiac, if he had taken himself for a black or a Jew rather than a pure Aryan, if he had not proved himself so competent in the management of his wealth, and if in his delirium he had not displayed a taste for the socius of an already fascisizing libidinal investment. As machines of subjugation, the social machines give rise to incomparable loves, which are not explained by their interests, since interests derive from them instead. At the deepest level of society there is delirium, because delirium is the investment of a socius as such, beyond goals. And it is not merely the despot's body to which the paranoiac lovingly aspires, but the body of capital-money as well, or a new revolutionary body, the moment it becomes a form of power and gregariousness. To be possessed by this body as well as possessing it; to engineer subjugated groups for which one becomes so many cogs and parts; to insert oneself into the machine to find there at last the enjoyment of the mechanisms that pulverize desire—such is the paranoiac experience.

Now Oedipus appears to be a relatively innocent thing, a private kind of thing to be treated in the analyst's office. But we ask precisely what type of unconscious social investment Oedipus presupposes, since psychoanalysis does not invent Oedipus; psychoanalysis is content to live off Oedipus, to develop and promote it, and to give it a marketable medical form. Inasmuch as the paranoiac investment enslaves desiring-production, it is very important for it that the limit of this production be displaced, and that it pass to the interior of the socius, as a limit between two molar aggregates, the social aggregate of departure and the familial subaggregate of arrival that supposedly corresponds to it, in such a way that desire is caught in the trap of a familial psychic repression that comes to double the weight of social repression. The paranoiac applies his delirium to the family—and to his own family—but it is first of all a delirium of races, ranks, classes, and universal history. In short, Oedipus implies within the unconscious itself an entire reactionary and paranoiac investment of the social field that acts as an oedipalizing factor, and that can fuel as well as counteract the preconscious investments. From the standpoint of schizoanalysis, the analysis of Oedipus therefore consists in tracing back from the son's confused feelings to the delirious ideas or the lines of investment of the parents, of their internalized representatives and their substitutes: not in order to attain the whole of a family, which is never more than a locus of application and reproduction, but in order to attain the social and political units of libidinal investment. With the result that all familialist psychoanalysis—with the psychoanalyst at the fore—warrants a schizoanalysis. Only one way to spend time on the couch: schizoanalyze the psychoanalyst.

We have maintained throughout that, by dint of their difference in nature with regard to the preconscious investments of interest, the unconscious investments of desire had sexuality as an index in their social scope itself. Which does not mean, of course, that one need only invest the poor woman, the maid, or the whore to have revolutionary loves. There are no revolutionary or reactionary loves, which is to say that loves are not defined by their objects, any more than by the sources and aims of the desires and the drives. But there are *forms* of love that are the indices of the reactionary or the revolutionary character of the investment made by the libido of a sociohistorical or geographic field, from which the loved and desired beings receive their definition. Oedipus is one of these forms, the index of a reactionary investment. And the well-defined figures, the well-identified roles, the clearly distinct persons, in short the image-models of which Lawrence spoke—mother, fiancée, mistress, wife, saint or whore, princess and maid, rich woman and poor woman—are dependents of Oedipus, even in their reversals and their substitutions. The very form of these images, their configurations, and the whole of their possible relations are the product of a code, or of a social axiomatic to which the libido addresses itself through them. Persons are simulacra derived from a social aggregate whose code is unconsciously invested for itself. That is why love and desire exhibit reactionary, or else revolutionary, indices; the latter emerge on the contrary as nonfigurative indices, where persons give way to decoded flows of desire, to lines of vibration, and where the cross-sections of images give way to schizzes that constitute singular points, points-signs with several dimensions causing flows to circulate rather than canceling them. Nonfigurative loves, indices of a revolutionary investment of the social field, and which are neither Oedipal nor pre-oedipal since it all amounts to the same thing, but innocently anoedipal, and which give the revolutionary the right to say, "Oedipus? Never heard of it." Undoing the form of persons and the ego, not in behalf of a pre-oedipal undifferentiated, but in behalf of anoedipal lines of singularities, the desiring-machines. For there is indeed a sexual revolution, which does not concern objects, aims, or sources, but only machinic forms or indices.

The fourth and final thesis of schizoanalysis is therefore the distinction between two poles of social libidinal investment: the paranoiac, reactionary, and fascisizing pole, and the schizoid revolutionary pole. Once again, we see no objection to the use of terms inherited from psychiatry for characterizing social investments of the unconscious, insofar as these terms cease to have a familial connotation that would make them into simple projections, and from the moment delirium is recognized as having a primary social content that is immediately adequate. The two poles are defined, *the one* by the enslavement of production and the desiring-machines to the gregarious aggregates that they constitute on a large scale under a given form of power or selective sovereignty; *the other* by the inverse subordination and the overthrow of power. *The one* by these molar structured aggregates that crush singularities, select them, and regularize those that they retain in codes or axiomatics; *the other* by the molecular multiplicities of singularities that on the contrary treat the large aggregates as so many useful materials for their own elaborations. *The one* by the lines of integration and territorialization that arrest the flows, constrict them, turn them back, break them again according to the limits interior to the system, in such a way as to produce the images that come to fill the field of immanence peculiar to this system or this aggregate, *the other* by lines of escape that follow the decoded and deterritorialized flows, inventing their own nonfigurative breaks or schizzes that produce new flows, always breaching the coded wall or the territorialized limit that separates them from desiring-production. And to summarize all the preceding determinations: *the one* is defined by subjugated groups, *the other* by subject-groups. It is true that we still run up against all kinds of problems concerning these distinctions. In what sense does the schizoid investment constitute, to the same extent as the other one, a real investment of the sociohistorical field, and not a simple utopia? In what sense are the lines of escape collective, positive, and creative? What is the relationship between the two unconscious poles, and what is their relationship with the preconscious investments of interest?

We have seen that the unconscious paranoiac investment was grounded in the socius itself as a full body without organs, beyond the preconscious aims and interests that it assigns and distributes. The fact remains that such an investment does not endure the light of day: it must always hide under assignable aims or interests presented as the general aims and interests, even though in reality the latter represent only the members of the dominant class or a fraction of this class. How could a formation of sovereignty, a fixed and determinate gregarious aggregate, endure being invested for their brute force, their violence, and their absurdity? They would not survive such an investment. Even the most overt fascism speaks the language of goals, of law, order, and reason. Even the most insane capitalism speaks in the name of economic rationality. And this is necessarily the case, since it is in the irrationality of the full body that the order of reasons is inextricably fixed, under a code, under an axiomatic that determines it. What is more, the bringing to light of the unconscious reactionary investment as if devoid of an aim, would be enough to transform it completely, to make it pass to the other pole of the libido, i.e., to the schizorevolutionary pole, since this action could not be accomplished without overthrowing power, without reversing subordination, *without returning production itself to desire:* for it is only desire that lives from having no aim. Molecular desiring-production would regain its liberty to master in its turn the molar aggregate under an overturned form of power or sovereignty. That is why Klossowski, who has taken the theory of the two poles of investment the furthest, but still within the category of an active utopia, is able to write: "Every sovereign formation would thus have to foresee the destined moment of its disintegration. . . . No formation of sovereignty, in order to crystalize, will ever endure this *prise de conscience:* for as soon as this formation becomes conscious of its immanent disintegration in the individuals who compose it, these same individuals decompose it. . . . By way of the circuitous route of science and art, human beings have many times revolted against this fixity; this capacity notwithstanding, the gregarious impulse in and by science caused this rupture to fail. The day humans are able to behave as *intentionless phenomena*—for every intention at the level of the human being always obeys the laws of its conservation, its continued existence—on that day a new creature will declare the integrity of existence. . . . Science demonstrates by its very method that the *means* that it constantly elaborates do no more than reproduce, on the outside, an interplay of forces by themselves *without aim or end* whose combinations obtain such and such a result. . . . However, no science can develop outside a constituted social grouping. In order to prevent science from calling social groups back in question, these groups take science back in hand . . . [integrate it] into the diverse industrial schemes; its autonomy appears strictly inconceivable. A conspiracy joining together art and science presupposes a rupture of all our institutions and a total upheaval of the means of production. . . . If some conspiracy, according to Nietzsche's wish, were to use science and art in a plot whose ends were no less suspect, industrial society would seem to foil this conspiracy in advance by the kind of *mise en scène* it offers for it, under pain of effectively suffering what this conspiracy reserves for this society: i.e., the breakup of the institutional structures that mask the society into a plurality of experimental spheres finally revealing the true face of modernity—an ultimate phase that Nietzsche saw as the end result of the evolution of societies. In this perspective, art and science would then emerge as sovereign formations that Nietzsche said constituted the object of his countersociology—art and science establishing themselves as dominant powers, on the ruins of institutions."[47]

Why this appeal to art and science, in a world where scientists and technicians and even artists, and science and art themselves, work so closely with the established sovereignties—if only because of the structures of financing? Because art, as soon as it attains its own grandeur, its own genius, creates chains of decoding and deterritorialization that serve as the foundation for desiring-machines, and make them function. Take the example of the Venetian School in painting: at the same time that Venice develops the most powerful commodity capitalism, bordering an Urstaat, that grants it a large degree of autonomy, its painting apparently molds itself to a Byzantine code where even the colors and the lines are subordinated to a signifier that determines their hierarchy as a vertical order. But toward the middle of the fifteenth century, when Venetian capitalism confronts the first signs of its decline, something breaks out in this painting: what would appear to be another world opens up, an *other* art, where the lines are deterritorialized, the colors are decoded, and now only refer to the relations they entertain among themselves, and with one another. A horizontal or transverse organization of the canvas is born, with lines of escape or breakthrough. Christ's body is engineered on all sides and in all fashions, pulled in all directions, playing the role of a full body without organs, a locus of connection for all the machines of desire, a locus of sadomasochistic exercises where the artist's joy breaks free. Even homosexual Christs. Organs become direct powers of the body without organs, and emit flows on it that the myriad wounds, such as Saint Sebastian's arrows, come to cut and cut again in such a way as to produce other flows. Persons and organs cease to be coded according to hierarchized collective investments; each person, each organ has a merit all its own, and tends to its own affairs: the infant Jesus looks from one side while the Virgin Mary listens from the other, Jesus stands for all the desiring children, the Virgin stands for all the desiring women, a joyous activity of profanation extends beneath this generalized privatization. A painter such as Tintoretto paints the creation of the world like a race represented in its whole length with God Himself on the sidelines, giving the starting signal across the track as the figures speed away in a transversal direction. Suddenly a painting by Lotto surges forth that could just as easily be from the nineteenth century. And of course this decoding of the flows of painting, these schizoid lines of escape that form desiring-machines on the horizon, are taken up again in scraps from the old code, or else introduced into new codes, and first of all into a properly pictorial axiomatic that chokes off the escapes, closes the whole constellation to the transversal relations between lines and colors, and reduces it to archaic or new territorialities (perspective, for example). So true is it that the movement of deterritorialization can only be grasped as the reverse side of territorialities, even the residual, artificial, or factitious ones. But at least something arose whose force fractured the codes, undid the signifiers, passed under the structures, set the flows in motion, and effected breaks at the limits of desire: a breakthrough. It does not suffice to say that the nineteenth century is already there in the middle of the fifteenth, since the same would have to be said of the Byzantine code underneath which strange liberated flows were already circulating. We have seen this in the case of the painter Turner, and his most accomplished paintings that are sometimes termed "incomplete": from the moment there is genius, there is something that belongs to no school, no period, something that achieves a breakthrough—art as a *process* without goal, but that attains completion as such.

The codes and their signifiers, the axiomatics and their structures, the imaginary figures that come to occupy them as well as the purely symbolic relationships that gauge them, constitute properly aesthetic molar formations that are characterized by goals, schools, and periods. They relate these aesthetic formations to greater social aggregates, finding in them a field of application, and everywhere enslave art to a great castrating machine of sovereignty. There is a pole of reactionary investment for art as well, a somber paranoiac-Oedipal-narcissistic organization. A foul use of painting, centering around the dirty little secret, even in abstract painting where the axiomatic does without figures: a style of painting whose secret essence is scatological, an oedipalizing painting, even when it has broken with the Holy Trinity as the Oedipal image, a neurotic or neuroticizing painting that makes the process into a goal or an arrest, an interruption, or a continuation in the void. This style of painting flourishes today, under the usurped name of modern painting—a poisonous flower—and brought one of Lawrence's heroes to speak much like Henry Miller of the need to have done with pouring out one's merciful and pitiful guts, these 'flows of corrugated iron.' "[48] The productive breaks projected onto the enormous unproductive cleavage of castration, the flows that have become flows of "corrugated iron," the openings blocked on all sides. And perhaps this, as we have seen, is where we find the commodity value of art and literature: a paranoiac *form of expression* that no longer even needs to "signify" its reactionary libidinal investments, since these investments function on the contrary as its signifier; an Oedipal *form of content* that no longer even needs to represent Oedipus, since the "structure" suffices. But on the other, the schizorevolutionary, pole, the value of art is no longer measured except in terms of the decoded and deterritorialized flows that it causes to circulate beneath a signifier reduced to silence, beneath the conditions of identity of the parameters, across a structure reduced to impotence; a writing with pneumatic, electronic, or gaseous indifferent supports, and that appears all the more difficult and intellectual to intellectuals as it is accessible to the infirm, the illiterate, and the schizos, embracing all that flows and counterflows, the gushings of mercy and pity knowing nothing of meanings and aims (the Artaud experiment, the Burroughs experiment). It is here that art accedes to its authentic modernity, which simply consists in liberating what was present in art from its beginnings, but was hidden underneath aims and objects, even if aesthetic, and underneath recodings or axiomatics: the pure process that fulfills itself, and that never ceases to reach fulfillment as it proceeds—art as "experimentation."*

And the same will be said of science: the decoded flows of knowledge are first bound in the properly scientific axiomatics, but these axiomatics express a bipolar hesitation. One of the poles is the great social axiomatic that retains from science what must be retained in terms of market needs and zones of technical innovation: the great social aggregate that makes the scientific subaggregates into so many applications that are characteristic of and that correspond to it—in short, the set of methods that is not content to bring scientists back to "reason" but anticipates any deviance on their part, imposes a goal on them, and makes scientists and science into an agency perfectly subjugated to the formation of sovereignty (for example, the way in which nondeterminism was only tolerated to a point, then ordered to make its peace with determinism). But the other pole is the schizoid pole, in whose proximity flows of knowledge schizophrenize, and not only flee across the social axiomatic, but pass beyond their own axiomatics, generating increasingly deterritorialized signs, figures-schizzes that are no longer either figurative or structured, and reproduce or produce an interplay of phenomena without aim or end: science as experimentation, as previously defined. In this domain as in the others, isn't there a properly libidinal conflict between a paranoiac-Oedipalizing element of science, and a schizorevolutionary element? That very conflict that leads Lacan to say there exists a drama for the scientist. ("J. R. Mayer, Cantor, I will not draw up an honor roll of these dramas that sometimes lead to madness . . . , a list that could not include itself in Oedipus, unless it were to call Oedipus in question."[49] Since, in point of fact, Oedipus does not intervene in these dramas as a familial figure or even as a mental structure; its intervention is determined by an axiomatic acting as an oedipalizing factor, resulting in a specifically scientific Oedipus.) And in contrast to Lautréamont's song that rises up around the paranoiac-Oedipal-narcissistic pole—"O rigorous mathematics. . . . Arithmetic! algebra! geometry! imposing trinity! luminous

*See all of John Cage's work, and his book *Silence* (Middletown, Conn.: Wesleyan University Press, 1961): "The word *experimental* is apt, providing it is understood not as descriptive of an act to be later judged in terms of success and failure, but simply as of an act the outcome of which is unknown" (p. 13). And regarding the active or practical notions of *decoding*, of *deconstruction*, and of the work as a *process*, the reader is referred to the excellent commentaries of Daniel Charles on Cage, "Musique et anarchie," in *Bulletin de la Société française de philosophie*, July 1971, where there is violent anger on the part of some participants in the discussion, reacting to the idea that there is no longer any code.

triangle!"—there is another song: O schizophrenic mathematics, uncontrollable and mad desiring-machines!

In the capitalist formation of sovereignty—the full body of capital-money as the socius—the great social axiomatic has replaced the territorial codes and the despotic overcodings that characterized the preceding formations; and a molar, gregarious aggregate has formed, whose mode of subjugation has no equal. We have seen on what foundations this aggregate operated: a whole field of immanence that is reproduced on an always larger scale, that is continually multiplying its axioms to suit its needs, that is filled with images and with images of images, through which desire is determined to desire its own repression (*imperialism*); an unprecedented decoding and deterritorialization, which institutes a combination as a system of differential relations between the decoded and deterritorialized flows, in such a way that social inscription and repression no longer even need to bear directly upon bodies and persons, but on the contrary precede them (*axiomatic: regulation and application*); a surplus value determined as a surplus value of flux, whose extortion is not brought about by a simple arithmetical difference between two quantities that are homogeneous and belong to the same code, but precisely by differential relations between heterogeneous magnitudes that are not raised to the same power: a flow of capital and a flow of labor as human surplus value in the industrial essence of capitalism, a flow of financing and a flow of payment or incomes in the monetary inscription of capitalism, a market flow and a flow of innovation as machinic surplus value in the operation of capitalism (*surplus value* as the first aspect of its immanence), a ruling class that is all the more ruthless as it does not place the machine in its service, but is the servant of the capitalist machine: in this sense, a single class, content for its part with drawing incomes that, however enormous, differ only arithmetically from the workers' wages-income, whereas this class functions on a more profound level as creator, regulator, and guardian of the great nonappropriated, nonpossessed flow, incommensurable with wages and profits, which marks at every step along the way the interior limits of capitalism, their perpetual displacement, and their reproduction on an always larger scale (*the movement of interior limits* as the second aspect of the capitalist field of immanence, defined by the circular relationship "great flux of financing–reflux of incomes in wages–afflux of raw profit"); the effusion of antiproduction within production, as the realization or the absorption of surplus value, in such a way that the military, bureaucratic, and police apparatus finds itself grounded in the economy itself, which directly produces libidinal investments for the repression of desire (*antiproduction* as the third aspect of capitalist immanence, expressing the twofold nature of capitalism: production for production's sake, but under the conditions of capital).

There is not one of these aspects—not the least operation, the least industrial or financial mechanism—that does not reveal the insanity of the capitalist machine and the pathological character of its rationality: not at all a false rationality, but a true rationality of *this* pathological state, *this* insanity, "the machine works too, believe me". The capitalist machine does not run the risk of becoming mad, it is mad from one end to the other and from the beginning, and this is the source of its rationality. Marx's black humor, the source of *Capital*, is his fascination with such a machine: how it came to be assembled, on what foundation of decoding and deterritorialization; how it works, always more decoded, always more deterritorialized; how its operation grows more relentless with the development of the axiomatic, the combination of the flows; how it produces the terrible single class of gray gentlemen who keep up the machine; how it does not run the risk of dying all alone, but rather of making us die, by provoking to the very end investments of desire that do not even go by way of a deceptive and subjective ideology, and that lead us to cry out to the very end, *Long live capital in all its reality, in all its objective dissimulation!* Except in ideology, there has never been a humane, liberal, paternal, etc., capitalism. Capitalism is defined by a cruelty having no parallel in the primitive system of cruelty, and by a terror having no parallel in the despotic régime of terror. Wage increases and improvements in the standard of living are realities, but realities that derive from a given supplementary axiom that capitalism is always capable of adding to its axiomatic in terms of an enlargement of its limits: let's create the New Deal; let's cultivate and recognize strong unions; let's promote participation, the single class; let's take a step toward Russia, which is taking so many toward us; etc. But within the enlarged reality that conditions these islands, exploitation grows constantly harsher, lack is arranged in the most scientific of ways, final solutions of the "Jewish problem" variety are prepared down to the last detail, and the Third World is organized as an integral part of capitalism. The reproduction of the interior limits of capitalism on an always wider scale has several consequences: it permits increases and improvements of standards at the center, it displaces the harshest forms of exploitation from the center to the periphery, but also multiplies enclaves of overpopulation in the center itself, and easily tolerates the so-called socialist formations. (It is not kibbutz-style socialism that troubles the

Zionist state, just as it is not Russian socialism that troubles world capitalism.) There is no metaphor here: the factories are prisons, they do not resemble prisons, they *are* prisons.

Everything in the system is insane: this is because the capitalist machine thrives on decoded and deterritorialized flows; it decodes and deterritorializes them still more, but while causing them to pass into an axiomatic apparatus that combines them, and at the points of combination produces pseudo codes and artificial reterritorializations. It is in this sense that the capitalist axiomatic cannot but give rise to new territorialities and revive a new despotic Urstaat. The great mutant flow of capital is pure deterritorialization, but it performs an equivalent reterritorialization when converted into a reflux of means of payment. The Third World is deterritorialized in relation to the center of capitalism but belongs to capitalism, being a pure peripheral territoriality of capitalism. The system teems with preconscious investments of class and of interest. And capitalists first have an interest in capitalism. A statement as commonplace as this is made for another purpose: capitalists have an interest in capitalism *only* through the tapping of profits that they extract from it. But no matter how large the extraction of profits, it does not define capitalism. And for what does define capitalism, for what conditions profit, theirs is an investment of desire whose nature—unconscious-libidinal—is altogether different, and is not simply explained by the conditioned profits, but on the contrary itself explains that a small-time capitalist, with no great profits or hopes, fully maintains the entirety of his libidinal investments: the libido investing the great flow that is not convertible as such, not appropriated as such—"nonpossession and nonwealth," in the words of Bernard Schmitt, who among modern economists has for us the incomparable advantage of offering a delirious interpretation of an unequivocally delirious economic system (at least he goes all the way). In short, a truly unconscious libido, a disinterested love: this machine is fantastic.

If one keeps in mind the tautological statement made above, one can then understand that people whose preconscious investments of interest do not, or should not, go in the direction of capitalism, can maintain an unconscious libidinal investment consonant with capitalism, or that scarcely threatens it. In the first case, they confine and localize their preconscious interest in wage increases and the improvement of the standard of living; powerful organizations represent them, which get nasty as soon as the nature of their aims is questioned ("It's clear that you're not workers, you have no idea whatsoever of real struggles, let's attack profits for a better management of the system, vote for a clean Paris—Welcome, Mister Brezhnev"). And how, indeed, could one fail to find one's interest in the hole where one has sunk it, at the heart of the capitalist system? Or else, in the second case, there is truly a new investment of interest, new aims that presuppose another body than that of capital-money; those exploited become conscious of their preconscious interest, and this interest is truly revolutionary—a major break *from the standpoint of the preconscious.*

But it is not enough for the libido to invest a new social body corresponding to these new aims, in order for it to perform a revolutionary break at the unconscious level with the same mode as the preconscious break. In fact, the two levels do not function in the same mode. The new socius invested by the libido as a full body can very well function as an autonomous territoriality, but one that is caught and wedged in the capitalist machine, and is localizable in the field of its market. For the great flow of mutant capital repels its limits, adds new axioms, and maintains desire within the mobile framework of its expanded limits. There can be a preconscious revolutionary break, with no real libidinal and unconscious revolutionary break. Or rather the order of things is as follows: there is first a real libidinal revolutionary break, which then shifts into the position of a simple revolutionary break with regard to aims and interests, and finally re-forms a merely specific reterritoriality, a specific body on the full body of capital. Subjugated groups are continually deriving from revolutionary subject-groups. One more axiom. This is no more complicated than in the case of abstract painting. Everything begins with Marx, continues on with Lenin, and ends with the refrain, "Welcome, Mister Brezhnev." Is this still a case of revolutionaries speaking to another revolutionary, or rather a village clamoring for a new prefect? And if one were to ask when it all started to go bad, how far back must we go for an answer, back to Lenin, back to Marx? So true is it that the various investments, even when opposed, can coexist with one another in complexes that are not the province of Oedipus, but that do concern the sociohistorical field, its preconscious and unconscious conflicts and contradictions, about which it can only be said that they fall back on Oedipus, Marx-the-father, Lenin-the-father, Brezhnev-the-father. Fewer and fewer people believe in all this but it makes no difference, since capitalism is like the Christian religion, it lives precisely from a lack of belief, it does not need it—a motley painting of all that has been believed.

But the reverse is also true: capitalism is constantly escaping on all sides. Its productions, its art, and its science form decoded and deterritorialized flows that do not merely submit to the corresponding axiomatic, but cause some of their currents to pass through the mesh of the axiomatic, underneath the recodings and the reterritorializations.

Subject-groups in their turn derive from subjugated groups by way of ruptures in the latter. Capitalism is continually cutting off the circulation of flows, breaking them and deferring the break, but these same flows are continually overflowing, and intersecting one another according to schizzes that turn against capitalism and slash into it. Capitalism, which is always ready to expand its interior limits, remains threatened by an exterior limit that stands a greater chance of coming to it and cleaving it from within, in proportion as the interior limits expand. That is why the lines of escape are singularly creative and positive: they constitute an investment of the social field that is no less complete, no less total than the contrary investment. The paranoiac and the schizoid investments are like two opposite poles of unconscious libidinal investment, one of which subordinates desiring-production to the formation of sovereignty and to the gregarious aggregate that results from it, while the other brings about the inverse subordination, overthrows the established power, and subjects the gregarious aggregate to the molecular multiplicities of the productions of desire. And if it is true that delirium is coextensive with the social field, these two poles are found to coexist in every case of delirium, and fragments of schizoid revolutionary investment are found to coincide with blocks of paranoiac reactionary investment. The oscillation between the two poles is a constituent aspect of the delirium.

It appears, however, that the oscillation is not equal, and that as a rule the schizoid pole is potential in relation to the actual paranoiac pole (how can we count on art and science except as potentialities, since their actuality is easily controlled by the formations of sovereignty?). This results from the fact that the two poles of unconscious libidinal investment do not maintain the same relationship, nor the same form of relationship, with the preconscious investments of interest. On the one hand, in fact, the investment of interest fundamentally conceals the paranoiac investment of desire, and reinforces it as much as it conceals it: it covers over the irrational character of the paranoiac investment under an existing order of interests, of causes and means, of aims and reasons; or else the investment of interest itself gives rise to and creates those interests that rationalize the paranoiac investment; or yet again, an effectively revolutionary preconscious investment fully maintains a paranoiac investment at the level of the libido, to the extent that the new socius continues to subordinate the entire production of desire in the name of the higher interests of the revolution and the inevitable sequences of causality. In the other case, the preconscious interest must on the contrary discover the necessity for a different sort of investment, and must perform a kind of rupture with causality as well as a calling in question of aims and interests.

In each case the problem is different: it is not enough to construct a new socius as full body; one must also pass to the other side of this social full body, where the molecular formations of desire that must master the new molar aggregate operate and are inscribed. Only by making this passage do we reach the revolutionary break and investment of the libido. This cannot be achieved except at the cost of, and by means of a rupture with, causality. Desire is an exile, desire is a desert that traverses the body without organs and makes us pass from one of its faces to the other. Never an individual exile, never a personal desert, but a collective exile and a collective desert. It is only too obvious that the destiny of the revolution is linked solely to the interest of the dominated and exploited masses. But it is the nature of this link that poses the real problem, as either a determined causal link or a different sort of connection. It is a question of knowing how a revolutionary potential is realized, in its very relationship with the exploited masses or the "weakest links" of a given system. Do these masses or these links act in their own place, within the order of causes and aims that promote a new socius, or are they on the contrary the place and the agent of a sudden and unexpected irruption, an irruption of desire that breaks with causes and aims and overturns the socius, revealing its other side? In the subjugated groups, desire is still defined by an order of causes and aims, and itself weaves a whole system of macroscopic relations that determine the large aggregates under a formation of sovereignty. Subject-groups on the other hand have as their sole cause a rupture with causality, a revolutionary line of escape; and even though one can and must assign the objective factors, such as the weakest links, within causal series that made such a rupture possible, only what is of the order of desire and its irruption accounts for the reality this rupture assumes at a given moment, in a given place.[50]

It is clear how everything can coexist and intermix: in the "Leninist break," for example, when the Bolshevik group, or at least a part of this group, becomes aware of the immediate possibility of a proletarian revolution that would not follow the anticipated causal order of the relations of forces, but that would singularly precipitate things by plunging into a breach (the escape, or "revolutionary defeatism"). In reality, everything coexists: still hesitant preconscious investments in the case of some people who do not believe in this possibility; revolutionary preconscious investments in those who "see" the possibility of a new socius but maintain it in an order of molar causality that already makes of the party a new form of sovereignty; and finally unconscious revolutionary investments that perform a real rupture with causality in the order of desire. And in the same people the most varied kinds of investments can coexist at such and such a moment, the two kinds of groups can interpenetrate. This is because the two groups are like determinism and freedom in Kant's philosophy: they indeed have the same "object"—and social production is never anything other than desiring-production, and vice versa—but they don't share the same law or the same régime.

The actualization of a revolutionary potentiality is explained less by the preconscious state of causality in which it is nonetheless included, than by the efficacy of a libidinal break at a precise moment, a schiz whose sole cause is desire—which is to say the rupture with causality that forces a rewriting of history on a level with the real, and produces this strangely polyvocal moment when everything is possible. Of course the schiz has been prepared by a subterranean labor of causes, aims, and interests working together; of course this order of causes runs the risk of closing and cementing the breach in the name of the new socius and its interests. Of course one can always say after the fact that history has never ceased being governed by the same laws of aggregates and large numbers. The fact remains that the schiz came into existence only by means of a desire without aim or cause that charted it and sided with it. While the schiz is possible without the order of causes, it becomes real only by means of something of another order: Desire, the desert-desire, the revolutionary investment of desire. And that is indeed what undermines capitalism: where will the revolution come from, and in what form *within* the exploited masses? It is like death—where, when? It will be a decoded flow, a deterritorialized flow that runs too far and cuts too sharply, thereby escaping from the axiomatic of capitalism. Will it come in the person of a Castro, an Arab, a Black Panther, or a Chinaman on the horizon? A May '68, a home-grown Maoist planted like an anchorite on a factory smokestack? Always the addition of an axiom to seal off a breach that has been discovered; fascist colonels start reading Mao, we won't be fooled again; Castro has become impossible, even in relation to himself; vacuoles are isolated, ghettos created; unions are appealed to for help; the most sinister forms of "dissuasion" are invented; the repression of interest is reinforced—but where will the new irruption of desire come from?[51]

Those who have read us this far will perhaps find many reasons for reproaching us: for believing too much in the pure potentialities of art and even of science; for denying or minimizing the role of classes and class struggle; for militating in favor of an irrationalism of desire; for identifying the revolutionary with the schizo; for falling into familiar, all-too-familiar traps. This would be a bad reading, and we don't know which is better, a bad reading or no reading at all. And in all probability there are far more serious reproaches to be made, which we haven't even thought of. As for those we have named, we hold in the first place that art and science have a revolutionary potential, and nothing more, and that this potential appears all the more as one is less and less concerned with what art and science mean, from the standpoint of a signifier or signifieds that are necessarily reserved for specialists; but that art and science cause increasingly decoded and deterritorialized flows to circulate in the socius, flows that are perceptible to everyone, which force the social axiomatic to grow ever more complicated, to become more saturated, to the point where the scientist and the artist may be determined to rejoin an objective revolutionary situation in reaction against authoritarian designs of a State that is incompetent and above all castrating by nature. (For the State imposes a specifically artistic Oedipus, a specifically scientific Oedipus.)

Secondly, we have not at all minimized the importance of preconscious investments of class or interest, which are based in the infrastructure itself. But we attach all the more importance to them as they are the index in the infrastructure of a libidinal investment of another nature, and that can coincide as well as clash with them. Which is merely a way to pose the question, "How can the revolution be betrayed?"—once it has been said that betrayals don't wait their turn, but are there from the very start (the maintenance of paranoiac unconscious investments in revolutionary groups). And if we put forward desire as a revolutionary agency, it is because we believe that capitalist society can endure many manifestations of interest, but not one manifestation of desire, which would be enough to make its fundamental structures explode, even at the kindergarten level. We believe in desire as in the irrational of every form of rationality, and not because it is a lack, a thirst, or an aspiration, but because it is the production of desire: desire that produces—real-desire, or the real in itself. Finally, we do not at all think that the revolutionary is schizophrenic or vice versa. On the contrary, we have consistently distinguished the schizophrenic as an entity from schizophrenia as a process; now the schizophrenic as entity can only be defined in relation to the arrests, the continuations in the void, or the finalist illusions that repression imposes on the process itself. This explains why we have only spoken of a schizoid pole in the libidinal investment of the social field, so as to avoid as much as possible the confusion of the schizophrenic process with the production of a schizophrenic. The schizophrenic process (the schizoid pole) is revolutionary, in the very sense that the paranoiac method is reactionary and fascist; and it is not these psychiatric categories, freed of all familialism, that will allow us to understand the politico-economic determinations, but exactly the opposite.

And then, above all, we are not looking for a way out when we say that schizoanalysis *as such* has strictly no political program to propose. If it did have one, it would be grotesque and disquieting at the same time. It does not take itself for a party or even a group, and does not claim to be speaking for the masses. No political program will be elaborated within the framework of schizoanalysis. Finally, schizoanalysis is something that does not claim to be speaking for anything or anyone, not even—in fact especially not—for psychoanalysis: nothing more than impressions, the impression that things aren't going well in psychoanalysis, and that they haven't been since the start. We are still too competent; we would like to speak in the name of an absolute incompetence. Someone asked us if we had ever seen a schizophrenic—no, no, we have never seen one. If someone reading this book feels that things are fine in psychoanalysis, we're not speaking for him, and for him we take back everything we have said. So what is the relationship between schizoanalysis and politics on the one hand, and between schizoanalysis and psychoanalysis on the other? Everything revolves around desiring-machines and the production of desire. Schizoanalysis as such does not raise the problem of the nature of the socius to come out of the revolution; it does not claim to be identical with the revolution itself. Given a socius, schizoanalysis only asks what place it reserves for desiring-production; what generative role desire enjoys therein; in what forms the conciliation between the régime of desiring-production and the régime of social production is brought about, since in any case it is the same production, but under two different régimes; if, on this socius as a full body, there is thus the possibility for going from one side to another, i.e., from the side where the molar aggregates of social production are organized, to this other side, no less collective, where the molecular multiplicities of desiring-production are formed; whether and to what extent such a socius can endure the reversal of power such that desiring-production subjugates social production and yet does not destroy it, since it is the same production working under the difference in régime; if there is, and how there comes to be, a formation of subject-groups; etc.

If someone retorts that we are claiming the famous rights to laziness, to nonproductivity, to dream and fantasy production, once again we are quite pleased, since we haven't stopped saying the opposite, and that desiring-production produces the real, and that desire has little to do with fantasy and dream. As opposed to Reich, schizoanalysis makes no distinction in nature between political economy and libidinal economy. Schizoanalysis merely asks what are the machinic, social, and technical indices on a socius that open to desiring-machines, that enter into the parts, wheels, and motors of these machines, as much as they cause them to enter into their own parts, wheels, and motors. Everyone knows that a schizo is a machine; all schizos say this, and not just little Joey. The question to be asked is whether schizophrenics are the living machines of a dead labor, which are then contrasted to the dead machines of living labor as organized in capitalism. Or whether instead desiring, technical, and social machines join together in a process of schizophrenic production that thereafter has no more schizophrenics to produce. In her *Lettre aux ministres,* Maud Mannoni writes: "One of these adolescents, declared unfit for studies, does admirably well in a third-level class, provided he works some in mechanics. He has a passion for mechanics. The man in the garage has been his best therapist. If we take mechanics away from him he will become schizophrenic again."[52] Her intention is not to praise ergotherapy or the virtues of social adaptation. She marks the point where the social machine, the technical machine, and the desiring-machine join closely together and bring their régimes into communication. She asks if our society can handle that, and what it is worth if it can't. And this is indeed the direction the social, technical, scientific, and artistic machines take when they are revolutionary: they form desiring-machines for which they are already the index in their own régime, at the same time that the desiring-machines form them in the régime that is theirs, and as a position of desire.

What, finally, is the opposition between schizoanalysis and psychoanalysis, when the negative and positive tasks of schizoanalysis are taken as a whole? We constantly contrasted two sorts of unconscious or two interpretations of the unconscious: the one schizoanalytic, the other psychoanalytic; the one schizophrenic, the other neurotic-Oedipal; the one abstract and nonfigurative, the other imaginary; but also the one really concrete, the other symbolic; the one machinic, the other structural; the one molecular, microphysical, and micrological, and the other molar or statistical; the one material, the other ideological; the one productive, the other expressive. We have seen how the negative task of schizoanalysis must be violent, brutal: defamiliarizing, de-oedipalizing, decastrating; undoing theater, dream, and fantasy; decoding, deterritorializing—a terrible curettage, a malevolent activity. But everything happens at the same time. For at the same time the process is liberated—the process of desiring-production, following its molecular lines of escape that already define the mechanic's task of the schizoanalyst. And the lines of escape are still full molar or social investments at grips with the whole social field: so that the task of schizoanalysis is ultimately that of discovering for every case the nature of the libidinal investments of the social field, their possible internal conflicts, their relationships with the preconscious investments of the same field, their possible conflicts with these—in short, the entire interplay of the desiring-machines and the repression of desire. Completing the process and not arresting it, not making it turn about in the void, not assigning it a goal. We'll never go too far with the deterritorialization, the decoding of flows. For the new earth ("In truth, the earth will one day become a place of healing") is not to be found in the neurotic or perverse reterritorializations that arrest the process or assign it goals; it is no more behind than ahead, it coincides with the completion of the process of desiring-production, this process that is always and already complete as it proceeds, and as long as it proceeds. It therefore remains for us to see how, effectively, simultaneously, these various tasks of schizoanalysis proceed.

Reference Notes

INTRODUCTION

1. Henry Miller, *Sexus* (New York: Grove Press, 1965), pp. 429–30.
2. Friedrich Nietzsche, *On the Genealogy of Morals,* trans. by Walter Kaufmann (New York: Random House, 1969), I, 17, p. 38.
3. Ibid., p. 46.
4. Gilles Deleuze, "Trois problèmes de groupe" in Félix Guattari, *Psychanalyse et transversalité* (Paris: Maspero, 1972, preface).
5. H. Miller, *Sexus,* pp. 425–26.
6. Ivan Illich, *Tools for Conviviality* (New York: Harper & Row, 1973).
7. Ibid., pp. 12–13.
8. Cf. in this respect Ivan Illich, *Medical Nemesis: The Expropriation of Health,* (New York: Pantheon, 1976).
9. R. D. Laing, *The Politics of Experience* (New York: Ballantine Books, 1971), p. 126.
10. Nietzsche, *On the Genealogy of Morals,* II, 24, p. 96.
11. Miller, *Sexus,* p. 427.

1 THE DESIRING-MACHINES

1. See Georg Büchner, *Lenz,* in *Complete Plays and Prose,* trans. Carl Richard Mueller (New York: Hill & Wang, 1963), p. 141.

1a. Ibid.

2. Samuel Beckett, *Molloy,* in *Three Novels by Samuel Beckett* (New York: Grove Press, 1959), p. 16. *Molloy* was translated from the French by Patrick Bowles in collaboration with the author. (*Translators' note.*)

3. Antonin Artaud, *Van Gogh, the Man Suicided by Society,* trans. Mary Beach and Lawrence Ferlinghetti, in *Artaud Anthology* (San Francisco: City Lights Books, 1965), p. 158.

4. On the identity of nature and production, and species life in general, according to Marx, see the commentaries of Gérard Granel, "L'ontologie marxiste de 1844 et la question de la coupure," in *L'endurance de la pensée* (Paris: Plon, 1968), pp. 301–310.

5. D.H. Lawrence, *Aaron's Rod* (New York: Penguin, 1976), ppl 200–201.

6. Henri Michaux, *The Major Ordeals of the Mind,* trans. Richard Howard (New York: Harcourt Brace Jovanovich, 1974), pp. 125–27.

7. Sigmund Freud, "Psycho-Analytic Notes upon an Autobiographical Case of Paranoia (Dementia Paranoides)," *Collected Papers: Authorized Translation under the Supervision of Joan Rivière* (New York: Basic Books, 1959), Vol. 3, p. 396.

8. Victor Tausk, "On the Origin of the Influencing Machine in Schizophrenia," *Psychoanalytic Quarterly,* no. 2 (1933), pp. 519–56.

9. Karl Marx, *Capital,* trans. Ernest Untermann (New York: International Publishers, 1967), Vol. 3, p. 827. See in Louis Althusser, *Lire le capital* (Paris: Maspero, 1965), the commentaries of Etienne Balibar, Vol. 2, pp. 213ff., and of Pierre Macherey, Vol. 1, pp. 201ff. (*Translators' note:* For the English text of Balibar's commentaries, see Louis Althusser and Etienne Balibar, *Reading Capital,* trans. Ben Brewster [New York: Pantheon, 1970], Part III, pp. 199–308. For contributions by Pierre Macherey, see footnotes in this edition on pp. 7, 30, and 251.)

10. Samuel Beckett, "Enough," in *First Love and Other Shorts* (New York: Grove Press, 1974).

11. Freud, "Psycho-Analytic Notes," p. 432 (emphasis added).

12. Beckett, *Molloy,* p. 29.

12a. Antonin Artaud, "Here Lies," trans. F. Teri Wehn and Jack Hirschman, in *Artaud Anthology* (San Francisco: City Lights Books, 1965), pp. 247 and 238 respectively.

13. W. Morgenthaler, "Adolf Wölfli." French translation in *L'Art brut,* no. 2.

14. Cited in Sigmund Freud, "Psycho-Analytic Notes," p. 415.

15. *L'Art brut,* no. 3, p. 63.

16. Freud, "Psycho-Analytic Notes," pp. 400–401.

17. Michel Carrouges, *Les machines célibataires* (Paris: Arcanes, 1954).

18. Antonin Artaud, *Le pèse-nerfs,* in *Oeuvres complètes* (Paris: Gallimard), Vol. 1, p. 112.

19. Samuel Beckett, *The Unnamable,* in *Three Novels by Samuel Beckett,* p. 452. The *Unnamable* was translated from the French by the author. (*Translators' note.*)

20. Pierre Klossowski, *Nietzsche et le cercle vicieux* (Paris: Mercure de France, 1969).

21. Ibid.

22. Friedrich Nietzsche, letter to Jakob Burckhardt, January 5, 1889, in *Selected Letters of Friedrich Nietzsche,* trans. Christopher Middleton (Chicago: University of Chicago Press, 1969), p. 347. (*Translators' note.*)

23. Klossowski, op. cit.

24. Klossowski, op. cit.

25. G. de Clerambault, *Oeuvre psychiatrique* (Paris: Presses Universitaires de France).

26. Beckett, *The Unnamable.*

27. D.H. Lawrence, *Aaron's Rod,* p. 162.

28. Immanuel Kant, *The Critique of Judgment,* Introduction, §3.

29. Clément Rosset, *Logique du pire* (Paris: Presses Universitaries de France, 1970), p. 37.

30. Henry Miller, *Sexus* (New York: Grove Press, 1965), pp. 262, 430.

31. Wilhelm Reich, *The Mass Psychology of Fascism,* trans. Vincent R. Carfagno (London: Souvenir Press, 1970).

32. Vladimir Jankelevitch, *Ravel,* trans. Margaret Crosland (New York: Grove Press, 1959), pp. 73–80.

33. See J. Laplanche and J.B. Pontalis, *The Language of Psycho-Analysis,* trans. Donald Micholson-Smith (New York: Norton, 1974). (*Translators' note.*)

34. Robert Jaulin, *La mort sara* (Paris: Plon, 1967), p. 122.

35. C. von Monakow and Mourgue, *Introduction biologique à l'étude de la neurologie et de la psycho-pathologie* (Paris: Alcan, 1928).

36. Jacques Lacan, "Position de l'inconscient," in *Ecrits* (Paris: Editions du Seuil), p. 843.

37. Maurice Blanchot, *L'entretien infini* (Paris: Gallimard, 1969), pp. 451–52.

38. All quotes from Proust are translated by Richard Howard. We also retain the title *In Search of Lost Time,* used by Richard Howard in his translation of Gilles Deleuze, *Proust and Signs* (New York: Braziller, 1972), p. 1. This title stresses the notion of search and voyage. (*Translators' note.*)

39. J.H. Rush, *The Dawn of Life* (Garden City, N.Y.: Hanover House, 1957), p. 148.

40. Melanie Klein, *Contributions to Psycho-Analysis, with an Introduction by Ernest Jones* (London: Hogarth Press, 1930), pp. 242–43 (emphasis added).

41. Ray Bradbury, *The Illustrated Man* (Garden City, N.Y.: Doubleday, 1951).

42. Antonin Artaud, "Je n'ai jamais rien étudié . . . ," *84,* December 1950.

43. Michel Foucault, *Madness and Civilization: A History of Insanity in the Age of Reason,* trans. Richard Howard (New York: Random House, 1971). The English version is an edition, abridged by the author himself, of his French text: Michel Foucault, *Histoire de la folie à l'âge classique* (Paris: Plon, 1961).

2 PSYCHOANALYSIS AND FAMILIALISM

1. J. Laplanche and J. B. Pontalis, "Fantasme originaire, fantasmes des origines et origine du fantasme," *Les Temps Modernes,* no. 215 (April 1964), pp. 1844–46.

1a. On the existence of a little machine in the "primal fantasy," an existence nevertheless always in the wings, see Sigmund Freud, "A Case of Paranoia Running Counter to the Psychoanalytic Theory of the Disease" (1915).

2. Sigmund Freud, *Three Case Studies* (New York: Collier, Macmillan, 1970).

3. Ibid., pp. 150–51.

4. Ibid., p. 154.

5. Ibid., pp. 152, 184–86.

6. Karl Marx, *Economic and Philosophic Manuscripts of 1844,* trans. Martin Milligan (New York: International Publishers, 1964), p. 145. See also the excellent commentary by François Chatelet on this point: "La question de l'athéisme de Marx," *Etudes philosophiques,* July 1966.

7. Sigmund Freud, " 'A Child Is Being Beaten': A Contribution to the Study of the Origin of Sexual Perversions (1919)," in *Collected Papers,* Vol. 2, Hogarth Press, London, pp. 172–202. (*Translators' note.*)

8. Ibid., p. 180.

9. On the importance of this controversy, see André Green, "Sur la mère phallique," *Revue française de psychanalyse,* January 1968, pp. 8–9.

10. See for example the (moderate) protest of Betty Friedan against the Freudian and psychoanalytic conception of "feminine problems," sexual as well as social: *The Feminine Mystique* (New York: Norton, 1963).

11. Pierre Klossowski, *Nietzsche et le cercle vicieux* (Paris: Mercure de France, 1969), p. 122. Klossowski's meditation on the relationship between drives and institutions, and on the presence of the drives in the economic infrastructure itself, is developed in his article "Sade et Fourier," *Topique,* no. 4–5, and especially in *La monnaie vivante* (Paris: Losfeld, 1970).

12. In *Standard Edition of the Complete Psychological Works of Sigmund Freud,* ed. James Strachey (New York: Macmillan; London: Hogarth Press, 1974), Vol. 23. (*Translators' note:* Hereafter this source will be cited as *Standard Edition.*)

13. André Green, *L'affect* (Paris: Presses Universitaires de France, 1970), pp. 154–68.

14. See Gilles Deleuze, *Proust and Signs,* trans. Richard Howard (New York: Braziller, 1972), pp. 120–22 ff. for a discussion in depth of the two Proustian series. (*Translators' note.*)

15. Translated by Richard Howard, and first appearing in Deleuze, *Proust and Signs,* pp. 121–22. Translation of Marcel Proust, *A la recherche du temps perdu,* Bibliothèque de la Pléiade (Paris: Gallimard, 1954), Vol. 2, 622 (emphasis added). (*Translators' revised note.*)

16. Luc de Heusch, *Essai sur le symbolisme de l'inceste royal en Afrique* (Bruxelles: 1959), pp. 13–16.

17. Immanuel Kant, *The Metaphysics of Morals,* Part I.

18. Green, *L'affect,* p. 167.

19. On the hysterical "question" (Am I man or woman?) and the obsessional "question" (Am I dead or alive?), see Serge Leclaire, "La mort dans la vie de l'obsédé," *La Psychanalyse,* no. 2, pp. 129–30.

20. *L'Art brut,* no. 3, p. 139. In his presentation, Jean Oury calls Jayet "the nondelimited," "in permanent flight."

21. Félix Guattari first develops this concept at length in "D'un signe à l'autre," in *Psychanalyse et transversalité* (Paris: Maspero, 1973). (*Translators' note.*)

22. Samuel Beckett, *Molloy,* in *Three Novels by Samuel Beckett* (New York: Grove Press, 1959).

23. Vaslav Nijinsky, *Diary* (New York: Simon and Schuster, 1936), pp. 20, 156.

24. A. Besançon, "Vers une histoire psychanalytique," *Annales,* May 1969.

25. Gregory Bateson et al., "Toward a Theory of Schizophrenia," *Behavioral Science,* Vol. 1 (1956). See the commentaries of Pierre Fédida in "Psychose et parenté," *Critique,* October 1968.

26. Sigmund Freud, *Group Psychology and the Analysis of the Ego,* Ch. 12, B.

27. Alexander Mitscherlich, *Society without the Father,* trans. Eric Mosbacher (New York: Schocken Books, 1970), pp. 296ff.

28. Marie-Claire Boons, "Le meurtre du père chez Freud," *L'Inconscient,* no. 5 (January 1968), p. 129.

29. Edmond Ortigues, *Le discours et le symbole* (Paris: Aubier, 1962), p. 197.

30. Jacques Lacan, *Ecrits* (Paris: Editions du Seuil), p. 813.

31. R. D. Laing, *The Politics of Experience* (New York: Ballantine, 1967), pp. 154–55.

32. On the interplay of races and intensities in the theater of cruelty, see Antonin Artaud, *Oeuvres complètes,* (Paris: Gallimard), Vols. 4 and 5: for example, the project of "La conquète du Mexique," Vol. 4, p. 151; and the role of intensive vibrations and rotations in "Les Cenci," Vol. 5, pp. 46ff. (*Translators' note:* For the English text of the latter, see Antonin Artaud, *The Cenci,* trans. Simon Watson Taylor [New York: Grove Press, 1970], pp. viiff.)

33. Arthur Rimbaud, *Une Saison en Enfer.*

34. Nietzsche, letter to Jakob Burckhardt, January 5, 1889, in *Selected Letters of Friedrich Nietzsche,* trans. Christopher Middleton (Chicago: University of Chicago Press, 1969), p. 347.

35. Jacques Besse, "Le danseur," in *La grande pâque* (Paris: Editions Belfond, 1969). The whole first part of this book describes the schizo's stroll in the city; the second part, "Légendes folles," progresses to the hallucinations or deliriums of historical episodes.

36. Wilhelm Reich, *The Function of the Orgasm,* trans. Vincent R. Carfagno (New York: Simon & Schuster,1973), p. 70. For a critique of autism, see Roger Gentis, *Les murs de l'asile* (Paris: Maspero, 1970), pp. 41ff.

37. Maurice Garçon, *Louis XVII ou la fausse énigme* (Paris: Hachette, 1968), p. 177.

38. Maud Mannoni, *Le psychiatre, son fou et la psychanalyse* (Paris: Editions du Seuil, 1970).

39. Ibid.

40. Jacques Hochman, *Pour une psychiatrie communautaire* (Paris: Editions du Seuil, 1971), Ch. 4. Also his article "Le postulat fusionnel," *Information psychiatrique,* September 1969.

41. David Cooper, *Psychiatry and Anti-Psychiatry* (New York: Ballantine Books, 1971), p. 44 (emphasis added).

42. Frantz Fanon, *The Wretched of the Earth,* trans. Constance Farrington (New York: Grove Press, 1968), p. 262.

43. Witold Grombrowicz, *L'Herne,* no. 14, p. 230.

44. Lacan, *Ecrits,* p. 870. With regard to the specific role of the rich woman and the poor woman in the Rat Man case, the reader may refer to the analyses of

Lacan in "Le mythe individuel du névrosé," *C.D.U.*, not included in the *Ecrits.*

45. Rimbaud, *Une Saison en Enfer.*

46. Gérard Mendel, *La révolte contre le père* (Paris: Payot, 1968), p. 422.

47. Friedrich Engels, *The Origin of the Family* (New York: International Publishers, 1942), preface, p. 10.

48. Friedrich Nietzsche, *Joyful Wisdom*, V, § 346. See also Marx, *Economic and Philosophic Manuscripts of 1844*, pp. 144–46.

49. Hochmann, *Pour une psychiatrie communautaire*, p. 38.

50. *Selected Letters of Malcolm Lowry,* ed. Harvey Breit and Margerie Bonner Lowry (Philadelphia and New York: J. B. Lippincott, 1965), p. 66.

51. "Letter to Michael Fraenkel by Henry Miller, May 7, 1936," in Henry Miller, *Hamlet* (Puerto Rico: Carrefour, 1939), Vol. 1, pp. 124–26.

52. Sigmund Freud, "The Dissolution of the Oedipus Complex" (1924), *Standard Edition*, Vol. 19, pp. 176–78.

53. Sigmund Freud, *Totem and Taboo*, trans. James Strachey (New York: Norton, 1950), p. 123.

54. D. H. Lawrence, "Psychoanalysis and the Unconscious," in *Psychoanalysis and the Unconscious* and *Fantasia of the Unconscious* (New York: Viking Press, 1969), pp. 11–30.

55. See the two classic accounts: Wilhelm Reich, *The Function of the Orgasm*, Ch. 6; Herbert Marcuse, *Eros and Civilization* (Boston: Beacon Press, 1955), the chapter "Neo-Freudian Revisionism." The question has been taken up more recently in some excellent articles in *Partisans,* no. 46 (February 1969): François Gantheret, "Freud et la question socio-politique" (pp. 85ff.); Jean-Marie Brohm, "Psychanalyse et révolution" (pp. 97ff.).

56. The two 1924 articles are "Neurosis and Psychosis" and "The Loss of Reality in Neurosis and Psychosis." See also J. Capgras and J. Carrette, "Illusion des sosies et complexe d'Oedipe," *Annales médico-psychologiques,* May 1924. Freud's article "Fetishism" (1927) does not go back on the distinction, despite what is sometimes said, but confirms it: *Collected Papers,* Vol. 5, pp. 198–204 ("I can thereby maintain my proposition . . .").

57. Jacques Lacan, "La famille," *Encyclopédie française,* Vol. 8 (1938).

58. Jacques Besse, *La grande pâque*, pp. 27, 61.

59. Gérard de Nerval, "Sylvie," in *Sfflected Writings,* trans. Geoffrey Wagner (New York: Grove Press, N.Y., 1957). (*Translators' note.*)

60. "El Desdichado," in *Selected Writings*, p. 213. (*Translators' note.*)

61. Jean Laplanche, "La réalité dans la névrose et la psychose," a lecture given at the Société Française de Psychanalyse in 1961. See also J. Laplanche and J. B. Pontalis, *The Language of Psycho-Analysis,* trans. Donald Micholson-Smith (New York: Norton, 1974), the articles "Frustration" and "Actual Neurosis."

62. C. G. Jung, *Contributions to Analytical Psychology* (London: Routledge and Kegan Paul, 1948), Ch. 1–4 and p. 345.

63. Gisela Pankow, *L'homme et sa psychose* (Paris: Aubier, 1969), pp. 24–26. The reader is referred to the very fine theory of the sign developed by Pankow in *Structuration dynamique dans la schizophrénie* (Paris: Huber, 1956). For Bettelheim's critique of regression, see Bruno Bettelheim, *The Empty Fortress* (New York: The Free Press, 1967), pp. 294–96.

64. Vincent Van Gogh, "Letter of September 8, 1888," cited in *Artaud Anthology,* trans. Mary Beach and Lawrence Ferlinghetti (San Francisco: City Lights Books, 1965), p. 150.

3 SAVAGES, BARBARIANS, CIVILIZED MEN

1. Lewis Mumford, "La première mégamachine", *Diogène,* July 1966.
2. Meyer Fortes, *Recherches voltaïques,* 1967, pp. 135–37.
3. F. Nietzsche, *On the Genealogy of Morals* (New York: Random House, 1969), II, 2–7. But these authors indulge in a strange gymnastics to maintain the existence of an Oedipal problem or complex, despite all the reasons they advance to the contrary, and although they say this complex is not "clinically accessible."
4. Ibid. Section 4.
5. Ibid. Section 3.
6. E. R. Leach, *Rethinking Anthropology* (London: Athlone Press, 1966), pp. 122–23.
7. L. G. Löffler, "L'alliance asymétrique chez les Mru," *L'Homme,* July 1966, pp. 78–79. Leach, in *Rethinking Anthropology,* analyzes the difference between ideology and practice apropos of the Kachin marriage (pp. 81–82); he greatly advances the critique of conceptions of kinship as a closed system (pp. 89–90).
8. Pierre Clastres, "L'arc et le panier," *L'Homme,* April 1966, p. 20.
9. Jeanne Favret, "La segmentarité au Maghreb," *L'Homme,* April 1966; Pierre Clastres, "Echange et pouvoir," *L'Homme,* January 1962.
10. Edward E. Evans-Pritchard, "The Nuer of the Southern Sudan," in *African Political Systems,* ed. Meyer Fortes and Edward E. Evans-Pritchard (London: Oxford University Press, 1958), p. 287.
11. Marcel Griaule, *Dieu d'eau* (Paris: Fayard, 1948), especially pp. 46–52.
12. Claude Lévi-Strauss, *The Elementary Structures of Kinship,* trans. James Harle Bell and John Richard von Sturmer, ed. Rodney Needham (Boston: Beacon Press, 1969), pp. 130–31.
13. Marcel Griaule, "Remarques sur l'oncle utérin au Soudan," *Cahiers internationaux de sociologie,* January 1954. Alfred Adler and Michel Cartry, "La transgression et sa dérision," *L'Homme,* July 1971.
14. Griaule, "Remarques sur l'oncle utérin au Soudan."
15. T. D. Lysenko, *La situation dans la science biologique,* French edition (Moscow, 1949), p. 16.
16. *The Elementary Structures of Kinship,* pp. 485–88.
17. Robert Jaulin, *La mort sara* (Paris: Plon, 1967), p. 284.
18. Lévi-Strauss, *The Elementary Structures of Kinship,* p. 309. Lévi-Strauss analyzes cases, abnormal or paradoxical on the surface, of beneficiaries of matrimonial prestations.
19. Löffler, "L'alliance asymétrique chez les Mru," p. 80.
20. Georges Devereux, "Considérations ethnopsychanalytiques sur la notion de parenté," *L'Homme,* July 1965.
21. Victor W. Turner, "Magic, Faith, and Healing," in *An Ndembu Doctor in Practice* (New York: Collier, Macmillan, 1964).
22. M. C. and Edmond Ortigues, *Oedipe africain* (Paris: Plon, 1966), p. 305.

23. Geza Roheim, *Psychoanalysis and Anthropology* (New York: International Universities Press, 1950), pp. 490–91.
24. E. R. Leach, "Magical Hair," in *Myth and Cosmos* (Garden City, N.Y.: Doubleday, 1967), p. 92.
25. Wilhelm Reich, *Der Einbruch der Sexualmoral* (Verlag für Sexualpolitik, 1932), p. 6. (*The Invasion of Compulsory Sex-Morality* [New York: Farrar, Straus & Giroux, 1971].)
26. Herbert Marcuse, *Eros and Civilization* (Boston: Beacon Press, 1955), p. 220.
27. Laura and Paul Bohannan, *The Tiv of Central Nigeria* (London: International African Institute, 1953).
28. Abram Kardiner, *The Individual and His Society* (New York: Columbia University Press, 1939), p. 248.
29. Victor Turner, "Themes in the Symbolism of Ndembu Hunting Ritual," in *Myth and Cosmos* (Garden City, N.Y.: Doubleday, 1967), pp. 249–69.
30. Michel Cartry, "Clans, lignages et groupements familiaux chez les Gourmantché," *L'Homme,* April 1966, p. 74.
31. Lévi-Strauss, *The Elementary Structures of Kinship*, p. 267; also, regarding his way of presenting Leach's argument, pp. 221ff. But with respect to this argument itself, see Leach, *Rethinking Anthropology*, pp. 60–64, 81–95.
32. Lévi-Strauss, *The Elementary Structures of Kinship*, pp. 193–95. See the statistical comparison with the "cyclists."
33. Emmanuel Terray, *Le Marxisme devant les sociétés primitives* (Paris: Maspero, 1969), p. 164.
34. André Leroi-Gourhan, *Le geste et la parole, technique et langage* (Paris: Albin Michel, 1964), pp. 270ff., 290ff.
35. Michel Cartry, "La calebasse de l'excision en pays gourmantché," *Journal de la Société des africanistes*, no. 2 (1968), pp. 223–25.
36. Pierre Clastres, *Chroniques des indiens Guayaki* (Paris: Plon, 1972).
37. *On the Genealogy of Morals*, II, 6.
38. Ibid., II, 17.
39. Ibid.
40. Ibid., II, 16.
41. Ibid., II, 21.
42. Jean Steinmann, *Saint Jean-Baptiste et la spiritualité du désert* (Paris: Editions du Seuil, 1959), p. 69.
43. Karl Marx, *Pre-Capitalist Economic Formations* (1857), trans. Jack Cohen (New York: International Publishers, 1965), pp. 69–70.
44. Nietzsche, *On the Genealogy of Morals*, II, 17.
45. Franz Kafka, "The Great Wall of China," *The Great Wall of China*, trans. Willa and Edwin Muir (New York: Schocken, 1948).
46. *On the Genealogy of Morals*, II, 12.
47. Etienne Balazs, *La bureaucratie céleste* (Paris: Gallimard, 1968), Ch. 13: "La naissance du capitalisme en Chine" (especially the State and money, and the merchants' impossibility of gaining an autonomy, pp. 229–300). Regarding imperial formations founded on the control of commerce rather than control over public works—in black Africa, for example—see the comments of Maurice Godelier and J. Suret-Canale, in Maurice Godelier,

Sur le mode de production asiatique (Paris: Editions Sociales, 1969), pp. 87–88, 120–22.

48. Michel Foucault, "La volonté de savoir", a course given at the Collège de France in 1971.

49. Lewis Carroll, "Peter and Paul," in *Sylvie and Bruno.*

50. Franz Kafka, "The Great Wall of China," pp. 163–64, 167–68.

51. *On the Genealogy of Morals,* II, 17.

52. Luc de Heusch, *Essais sur le symbolisme de l'inceste royal en Afrique* (Brussels, 1958), pp. 72–74.

53. Jacques Derrida, *De la grammatologie* (Paris: Editions de Minuit, 1967), and "Freud et la scène de l'écriture," in *L'écriture et la différence* (Paris: Editions du Seuil, 1967).

54. Andras Zempléni, *L'interprétation et la thérapie traditionelles du désordre mental chez les Wolof et les Lebou* (Paris: Université de Paris, 1968), Vol. 2, pp. 380, 506.

55. Jean Nougayrol, in *L'écriture et la psychologie des peuples,* (Paris: Armand Colin, 1963), p. 90.

56. Guy Rosalato, *Essais sur le symbolique* (Paris: Gallimard, 1969), pp. 25–28.

57. Nietzsche, *On the Genealogy of Morals,* II, 17.

58. Kafka, "The Great Wall of China," p. 167.

59. Neitzsche, *On the Genealogy of Morals,* II, 17.

60. Ibid.

61. Concerning the régime of private property already present in the despotic State itself, see Karl Wittfogel, *Oriental Despotism* (New Haven, Conn.: Yale University Press, 1957), pp. 78–85, 228–300. On private property in the Chinese state, see Balazs, *La bureaucratie céleste,* Ch. 7–9. Regarding the two paths of transition from the despotic State to feudalism, according to whether or not commodity production is joined with private property, see Godelier, *Sur le mode de production asiatique,* pp. 90–92.

62. Jean-Pierre Vernant, *Les origines de la pensée grecque* (Paris: Presses Universitaires de France, 1962), pp. 112–13.

63. Karl Marx, *Grundrisse,* trans. Martin Nicolaus (New York: Random House, 1973), p. 102.

64. Gilbert Simondon, *Du mode d'existence des objets techniques* (Paris: Aubier, 1969), pp. 25–49.

65. Nietzsche, *On the Genealogy of Morals,* II, 22.

66. Karl Marx, "Reply to Milkhailovski" (Nov., 1877), in Karl Marx and Friedrich Engels, *Basic Writings on Politics and Philosophy* (Garden City, N.Y.: Doubleday, 1959), p. 441.

67. Fernand Braudel, *Capitalism and Material Life, 1400–1800,* trans. Miriam Kochan (New York: Harper and Row, 1973), p. 308.

68. Karl Marx, *Economic and Philosophic Manuscripts of 1844,* (trans. Martin Milligan (New York: International Publishers, 1964), p. 148.

69. See Balibar's commentary, in Louis Althusser and Etienne Balibar, *Reading Capital,* trans. Ben Brewster (New York: Pantheon, 1970), p. 281: "The unity possessed by the capitalist structure once it has been constituted is not found in its rear. [It requires] that the *meeting* should have been produced and rigorously thought, between those elements, which are identified on the

basis of the result of their *conjunction,* and the historical field within which their peculiar histories are to be thought. In their concepts, the latter have nothing to do with that result, since they are defined by the structure of a different mode of production. In this historical field (constituted by the previous mode of production), the elements whose genealogy is being traced have precisely only a marginal situation, i.e., a non-determinate one."

70. Maurice Dobb, *Studies in the Development of Capitalism* (London: Routledge and Kegan Paul, 1959), pp. 177–86.

71. Marx, *Grundrisse,* pp. 104–106.

72. Karl Marx, *Capital,* trans. Ernest Untermann (New York: International Publishers, 1967), Vol. 1, p. 154.

73. Suzanne de Brunhoff, *L'offre de monnaie, critique d'un concept* (Paris: Maspero, 1971); and *La monnaie chez Marx* (Paris: Editions Sociales, 1967) (see the critique of Hilferding's arguments, pp. 16ff.).

74. Jean-Joseph Goux, "Dérivable et indérivable," *Critique,* January 1970, pp. 48–49.

75. Samir Amin, *L'accumulation à l'échelle mondiale* (Paris: Anthropos, 1970), pp. 373ff.

76. Maurice Clavel, *Qui est aliéné?* (Paris: Flammarion, 1970), pp. 110–24, 320–27. See Marx's great chapter on automation (1857–58) in the *Grundrisse,* pp. 692ff.

77. Paul Baran and Paul Sweezy, *Monopoly Capital* (New York: Monthly Review Press, 1966), pp. 93–97.

78. Regarding the concept of depreciation implied by this proposition, ibid., pp. 99–102.

79. *Capital,* Vol. 3, p. 244.

80. André Gorz, *Strategy for Labor* trans. Martin Nicolaus and Victoria Ortiz (Boston: Beacon Press, 1967), p. 106.

81. Baran and Sweezy, *Monopoly Capital,* p. 344.

82. Bernard Schmitt, *Monnaie, salaires et profits* (Paris: Presses Universitaires de France, 1966), pp. 234–36.

83. Ibid., p. 292.

84. Michel Serres, "Le messager," *Bulletin de la Sociétfrançaise de philosophie,* November 1967.

85. Jean-Francois Lyotard, *Discours, figure* (Paris: Klincksieck, 1971).

86. Ibid.

87. See Herbert Marcuse's analysis of the functional language of "total administration"—especially in abbreviations (e.g., S.E.A.T.O.), the floating configurations formed by letters-figures): *One Dimensional Man* (Boston: Beacon Press, 1964), Ch. 4.

88. Marx, *Capital,* Vol. 1, p. 150.

89. Schmitt, *Monnaie, salaires et profits.*

90. For a discussion of all these points, see Dobb, *Studies in the Development of Capitalism,* pp. 23–25, 161–67, 193–210.

91. G. Plekhanov, "Augustin Thierry et la conception matérialiste de l'histoire" (1895), in *Les questions fondamentales du marxisme* (Paris: Editions sociales.).

92. Marx, *Capital,* Vol. 1, p. 592.

93. Jean-Paul Sartre, *Critique de la raison dialectique* (Paris: Gallimard, 1960).

94. Wilhelm Reich, "What Is Class Consciousness?" (1934), trans. Anna Bostock, *Liberation,* Vol. 16, no. 5 (October 1971), p. 22.

95. Marx, *Grundrisse,* p. 104, and *Economic and Philosophic Manuscripts of 1844,* pp. 128–31.

96. Marx, *Capital,* Vol. 3, pp. 249–50.

97. See Emmanuel Terray's differential analysis of production modes, *Le Marxisme devant les sociétés primitives,* pp. 140–55 (why, in precapitalist societies, "the reproduction of the economic and social structure depends in large measure on the conditions under which the physical reproduction of the group is maintained").

98. Regarding the production of *the* capitalist, etc., see Márx, *Pre-Capitalist Economic Formations,* pp. 118–19, and *Capital,* Vol. 1, pp. 591–92.

99. Jacques Lacan, *Lettres de l'école freudienne,* March 7, 1970, p. 42.

100. D. H. Lawrence, "Art and Morality," in *Phoenix* (New York: Viking Press, 1936), pp. 522–26. On the "reality" of modern man as a composite and motley image, see Nietzsche, *Thus Spake Zarathustra,* II, "Of the Land of Culture."

101. Marx, *Grundrisse,* pp. 104–108.

4 INTRODUCTION TO SCHIZOANALYSIS

1. Claude Lévi-Strauss, *The Raw and the Cooked,* trans. John and Doreen Weightman (New York: Harper and Row, 1969), p. 48.

2. Joseph Gabel, "Délire politique chez un paranoïde," *L'Evolution psychiatrique,* no. 2 (1952).

3. Abram Kardiner, *The Individual and His Society* (New York: Columbia University Press, 1939), pp. 223ff. And concerning the two possible paths, from the child to the adult or from the adult to the child, see Mikel Dufrenne's commentaries in *La personnalité de base,* (Paris: Presses Universitaires de France, 1953), pp. 287–320.

4. For a rigorous philosophical discussion of the notion of *repetition,* both the radical repetition of the Same and of Difference (the Eternal Return), and the normative repetition of Habit and Representation, see Gilles Deleuze, *Différence et répétition* (Paris: Presses Universitaires de France, 1972), pp. 128–67. (*Translators' note.*)

5.

6. Allen Ginsberg, "Kaddish," IV, in *Kaddish and Other Poems,* , (San Francisco: City Lights Books, 1961), pp. 34–35.

7. Samuel Butler, *Erewhon, Everyman's Library* (New York: E.P.Dutton; London: J. M.Dent, 1965), pp. 146–60.

8. Ibid., p. 148.

9. Ibid., p. 156.

10. Ibid., p. 159.

11. Karl Marx, *Critique of Hegel's "Philosophy of Right",* trans. Annette Jolin and Joseph O'Malley (New York: Cambridge University Press, 1970), pp. 88–90. And on this text of Marx, see the fine commentary by Lyotard (see reference note 12), pp. 138–41.

12. Jean-François Lyotard, *Discours, figure* (Paris: Klincksieck, 1971).

13. Henry Miller, *Hamlet* (Puerto Rico: Carrefour, 1939), Vol. 1, pp. 124–29.

14. Michel Foucault, *The Order of Things* (New York: Random House, 1970), pp. 208–11 (on the opposition between desire or desiring-production and representation); pp. 253–56 (on the opposition between social production and representation, in Adam Smith and especially Ricardo).
15. On myth as the expression of the organization of a despotic power that represses the Earth, see Jean-Pierre Vernant, *Les origines de la pensée grecque* (Paris: Presses Universitaires de France, 1962), pp. 109–16; and on tragedy as the expression of an organization of the city-state that represses in its turn the fallen despot, Vernant, "Oedipe sans complexe," *Raison présente,* August 1967.
16. Octave Mannoni, *Clefs pour l'imaginaire ou l'autre scène* (Paris: Editions du Seuil, 1969), Ch. 1 and 7.
17. Louis Althusser and Etienne Balibar, *Reading Capital,* trans. Ben Brewster (New York: Pantheon, 1970).
18. Serge Leclaire, *Démasquer le réel* (Paris: Editions du Seuil, 1971), pp. 28–31.
19. Elisabeth Roudinesco, "L'action d'une métaphore," *La Pensée,* February 1972. See in Jacques Lacan, *Ecrits* (Paris: Editions du Seuil), p. 821, the way in which Lacan raises the idea of a "signifier of the lack of this symbol" above the "zero symbol," taken in its linguistic sense.
20. Sigmund Freud, "Analysis Terminable and Interminable," *Standard Edition,* Vol. 23, pp. 251–52.
21. Miller, *Hamlet,* pp. 124–25.
22. Wilhelm Reich, *The Function of the Orgasm,* trans. Vincent R. Carfagno (New York: Simon & Schuster, 1973), pp. 167–68. See also Wilhelm Reich, *Character Analysis* (New York: Simon & Schuster, 1974).
23. Gisela Pankow, *L'homme et sa psychose* (Paris: Aubier, 1969), pp. 68–72. And on the role of the house: "La dynamique de l'espace et le temps vécu," *Critique,* February 1972.
24. Michel Cournot, *Le Nouvel Observateur,* Nov. 1, 1971.
25. D. H. Lawrence, "Psychoanalysis and the Unconscious," in *Psychoanalysis and the Unconscious* and *Fantasia of the Unconscious* (New York: Viking Press, 1969), p. 30.
26. Serge Leclaire, "La réalité du désir," in *Sexualité humaine* (Paris: Aubier, 1970), p. 245. And *Séminaire Vincennes,* 1969, pp. 31–34 (the opposition between the "erogenous body" and the organism).
27. Jacques Monod, *Chance and Necessity,* trans. Austryn Wainhouse (New York: Knopf, 1971), p. 98.
28. On "the double death," see Maurice Blanchot, *L'espace littéraire* (Paris: Gallimard, 1955), pp. 104, 160.
29. Arthur Rimbaud, letter to Paul Demeny, May 15, 1871.
30. Reich, *The Function of the Orgasm.* A correct interpretation—marked throughout by idealism—of Freud's theory of culture and its catastrophic evolution concerning guilt feeling, can be found in Paul Ricoeur: on death, and "the death of death," see *De l'interprétation* (Paris: Edition's du Seuil) pp. 299–303.
31. Sigmund Freud, *The Problem of Anxiety,* trans. Henry Alden Bunker (New York: Psychoanalytic Quarterly Press, Norton, 1936); or *Inhibitions, Symptoms, and Anxiety,* trans. Alix Strachey (London: Hogarth Press, 1936).
32. Nietzsche, *On the Genealogy of Morals,* II, 13.

33. D. H. Lawrence, *Aaron's Rod* (New York: Penguin, 1976), p. 101.

34. Henry Miller, *Sexus* (New York: Grove Press, 1965), pp. 429–30 (words in brackets added). One would do well to consult the exercises of comic psychoanalysis in *Sexus*.

35. L.-F. Céline, in *L'Herne*, no. 3, p. 171.

36. Ibid.

37. Maurice Blanchot, *L'amitié* (Paris: Gallimard, 1971), pp. 232–33.

38. See Sigmund Freud, "The Unconscious" (1915), in *Collected Papers*, Vol. 4, pp. 131–34: the two uses made of the sock—the psychotic use that treats it as a molecular multiplicity of stitches, and the neurotic use that treats it as a global object and molar lack.

39. For a first formulation of this notion of clothed and naked matter in terms of the repetition of difference and the Eternal Return, see the conclusion of Gilles Deleuze, *Différence et répétition* (Paris: Presses Universitaires de France, 1972). (*Translators' note.*)

40. Pierre Klossowski, *Nietzsche et le cercle vicieux* (Paris: Mercure de France, 1969), pp. 174–75. Klossowski's commentary on the formations of sovereignty according to Nietzsche (*Herrschaftsgebilde*), their absurd power without purpose, and the ends or meanings they invent for themselves in terms of a degree of development of energy, is essential in every respect.

41. D. H. Lawrence, "We Need One Another," in *Phoenix: The Posthumous Papers of D. H. Lawrence* (New York: The Viking Press, 1936), p. 191.

42. Sigmund Freud, *Three Case Histories* (New York: Collier, Macmillan, 1970), p. 162.

43. On the first point, Ernest Jones, *The Life and Work of Sigmund Freud* (New York: Basic Books, 1953), Vol. 1, Ch. 1. For the second point, Freud, "The Familial Romance of the Neuroses" (1909). For the third point, *The Rat Man*, passim, and Jacques Lacan, "Le mythe individuel du névrosé," *C.D.U.*, pp. 7–18 (and p. 25 on the necessity of a "critique of the entire system of Oedipus"). For the fourth point, see Freud, "The Wolf Man," *Three Case Histories*, pp. 205, 285, 286.

44. Freud, *Three Case Histories*, p. 291. See also pp. 205, 286.

45. R. D. Laing, *Self and Others* (New York: Pantheon, 1970), pp. 113–14, 125.

46. Maud Mannoni, *Le psychiatre, son fou et la psychanalyse* (Paris: Editions du Seuil, 1970), Ch. 7.

47. Klossowski, *Nietzsche et le cercle vicieux*, pp. 175, 202–203, 213–14. The opposition between aggregates of gregariousness and multiplicities of singularities is developed throughout this book, and then in Pierre Klossowski, *La monnaie vivante* (Paris: Losfeld, 1970).

48. The authors are referring here to D. H. Lawrence's "We Need One Another" (see reference note 41) and to the comical psychoanalytical scene in Henry Miller's *Sexus*, pp. 429–31. (Translators' revised note.)

49. Lacan, *Ecrits*, p. 870.

50. On the analysis of subject-groups and their relations with desire and with causality, see Jean-Paul Sartre, *Critique de la raison dialectique* (Paris: Gallimard, 1960).

51. André Glucksmann has analyzed the nature of this special counterrevolutionary axiomatic in "Le discours de la guerre," *L'Herne* (1967).

52. Maud Mannoni, *Lettre aux ministres*.

INDEX

THE STORY OF PENGUIN CLASSICS

Before 1946 . . . "Classics" are mainly the domain of academics and students; readable editions for everyone else are almost unheard of. This all changes when a little-known classicist, E. V. Rieu, presents Penguin founder Allen Lane with the translation of Homer's *Odyssey* that he has been working on in his spare time.

1946 Penguin Classics debuts with *The Odyssey*, which promptly sells three million copies. Suddenly, classics are no longer for the privileged few.

1950s Rieu, now series editor, turns to professional writers for the best modern, readable translations, including Dorothy L. Sayers's *Inferno* and Robert Graves's unexpurgated *Twelve Caesars*.

1960s The Classics are given the distinctive black covers that have remained a constant throughout the life of the series. Rieu retires in 1964, hailing the Penguin Classics list as "the greatest educative force of the twentieth century."

1970s A new generation of translators swells the Penguin Classics ranks, introducing readers of English to classics of world literature from more than twenty languages. The list grows to encompass more history, philosophy, science, religion, and politics.

1980s The Penguin American Library launches with titles such as *Uncle Tom's Cabin* and joins forces with Penguin Classics to provide the most comprehensive library of world literature available from any paperback publisher.

1990s The launch of Penguin Audiobooks brings the classics to a listening audience for the first time, and in 1999 the worldwide launch of the Penguin Classics Web site extends their reach to the global online community.

The 21st Century Penguin Classics are completely redesigned for the first time in nearly twenty years. This world-famous series now consists of more than 1,300 titles, making the widest range of the best books ever written available to millions—and constantly redefining what makes a "classic."

The Odyssey continues . . .

The best books ever written

PENGUIN CLASSICS

SINCE 1946

Find out more at www.penguinclassics.com

Visit www.vpbookclub.com

CLICK ON A CLASSIC
www.penguinclassics.com

The world's greatest literature at your fingertips

Constantly updated information on more than a thousand titles,
from Icelandic sagas to ancient Indian epics, Russian drama to
Italian romance, American greats to African masterpieces

•

The latest news on recent additions to the list, updated
editions, and specially commissioned translations

•

Original essays by leading writers

•

A wealth of background material, including biographies
of every classic author from Aristotle to Zamyatin, plot
synopses, readers' and teachers' guides, useful Web links

•

Online desk and examination copy assistance for academics

•

Trivia quizzes, competitions, giveaways, news on
forthcoming screen adaptations